Franklin 1845 ~ 1872 ca.

1. Presbyterian Church
• 2. Peter Van Every Mill
3. Van Every Steam Flouring Mill
   1851~1856
• 4. Pickering Farm house
5. Van Every Potashery
6. Distillery - closed 1877
7. Harvey Lee - shoe shop & home
8. Pratt Distillery (Evans, operator)
9. A. J. Reid - J. Bouton
   blacksmith shop (Mattie Cox later)
• 10. Peter Van Every house
   (possible location of Franklin
   Cottage?)
• 11. Barnum House
12. Smith House
• 13. Midgley House
• 14. Franklin Hotel
15. Broughton store
16. J. Grace store
17. H. S. Cox office
18. J. German residence
19. Kyle/Broughton house - 1800
• 20. Zlet House
• 21. Berger - Smith House
22. Brick school - 1809
• 23. Frame school - 1845
   (H. S. Cox residence)
• 24. J. Grace house
• 25. William Hall House
26. Broughton's wagon shop
• 27. Charles Coder House
   (Post Office in 1800's)
28. A. A. Rust House
   (moved to 26800 German Mill)
• 29. Church
30. A. A. Rust store & Post Office
31. German, Pratt, Delling, M'Crumb Mill
32. Mill Property ~ J. German House
33. J. B. Rust House
34. Dr. H. S. Buel House (D. Stoughton)
35. Odd Fellows Hall - built 1872
• 36. J. A. Buel House - ca. 1870
37. Peter Van Every House
• 38. Congleton House & Wagon Works
• 39. Temperance Hotel

• = still standing

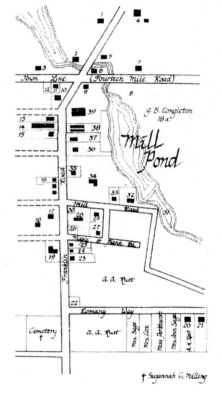

Town Line   (Fourteen Mile Road)

J. B. Congleton
18 a?

Mill Pond

A. A. Rust

Romany Way

Cemetery   A. A. Rust   Mrs. Sage Mrs. Cox Miss Jerthurst Mrs. Ann Sage A. H. Yet

† Suzannah C. Milling

Tansy Bitters,
Tansy Sweet

by

David Lee Roberts

authorHOUSE™

1663 LIBERTY DRIVE, SUITE 200
BLOOMINGTON, INDIANA 47403
(800) 839-8640
WWW.AUTHORHOUSE.COM

First published by AuthorHouse 03/16/05

ISBN: 1-4208-0246-1 (sc)
ISBN: 1-4208-0247-X (dj)

Printed in the United States of America
Bloomington, Indiana

This book is printed on acid-free paper.

Cover: (top to bottom)
Colt 1847 Walker Revolver, caliber .44
Daniel Moore 1860 Revolver, caliber .32
Christian Sharps 1859 Derringer, caliber .22

United States Copyright Office
Registration number
TXU 1124729

ACKNOWLEDGMENTS

The greatest assistance of all to me has been the great and long-suffering patience of my wife of forty-seven years, Jane, as she waited for me to finish writing and get back to the accomplishment of a number of delinquent projects that have been put of the back burner for lo! these many years. She only rolls her eyes when I mention that I have ideas in my head for another book, and then another after that. Jane is also my resident in-house expert on all things feminine....an area in which I am sadly lacking in knowledge. I never did, and doubtless never will, understand the inner workings of the female mind.

The Reverend Doctor Richard Cheatham helped me to change from the mind-set of play writing to the techniques of the novelist. On the stage, he explained, actors are seen by the eyes of the audience....which makes the task easier for the writer. In a book one has to paint the complete picture of the characters so that they may be seen by the minds of the readers. Hmmm! Sounded like a lot more work. It was. Dr. Cheatham also coached me in the endless battle against the notorious split infinitive. I find myself to be a slow learner in that regard.

Nationally known Lincoln expert, Dr. Weldon Petz, has offered invaluable advice during the post-writing area. Reverend Jim Greer is not only an expert proofreader, he also as a pastor questioned the propriety and frequency of extramarital sex, especially during the Victorian Era. He was finally convinced that such things were bound to have happened at least once in a while.

A big thank you to Lori Grundy, Franklin's own and only genuine Chippewa princess for the loan of her ancestors on Mackinac Island. I had fun chasing them down and coaxing them to live again. Thanks also to all of the people, historic and contemporary, who loaned bits and pieces of themselves to take part in the tale....even though they had no choice in the matter.

An especially grateful pat on the noble heads of Horrid, Noel, Casey, Maggie, and Whitney....Labrador Retrievers all....who helped me to sniff out that silly, stumbly old dog Tansy.

Table of Contents

PROLOGUE

The Village of Franklin is a tiny bedroom community situated in southeastern Michigan. Its claim to fame, as the "Town that Time Forgot" is that its quaint circa 1840 business district still marches sedately, just as it always did, along Franklin Road to the south of the Franklin River and terminates at the base of the abrupt ridge which boundaries the valley of that crystal clear and remarkably pristine little stream. Franklin was established in 1824 when pioneers Dillucena Stoughton, and in 1825, Elijah Bullock purchased the land from the United States Government and settled there. At the top of that sandy, gravely drumlin, to the south of town, is the little Franklin Cemetery which is appropriately protected by fancy, ancient iron fencing. To the north of town, across the river and in Bloomfield Township, stands the Franklin Cider Mill. Originally constructed by Colonel Peter Van Every as a grist mill, it attracted farmers from all over Oakland County to bring their grain to be expertly ground by the mill's fine, water powered stones. The success of the Van Every Mill brought prosperity to the little village. At one time, the town sported at least five taverns and a couple of hotels to serve the prosperous and often thirsty farmers.

The little cemetery is populated not just by the mix of both historic and contemporary stones marking the graves of former residents, but also by the beautiful white oak trees that gave Oakland County, Michigan, its name. Originally, in 1824, this cemetery overlooked vistas of white oak trees interspersed with newly cleared farmlands. Today, it looks over many of the same white oaks....but now interspersed with fine homes, ball diamonds ,and the spires of the Franklin Community United Methodist

Church. This cemetery serves as the locus of inspiration for this tale of the tansy.

Ever since the War Between the States, the Village of Franklin has held touching morning Memorial Day services to honor those who have fought for our country. Veterans from as far back as the War of 1812 are buried there. Some time ago I was asked to speak at a Memorial Day service. Wandering about the cemetery in search of inspiration, I came upon the grave of one Richard Trick, Company E, 30th Michigan Infantry, who died October 29, 1865. Something attracted me to his grave....just one of many of the honored veterans upon whose final resting place the stars and stripes fluttered in the pre-Memorial Day springtime sunshine. Pretending that I was Mr. Trick for the occasion, I gave my speech (which I considered to be cleverly contrived), and promptly forgot about the whole thing. A few years later, as I was contemplating the writing of this novel I again thought of Richard Trick. Leaving my bicycle at the edge of the little road that winds through the cemetery, I attempted to find his grave but could not. Some voice from within cried out to me that there could be a story to be told. "Silly!" I thought I as I returned to pick up my bike. Then, a crazy whim struck me. "Dick Trick!" I cried, "Where the hell are you?" Without hesitation, I then laid down my bicycle and promptly walked directly to the grave that I had just been unable to locate during a half-hour search. I sat in the grass and stared at the stone. Perhaps there was a tale to be told here. Perhaps Richard's spirit was restlessly hanging around his grave, waiting for his real story to be told. Damned if I know. Dick had died at age nineteen, just a few months after the close of the American Civil War. A few feet, probably two grave widths to the north his sister Ellen was buried who had also died at age nineteen but ten years earlier. I resolved at that moment to tell their story even though I could not possibly do so unless their spirits would be so kind as to guide me in the telling. I have no idea whether they did or did not, but I will say that the story was remarkably easy to write....at some times even seeming to write itself as the characters had their own way as to what would or would not happen, or as to what would be said, or what would occur. They seemed to refuse to do things that I would have them do if it were not within their psyche to do so.

I researched Richard Trick. The only record of him in either the archives of the State of Michigan or in the National Archives was of his grave. He did not appear in the roster of Company E, 30th Michigan Infantry. Richard Trick appeared to be something of a fraud.

So....would you call this a ghost story? Well, maybe. Now then, we'll discuss ghost story number two. My cast of characters needed a local, wholesome, grain fed *femme fatale*. I dreamed her up, beautiful, young, and sweet, and seductive enough to make the nose hairs of the local young men stand at attention when she walked by. I named her Hannah Midgley. The Midgley part was easy because well digger Tom Midgely had built the house that still stands on Franklin Road and currently houses a very excellent dental office which I am occasionally unable to avoid. The name of "Hannah" was picked simply because it had a nice sound to it....or so I thought.

A year or so into the writing of this tale (yes, I am admittedly very slow), the original handwritten records of the Franklin Methodist Protestant Church, which had been briefly lost, were returned. I was privileged to examine the treasured documents. They were the records of the annual church meetings, complete with attendance records. Guess who was there every year from 1873 to her death on October 25, 1887? You got it. Hannah Midgley! The document noted that she was "removed by the messenger of death. Truly, she hath done what she could." One would suspect that perhaps Hannah was not well liked in her later years. It is obvious that she never married. But, why? Perhaps, no gentleman ever came along who could measure up to a love that she had lost early in her life. Perhaps she mourned him to the end of her own life. True love has no end....it has only a beginning.

And so, the story of Dick Trick and Hannah Midgley is told. If it didn't happen quite the way that I have written, it probably should have. Perhaps now their souls will be at peace.

CHAPTER ONE

Franklin, Michigan
August, 1861

The old dog was snoring contentedly when the first yellow rays of the sunrise slipped through the open window and caused her to blink, yawn, and stretch. She always slept on her own soft, frayed, rug next to her master's bed. She creaked to her feet and placed her muzzle on the edge of the quilt that covered his sleeping form. Her tail wagged hopefully as she watched for signs of his awakening. It was, after all, nearly time for breakfast. Happily, it had been a quiet, peaceful night. She had detected no suspicious sounds in the darkness that would have obliged her to bark a warning. There had been no sign that unknown evils might have been lurking about. If the raccoons and skunks had paid their usual nocturnal visits, they had been extraordinarily quiet about their respective rattlings and diggings. She had no reason to believe that there was anything unusual or different about the wispy August morning. It was simply time for breakfast....or, to be more practical....time for her morning constitutional before breakfast. She sighed. There was no response. She yawned, producing a loud squeak. That worked better. Matthew rolled over to look at her, smiled, and patted her head. "Good morning, Tansy. You must have slept well. You snored like an old threshing machine!" His bare feet hit the floor with a thud. "Come along, old lady." He padded to the kitchen door, lifted the latch, and let her out into the early sunshine. "Hurry back, Tansy!"

The old dog momentarily forgot her hunger as she became captivated by the fresh smells of the morning. "Hmmm!" she thought. "Rabbit was here. And squirrel was digging right there, and just ran up that tree!" She looked up to see the annoyed, bushy tail flicking high in the branches. Tansy wandered a little way down the road. "Aha! That mangy cur from the other side of the river has been watering our fence posts again! Got to teach him to stay away from here. One day I will catch him lifting his leg in my territory and give him a bite that he will not soon forget! Mr. Stud Dog had best just stay home and pee on his own posts." She snuffled her way a little farther to where the road overlooked the Van Every Mill. Little tendrils of mist, following their standard morning choreography, tried to hug the river as it coursed past the mill and squeezed under the rickety Franklin Road bridge.

There had been a mild chill to the night, as if to prophesy the arrival of another beautiful, golden Michigan autumn that was now just weeks away. The sleeping residents of the rural southeastern Michigan town had enjoyed the warmth of a coverlet over their toes during the night, but were soon obliged to uncover them again as the chill fled before the first warmth of the sunrise and the promise of another hot and dusty day.

The rumble of the cannon, and the rattle of the musketry, of the American Civil War....the War Between the States....was far to the south and east. Most of the villagers had slept undisturbed, smug in the belief that the horrors of war would never reach their soil. Their assumption was, in part, correct. The significant battles between the blue and the gray would remain hundreds of miles away. A few of the townspeople, however, were not so fortunate as to sleep quite so comfortably. They were the parents, wives, and sweethearts of the many young men who had either already marched away to war, or who were preparing to do so.

All of the villagers, with the exception of just one person, were oblivious to the fact that the war would touch their community in an entirely different, shadowy, and unexpected manner. Much to the surprise, and disbelief, of that rural community, a clandestine war would be quietly fought within the boundaries of their own little village. They could not have known that even early in the war the leadership of the Confederate States of America had realized that operatives must be placed in the north to glean essential military information, and to prepare the way for operations that could disrupt the Union from within. The Village of Franklin was already

2

indicated on secret maps and lists that were kept under lock-and-key in the secure offices of what soon would become the Confederate Secret Service Bureau.

The yellow sunrise glinted into Tansy's fading eyes as she sat in the middle of the Stoughton Road and scratched laconically at a persistently irritating flea. Some of her favorite mornings had been spent traveling that road as she helped her master to deliver farm produce to the Village of Piety Hill. Piety Hill, which would one day be renamed Birmingham, was just another quaint, clap boarded community located about ten miles to the east and an easy two hours travel by Congleton wagon along the Stoughton, or Fourteen Mile, Road.

Piety Hill had won the railroad. Franklin Village had not. The road grades were more manageable in the Piety area, and the line was more direct between Detroit and Pontiac. The old dog had traveled to that prospering little railroad town many times. She was usually allowed to ride, but was occasionally forced to trot alongside should the wagon be so heavily loaded with sacks of corn meal, or wheat flour, or barley flour, that there was no room for her. Even the seat alongside the driver would be often filled with cargo. On such an occasion it was clearly her duty to deliver well-timed and businesslike nips to the heels of the sweating team as they groaned, snorted, and flatulently defecated their way up and down the sandy rises and falls of the road. The product, after all, had to be delivered to the railroad where it would be transported north to Pontiac or south to Detroit. Wherever. Just so it made her master happy.

The return trip to Franklin was always pure heaven. The team was headed for home....and all horses love to go home....especially if all they have to pull is an empty wagon containing nothing more than a cheerful driver and his snuggling dog. The high quality flour from the Van Every Mill always fetched a good price from the Piety Hill agents. This happy circumstance often produced lots of whistling, singing, and ear-scratching along the way. Interestingly, there was a mysterious, glazed earthenware jug which was stowed in a carefully protected spot under the driver's seat. The contents of the mysterious jug apparently pleased the farmer considerably. He referred to it often, and with a celebratory flourish that was well-timed to prevent spills amongst the bumps and jumps of the wagon. The old dog could not understand how any living thing, human or otherwise, could drink the vile liquid. Matthew, her master, had let her taste some once.

3

He had poured a little into his hand for her one hot and thirsty day. One trusting lap had caused her to shake her head and to drool for at least a mile. The concoction smelled like dirty feet--people feet. "Tansy Bitters" the boss called the stuff. He was proud that he had fermented and prepared it himself according to his own secret, carefully guarded, recipe. Matt frequently shared his liquid treasure with his friends and neighbors, who always smacked their lips in appreciation. It was obvious, even to a dog, that people have extremely weird taste buds.

This morning, however, no trip to Piety Hill seemed to have been scheduled. Tansy turned to trot back up the hill toward the farmhouse. Breakfast, no doubt, would soon be served. She knew that on a normal morning, which this one appeared to be, it would take quite a while before matters reached the breakfast stage. She had no real reason, except for the increasingly persistent pangs of hunger, to hurry home. Normal mornings, for Matthew, were slow and reflective. He would roll out of his lonely bachelor bed at sunrise, starting a small kindling fire in the corner of the big cast iron cook stove in preparation for his breakfast coffee. He would often kneel in the sparsely furnished parlor near the picture of "Jesus In the Garden" which hung unobtrusively in the corner.

Matt always thanked his Creator for the new day. He frequently spoke sadly to Him as he asked for relief from the sorrow which for years had consumed his heart. His heart and his prayers still cried for Ellen. Ellen Trick. Beautiful, nineteen year old, sparkling, intelligent, witty Ellen. They had been hopelessly in love. Their devotion to each other had been so complete and consuming that at times they had seemed to exist within their own, private little world....to the exclusion of all else. They had planned to be married soon. Everyone knew that. The marriage date had been set. Even her staid, and somewhat grumpy, father was so comfortable with the arrangement that he turned his head with a muffled "harrumph", pretending to not notice that she did not return home on some nights. At least, he knew that she was safe in Matthew's arms, even though the behavior of the two love-birds would definitely not fit into the Victorian rule book. The prospect of a son-in-law of that caliber was well worth the risk.

Sadly, their beautiful love story did not have a happy ending. Instead, there was the unspeakable agony of Ellen's death. She had been tucked into her own bed, where she dutifully belonged, on that horrible night in 1851

4

when the Trick family home literally exploded in flames. A spark had crept through a crack in the masonry of a faulty chimney and sneaked upon the sleeping family like a rapist in the night. Mercifully, her sweet dreams were snuffed by the smoke and carbon monoxide before the beauty of her youthful body was consumed....never again to please the eye of mortal man, except in wistful memory.

Ten years of self-imposed loneliness and mourning had passed since Ellen had been taken from Matthew. He could not, and would not, forget her.

There were two kinds of nights for him in those lonely years. Sometimes, his dreams were so troubling that he was afraid to close his eyes after slipping under the quilted comforter. The old dog always circled in the darkness to prepare her sleeping place, then thumped, with a sigh, upon her rug. At least the dog was still there. He was not entirely alone.

During the good nights, exhausted from the labors of farming, he would fall asleep almost as soon as he pulled up the covers. His limbs would feel like lead, aching for rest. As sleep claimed him he could feel the warmth of Ellen's lithe body pressed against his. The excited nipples of her perfect breasts nestled against the bareness of his chest. Matthew could smell the faint fragrance of rose water in her hair. His tongue remembered the evenness of her teeth, the sweetness of her breath. He slept like a child in the arms of an everlasting love.

The other nights had left him exhausted and tearful by the time the first light filtered through the panes of the little farm house. The pretty morning songs of the cardinals and of the robins had struck him as the irritating utterances of creatures too stupid to realize that one should not sing during a time of tragedy and sorrow. When his eyes closed, he could not help but visualize the cluttered dwelling and outbuildings of the Trick farm. The humble farm was scattered along a slope overlooking the rutted trail that lead, eventually, to the little village of Inkster, a nondescript town which was struggling to justify its own existence somewhere far to the south. His dreams had watched, in horror, as the wooden house burst into flames in the night. It had ultimately collapsed upon itself into a funereal pyre of ashes and coals which was not more than three feet high.

In his persistent dreams, he could see Ellen's mother, blackened in singed night clothes, collapsed into the arms of their weeping neighbors. Grace, the miraculously unscathed middle child, clung to her swooning mother in silent, wide-eyed terror. Ellen's father was standing alone in his ridiculous long underwear. An empty bucket hung from his hand in useless testimony to the firefighting techniques of the time. Ellen's father's eyes only dully perceived as the flames licked away his labors, his dreams, his daughter. His dear, sweet daughter was gone.

In the firelight of his dreams Matt could still see Ellen's little brother writhing in the dirt just outside of the circle of flame. Young Dick was screaming from the pain of the deep, disfiguring burns which covered most of his charred body. "Sister! Sister!" he had cried with his seared lungs. "Help me!"

Ellen could not provide comfort. She was no longer there.

Now, ten years after the tragic fire, Matthew had finally begun to heal the painful slashes which had torn his heart, and very nearly killed his soul. Christians of the nineteenth century walked daily with their God. They spoke to Him often in prayer and read His Word in the Bible. They marveled in the gift of eternal life promised by Jesus. Matt was no exception. He took great comfort in the belief that someday he and Ellen would again walk hand-in-hand along the banks of the river. At the very least, they would walk along some river, somewhere.

He was somewhat surprised, almost ashamed on that particular morning, when his thoughts did not turn to prayer, or to Ellen, but to the young townswomen whom he playfully knew. His dark good looks and gentle, quiet manner had certainly attracted their attention. They sighed and giggled about him in their private, girlie conversations. They cautiously flirted with him whenever they were out from under the stern and watchful eyes of their parents. He was older, of course, and probably not to be trusted in the presence of virginal innocence.

He was not only handsome, but he seemed to be well-fixed financially. This was truly a winning combination for budding females who were in search of love and security. He politely enjoyed their attentions, and even returned them sometimes, but never allowed himself to be drawn into any meaningful relationship. The townspeople clucked sympathetically among themselves as they watched him make his daily climb to the little cemetery where he would kneel at Ellen's grave. He could often be seen running his fingers over her name, which was engraved upon the simple, flat stone, as though, somehow, he were actually caressing her in his memory. He always left something at her grave. Sometimes it was a prayer, sometimes a tear, sometimes a flower. His many friends feared that his grief was pushing him into insanity. Perhaps it was. Oh, he could still be fun. He could sing, drink, smoke, and be mischievous along with the best of them...but always there was that sadness that smoldered deep within his brown eyes. Even when his face smiled, his eyes did not....not until Bethany came to town.

Bethany was something of a mystery. She had somehow learned that Franklin was in need of a schoolmistress and had appeared, in person, to apply for the position. Her application was immediately accepted by the parents of the community, based upon her sweetness and upon her obviously well-educated intelligence. Credentials were not necessary in those days as capable teachers were in short supply. This was especially true for a school in such a rural location. Bethany was somewhat vague about her origins, but indicated that she was from somewhere in the south. Strangely, she did not speak like a southerner. There was no drawl, no "y'all". Instead, she spoke with a Midwestern twang that was charmingly seasoned with good grammar. Even though many of the villagers had no idea as to what was good grammar, and what was bad, they liked her "fine way of speakin'". They hoped that some of her language skills would rub off onto the little darlings over whom she would have charge.

Much to his chagrin and emotional confusion, Matthew was immediately attracted to her and she to him. She was slender, serious, and deeply religious. She was twenty years of age and appeared to be something of a late bloomer. At that age, Bethany teetered on the brink of spinsterhood, and by choice. She had simply not met a prospective mate who could meet her stern prerequisites for intelligence, education, and moral fiber. In Matt, she found everything of which she had ever dreamed, and set herself to capture him. In addition to her teaching duties, she had accepted the volunteer position of organist for the tidy new Methodist Protestant meeting house that was located down on the Mill Road. Bethany could sing like a sweet little bird. When her smoky blue-gray eyes looked directly into Matthew's, it was as though they were determining the depth of his soul. He would involuntarily tremble, just a little, when she locked her gaze into his. He had hoped that she would not notice his involuntary reaction....but notice, she did.

Bethany smiled to herself as she observed that her feminine wiles were finding their mark. She also knew, courtesy of her new and gossipy female friends, of Matthew's devotion to his deceased love. That devotion impressed her as sweetly, sadly charming. She began to dream that she might spend her life in the arms of a man who knew how to love that deeply. However, the thought that she would not be able to measure up to Ellen's mystical, amplified memory gave her a shudder. Bethany tortured herself with the thought that were Ellen alive, she, Bethany, would not have the slightest chance of winning the handsome prize. Oh well! Ellen was indeed gone. The slightly smug appreciation of that fact gave Bethany occasional little twinges of conscience. But, they were just that....twinges....and she could easily brush them aside. Ellen was good and gone...and that's that!

Tansy wearily climbed the wooden steps to the back porch and nosed open the kitchen door which she found to be unlatched, and slightly ajar. She sniffed a quick survey of the kitchen. Her bowl still stood empty, and no breakfast was as yet to be seen. She sought out her master, watching as Matthew selected his second best shirt from the collection that hung, washed and ready, in the armoire. She sat, and waited patiently, as he looked into the mirror and ouched his way through his shave. Sensing that nothing interesting was going to happen for a while, she curled up for a short nap to rest from the exertion of her morning excursion.

Matthew was having difficulty concentrating on his tonsorial efforts. Visions of Bethany danced in the mirror. He knew of many young and attractive women who were certainly available to respond to his charms, should he choose to apply them. Nevertheless, skinny little Bethany danced in the mirror and obscured them all. "How does she do that?" he mused aloud.

Tansy raised her head at the sound of his voice. Realizing that he was not speaking to her, she curled back to her watchful snooze. Apparently, he was not even speaking to anyone who was actually in the room. "Strange! Humans can be very strange." The old dog closed her eyes. "Perhaps" she thought "we are skipping breakfast and going straight to lunch!" Her stomach rumbled a protest as her master continued to stare into the mirror.

Matthew had recently made two major decisions which would forever change his life. First, he would respond to President Lincoln's call to arms. The president was pleading for men to join in the fight to save the Union. As an experienced cavalryman, he felt obliged to answer the call. In the jargon of the times he would "jine the cavalry". A Colonel Thornton Brodhead was in Pontiac, organizing a unit to be called the First Michigan Cavalry. Matt had already sent a written application to the colonel. It had been promptly accepted.

His second decision was one of the heart. He had resolved to ask Bethany to become his wife. Formerly, he had briefly considered two other local females as candidates for the wifely position. Smiling at his own half-shaven face in the mirror, he was startled to see that the smile that reflected back to him seemed to look just a little bit wicked as thoughts of the rejected females flitted across his mind.

Be it wicked, or be it not, he decided to entertain himself by reviewing, for the benefit of the face in the mirror, the womanly attributes of the ladies whom Bethany had so handily eliminated from the contest. "First, there is Mary Beth, with her long, beautiful, golden hair and her, well, ah, substantial physique. Strong, for a woman, too. A body that sings of good health and great promise!" He chuckled to himself. "She can work the farm like a man. She even knows some choice words and can cuss real colorful if she has to." Matt laughed out loud, causing Tansy's ears to twitch. "Nothing works better that a few fine cuss words, and some whacks with a big stick, to get a stubborn mule movin', or to pry a pig from under the porch!" He waved his razor for emphasis as he continued his mirrored observations. "Mary Beth can be sweet, cuddly, and giggly when she's of a mind to. She has bosoms that press so tight against the inside of her bodice that it appears that they will, one day, burst their way out!" He cackled at the bizarre thought. "Her buttocks have the very same problem. They may just gain their freedom, by the same means, but in the opposite direction! Lots of woman there," he mused "but the only way she's got Bethany beat is if you figure 'em by the pound!" He turned and addressed Tansy. "So much for Mary Beth." Tansy thumped her tail in uncomprehending reply.

Matt turned his attention back to his shave for a moment. "And, ah, ah, there's beautiful Hannah. Just a child. A lovely, lovely child who has all the tools of her trade, and then some! Her body is proportioned perfectly, and she moves with a natural grace that makes men and boys alike melt into helpless lumps! And she is only fourteen. Good maryin' age. I 'spect

Hannah knows very well how remarkable her assets are, and just how to use them to advantage." Matt snickered into the mirror as further thoughts struck him. "The lightest touch of her hand, the slightest brush of her breast, might just be enough to send a young man scurryin' to the outhouse for a few moments of reflection! I confess she's the best lookin' woman-child that has crossed my path since Ellen went away." He gulped as thoughts of Ellen guiltily returned to his consciousness. The smiling face in the mirror had turned sober in the realization that he was not just goofily titillating himself with thoughts of the two young women. He was really trying to deal with the fact that he was being untrue to his first love. He was not sure that he could handle that thought. Matthew swished his razor in the washbasin to remove the lather that clung to it, tapped it until it made mournful music on the rolled edge of the porcelain, then continued his shave, and his deliberations. For a moment, it seemed that it was Ellen who looked back at him from the mirror. The face looked sad, but kindly and approving. Her face, fading in the mirror, seemed to want him to go on with his thoughts. He shuddered. He had heard that talking to oneself was one of the first symptoms of impending insanity. Yet, there he stood, talking to a mirror, and to a dog. He shrugged away the notion of madness and stared hard into the mirror, hoping that Ellen would talk to him and tell him that she approved of his going on with his life. She would not, or could not, speak to him.

Matt made faces at the mirror as he inspected his shave and found it to be satisfactory save for a few minor nicks and scrapes that would soon heal. He paused, for a moment, to stare into the parlor at the picture of his Savior, then plopped into a chair at the kitchen table to savor his coffee. The dog followed as she tried to figure a way to communicate to him that he had forgotten about her breakfast.

Matt tipped his chair and stared out of the window at the neatly-maintained farmscape. Bethany, he mused, had gently, softly glided into his heart, and, just as gently and softly, pushed the image of Ellen further and further away. The recurring vision of Ellen, lying cold under all that dirt, had nearly driven him mad.... just as everyone had suspected. Bethany had caught him by the hand and brought him back to life, away from the precipice of insanity. He began to fully realize the true depth of Bethany's love for him. Perhaps, now, he no longer needed Ellen's approval. Bethany had already given him all of the answers....he had heard her speak but had not listened to her words....until now. He resolved to listen more closely to what his new love had to say.

Beth seemed to have a knack for understanding deeper concepts more quickly than he could. Her superior intelligence made him feel just a little embarrassed, once in a while, but he could deal with that fact even though women were not supposed to be as smart as their male counterparts. She knew her Bible well, and interpreted the teachings therein to be fresh and full of happiness. Further, she rejected hellfire and damnation as things that her loving God would not allow to exist. Her God, instead, would allow only forgiveness.

He had bravely shared the despair of Ellen's death with Bethany, even though he feared that she would consider him to be a fool....and walk away. She did not. Instead, she had added her tears of sympathy to his tears of sorrow. The living, she had said, must play the dealt hand. The dead must wait until all are united in heaven to work out the details of life and love. It was clear that Bethany intended to become a major player in both scenarios.

Now, he must go to war and leave his new love to long for him in his absence, or to grieve for him if he did not return. He was at once saddened, frightened, and excited. Nevertheless, he would serve his flag and his country. Matt could not help but worry that Beth would find some other love while he was gone. He worried about his little farm even though he had made appropriate arrangements for its operation. The poor, seared cripple, Dick Trick, Ellen's little brother, had been engaged to serve as caretaker. Matt sincerely hoped that Dick would be equal to the task. Surely, Bethany would supervise him to ensure that reasonable order would be maintained. The crops were already mostly gathered. Dick seemed capable enough to feed the animals and to mind the house. Matt had arranged for his neighbors to sharecrop most of the carefully drained and maintained acreage, starting in the spring.

The horrible defeat of the Federal forces at Bull Run near Manassas Junction, Virginia, had just occurred on July 21st. Brigadier General Irvin McDowell had been dishonored and removed from command as scapegoat for the fiasco. Major General George McClellan was subsequently appointed by President Lincoln to replace poor McDowell. McDowell was actually a very good general. Politicians had ordered him to the offensive without time or materiel for adequate preparation. Someone had to take the blame. Apparently, Lincoln and his cabinet would not do so. The delighted and serious McClellan was already busily arranging to rebuild the shambled army near Washington. The nation was sundered and in despair. Washington, D.C., could very soon be overrun by the rebels. Congress was calling for thousands of volunteer soldiers. Matthew Greyson would be one of them.

Matt would ride to Pontiac, that very morning, to complete the terms of his enlistment. He finally remembered to feed the waiting and appreciative dog her long-awaited breakfast. He thoughtfully fed her an unusually large helping of scraps and leavings from the kitchen. As he stepped off of the back porch, Matthew gazed wistfully across the harvested fields and at the neatly red-stained barns and outbuildings of his farm. Now, he had to leave it all behind and go to war. There was no way to know whether he would be gone just for the duration of a short enlistment....or whether he would be gone forever. The sheep and a pair of beef steers were on the far side of the pasture blissfully munching their own dew-moistened breakfast. The two draft horses, along with Matt's handsome sorrel gelding, leaned across the wooden fence and whinnied loudly for their morning oats. He grained Molly and Moe only lightly, for they had no work to do that day. A full ration might give them a bellyache. The sorrel received a little extra as fuel for the trip to the north.

Chores finished, he curried, saddled, and bridled the gelding. Swinging easily into the saddle, he rode down the hill and turned left across the bridge. As he passed the mill, and trotted his mount up the sandy hill beyond, he noticed that the old dog was plodding, as best she could, at the horse's heels.

"Go home, Tansy!" His voice was stern as he pointed back across the bridge. "You can't come along this time."

The poor dog acted as though she had been struck by a switch. Her tail drooped and her chin nearly dragged the surface of the dusty road as she turned back. Tansy's faded brown eyes turned to look at Matt several times, just in case he might change his mind. No such luck. Matthew dug his heels into the sorrel's flanks, and they were gone. There was only a curl of dust mixing with the morning mist to mark where they had been.

A small rise on the southwest corner of the intersection afforded a good view of the road upon which her master had disappeared, and upon which he would certainly return. The blue flowers of chicory and the yellow blossoms of her namesake tansy mixed there in profusion. Tansy struggled up the bank and settled into her selected observation post. Surely, he would not be gone long.

The cardinals were chirping their happy "pit pit pit" as they went about their morning business. The mourning doves moaned about a sadness which only they understood. There were a few preliminary thumpings and clankings from within the bowels of the mill. The long day had only begun.

CHAPTER TWO

Come Jine the Cavalry!

The gelding trotted easily up the long hill from the river. At the summit, Matt pulled up to stare at the small, weather-beaten Presbyterian Church that sat, unpretentiously, on the west side of the road. Matt had worshipped there many times with Ellen. It had been her church home. The last service that he had attended there was Ellen's funeral. He had not been back since for fear that the shadow of her coffin and the echoes of mourning would feed his sadness, his sense of loss, his depression. Shutters closed, and door pulled firmly shut, the church seemed to be resting from the labors of the previous Sunday. Nevertheless, the gilded cross on the abbreviated steeple seemed to beckon to him to come inside.

Matt shook his head. "I'm not ready yet." He patted his horse's neck. "Great day for a nice ride, hey Saber?" He held the horse to a leisurely walk for a few minutes. "Should have gone in that church, seein' as nobody is around to watch me fly to pieces, and get it over with. Well, maybe next time I go by. Saber boy, let's go for a little ride to take us away from here." From the church at the top of the hill all the way to Wing Lake the Franklin Road was fairly level and quite smooth. Matthew eased him through the trot and into an easy rocking-chair canter. Satisfied, he loosened the reins and lightly touched his heels to the animal's flanks. Saber was off like a reddish streak, his rider leaning low over his neck.

Henry Cox was riding in the same direction but at a much more leisurely pace. He looked over his shoulder and was startled to see Saber's speedy approach. He pulled up and moved his mare to the side of the road to watch him thunder by. "Golly whoppers!" whistled Henry as both he and his startled horse stared after the fast-disappearing duo. "Matthew sure as hell is in a hurry to get somewhere!" Henry spurred to follow at a brisk trot. It did not take long to catch up with them as Matt had pulled up and dismounted just before the road began to slope downward toward Wing Lake. He had tried to walk Saber down the hill, while they both caught their breath, but the horse danced and pranced--still feeling the excitement of the exhilarating run. He then led him into the lake where he could enjoy the coolness of the shallow water on his hoofs. Saber was being allowed a few sips of water when Cox, astride his sturdy mare, trotted toward them.

"Halloo, Matt!" I've seen some chaps in a hurry before but I believe you win the prize!" He rode into the lake to join them but stayed mounted as he did not wish to either remove his boots or to get his pant legs wet.

"Halloo to you too, good Doctor Sawmill Sawbones!" Matthew was up to his knees in the water, pant legs and all. "Sorry about the dust. Both Saber and I needed to work out a few kinks this mornin'."

Henry looked Saber over with an appreciative eye. "Indeed! If he can go that fast with kinks imagine what he could do without kinks! I believe I would wager a greenback or two on him if he were put up against almost any horse in the county."

"And it would be money well wagered, Henry." Matthew wore a pleased smile as he fussed with Saber's mane. "I'm right proud of this boy. C'mon in. The water's nice and cool."

"Thank you, no. I'll just stay up here high and dry while I watch you slosh around. I hear we may be soldiering together in Brodhead's Cavalry. I suppose that is where you are heading in such a hurry?"

"Yep. This morning I'm to find out if they meant what they wrote about wantin' me to join up. Might just change their minds when they get a good look at me."

Cox cackled from his vantage point in the saddle. "Of course they'll want you." He scratched his chin in mock thoughtfulness. "But if they don't they will at least take your horse."

"Very funny. You all signed up?"

"Indeed so. For three years of military bliss. Do you expect that the war will last that long? Three years?"

"Could just be that long, Henry. I know some about those southern folks. They're a tough breed."

"Aw, we can whip those bad boys with no problem." He was a short, stocky, but well-muscled Englishman who had been in his adopted country for about twelve years. His speech was clipped and rather aristocratic compared to Matthew's backwoods drawl. Cox was known to be an excellent equestrian having been brought up riding to the hounds across the British countryside. His skill made him a perfect candidate for service in the cavalry. This fact was not lost on Colonel Brodhead who had signed him speedily upon learning of his qualifications. Henry Cox was honored to be enlisted as a corporal. Strangely, either by design or by clerical error, his age at enlistment was entered in his military records as twenty-five. He was actually thirty-five years of age at the time and was married to Grace Trick. Grace was Dick Trick's surviving sister. She and Henry would manage to produce five daughters before she met her own untimely death at the age of twenty-eight. In 1861, however, she was very much alive, in good health, and not to be ignored. Henry loved her deeply and forever.

Cox was never to experience combat in the war. He was with the First Michigan Cavalry when they marched from Washington toward Frederic, Maryland. When their supply wagons became mired in the mud he suffered a leg fracture in the process of trying to free them. To this injury was added a nasty case of dysentery. His problems required him to be hospitalized. The military doctors learned of his medical training while he was in their care. Upon sufficient recovery, he was ordered into the hospital service rather than being returned to the cavalry.

Henry was commissioned Assistant Surgeon in 1864.

After the end of the war he enrolled at the University of Michigan in order to complete his medical education. The admired and respected Dr. H.S. Cox subsequently looked after the health needs of the Franklin villagers until his own body failed in 1910. His many friends laid him to rest in the Franklin Cemetery next to his beloved Grace who had predeceased him by many years. They lie within the pleasant grassy knoll roughly fifty paces north of where Ellen Trick had been interred so many years before them.

Matthew retrieved his boots and the two rode north together. "What about your sawmill, Henry? I hear its doing well."

"It is. I just sold it."

"Now, why would you do that?"

"Simply because it is doing well. That's the time to sell for the best price."

"Makes sense, I'd guess, but only if you don't want it anymore."

"Precisely. I scratched that itch and now its time to move along. I believe I'll go back to medicine after the rebellion is put down."

Matt thought a moment as they cantered side by side. "Makes sense to me. Be a shame to waste your education as a surgeon."

"Precisely."

Henry, if you don't mind my askin', how is Grace taking all this? She can't be too happy being left alone to care for the children while you run off to serve Father Abraham!" Grace had grown into a pretty, no-nonsense wife and mother. Matt could not help but notice how much she resembled Ellen even though she was not quite so lovely, not quite so caring, and not quite as sweetly charming as her sister had been. Grace had sometimes noticed Matthew staring at her but she did not seem to mind. She had intuitively understood that, although he was looking at her, his sad eyes were really seeing Ellen. She pitied his despair. She shared his sorrow.

Henry shrugged. "Well, as you know, my Grace has strong opinions. She feels that this is a stupid little war that will soon be over. Hope she's right. When the war is done I'll come back and make some more babies with her."

They slowed their horses to a walk. Matthew threw one leg affably over the pommel while he shot his friend a mischievous grin. "More babies, eh? My goodness, Henry! I can't believe how many things you are good at. Sawing boards, fixing broken bones, riding horses, and making babies. Maybe you should write a 'how to' book."

"Perhaps I should!" grinned Cox. "And you can be the first to read it. Maybe even you can learn to do those things. We'll start with the lovemaking part."

Matt snickered. "Already know how, Henry."

"Do you? I'm relieved to hear that. Now all you need is someone to do it with. Its a lot more fun that way."

Matthew howled with delight at the witticism. "Surely, you are right about that one, Henry. Guess its no secret that I'm hoping Bethany will share her love. Think she will have me?"

"I'm sure she will. I can tell by the way she looks at you. She's sweet on you as could be."

"Hope so." Matt scratched his head reflectively. "Least I think I hope so."

"You better hope so or you will have a problem. Beth is surely stuck on you." They resumed their canter. "One can tell a lot by the way a woman looks at a man." Henry was happy to share his knowledge of the machinations of the fair sex. "For instance, I could tell by the way Grace looked at me, when I bid her good-bye, that she was thinking of the possibility that I might be returned to her in a box."

"Pish. You're too mean and ornery to die young."

"Right. I hope you are right." Cox smiled with a bravado that he did not really feel. Henry was not a fighter by nature. He was, instead, a healer. His instinct was to save lives, not to end them. However, his adopted country had called to him to help defend the glorious flag. He would fight if he must. "Best of luck to both of us!" Henry guided his mare so that they rode stirrup to stirrup while cantering along the dusty road. He extended his hand. Matthew warmly grasped it. It was the hand of an old friend and of a new comrade-in-arms.

"Good luck to you too, old friend. May God be willing that we will do our duty and return in one piece!" Matthew knew first hand of the horrors of war. He had seen the grotesque, decaying forms of too many brave men being covered with charcoal and nailed into pine coffins. The two rode on in silence.

Pontiac was a hot, dusty, bustling place that August morning. It rang with the sounds of growth. Heard were the sawing and banging of construction, the rumble of iron-shod wheels on the bumpy streets, and the countless clip-clops of horses going at various speeds in every conceivable direction. Matt and Henry wound their way through the remarkable mix of traffic. There were heavy six-horse drays, buggies, wagons, scurfy-looking workers, Indians, mounted soldiers, gents in top hats, and ladies parasoled against the heat of the sunshine. The ladies, of course, took the greater part of their attention as they busily tipped their hats to the pretty, and even sometimes to the not quite so pretty, young damsels in hope that they would be rewarded by a coquettish smile.

Sam Brotherton's Railroad Hotel was a homely place, but rather large, thus suiting the purposes of the military. The proprietor himself greeted them at the front desk and directed them into the tavern room. They blinked for a moment at the door while their eyes adjusted to the dimness within. In a corner sat a contingent of blue-clad officers, each nursing a neat whiskey, while they attended to their military affairs. The table was covered with lists, manifests, requisitions, and the like.

Colonel Thornton Brodhead threw back his chair at their approach and hustled around the table to greet them with a smile and an extended hand. "A pleasure to finally meet you, Matthew Greyson. And a pleasure to see you again, Corporal Cox."

"Thank you, sir!" they chorused.

Colonel Brodhead was a proven warrior having served with distinction in the Mexican War. The popular fifty-six-year-old was a native of New Hampshire but had resided in the Detroit area for nearly twenty years during which time he had attained great popularity and respect. He had offered his sword to the service of the federal government at the outset of the rebellion and was almost immediately placed in command of the First Michigan Cavalry. The unit was thereafter affectionately known as "Brodhead's Cavalry".

Thornton Brodhead was fiercely loyal to the flag. He had no patience with those who would defile it, be it by secession, or by any other disloyalty. Instances of poor leadership within the military could throw him into a sputtering rage. Yet, he was a kindly man and friendly by nature. He was genuinely concerned for the welfare of those who would serve with him. His face was clean-shaven as he chose to display its natural features rather than to hide them under a bristling mustache or itchy whiskers. Thinning brown hair and a receding hairline bespoke his age. Matthew liked him instantly. Henry was a little awed by the sight of the impressive group of officers who were assembled at the conference table.

The colonel turned his attention to Henry. "Corporal Cox, have you brought your horse?" He chuckled. "Or rather, has he brought you?"

"Indeed he has, sir" quaked Henry.

Matthew struggled to control a guffaw which almost escaped his lips. "So!" he chuckled to himself "it appears that the cavalry wants Cox's horse as much as they want Cox!" At the earliest opportunity he would remind Henry of his previous smart remark regarding Saber's enlistment to the cause.

The colonel was obviously pleased to see his command forming around him. "Good! Corporal, please report immediately to Captain Angelo Paldi of Company G. He is most eager to meet you." A wave of the hand indicated the stiff young sentry at the door. "Private Adams, also of Company G, will direct you."

Brodhead took Matthew by the shoulders. "Welcome, and congratulations, Captain Greyson." Matthew's eyebrows raised in surprise as he absorbed the colonel's unexpected congratulation. "Captain, sir? I did not expect to enlist as an officer."

"Captain indeed! A man of your experience and military talent should expect nothing less. Let me introduce you to your comrades. Gentlemen--". They all scraped back their chairs and rose to meet their new associate. "Gentlemen, may I introduce Captain Matthew Greyson. He is a resident of the Village of Franklin which is situated in the Township of Southfield. Matthew is a decorated veteran of the War on Mexico, having been twice wounded. He has been commended for bravery by General Winfield Scott himself. Captain, meet the staff of the First Michigan Cavalry: Lieutenant

Colonel Joe Copland, Surgeon George Johnson, Adjutant William Brevoort, and quartermaster James David. Please resume your seats, gentlemen." Brodhead pulled a chair to the table for Matt.

"Now, my friends," said the colonel once they were seated "it is important that you know, right from the start, that Matt was born of southern parentage, raised, and educated in the south. I wish to dispel any problems or speculations before they may begin. Specifically, you are advised that Captain Greyson has received his initial military training as a cadet at the Virginia Military Institute. Like many other southerners in the federal service, both leaders and men, Greyson has fortunately elected to remain with us in the fight to preserve the Union. His loyalty is unquestionable. We are most fortunate to have a man of his military experience on our side. Believe me, I am delighted to have him with us! Matthew, have you anything to add?"

"No, sir." Matt was feeling a little uncomfortable. "You have covered my history very nicely. I am, of course, open to any questions that you gentlemen might have."

Surgeon Johnson cleared his throat and spoke first. "Captain, please tell me about your wounds. Have they left you with any problems?"

Matt managed a shy grin. "Fortunately, Surgeon Johnson, there is nothing for you to repair. One wound was by lance that was delivered to my shoulder by a dying Mexican horseman. The second was caused by a musket ball which penetrated the width of my horse, killing him, and then lodged in the calf of my leg. Neither was serious enough to cause lasting difficulty and both are completely healed. I'm ready and rarin' to fight, doctor, and promise to stay as far away from your services as I possibly can."

There was considerable chuckling and a few guffaws at the surgeon's expense. He did not seem to really mind, but pretended that he did. "Just remember, all of you, you'd best be nice to me. I'm the gent with the knife and saw who may or may not be called upon to save what's left of your sorry asses. The level of my expertise, in your cases, might just depend on how well you behave."

"Oooooo!" they cried in mock fear.

"You can bet I'll behave!" exclaimed Matt.

"Mr. Greyson" interrupted a more serious Lieutenant Colonel Copland. "May I tear you away from the current unpleasant subject long enough for you to explain why and how you happened to attend V.M.I.? It is my understanding that many of the students and faculty of that institution have sworn their loyalty to the Confederacy."

"Certainly, colonel. I understand your concern." Greyson shifted a bit uneasily in his chair. The unsmiling officer seemed intent on questioning his loyalty. He could sense the beginnings of an inquisition. "I hope I can answer, sir, without boring you. I'll try to be brief. I was born in Halifax, Nova Scotia, the son of North Carolinians who had moved there to engage in the tobacco export business. In my infancy my mother died. A few years later my father, who was a veteran of the War of 1812, died also. This left me in the care of an aunt who still lived in North Carolina in a little tobacco-farming community called Durham Station. As my father was a military man my aunt determined that I should be given the opportunity of a military career also. So--she enrolled me at V.M.I. when I came of age."

"I see" mused Copland. "And just how did you get from there to here, if I may ask?"

"You may, indeed, but I fear that you will not find the story very interesting. Immediately after graduation I joined the U.S. Cavalry and served in the Mexican war as Colonel Brodhead has mentioned. After the war I decided to pursue a gentler life. One in which nobody would be trying to run a lance up my backside."

"Aha! We're back to your ass again!" chortled the surgeon.

"Really, Surgeon Johnson, perhaps you should try to control your warped humor for a moment!" chuckled Colonel Brodhead. "Go on, Greyson."

"Not much more to it. On a whim I traveled here to the Great Lakes area and took employment as an able seaman on various commercial vessels that were plying those waters. I worked long enough, and studied hard enough, to rise to the levels of first mate, and of navigator before I became bored with the maritime life. After about three years on the water I felt like I had visited every Great Lakes port worth visiting. To make a long story short, I then bought a small farm in Franklin and have worked it for some years since. And, I hope to work it for some years more after the unpleasantness of the war is over."

Matthew looked the Lieutenant Colonel straight in the eye. "If you will, a part of me is definitely southern. If you have a problem with that, kindly tell me now." He switched his gaze to Colonel Brodhead who smiled approvingly.

"Well done, Greyson. Are you satisfied with what you have heard, Joe?"

The lieutenant colonel, who had been sitting ramrod-straight in his chair during the questioning, glanced around the table at his fellow officers. Several smiled and nodded their approval. Joe Copland relaxed and leaned back in his chair. "Quite satisfied, thank you. Welcome, Captain Greyson."

"To Captain Matthew Greyson!" called Brodhead as he rose to his feet and held his glass aloft.

"Greyson!" They all followed suit. Sam Brotherton, the omnipresent proprietor, circulated to quickly refill the glasses. Visions of a nice fat bar bill danced in his head as he tried to keep track of the number of shots poured.

It was Matt's turn to rise. "To Brodhead's Cavalry! May we be the pride of the State of Michigan as we strive to serve our country!"

"Hear hear!" Sam scuttled to refill the glasses yet again until Brodhead called a halt to the impromptu celebration.

"Gentlemen, this meeting is ended. We'll meet again tomorrow. Be prepared for a little more work and a little less whiskey. There is a great deal of preparation to be done before we move to Detroit. You are excused to attend to your duties. Greyson, please remain. We have some details to attend."

Matthew remained in his chair while the cavalrymen filed out of the room. Colonel Brodhead clasped his hands behind his back and watched through the window as his officers clustered for a moment in front of the hotel. The glittering gold of their insignia and the deep blue of their uniforms made a splendid sight as they adjusted their hats, lit their cigars, and bid each other good-day.

"Matt, I have special duty for you. For the time being I am assigning you to my headquarters staff rather than to a specific company. As a former army regular, I need you to organize and to train. Our officers mostly don't know Hardee's Tactics from Aesop's Fables. Our recruits haven't a clue as to what is going on. I'm counting on you to transform a collection of country boys into a fighting unit second to none. I believe that you are the man who can do just that."

Matt was somewhat overwhelmed by his new and challenging responsibilities. "I'll do my very best, sir, but over a thousand men and horses could be something of a chore."

"Of course. Care for a cigar?"

"Thank you. I believe I will."

Brodhead scratched a match on the bottom of his chair and lit both cigars. "This would be nearly impossible for only one man. I have, however, good news. A skilled drillmaster, Sergeant William McEwan, has been detached from regular service and assigned to our regiment. Should work beautifully. You can teach tactics and command. He can instruct in formation, drill, and such. Sound reasonable?"

"Um, quite reasonable, I think, sir." Matthew was still a little dubious. "When do we get to work?"

"Just as soon as you go home,. say your good-byes, and collect your effects. Are we agreed?"

"Of course. If I may ask, what about uniforms, tack, side arms. and the like?"

"Quartermaster David is fitting officer's uniforms as we speak. He also has a good supply of regulation leather for your mount. I assume that you have no problem with committing your own personal horse to the service?"

"No problem at all, sir." Again Matt had to suppress an inward chuckle. Here was the horse thing again! "Saber is well-trained and ready to report for duty. I'll appreciate the opportunity to have him serve with me."

"Saber, eh? That is a fine martial name for an officer's horse. As he is yours I expect that he is a good one. The only problem we have is with side arms. I have requested a quantity of the new Colts, as well as regulation sabers, but they are not, at present, available."

"With your permission, colonel, I have both my Colt Walker and the saber that I used in Mexico."

The colonel puffed on his cigar. "Really! How fine! How is it that that you are still so well-armed?"

"I personally purchased the revolver. The saber was engraved and presented to me by General Scott."

"Wonderful!" The colonel reflected for a moment, the cigar smoke curling above his head. "A Walker, eh? You are better armed than most. We'll issue you a new 1860 Model Colt as soon as we can get our hands on some. The new Colts are smaller, lighter, and have provision for a shoulder stock. They make a dandy little carbine for cavalry operations."

Matt flicked the ash from his cigar onto the floor next to his chair. "Yes, sir, but I'm sure you know that the Walker is more powerful than the new model."

"So I have been given to understand. Fully charged, the Walker is said to be practically akin to artillery!"

"Well, not quite. But, maybe pretty near!" chuckled Matthew.

Colonel Brodhead shrugged and rose to leave. "You may carry whatever you wish. If we lose a Parrot we'll call upon you to provide covering fire!" The colonel turned back to the business at hand. "Why don't you look up McEwan and take him with you to Franklin? Might give you a chance to get acquainted while you go home to pick up your gear and say your good-byes."

Matt stood to salute his commander. "I'll do that. Thank you."

"My pleasure. I'll see you in the officers' car on the way to Camp Lyon."

"Camp who?"

"Camp Lyon. Its actually an old race track in Hamtramck. You'll find it less than charming."

CHAPTER THREE

A Silly Old Black Dog

The workers at the Congleton Carriage Shop were, as usual, hard at their tasks that afternoon. The soothing music of the blacksmith's hammer-upon-anvil echoed up and down Franklin's main road as though to announce that another fine carriage, or a wagon, or a buggy, was under construction.

"'Scuse me, Mr. Congleton." Dick Trick stood nervously at attention before his employer with his broom held as though he were a rifleman on a parade ground..

"Richard, my boy, what'll it be?" George Congleton did not bother to look up from his work. A thin curl of white ash blossomed over the blade of his spokeshave as he coaxed a graceful buggy wheel spoke out of the rougnsawn blank that was clamped into his vise.

Dick tried to make himself look tall, and important, but with little success. "Can't work here no more, sir. Least not for a while. Mr. Greyson is goin' to war and I'm to run his farm. He left this mornin' to jine himself up."

"Really?" Congleton puffed away the shavings and ran his fingers over the wood. Those fingers seemed to marvelously know which part had to stay and which part had to be whittled away. He turned to fix the nervous youth in a kindly stare. "Are you sure you can handle it?"

"Yessir. He already taught me all I'm to do and I remember what he said real good. Matthew says this job will be the next best thing to goin' to war

26

myself, 'cause if I do his chores for him, then he can go. He knows better'n me how to be a soldier....and he ain't slowed up like I am. Dick shuffled his toe in the sawdust and shavings that already littered the floor that he had just swept. "Rather, though, I'd like to go with him and have me one of them fine blue uniforms with all the gold an' such."

George patted the boy on the shoulder and tousled his hair. "Don't guess you'll get a uniform just yet, son. You're still a mite young. Give yourself a couple more years."

Dick looked distressed. "But....but in a couple more years the war may be over and I'll have missed it!"

"Well, I suppose that could happen. It wouldn't be all bad if it did. Look on the bright side. Perhaps Matthew will pay you enough to afford a new set of trousers. Those you are wearing are right disgraceful."

"Yessir. Haven't given much thought to the way they look." Dick gave an embarrassed hitch to his baggy and patched pants which dangled from the ends of a very tired pair of galluses. "Says he will pay me with real greenbacks. By war's end, I could be rich enough for a whole new suit."

"Maybe so. Maybe so." chuckled Congleton. "In any case I'll keep your job open should you need it, sometime. War shouldn't last more than a few months once McClellan gets our boys whipped into fightin' trim." The spoke shave produced another curl. "You'd best get to it, son. You'll have evening chores to do."

Dick ceremoniously placed the broom into its assigned corner. "'Bye, broom!" He gave it a mock caress. "Don't guess I'll miss you too much." His belongings were few. It took only moments to gather them from the storeroom at the back of the buggy works where Mr. Congleton had kindly allowed him to stay. His heart was light as he limped at full speed up the Stoughton Road. He had never had any real responsibility before. No one except Matthew, and perhaps his schoolteacher, Bethany, had realized that within his scarred body lived an intelligent person who was perfectly capable of good judgment and reliable behavior. His greatest hurt came from beautiful Hannah, who deemed him to be beneath her consideration. He secretly worshipped her, but did not dare to let his feelings show for fear that she would laugh at him. He put such thoughts out of his mind as trudged up the hill. He had work to do.

Molly and Moe, the draft horses, watched skeptically over the fence as the whistling ragamuffin, toting his sack of meager belongings, clumped onto the porch and into the house. The paddock was pretty well devoid of grass, as it was late in the year, and the pickings were small. Lots of nibbling yielded little solace to their huge tummies. They whinnied their hopeful impatience, and were soon delighted when the evening hay was served promptly by their new benefactor who zipped through his chores like a lopsided whirlwind in accelerated slow motion.

It was not until Dick sat panting in the squeaky rocker on the porch, after pumping the stock tank full, that he realized that Matt's dog was missing. Tansy was nowhere to be found. She was not on the porch, under the porch, in the kitchen, in the bedroom, in the barn, or anywhere. His whistles and calls were answered only by the silence of the deepening shadows.

"Damn. Damn, damn!" he shouted into the darkness. "First day on the job and things are already shitty!" The rocker squeaked furiously. "Ol' dog never goes anywhere. Whup! Tried to follow Matthew to Pontiac? Oh no! Too old. Shit. She'll never make it. Matt will fire me if something happens to that dog. 'Sides I love her 'bout as much as he does. Tansy! Tansy!"

He strained to listen, but could hear nothing. There was not a sound, not a bark, not a whimper. Dick might have to walk all the way to Pontiac to look for the stupid dog. A lantern hung next to the door, and a spouted can of coal oil sat nearby on the porch. His clumsy efforts to fill the lantern spilled nearly as much oil as he managed to get into the reservoir. Dick reached into his shirt pocket for a match but, fortunately, decided against striking it so close to the spilled coal oil. He knew of the dangers of fire more acutely than did just about anyone. Moving to a safe distance out in the door yard, he scratched the match on a stone, adjusted the wick, and set off down the road. He carefully checked the ditches on both sides, but with no success.

He decided that, next, he had to check the possibility that she might have fallen down the bank and/or ("Oh no!") tumbled into the river. Dick was lying on his belly in the dust, calling her name while hanging his head and his lantern over the side of the bridge, when he became aware of a feeble, answering bark. The sound seemed to be coming from near the intersection that he had just passed. After some searching, he finally found her. She was still stationed, dutifully, at her post on the little rise above the road where she lay nearly hidden by the tall grass and the flowering weeds. The old dog's black coat had soaked up the hot August sun like a sponge. Now, even in the coolness of the night, she was still hot to the touch, her tongue hanging and dry, and her chest heaving for breath. Still, her nose pointed northward like the needle of a compass. Even as she lay on her side, barely able to move, she strained for the sound and sight of her master's return.

"Tansy, Tansy! Why didn't you come back home?" Dick knelt beside her and tearfully stroked her feverish head. "You're burning up, girl." There was a feeble wag in reply. He gave her a reassuring scratch under the chin. "Be right back, Tans."

A small home was just a few rods away. Peter VanEvery had dug a wondrously deep well there. It always contained sweet, cool water.... even in the driest of seasons. Dick turned the lantern low, and rotated the windlass of the well as quietly as possible in order to avoid arousing the sleeping occupants of the house. Finding no handy container, he untied the bucket and took it with him. The VanEverys, he told himself, would not mind all that much. He would return the stolen vessel in the morning.

He tenderly supported Tansy so that she could drink. When her lapping slowed, he ladled the cool water over her head with his cupped hands. Dick knew that he could not possibly carry her back up to the house by himself. He looked to the south along Franklin Road. The whole town seemed to be asleep. No assistance would be available unless he awoke someone....and that did not seem to be a good idea. "Guess we'll rest here tonight, Tansy. Don't you worry. I'll not leave you here alone."

He curled up to sleep next to the wet, trembling dog. Together, they nestled into the sweet-smelling weeds. Thankfully, there were no hungry mosquitoes to bother them. The late summer dryness had caused the annoying little creatures to disappear. The lantern flickered and went out, its fuel exhausted. No longer thwarted by the lantern's glow, the summer night folded around them. There was no disturbance save the soft, eerie warble of a little screech owl who was singing his spooky song from somewhere down by the river.

+ + +

The first light of morning found Mrs. Pitts Lanning already stirring. She loved to arise early and well before the bustle of the day began. Weather permitting, she would perch her plump self upon the front porch swing with her current sewing project spread across her ample lap. From her vantage point aboard the wooden two-seater, she could keep a sharp watch for anything of interest that might occur up or down the Mill Road. Looking directly across from the porch of the parsonage, she could admire the new, little, white Methodist church as the rising sun made it seem to glow. She was proud of that church, and for good reason. Her husband, the Reverend Pitts C. Lanning, had shepherded the little Methodist flock during its construction. Of course, in her unbiased opinion, the project never would have been properly completed had she not been there to advise and to counsel.

Mrs. Lanning smiled to herself, in sweet satisfaction, as she expertly repaired a tear in the bodice of Bethany's blue and white striped gingham dress. Bethany, who had boarded with them since she had been hired two years previously, was a fine teacher and musician. Her sewing abilities, on the other hand, certainly left something to be desired. "Ah!" she suddenly exclaimed. Her alert eyes had spotted a figure approaching along the road. "My goodness! Its the Trick boy. Now why would he be out and about this early?"

Dick shuffled warily up to the porch steps. "Mornin' Missus Lanning." He looked mostly at his feet.

Mrs. Lanning set aside her mending. An investigation was unquestionably in order. The boy's suspiciously early arrival coupled with his nervous manner indicated that he probably had a problem that he could not handle by himself. "Now why aren't you doing your chores, boy, instead of wandering around town? Don't you try to tell me that you have all of Mr. Greyson's critters fed and watered already."

Dick squirmed. He suddenly had the desire to run away but somehow managed to control the urge. "No, ma'am." he blurted.

"Humph. And what about the chickens? Did you feed the chickens yet?"

Dick struggled to gather his fading courage. "No, ma'am. Not just yet. I've come to see Miss Bethany."

"What in the world for? I don't believe that she is even up yet."

"Surprise! This sleepy head is out of bed!" Bethany smiled from the front door as she tied her soft black hair with a ribbon.

Dick watched as the long hair fell fetchingly over one shoulder. He had never thought of her as being a pretty woman before. He had always regarded her as just the skinny, not very tall, and stern but pleasant schoolmistress who always had her hair drawn into a severe bun, befitting her position of academic authority. Somehow, the morning light seemed to make the schoolmistress part of her vanish. She stood in the doorway as a lovely, slender girl who was a pleasure to behold. Dick was entranced.

Mrs. Lanning caused the springs that supported the porch swing to chirp in protest as she swiveled on her fanny to face the doorway. "My goodness, child, you're up early. Don't usually have the pleasure of your company at this bright hour."

Bethany stretched and yawned, holding her hand properly in front of her mouth as she did so. "I have managed to get myself out of bed early to practice the hymns for Sunday before too many folks are around to hear my mistakes." explained Bethany with a fetching smile. She took a look at the awestruck youth. "Something wrong, Dick? Your mouth is hanging open wide enough to catch a passing fly or two."

Dick's mouth slammed shut. "Sorry, Miss Bethany" he stammered. He forced himself to get back to the business of the morning. "Miss Bethany, Matt's dog is awful sick. Wish you'd come and take a look."

Bethany instantly read the boy's sincere concern. "Oh dear. Of course. Mrs. Lanning, if I'm not back in time for breakfast I'll just fix my own. Please don't wait for me."

Mrs. Lanning adjusted her avoirdupois on the swing. Again, the springs registered their squeaky complaint. "Very well, love. But, don't forget to start the day right. I'll have a good breakfast waiting for you. You're skinny as a fence rail now, dear. You mustn't miss any meals, or you will blow away with the first good wind."

"Well now. I just don't believe that I look quite that bad!" Bethany twirled to display her trim figure.

Dick tried to stifle a giggle as he looked from plump Mrs. Lanning to slender Bethany and back again. Mrs. Lanning seemed to read his thoughts. A stern look from the annoyed lady wiped the smile off of his face. She was obviously about to mount an attack upon his imperfect manners even though he had not said a single word that was out of line.

The best defense, he thought, would be accomplished by means of a speedy retreat. Dick called a polite good-bye over his shoulder while his feet, not failing him, carried him out of range of any possible unpleasantness. Bethany followed. Dick could not help but notice that she picked up her skirts, ever so daintily, to keep them out of the dust of the road. He was delighted to see glimpses of trim ankles visible just above her slippers. Tansy seemed to be anxiously awaiting them when they came to her. She was a little stronger, but still too weak to stand. She could, however, lift her head while her tail wagged a feeble greeting.

"Looks like the heat stroke, I'd guess" pronounced Bethany as she took charge of the situation. "And maybe a little broken heart thrown in for good measure!" She knew first hand about broken hearts. She had done little but think about, and pray for, Matthew during the last twenty-four hours. The specter of his possible death or injury, as a result of the horrible new war, hung over her. She had not really been out of bed early that morning to practice on the church organ. She simply had not been able to sleep for fear that she would never see Matthew again.

Tansy seemed to gather more strength as Bethany cradled the dog's panting head on her lap. The heat of the summer sun was intensifying rapidly and soon would be directly upon them, certain to rekindle Tansy's discomfort.

"Dick, run to see if Mr. Congleton can help us. Maybe he can hitch up his buggy and carry her up to the house for us." Dick obediently limped his way across the road to Mr. Congleton's shop.

Bethany cooed comfortingly to the old dog. "Don't you worry, Tansy. Your master will come back. I've prayed, and prayed, and just know that he will." Tansy seemed to understand. She, too, was certain that he would return. After all, he always did. Beth was not really quite as confident as she pretended to be for the benefit of the listening dog. Her hands, white as ivory, caressed the blackness of the fevered ears. "Here we sit, Tansy, the two charter members of the local 'Broken Hearts Club'." Bethany sighed a shuddery sigh. She lifted her eyes to the heavens to offer yet another prayer. The prayer was barely upon her lips when it was interrupted.... or perhaps answered....by the sight of two horsemen riding down the hill, past the mill, and toward them.

"Oh, Tansy, look!" She supported the dog's head so that she too could see.

Tansy looked. Even at that distance, her failing sight could still recognize Matthew and Saber returning home. She started to bark, as best she could, in her hoarse, whispery voice. Her master had indeed returned, just as she knew that he would. Both riders were resplendent in regulation blue army uniforms. Their kepis sparkled with the golden crossed sabers of the cavalry. The sparkle was echoed by the gold-embroidered captain's bars on Matt's shoulders. The horses seemed to sense the proud spectacle that they displayed. They held their heads high, dressed as they were in new black leather, including the latest in McClellan saddles. At the bridge they began to prance, Matt's sorrel acting the more giddy of the two, knowing that he was nearly home.

Bethany wanted to call out, to applaud, or to cry...but did not know which to do first. There seemed to be no breath left in her body. The tears that welled from her eyes were the only response that she could muster, try as she might.

Captain Greyson spotted the swirl of gingham on the little rise above the road. There was something about the cascade of the long black hair, which matched the blackness of the dog on Bethany's lap, that raised a lump of concern in his throat. He spurred forward and made an unconsciously flashy dismount in the rising dust. Passing the reins to his sergeant, he hurried up the little hill.

"Bethany? What's wrong?" He dropped to his knees beside the trembling pair. "It's Tansy. She's really sick." Their eyes met, his brown and questioning, hers blue and urgent.

Dick returned from his mission, scrambled up the rise, and collapsed dramatically next to them. He was a puffing, sweaty mess. "Oh, Matt! You're back. Thank God!" Dick was wheezing uncomfortably.

"Yes" said Matt calmly "I am indeed back. Would you two mind telling me just precisely what the hell is goin' on?"

They both overlooked his profanity and proceeded to babble in chorus. "Heartsick dog. Heat stroke. Out all night."

"Mr. Congleton is coming to take her back to the house!" panted Dick.

"I see." Matthew was beginning to decipher the situation. "Dick, please go tell George that we needn't bother him. An' don't forget to thank him for his kindness."

Dick heaved wearily to his feet. "I will. I will. I surely will. Geez. Are we sure we don't need him?"

"We're sure, Dick. Now get goin', son."

"Yessir." Dick scrambled down the little hill.

"Dick."

Dick paused in mid-scramble. "Aw, what?"

"Whose bucket is that?"

"VanEvery's, sir."

"Did you steal it?"

"Kind of." Dick tried to look ashamed of himself. He didn't feel ashamed but he attempted to look that way, anyhow. "From VanEvery's well" he confessed.

"Best take it back to where you found it. Mrs. VanEvery will be looking for it by now so you'll be obliged to knock at the door and explain yourself."

Dick stood at attention. "Yessir."

"Then, take Sergeant McEwan up to the house and get him settled in the spare room."

"Yessir."

"And the horses will need to be curried and brushed before you turn 'em out. The sergeant will show you how to properly care for military tack."

"Yessir." Dick reached for the bucket.

"And, Dick...."

"Sir?" He was again standing at attention.

"Thank you for taking good care of Tansy. You've done well and I'm right proud of you."

Dick's scarred face blushed under its tan. "Thanks, Matt. I sure done my best." He grabbed the bucket and scrambled over to McEwan who was still sitting his horse. "Name's Dick, sir." He was at attention again and attempted a snappy salute. Sadly, his arm was just too stiff to present a proper military appearance no matter how hard he tried to overcome his handicap.

The sergeant was quick to understand. He returned the salute and then leaned down to shake Dick's hand. "Pleased to meet you, Dick. I'm Willy McEwan. I believe that you and me will be the best of friends."

"You bet, sergeant." Dick was thrilled.

"Call me Willy." Dick had never had a real soldier for a friend before, except Matthew. He wiggled with excitement, but suddenly realized that he was about to wet his drawers.

"'Scuse me. Got to go." Dick was undergoing a real outhouse emergency but tried, with all of his might, to keep his composure, and with his composure, the appearance of his trousers. "Be right back, Sergeant Willy. Got to return this here bucket."

"Take your time, son." McEwan swung out of the saddle to stretch his legs.

Dick hurried behind the nearest bush that would screen him while he discreetly relieved himself. This urgent chore completed, he hustled to make his confession to Mrs. VanEvery.

Bethany struggled to twist a tough stalk of Queen Anne's Lace from its firm anchor in the ground. With the flower as her weapon, she went on the attack. She tickled Matt's face, neck, and ears with it in mock fury. McEwan chuckled at the sight of his newly-acquired, obviously distinguished

35

captain being teased by a slender little girl. Best of all, the captain looked flushed and embarrassed as he tried to gain control of the little creature. Bethany wielded her flowery ordinance skillfully. "How come you can't just stay at home and stop causing everybody so much trouble?"

Matt caught her graceful hand and held it trapped against his heart...flower and all. "These are just not stay-at-home times, little missy."

"Poo!" Bethany coyly retrieved her hand.

"Poo? Poo to you too, young lady. Whew! I believe its getting hot here. Shall the three of us seek a cool spot?"

"By all means, sir."

Matt easily lifted the sixty-pound dog off of her lap. Tansy loved the additional attention and wagged with renewed strength. Bethany ruefully surveyed her ruined dress.

"You owe me a dress, Your Majesty, Captain Matthew Greyson." She curtseyed while holding the splotched skirt so that he could see the damage.

"Tell you what. I'll owe you a bar of soap so's you can wash it."

"It would appear that generosity is not your long suit."

"I don't even own a long suit."

"Oh, stop! Let's go before you drop the poor dog." Bethany dismissed his idiocy with a wave of the hand.

"Stop! Go! Stop! Go!" muttered Matt as he plodded up the hilly road. The incline seemed to increase the weight of his burden. "I swear, it seems as though we are already married."

"Careful, captain. That almost sounded like the edge of a proposal."

"Don't flatter yourself, lady. Nothing could be further from my mind than marriage."

"Fine. And don't you flatter yourself, either, mister. I haven't yet seen anybody around here worth marrying," she lied, "present company included."

They stopped in the middle of the road to look into each other's eyes. Matt was beginning to tremble under the weight of the dog. "Excuse me, ma'am, but could we continue this discussion some other time?"

"Maybe yes. Maybe no. Straighten up there, young man, and don't drop that dog!" Bethany gave him a daring pat on the rear, then danced and skipped impishly while he groaned his way up the hill. Her ribboned hair, falling to the middle of her back, made her feel particularly frolicsome.

"Young lady," puffed Matt, as she gave him a quick hug from behind, and then twirled away, "I'm going to send you home for your snood if you don't behave. You are looking, and acting, more like twelve, than twenty. Got to admit, though, you do have a certain charm about you."

She stood in his path, arms akimbo, effectively blocking his progress. Her pretty eyes blazed into his. "That doesn't sound like a compliment to me."

"It wasn't." Matt shifted the weight of the dog in his arms. "If I tell you the truth, will you get out of the way?"

"Depends."

"You are the prettiest twelve-year-old I ever saw."

"Not good enough."

"You're the prettiest twenty-year-old I ever saw."

"That's a little better. But you forgot sweet, witty, charming, intelligent. Stuff like that."

"Yeah. I did, didn't I? Now kindly move out of the way or Tansy and I will run over you."

She reached across the dog and took Matt's face in her hands. She kissed him, her lips hungrily parted, fully on the mouth. "Still think I'm twelve?"

"Goodness me! That kiss was as grown-up as could be! You just wait, my sweet, until I can put this dog down. I aim to find out if you have any more of those."

"Judging from the way you are struggling up this little hill, I doubt that you'll be much of a kisser when, and if, we get to the house."

"You could be right." Matt was starting to pant with the exertion. "Care to carry Tansy for a while?"

"Thank you, no. Nice of you to ask, though." Bethany skipped on ahead, brazenly making certain that he would have the opportunity to admire the way her slender fanny could move.

Dick and Willy watched the lovers' antics from a distance as they followed, leading the horses. Dick was waving and pointing as he acted as a tour guide for his new friend. The VanEvery mill, the potashery, and the distillery were all clustered by the river. The remains of an old, abandoned, steam-powered flouring mill were on the flats below. To their left, and above the road, was the Barnum's little home. Next-door to them stood the Smith family's cottage.

"This road got a name?" asked McEwan.

"Got three."

"Pshaw."

"But, its true. Called Fourteen Mile Road 'cause its fourteen miles from someplace or other. Called Townline Road 'cause it runs between the Town of Bloomfield and the Town of Southfield. An' called the Stoughton Road after some of the first folks who settled here some thirty, or maybe forty, years ago."

"My! You're a regular walkin' 'cyclopedia." Sergeant Willy was impressed. "How'd you get to be so smart?"

"I have a good teacher. Miss Bethany."

"Bethany is the schoolmistress? Do tell! Don't act like no teacher I ever saw. Most of 'em are mostly stiff, stodgy, and spinstery."

Dick chuckled. He was happy to share his inside information. "Well, I 'spect she's near old enough to be a spinster. Could be she figures Matt might just fix that."

38

McEwan threw back his head with a hearty laugh. "I believe you could well be right, son. Appears to me that she's about got the captain whipped into shape."

Dick was quick to come to Bethany's defense. "She don't need no whip. Everybody loves her. Even them rough, big boys in the school don't give her no trouble. They just sort of wilt when she speaks to 'em. She tells 'em what they are to do, and they just up and do it....right quick."

Will was getting some amused insight into the relationship. "Sounds like she is a good match for the captain. I've only known him for a day, you understand, so I could be wrong. Seems, though, that nobody dares to sass him 'cept her. He's got a tigress by the tail in that little lady."

While Matthew plodded the last few yards up the road Bethany ran ahead to find Tansy's rug in the bedroom, carry it to the porch, and neatly spread it for her on the coolest and most shaded portion of the porch floor. The porch itself was comfortable and spacious. It was constructed to provide shade and shelter on three sides of the house, leaving only the back of the dwelling unprotected. One could, therefore, select the best conditions for sitting, depending upon the time of day. Matt gently placed Tansy on the rug and offered her water, which she took, and food, which did not interest her. The porch had no railing between the white-painted posts which were spaced regularly along its perimeter to support the roof. The flooring was a good example of Matthew's fussy pride in his dwelling. It was sanded smooth and painted a shiny, cool gray.

Matt and Bethany sat next to the dog, with their legs comfortably over the edge of the porch, and talked softly about the war, about where he would go, and about when he would return. Bethany tried, but unsuccessfully, to be brave. Their parting was now so close upon them that she began to cry on his shoulder. He stroked her pretty hair. No one could know when, or where, the war might end. They spoke, tenderly, of the bond that had formed between them, of the painful separation which they now faced, and of their love, a love which was surely so deep that it could easily transcend any and all of the wartime trials which might come their way.

Matthew turned her face toward his, with his fingers gently under her chin, and kissed the tears from her eyes. He struggled to find the words which would best express the feelings of his heart. "I reckon that everything's been said between us except the one thing that I figure can't be left unsaid any longer. Bethy, will you be my bride soon's the war is over?"

Bethany sat there, wide-eyed, for a moment. The startled, almost mesmerized, look on her face betrayed the depth of her love as her very soul locked itself into a study of his tender smile. He knew her answer before it came. Had Matthew been wearing his cap, it would have gone flying. Beth emerged from her trance with a hug that was almost a tackle, bowling him over onto his back while his knees remained dangling over the edge of he porch. She covered his face with kisses. "Oh, yes! Yes. Yes!" Each "yes" was punctuated with another kiss.

Matt laughed when she let him up for breath. "May I take that to be an affirmative answer, my love?"

"You may indeed, sir." She pushed him back to the floor, her soft breasts a delight against his chest. They kissed some more. Each caress had more meaning than the one just preceding as their bodies drew tightly together. Matthew could feel her nipples growing firm as he ran his fingers over the bodice of her dress. Beth, giggling, wiggled her way on top of him. His manliness was growing erect as they became aware that their bodies were separated by only a few intervening, annoying, layers of cloth. Bethany paused in her seductive ministrations long enough to regard him from nose-to-nose range. "Tell me that you love me."

"I do love you."

"How much?"

"With all my heart."

"Good answer, Mister Soldier. And, in case you might be interested, I love you with all my heart, too!"

"I knew that."

"My, you are so smart. Oh, Matthew, please don't go away."

"But, I must."

"Yes, I know. You must." She wiped some tears away and replaced them with an impish look. "Say, Captain Wonderful, aren't you supposed to give me a ring, or something, on such an occasion as this? I mean, after all, I have just promised to give my whole self to you forever."

Matt sighed, his passion momentarily stilled. "Goodness! You are indeed a quick little woman!" He hugged her so tightly that she could barely breathe. "To tell the truth, I didn't really plan on this happening today, so I'm not well prepared."

Bethany teased as she put her fingers over his lips to quiet him. "You are forgiven. I suppose I can wait until you are better equipped for the occasion!" she sniffed, pretending to be annoyed.

"Are you telling me that you think there is something wrong with my equipment?" He pulled her hand to his groin so that she might check... which she did with some considerable attention to detail.

"Um," she breathed "I don't seem to be able to find any problem at all!" They snuggled and kissed some more. "Matt, love, I want you now. Right now."

Matthew was more than willing to oblige.

"But..." Beth interrupted his concentration.

"Oh, Lord! But what?"

"Don't be grumpy. I just want to go into the house before you have me completely naked for all the world to see."

"I don't guess the world is ready for such a pretty sight!" She sealed his lips with a giggly kiss. "But, I certainly am....whoops!" Matt had caught a glimpse of someone rounding the corner of the porch and walking toward them.

"My! Such behavior for so early in the day!" It was Sergeant McEwan, who was wearing his widest grin. Beth raised her head and smiled at him without moving from her position of advantage.

"Sergeant," admonished Bethany, "Surely you can see that we are busy at the moment."

"Yes, ma'am. Indeed I can see that. 'Deed I can! It does appear that I'm definitely not needed around here at this particular moment. I 'spect I'll go poke around town if it's all right with you, captain."

"Fine!" exclaimed Bethany, as though the permission were up to her. She brazenly returned to her kisses. Matt could only wave his hand in a "go away" gesture. Willy chuckled to himself as he strolled down the path that was a shortcut to town. With an accuracy that would put a homing pigeon to shame, he located, without hesitation, the cool depths of the well-stocked tavern within the Franklin Hotel. Will immediately made the acquaintance of the proprietor and bartender, George Green, who was busily organizing the bar in preparation for the slaking of the many thirsts which would soon be arriving when the sun climbed closer to noon.

Sergeant McEwan was a man who knew how to enjoy the finer things in life, most particularly, a good cigar and a nice morning whiskey. Mr. Green happily supplied both. Will settled himself into one of the scarred, oaken chairs and made ready for a late morning of pleasant conversation with whomever happened to wander within range.

The sergeant had barely rounded the corner of the porch before Matthew and Bethany pushed, shoved, giggled, and hugged their way into the farmhouse. Tansy looked disappointedly after them, but did not try to follow. She stretched, with a sigh, upon the rug that Bethany had so thoughtfully provided for her comfort. "After all," thought Tansy, "they don't seem to have time for me, right now, anyway."

The lovers' headlong dash for the bedroom halted for a moment at the kitchen window just long enough to check on Dick's whereabouts. They were pleased to see him still busily grooming the horses. "Hope he stays busy for a while!" smiled Matthew.

"A good while!" cooed Beth, as she planted more kisses.

Bethany pushed the bedroom door closed. The tiny click that it made, as the latch fell into its notch, seemed to mark the end of one world and the beginning of another. There was no room for wartime concerns as their minds, their souls, and their bodies focused entirely upon each other. Their universe, to the exclusion of all else, began and ended in that little, humble room. Each button, unbuttoned, seemed to sing a tiny, unforgettable symphony as they undressed each other. Matt, at last, lifted her, beautiful in her nakedness, and placed her tenderly upon the quilted coverlet. Their love was fulfilled as they were united in the sweetly savage rhythm of passion that has delighted man and womankind since that fabled affair in the Garden of Eden....and, hopefully, will continue to delight the children of God until He allows the very last star to fade into the blackness of eternal night.

"Oh, Matt, I love you so! Let's do some more!" gasped Bethany. Matthew supported himself above her and kissed her eyelids, her nose, and her pale, pink nipples that were moving with each excited breath.

Matthew murmured as he kissed her again and again. "Oh, we will, my love, we will! But, if you don't mind, you'd best allow me a little time for reloading!"

"Humph. You sound like a soldier....even at a time like this."

Matt held her close as they rolled across the bed in snickery happiness. "Bethy, I have something for you."

Really? I do like what you have given me so far. I'll have another helping, please."

Matt gave her a sweaty smile. Their bodies were wet with the perspiration that sprang from the heat of love which, in turn, was amplified by the sweltering temperature of the August day. He paused for a moment to look at her. A drop of perspiration fell unromantically from the end of his nose and landed squarely between her eyes. "Oops!" he chuckled. "Sorry, my love!"

Bethany burst into uncontrollable gales of laughter as she tried to wipe the offending droplet away. "You're quite a lover, captain. I guess I'll just have to keep you!" She struggled, rather unsuccessfully, to control her merriment. She could see that he was trying to be serious. "Tell me, my sweet, in-between drips if you can, what is it that you have for me?"

Matthew was just a little peeved. "Well, you can laugh at me all you want.... but I do have something special for you. It's meant to go right here." He kissed a spot that was between and just above her breasts.

"You do?" Her eyes were wide. "I can't imagine what else you possess that might go there. I mean, so far things have been pretty straightforward, if you don't mind the pun, but...." she tapped the indicated spot on her chest...."right here?"

"Yes, I do mind the pun. And yes, right there!" He tapped the same spot with an emphatic finger. "Life will be full of pleasant surprises should you care to share it with me!" Matthew vaulted off of the bed and rummaged through the contents of the top drawer of his bureau. He returned to kneel next to her on the bed. His hand held a small gold cross, which was suspended on a delicate chain, for her inspection. The cross was of finely-crafted solid gold and was exquisitely carved. "Will this do as a token of my love? I mean, will it do for now? It belonged to my mother."

Bethany looked at the sparkling treasure as he placed it in her hand. "Oh, Matt, it is absolutely beautiful!" She suddenly felt a little ashamed that she had been so brazen. "You don't really have to give me anything right now. I was just having fun with you. Knowing that you are mine is all that I need! Really! This must be very precious to you if it belonged to your mother."

"It is, and so are you. Mother would have wanted you to have it. I want you to wear it always. When I'm off to war, and far away, I want to be able to think of this cross pressed close to you....right where I'll always wish I could be." There were tears of happiness in her eyes as he lifted her to fasten the clasp behind her neck, then gently lowered her head back upon the pillow. The cross glowed brightly as it nestled close to the beauty of her breasts. He kissed away her tears. "Bethy, I'll be traveling through some big towns before our unit has to get down to serious business in the south. Those big towns, like Baltimore or Washington, will certainly have some fine jewelry shops. I promise that I'll bring you an engagement ring on my first leave, or I'll send it to you if I can't deliver it in person. It'll be a ring that will make you the envy of every lady in Oakland County!"

Bethany giggled. "Silly, I am already the envy of every lady in the county. They just don't know it yet! I have you, and they don't!" She snuggled into his neck. "My own little soldier boy! You are all that I've ever wanted, ever prayed for. But," she chirped brightly, "you can bring me a ring, anyway, if you really want to." She raised up to flash her mischievous smile at him. He was so filled with love that he did not notice that the smile was, at that moment, just a little empty, just a little forced. Her own heart had suddenly begun to ache as his mention of travel toward the war zone brought back to her the reality of their impending separation. She kissed him desperately. "Oh, Matthew, love me some more. Oh, please love me some more!" She wiggled herself under him. His love again expressed itself deep within her slender body.

Matt dozed, when they finally rested, his passion for the moment exhausted. Bethany, on the other hand, was totally alert. Her body was finally released from her long pent-up desire for fulfillment. "Hmm," she soliloquized, "Mrs. Matthew Greyson. My, what a pretty name! Mrs. Bethany Dodge Greyson." She sighed a happy sigh and snuggled tightly against Matt's sleeping form. "I love my new-name-to-be! It has a nice sound doesn't it? Matt?" She shook him, not wanting to lose a moment of his attention. "Doesn't it?"

Matthew groaned. "It does, my love. Indeed, it does have a fine sound to it."

She was quiet for a moment, then shook him again to ensure his attention. "Matthew, please don't let those Johnny Rebs hurt you."

Matt stroked her dampened hair. "Believe me, my little one, I'll do my very best to stay in one piece. It would take one hell of a tough reb to take me away from you!" Her concern brought a pensive shadow across his thoughts. This, indeed, would be a very inconvenient time to die, especially in a war that was probably unnecessary, and certainly was the product of political stupidity. The promise of life with the little dark-haired beauty in his arms was unquestionably more important to him than was any war ever fought. The shadows in his mind deepened. He began to regret that he had offered his services to the First Michigan. Nevertheless, Greyson was both a patriot and a man of his word. He would go, and he would serve his country to the best of his ability. Bethany stirred in his arms and delivered a smiling kiss that caused the gray shadows to fly and the sunshine to return to his mind. His body would go, but his heart would stay in Franklin, in Bethany's care, until he could return. "Bethy, would you please promise to pray for me every day that I am gone?"

"Oh, I will. I do promise. And will you pray for me? I'll need prayers, too."

"You will?" He looked at her quizzically for a moment. "Well, you can bet I'll remember you in my prayers every single day. And that'll be easy, as

I'll be thinking of you all the time anyway! And, I'll take great comfort in the fact that you'll be safe here and far away from the war. I'll thank the Lord for that, while I'm at it."

Bethany took him by the chin and looked deep into his eyes, then looked away. "Just don't forget to pray. I may well need all the prayers I can get while you are gone."

"Why? You're not planning to get sick, or to let Molly or Moe step on you, or anything like that, are you?" A vision of the Trick's farmhouse, in flames, raced across his eyes. Matthew was suddenly alarmed. "I couldn't stand it if anything would happen to you. Are you worried about something that I don't know about? If you are, tell me. I want to know right now."

Beth smiled and patted his cheek. "Never mind. It's nothing." she lied. "And, I'll be careful as can be. It's just that I will miss you terribly."

"And I, you."

She pointed a finger comically at his nose as though her hand were a pretend gun. "See that you don't forget me while you are off soldiering, or I'll find you wherever you are."

"And whip me with a flower?"

"Probably."

Dick was finished with his chores. The horses were curried and brushed to perfection. He admired his own handiwork as he turned the handsome, shiny creatures into the paddock, put his tools away, and headed for the kitchen. It was high time for a snack. Dick was surprised to see that the bedroom door was pulled firmly shut. Bethany and Matthew were nowhere to be seen. It took only an instant to put the two bits of information together. He smiled to himself, and even blushed a little at the thought of what he suspected might be happening behind that closed door. After quietly cutting for himself a slice of bread, and a thick wedge of cheese, he took up his crude fishing pole and set a course for the river. He paused to give Tansy a reassuring pat as he passed where she lay, still waiting patiently, on the porch.

"Surely, Tansy, they'll come out of there sometime." He thought for a moment. "Well, maybe they will and maybe they won't! We'll see. They're

46

bound to need food or water sooner or later. They'll be along, Tans. Just don't you worry."

The old dog watched him shoulder his pole, shuffle across the road, and disappear into the woods beyond. She knew that the familiar path led to the edge of the bluff and then slid down to the river where the hungry fish lurked in the deep pools. She was alone again, but not quite. Her sharp ears could hear the whisperings of familiar voices from within the house. Again she settled herself to wait. Faithful dogs sometimes have to put up with a whole lot of waiting.

There were two white oak trees shielding the house from the summer sun. One stood on either side of the little dwelling. Their trunks were straight, and silvery gray, and measured at least four feet in diameter. Their broad, strong bases had allowed them to defy winds and storms for several hundred years. Their lowest branches were high enough to interlock over the ridgepole without touching it. Somehow, probably by chance, they had survived the onslaught of the settlers who had perceived the magnificent trees as the enemy. They had survived those who would girdle, slash, and burn them in huge funereal pyres in the headlong rush to till the fertile Oakland County soil. The pioneers knew that it was soil that could produce apple trees and cornfields second to none....anywhere.

One hundred years later, this same soil would be buried and wasted by a new frenzy: The construction of obscene-sized houses, parking lots, shopping malls, asphalt paving, expressways, and whatever else would accommodate the greedy for profit. This latter-day exploitation would be fueled by the rabbit-like expansion of the human population....this in itself obscene and uncaring. The Creator would have been better served if more of the space could have been reserved for oak trees, or for bloodroot, or for the monarch butterflies who would travel thousands of miles from Mexico to nest in milkweeds that were no longer there. Yet, butterflies or no, it seems that man must have his place in the sun.

In spite of the deep shade provided by the giant oaks, the noonday heat finally flushed the lovers from their secret place. Beth and Matt emerged to giddily splash at each other with the cool water from the well as they attempted, rather unsuccessfully, to set their disarrayed selves aright.

They were ready to tell the world of their love, even though most of their world could hardly help but already know. They resolved to spread the happy news of their engagement immediately. They would start with their dear friends, the Reverend and Mrs. Lanning. First, however, it would be kind to check on the old dog who still lay, waiting expectantly, upon the porch. They went hand-in-hand to her. She responded with a happy look and a wagging tail.

"Tansy, we are to be married, and you will be with us always." Bethany delivered the news as though the dog could understand.

The black tail made a seemingly comprehending thump upon the gray-painted boards.

"Tansy, do you approve? Surely, you do!"

She wagged another thump.

Again, they sat together on the edge of the porch. Tansy lay her head on Bethany's lap with a sigh of contentment. Matthew scratched the soft ears and looked into the eyes that once were sparkly brown, but now were dull and cloudy with age. But, cloudy or not, within those eyes still burned the sweet fire of love for her master. She was already in heaven. She could hear kind words, uttered by familiar voices, and feel the kind caresses of familiar hands. No dog could ask for more.

Matt lay back upon the hard flooring, closed his eyes, and was momentarily lost in wistful thought. He was disturbed by his dog's weakened condition. He was convinced that such a faithful dog must have an eternal soul. Surely, his God would not ignore the sharing of love between man and beast, nor would He allow such love to end forever. Perhaps sooner, perhaps later, perhaps bullet, perhaps old age, Matt would one day knock at the heavenly gates and ask to speak with his Savior. Tansy would certainly be there, wagging, to welcome him home. "Such sweet love could never die!" he mused aloud, suddenly breaking the silence and causing the mutual raising of both Bethany's and Tansy's eyebrows. "I mean, there must be a lot of rompin' goin' on up there. Seems to me that if you can take human friendship with you beyond the grave then, surely, a person should be able to find the spirit of his dog in eternity."

Bethany shot him a wry, sideways look. "Pardon me? I have the feeling that you are letting me in on the middle of a conversation. Care to start over so I can know what in the world you are babbling about?"

Matt looked a little sheepish. "Sorry. I 'spose you'll think me a little crazy, but I was just thinking about dogs' souls."

"Dog souls? Hmm. Maybe you're just a little strange, Matthew Greyson. Perhaps your Christianity is seasoned with a little touch of Buddhism."

"A touch of what? Buddhism? Who are Buddhisms? Don't think I ever met any of those." Matt sat up and scratched his head in wonder. The thought returned to him that, perhaps, his lady was an uncomfortably smart person. "Now, love, how do you know about Buddhisms?"

"I'm a schoolteacher, remember? Hello? If I didn't have a little extra knowledge, then I wouldn't have anything to teach. Everybody would already know everything that I know." Bethany snickered. "I'd have to take up a new trade....like farming or soldiering."

"Very funny." Matt pretended to be hurt by her unseemly aspersions upon his occupations. Actually, he really was a little miffed. "So, what is so wrong with being a farmer, or a soldier?"

She gave him a laughing peck on the cheek. "Nothing, of course. I happen to love somebody who is both of those! Now, let me tell you about Buddhisms....I mean Buddhists. Goodness! You've got me saying it wrong. Buddhists are gentle people who, unfortunately, worship big, fat idols. The good part is that they believe that all creatures," she patted his arm to emphasize her point, "including dogs, yaks, and all matter of beasts....including people....enter eternal paradise when their life on earth is over. How about that? You see, we are not the only ones who hope and pray that it is so."

Matt's eyes searched Bethany's face as he mulled the earnestness of her little discourse. He brightened. "Aha! There! See, Tansy, we are all saved! Even the Buddhisms think so. Tansy? Aw, damn. Tansy?" He shook the dog, gently, as though to awaken her. The sensitive, caring nature of the man sprang to the surface as tears began to flow down his cheeks upon the realization that the light that had been in her faded eyes had finally flickered out. Tansy--gentle, sweet, loving Tansy--was gone.

There was a hush around the farmhouse. It was as though every living thing was suddenly holding its breath. Even the breeze stilled, and the protective branches of the old oaks were silent. It seemed that even trees could pray when a soul is freed from its cares and takes wing to fly happily away.

Matthew's and Bethany's tears mingled as they mourned the passing of their friend. They cried quietly together as they cradled her, and stroked her head, as though to give her enough love to last her on her journey. Love, after all, was love. Love united all creatures fortunate enough to experience it. Love was life. Love was eternity.

Matthew and Bethany looked through their tears into each other's eyes. They could feel that something sacred, something holy, had just taken place. Their love for each other had been forever blessed by, of all things, a silly old black dog.

THE FRANKLIN HOTEL ca 1840
Courtesy of Franklin Historical Society
Artist: David Johnson

CHAPTER FOUR

John Brown's Body

The Reverend and Mrs. Lanning shared a great joy for life, a great love for their parishioners, and a great fondness for celebrations. They adored their every opportunity to organize and sponsor picnics, parties, dinners, parades, or anything else that was fun. Now, they had two real occasions to celebrate but very little time for arrangements. Unfortunately, McEwan and Greyson had to report back to Pontiac on the very next day in order to entrain with their unit for Detroit. The soldiers could not be present at the coming Sunday service to hear the prayers that would be intoned on their behalf. There was no time for the traditional "dinner on the church grounds". However, the men were delighted to settle for an invitation to breakfast with the Lannings on the morning of their departure. It was not to be just an ordinary breakfast. It would be an ENGAGEMENT BREAKFAST. Bethany was thrilled.

Various plans and arrangements were hastily made. Reverend Lanning would announce even more good news than usual from the pulpit on Sunday. He would make the official announcement of the betrothal. All were saddened that Matthew could not be present to share in the congratulations. Bethany would have to receive the good wishes without him.

Matthew and Bethany had settled upon a new, and perhaps controversial, arrangement. Bethany would move into the farmhouse immediately after Matt's departure....gossips and raised eyebrows be damned. They were determined to do what seemed right for them. She would brighten the otherwise empty home alone until such time as, the Lord willing, she could share it with her beloved.

Dick would be banished to the barn. The three of them swept and dusted the cozy little tack room that adjoined the horse stalls. It was to be his new home. They cleaned the wood-burning stove and removed the cobwebs from the nickel-plated finial that decorated its top. A loosely-organized group of sullen and objecting spiders were evicted from their chosen homes and swept out of the door. The flyspecks and dust were washed from the single, small window. The bunk was supplied with a cheerfully colored quilt. Dick was more than pleased. The back room at Congleton's had not been nearly so snug and pleasant. He carefully hung the framed, formal portrait of his parents on the wall where he could see it from his bunk. He recalled that they had left the picture with him, and with his sister, Grace, when they had gone away. They had thought, perhaps, that the portrait would help their surviving children to remember them until such time as they could return. Dick did not really need the portrait to jar his memory. His recollection of his parents was vivid and clear. Nevertheless, it gave him a feeling of comfort when he looked at it. He remembered how they had cared for him until his burns had healed and it was determined that he would live to breathe adequately enough to sustain a reasonably normal existence. His parents had arranged with a neighboring family to care for Dick and Grace until they could return to claim them. They had sold the burned-out farm and left enough money to cover the children's' expenses. The elder Tricks had looked back, smiled, and waved good-bye to the sobbing six-year-old and his sister as they stood in the middle of the Townline, or Inkster, Road. His dry-eyed, seething sister had tried to comfort Dick by holding his hand. With his free hand, he had held the portrait to his scarred chest. Dick was convinced that surely, one day, his parents would return to take them away to some wonderful new home. Sadly, Mr. and Mrs. Trick were never seen again. The neighbors were convinced that the fiery loss of their favorite daughter, Ellen, had driven the Tricks to some pernicious form of shared depression. It was gossiped, and rightly so, that the parents had reasoned that the horrible recollections of the fire, and of the tragic loss of their daughter, would lessen if they moved away. Their intentions, very probably, were good. The result, however, of their faulty decision was indescribably unfortunate. Their two abandoned children would forever weep for their return. No one seemed to know where the Tricks had gone. Perhaps they had gone to St. Louis. Perhaps they had traveled even farther west, seeking to lay claim to a slice of the new land that was becoming available as it was being systematically stolen from the sometimes fiercely resistant Native Americans.

Grace had been old enough to understand the fact, but not the reason for the abandonment. She had managed to conceal her painful anger and disappointment, albeit betrayed by a secret tear or two, until the clopping and rattling of her parent's homely wagon had faded into the distance. The unbelievable had become a sudden, screaming, reality. Her parents were actually gone! A long, agonized wail was the only belated protest that she could muster. Dick, trying to understand, wailed in chorus with his sister. Only the croaking of an unsympathetic old crow, who had happened to have stationed itself at the top of a nearby tree, was there to give answer to their sorrow.

Grace had snatched the parents' portrait from Dick's grasp, looked at it for a long moment through her tearful eyes, then disgustedly sailed it into the roadside ditch. "I hate them! I hate them!" she had screamed as she stamped her foot in the dusty road. Dick was trembling with fear as his sister turned and ran to the charred remains of their former home. The tree that stood next to the house had died from the scorching heat of the fire, but the swing that it supported was still there. Grace had swung herself furiously as she tried, without success, to suppress the disappointment that sobbed within her broken, young heart.

It was obvious, even to a six-year-old, that Grace did not want to have anything to do with the portrait. Dick had retrieved it from the ditch and had dusted it carefully with the tail of his shirt. Handy thing, the tail of a shirt. It was an easily accessible wiping cloth that was usually just hanging there, anyway. Thereafter, the picture was his and his alone. Grace refused, for years, to even look at it.

To Dick, having Grace near him was comforting even though she was frequently temperamental. At least, he could still look at, and to, his surviving sister when he wanted, or needed, to do so. Sadly, no one had a likeness of Ellen. Even Matthew, who loved Ellen more than life, had only the bittersweet pictures of her in his heart. All that Dick had to remind him of his sister Ellen was her simple tombstone that stood, as a sad and lonely remembrance, in the little cemetery on the hill above town. Like Matthew, there had been no solace for Dick in the coldness of the stone.

But, now, never mind all that. Wonder of wonders, the lovely Hannah had actually stopped to talk to Dick as he was hurrying through town on an assignment to retrieve some of Bethany's belongings from the Lanning's house. "My!" sweet Hannah said, flashing her enchanting smile, "You must be right proud to manage Mr. Greyson's farm while he goes to fightin'."

Dick tried to appear nonchalant. "Surely am. I'm proud as could be, Hannah. And, I believe that I will handle the job just fine."

"Well now, I guess I'm sure you will. An', maybe, you'll one day have a handsome uniform an' be a hero just like Captain Greyson and Sergeant McEwan." Hannah was surprised to feel herself being warmed by a sudden realization. Perhaps, she decided, the young man standing before her would not be such a bad catch, after all, given that he could be cleaned up a bit.

Dick stood ramrod-straight as he tried to achieve a military appearance. "I plan to try my hand at soldierin' soon's I can."

"I believe you will look quite nice in blue!" beamed Hannah. Her soft eyes flickered over his face, and over the portions of his body that were available for inspection, as she took a quick inventory of his assets. "Don't look too bad," she thought to herself, "if a person could just get by them scars." She smiled coquettishly. "I believe I could enjoy bein' on the arm of such a fine-looking soldier as you might become!" She touched his sun-browned arm to emphasize her point. "'Bye now, Richard." She turned to walk away from him, deliberately allowing her hips to sway seductively. She knew exactly where he would be looking. In fact, it would be quite some time before Dick would be able to think of anything other than the way her shapely body had moved. She was girlish and graceful, not crass, but with a powerful message. Excited thoughts ran though his head. "Golly," he mused "maybe someday she will come to me. Oh my! This is the stuff that dreams are made of!"

Hannah scampered up the steps of the Midgley house that was her adopted home, then turned to smile at the tanned boy who still stood in the road looking after her. His trousers still drooped, as they always did, on the ends of his stretched-out suspenders. Still, there was something new in her perception of him. There was a manliness, now, about his shoulders and about the maturing bulges of his biceps. He returned her smile, the whiteness of his teeth contrasting alluringly with the sun-swept darkness of his face. He waved good-by. She answered his wave by blowing a kiss to him....which he delightedly pretended to catch and to press to his lips. Hannah tried to suppress the warm feelings that welled within her, but without success. A realization at once alarmed and pleased her. She, who could have almost any man that she wanted, was falling in love with the shy, scarred boy who seemed to be calling to her from the center of Franklin's dusty main street.

Later that same day, Dick went with Sergeant McEwan to the pond above the VanEvery Mill. They threw bottles into the water and blazed away at them with Will's brace of horse pistols. The handsome weapons, Dick was quick to learn, were normally carried in holsters attached to the saddle just ahead of the rider, one on each side. The pistols were big, single shot, flintlock affairs that fired a .54 caliber round ball of soft lead. Ignition produced a bellow of white smoke that pleased the nose of the shooter with its businesslike acridity. They recoiled smartly, when fired, but not enough to frighten the boy in the least. He seemed to be a natural marksman. A number of the hapless bottles exploded in geysers of water as they tried their best to float their way out of danger.

"Well!" The sergeant was impressed. "My boy, you might just make a fine dragoon soldier, someday! Pretty damn' good shootin' I'd say."

Dick's face showed a curious mixture of "aw shucks" modesty along with a considerable measure of pride in his own marksmanship. "Thanks, Will." He caressed the walnut stocks and wiped at the black powder residue on the shiny steel barrels with the sleeve of his shirt. "You say these are Johnson pistols?"

"Right you are, son. They've served me well through the Mexican War, but now they're pretty much old-fashioned. Sam Colt has seen to that."

"Sam who?"

"Colt. Inventor fella from out east. Makes pistols that shoot six times without reloading."

"Y'know," recollected Dick "I believe Matt has one of those. Showed it to me once. Has a saber, too."

"Bet he does. I'm sure that's why he told me that he wasn't upset when Colonel Brodhead allowed as he didn't have any sidearms available for issue right now." The sergeant gathered up his equipment. "What say we go up to the house and make him break out his stash so's we can see just what he's got."

"Let's do that, Will, now that I've showed you how to shoot these here things."

"Pshaw! Sure don't take long for you to get too big for your britches. After you, my boy. By the way, don't be thinkin' about sneakin' off. You and me....'specially you....have some pistols to clean."

"Figured as much."

When they returned to the farmhouse, the stash about which they had speculated was already on display. Matt was seated at the oak pedestal table in the kitchen while Bethany was busily preparing supper. Dick was immediately wide-eyed at the array of wonderful items to be seen. There were canisters marked "Pistol Powder", cleaning rods. cleaning patches, and bottles of gun oil. The freshly polished cavalry saber gleamed where it lay on the table. Tins were marked with mysterious inscriptions reading "Caliber .44 Conical Bullets ½ oz. wt." and "Caps, Percussion". The heavy cylinder of the Walker Colt had been separated from the rest of the weapon. It was engraved with the scene of an army vs. Indian battle. Dick was immediately engrossed in the examination of all those things military. Willy drew up a chair, careful placed his pistols on the table, and made ready to enter the cleaning bee.

"Excuse me, gentlemen." Bethany interrupted their male industry. She waved a large spoon for emphasis, or perhaps for intimidation. "You will kindly remove your armory to the parlor. I wish to set for dinner."

The response, appropriate for three hungry men, was immediate. They exchanged knowing glances and tolerant little smiles. Their equipment was hastily gathered and transferred from the kitchen to the parlor table.

Sergeant Willy carefully instructed Dick as to the finer points of cleaning the dragoon pistols. Once satisfied that Dick was carefully and industriously engaged in his assigned task Willy examined Matthew's disassembled Colt. He knew that the weapon had been designed as an improvement on the earlier Patterson Model that had been manufactured by Colonel Samuel Colt, the improvements made in accordance with the suggestions made by Texas Ranger, and Mexican war hero, Captain Samuel H. Walker. The big pistols had been manufactured for Colt by one Eli Whitney, the son of the famous cotton gin inventor. It was common knowledge that these Whitneyville-Walker Colts could sometimes malfunction. Occasionally, they could even fail catastrophically. "Ever have any trouble with this thing?" asked Will as he held the cylinder toward the light and squinted through the chambers.

"Nope." smiled Matthew. "Never once let me down."

"What size charge you put in her?"

"Thirty-five grains for target practice, shootin' hogs, an' such. Fifty grains for serious work. That's ten or fifteen grains of powder more than used in the new Colt."

"My, my!" murmured Willy. He knew that that much black powder behind a ½ ounce .44 caliber conical bullet meant devastating effect upon the unlucky recipient....not to mention the considerable recoil discomfort to the shooter.

"That's a lot?" queried bewildered Dick as he glanced up from his work. He was not about to miss any of the conversation. He was soaking up information like a sponge.

"That's a lot!" answered Will. "Reckon I'll just stick to my nice, safe flintlocks."

"Pish!" guffawed Matt. "Here, Dick, heft this little darlin'." He deftly reassembled the gigantic revolver and handed it to the boy.

Bethany watched from the kitchen as Dick struck an heroic pose while aiming the big Colt in the direction of the window. The weapon weighed close to five pounds when it was loaded. Even unloaded, the weight made it very difficult to hold steady at arms-length.

"Might try using two hands, son." smiled the sergeant.

"No, sir." Dick renewed his efforts, determined to hold the weapon steady. "Rather learn to shoot like a man."

Bethany shuddered. "Strange," she thought "how men of any age seem to gravitate toward weapons of war....even to war itself." She suspected that there was something primordial involved. She had recently read Charles Darwin's newly published, provocative treatise *The Origin of Species* and had been disturbed by its many implications, implications which flew in the face of her own comfortable understanding of the Garden of Eden. She wondered if this male preoccupation with martial violence could be related to an inherited instinct for survival that had protected mankind since more primitive times. "Just look at those three little boys!" mused Bethany with a sad smile. "The determined hunters. The brave defenders. War makes them cuss and spit and swagger when they walk. Makes them squint, flinty-eyed, down the barrels of guns. Makes them heft and caress a saber as though it were an art-form instead of an horrible engine of destruction. God grant," she prayed, "that they may never feel the screaming pain that such weapons could inflict." She knew that Matthew had already felt that pain more than once. Yet, he was willing to expose himself to it again. She wilted, bracing herself against a kitchen chair, as tears of fright welled into her eyes. She had to turn away, to pretend that she was busy with her dinner preparations.

Matthew slipped away from his comrades, stole into the kitchen, and encircled her from behind with his strong arms. Somehow, he had felt her distress, even from the other room. He could tell that she needed to be cheered. "I'll let you in on an important observation" he chirped.

"Let me guess. Your big nose has observed that dinner smells good." She reached back to pat his cheek.

"Well, that too. But what I really wanted you to know is that there is nothin' quite so warm and sweet as the sight of a good-lookin' woman busyin' 'round in the kitchen. Especially if she is fixin' good things to eat. 'Specially if she is you."

"Goodness, you are indeed a smooth talker!" She wiggled out of his grasp, dabbed at her eyes with the corner of her apron, and quickly regained her composure. "You fierce warriors get washed up and presentable for supper. Now!" She gave Matthew an exaggerated, passionate kiss, much to the delight of the onlookers who stood, grinning, in the other room. "And, you'd all better say supper is the best you've eaten or I'll be parking the leftovers on your heads."

"Oops! Go, boys." Matt waved and pointed them toward the washstand. "I can already tell that it is the best I ever ate....and I ain't even tasted it yet."

"Smart soldier boy!" observed Bethany. "I have great hopes for you as a husband."

Dick dutifully splashed in the washbasin. Suddenly, it seemed that he was wise for his years. "Seems like," he whispered to Will, "this here is a piss-poor time to fall in love. I mean with the war and all."

McEwan smiled condescendingly. "Don't know much about such things, myself. Guess it just happens when it happens irregardless of what's goin' on around you."

Dick dried his face as he contemplated the sage answer. He realized that more essential information might be gleaned from his worldly new friend. "You got a girl, Willy?"

"Nope." McEwan was not volunteering any information.

Dick persisted. "Ever have one?"

Will talked through his towel as he, too, was drying his face. "If you must know....lots of 'em. But, not like that!" He jerked a thumb toward the cuddly scene in the kitchen. "Maybe someday the right one will grab me by the ear an' drag me off. Maybe when I'm through soldierin'."

Dick shrugged. "Likely will happen to you, I'd guess, but probably never will happen to me." He brightened, his face softening at a recollection. "A nice thing did happen today, though. A really pretty girl stopped to talk to me. An', I swear, Will, she even threw me a kiss!"

Will chuckled. "You don't say!"

"Yep, she did. But I doubt anything will come of it....I mean, between me and her."

"And why not?"

"'Cause I'm scarred, and slowed, and ugly."

"Ain't so. Just ain't so, son. One day a fine young woman won't even see those little scars of yours. She'll be lookin' to see who you really are. Don't take much smarts to tell that you are a bright young feller with lots of good future. Any woman worth her salt will see that ten times quicker than me. And it didn't take me no time a'tall."

Dick blushed at the compliment. "Thanks, Will."

McEwan leaned over the washstand with a whispered air of confidentiality. "One day, Dick, a woman will want you inside her so bad that she will practically help herself to you!"

"Really? Could that really happen?" Dick blushed some more. A beautiful picture danced across his mind.

"Surely!" Will was suddenly struck by a dark thought. "Uh, Dick, you can do that, can't you?"

"Do what?"

"Get inside a woman."

"Sure. I mean, I think so."

"You *think* so?" Willy stepped back, his eyes closed in sorrow. "Oh, don't tell me that your privates got roasted in that fire you told me about."

Dick snickered at his concern. "Just a little 'round the edges. But I can stand up like a real man should I be called upon."

"Whew!" Will shook his head in relief. "Then, my boy, you haven't a care in the world. Just you sit back and wait for that woman to come along. 'Course you could put out a little bait, now and again, just to see what kind of bites you might get."

"Bites?"

"Just a figure of speech, son."

Bethany was at the kitchen door, smoothing her apron. "Are you girls ready to stop whispering and come to supper?"

"Yes, ma'am." They both hoped that she had not overheard their conversation, but suspected otherwise. They could see a funny little smile on her face as she trundled them into the kitchen.

Supper was consumed with gentlemanly good manners. Beth presided over the table and was rewarded with the good behavior, and with the mumbled compliments, that she clearly expected. Afterwards, her request for assistance with the cleanup precipitated an hilarious cacophony of outrageous behavior as her companions flounced about the kitchen dressed in towels and aprons. They sailed the dishes to each other, as they were dried, and deposited them into the sideboard. The resulting clashes and clatters made the lady wince. Strangely, nothing was broken and the kitchen quickly regained its clean and tidy appearance. Their housekeeping tasks completed, Dick and Will excused themselves, giving each other a knowing wink. Each retired to his own quarters to turn in for the night. Bethany and Matthew were finally left alone in the soft glow from the coal-oil lamps.

"Bethy, stay with me tonight."

She pinched his lips closed with her fingers. "Much as I would like to do so, I must not. Soon, you'll be gone and I'll be left to listen to the whisperings about Miss Dodge, the whore schoolteacher, who sleeps with soldiers."

"Oh, they wouldn't say such a thing!"

"Oh, yes they would. But never you mind. Walk me home. I'll move in tomorrow after you are gone. Oh, I hate that word....gone! Please, please take me home. I can't take much more of this parting."

They walked down the trail and turned along the darkened main street. The houses and the businesses were all dark except for a single lamp in a bedroom at the Midgleys' and a couple of lights in the hotel next door. The August moon had transformed itself from a huge, orange ball on the horizon to a bright, white disc as it rose. The moonlight turned the dusty road into a ribbon of silver. The chimneys, lighted and shadowed into quaint silhouettes, looked even more whimsical than they did in the daylight.

"Look at that man in there!" giggled Bethany as she pulled Matthew to a halt. She indicated a gentlemen who could be seen reading his paper in the parlor of the hotel. "He looks like all of his hair has slid off his head and landed on his face!" She giggled louder.

"Shhh!" Matt clapped his hand over her mouth. "He might hear you! And, he looks big enough that he might just be able to keep me busy 'till breakfast, should he become irritated."

As they watched, the magnificently-bearded fellow set aside his newspaper and rose to stretch himself to his full height. Matthew was correct. The man's full stature was of considerably large proportions. They saw him consult the watch from his vest pocket and then move out of the circle of yellow light that emanated from the dim parlor lamp. His bulk became a large shadow, then disappeared altogether. They sincerely hoped that he had not heard the snickered comments from outside of the window and that he really was just going to his bed.

Matt tugged at Bethany gently. "Come along now, and mind your own business. Baldheaded, bushy-bearded persons are allowed at the hotel the last I heard. 'Long as they can pay for the bed they are welcome. He's probably a snake oil salesman. Or, could even be a lizard tongue salesman! Or, maybe he is a whiskey dealer....or a grain dealer. You just never know who might be in this town."

Bethany looked up at him in the moonlight. "Surely, you are right. A snake oil person. Take me home."

"I'm trying to."

"Well, try harder." She put her arm around his waist and hustled him along the road. Bethany fought with herself as she tried to replace the dark thoughts of their parting with the joyful thoughts of their engagement. "There is much to be done." She even managed to skip and hop in order to demonstrate her happiness. "Our engagement breakfast! I must rise early to help Mrs. Lanning with the preparation. And, I must have a little time that I may pick out just the right dress to wear."

"Really, your highness? Do you have a vast collection of engagement breakfast gowns?"

Beth smiled to herself in the darkness. "Might just surprise you there, Little Sir Matthew."

Matt paused abruptly, in the middle of Franklin Road, to perform a courtly bow in her direction.

"Pardon me, my lady. Did you bring handmaidens too?"

"I tried." She answered his moonlit bow with a sweeping curtsy. "But, they wouldn't get into my trunk."

"Oh, really, my princess? Sounds like tomorrow will be a busy day for you. I suppose that you have other, similarly important things to do, tonight, before you put your tender body to bed."

"I do, indeed."

"And, what would that be?"

"To cuddle with you on Mrs. Lanning's porch swing."

"Now! There's something to hustle for!"

They playfully jostled around the corner and hurried, hand-in-hand, up the Mill Road. Bethany tripped on the hem of her skirt as they giggled their way onto the porch. Matthew caught her arm and together they plopped onto the swing. The sudden weight caused the supporting springs and chains to squawk loudly, as was their habit, in protest. Even Mrs. Lanning's landings did not produce quite that much music.

At the unexpected sound, The Reverend Lanning's sleeping eyes opened wide as he lay in the upstairs bedroom. He could hear the laughing of happy whispers. He could hear them saying something about not wasting any more moonlight. Pitts smiled at their joy as he glanced out at the bright and beautiful moon. "How wonderful!" he thought. "Young folks are able to put their cares aside and lose themselves in each other. Hmmm. In the face of love, even war is inconsequential. Must be a sermon in there, someplace." His smile faded back into sleep as he tenderly placed his arm over his own beloved who was breathing softly as she slumbered peacefully by his side.

+ + +

The morning sky was already bright when Mrs. Lanning's eyes flew open at the sound of the Seth Thomas mantel clock in the parlor as it dutifully hammered out the hour of six.

"Mercy sakes!" she exclaimed loudly enough to turn her husband's purring snore into an explosive snort. "All those beautiful men coming for breakfast and here I lie like a lazy, fat old sinner!" It took two or three strained grunts from her, each with an answering snort from the startled reverend, before she was on her feet and in front of the mirrored bureau. "Hmmm!" She smiled as she ran her hands over her ample thighs. "Maybe lazy, a little old, and a bit plump, but still quite a sweetly handsome little sinner!"

Her girlish chuckle caused Pitts Lanning to open an appreciative, if sleepy, eye. He watched as she dropped her nightgown and primped, for a moment, in front of the mirror. Indeed, that secretive eye, camouflaged by the jumble of coverlets, could easily have been that of an alligator awaiting the moment when his prey would get close enough for capture. The telltale eye blinked quickly shut when the dear lady turned her stern gaze upon his prostrate form.

"Out of bed, Mr. Lazy Lout Lanning! There is much to be done this morning."

Pitts groaned pitifully as he sank deeper into the feather ticking. "This is, indeed, the day the Lord hath made, my love." His voice was muffled as he turned his face into the depths of the mattress. "Bless you, my sweet."

"Don't you try to butter me up with your blessings. Blessings indeed! Up! Up! Up! I need the stove lit, and I need it lighted now." The lady of the house hustled her bulk down the stairs and headed for the "necessary shed" behind the house

Bethany was already awake. Lying in her room, she was hardly surprised by the familiar rustling, whispering, thumping, and grunting that routinely signaled the start of the day in that household. She had slept only fitfully.

When she had managed to sleep, she still tossed, turned, and flapped the covers as she dreamed vividly of Matthew. Each dream was a variation of the one preceding. Sometimes, she would throw herself in front of him as she tried to protect him from danger. Sometimes she would try, with leaden arms, to drag him away as the cannons roared and the sabers clashed. The sounds of conflict would startle her awake and leave her to stare, wide-eyed and exhausted, into the gray shadows of the ceiling. The chill from the tear-soaked pillow against her cheek worsened the shivering of her body that had trembled with fear, even as she slept.

She lay in her bed, quietly trying to stifle her despair, as she listened to the morning routine. The door of the outhouse banged. There were splashing and gurgling sounds as Mrs. Lanning used the pitcher and basin. Bethany heard her softly coo "biddie, biddie, biddie!" as she scooped the little basket of orphan chicks from next to the kitchen stove where they had been sheltered by its residual warmth from the chill of the night air. She could hear the tiny, excited peeps as the chicks piled out of their warm basket and attacked the cracked-corn breakfast that their mistress had spread for them. The reverend had resumed his snoring. He was obviously unimpressed by the importance of the morning.

Mrs. Lanning creaked back up the stairway and knocked softly at Bethany's door. Opening it, she caught Beth wiping her tears away with a sodden handkerchief. She flew to the distressed young woman's bedside in an instant.

"Oh, you poor, sweet thing! You mustn't cry. This is a time for joy. You are betrothed!"

Bethany shuddered. "But, Mrs. Lanning, I'm so afraid. I'm afraid that he will be killed. I'm afraid to let him go away from me."

"I know. I know, dear. You must pray for him. We all must."

"I do pray. I pray for him constantly."

"Then, you must trust in the Lord that all things will happen according to His plan for us."

Bethany shook her head. Her eyes were red from the distress of the long night. "I know all that. It doesn't help. What if, in His plan, Matthew would

66

have to die? What of that?" She began to sob. "It wouldn't be fair that I should lose him just when the love between us is so beautiful."

Mrs. Lanning perched carefully on the edge of the bed, hoping that it would not tip under her weight. "Child, it seems that men must fight to protect us from whatever danger they think is out there. We can only pray for their preservation."

Bethany's eyes changed from the tearfulness of sorrow to a blaze of fire. "Do you really think that all we can do is sit home, work our knitting needles, and pray? I think not! Perhaps we should go and fight alongside them."

Mrs. Lanning patted Bethany's hand. "I'm sure! And just what would you have us ladies do? Would you have us go forth and smack the rebels with a feather duster? I think not. The best we can do is to let our men know that we will be waiting for them when they return." She stroked Bethany's tousled hair.

"You mean if they do return! I dreamt of him fighting. I dreamt of him being wounded....or perhaps killed." She sobbed, uncontrollably, as Mrs. Lanning held her in a comforting hug. "Do my dreams mean that he will die?"

"Of course not, dear. You are a very sweet, dear person but I doubt that you are a prophet. My husband believes that when you dream you are just listening to the feelings of your eternal soul. Your dreams are your contact with your real self."

"That could well be." Bethany dabbed at her eyes. "My real self really loves Matthew. My real self is just plain scared silly!"

Mrs. Lanning enveloped her in another motherly hug. "I understand your feelings, dear. Matthew is strong and experienced. I'm sure he will take care of himself and will come safely back to you just as soon as he can. Now, enough of all this. Dry your tears and help me to prepare breakfast."

Bethany showed the beginnings of a smile on her face. "Thank you for being so nice, and so understanding. I never knew my mother, but I think that she would have been just like you."

Mrs. Lanning grunted as she pushed herself to her feet, her posterior rising with difficulty off of the low bed. "That's a sweet compliment! Tell you what. I'll be your mother and you can be the daughter that I never had."

It was Bethany's turn to do the hugging. "That sounds like a fine arrangement to me. I surely need a mother, right now."

Mrs. Lanning strutted to the bedroom door. "Well, here I am in all my glory! If ever there was a mother, I am she! Now, enough of this. Time to stop blubbering and get to work. Your fat mother has some handsome young men to feed."

Beth dressed hurriedly and joined her newly-appointed mother in the kitchen. Mrs. Lanning was determined that her husband would rise, immediately, and make himself available to help with the kitchen chores. It took two or three loud calls up the stairs, and the threat of the application of a pancake spatula to his body, before the reverend stumbled down to join them. "Bless you on such a beautiful morning, ladies." His eyes were mere slits in his face.

His wife glared at him from in front of the cook stove where she was busily encouraging a small flame to spring to life among the kindling. "We are well-blessed today. And so early, too! I've already managed to do part of your job, Pitts. We would have trouble making dinner, let alone breakfast, if we waited for you. Kindly take yourself to the woodpile and split some more kindling before this fire goes out. And, for mercy sakes, open your eyes so's you don't chop your fingers off."

Pitts shuffled sleepily out of the back door. It was clear that he was unaffected by the criticism, but was drowsily resolved to tend to his duties....at his own pace, of course.

"Men!" snorted Mrs. Lanning. "Are you certain that you want to marry one of those pitiful creatures?"

"Oh, I'm sure. I'm very sure. I can hardly wait to try my hand at swatting my man with a pancake turner." Her eyes twinkled. "My, there is so much that I can learn from you!"

"Yes, dear. I have much to teach you. Now, please set the table. Use the linen cloth and napkins. Use the pressed glass goblets for water and juice...."

that's the best we have in the way of glassware. The silver is already polished. I did that yesterday."

"You really mean to use the Irish linen? I never saw you get it out before except to just look at it."

"And, you might never see it used again. First person that spills grape juice, or decorates the cloth with strawberry preserves, will die an instant and painful death at my hands." Mother Lanning waved her long-handled spatula as though it had the lethal qualities of a saber. Beth very nearly believed that the dear lady might well make good her threats of violence.

In a remarkably short time, the dining table was transformed into a glittering display. Sparkling glassware, gleaming silver plate, and blue and white Staffordshire china graced the Irish linen. Freshly cut flowers added a truly festive air as they were arranged in a vase that matched the goblets. The vase was actually a spooner, a little chipped and a bit worn, but with no glaring defects that anyone would notice among the cheerful blooms. Nearly all of the tableware were heirlooms. The flowers themselves, not to be outdone, were treasures that had been carefully selected from the backdoor garden. The beautifully appointed table seemed to echo the joyful life that flourished in that household.

"Menfolks probably won't even notice all the trouble that we've gone to" sniffed Mrs. Lanning.

Bethany patted her shoulder appreciatively. "Well now, I'll bet that you are wrong there. I'm certain that they can't help but notice such a beautiful table in such a beautiful home. Surely, at least Matthew will be dazzled by it all. I guess I can't really speak for the other two, but they will probably be just as thrilled. I'd be surprised if either of them has ever sat at such a table before." She fussed with the napkins to make sure that their placement was perfect. "This is such a lovely way to celebrate our engagement. You are so sweet to do all this for us." Bethany made a mental note to surreptitiously prompt Matthew so that he would not fail to show his appreciation for the Lanning's efforts. She would also tell him to pass the instructions along to the other two. Be complementary. Eat daintily. And, for heaven's sake, don't you dare drip on the tablecloth!

Bethany cracked a full two dozen eggs in preparation for the huge bowl of scrambled, soft, yellow delight. Mrs. Lanning chucked a few of the eggshells into the boiling coffeepot to settle the grounds. The salt pork simmered in water and the mush was sliced....both of them in preparation for frying. Baking powder biscuits plumped in the oven of the trusty black "Farmer's Friend No. 9" stove. Bacon sputtered and spat deliciously in the cast iron skillet. Beth spooned apple butter into some glass serving bowls and strawberry preserves into others. All seemed to be in order.

The lady of the house beamed with a motherly smile of satisfaction as she gave Bethany a sideways hug. "Time to get yourself prettied up, bride-to-be. The gents will be arriving soon."

The Seth Thomas laboriously counted the hour of eight as Beth hurried up the stairs, pulling her apron off as she retreated to her room. Bethany was, without even trying, a very pretty young woman. On this special morning, however, pretty was not nearly good enough. She was determined, as she closed the door to her room behind her, that she would not emerge until pretty had been transformed into beautiful.

Pitts Lanning had, somehow, managed to survive his assigned kindling-splitting duty with all appendages intact. Additionally, he had survived an egg-gathering assignment as well. ("Humph! Woman's' work.") Further, he was the clear winner after successfully fending off two flapping, squawking, and spurring attacks by their belligerent rooster. ("That bird has a poor attitude! I'll see his little butt plucked clean, and in the fry pan, one glorious day.") Finally, his menial tasks were completed. It was time for him to resume his position as cleric and community leader. He smiled at his image in the mirror as he carefully combed his hair. "Ah! I must look my very best for this exciting day that the Lord hath made. Thank you, Lord, for the opportunity to help our friends and neighbors." He chuckled to himself. "And, if I may say so, good planning, Lanning!" He dressed in his Sunday finest, even though Sunday it was not. His gleaming white shirt contrasted nicely with his black ribbon tie, black vest, black trousers, and similarly black, wide-brimmed hat.

He was feeling quite good about everything, including his own appearance, as he hustled out of the parsonage and hurried toward the schoolhouse to check on his premiere project of the day. He was delighted to see that there were two unfamiliar rigs tied to the hitching rail in front of the school. The spiffy one-horse buggy and the somewhat dilapidated two-horse farm wagon were definitely not of Franklin origin. "Ah, yes!" he cried. "They are indeed here!" He burst through the schoolhouse door. "Good morning! Good morning! Thank you, gentlemen, for joining our celebration!"

The musicians of the Clarenceville Patriotic and Military Band were impatiently waiting inside. They returned his greeting warmly. The band had been engaged, on an emergency basis, with only one day's notice. The short notice, of course, had been somewhat unavoidable as the Lannings had conceived the idea of a Franklin Village parade only on the previous day.

Upon learning of the betrothal of the two favorites of their flock, the Lannngs had immediately convened themselves into a kitchen table Council of War. They had been determined to make the most of the situation. Perhaps, a breakfast in honor of Bethany and Matthew? Certainly! What a fine idea! And, after breakfast, how about a real, honest-to-goodness parade? Of course! With all of the boys that were about to leave to go to war, a proper sendoff in the form of a gala parade would be most appropriate. They would honor Matthew, Bethany, Sergeant McEwan, the other soldiers, and the glorious flag! Yes! All would be saluted by one, really nice, PARADE! Mrs. Lanning had sallied forth to notify the populace, and to arrange the details. Pitts had saddled his mare and had headed for the Village of Clarenceville from whence had come rumors of the existence of an excellent, and generally available, marching band. His journey had been a rather long one....one that had produced two rather painful saddle sores upon his tender behind. He had ridden his mare through the Village of Farmington, and along the Grand River Road, with only one brief stop to rest at the bustling Botsford Inn where he received both refreshments and information. His persistence had been rewarded when he had finally managed to locate the leader of the fabled band. The bandmaster had turned out to be a handsome fellow with a wonderfully curled mustache and an even more wonderful silver trumpet. Terms were swiftly arranged. A two-dollar contribution to the "Clarenceville Instrument Acquisition and Sheet Music Fund" would make available, to the people of Franklin, the services of the very best parade musicians that money could buy.

Gloriously, The Reverend Pitts Lanning's heroic efforts had come to fruition. All six of the Clarenceville musicians were lounging in the schoolroom awaiting their day in the Franklin sun. The tuba player was an extremely plump, red-cheeked youth who had taken residence in a corner of the room where he was cuddling his fractured-looking instrument. Perched next to him, and in remarkable contrast, was a consumptive-looking figure who held an Euphonium which still proudly displayed a few traces of its former silver plating. Scattered around the room were two farm lads with pitifully patched and stitched snare drums, and an octogenarian fife player who looked as though he might have piped for George Washington. Their handsome leader sat, silver trumpet and all, with his feet parked upon Bethany's desk. He stood politely, if a little grudgingly, when Reverend Lanning burst into the room.

Lanning surveyed the motley group with eyes that widened with alarm as their unkempt appearance registered in his mind. Fortunately, being a trained and skilled professional, he could quickly regain his Christian composure. "My!" he gushed. "What a nice-looking group! And nice hats, too!" The gentlemen were devoid of uniforms, but each sported a tall, maroon, cockaded hat. The hats, unfortunately, were in various stages of disrepair....a disrepair that, in some of the examples, bordered upon decay.

The leader, now standing beside Bethany's desk, assumed a proud, military posture. "Thank you, sir. The hats are vintage 1812, we believe. They are truly historic regalia."

"How nice. Now, what fine tunes may we expect to hear this morning?"

"Just one, reverend."

"Excuse me?"

"Just one. We only know just one."

Lanning blanched, perceptibly, as the true image of his musicians dawned upon his increasingly fevered mind. "Now, sir, which tune would that be?"

"*John Brown's Body.*"

"*John Brown's Body*? You mean, as in 'a-moulding in his grave?"

"Yes, sir. That's the one. That's all we know at this time."

"I see." Pitt's newly-regained Christian strength was, alarmingly, fading again. "Well, then!"

He inspected the brim of his hat so that he did not have to make eye contact with the musicians. "I'm sure that you will play it well."

"We will. Indeed we will." The bandmaster stroked his mustache as he turned to address the tuba player who remained, skulking, in the corner. "Show the reverend what we can do, Herman."

Herman obligingly unlimbered his fractured tuba and began to demonstrate his prowess.

"Umph umph umph umph umph umph!" He then skillfully transitioned up two full tones. "Umph umph umph umph!" Then, again showing consummate skill, he went back to the original note. "Umph umph umph!" During the entire demonstration, Herman managed to look both exhausted and bored at the same time.

"Thank you, ah, Herman. That was very nice." Pitts was feeling faint.

"Yer welcome!" panted Herman.

"Gentlemen, I have good news." Even in the face of adversity, the reverend was determined to be a good host. "Some ladies of our community will be here, shortly, with sustenance for your efforts."

"Huh?"

"Breakfast."

"Aha!"

As if on cue, the door flew open and through it flounced Mary Beth. Her flags were flying, and her impressive pulchritude was nicely on display. She was followed, much more daintily, by Grace Trick Cox who was blushing prettily at the sight of all those men. Each carried a towel-covered wicker basket, the delicious contents of which had been carefully crafted for the satisfaction of the honored musicians from distant Clarenceville.

Herman, still safely ensconced upon his corner perch, viewed the pretty ladies with some degree of annoyance, that attitude only slightly tempered by his interest in the food that they carried. The food was of major interest to him, but the ladies were of no consequence, whatsoever, in his mind. Adequate levels of testosterone had not yet graced his young and plump body in meaningful concentrations. Perhaps, they never would. Now that the food was delivered, the women who had so graciously provided it were of no further practical use. In fact, their presence might actually impair his instantly-planned assault upon the fragrant contents of the picnic baskets. The prompt departure of the ladies, Herman reasoned, would serve his purposes nicely. He snickered to himself as he drew a deep breath, placed his floppy lips upon the mouthpiece, and produced a disgustingly wet, and flatulent, salute that echoed from the bowels of his tuba.

There was a moment of stunned silence. Then, quickly recognizing Herman's obtuse performance, the farm boys broke into howls of foot-stomping laughter. The startled young women recoiled in horror, dropped their baskets upon the schoolhouse floor, and fled. They were closely followed by the apologetic minister who vainly tried, hat in hand, to persuade them to return.

The Clarenceville Patriotic and Military Band would breakfast without benefit of feminine companionship that morning.

Pitts managed to calm himself during the short walk back to his home.... only to face a new crisis. He discovered that, very likely, he could expect criticism from his none-too-patient spouse. "Oh, dear!" It was at once clear that their breakfast guests had already arrived, and that he had not been present to greet them. Gleaming with military tack and ominous, holstered weapons, their horses swished and stomped at flies as they waited at the hitching posts in front of the parsonage. He hustled inside to find that the gentlemen were happily sipping coffee in the parlor with his, as expected, somewhat irritated wife.

"Pitts, my love, where have you been? We have been waiting for you for some time."

"Sorry. I have been making final arrangements for the parade, dearest."

"What parade would that be, pastor?" asked Dick from his uncomfortable perch on a carved and brocaded Victorian chair.

The reverend looked, in surprise, at the youth. "Well, well! My goodness, Dick, is that really you? You look so, um, so even more handsome than usual."

Dick giggled. "Yes, sir, it's me!" Dick had been forced by his companions to scrub, and to comb, to as near a state of perfection as he could attain. He was nervously balancing a cup and saucer which contained some of the most vile stuff that he had ever tasted. He manfully smiled, and pretended to enjoy the brown substance that he was sipping. He repeated the question. "What parade, Mr. Lanning?"

"The magnificent parade that we are having, this morning, in honor of Matt, Will, and all of the other heroes who are going off to preserve the Union."

"What a wonderful surprise!" Matthew rose from his chair and bowed to express his appreciation. "We are, indeed, honored. I'm sure that you folks have gone to a great deal of trouble. Thank you."

"No problem." lied the reverend. He resisted the impulse to rub the saddle-sores that still smarted on his behind. "No problem at all. Its an honor to salute our heroes."

Bethany picked that strategic moment to sweep down the stairs in a swirl of rustling, black taffeta. Her goal was achieved. She was, indeed, breathtakingly beautiful. The men stared in mute appreciation. She flew into Matt's arms murmuring "good morning! Good morning, all!"

Matthew stepped back to look at her, then embraced her again. "You look lovely, Beth. You weren't joshin', were you? You do have gowns for all occasions!"

Bethany smiled and twined her arms around his neck as she shamelessly ignored the audience that was seated, entranced, around the room. "Not too bad, hey?"

"Not too bad a'tall! Are you sure that you don't have a lady-in-waiting hidden upstairs?"

"Poo! You must realize that these are hard times. I must do the best that I can without my servants." Everyone in the room was convinced that she was joking. She, secretly, was being perfectly truthful.

Pitts sprang to his feet. "Please excuse me for a moment. Everyone stay right where you are." He hustled into the kitchen and returned with a tray of sparkling stemware which he had hurriedly filled with a ruby-red wine.

He looked each of his assembled guests in the eye, one at a time. "Don't any of you dare tell our parishioners of this little treat or I shall personally see that you suffer hell and damnation!"

"Our lips are sealed!" grinned Willy.

"The old sinner brews this devil's drink out back in the shed!" smirked the hostess.

"Hush, darling." He raised his glass to the bride and groom-to-be. "May your union be blessed by the love of Christ Jesus. And, may your love produce many healthy children. And, may...." he stifled a sigh "this damnable war spare you pain."

"Hear, hear!" Willy downed his wine. "Reverend, this is really tasty stuff." He looked, wistfully, at his empty glass.

"Thank you, Will. You won't often taste Methodist wine. I prepare it primarily for sacramental use, of course."

"Of course!" Mrs. Lanning winked as she daintily drained her glass and then strained to free herself from the grip of her embroidered chair. "Everyone to the table, please. I fear that the eggs are getting cold."

The grace, as offered by The Reverend Lanning, was long and impassioned. It was so long, in fact, that it caused both Mrs. Lanning and Bethany to glance, fearfully, through the kitchen door at the faithful "Farmer's Friend No. 9" within the bowels of which the biscuits were beginning to desiccate.

During the sumptuous meal, and between bites, Pitts waved his fork, and pointed emphatically with it, as he finalized his parade instructions to the key participants. "Dick, I have asked little Jimmy Barnum to help you to lead the military horses. Jimmy is quite young. Will you be so kind as to keep an eye on him?"

"I will, sir."

"Thank you." He turned to the sergeant. "Will, I have hazardous duty for you."

"You do?" McEwan paused with a fork-full of scrambled eggs in midair. "That sounds just a bit scary."

"Well, it is....a little! I'm asking you to escort Grace Trick Cox and her small daughters in the parade. Her husband, Henry, is already on duty at Camp Lyon and can't be here. Yet, we want her to be a part of the celebration. Will you offer her your arm?"

Willy breathed a sigh of relief. "Of course. Be happy to do that. Doesn't sound all that hazardous to me."

"Good! Be advised that she may not be in a really good mood. Things have not gone well for her, so far, today."

Will leaned back in his chair with an air of confidence. "This is not a problem. I am an expert in the un-grumping of grumpy women."

The reverend looked a bit skeptical. "I'm relieved to hear that the matter is in the hands of an expert. Good luck to you, my friend. Now, I believe that it is time to go. If God and the Clarenceville Band are willing, the parade is to start in just ten minutes."

The parade was remarkably well-organized for such an impromptu affair. Patriotism was at an all-time high. Red, white, and blue bunting sprouted from the residences and businesses along the short parade route which ran from the German Mill Road to Fourteen Mile.

The Clarenceville boys were assembled, in a loosely-organized gaggle, in the German Mill-Franklin Road intersection. They were already facing, mostly, north. Their leader waved his trumpet imploringly as he begged them to try to look sharp. Behind the band were assembled a dozen, or so, uniformed members of the local veterans' association who were to serve as the color guard. After a heated discussion, it was determined that the oldest of their members, a veteran of the War of 1812, would have the honor of carrying Old Glory even though there was some grave doubt as to whether he would survive the entire length of the parade.

Matthew, Bethany, Willy, and Grace Cox were to be positioned behind the veterans. Grace, however, was nowhere to be seen. In the next rank were assigned Dick and the very young Jim Barnum who were to lead the two cavalry horses. Behind them were a group of newly-volunteered soldiers along with their wives, sweethearts, and/or mothers. Following this chatty group was a squad of grim-appearing ladies who displayed a bipoled banner which proclaimed their membership in the "Women's' Temperance Alliance of Oakland County".

"Those ladies look as though they could use a drink!" opined Sergeant Willy to Reverend Lanning. "Perhaps, you could serve them a little of your Methodist grape."

"Hush!" winced Lanning. "Not funny, Will."

"Sorry!" grinned Will. He clandestinely assessed the women. "I could be wrong, of course, but instead of needing a drink, I suspect that they could just be lacking in the services of a gentleman who might find a way to put a smile on their faces....but I surely can't imagine a man who would be willing to service such a surly-looking group!"

Pitts gasped. "Really, Will, you must learn to control the expression of your opinions." The reverend sneaked a look, for himself, and turned away to suppress a chuckle. "You might, however, be absolutely right."

"Now," said Will as he attempted to suppress his merriment, "where is this Grace person? Don't tell me that she is among the temperance females!"

"No, she is not with them. I'm afraid that I just don't know where she might be. She was supposed to be here. Oh! There she is! See her?" Pitts pointed secretively. "She's the one under the oak tree, on the corner, wearing a yellow bonnet. There are two little girls with her."

"Aha!" exclaimed Will. "The target is in my sights. I shall be right back." He wore a cavalier smile as he strode to confront the little feminine group that was clustered, prettily, under the oak. "Ma'am," said he as he respectfully touched the visor of his kepi, "I'm Willy McEwan. I'm a member of the First Cavalry, same as your husband. I would be greatly pleased if you would allow me the honor of escorting you, and your children, in the parade." He removed his cap and bowed in his most gentlemanly fashion.

Grace had lovely, ice-blue eyes. They transfixed him with a glare that very nearly cut him in two. "Sir, I would not march in the same parade as that group of Clarenceville hoodlums if my life depended on it!" She stamped her foot at him, in a most unfriendly manner, effectively emphasizing the sincerity of her feelings.

Sergeant McEwan recoiled in disbelief. His eyes were wide at the ferocity of the rebuff. "Really? Oh, I see....or at least I think I do! Ah, well." He spun on his heels to escape. "Thank you, anyway, madam." Willy beat a dismayed retreat. Feminine rejection was not something that he often experienced.

Hannah Midgley was standing nearby. She was combed, primped, and dressed in her favorite blue dress. The garment was her favorite because it fetchingly intensified the color of her eyes. It was, also, carefully home-tailored to emphasize the fullness of her beasts while showing, at the same time, the trimness of her tiny waistline. She had not missed any detail of the unfortunate exchange between the unlucky sergeant and the irate Mrs. Cox. Hannah perceived an irresistible opportunity and impetuously decided to take advantage of it. The warm thoughts of Dick Trick that had been intermittently dancing through her mind suddenly vanished, for the moment, as she contemplated the challenge of a tempting new conquest. She intercepted Willy as he, stinging in defeat, was making his way back toward his appointed parade position. The light touch of her hand upon his arm stopped him in mid-stride.

"Excuse me, sergeant. It 'pears to me that you have need of someone to march with you in the parade. I would like to apply for the position, if I might."

Will was instantly enchanted. The hand of an angel, unexpectedly, was suddenly resting upon his arm. "Dear me....yes, of course, miss! I would be most honored. Thank you!" He was quick to gently cover her hand with his. "May I ask your name?"

"You may, indeed!" she giggled.

"Well then, what is it?" Willy was too awestruck to realize that she was playing a coy little game with him.

"I'm not sure that I'll tell you."

"Good heavens!" Will could not believe that he had encountered a second impenetrable female within the span of a few confusing minutes. "And.... why not, may I ask?"

"'Cause, we have not been properly introduced."

"But, how could I do....I mean, who could do that....I mean....aw, shucks." McEwan's ears were turning red in frustration.

Hannah demurely held her hand over her mouth to conceal her laughter. Her eyes, however, spoke the truth. They twinkled with mischievous hilarity at his obvious discomfort. She yanked at his arm for emphasis. "If you'd really, really like to know my name then maybe I'll just tell you what it is!"

Will laughed heartily. "I'd really, really like to know. I'd be honored to make your acquaintance, ma'am. Be nice to know what to call you as it seems we are to be friends."

"Well, then, my name is Hannah. Hannah Midgley." She frowned at him. "I'm only telling you so's you won't have to call me 'ma'am'! 'Hannah' will do. Or, even 'Miss Midgley' would be fine!"

"Yes, ma'am....er....Miss Midgley." Willy's grin had returned.

Hannah gave his arm another yank of disapproval at the second "ma'am".

Will grinned even wider. "Do I dare ask if you live around here?"

She was coy again. "Well, I 'spose. I live, over there, with my brother and his wife." She pointed up, and across, the Franklin Road toward a little house that really could not be seen from where they stood.

Willy strained to see. "Where?"

"Right up there. You'll see when we go closer. You needn't tell me your name 'cause I already know what it is."

The sergeant chuckled. "Oh, do you? Bet you don't. Name is Alfred William McEwan."

"Oh, I thought it was just Willy. Sergeant Willy."

"That's me, too. See, you are not quite so smart as you thought." It was his turn to do a little joshing. "Reckon you can't help not bein' very smart.... but a person looks as nice as you do don't have to be! Would it be proper for me to tell you that you are a very beautiful young woman?"

"Proper as could be, if you think you are speakin' the truth about the beautiful part, and not about the not smart part."

"Huh? Oh, I see. I give up. You win. You are both beautiful and smart! Thank you for offering to walk with me. I will be honored." He held her hand, which still rested on his arm, as they walked back toward where Reverend Lanning was staring at them, from a distance, in puzzled dismay. "Hannah, I'm probably going to be in trouble again, but I have to ask. How old are you?" He looked, in wonderment, at her as though she were some lovely apparition.

She released his arm. "Yep, you are in trouble. That's not a polite question to ask of a lady. Besides, I didn't ask your age, did I?"

"Nope. You didn't. I'm thirty-one."

"And, I'm almost fifteen. But, I intend to get older."

"Don't do that too soon. I surely like you just the way you are. Shall we take our place in the parade before they leave without us?"

Lanning was waiting for them. "What happened? Where is Grace?"

McEwan, a little embarrassed at his failure, chuckled self-consciously. "She ain't comin'. Surely don't bother me, though, as this sweet lady offered to take her place."

The reverend knew flirtatious Hannah well. He was not surprised at all to see her seeking the sergeant's attentions. "Welcome to the parade, Hannah. Grace's loss is our gain!"

Dick, dutifully holding Saber's reigns in the middle of the road, was seething with jealousy as he watched Hannah and Will. He wished, desperately, that he possessed a fine uniform, like the sergeant's, so that Hannah would be attracted to him instead. He watched and listened as the pair chatted cozily. Finally, he could stand no more. He forcefully handed the reins of Matthew's horse to the Barnum boy and stalked away from the parade. Little Jimmy, confronted with the specter of being trampled by two very large horses, and without Dick to save him, burst into screams of terror. His howls worked wonderfully to his advantage as the chatty foursome, who were positioned just ahead of him, flew to his rescue. Matt took Saber's reins in one hand while Bethany clung to the other. Jimmy was hoisted to Will's shoulder whereupon his screams, thankfully, subsided. His fright was almost immediately replaced by a happy grin. Hannah, not relinquishing her new friend's arm, took the reins of his mount with her free hand.

"Let the parade begin!" shouted Reverend Lanning. The Clarenceville Patriotic and Military Band stepped off, rather smartly, and in surprisingly synchronous precision. The strains of *John Brown's Body* echoed up and down the little main street. This was, unquestionably, Franklin's finest, proudest hour.

All of the little boys and girls had been given quantities of small United States flags to distribute to both the parade participants and to the spectators as well. Bethany waved hers with such enthusiasm that if flew from her hand and landed in the dust. Before she could retrieve it, a very large gentleman stepped from the edge of the road and picked it up for her. He slapped the flag against his leg, to remove the dust, and handed it back to her. Their eyes met for only an instant. Beth smiled a polite "thank you" and then tightened her grip on Matthew's arm. For some reason, she felt uncomfortable in the presence of the big fellow. He was, she recollected, the stranger whom they had seen through the hotel window the night before. Perhaps, he really was a traveling snake-oil salesman....but then, again, perhaps he was not.

Hannah and Sergeant Willy thoroughly enjoyed the parade even though they did not really pay much attention to the activities that swirled around them. They were much too busy chatting, and getting acquainted, to focus upon anything except each other. Hannah was both excited and proud to find herself clinging to the chevron-decorated sleeve of a real, honest-to-goodness soldier. "Will," she flirted, "if you were to write to me from the war I would be pleased to answer your every letter." The pledge of a man and a woman to correspond was not just a pen-pal arrangement during those war-torn times. It had much more meaning. It meant that love was possible, even probable.

82

The implication was not lost upon Will. He slipped his arm around her waist and hoped that no one, except her, would notice. "I will write to you as often as I possibly can, I promise. And, I will 'specially look forward to calling on you whenever I have a furlough. Would that please you?"

For answer, Hannah removed the silk scarf that she wore and offered it to him. Will pressed the bright cloth to his lips and then tied it to the hilt of his saber. He, of course, did not know that she had filched it from her sister-in-law's bureau drawer just before the parade. As they parted, Hannah favored him with a little kiss that left a treasured sweet spot upon his tanned cheek. She hoped, secretly, that her kiss would haunt his memory as he sat, dreaming of her, by many a wartime campfire. As usual, in such matters of the heart, she was correct. Will would not, and could not, easily forget her.

Bethany clung to Matthew for as long as she could. She prayed that, somehow, God would tell him to abandon his military plans and to simply stay with her. Then, when there was no answer to her prayer, she kissed him good-bye and then fled to Tansy's little hill that rose above the Fourteen Mile intersection. From there, she could watch him ride away. The yellow tansy and the blue chicory still bloomed there as though they had waited to witness just one more sadness. She stood on that little hill, and waved farewell, as tears streamed down her face and fell to stain the taffeta of her stylish dress. She remained there, like a pitiful, lonesome, and heartbroken child, long after Matt and Sergeant Willy had crossed the bridge, trotted their proud horses up the hill, and disappeared from her sight. The love of her life had just ridden away, perhaps never to return, and taken her broken heart with him. "Oh, God!" she cried at the blue of the August sky. She shook her fist in frustration. "Why must this damnable war be? Why? Why?" She turned and walked, sad and alone, toward Matthew's empty house.

The men cantered their horses to the north in silence. It was a silence that weighed heavily upon them both. Willy finally intruded into Matthew's gloomy thoughts. "Sir?"

"What is it, Will?"

"Are you sure we have to do this?"

"Do what?"

"Leave this place. It just don't feel right to do that, just now."

Greyson clucked sympathetically. He had noted the sergeant's tender parting from his new love. He could easily understand the sadness. "There's some considerable pain to such a parting, I reckon." There was a lump rising, uncomfortably, in his own throat as he thought of Bethany. He realized that there was a good chance that he would never see her again.

"'Deed there is. First time in my life that I don't seem to feel like goin' to war."

As they continued to canter their horses, Captain Greyson turned to give his sergeant a hard look. "Sure hope that you'll get over that notion real quick, Will. Like it, or not, we got us a war to fight!"

"Shit! This ain't no fun a'tall."

Greyson held up a gloved hand. "Pull up a minute, Will. Listen."

The sounds of the ongoing celebration in Franklin could still be heard even though they were nearly a half-mile up the road. The silver trumpet still sang sweetly: "John Brown's body lies a'moulding in the grave...."

And Herman, for some unfathomable reason, was still giving his all to his music.

"Umph umph umph."

"Umph."

CHAPTER FIVE

Tansy Too

The first week of Matthew's absence went by quickly. There was much to be done. Bethany worked hard to convert the former bachelor-pad farmhouse into a residence appropriate for a lady to occupy. She lovingly investigated and scrubbed every dusty corner. Matt was actually a very tidy person, for a man, and therefore her tasks were reasonably easy to accomplish. There were only occasional clucks of dismay when she found dirty socks in unkempt bureau drawers and smelly shirts stuffed into a basket. She had already received her first letter from Matthew wherein he had described the tumble-down, rat-infested, Camp Lyon and how they were working to convert it into a decent military facility.

Dick worked from dawn to dusk assisting the neighbors as they picked the stock corn and stored it in the granary. He swung the scythe until his shoulders ached. The cornstalks were bundled into neat shocks which he then stood, rank on rank, in the fields like brown, leafy soldiers.

Nighttime found Bethany dragging the big copper bathtub from its storage place in the washroom. She placed it near the kitchen stove so that it could be conveniently filled with water from the kettles and buckets which steamed and whispered from their perches upon the neatly-scrubbed cooking surface. It was dark and it was late. Beth could observe Dick's tack room-cum-bedroom window in the barn from her kitchen vantage point. She smiled smugly as she watched his lamp extinguished. Dick had turned-in for the night. It was, at last, time for a nice, private, luxurious bath as a reward for her labors of the day. She stripped, assembled her sponge and soap, and slipped into the warm water for a delicious soak.

As the bath water began to cool, she decided that her personal luxury was complete. She had just stepped out of the tub, and was drying with her large, soft towel, when her eyes opened wide at the sound of heavy footsteps treading on the porch outside of the window. She gasped in horror. Someone else had been enjoying her bath! Perhaps they had enjoyed it even more than she had! She could hear the footsteps heading toward the unbarred kitchen door. Bethany stifled a frightened cry as the reality of the situation dawned upon her. Quickly gathering both her wits and her towel about her, she ran into the adjacent bedroom. Just as she hurriedly slammed the bedroom door, behind her, she was horrified to hear the outer door, that led from the porch to the kitchen, burst open. She hurried to the bureau, tripping and scrambling, not pausing to notice that the towel had fallen from her grasp. She frantically scattered her neatly-arranged articles of feminine undergarments as she searched for her little Sharps four-barreled "pepperbox" derringer that she had hidden in the bureau drawer. The tiny weapon was fully loaded with four .22 caliber rimfire cartridges. The frightened lady thumbed the hammer to full cock as she swung to face the door. In a heartbeat, the latch splintered away, and bounced across the floor, as the intruder forced the door without bothering to lift the handle. The huge, big-bearded, baldheaded snake-oil salesman from the hotel lunged into the room. The hungry grin of a rapist split his unkempt beard as he ogled her nakedness and reached to clutch her.

The Sharps bucked in her hand as it spoke a loud "pank", the sound echoing flatly within the small room. Bethany gasped as she observed her attacker's upper incisors disappear in a gush of blood. The big man screamed with rage as he paused in his attack only long enough to reflexly hold his hand momentarily to his mouth, then to spit bits of bloody teeth at her. Beth instinctively aimed and fired again. A jagged hole appeared between the bushy eyebrows as the second tiny projectile mushroomed against his massive skull but failed to penetrate the heavy bone. He staggered, but continued to move toward her. His bloodied hands were outstretched, and reaching for her throat, until a third shot found its mark. His left eye exploded in a pink fountain of blood and ocular fluid that splattered across his face. Penetrating the relatively thinner skull behind the eye, the slug punched its way into the fragile tissue of his brain. Slivers of bone and lead, plus the destructive force of hydrostatic shock, instantly ended his life. The would-be rapist's arms flailed helplessly. His legs buckled beneath him as he, suddenly silent, sagged to the floor. Momentum caused his nose to plow a furrow in Tansy's rug as his head came to rest just short of Bethany's bare and trembling feet.

The Sharps .22 caliber pepperbox was really not much of a firearm. It was a gambler's hideout gun designed to discourage cheating at under-the-cardtable range. Its diminutive ammunition was almost laughably under-powered for serious self-defense. Detractors considered it to be more of a tool for intimidation rather than a true weapon.

However, on that frightening night, the genius of Christian Sharps was confirmed. The effectiveness of the derringer, in Bethany's obviously capable hands, was beyond criticism. The horror of sexual attack, and of possibly even greater harm, had been quickly and effectively averted. The big man lay dying upon Tansy's rug....his terminal gasps agonal and autonomic. The bullet had managed to penetrate the heavy skull only because the range was very short. Energy delivered to the point of impact was nearly the same as the energy carried by the bullet as it left the muzzle of the gun. The world would have to find another snake-oil salesman.

Bethany jumped onto the bed to kneel and cock the weapon for a fourth shot should her adversary resume his attack. She need not have worried. His respiration ceased and his huge body twitched in the final dance of death.

The horrifying sounds of combat caused Dick to fly out of his tack room bed, and from his deep sleep, as though he were raised by an unseen hand. At first, he had no idea as to what was taking place. Nevertheless, it immediately seemed obvious that, whatever it was, it was likely that Bethany was having some sort of a serious problem. Dick jumped into his trousers, grabbed a pitchfork, and ran into the house. As he entered the bedroom, pitchfork at the ready, his sleep-fogged mind was totally bewildered by the scene.

Bethany was kneeling, stark-naked, upon the bed. Her shaky two-hand hold pointed a cocked derringer at a bear-like object which lay nearby. At first, Dick's sleepy eyes could discern only the soles of two very large shoes which were ludicrously positioned, toes down, on the floor. As the scene came into focus, he was amazed by the realization that the shoes were attached to a man who lay, face-down and motionless, next to the bed.

"Miss Bethany, what...."

"Never mind what. See if he's dead."

"See if he's what?"

"Dead! For heaven's sake, Dick, poke him with your pitchfork!"

"Poke him with...."

"Yes, you dummy, poke him!" Beth, in her excitement, waved the gun dangerously.

Dick, frightened out of his wits, obediently, but gingerly, jabbed the man in the buttocks with his fork. Fortunately, there was no response.

"Good!" Bethany scrambled from the bed and found her robe....in the process of which she inadvertently presented Dick with a series of appealing views that he was much too upset to appreciate at the time.

"Miss Bethany, who in hell is that?"

Beth shrugged and shivered at the same time. "You mean, who *was* that! And watch your language." She pointed at the prostrate form with her weapon. I don't know who he was, but he tried to attack me. I had to defend myself. Now, Dick, run and get somebody. Anybody. Get Mr. Lanning."

"But...."

"Right now, Dick. Now!"

Dick dropped his pitchfork and ran frantically out of the door, then down the dark path toward town. Bethany lowered the derringer's hammer to its safety notch, unlatched the barrel assembly, carefully slid it forward, and replaced the spent rounds with some fresh ones that she retrieved from her drawer. She forced herself to take several deep breaths, hoping to control her trembling and to regain her nearly shattered composure. Beth's thoughts flashed, in gratitude, to her father who had wisely provided her with the little weapon before allowing her to leave their South Carolina home. Her self-control nearly restored, she coolly dropped beside the bleeding hulk of her ex-attacker. She had to pull and tug, rocking him back and forth, as she forced herself to search his clothing in order to find a clue as to his identity. Pinned inside his coat was a badge which was inscribed "Pinkerton Detective Agency". An inside pocket yielded an envelope which contained a page of meaningless-appearing gibberish that she recognized as cipher. She secreted the message in her bureau just as shouts of alarm and running footsteps approached the house. The envelope had only one word on it as an address. The word was "Tansy".

Mrs. Lanning ran a sweaty, but fairly respectable, third place behind Dick and the reverend. She even managed to retain enough energy, upon arrival, to immediately envelop Bethany in a protective embrace....notwithstanding the fact that she had to give a somewhat ponderous hop over the corpse in order to do so. "Come with me into the parlor, and away from this, dear. You poor thing! You must be scared to death!"

"I am. Oh, yes, I am!" shuddered Beth.

"Thank heavens you had a gun! I see that the beast got what he deserved!" Mrs. Lanning was trying to comprehend the bizarre situation. "Ah, dearest, where in the world did you get it?"

"Get what?"

"The gun, of course. I had no idea that you owned such a thing."

"My daddy gave it to me just in case I needed it to protect myself."

"How sweet of your daddy! He must be a very thoughtful man, I would suppose." She continued in the struggle to collect her thoughts. "And protect yourself you did. Bless you, poor child. I'm so relieved that you are unharmed."

"As am I. Believe me!" Beth was forcing herself to recover from the fright of her narrow escape. A frown, nearly hidden by her disarrayed hair, touched her forehead. "Mother Lanning, what do you suppose will happen now? After all, I have just killed a man. Do you suppose that I will be accused of his murder? Do you think I will be prosecuted?"

"Of course not, my dear. You acted, clearly, in self-defense. Don't you worry about such a thing. No one could possibly blame you. Now, this instant, you are coming home with me. I believe that we both deserve a nice cup of tea." Mrs. Lanning hugged her again and then drew back to look into her eyes. "That thug didn't harm you, did he?"

"No, praise the Lord, but he certainly meant to do so. He watched me take my bath by peering through the kitchen window."

Mrs. Lanning clutched at her heart in horror. "Oh, the beast! The disgusting beast! The Lord forgive me for saying so," she fanned her flushed brow with her hand "but I hope that his soul burns in hell."

Bethany's frown deepened. "I could care less what happens to his soul. Just so that he can't get to me again." She called into the bedroom where Pitts and Dick were gawking at the corpse as they tried to decide on a course of action. "Do you suppose that Matthew could be notified of this? I believe he is still at Camp Lyon, in Hamtramyck."

"Of course, Bethany." Reverend Lanning was shaken but was still perfectly capable of handling even this most extraordinary situation. "We'll see to it. Dick, you have a mission."

"A mission reverend? What mission?" Before Pitts could explain, they were both distracted by the dark, crimson stain what was spreading on Tansy's rug. Dick rolled the man over and examined the destroyed face from which the dark blood was seeping. "Sure is dead, ain't he?"

Lanning forced himself to take a quick look. "Yes. Dick, he is very dead. Dead indeed! And, thankfully, it is him and not Bethany!" A compassionate thought caused the clergyman to pause. "Dick, we must pray that God will forgive this man, lest he burn in hell."

Dick stared, open mouthed, at the pastor. He could not believe what he was hearing. "Pray for that bastard? I surely don't think so." He was bristling, almost shaking, in disagreement. "I hope he does burn. He *should* burn in hell! He meant to harm Miss Bethany! Nobody should ever dare to do that!"

That made it two votes for hell, one against, and one abstention. If it were up to the voters the terminated rapist would not have the good fortune to enjoy a pleasant hereafter.

Lanning struggled to make his face wear a benevolent smile. "You are right. No one should dare to do such a thing. Yet, eternity, and who gets to live in it, is up to the Lord and not to us. Let us bow in prayer, Dick." Pitts bowed his head but Dick stared, pointedly, at the ceiling. "Dear Lord, we pray that you will be merciful unto this depraved man's soul. And we thank you that Bethany is unharmed." Dick ducked his head just in time to join the last part of the prayer....the "thank you" part.

"Amen" intoned the reverend.

"Amen" echoed Dick, keeping his reservations to himself. "Whup! Look at this, Rev. He's got a pistol in his belt. And danged if there ain't a badge in his coat. Says 'P-i-n-k-e-r-t-o-n' on it."

"Pinkerton, eh? I've heard of that outfit. A detective agency. Word is that Mr. Alan Pinkerton has the confidence of President Lincoln and is advising him on security matters in Washington. Well! This makes things a bit more complicated. It appears that this man is not your average, run-of-the-mill criminal. I shall see that Mr. Pinkerton is strongly advised that he must pick his employees more carefully."

"Give 'em hell, Rev."

"Not funny, Dick."

"Sorry, sir." Dick smirked. "Now, you mentioned that you have a mission for me. What might that be?"

"Your mission is to saddle my mare and ride to Hamtramyck to notify Matthew that he should immediately return to comfort and care for Bethany."

"Yessir."

Pitts waved a finger at the youth. "Mind you, you are not to allow any harm to come to that mare. She is all that I have. She is my friend." A little smile played across the corners of the reverend's mouth. He leaned forward to speak in confidence. "We even talk, sometimes."

"You talk to your horse?" Dick was by now sitting on the side of the bed as the two blithely conversed across the remains of the late Pinkerton agent. "You're joking, of course."

Pitts chuckled. "Well, I confess that I do talk more than she does. At least, she doesn't argue with me or take pleasure in pointing out my inadequacies."

"Oh! I see." Dick scratched his head in puzzlement. "I guess I see. I will certainly be careful not to lame your talking horse friend."

Pitts brightened. "Thank you, Dick. In the meantime, I will send someone to notify Snuffy Smith." Snuffy Smith was an extraordinarily annoying person who served as the local constable. He was not noted for his constabulary expertise. He was, however, indeed noted for his unconscious, nervous snuffing which bothered everyone except him. "Perhaps," continued the reverend, "Snuffy will know what to do with this dead person. It's a little warm to let him lay around here for very long. Yet, I don't think we want him in our blessed little cemetery."

"What if we just dig a hole back by the manure pile, dump 'em in, cover 'em up, and forget the whole thing....including Constable Smith?" Dick was convinced that he had the perfect solution to the disposal problem.

"Actually, Dick, that's really not such a bad idea. Unfortunately, it won't work because his fellow agents will soon come looking for him. Might be a little hard to explain if they find him under Matthew's manure pile." Mr. Lanning stepped over the body and plopped onto the bed next to Dick. "Certainly wonder what he was doing here in the first place. I believe that I'll take that up with Mr. Pinkerton, too."

"And well you should!"

Lanning, deep in thought, swung his feet up and lounged, prone, on the bed with his hands comfortably folded behind his head as he rested on the pillow. He carefully considered the courses of action that could be taken. "Lets see. Snuffy will notify the county coroner in Pontiac who hopefully will arrange to remove the body in a timely fashion. Only thing is, I expect it will cost money for that service. Could be as much as five or ten dollars."

Dick whistled in dismay. "That's a bunch of money, I reckon. Maybe we should go back to my manure pile idea. Hmmm. I gotta new idea. Why don't you take that five or ten dollar fee up with Mr. Pinkerton, too?"

"My boy, you have flashes of brilliance. You have a good mind when, and if, you choose to use it. That's a grand idea. If Pinkerton can't control his men, the very least he can do is to pay to bury them."

"S'pose you can even get him to pay for Bethany's bullets? Seems to me that would be fair seein' as the bullets will go with him when they cart him off to Pontiac."

"That may just be a little too much to ask" chuckled Pitts. "I take back what I said about your bright ideas!" As he spoke, he sat up to take another look at the corpse. "Poor, ugly fellow!" he observed. He gave the body a push with his foot so that the perforated visage returned to its original face-down position. He had seen quite enough of the one, remaining, glazed eye that was staring at, or perhaps through, him. A wave of sadness and sympathy for the unfortunate man swept over him. When he looked at the unseeing eye, he could almost feel that the eye was looking back at him, seemingly asking for forgiveness. Pitts found himself listening to a voice that no one else could hear. It was the voice of the departed felon. He was crying for mercy....mercy that might give, even him, a place in eternity.

+ + +

The morning after the demise of the offensive Pinkerton agent found the villagers aflutter with excitement. The ladies of the Methodist Church felt obligated to do something to show their support for Bethany in her hour of need. The delightful fragrances of baking pies, cakes, cookies, and other culinary delights wafted about the village. These offerings would be carried to her, many of them still warm and steaming, in order to ease the distress that they assumed she would be suffering after her traumatic experience. Beth, actually, rarely ate little more than bird-like amounts of such foods. Nevertheless, she accepted them gracefully, and with happy expressions of delight. Her neighbors descended upon her in skirt-rustling waves to pat her hand and to assure her of their support for her heroic deed. She was already well-known, loved, and admired within the community before the shocking incident. Now, she had suddenly achieved celebrity status and was practically smothered with attention. She was transformed into the figurehead of a small, spontaneous, "women's' rights" movement.

Subsequently, the men of the village rolled their eyes in dismay as their wives demanded the installation of bars and locks for their doors. Some of the females even pressed to be provided with their own personal firearms with which they could defend themselves should a fate similar to Bethany's be foisted upon them. Most of the males recoiled from the gun-toting idea as they considered it to be inherently dangerous to anyone within range.... including to the would-be feminine gun wielders. Some of the gents had visions of being mistakenly bushwhacked by a panicked, armed female. An innocent trip to the outhouse, in the middle of the night, could well become an hazardous experience should their spouses happen to mistake them for a night-creeping felon.

Petite Bethany had defended herself against the perpetration of an unspeakable crime. As a direct result, over the next few weeks, many a pie plate, and other improvised targets, were terrorized by the whine and spat of bullets and shot. The time had come, at least at that moment in Franklin, for women to learn to defend themselves. Many of the men, mostly out of fear for their own safety, gently provided the requested firearms instruction. Shooting expertise became the favored topic of conversation at ladies' card, quilting, and/or circle meetings. Exclamations of admiration were favored upon those who had the largest contusions on their shoulders caused by the recoil of the family shotgun or rifle. Many of the ladies demanded to have their own weapon, such as the appealing Sharps derringer which had been so effective in Bethany's manicured hands. Few, however, could afford such a luxury.

George Congleton was assured payment for an appropriate wooden coffin to be crafted for the accommodation of the deceased Pinkerton agent. The construction of the macabre container took the expert craftsman only an hour, or so, to cut and assemble. By midmorning, the hefty corpse had been sealed therein and loaded upon Congleton's wagon. Per instructions from the coroner's office, it was promptly sent on its way to Pontiac. Haste was of essence as it was, obviously, desirable to avoid the odors of decomposition which would easily have become a problem on a warm, early September day. Irreverent little boys skipped alongside, and made snickery comments, as the wagon crossed the bridge and made its way out of town. Constable Snuffy Smith, in all his official glory, was at the helm. Justice of the Peace Harvey Lee rode next to him. His presence provided the necessary official solemnity to the occasion.

By early afternoon, the excitement had diminished. Bethany freed herself from the protective custody of Mrs. Lanning and returned to Matthew's house. Kind souls had already washed Tansy's rug, cleaned up the blood that was spattered over the bedroom floor, and generally set the house to order. The church women of the community had done something to help Bethany that was infinitely more horrifying than to just bake a pie. They had cleaned and scrubbed away the gore bravely, and well. Beth looked about the now tidy bedroom and thanked her Creator for providing such wonderfully supportive friends. Now, she was, at last, alone. Even Dick was gone. He had departed early, aboard the minister's treasured mare, on the way to Camp Lyon.

Bethany retrieved the "Tansy" dispatch from where she had hidden it in her bureau. Further rummaging produced an unusual object known as a "cipher wheel". The dispatch had no apparent meaning to anyone who did not know how to decipher it. It read:

"EBFR NEEFGQ LBH JNGPUQ FBGC QFCGPU JNVG SEGUE WAFG WQ"

More than two years before, when Bethany had announced to her father her intention to seek broader horizons, Jared Dodge had strongly objected to the proposed adventure. In the end, however, he had given her his misty-eyed blessing, funds more than ample for the occasion, the brand-new Sharps derringer, and the strange little brass cipher wheel. The cipher wheel was a primitive encoding/decoding device for use in the sending of private communications.

Major Jared Dodge, of the South Carolina Palmetto Guards, was a lonely man. He had lost his wife in childbirth when Bethany, their only child, was born. Beth was a great comfort and joy to him. It was most difficult for him to let her go away. The adventurous girl was aristocratic enough in behavior but, at the same time, was uncomfortable within the likewise aristocratic society of "Old South" Charleston. She considered most of the young, would-be cavaliers who called upon her to be self-centered, foppish, and not very smart. She had desperately needed a look at the rest of the world.

Granting permission for her to go was, for the major, an act of love and of courage. Jared had tried to hide the anguish that he was feeling....but with little success. She would look into his eyes, see the sadness there, and then force herself to look quickly away before her resolve to leave him could melt.

Sad as he was at the parting, Major Dodge was a practical person. As long as Bethany was determined to go north, she, in his mind, might just as well be of some use to the "Southern Cause" in the process. Consequently, he had arranged for her to make an extended visit to his good friend, Rose O'Neill Greenhow, who resided in Washington, D.C. Rose became delighted with her charming young guest. In no time, the two became fast friends. Bethany was thrilled to be thrust into the center of Washington's sometimes rough-and-tumble society. There was a seemingly endless supply of handsome, dashing West Point cadets, and a similarly appealing supply of recent graduates, who all vied for her attentions much as the older men vied for Rose Greenhow.

Jared had hoped that Bethany would become bored with the extravagances of Washington and would soon run back to the safety and glow of Charleston where she belonged. There was no such luck. Beth had thoroughly enjoyed her stay in the capitol. When she had tired of Washington she would go further north, not back to the south.

Well before the firing on Fort Sumpter by the Palmetto Guards, on April 12. 1861, the people of the south had realized that conflict, of some sort, was inevitable. The disparity of opinion, and of style, between the north and the south was on a collision course. Consequently, forward-thinking heads in Virginia, and in the Carolinas, began to enlist the aid of southerners in Nova Scotia, Canada, and in the northern states to form a loose network of espionage and communication. The lovely and seductive Rose Greenhow, with her numerous friendly contacts in Washington, was the most effective informant of all at the time.

Although Bethany was not interested in learning Rose's expert boudoir espionage techniques, she did greatly admire her mentor and aspired to follow, at least in spirit, her covert footsteps so that she might aid the cause of the southern states. Rose was a remarkably advanced instructor for her time. She had taught Bethany how to defend herself, how to use concealable weaponry, and how to turn off her sweet-as-honey Charleston, South Carolina, manner of speaking and to substitute the twang of a midwestern Yankee.... just in case her travels should require such concealment.

The joys of the new style of life had inspired Beth to become an apt pupil. The major, although disappointed that his daughter would not immediately return home, was proud of her new-found dedication to her southern homeland. In the absence of a yet to be formed Confederate Secret Service, it was arranged that should Bethany happen to gather any possibly important military information she would be obliged to communicate her findings directly to him. Major Dodge would then pass the intelligence along to President Davis, or to his staff, for evaluation. Bethany, at the time, had been more than happy to oblige. Although minor, her covert position had given a new excitement to her life.

Now, after two years of living in the north, and with Matthew serving as a Union cavalryman, Bethany was certain that she did not want to continue to be an informant for the south. She had been dutifully sending clippings from the *Detroit Free Press* that had pertained to troop movements and to other pertinent military information. Happily, she had very little access to any news of significant value. This lack of information had been especially pleasing to her in the light of her newfound conflict of interest. She had communicated, to her father, that her code name would be "Tansy". That code name had been inspired by Matthew's sweet dog. She had been certain that no one would make any tangible connection between her and a stumbly old black dog that was named, for some strange reason known only to Matthew, after a fragrant yellow flower. By previous arrangement she knew, because this was the third communication that she had received in the year 1861, that the "N" in Tansy was the key letter. The cipher wheel contained the alphabet engraved around its perimeter. A smaller, moveable inner wheel also displayed the alphabet. By moving the "A" on the inner wheel to correspond to the "N" on the outer one she could easily decode the message. It read:

"ROSE ARRSTD YOU WATCHD STOP DISPATCH WAIT FRTHR INS JD"

Bethany was distressed to learn that her friend, Rose, was incarcerated in Washington. At the same time, she was extremely happy to be effectively relieved from the covert service of the Confederacy. Now, she was reasonably certain that nothing that she had to do could hurt Matthew. She breathed a happy sigh of relief, at least until the dark shadow of the Pinkerton Agency flowed across her mind. Bethany was concerned, and frightened, by the probability that her disgusting Pinkerton attacker had intercepted, and possibly killed, the southern courier who was supposed to deliver the encoded message to her. The fact that the other agents could pick up on the lead established by the so-called snake-oil salesman was a worry of no small proportions.

The thought that Matthew might discover her covert activities caused a cold shudder to crawl up her spine. She became afraid that his love would quickly turn to hate should he discover her southern connection. Further distress was caused by the realization that spies are often hanged during wartime. Involuntarily, her hand went to her throat as though to check to see if it was still intact. She cradled her head on Matthew's oaken kitchen table and tried, with all her might, to be brave.

Dick Trick arrived at Camp Lyon with as much speed as he dared to coax out of the minister's mare without causing her discomfort. He even felt obligated to talk to the horse along the way, thus ensuring that she was happy and comfortable with his demands. Unfortunately, he arrived too late to intercept Captain Greyson.

The First Michigan Cavalry had been mustered into Federal service, by General Backus, and had promptly entrained for the "seat of war". They were well on their way to Washington, D.C., by the time Dick trotted the mare into Camp Lyon. Dick did, however, manage to locate Adjutant William Breevort whom he found to be busily organizing his paperwork in preparation for his own departure. Adjutant Breevort was instantly cooperative upon learning of the perilous situation into which Greyson's fiancee had been thrust. He telegraphed his intentions to Colonel Brodhead, and promptly arranged to accompany Dick back to Franklin. Once there, his stern military presence soon squashed any inclination to examine the incident further. Constable Snuffy Smith was no match for the army officer. Consequently, Snuffy took what he considered to be the honorable course of action. He simply slunk away. Even Justice Lee was relieved, and pleased, to be free of the whole affair.

Dick Trick and Bethany Dodge returned to the peaceful management of the farm. They were blissfully unaware that another Pinkerton agent was already sniffing around the village.

CHAPTER SIX

Alphaeus Plotkin

Near Washington

October 6, 1861

Dearest Bethany,

We arrived in good order and are encamped in the fields near a bristling fortress which overlooks the confluence of the Potomac and Anacostia Rivers. The view of the naval and commercial shipping is quite spectacular. I never saw so many ships, under sail or steam, honking and hooting at each other as they push and shove their way up and down the rivers.

We are quartered in row upon row of conical Sibley tents which are arranged upon muddy, but militarily precise, impromptu streets. Each tent has a stove in the center and is quite comfortable. We spend all of our time in organization and training as our command gradually arrives. All is amazingly well organized thanks to General McClellan and, of course, Colonel Brodhead.

I recently enjoyed the rare privilege of shaking the hand of General McClellan, himself! He stopped to speak with the colonel and spent some time with us in pleasant conversation. He is, truly, an impressive soldier. I believe that every hair on his head, as well as every hair on his horse, is combed separately to perfection. I had heard of his heroic exploits in Mexico, while I was there, but had never met him before. If anyone can lead us to victory over the secesh, I believe that he is certainly the one who can do it. His abilities to organize, and to train, are truly remarkable. I believe, as do many, that he seeks to emulate Napoleon. He appears to be doing a pretty fair job of it!

Saber has learned to hold steady in the face of the booming artillery and musket fire which are touched off on the training field for that purpose. He does not, however, like trains. He refused to load when we left Detroit. I had to catch (and twist a little) the arm of a private who was whipping him in order to get him to walk up the ramp and into the car with the rest of the mounts. Poor Saber was trembling like a scared puppy when I took his lead and spoke to him. His trembling immediately ceased and he followed me into the car without further protest. He made funny little trusting, flappy sounds with his nostrils as he went. Bethy, you would have cried to see the great beast so frightened, and yet so sure that I would not lead him to harm. I certainly hope that his trust was well-placed. I fear that I am really not quite so sure that he will not come to harm. The dangers, to both man and beast, will be many.

I pray that all is well with you, and with Dick, and with the farm.

I love you, forever, and miss you terribly! I sleep only fitfully. My mind and my body seek to caress you in my dreams.

Matthew

The capitol of The United States, in late 1861, was a sordid little city which was struggling to become worthy of the great nation which it represented. Monuments and edifices were being raised amongst the stench and flies that were associated with too many horses and mules, and too many people. The army quartermasters were on the verge of a cussing and spitting panic as they tried their best to accommodate, and to supply, the thousands of ill-equipped and ill-trained recruits who were arriving by the trainload. President Lincoln had called for a volunteer army to preserve the Union. The response was far in excess of the preparations that had been made for them.

The threat of attack by the recently victorious, rag-tag, butternut-and-gray army that skulked, appeared, disappeared, and reappeared across the

Potomac River was very real. A defensive perimeter of forts and redoubts were being hastily constructed and armed. Vast tent cities, parade grounds, and stables appeared everywhere. Teamsters shouted vulgarities as they whipped their straining teams through the mud, trying desperately to deliver the mountains of needed supplies.

The flashy and brilliant General George Brinton McClellan had been transferred from his former post in Ohio. He slashed his way into the reorganization of his new command with the fury of an avenging angel. The general was fresh from victories in western Virginia where he had captured Parkersburg and chased the boys in gray across the Kanawha River. His successes had stimulated the people of the area to desire separation from the Confederate State of Virginia. They, eventually, entered the Union as the State of West Virginia, by act of congress, in December of 1862.

General McClellan's star shone brilliantly and rose at an unprecedented rate. In the course of only a few months, he proceeded from commander of the Department of the Ohio, to commander of the Department of Washington and Northeastern Virginia, to commander of the Army of the Potomac, to commander of all armies of The United States. The none-too-humble "Little Mac" considered his amazing ascendancy to be totally appropriate....and a desperate nation concurred. Even Republican President Lincoln had to reluctantly ignore, at least for the moment, the fact that this Napoleon-inspired hero was a ferocious Democrat.

When the First Michigan Cavalry arrived at "the seat of war", McClellan's handsome, droopy mustache seemed to be everywhere. The officers and men were in awe of the charismatic general and leapt to follow his orders. Under his watchful eye, the Army of the Potomac was rapidly becoming a proud and formidable fighting force. Meanwhile, McClellan planned his famous, but ill-fated, Peninsular Campaign. He had little difficulty in convincing President Lincoln of the merits of the plan. He would transport almost one hundred thousand men, by water, to Fortress Monroe. The fortress was a federal bastion situated at the tip of the peninsula separating the York and James Rivers. Once there, he planned to sweep the rebels before him as he marched on the City of Richmond, the saucy Confederate capitol, and swiftly end the war.

Bethany read each of Matthew's none-too-frequent letters over and over again. She could almost recite their contents word for word. She saved each one, carefully adding it to the neat, ribbon-tied bundle that she kept in a drawer next to her bed. She usually wrote to him daily, and often sent packages of cakes and cookies in the sometimes vain hope that they would reach him intact....or even reach him at all. She prayerfully sent to him the miniature Bible that her father had given to her during her girlhood. She entreated Matthew to carry it close to his heart as she had heard that Bibles carried in breast pockets were known to stop bullets. Such body armor was probably more spiritually than physically effective....but, at the very least, it was worth a try.

Unbeknownst to Bethany, her worst fears were actually being confirmed. A second Pinkerton agent had been dispatched to Franklin, under orders from Allan Pinkerton himself, to uncover any facts which might shed more light upon the untimely demise of their deceased operative. Mr. Pinkerton had been informed that a Miss Bethany Dodge had killed his employee. The first agent had been assigned to the task of ferreting-out suspected Confederate couriers and spies, and to follow them in an attempt to expose any southern sympathizers who might be secretly working to damage the Union cause. The question to be resolved: Did Miss Dodge shoot the man in simple self-defense or was he shot because he was investigating her activities and was getting uncomfortably close to the truth? Agent #2 was dispatched to Franklin Village to find the answer. Pinkerton had definitely picked the right man for the job.

It was known to the agency that Agent #1 had been following leads in Detroit just before he had traveled to Franklin. Accordingly, Agent #2 checked on his late colleague's activities in that city hoping to learn what sort of trail had led him to Franklin. He uncovered no hard evidence, but had laughed out loud when he discovered a remarkable coincidence. Perhaps, it seemed, Agent #1 had been just a trifle overzealous in the prosecution of his investigative assignment. A young man, known to be from Richmond, Virginia, had been found floating in the Detroit River. The poor fellow had not had the opportunity to drown peacefully. His throat had been expertly slashed sometime before he was tossed into the dark waters. There were no suspects. Detroit police, with a shrug, had closed their investigation of the murder, considering the crime unsolvable.

With the onset of war, the Pinkerton Detective Agency had suddenly become a very busy organization. Allan Pinkerton's carefully cultivated friendships with General McClellan, and with President Lincoln, were bearing fruit. Covert assignments were causing his small gumshoe operation to blossom into a respectable, and profitable, counterintelligence agency. New operatives were hired as fast as they could be found. There was no effort to evaluate the moral fiber, nor to examine the police records, of the new men. To become, and to remain, a Pinkerton agent one had only to produce results--the completion of assignments within a reasonable length of time, at nominal expense, and with a reasonable degree of accuracy--all of this while attracting as little public attention as possible.

Agent #2, whose real (but rarely used) name was Alphaeus Plotkin, was more than pleased to be a part of this new game. Snooping for profit was the delight of his life, his *raison d'etre.* To him, the perfect day would be one during which he would expose someone--anyone--to the fact that they were not nearly as smart, nor as clever, nor as ruthless as Alphaeus Plotkin. His acute case of "small man syndrome" could even take a murderous turn on occasion. Still, he did occasionally have some human feelings. Alphaeus was both saddened and irritated by the fact that Bethany had snuffed his fellow agent. Vengeance, he gloated, would be his.

He was a sleazy little fellow with scraggly, thinning hair the remains of which hung down the back of his neck in a pathetic and greasy display. The none-too-subtle investigator soon became well-known to Franklinites as he drifted in and out of town for several weeks while seeking information. Much to his chagrin, everyone soon learned of his true identity and stonewalled his attempts to gain information out of concern for Bethany's safety. The villagers had witnessed the results of one Pinkerton agent's activities and did not care to encourage the efforts of another. Eventually, he disappeared....giving the impression that he had given up his quest. The villagers in general, and Bethany in particular, breathed a sigh of relief when they discovered that he had finally gone away. Unfortunately, they had grossly underestimated the mettle of Alphaeus Plotkin.

Even though he had received little cooperation, his investigative efforts had not been totally in vain. By piecing together bits and snatches of conversation, he had discovered that church choir practice was always held on Wednesday evenings and that both Bethany and Dick were sure to be in attendance. The perfect window of opportunity had presented itself. Accordingly, he slipped, unnoticed, into town on a Wednesday evening and ransacked the Greyson farmhouse at his leisure. He found Bethany's derringer in the drawer by the bed and pocketed it. He would have been delighted to find her cipher-wheel decoder had he known that she possessed such a device. Fortunately for Bethany, he did not find it. She had cleverly hidden that potentially damning evidence of her southern connection under a loose floorboard in the washroom. Plotkin was disappointed. He had uncovered no hard evidence of spy activity. He was uncertain, for a moment, as to what his next move should be. Thoughts of revenge still smoldered in his mind. Still undecided, he stationed himself, in good ambush position, next to the narrow path that wound down the hill between the farm and the downtown area. Alphaeus smiled smugly as he made himself indistinguishable from the other shadows. The trunk of an old apple tree provided additional cover for him as he waited for Bethany to pass along the path. She would probably be alone, and very likely would not bother to carry a lantern to light her way along the familiar path, even though it would be very dark before choir practice was over. Dick Trick, the agent had learned, had the habit of visiting with friends in town, after choir, and usually would not be along until later.

The detective heard Bethany's approach long before he could distinguish her as a deeper shadow against the barely perceptible whiteness of the sandy trail. She was still engrossed in her choir music. Little snatches and shards of hymns softly preceded her on the trail as she hummed her favorites. Alphaeus stopped chewing his quid of tobacco, and held his breath, as she passed so close to him that the swishing of her skirts seemed extraordinarily loud. When she was a few steps past his position, he could safely start to breathe again without fear of detection. The faint fragrance of roses lingered behind, in the darkness, to prove that she had really been there.

Plotkin flitted silently onto the path and followed Bethany, undetected, at a short distance. He nervously fingered the wire garrote which was always carried in the side pocket of his coat just in case the emergency silencing of an unfortunate subject should ever become necessary. Dark thoughts flitted across his mind. He could end the investigation, terminate Bethany, and avenge the death of his friend, all with one swift twist of the shiny wire around her pretty neck. He smiled to himself as he envisioned that there would be nothing pretty about that neck when he got through with it. However, he recalled, it was known that he had recently been spending a suspicious amount of time in the Franklin area. There was a good chance that he would be immediately connected to such a crime, especially considering the fact that local opinion was currently running very high against all things Pinkerton. As an instant, prime suspect, he would very likely have to suffer the inconvenience of flight from a lynching party, let alone from the law. Agent #2 silently ejected a stream of tobacco juice as he padded along behind Bethany in the darkness. Alphaeus was a man of patience. He could wait for a better opportunity. He left the silvery wire in his pocket.

Bethany found the door of the farmhouse standing open in the darkness. She started to walk in....but quickly changed her mind in fear that danger might be lying in wait for her should she be so careless as to step inside. Instead, she lit the porch lantern and held it high before her as she peered through the open door. The house had been trashed. Bethany gasped, in horror, at the sight of broken dishes, pulled-out drawers, and overturned furniture. Alphaeus chuckled silently in the shadows as he enjoyed her pain. He congratulated himself for a job well done.

He may not have found any hard evidence to the young woman's covert activity, but he had thoroughly enjoyed the process of looking for it. Most especially, he had enjoyed ripping open the ribboned bundle of Matthew's letters and snickering at the loving prose that they contained. He had made a point of crumpling, tearing, and scattering the precious letters as he finished scanning each one, looking for incriminating evidence.

Looking for a makeshift weapon, Bethany selected a stout piece of kindling from the firewood box on the porch. She cautiously made her way into the bedroom, holding the lantern before her, and made straight for the drawer where her derringer had been kept. The little weapon was no longer where it belonged. In fact, the drawer was no longer there, either. Suddenly realizing that she was nearly defenseless, and could be easily trapped in the house, she ran back to the porch, took a quick look around, extinguished the lantern, and slipped quietly into what she considered to be the safety of the darkness. Her plan was to run back down the trail toward town where she could easily find someone to protect her.

Alphaeus had anticipated such a move and stood, unseen, waiting for her in the darkness. The fevered brain of a born assassin could no longer resist the temptation presented by such an easy mark. She was hurrying straight into his clutches. Instinctively, he retrieved the garrote from his pocket, wound it around his wrists, and stretched it between them in anticipation of the moth fluttering into the web. Done properly, she would die without a chance to scream....but with ample time to realize the terror as her windpipe would be crushed and very nearly severed by the sharp wire that he would loop, and pull tight, around her neck. He wanted, desperately, to experience the completion of his murderous plan. He began to rationalize about his chances to escape retribution for his intended crime. Surely, one as expert as he in such matters could be far away before anyone would find her body. It would be inconvenient, but he could find a new place to do his work, a new job, and a new identity if necessary. A cruel smile twisted his lips. He had no shortage of spare identities upon which to draw. He stepped to the side of the trail and waited for his victim to come within reach. He was poised to strike, the wire strung between his wrists like the string of a violin, when he was startled to observe both the light of a lantern and he sound of footsteps approaching along the path from the opposite direction. Dick was returning from town. Plotkin, disgusted and disappointed, forced himself to move away from the path and into the deeper shadows.

Bethany nearly scared Dick out of his wits when she called to him from the darkness of the trail. "Dick, is that you?"

"Why....why yes, Bethany!" Dick tried to calm his suddenly jangled nerves. "You 'bout made me jump out of my skin! Why are you running around in the woods scaring people?"

Beth ran to the circle of light from his lantern. Her voice was quavering with fear. "Someone has been in the house. Tore it all apart! I'm afraid they may still be near!"

Dick was incredulous as he put a protective arm over her shoulders. "What are you talking about? Why would anybody get into our house? We haven't anythin' much worth stealin'!"

"I guess I just don't know, Dick," she lied, "but I'm afraid they might still be around here. I'm really scared!" Bethany clung to the boy for protection while Dick raised the lantern and tried to see into the darkness.

"Miss Bethy, we'd best run right down to get Constable Smith. He ain't worth much, but it's his job to protect us from such happenings."

Bethany nodded assent as tears of fright streamed down her cheeks. "Yes! Of course!" They had hurried just a short distance down the trail toward town when Bethany suddenly pulled Dick to a stop. Her bravery was returning, and her panic was subsiding, now that she was no longer alone. "Maybe telling the constable is not such a good idea. I think we should handle this ourselves."

Dick looked around, nervously, and then held the lantern so that he could see her tear-streaked face. "Now, why would we do that? Smith gets paid to handle such things....even though nothing like this has happened 'round here....'till now!"

"Let's just keep the constable out of it. People will talk."

"So?"

Beth was concerned with the distinct possibility that both Dick and the local residents would begin to raise their eyebrows at the unlikely coincidence that two strange occurrences had taken place, at her residence, within a few weeks of each other. She worried, and with good reason, that folks would begin to speculate about a possible golden thread running through it all. Such peculiar happenings were, to say the least, most unusual in the little village. Speculation was, indeed, a likely possibility. She feared that her cover was about to be blown. The worst thing that could possibly happen, especially if the news got back to Matthew, would be that word would get out that she was suspected to be a Confederate spy. She had survived the first Pinkerton occurrence in good order. She was not at all sure that her secret identity could survive a second incident without being detected. The unpleasant fear that she might end up dangling from a hangman's rope was a persistently terrifying possibility. "Never you mind, Dick. I'm going to ask you to rely on my judgment."

Dick shrugged. "Whatever you say, Miss Bethany."

"Good. Thank you. Do you still have that old double-barrel shotgun that Mr. Congleton gave you after that Pinkerton thug attacked me?"

Dick assumed the posture of a manly defender of the fair sex. "Yep! Its loaded and ready to go to work, should it be called upon. It stands behind the door to my room. Got it stuffed full of a nice load of buckshot just like Mr. Congleton told me to do."

"You're a good lad, Dick, and a real comfort to have around. Let's go and get it. We'll light all the lamps, check all the doors and windows, and stand guard for ourselves." She give him a stern look in the yellow glow of the lantern. "Now, listen to me. This is important. Unless we get into more trouble, we'll not mention this little problem to anyone. Clear?"

Dick rolled his eyes. He knew better than to cross the feisty schoolmistress. "Clear. Yes, ma'am, clear as could be. I'm sure that you know best."

Alphaeus Plotkin could hear their every word as he cowered in the darkness of his hidden position. Bethany's decision to keep the incident a secret confirmed his already firm suspicions. She must, indeed, be a Confederate undercover agent. No question, at all, now. He would file his report to the home office and subsequently receive appropriate accolades, as well as financial compensation, for his expert sleuthing. He, sadly for him, would not have the immediate pleasure of killing Bethany with his own hands. He was certain, however, that once his report was filed, someone else would see to it that she was properly punished for her treasonous activities. He, like Bethany, was aware that spies are normally hanged in time of war. He was, at the same time, both disappointed and gleeful as he coiled his garrote and returned it to its secure place in his pocket. Perhaps, with a little luck and a bit of effort, he could manage to be present to watch her final dance on the end of the executioner's rope. Agent #2 silently slipped away.

CHAPTER SEVEN

February, 1862

1st Mich. Cav. Camp, Washington

February 3, 1862

My Dearest, Sweet Bethany,

Oh! How I long for the sound of your voice, the gentle promise of your touch! Thank you for sending to me your little New Testament. I read it daily and carry it next to my heart as you have wished. I see, by the inscription, that it was given to you by your father when you were a child. I am deeply touched that you would give such a precious gift to me.

We are now a fairly well-disciplined fighting unit. The younger fellows revel in the pageantry, and consider themselves to be invincible. However, they have yet to know the horror, and pain, and suffering, of battle. I pray for their safety. I know that you are praying for all of us, too. I can often feel the comfort and strength of your prayers.

The southrons are proving themselves to be fierce warriors, just as I predicted. I'm afraid that this is going to be a long, horrible, and bloody mess. More and more brave men are going to be sacrificed on the altar of this war just to please the politicians. As far as I'm concerned, the rebs should be allowed to keep their precious Southland. It isn't worth much, anyway. But yet, the Union must be preserved, I am told. So....

I will serve my flag as I must. Be brave and patient, Bethany! I will endeavor to do the same.

Washington is a nasty town. It smells. It is filled, for the most part, with charlatans, prostitutes, and the ever-present politicians. They are good company for each other and all seem to be immensely enjoying themselves. The capitol building has a big crane and a lace work of scaffolding protruding from it as workers attempt to finish its construction.... even in the face of war. It seems to be our duty to protect this edifice so that it may be completed and dedicated to the honor and glory of our country, and to Father Abraham.

Speaking of our president, I had a glimpse of him as we passed in review before the grandstand where he stood along with an assortment of other dignitaries. He is very tall, very plain, and wears a tall dress hat which makes him appear even taller. He did not smile, at all, during the short time that I could see him.

I was recommended to a jewelry store, the proprietor of which was, of course, (forgive me) a Jew! I had misgivings, but was soon impressed by the gentleman's expertise and perception. He listened to my loving description of your hand and, somehow, immediately figured out your size. I hope that he figured correctly! He is a remarkable little man and seems to be trustworthy. I purchased a beautiful ring which I am sending to you, forthwith. I believe that it will fit your lovely finger as a long-overdue token of our engagement. I hope that the mails will safely convey it to you. Please write to me, truthfully, as to whether or not you like the ring. If (oh sorrow!) you do not, I will send another at first opportunity....whenever that may be. The disposition of our unit is uncertain at this time. I suspect that we will soon be on the march.

Your faithful, and lonely, love,

Matthew

The "Michiganders" were ready. They were itching to fight, to put the upstart Confederates in their place. Even the horses were proudly head-high as they pranced through their seemingly endless drills. They too could sense the excitement in the air. McClellan was finally about to make his move. The First Cavalry was poised to serve with "Little Mac" in the grand Peninsular Campaign. But, in spite of Colonel Brodhead's considerable influence, it was not to be. Instead, they were attached to the forces of General Nathaniel Prentiss Banks and sent northwest. General Banks was ordered to take, and hold, the valley of the Shenandoah River. They marched to Frederic, Maryland, and from there to Harpers Ferry, Virginia, where a large Federal armory was situated at the confluence of the Potomac and Shenandoah Rivers.

+ + +

In Michigan, February is a time of intense, delicious beauty....at least in the eyes of those who are programmed to love howling winds, drifting snow that could pile itself higher than a belt buckle, and snowflakes that can become icy butterflies that flutter around one's face as though to brighten the gray of a frosty morning. Sometimes, a frolicsome northerner could catch some of the plumpest flakes on his tongue, were he willing to throw himself, tongue first, into the sport. When the sun would show itself, which it seemed to do only occasionally, the world would be transformed into a spectacularly blinding crystal palace of frosty diamonds, the beauty of which could hardly be equaled by any dusty rock that was dredged from the bowels of the earth.

Dick Trick loved the winter. He loved the challenge of the snow and ice as he labored to keep the livestock fed and comfortable. His animal friends, who seemed to be both frosty and steamy at the same time, rewarded his efforts with soft nickers, happy moos, and bleats of recognition whenever he appeared to provision them. His mildly crippled body, once considered to be nearly hopeless, responded to the healthy exercise by becoming more supple, more manly.

He watched, with concern, as the neatly split and stacked piles of stove wood near the house were depleted at an alarming rate when the temperatures stubbornly remained below zero for days at a time. The big kitchen stove in the house, the parlor stove, and the comforting little tack room stove that kept him warm at night, all seemed to have voracious appetites. Winter had the bit in her teeth and seemed to be determined to trample the whole world into icy oblivion.

Farmers are supposed to take their rest during the winter as they restore their energies to make ready for the time of spring planting. Dick had no such luxury. He spent many hours in Matthew's expansive wood lot as he cut previously stockpiled timbers into manageable lengths and then loaded them onto the heavy wooden sledge for transport to the house. Molly and Moe waited patiently as he assembled the load, then grunted, steamed, and scrambled on the slippery footing as they strained to break the runners free from where they had frozen into the ice. Once free from the icy grasp, the sledge glided easily to the house where Dick unhitched the team and then faced the monumental task of unloading, sawing, splitting, and stacking. Bethany would help where she could, often handling the stacking part of the operation.

The cold always intensified in the evening when, if it could be seen at all, the sun slipped below the horizon and pulled its frost-pink afterglow with it. Dick generally finished his chores by lantern light. Bethany would hold the palm of her hand to a kitchen windowpane, defrosting a transient observation post through which she could watch his progress. She could see his lantern flit from harness room, to water trough, to haymow.... looking, for all the world, like a giant, orange firefly that had lost its way. By watching the movements of his light, Beth could determine the exact, optimum moment to pop the biscuits into the oven and to make ready to ladle her specialty, a tangy and chunky vegetable-beef soup, into the waiting preheated bowls. Dick would invariably be famished at the end of a hard day's work out in the cold. Given the opportunity, he would try his best to snatch a plump, hot biscuit from the table before Bethany could forcibly divert him in the direction of the wash stand.

Dick and Bethany shared a common goal. Together, they would manage the farm to the very best of their abilities. They talked, often, of how pleased that Matthew would be when he returned from the war to find the fences mended, the livestock fat and healthy, and the buildings all painted and tidy. The togetherness necessitated by the shared tasks of the long winter had forged a warm bond between them.

Bethany considered herself to be Dick's older sister. She treated him with the firmness and love that would befit such a relationship. That was fine with Dick....at first. However, as his manhood began to assert itself, he began to find that he was thinking of her in other terms. He became more acutely aware of her sexuality when she leaned close to him to help him with his school work, or to serve his breakfast. He began to feel a strange new warmth, from deep within, as he watched her busily attending to her work around the house, or when she combed her long, black hair. He noticed that when she perched on the parlor sofa to mend his clothes, or to cross-stitch a gift for a friend, she would always tuck her bare feet under her skirt like a contented cat. "Helps to keep them warm" she would say. Beth would hum a soft little tune while she stitched. "Music" she told him "helps to make the stitches fly."

Dick was feeling the pangs of a first love. He hated himself for his disloyalty to Matthew, his friend and mentor, who had entrusted him with his woman, and with his farm. His guilt was strong, but was finally burned away by the intensity of his desire....desire fueled by recurring visions of Bethany kneeling on the bed, naked, with her derringer in her hand. He had thought that he had been too distracted by the bizarre situation that was caused by the felonious Pinkerton agent to pay much attention to Bethany's nakedness, but he was wrong. His mind had recorded the scene with the accuracy of a fine tintype. He could envision every detail of her perky breasts, her beautiful nipples, her sensuously slender fanny. Dick could stand the pressure on his heart no longer. He had to tell her....he had to make his play.

Bethany sensed a change in Dick's behavior. Her adopted "little brother" was getting to be a little too attentive, a little too interested in her activities. Her teaching experiences had taught her to recognize such symptoms. She was well-prepared to deal with such a problem. In fact, she had become something of an expert in the field of aberrant love as her youthful beauty, and the nearness to her age of some of her pupils, had caused her to learn to deal with the same problem....more than once. When Dick appeared for dinner, presenting an unusually washed and combed appearance, she began to suspect that her male-handling skills were about to be tested.

Dick did not waste any time in confirming her suspicions. "Bethy, I got to tell you something." He reached across the table to take her hand. "Promise you won't be put out?"

"Now, how can I promise that? I don't know what you're going to say, yet." She smiled at him, concealing her alarm, as she freed her hand from his grasp. "Oh, Dick, my dear little brother, don't tell me that you have done something that you should not have done!"

Alarm bells rang in Dick's ears as his thoughts reeled from the impact of the "little brother" reference. He dropped his eyes from her gaze. "Well, no. I ain't done nothin' wrong."

"Well now, that's a relief!" As usual, she could not resist correcting his grammar. "You mean to say, of course, that you have not done anything wrong?"

"Uh, yeah. That's what I mean. I, well, um, I just got me a man-to-woman problem."

"Oh, of course!" Bethany was brightly sympathetic. "I guess that I have suspected as much, what with your growing up so much, lately. Let me guess. You are lonesome for the company of a girl of your own age. Right?"

"Well, something like that." Dick was getting the picture. His mind began to cast about for a way to get himself out of an embarrassing situation.

Bethany saved him the trouble of having to contrive an escape. She excitedly clapped her hands. She had a funny way of applauding when something really delighted her...she always held her wrists together and clapped, in a most ladylike fashion, with just her fingertips. When she did that, Dick knew that she was really pleased about something but was at a total loss, this time, to figure just what that something might be. "Well, little brother," she summoned her most impish smile "I have good news for you!"

"You do? And what, in the world, could that be?"

"You have an admirer." Dick's jaw dropped in surprise. Bethany's grin widened as she reached to pat his hand. "Its Hannah! I believe that she is beginning to feel that you are God's gift!"

Dick ducked his head in fear that he was being put upon. "I hardly think so, Beth. I want you to know that I am not in a mood to be joked with."

"But, I'm not joking. I talked, for a long time, with Hannah during the quilting party last week. She spoke very highly of you."

Dick's eyes were wide, his face skeptical, at the new revelation. "I can't believe that a beauty like Hannah could be interested in a scarred and ugly person like me."

"Well, its true. I wouldn't make up such a thing." Beth, actually, was not lying. Indeed, she had discovered Hannah's interest in Dick when she had deliberately cornered the pretty child and held a lengthy conversation with her during the quilting bee. "And, for heaven's sake, stop hiding behind that 'scarred and ugly' thing. You've grown to be a handsome young man."

Dick's ears turned red at the compliment. "How's come you didn't tell me about this right off?"

"Because, I wanted to give you some advise, first. You have no man to instruct you in the fine art of girl-catching, so I guess it is up to me to tell you how its done. Hannah would probably be thrilled if you were to call on her."

"She would?"

"Yes, but don't do it."

"Huh? And, why not? How can I get to know her if I don't go to court her? Are you really sure you know what I should do?"

"Of course I'm sure. I'm both your teacher and your big sister, you know. You need to trust my judgment as I am older, and more experienced, than you. I know what kind of a girl she is. Ignore her. Make her come to you."

"What if she don't?"

"Doesn't."

"What if she doesn't?"

"She will. I'm certain that she will. Now, go to bed. Its going to be clear tomorrow. Dawn will come early and you need your rest."

Dick's head was reeling from all of the new, bittersweet revelations that he needed to sort out in his mind. Obediently, he bade Bethany goodnight and followed the narrow path of trampled snow, that was just barely two boots wide between the drifts, to his tack room sanctuary. The swath of the Milky Way that twinkled across the sky was so bright that he could see his shadow in the snow. Beth was right....tomorrow would be a clear day. Molly and Moe nickered soft, sleepy greetings as he passed their snug, warm stalls in the barn. He was so full of both wonderful and confused thoughts that sleep was definitely out of the question. He sat, long into the night, and watched as the little flickers of light from the dying embers in the stove pirouetted and curtseyed charmingly across the floor.

Bethany had swung the door shut against the coldness of the night after watching Dick disappear into the darkness. She stood for a moment, staring at the closed door, feeling tragically alone. She understood, perfectly, the feelings of the distraught boy. The prospect of another solitary, chilly night made her breath quiver a little. She almost wished that she could put on her shawl and follow him to the warm coziness of his bedroom.

+ + +

When the new day did creak and shiver itself awake, the dawning was spectacular. The deep blackness of night gradually shaded into frozen gray, then to red, then to a bright and startlingly cold cobalt blue.

Mail delivery to Franklin was, at best, regularly irregular. But this day, the villagers were treated to a midmorning delivery. The mail sleigh jangled along the main street. Then, runners squealing on the subzero snow, it turned onto Plank Road and stopped at the little cobbler's shop which doubled as the post office. Delighted and surprised, Postmaster/shoemaker Charlie Coder looked up from the new boot that was taking shape upon his cobbler's last as the sleigh groaned to a stop at his door. Without bothering to put on his coat, Charlie jumped from his stool and plunged into the frosty outdoors to receive the mail. His cheery greeting to the mailman was followed by an invitation to dismount and to join him in the warm shop for a spicy cup of hot cider. Coder's cider, which was expertly spiced with just the right amount of cinnamon, was guaranteed to improve even the thermally-compromised circulation of the frost-encrusted delivery man. The driver was tempted by the neighborly offer, but reluctantly declined the invitation in consideration of the possibility that his horse might freeze into an icy lump and thus be unable to pull the mail sleigh back along the frosty road to Piety Hill from whence he had just come. He considered it to be prudent to remain cocooned within the furry warmth of a monstrous bearskin robe from which only his cap, his nose (very red), and his mittened hands protruded.

Bethany had been a frequent visitor to the post office, always hoping that a letter from Matthew would have arrived. Lately, she had been looking for a special package that would contain the long-anticipated, and lovingly promised, engagement ring.

The bundle of mail was so cold that it caused Charlie's hands to hurt as he sorted through it. "Oh, how nice!" he exclaimed, with a happy smile. There, amongst the letters and newspapers, was a small package addressed to Miss Bethany Dodge. "Miss Bethany will be more than pleased. I will deliver this to her personally!" he announced. His fuzzy cat, the only available listener, was totally uninterested in the news as she curled close to the warmth of the stove. Charlie next spotted a letter that was addressed to Miss Hannah Midgley. The return address displayed the identity of the sender. It was from one Sergeant Will McEwan, and was postmarked "Harpers Ferry, Va." He decided to deliver it, too, even though the mail was normally picked up at the post office. In a small town, everyone seems to know the more important aspects of everyone else's business. Charlie was especially proud that his fingers were always on the pulse of the community. He was well aware that Miss Midgely was hoping to hear from her soldier beau, and that Bethany was anxiously awaiting her little package.

His sorting carefully completed to his satisfaction, Postmaster Coder bundled himself against the cold and trudged through the drifted snow to the Midgley home. Hannah sang little squeals of happiness when he placed the letter in her trembling hand. She held it to her breast as she thanked Coder, over and over again, for his personal and caring service. When Hannah had calmed sufficiently, the postmaster told her of the arrival of Bethany's package. Hannah responded with even more squeals, accentuated, this time, by jumping up and down in childish delight. "Please, please, Mr. Coder! Could I take it to her? I know she is home this morning. Bethy will be so very happy! I want to see her face when she gets it. Please?"

The big blue eyes were just too much for Charlie to resist. "Well....yes, miss. I reckon that it will be just fine for you to do that. Mind that you go right away....and be certain you don't lose it in the snow."

"Oh, I will. I will! I mean, I won't. I won't lose it, I promise. I swear, I don't know what I mean! Oh, this is so exciting!" Hannah was already pulling on her boots. He helped her to don her heavy coat, then handed the little package to her. She smiled up at him with a sweetness that could melt the stoniest of hearts, let alone Charlie Coder's soft and caring one, as she wrapped a shawl over her golden curls. "Thank you again, Mr. Coder. This will be a quick delivery. I'll run all the way up the hill!"

Charlie chuckled at her antics. "I expect you will do just that, miss. Good morning." His cupid duties were successfully completed. Now, he could return to the fragrant, leathery warmth of his shop. It was nice to be able to deliver some happiness, to create some little bright spots, in that foreboding time of war. All too often, the mails contained messages of despair and of sadness as tearful families learned of the incapacitation, or of the death, of the young men who had marched so heroically away, only to be sacrificed on the altar of the gods of war.

Hannah found Bethany and Dick seated at their kitchen table. Accounts, ledgers, and papers were sorted into neat piles as they planned for the purchase of the seed, supplies, and equipment which would be needed when it came time for spring planting. Startled, they looked up with surprise as she burst through the door in a snowy flurry. "Bethy, its here. Its here!" With a dramatic flourish, she placed the small package on the table and seated herself expectantly, opposite Bethany, without taking the time to remove her coat.

"What? Oh! How nice of you to bring it up here through all the snow. Thank you, Hannah. I can hardly believe that its really here." It was addressed in Matthew's familiar handwriting. The sight of his bold script made her feel warm inside.

"Open it, Bethany, open it!" shouted Hannah, impatiently.

"Goodness, child, contain yourself." Bethany unwrapped the box with painstaking slowness, taking care not to tear the wrapper. She gasped when she saw the ring. "Oh my! Oh dear! It is absolutely beautiful!" She stared at the large, many-faceted diamond that was surrounded by smaller ones and set in yellow gold. Both women burst into tears of happiness. Dick, on the other hand, viewed the scene in openmouthed amazement. Bethany slipped the ring upon her finger. It fit perfectly, just as Matt and his Jewish

118

friend had said that it would. "I only wish Matt could have been here to give it to me in person." she sighed. "Oh well. Can't have everything." Her young friends were staring at her, their smiles fading. "Sorry, you two. I'm really very, very happy. How could I not be with such a beautiful treasure on my finger?"

Hannah nodded, knowingly. "'Spect you'd rather have Matthew here.... ring or no ring."

Beth patted Hannah's hand. "You are so right! I'm glad that you understand." Bethany jumped to her feet. "I believe its time to celebrate. How about fresh apple pie, cheese, and milk for lunch?"

"Now we're gettin' somewhere!" Dick hitched his chair closer to the table. "I could eat that whole pie by myself."

Beth pretended to scold. "Mind your manners, Dick." She brought a pitcher and glasses to the table. "You may pour the milk, if you can stop thinking about the pie for a moment."

"Yes'm."

It was the perfect time for Hannah to display her own triumph. "Guess what else came in the mail today!" She produced Will's unopened letter from her pocket and waved it at them. "Its a letter from Sergeant Willy, at last! Whew! I'm getting hot, what with all this excitement."

Dick looked up from his milk detail and gave her a grumpy stare. "Why don't you try taking your coat off?"

Hannah ignored him, hastily opened the letter, and began to read. Her lips moved as she sounded out the words. "What a sweet man! He says he thinks of me, often, and can't wait to see me again."

That was quite enough for Dick. Without a word, he took up his coat and made his exit, slamming the door behind him as he clumped away. The women watched, in surprise, as he stalked by the window and turned up the road, his appetite forgotten as disappointment and hurt wrenched at him. The only two women in the world that he really cared about had already been claimed by other men.

"Surely don't seem fair, somehow" muttered Dick to the unconcerned snowdrifts. "I 'spect I'm doomed to be forever alone!" He kicked savagely at the drifts as he slogged along the nearly impassable road. "No folks, no girl, no nothin'. Guess I might have known it would be this way. Bethany says I'm growin' to be a little better to look at....but I think she's just tryin' to be nice to me." He clapped his mittened hand to his forehead in anguish. "An', I even managed to make a fool of myself over her, besides!" He delivered a sweeping kick to a perfectly innocent drift that happened to be within reach of his boot, decapitating it in a spray of snow.

At Dick's sullen departure, Hannah dropped her suddenly-not-so-precious letter and ran to the window. She pressed her face to the glass as she tried to see where he was going. Tears sprang into her eyes as she watched him trudge out of her sight. "Oh-oh!" whispered Hannah as her breath mingled with the frost already on the window, "he didn't even get to eat the pie he wanted so bad. Beth, what's wrong with me? I'm so thoughtless! Oh dear, what have I done?"

"Oh dear, indeed, Hannah! I'll tell you what's wrong with you." Bethany gently pulled her from the window and plunked the woman-child into a chair from which there was no way to escape the lecture that she was about to deliver. Stern, smoky-blue eyes locked into the startled, more intense blue of the girl's gaze. Hannah tried to look away, but Beth would not let her do so. "Look at me! Listen to me for a moment! You have found this man whom you can really love--I'm talking real, grown-up love-- but you just haven't quite figured how you should behave. Hannah, you must not torture the man that you love by gloating over the attentions of those that you don't. It's time for you to grow up lest you hurt someone deeply....including yourself." Bethany knelt before her, resting her arms on Hannah's knees. "You once told me that you cared for Dick. Did you, or didn't you, mean what you said?"

Hannah nodded, tearfully. "I guess I meant what I said when we talked, before. I just didn't realize, 'till now, what I was saying. Bethy, how come you are so wise? I just come to know how much I care for Dick, an' you knew it all along. And now, I have hurt him deep by reading, with such pleasure, Will's words." Hannah tried to wring her hands and to dab at her eyes all at the same time, utilizing a linen napkin that she had snatched from the kitchen table.

120

Bethany patted Hannah's cheek, trying her best to ward-off the sobs of despair which she could see were just on the verge. "All is not lost, poor little dear. I think that it might just be wise for you to go after him. Why don't you go after him right now?"

Hannah soiled the napkin a little more with her tears. "But, should I manage to catch up with him, whatever will I say? He'll think I'm stupid, or something."

"He won't think any such thing....believe me. And, don't you worry. You'll say the right thing. I'm sure you'll think of something." Bethany was not really quite as positive in her mind as she tried to sound. "If you really do care, Hannah, you must go and catch him right now." Beth pulled the tearful girl to her feet and propelled her toward the door.

Hannah needed no further prompting. Snatching up her shawl, she flew in hot pursuit of the quarry that she had just determined must not get away. Bethany stepped out onto the porch and watched, with amusement, as the little figure scampered through the snow and disappeared up the road trailing clouds of breath and the tail of her shawl behind her.

Dick was nearly at the intersection of the two Townline Roads when Hannah overtook him. She did not present herself as a particularly romantic figure when she breathlessly called for him to wait for her. Amazement, delight, and a warm, excited glow instantly pushed his bad mood away as he turned and waited for her to struggle through the snow, to finally reach him, to catch his arm. He had never seen her look quite so messy before.... but that mattered not a bit. Her hair hung in sodden ringlets. She was panting from exertion like an overworked steam engine. Her once pretty nose was reddened, and was dripping at an embarrassing rate.

"Hold me while I get my breath!" she gasped. He obligingly put his arms around her and supported her, gently, while her respirations returned to something near normal. She made an attempt to regain her composure by blowing her nose in a rather unladylike, but noisily effective, fashion.

Dick marveled that she could look so soggy and so beautiful at the very same time. "Where are you running to in such a hurry?"

"To catch you, silly. I want to walk through the snow with you."

"You do?" Suddenly, the angels were singing in his ears. Having never been in such a wonderful situation before, he really had no idea as to what he should do. Bravely throwing caution to the winter winds, he lifted her chin and shyly kissed her. Hannah did her best to give a meaningful response, but unfortunately, his tender ministration was not too successful as by now she was trembling from the cold. Her lips were turning blue and her nose insisted upon continuing to drip. Dick, instinctively, assumed the manly role of protector. "Hannah, you're about to freeze up. Best we get you right home."

"Oh, yes! Please!" She cuddled against him. He could sense the shivering softness of her body right through the thickness of her heavy woolen coat. "If you will just keep your arm around me, I'll get nice and warm in no time."

Bethany had pulled her wooden rocker to the parlor window. The window, a bay, gave a good view up, down, and across the snowy road. From her snug vantage-point, she hoped to see evidence that Hannah's frantic pursuit had ended successfully. She did not have long to wait. The happy couple emerged from the blowing snow and traipsed, arm-in-arm, past the house as they headed toward town. Beth could see that they were chattering gaily as they flounced their way through the drifts. "Hurrah!" she exclaimed to the empty parlor, "the rabbit has caught the hound and is returning, victorious, with her prey in tow!"

She shivered and pulled her shawl around her shoulders. The parlor was not nearly as warm as the kitchen. Returning there, she put extra wood into the big iron stove and filled the teakettle. She would treat herself to a nice, steamy cup of tea in celebration of her successful counseling. The emptiness of the house, however, seemed to be folding around her. She lit a lamp, to dispel the deep winter gloom, and held her hand in its light. Bethany moved her fingers to make her new ring twinkle in the lamplight. She could feel the comfort of Matthew's prayers as she admired the beauty of his gift of love. "Perhaps," she thought, "I should put on my coat and run down to the parsonage to show off my new ring! I know Mother Lanning will squeal with delight when she sees it!" She smiled at the thought, but the smile was chased away when a frown knitted her pretty brows. She wanted to go, but was afraid to go outside. The winter storm was causing the darkness to come early. Anxiety and fear had grown within her ever since the Pinkerton incidents, never giving her rest. She shrugged as she glanced out of the windows. All seemed peaceful and quiet as the snow swirled and danced in the darkening yard. With a sigh, she barred the door and returned to her tea. "It will be brighter tomorrow, I'll guess. I'll show them then." The chill from the parlor seemed to have followed her into the kitchen in spite of the best efforts of the sizzling stove.

Hannah and Dick pushed their way through the drifts to the Franklin Road, then followed the wagon-wheel ruts to the Midgley house where they tramped the snow off of their boots on the front porch, then burst through the door and into the foyer where they struggled, giggling and chattering, out of their wet and frozen outerwear. Hannah's sister-in-law emerged from the kitchen to determine the nature of the disturbance. The delicious odor of baking gingerbread cookies wafted along behind her.

"My goodness, children, what have you been doing? Hannah, you look as though you have just been fished out of the mill pond!"

"Guess again, dear sister. I've just been havin' a fun time with my friend." She reached for Dick's hand and gave it a squeeze.

The maneuver was not lost on Mrs. Midgley. "Oh my!" she thought, "Hannah has another new beau. Wonder how long this one will last!"

Hannah led Dick into the kitchen and pulled a chair in front of the big range where he could thaw in comfort while she went upstairs to change her clothing, and to attempt to repair her appearance. Dick chatted affably with Mrs. Midgley until Hannah reappeared. She looked, for all the world, like a golden-haired angel. Dick tried to conceal his awestruck admiration by acting casual....but his heart almost stopped when he looked at her. Hannah sensed, a bit smugly, the love in his eyes.

Suddenly and magically, it occurred to Dick that he had been transported to a heaven on earth. He was in the company of a beautiful young woman, a warm stove, a plate of scrumptious gingerbread cookies, and a mug of hot mulled cider. Could one ask for anything more? Not in this life.

Mrs. Midgley excused herself and disappeared into the adjacent parlor. As soon as she was gone, the youthful lovers held hands until the chill was entirely gone from their fingers, and then held them just a little longer to make sure that the warmth would remain. They chatted happily as they laid plans to do many fun things together: Skating on the mill pond, a sleigh ride to visit friends in North Farmington, sledding down the cemetery hill, making a snowman....the list appeared to be endless.

They began to wish that they could have been left completely alone....but Mrs. Midgley was far too wise to allow that. They could hear her rocker squeaking softly as she sat, out of sight, in the next room.

"Sounds like you got a little bird in your parlor." whispered Dick. "A squeaky one."

Hannah giggled. "Maybe we do. Must be spring!" She kissed him, sweetly, but kept one eye open to monitor the parlor door.

The howls of the winds that curled and rattled around the Midgley house seemed to fade and to change their tune to play a softer song. The sound of the sleet that had just begun to tap upon the windowpanes went unnoticed. Perhaps, the sleet was just noisy sunshine. Hannah was correct. Spring did seem to come early to Tom Midgley's home that day.

CHAPTER EIGHT

John Chandler

During the winter of 1861-1862, the military genius of Confederate Major General Thomas Jonathan Jackson was yet to be recognized. In fact, he had demonstrated quite the opposite by sacrificing his men and materiel in an exhausting winter campaign that, although reasonably successful, accomplished little except to earn him the ire of his subordinates. He was, however, already a hero throughout the south as the famed "Stonewall" who had stopped the Federal offensive at the Battle of First Manassas. The officers and men of his little Army of the Valley considered him to be a grumpy, secretive, stubborn, Bible-thumping, and rather odd ex-professor of physics whose negative qualities far outweighed his "Stonewall" mystique.

Union leaders in Washington were likewise unimpressed with either Jackson or his army. They were impressed, however, by the fact that his rebel forces were camped for the winter at Winchester, Virginia, just sixty miles northwest of Washington. Jackson's position was at once both annoying and somewhat alarming. First, the proposed Federal invasion of the prized Shenandoah Valley would require the commitment of a large body of troops in order to assure success. Second, the somewhat meager defenses around Washington were about to be further weakened by the departure of McClellan's 100,000 man army which was preparing to sail to Fortress Monroe in preparation for the Union general's treasured Peninsular Campaign. An attack on the capitol city by the brash General

Jackson, given the present circumstances, was an embarrassing possibility. Lincoln worried that his blue line of defense was about to get a little thin in spots.

The Federal grand strategy was generally well-conceived. Based upon old General Winfield Scott's "Anaconda Plan", they sought to strangle the rebellious south within a coil of military might. The Blockade Fleet began to assemble along the Atlantic Seaboard and the Gulf of Mexico. Naval forces were concentrating at Ship Island, near the mouth of the Mississippi River, in preparation for the capture of New Orleans. Defenses were being strengthened along the Ohio and the upper Mississippi.

General Banks' 8,000 man Union army crossed the Potomac River at Harpers Ferry, Virginia, in late February under orders to sweep Jackson's forces south, up the valley, and safely away from Washington, thus removing that city from the "endangered species" list. As a further benefit of the plan, Federal control of the Shenandoah Valley would deny the Confederates access to the rich agricultural resources of that lush and beautiful region.

General Banks' forces, which included the First Michigan Cavalry, encountered few difficulties as they chased Jackson's 5000 man army out of Winchester, Virginia, and beyond. They would have been a little less jubilant about their apparent success had they known the orders under which General Jackson was operating. His orders had come straight from President Davis. Jackson had been instructed to harass Banks, to the best of his ability, without exposing his own forces to significant losses. He was to keep Banks too busy to even think about leaving the valley, thus denying the possibility that he could spare any of his troops for the reinforcement of McClellan's Peninsular Campaign which was about to threaten Richmond.

On May 17, 1862, General Banks, having marched as far south as Harrisonburg, was ordered to retrace his steps and to return north to Strasburg. Lincoln's strategists no longer considered Jackson to be a threat. The Federal forces would concentrate and then leave the Shenandoah Valley for a coordinated assault upon Richmond from the west. The Confederates, of course, were delighted by the move. Spearheaded by Colonel Turner Ashby's splendid cavalry, they proceeded to nip at the heels of the departing Federal columns as they moved back down the valley and away from the southern heartland. The First Michigan Cavalry, along with the rest of the mounted forces commanded by Brigadier General John P. Hatch, drew the hazardous task of protecting the long line of march from the fierce depredations of the rebels who focused their slashing attacks upon the flanks and rear of the re-deploying blue-clad soldiers and their rolling materiel.

In spite of the Confederate's best efforts, the re-deployment of Bank's Federal forces was successfully completed. General Banks, left with about 6000 men, along with General Hatch's exhausted cavalry, were bivouacked in and near Strasburg. A few miles to the east, at Front Royal, another 1400 men, under a Colonel Kenly, were encamped.

Defensive perimeters were thrown up by the infantry at Strasburg and the area seemed secure. At last, the cavalrymen were allowed a well-deserved rest. Those whom they had protected were now protecting them....at least for the moment.

"Colonel Brodhead?"

"Here, sir." Thornton Brodhead excused himself from a chatty circle of fellow officers and quickly approached the general. The guards flanking the commander snapped to attention and saluted as he strode toward them.

Brigadier General John Hatch puffed on a well-chewed cigar as he tipped precariously on his battered chair. A hesitant spring breeze fluttered the flaps of his headquarters tent and ruffled the reports and dispatches on the table before him. In response to his kind invitation, the ranking officers of his cavalry command were swapping stories and telling jokes as they clustered near the commander's tent. They were thoroughly enjoying a moment of sanctioned relaxation, a few cups of quality (for a change) coffee, some piping-hot, sweet, cinnamon bread that was prepared on the special order of the general, and a relaxing smoke.

Colonel Brodhead returned the sentries' salutes, then saluted his commander. Hatch barely acknowledged the gesture. "Relax, Thornton. Did you enjoy the coffee and bread? It was the best I could summon, considering we are in the field."

""Just fine, sir. Thank you." The colonel remained at attention.

"Will you kindly be at ease, colonel?"

"Yes sir."

"Now, go and get another cup of coffee and pull up that other chair. I need to have a word with you." Brodhead was pleased to do as ordered. "Now, colonel, thanks particularly to the excellent rearguard activity of your First Michigan, the army has safely completed its withdrawal from Harrisonburg, and in good order." Hatch retrieved a dispatch from the table in front of him and waved it at Colonel Brodhead. "I'm pleased to tell you, Thornton, that glowing reports of the effectiveness and aggressiveness of your command have been forwarded to me from General Bank's headquarters. General Banks personally sends his congratulations for a job well done." Please accept my congratulations, also. I hope that you will not be tested so severely in the future."

Brodhead sprang to his feet and again stood at attention. "Hope not too, sir, but I'm not expecting any vacation....not any time soon! My regards to General Banks. On behalf of my troopers, I'm most pleased to accept the recognition of our efforts." Every inch of him--from his immaculate uniform to his boyish grin--was of an officer of the highest caliber. "I'm proud to report that my Michigan boys have proved themselves to be mighty brave and mighty tough! I must say, the more the rebs increased the pressure on us, the harder we pushed 'em back!" The polished brass buttons on his tunic seemed to be straining to stay where they belonged.

General Hatch grinned as he munched his cigar. "For heaven's sake, colonel, relax and sit down! Indeed, Thornton, you have every right to be proud of your sabers. They have obviously done very well. Now, I need your help. What is your assessment of the enemy forces? Do you believe that they're being reinforced in significant numbers?"

"Yes. sir. No question about it. There are more and more rebs out there every day, and they are certainly aggressive. I believe that they intend to do something more than just raise a little hell."

The general removed his cigar from his mouth and gazed reflectively at the soggy, smoldering mess while he scratched at his beard with his other hand. "'Fraid you could be right about that. Other units are making similar reports. There's trouble in the air. I can smell it."

Brodhead repressed a chuckle. He could not imagine that anyone could smell anything with such an awful cigar under his nose. He leaned forward in his chair. "It appears to me, sir, that the southerners consider our withdrawal to Strasburg to be a retreat."

Hatch propelled his chair to an even keel with a thump that startled the colonel. "We are not in retreat, colonel. It should be obvious, even to the rebs, that we are proceeding with an orderly withdrawal! There is, after all, a big difference between the two!"

"I do understand that, sir." Brodhead had not intended to ruffle the general's feathers. "In any case, the rebs are pressing us hard....and in good strength. We have observed significant columns of General Jackson's infantry moving north along the Valley Pike. They have very good cavalry support, to say the least. That reb, Colonel Ashby, has some fine fighting men on fine Virginia horses. He's a man to be reckoned with, I'll tell you. The First Michigan has been pushed mighty hard during the last few days."

"And, I know that you have fought well, colonel. Be advised that I have sent several dispatches to General Banks regarding the suspected enemy buildup, but our commander does not seem to react to the information." General Hatch relaxed in his chair, letting his posterior slide forward to a more comfortable position. "I'll send yet another dispatch, and in it I shall mention your report as reinforcement to the observations of the other cavalry units. I'm not sure that, as yet, he understands that we could be out gunned, and possibly even flanked, should the rebs be smart enough to try their luck."

Brodhead flashed a knowing smile. "The rebs may not look like much, at first glance, but that doesn't mean that they aren't smart! It would be most dangerous to underestimate Stonewall Jackson, or Turner Ashby....either one. Seems to me we are up against the best the South has to offer."

"Yeah, I know." The general flicked an ash and leaned inquisitively toward the colonel. "Tell me. Is it really true that you attacked, and drove off, Turner Ashby's horsemen on several occasions during the last few days?"

Brodhead's smile grew wider. "True indeed, sir. We blunted several of their attacks and chased them off before they could do much damage."

General Hatch reached to give the colonel a congratulatory clap on the shoulder. Brodhead struggled to stifle a cough. At close range, his commanding officer really did smell like a giant, stale cigar. The soggy stogie that Hatch had returned to his mouth, and held clamped in his teeth, was not contributing anything pleasant to the ambient air quality. The colonel repressed another chuckle. The general's nose had to be dead. It would seem that he probably could not smell a passing shit wagon, let alone catch the odor of trouble in the air.

"Thornton, as you know, we are ordered to quit the Shenandoah and march east to assist in the effort upon Richmond. In fact, General Shield's division has already departed in that direction. I'm concerned that Washington has made a grave error in this regard. May I ask your opinion?"

"Sadly, I have to agree with your concern. I don't mean to be disrespectful of Mr. Lincoln's orders, but I firmly believe that we still have our work cut out for us here." The worrisome thought furrowed the colonel's brow.

"Excuse me, General Hatch, sir." A very young-looking corporal had been nervously waiting for the opportunity to gain the general's attention, fearing to interrupt the conversation.

"Just a moment, son. I'll be with you as soon as I finish talking to Colonel Brodhead."

"Yes, sir, but...." The general's glare caused the boy to step back a few paces.

"What's the condition of your men and horses, colonel?"

"Not surprisingly, my men are worn. They have had only short naps dozing in the saddle, or lying on the reins, for several days. The animals are looking thin and themselves fall asleep, where they stand, whenever they are allowed to be still for a moment. We're grateful for this opportunity to rest behind the infantry positions."

The general shrugged. "There should be ample time for rest while the remainder of the army forms in preparation to move east, or to wherever the hell we are ordered to go. I doubt that General Banks will allow the reb trash to keep him from joining McClellan's Richmond tea party, if he can help it."

The courier's lips were quivering with fear. Nevertheless, he bravely reasserted himself. "Excuse me again, sir! I respectfully apologize for the interruption, sir, but I believe this dispatch is a matter of most importance!" The boy's quaking speech was punctuated by repeated awkward salutes that the general did not bother to acknowledge.

Hatch was looking irritated, his whiskers seeming to bristle. "All right! What is it, son?"

"I have an urgent dispatch for you, General Hatch. I was told to deliver it with all possible speed."

"Very well, then." Hatch snatched the paper from the courier's outstretched hand. He chewed furiously on his cigar as he read the dispatch, deftly causing the saliva-laden stogie to migrate back and forth across his whiskered face. "Hmmm! Pickets on the ridge to the east report weapons-fire from the direction of Front Royal." His eyes flickered along the scrawled message. "They believe that a major action is taking place! This is no minor skirmish, they say. Artillery and massed musketry. It seems that the detachment at Front Royal is under major attack." The general looked a little pale as he leaned on his table. "Thornton, our concerns may be already vindicated. A large rebel force could be flanking us to the east."

Colonel Brodhead looked puzzled. "How do you suppose they got to Front Royal? I was under the impression they were marching along, behind us, down the Valley Pike."

Hatch took up his pen. "Like you just said, don't underestimate the enemy. I'd guess Jackson has split his command and has marched some of 'em up the east side of the Blue Ridge.... the crafty bastard! Well! This news ought to get our commander's attention!"

> May 23, 1862
> 12:00 Noon
>
> To: Major Gen'l N.P. Banks, Strasburg
> From: Brig. Gen'l J.P. Hatch
>
> Significant weapons-fire reported from direction of Front Royal. Concerned for safety of detachment garrisoned that location.

Respectfully suggest enemy may be in the process of flanking our position. Will immediately dispatch reconnaissance. Will report observations earliest possible instant. Will proceed unless receive your orders to the contrary.

Respectfully,

Hatch

The general was not about to wait for a reply. "Thornton, your men are the most available, and currently unassigned. I know they're fatigued. Nevertheless, please immediately assemble four companies for a reconnaissance-in-force toward Front Royal. We must know the strength and the intentions of the enemy. Sorry that some of your men won't have a chance to rest. Pick some good ones. This could be a most urgent situation!"

Brodhead grinned as he saluted his commander. "We're practically on our way now, sir!" The colonel knew instantly to whom he would entrust the command of such an important reconnaissance. He sent an orderly running at top speed to inform Lieutenant Colonel Greyson of the assignment. On Brodhead's recommendation, Matthew Greyson had recently been brevetted to his new rank in recognition of his coolness under fire, his clearly superior abilities as an officer, and as a leader of men. His recent victories over Turner Ashby's gray-clad cavalrymen had clearly illustrated Greyson's abilities.

Within the hour, four-hundred men and horses jangled out of camp, pennants flying. A small, bronze mountain howitzer bounced along in their midst. Greyson assigned three groups, each consisting of three horsemen, to point duty. These scouts were to carefully sweep the intended route by riding roughly one-half mile in advance of the blue column. One group would travel on the trail, the other two would ride parallel courses to the left and right as they looked for the presence of the enemy. The colonel wanted no unpleasant surprises.

Greyson and Sergeant McEwan rode at the head of the column of blue-clad troopers. Together, they anxiously scanned the surrounding ridges for signs of enemy activity as they trotted along the narrow trail. McEwan, who was, as usual, totally relaxed in his saddle, was just happily observing that the horses were raising very little telltale dust, thanks to a recent light rain, when his chatter was interrupted by the sight of several of the scouts cantering toward them, their horses lathered by the exertion.

The scouts reined to a skidding, snorting stop. "Colonel, we just snuck up on a hunner'd, or so, dismounted reb cavalry 'bout five hunner'd yards ahead!" He anxiously pointed in the direction of the enemy position as his excited horse wheeled under him. "They 'pear to be planning an ambush from a heavy timbered ridge just to the north of this here trail."

"Thank you, private." Colonel Greyson calmly returned the salute that the excited horseman had forgotten to give. "They see you?"

"Don't believe they did, sir."

"Good work, trooper. Now, slip back up there and report any changes in their position. Do you believe that they are supported by any artillery?"

"Not that we could see, sir."

"Very well. I guess we'll have to mount a little surprise for those gentlemen. Please glass their position for sign of significant ordinance. I'll give you a few moments to confirm. Now, off with you!"

"Good luck to you, sir!" The scouts saluted as they wheeled their mounts and trotted back up the trail toward the hidden enemy position.

Greyson chuckled at the audacity of the rebel cavalrymen. "They figure they got us good, I reckon. Almost a shame to cause them disappointment. Willy, I don't suppose that we have any detailed maps of his area, by any chance?"

"My, my, Matt. Don't we wish! All we got is a map shows us the direction to Front Royal." McEwan had one leg casually slung across the saddle and was carefully inspecting the priming charges in his flintlock pistols.

Lieutenant Colonel Greyson quickly formed his battle plan. Companies A and C, under Captains Stebbins and Fisher, would dismount their men, hide and mount a proper guard over their horses, then proceed to the right and to the left of the trail. The plan was to flank, and if possible, get to the rear of the enemy without being detected. The rest of the command would travel leisurely along the trail, giving the impression that they were about to march, unaware, into the Confederate trap. The rebels would very likely have their horses held safely behind the planned line of combat. Hopefully, once the rebels were routed from their position, the flanking companies would be able to interdict the escape of the would-be ambushers. Matthew intended to open the festivities with a showy shower of howitzer shells that was calculated to cause, if nothing else, the enemy to cower unhappily in their positions. When the barrage would be completed to the colonel's satisfaction, and the little howitzer ceased to sing its song of death, the rebels would be attacked from several sides at once.

Matt figured that the Confederate scouts who had discovered the approach of the Union troopers probably had not noticed the little artillery piece that was trundling inconspicuously along, and nearly hidden from sight, within their column. Had the rebs discovered the howitzer, they probably would have decided against a dismounted ambush. The relative immobility of such a tactic could, and would, expose them to considerable danger from artillery fire. Rather than to attempt a dismounted ambush, a more logical, and safer, tactic would have been to organize a surprise, slash-and-run mounted charge. They could have inflicted heavy damage, and been long out of range, before the howitzer could have been unlimbered and brought into action. The advantage of surprise could have canceled, at least temporarily, the four-to-one numbers advantage enjoyed by the Union horsemen.

"Give 'em the benefit of the doubt, I suppose" muttered Matt as he tried to outguess the enemy. "Chances are the rebs didn't see our little brass friend." A mountain howitzer can be difficult to spot from a distance. The little smoothbore had a barrel that was only 31" long and was light enough to be packed on top of a horse, if necessary. The little 12 pounder accompanying Greyson's command, however, rolled along on its own carriage....an arrangement that allowed it to be quickly placed into action when necessary.

Several horses each carried two ammunition chests. Each chest contained eight 4.52" rounds, most of which were of the spherical case type, designed to fit easily into the 4.61" bore of the weapon. Spherical case rounds were murderous ammunition if they happened to explode when, and where, they were intended to do so. British General Henry Shrapnel had designed the round for use against Napoleon and his enterprising French army. The round, hollow case of the shell was filled, in the 12 pounder, with seventy-eight .69" lead balls. It also contained a charge of black powder which, when ignited by the timed paper fuse, would explode above, into, and/or among whomever might be unfortunate enough to be in the vicinity at that particular moment.

Colonel Greyson ordered his column, minus the two companies assigned to flank the enemy position, to trot noisily along the trail and to halt behind a low rise which served to screen them from the sight of the rebels who were hidden on the ridge beyond. Matt could imagine that the gray-clad troopers would be gleefully moistening the front sights of their carbines in anticipation of a turkey shoot. "Will, reckon its a damn shame to spoil their fun....but, doggone....somebody has to do it! Care to direct the howitzer fire?"

"Be honored, sir." McEwan's grin showed his delight.

"Go to it, sergeant. Fire soon as you get into position."

The Confederate cavalrymen were not as easily fooled, however, as Matthew had hoped. The battle-wise, detached company of Ashby's horsemen were quick to note that the Federal column did not top the rise, which screened their approach, within a reasonable length of time. The southerners were already nervous about the relative numbers of the approaching Federals, the thought of which made them especially concerned about anything which might indicate that they had lost the advantage of surprise.

The CSA commander lowered his telescope when the Federal flags did not appear over the rise in the trail. "Sergeant!"

"Suh?"

"You will instruct an immediate withdrawal. I don't rightly care for the smell of this. I do believe we've been spotted! And, there 'pears to be too many of them for us to just sit here and wait to be surrounded. We'll mount and fall back toward Front Royal. Move right smart, sergeant."

"Yes, suh!" The sergeant hurried along the concealed gray and butternut-clad line, whispering the order. "Y'all git outah heah, right quick! Fall back to the horses. Now!"

The Confederate troopers grumbled and muttered as they thumbed the hammers of their carbines to half-cock and slithered out of their positions. "We could of had 'em good, sarge." The trooper's complaints were silenced when the first round from the Union howitzer whistled over their heads and exploded, harmlessly, in the woods just behind the ridge.

The sergeant ducked, instinctively, as the round passed over them. "Well now! Y'all get the picture? Move out. Double quick!"

One of the tall Virginia horsemen grinned nervously as he slid behind the protection of a nearby tree. "Ain't nobody has to tell me twice!" He, and the rest of the rebels, scrambled through the timber toward their horses.

In the Federal position, hidden from the view of the Confederates, the recoil caused the wheels of the gun carriage to leap clear of the ground each time the little piece roared. One of the Union cavalryman-turned-artilleryman whistled a happy tune as he swabbed the bore in preparation for the next shot. "She's jumpin' for joy, McEwan! She's happy to serve them rebs some lunch"

"Be a lunch that's hard to swallow, I'll wager!" chuckled Sergeant McEwan as he directed the gun crew to fire along the ridge by increments. The barrage, however, had little effect upon the enemy as most of the Confederate cavalrymen had vacated their positions by the time that the shells were bursting along their former hiding places.

Many of the southerners had just reached their horses when they came under fire from the flanking Union dismounted cavalry. The fire fight produced numerous casualties on both sides. The net result, however, was that those of the Confederates who could leave the field did so in the greatest of haste. Some suffered the indignity of fleeing on foot, having been unable to reclaim their horses, thanks to the efforts of the Yankees who peppered the retreating troopers with rounds from their Colt revolvers. Even worse than the stinging defeat was the inglorious and embarrassing prospect of a long walk back to join the main body of gray troops at Front Royal.

When Colonel Greyson had first been informed that the rebels were blocking the trail to Front Royal, and before engaging them, he had dispatched several horsemen to skirt the enemy position and to continue toward the village in an effort to discover what had happened there. His men had accomplished their mission and now returned, safely, without having been discovered by the enemy. Their report was disturbing, to say the least. They had found that Front Royal had been overrun by a very large body of Confederate soldiers. They could only guess at the size of the enemy force....reporting it to be "huge". "Never saw so many damn rebs in one place before, colonel!" What they had seen, in fact, was an army that had grown to approximately 17,000 men, supported by at least fifty artillery pieces. Nearly all of Union Colonel John Kenly's 1,100 men, who had been posted at Front Royal, had been either killed or captured. It was obvious that Stonewall Jackson was wasting no time in his effort to surround and destroy General Banks' depleted Federal command. Greyson sent couriers galloping to General Hatch to inform him of the presence of the large and dangerous flanking force.

"Sergeant McEwan!"

"Yes, sir?" Will's face was streaked with a combination of sweat and black powder residue from the clouds produced by the firing of the howitzer.

Matt swung aboard Saber. "Inform the captains to reassemble their companies on the trail....facing them back toward Strasburg. Have Captain Stebbins deploy his company as rear guard. Have him post vedettes on the trail to the east."

"Consider it done, sir."

Matt was not through barking commands. "Have Captain Pauldi take the advance. And, have him deploy flankers immediately. There could be more rebs around here."

McEwan grinned through the powder stains and saluted. "Right away, colonel." Will jumped into the saddle, without bothering to use a stirrup, and dashed off to accomplish his orders.

Greyson spotted Captain Fisher, who was busily collecting his men around their Company C pennant, and trotted Saber over to them. "Jim, as soon as you get organized, I want your men to sweep the area for casualties. Have them brought here to the side of the trail to be counted. I have sent word to General Hatch to send six ambulances. I want to be sure that that will be enough."

"What about the reb wounded, colonel?"

"Gather them up, too, of course. We'll take them with us."

"What about the dead?"

Matt looked off into the distance, for a moment, before he answered. "Bring ours, leave theirs. And, Jim, shoot any wounded horses." Even though he was hardened to the horrors of war, Matthew could not bear the thought that wounded men, or even injured and suffering horses, would be left, unattended, in the skirmish area. He decided to join Company C to personally assist in their errand of mercy....but stayed at a distance so that the soldiers could not see the tears that welled from his eyes as he paused to look down, sadly, upon the fallen animals and gray-uniformed men who were now growing cold as they lay in the dark crimson puddles of their own congealing blood. He winced as occasional pistol shots rang out, signaling the merciful death of the injured animals. "Oh! Lord!" He prayed, silently. "Why must this horror be?" No answer came forth from the dark Virginia woods to comfort either him or the fallen warriors who lay so still, silent, and tangled within the brushy undergrowth. The blood-spattered leaves of the laurel and ivy nodded silently in the breeze that sighed over the wooded ridge. If those sad, green witnesses would have had tongues, they would have spoken words that Lieutenant Colonel Greyson would not have wanted to hear. He let his horse wander aimlessly over the battleground.

When Saber's ears suddenly swiveled forward, Matt jerked upright in the saddle, instantly on the alert. His handsome gelding pranced nervously, and nickered loudly, as though expecting an answer. The answer was almost immediate....a soft nicker from within a nearby thicket of downed timber. Alert to the possible danger of the presence of a stray rebel who might thoroughly enjoy the opportunity to bag a Union officer, Matt drew and cocked his big Colt revolver. There was no further sound from the dark copse, even though Saber's biological radar indicated that there was a presence there. Greyson dismounted, and, keeping his weapon at the ready, peered under the branches. He was startled to see a fine-looking bay horse that was standing quietly in the shadows. Thumbing the hammer carefully down onto the one chamber that was carried empty, for safety purposes, Matthew reholstered the Colt and worked his way through the brush. His hand rested upon the butt....just in case is should become necessary to draw the weapon again.

Greyson caught a glimpse of butternut and gray on the ground before him, nearly obscured by the foliage. Again, he hastily drew and recocked his weapon....his trigger finger trembling within a heartbeat of firing. But, there was no movement, no apparent threat of danger. A southern cavalryman lay in the underbrush, very still, and not hearing, much less caring, about Greyson's approach. The severely wounded trooper, his tan-colored shirt stained with blood, was jammed, prostrate, within the woody tangle with his booted foot caught in the twisted stirrup of his russet saddle. The beautiful bay mare had halted, for fear of injuring him, and was awaiting instructions from her fallen master. She could not have known that those instructions would never come.

Matt spoke softly to the quivering horse while he disengaged the boot from the tangled stirrup. The faithful animal stood quietly, but still quivering.... for a moment.... then came forward to sniff the face of her fallen beloved. The rebel trooper stirred, then reached to stroke the muzzle of his equine friend. Slowly, his clouded eyes focused upon Matthew. Understanding came upon the fallen warrior's face as he again reached to stroke the muzzle that was inquiringly touching his cheek. Tears began to trickle down the young cavalryman's face, making streaks in the dust and grime of battle that clung there. Sympathetically, Matt felt his own eyes fill. Before he could wipe the tears away, a few renegade drops escaped, fell, and became lost as they mixed with the growing, crimson stain on the man's blood-soaked shirt.

The man struggled to speak. His voice was so soft that Matt had to lean close to hear his words. "Suh, who might you be, suh?"

"Matthew Greyson, First Michigan Cavalry."

The Confederate tried to focus on Matthew's uniform. "You 'pear to be an officer, suh."

"I am, son. Lieutenant colonel."

"Well now, I'm honored, colonel. I'd salute, and stand at attention, but I just don't believe I'm able."

Matt smiled down at him, patting his shoulder. "Don't you worry 'bout that, trooper. Here, let me see if I can't untangle you from this mess of branches." The colonel tried to make the soldier more comfortable by removing his pack and placing it under his head to serve as a makeshift pillow.

"Colonel, suh, if you'll excuse me for saying so, I believe I am killed."

Matt replied quietly....the way one would speak were he in church. "I'm afraid you well could be." He eyed the red-rimmed hole in the center of the butternut shirt. "I'm truly sorry."

"Not half as sorry as I am!" The rebel's body was wracked with a fit of frantic coughing that produced a froth of blood on his lips. When he regained his breath, he managed a little smile.

"Don't reckon you should feel too bad. I would of killed you, if I could, you can bet!"

"I know."

The dying trooper drifted away, for a moment. Matt thought that he was gone, but he rallied once more. "Colonel, I believe I would have preferred it the other way "round!"

"Matt chuckled sadly. "Can't hardly blame you for that preference!"

The rebel struggled to rise to his elbows, but fell back, coughing, as the blood continued to fill his lungs. "You reckon you could patch me up so's I could live to fight you again....man to man?"

"I'll surely try to do that. I'd be honored to fight you again."

The dying eyes glowed, for a moment, with a fierce fire, and then softened. "I believe you are a true gentleman. I'm proud to make your acquaintance even if you are a Yankee." He reached, weakly, for Matthew's hand. "Want you to know I've got much to live for. Got me a nice farm, a pretty wife, and a fine, sweet daughter. Colonel, what you got?"

"I, too, have a farm, and a lovely lady waitin' for me, but no child."

"Then you should be lyin' here 'stead of me." Tears again followed the streaks on the grimed face. "I got nobody to care for 'em. Things bein' as they are, I fear they will starve if I don't come home to work the farm." The reb squeezed Matthew's hand. His eyes were fading again. "I just don't know why Jesus has gone and left me. Why would He do such a thing? I never crossed Him, much." He coughed some more blood. "Leastaways not very much."

Matt clasped the hand of his former enemy in both of his, trying to warm it. He was enemy no longer....strangely, he was now a treasured friend. Matt could feel the coldness of death creeping into the work-hardened fingers. He spoke slowly, seeking to speak words of comfort. "Jesus hasn't left you, friend. He's here. Right here with us. He might have even sent me so that you wouldn't die alone. Might just have sent me so that you and me could be friends through His eternity."

"You think that could be?" The failing man looked frantically around. "Can't see Him. Surely wish I could."

"You will. I expect you will. Right now, listen real close. He'll be telling you he loves you." Matthew began to feel a peace, a warmth, spread through him as he knelt there among the leaves and brambles. He drew a deep, quiet breath. He could very nearly hear the words himself.

The soldier was quiet for a moment, then smiled. "I hear! I do hear.... just as you said! He seemed to drift off to sleep, then startled awake. "Is it gettin' dark? I can scarce make you out. I can feel the dark closin' in. Scares me, some."

"Don't worry, son. Gettin' dark right early today" lied Matthew. "You haven't told me your name." He shook the reb gently. "What is your name, trooper?"

The reply was barely audible....a rattling whisper. "Name's John. John Chandler. Wife is Charity Jane." He coughed weakly. "But, I calls her 'Melody Jane' 'cause she can sing so sweet. My daughter is called Mary Sue. Sure wish I could see them, just once again. Colonel, you still there? Can't scarce make you out."

"I'm here, John."

"My horse still here?" Chandler was staring, hard, into his own darkness.

"She's right here, John, right here next to me."

"Can you put me on her so's I can go home?"

"Right soon, John, soon's you gather a little strength."

"I'll try to do that. Gather some strength. Matthew....Matthew....can I call you that?"

"'Course."

"I case I can't make it, will you see that my Bible gets taken to my Melody? It's just a little old New Testament, but she will take comfort in its return."

"I will surely do that, but I don't know where to find her."

"Middleburg. Close by Middleburg. Little farm sets by Goose Creek. Book's here. In my shirt pocket. Here." He pulled Matt's hand to direct him to the tiny volume. Settling his head upon his makeshift pillow, John managed a weak smile. "I believe its right comfortable here, but I'm just a mite cold." He relaxed, just as though he were pulling up the comforter on his own bed....with Charity Jane at his back. "You reckon we could say the Lord's Prayer together?"

"I'm honored to pray with you, John." Greyson smoothed the dark, tangled hair on the Confederate cavalryman's brow. "Our Father...." Matthew finished the prayer alone.

Gently, he freed his hand from the faded grip and lifted the Book from John's pocket. The bullet that had killed the reb had missed it only by inches. As he glanced at the stained pages he could not suppress a shudder. It looked just like the New Testament that Bethany had sent to him not long before. Matt led the mare from the now-sacred spot and swung wearily into Saber's saddle. He could not look back at the still, forlorn figure who was lying there, alone, in humble and unsung testament to the foolishness of mankind. The unseen, and the unheard, had pronounced an holy benediction.

Lieutenant Colonel Matthew Greyson would never be quite the same again. That young trooper would ride with him, stirrup to stirrup, even unto his own death.

+ + +

Colonel Greyson's Michigan detachment returned to the Strasburg area without further incident, but only to find that the army there was mobilizing and moving out. General Banks, now realizing the danger, had ordered a full retreat to the north.

Subsequently, feisty Confederate General Thomas Jackson accomplished his own orders with a brilliance that distinguished him as one of the best military commanders who had ever taken the field. By marching, and counter-marching, and with the assistance of Colonel Turner Ashby's cavalry, Jackson eventually drove the Union army totally out of the "bread basket of the south". Banks was clearly outguessed and hopelessly outgeneraled. Brigadier General John Hatch's mounted command, which included the First Michigan Cavalry, again drew the dangerous task of screening the retreating columns from the yipping rebels until the Union force crossed the Potomac River and rested, in relative safety, in Maryland.

CHAPTER NINE

Cuppie

The frightening events of the previous autumn, when a member of the Pinkerton organization had brutishly tried to uncover Bethany's suspected involvement with the Confederate States of America, had continued to leave their mark upon her. Brave as she had been, and brave as she remained, the uneasiness persisted to the point where it undermined her sense of well-being, and even shadowed her once exuberant love of life. As the long Michigan winter ceased its shivering and blustering, and finally gave way to the blessed warmth of spring, Bethany tried to hide her continued apprehension as she immersed herself in her work at church and at school. As the spring days ticked across the calendar, and there were no apparent further incidents, she began to allow herself the somewhat optimistic glimmer of hope that perhaps, just perhaps, she was no longer under suspicion.

Dick seemed to have forgotten the house-trashing incident and cheerfully went about his chores. He never approached Bethany for an explanation of the mysterious affair, even though there were many questions in his mind. He suspected that there might be much, much more to the story than he knew, but his loving respect for Bethany prompted him to mind his own business.

Bethany struggled to control the fright, the panic, that sought to destroy her from within. She began to hope that the whole Pinkerton problem was just some sort of surreal nightmare that had not really happened. Much as she tried to comfort herself, however, the reality would not go away. She tossed and turned through many a sleepless night. Always, in her mind, there was someone lurking in the shadows, waiting to pounce. The fear of bodily harm, or of being arrested, gnawed at her with uncomfortable persistence. When she could sleep, it was only fitfully....and she frequently startled awake at the slightest nocturnal sound. She would cry out in her sleep, begging for Matt to come home to save her, but then would shudder awake with the realization that he, too, could become her enemy if he were to learn that she had been a rebel spy. She would sob, night after night, into her pillow. Her beloved Matthew could well be lost to her, and lost forever. Her sorrow was almost too much to bear. She dared not seek comfort from anyone. Bethany was trapped within her own, private hell. Her frequent prayers for help from her Creator were unanswered. It seemed that her God, too, had turned away.

Bethany's many friends could sense that something was wrong. They whispered among themselves as they observed that her pretty face was growing haggard and thin. The sparkle was gone. They feared, naively, that she was not dealing well with Matthew's absence, but they could not convince her to share her problems with them. Bethany longed to cry on someone's shoulder, especially Mrs. Lanning's, but felt that she could not entrust even her with her dark secret.

There had been very few strangers present in Franklin during the cold and quiet winter. Now, as the roads improved with the coming of spring, more travelers appeared. Bethany made it her business to clandestinely scrutinize each one, seeking to determine if their business appeared to be legitimate. At that time, fortunately for her, no agents had been assigned to snoop into her affairs as a follow-up to the previously botched investigation. However, contrary to her hopes, it would not be long before Alan Pinkerton would get around to sending his investigators to tend to the unfinished business.

Bethany, much as she prayed that they would leave her alone, knew that she must expect the worst....that the Pinkertons would come after her again. She was not a Confederate soldier, but, nevertheless, she would fight....not necessarily for the Southern Cause....but for her own survival. She forced herself to remain alert to any possibility of danger during the day, and carefully barred her doors each night. Ignoring Dick's vehement objections, Beth commandeered the lad's treasured shotgun. Every night, it became a part of her bedtime ritual to take it from its assigned place behind her chamber door to check that the percussion cap was in place and that the hammer was safely at half-cock. The piece could quickly be put into firing mode by simply pulling the stiffly-sprung hammer the rest of the way to the rear. Anyone who was brash enough to force their way into her bedroom would pay dearly for their transgression.

Matthew's letters did not arrive often, but did so with at least enough frequency to provide her with a measure of comfort. She continued to write to him daily. Her letters jabbered happily of the local news, and gave no hint of the fear that was hidden behind her words. Each day, after her schoolmistress duties were done, she would rush to the post office in the hope that a letter from him would have arrived. More often than not, Postmaster Coder could only shake his head, sadly, when she hustled expectantly through the door. When a letter did finally arrive, Mr. Coder's face would be wreathed in smiles as he handed it to her. She would then hurry home, shut herself in her bedroom, curl up on the bed, and read.... and reread....Matthew's every word. For the moment, at least, he seemed to again be at her side. The vision of his handsome face swirled before her as his words tumbled off of the paper and into the depths of her frightened heart.

Williamsport, Maryland

June 10, 1862

My Dearest Bethany,

Well! It looks as though we will again have something to do. I hear that we are to have a new commander. He is a newly-promoted major general, from out west, named John Pope. The word is that he will order us, under General Banks, to re-cross the Potomac and avenge our embarrassing retreat to this boring place. Two weeks of watching the rebels thumb their noses at us from across the river has been quite long enough. It appears that a major campaign against Jackson and Lee is finally at hand. I certainly hope so. It's high time to get this mess over with!

Do you recall my writing to you of the bay mare that I captured in Front Royal? She is still in my possession, thanks to the increased clout that my lieutenant colonelcy gives me. Splendid mount as she is, I have resolved to try to return her to the family where she belongs. Colonel Brodhead is touched by my wishes and will help me to accomplish that goal if he can do so without stirring up too much trouble. My faithful Saber is still holding up well, in spite of the severe strains that cavalry action puts upon him, so I guess the two of us can get along without her company, and without her use as a reserve mount, I hope.

I have not given the mare a name because I figure she already has one. I just don't know what it is. I asked her, but she just wont tell!

I am pleased to learn, from your sweet and informative letters, that the spring planting has gone well. Please tell Dick that I am proud of him. I knew that there was a strong and husky farmer inside of that boy. my next letter will be from somewhere in rebel Virginia. I hope that we do better against the secesh than we did last time. I do think we will, as we are to be heavily reinforced by Generals McDowell and Fremont.

I love you with all my heart, and long for the day when we are together again.

Your faithful "Soldier Boy",

Matthew

On June 12, 1862, General Banks' forces crossed the Potomac and swept back up the Shenandoah Valley. Matthew, happily astride Saber, was delighted to be back into the fray. They met only token resistance from the slippery General Jackson. He had gathered his little army and disappeared. Jackson, fearing the trap that had been set for him, was not about to be caught between the forces of Fremont, Banks, and McDowell. The rebel army was force-marched up the valley, to the south, and away from danger, much to the disappointment of the Union command. General Banks, with his 8,000 men, and General Fremont with his 11,500, concentrated at Middletown, Virginia, to await further orders from Major General Pope.

It was in Middletown that Lieutenant Colonel Greyson perceived the dawning of an opportunity to carry out his plan. When he had entrusted his Bible to Matt's care, the dying rebel cavalryman had confided that his home was near Middleburg, Virginia. Now, Middleburg was just across the Shenandoah River and only a day's ride away from the present Union position.

Greyson conferred with Sergeant McEwan on the possibility of visiting the dead reb's family. Willy, as usual, was game for any kind of excitement. "Middletown, Middleburg. Middleburg, Middletown! Never saw such a place where everything seems to be in the middle!" snorted McEwan. Might even lose us in the middle."

"In the middle of the muddle?" grinned Matt.

"Or, the muddle in the middle. Shucks, Matt, I think we're both losing our minds. I'll try to find somebody we can trust who knows the area so's we can keep ourselves out of the m....!" McEwan stalked away, holding his head as though he had a severe headache.

Matt chuckled as he watched the sergeant depart. "Well now, Mrs. Charity Jane 'Melody' Chandler," he mused, "you might just get your horse and your Book back." Something in Matthew's soul told him that, indeed, he must give it a try. The death of Confederate Trooper Chandler often haunted him, especially when he sat, alone, by the campfire after his men had turned in to take their rest. The sound of Chandler's last, agonal breaths would sometimes echo in his ears and mingle with the sleepy sounds of the night. Colonel Greyson had made a promise to the deceased rebel. He would keep that promise if he could possibly do so without endangering his men, and without compromising his obligations to his flag and his country. Matthew was a man of his word. Even in the face of an insane war, he was determined that at least some measure of love and compassion could survive.

The cavalry was the eyes and ears of the armies. It was the horsemen who would provide advanced warning of any concentrations of enemy forces which could endanger the main body of troops. General Banks had learned his lesson, and General Fremont concurred. Their cavalry would be utilized to its fullest potential. Accordingly, cavalry units were dispatched in various directions to ensure against any of Stonewall Jackson's unwelcome surprises. Colonel Brodhead, who met regularly with General Banks' staff, cleverly arranged to have elements of the First Michigan assigned to reconnaissance of the area east of the Shenandoah....

the area which, of course, contained the delightful little community of Middleburg.

Major General John Pope, whom President Lincoln had appointed to overall command of the operation, was an unusually self-assured man. He also had a remarkable propensity for making himself unpopular with nearly everyone.... from his general officers down to the lowliest, most footsore soldier. Nearly every move, from the moment Pope assumed command on June 27, seemed deliberately pointed toward the assurance that he would be universally disliked. He had been assigned command of three corps which were made up of a total of over 40,000 men. It did not take the army long to discover that their new general was both inept and annoying. Morale plummeted. General Fremont tendered his resignation almost immediately. Just a few weeks later, General Hatch was removed from his cavalry command as Pope was displeased by his failure to occupy Gordonsville, Virginia, which was an important railroad hub and vital to the Confederacy. The First Michigan Cavalry was soon to be assigned a new commander....a remarkably capable cavalryman and leader.... Brigadier General John Buford.

The camp at Middletown bustled with activity as Col. Brodhead split his cavalry into three sections and prepared to send them off on their respective reconnaissance missions. Brodhead would remain in camp with his headquarters staff, minus Lt. Col. Greyson, to await their return. The acrid smoke from the charcoal fires in the farriers' portable forges drifted around the camp, while their anvils clanged. The horses' hoofs were trimmed and reshod as necessary. Supply wagons trundled to and fro, delivering food and ammunition to the assembling companies.

Greyson was checking supplies, as they were being unloaded and distributed, when Sergeant McEwan suddenly appeared at his elbow. "'Pears you're a bit busy, colonel, but I have some good news."

Matt looked up from his papers in surprise, then glared at his friend. "Where have you been, sergeant? I could use a little help around here."

McEwan, poker faced, saluted apologetically. "Sorry, sir, but I do have some good news."

Greyson straightened. "Good for you! What is it?"

"It is a him, sir. Corporal Tom Downs." Willy jerked a thumb at a shy young infantryman who was standing, respectfully, a few paces away.

The colonel raised his eyebrows. "Corporal Downs?"

The man stepped forward and saluted smartly. "Yes sir, colonel sir. Thomas Downs at your service, sir."

Greyson returned the salute. "Thank you, corporal. Sergeant, do you care to explain?"

Will grinned. "You bet! Downs used to live in Middleburg 'till he decided he wanted to stay with the Union. Says he knows his way 'round there real good. Took some doin' to find him, but find him I did."

Matt was delighted. "Good work, as usual, sergeant. Corporal Downs, thank you. I imagine that you'd rather ride than walk. I'll arrange to detach you from your unit and take you with us to Middleburg as a guide. What would you say to that?"

The soldier looked uncomfortable. "Yes, sir, but no, sir, please, sir!"

Greyson raised his cap and scratched his head in confusion. "I'm not sure I understand. Do you mean that you'd like to ride a horse, 'stead of on your feet, but you don't want to go with us? Is that right?"

The man lowered his eyes and traced a circle in the dust with the toe of his shoe. "That's right, sir."

"May I ask why you don't want to go?"

"'Cause some of the folks around Middleburg would shoot me should they see me in Yankee blue. They figger me as a traitor 'cause I chose to stay with the Union."

Colonel Greyson, his military stiffness relaxing, reached to shake the soldier's hand. "I see! I want you to know that we are all grateful that you chose to defend our great flag. We're honored to have you serve with us. May I ask, corporal, how you, as a Virginian, chose to support the Union?"

"Yes, sir. My grandaddy died fighting for the stars and stripes in 1812. It would be a dishonor to his memory were I to fire upon it. I just couldn't do it, much as I wanted to defend Virginia. I hope y'all can understand that."

Greyson and McEwan nodded their heads in support of the earnest young man. "Well, now," said Matt in a quiet, respectful tone, "I understand perfectly. No question that you should stay with your unit. Do you reckon you could draw us a map?"

"Surely."

"Would you happen to know, by any chance, where a farm is belonging to some folks named Chandler?"

"I do. Over by Goose Creek. I know it well."

"I'll be damned!" Greyson was incredulous at the good fortune.

McEwan guffawed. "Careful, colonel. You might just be!"

"Thank you, sergeant, for your kind words!" The corporal sketched a crude, but nicely detailed, map of the Middleburg area. He then excused himself, and amid a shower of thanks, left to return to his unit. Matt thought he saw a tear in Downs' eye when he had turned to leave. He waited to speak until the corporal was out of earshot. "There walks an unhappy man. He'd give anything to go home to Middleburg, if he dared."

McEwan shook his head. "Saddest part is the chances are he can't never go home."

By sundown, Greyson's two companies had splashed across the Shenandoah and set up camp for the night on the high ground just east of the river. The men were in high spirits, laughing and joking, as sentries were detailed, horses picketed and grained, and rations cooked. They had been ordered to travel fast, light, and to return as quickly as possible with the results of their reconnaissance. Accordingly, there were no clumsy supply wagons to lumber along with them, the presence of which would impede the speed of their march. With no wagons, there were no tents, rifles, or other comfortable amenities. The troopers did not seem to mind in the least the slight inconvenience of sleeping under the stars in the pleasant spring weather.

Armament was limited to that which they could easily carry on horseback. At that time, the saber was the accepted primary weapon of the cavalry. The other standard issue was the Model 1860 Colt caliber .44 revolver which the troopers carried in belt holsters, worn butt forward, and situated on the side of the strong hand. The Colts had been issued with a detachable shoulder stock designed for use in dismounted operations where a longer-range weapon might be desired. These rather unpopular accessories were sometimes "lost" by the cavalrymen who, understandably, preferred to keep their eyes and faces intact. The use of the short rifle-type stock brought the cylinder of the weapon almost under their noses....creating a most uncomfortable and dangerous situation for the soldier. When fired, with arm extended, the powder granules, gasses, and lead shavings which flew laterally from the cylinder-to-barrel gap were of little consequence. Holding that mini-inferno close to the face, and under the nose, was quite another matter.

A few personal weapons were also carried. A diverse assortment of derringers and small pistols were tucked under trouser belts, or into pockets, for emergency use. Col. Greyson was not convinced that such small weapons were of much value. Instead, he carried his treasured, giant Colt Walker revolver in a saddle holster that rode just forward of his right knee. Sergeant McEwan toted his flintlock Johnson pistols, likewise in saddle holsters, one on each side.

As darkness fell, the men gathered around small fires to enjoy (somewhat) their rather uninteresting, standard issue, evening meal. Supper consisted of "hardtack" [an amazingly hard biscuit that threatened dental health], "sowbelly" [salt-preserved pork that puckered the lips and parched the tongue], and boiled coffee [usually brewed strong enough to corrode the pot in which it was prepared]. They were fortunate in that they had drawn relatively fresh rations just before their departure from the main camp. There were, happily, only a few maggots crawling upon the crackers and/ or popping from the meat as it was cooked over the campfires.

Not long after supper, the troopers snuffed their cigars, tapped out their pipes, and turned in for the night. A chorus of snores rose to meet the moonlight as it filtered through the smoke from the dying campfires on the bluff then sparkled on the rippling Shenandoah River below. Matt wandered, sleeplessly, among the blanket-rolled men who lay clustered around each flickering campfire. He checked and rechecked the sentries,

152

making certain that they would be properly relieved at the end of their four-hour watch. He noted, with a chuckle, that his trusty Sergeant McEwan was sleeping on his reins even though he had not been ordered to do so. "Willy," he mused, "is a true professional. He's always prepared for a fight....even in his sleep!" The sergeant's horse kept jerking at the reins as it tried to reach the grass that was just a little too far away from his hungry lips. Willy unconsciously jerked the reins back again, and without missing one beat of snore. Matt knew that the sergeant's venerable flintlock pistols were cuddled, warm and dry, under the blankets with him. They were, Matthew believed, Willy's favorite mistresses.

The colonel paused to caress the soft muzzles of Saber and the Chandler mare. Both were picketed, still saddled in case of emergency, under the watchful eyes of their own, assigned, sentry. Matt was missing Bethany, terribly. Oh! If he could just touch her hand, could run his fingers once more through her soft, black hair! He rolled into his blanket, lonesome and alone, to await the dawn.

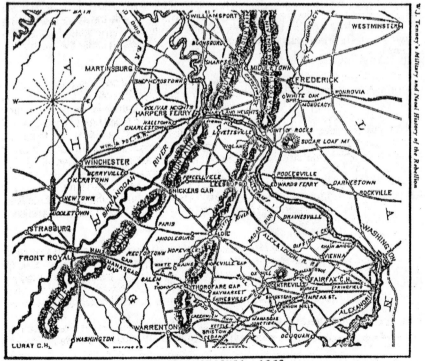

NORTHERN VIRGINIA 1862

The fresh spring leaves that rustled above the camp were barely visible in the first gray of the new day when Captains Angelo Paldi and George Acker reported to their colonel for their morning briefing. Matthew was already drinking his second cup of coffee when they arrived. The delicious aromas of breakfast cookery wafted pleasantly around the camp.

"Gentlemen, here is our plan." Matt spread his map close to the flicker of the fire so that they could see it in the dim morning light. "We are ordered to reconnoiter this little chunk of northern Virginia." His finger traced a rough circle on the map. "We are here, as you know." He indicated their present position on the east bank of the Shenandoah. "We'll cross the ridge through Ashby's Gap, then make our presence known in Paris. From there we'll go east to Middleburg and Aldie, then southwest to White Plains and Salem. Salem, as you can see, is on the Manassas Gap Railroad. As you would expect, we may well find enemy resistance in that area. The rebs won't take kindly to folks messin' with their railroad! We'll then, God willing, follow the rails back west through Front Royal, and then back to camp." The colonel stood, clasped his hands behind his neck, and stretched, looking down on his captains who were intently studying the map. "Any questions, gents?"

Captain Acker seemed pleased with the assignment. "Looks like a nice ride, Matthew. You 'spect we'll be just lookin', or will there be some fightin' involved with this little stroll? My men are itchin' for some real action."

Matt poured the dregs of his coffee on the fire. "Might be more action than we really want, George. No way to tell 'till we take a look. If we find a sizable reb force, we are ordered to scoot back an' tell about it....if we can. What do you think, Angelo?"

Captain Paldi glanced over his shoulder to see if anyone seemed to be listening, then leaned close to talk quietly. "Matt, the word is that you plan to return that fine horse you captured to some rebel lady. The troops are whisperin' about it. You really think that's a good idea? That mare could end up under some reb cavalryman's bottom in no time. Could be used against us."

The colonel had been expecting some resistance to his somewhat quixotic project. "You're right, of course, Angelo." Matt looked away, for a moment, as he weighed his words. "Right or wrong, I feel I would like to help the family of that reb I watched die over by Front Royal. Seems to me that gettin' that horse back to them might ease their pain, some. Likely they'll need her to pull a plow and to get their spring plantin' done. Plantin' is already some late. Guess the farmer in me makes me worry about such things."

"But....Matt....they're just southern trash!" Angelo's brown eyes flashed with the fire of his Italian heritage. "You're gettin' soft, Matt. I've watched my share of my own men die, and I didn't send their widows no horse.... let alone send one to a reb! Paldi's voice was rising. Nearby cavalrymen pretended to not hear, but nevertheless strained to eavesdrop on the conversation as they scattered their fires and bustled to organize their equipment.

Captain Acker nudged Captain Paldi. "Better keep your voice down, Angelo. Seems there's many an ear, close by, that needn't hear what we have to say. Now, I just don't see no harm done, if that's what Matt wants to do. Ain't Union horseflesh, anyhow. Besides, this ain't an official act, and needn't be talked about. Right, Matt?"

Greyson looked relieved that he had some support for his venture. "Right, indeed! Angelo, tell you what. I'll make you a deal. If it turns out that the lady can't, or won't, keep the horse to use for farming, we'll just bring it on back with us. I'll just give her her husband's Bible and wish her a good day. Deal?"

Paldi was unconvinced. "Whatever you say, colonel. You're in charge."

Matthew put his hands on the captain's shoulders and looked him in the eye. "More important than who's in charge....we're friends. I want us to agree before we start."

Paldi unflinchingly returned his gaze, faltered, then surrendered to his peers with a sheepish grin. "I guess it don't matter all that much, one way or the other. I'll go along with your silly game, if only to just see what happens. Still, I think you're gettin' soft in the head. You should have been a preacher instead of a horse soldier."

George Acker laughed loudly as the three shook hands. "Don't believe I'd go along with the preacher idea, Angelo. Never yet saw a preacher who could fight, cuss, ride a horse, and comb his hair....all at the same time!"

"You'r exaggerating, George!" snorted Matt, with a haughty air. "I don't generally comb my hair at times like that! After all, I'd have to take my pretty blue hat off." He struck a mock-heroic pose.

The nearby troopers abandoned all pretense of being out of earshot and burst into howls of laughter. It was good to have officers who could joke, so early in the morning, and in the face of so much serious work to be done. It was good, indeed, to be in the ranks of the First Michigan Cavalry.

Colonel Greyson shook the dust, and a scattering of campfire ash, off of his map. He folded it carefully as he waited for the horsemen to cease their chuckling and to get back to their morning chores. "Captains, kindly have your men mounted and ready to move out in ten minutes. Acker, I Company will head the column this morning. Please deploy your scouts right away, if not sooner." He returned the captains' snappy salutes, then buckled on his saber. "Well now, Will, shall we scare us up some Johnny Rebs?"

Sergeant McEwan flashed his trademark grin. "Might's well, sir. Might even be some pretty ladies to look at in them towns!"

"You'll live longer if you'll keep your eyes peeled for the rebs in britches.... not just the ones in skirts."

Willy spat a juicy stream of brown tobacco juice, adjusted his first quid of the day into a comfortable position inside of his cheek, and clambered into the saddle. "Shucks, colonel, you ain't no fun at all."

The small blue column, barely 200 strong, rapidly traveled their predetermined route by alternately cantering, walking, and trotting their horses to avoid tiring them. It was a complete surprise to the inhabitants of the Village of Paris when the dusty horsemen formed a skirmish line at the west end of town, then swept down the main street, pistols at the ready, as they searched for military personnel and stores. Finding nothing of importance, and meeting no resistance, they reformed their column, tipped their hats to the ladies who peeked at them from behind curtains and shutters, and trotted eastward.

The dust of their departure had barely settled before the townspeople dispatched gallopers to neighboring communities, warning their fellow Virginians that the Yankee cavalry was on the prowl. The citizenry, at that moment consisting primarily of women, children, and old men, hustled to hide their treasures, their horses, and as much of their other livestock as they could on such short notice. In spite of the First Michigans' genteel handling of the brief occupation of Paris, the inhabitants, being nearly defenseless, were expecting the worst. All men of military age, who were worthy to be called real men, were "gone to fightin'". Those males that were still in the area, for whatever reason, made up the ranks of the "home guards" throughout the Confederacy.

The Upperville Home Guard and the Middleburg Home Guard were mobilized to meet the emergency of the Yankee intrusion. They combined forces to establish a defensive line across the Ashby's Gap Road just west of Upperville. They had little time to get organized before Greyson's scouts discovered them, then galloped back to report the presence, in the road ahead, of the would-be blockaders. The Virginians, they reported, were hard at work constructing a barracade consisting of overturned wagons, fence rails, and whatever else they could find....in their haste.... that might serve to turn away a bullet or a horse. The heroic defenders were armed with a diverse assortment of flintlock muskets, squirrel rifles, old shotguns, and even a few pitchforks. There was only a single ragtag line, with no reserves, no bayonets, and no artillery. A few swords and sabers swung proudly on the hips of a chosen few.

The southern men and boys crouched behind their barrier as they witnessed a frightening spectacle. The Union cavalry appeared, switched expertly from column of twos to column of four abreast, colorful pennants and the stars and stripes flying, drew their sabers, and charged down the road toward them at full gallop, screaming blood-curdling yells. It was enough to unnerve the bravest of men. The Confederates fired one hasty and ineffective volley, then dropped their weapons and ran for their lives. The cavalry easily jumped the barrier and proceeded to accelerate the rebs' departure with the points of their sabers. Captain Acker spurred to Matthew's side. "Shall we round 'em up, sir?"

"We needn't bother, George. Appears to be just old greybeards and little boys. Not much of a threat, as I can see. Have your men set fire to the barracade. Gather up all the weapons and ammunition that they have dropped and pitch 'em into the fire. Then, my friend, let's see what they might have in town that they were supposed to be guarding!" With the fire burning merrily, the troopers rode, without further opposition, into Upperville.

Upperville was a wispy little hamlet that lay scattered along the road on the high ground above Middleburg. Except for a few brave, barky, dogs the place appeared deserted. The occupants had disappeared into the surrounding forest in a frantic hurry upon perceiving that their home guard had failed to turn back the advancing Yankees.

Colonel Greyson had ordered that private residences were not to be molested. The order was strictly obeyed, even though many doors had been left invitingly swinging open in the haste of the departure of the residents. Two small barns, however, were found to contain barrels of flour, bags of oats, and a few casks of gunpowder. They were summarily put to the torch. The blue column was well clear of Upperville, having descended into the valley that marked the course of Goose Creek, and were crossing the stone bridge that spanned that stream, when the first thunderclap of exploding gunpowder caught up with them. Matt worried that the citizens had not remained in hiding, and might have been stupid enough to attempt to extinguish the flames. "Hope those folks stayed behind their trees, or under their stumps, or wherever the hell they were hidin'!"

Willy, riding alongside Greyson at the head of the column, nodded in assent. "They surely got their heads blowed off if they didn't!"

The reports of the hard-riding scouts that preceeded them on the road toward Middleburg were favorable. They had found no evidence of organized military activity in the area. The locals were apparently unable to offer any further resistance to their approach. Matthew elected to take advantage of the momentum that they had attained, and to march immediately upon Middleburg. Well before nightfall, their dusty column trotted into the downtown area of the charming little city, opposed only by the unhappy stares of the residents who cautiously gathered on porches and street corners to witness the arrival of their unwelcome visitors.

Acker's and Paldi's men conducted as detailed an inspection of the city as the fading light allowed, collecting arms and unnerving any groups who might be considering resistance. Watchful vedettes were posted on the roads outside of town, while picket posts sealed the perimeter. Middleburg was effectively isolated from the rest of the Confederacy. Michigan horsemen patrolled the streets, in a show of force, while Greyson established his headquarters on the pleasant lawn in front of the handsome, brick Methodist Church which stood near the center of town.

Local merchants were encouraged to provide the Yanks with firewood, and with forage for their hungry and tired horses. They were not happy with the requests, but complied, for fear of punishment under martial law. Their sullen faces blinked in amazement when they were promptly paid, with real Federal greenbacks, for their provisions.

Campfires blossomed along the main street as the troopers cooked their usual meager supper, and then rolled into their dusty blankets in the hope of enjoying a few moments of rest before being called to their turns at watch. One by one, the yellow lights in the windows of the town winked out as the residents, too, attempted to sleep. Unaccustomed to being in enemy hands, few slept well. The quiet cries of frightened children, promptly shushed by their mothers, made Colonel Greyson shiver. Sleep, for Greyson, was impossible. He wrapped himself in his blanket and leaned against a tree, staring into the fire that his men had prepared for him.

He could kill a man, if he had to. That was war. To frighten women and little children was quite a different thing. It was a role that he did not, in the least, relish. He began to pray for forgiveness. He began to wish that he was somewhere....anywhere....else. He threw back his blanket, took paper and pen, and began to write to Bethany, even though he would be unable to post it for days....if ever.

+ + +

Most travelers knew, or soon learned, that an agreeably pleasant place to stop in Middleburg, if one were seeking a comfortable bed and tastily prepared food, was a Federal style hotel called the Colonial Inn, a fine establishment run by a gracious lady named Catherine Broun. The inn was located just across a sidestreet from the Red Fox Tavern, in the heart of the city.

Very early in the morning following the occupation, Catherine Broun stepped out onto the porch of her hotel. She trembled nervously as she smoothed her starched white apron with the palms of her hands. The calls of the changing watches pierced the grayness of the Middleburg dawn as the Union soldiers went about their duties. She, also, had not slept.... uncomfortable in the realization that the dreaded Yankees, by force of saber and gun, were camped at her doorstep. No southerner could sleep well in the face of such of a barbaric affront. Wistfully, she watched as the men in blue struggled to light their breakfast fires and to cook their none-too-appetizing rations. They had been ordered to respect the rights of the citizenry by refraining from requisitioning food, but rather to subsist upon whatever they still carried in their knapsacks. Should they desire to supplement their diet with local food, they would be obliged to pay for it, and at a fair price. As most of the troopers had little money to spare, the majority chose to make do by eating just that which they had brought with them.

From her vantage point, overlooking the Ashby's Gap Turnpike which served as the main street of town, Mrs. Broun could see the grimy faces and tousled hair of the Federal troopers....some handsome, some homely, some who appeared to be kind and patient, some who did not. She was surprised by, and began to appreciate, the gentlemanly behavior of the occupying force. They seemed to refrain, for the most part, from profanity. They retired, discretely, to tend to nature's calls. In spite of her dislike for Yankees in general, and these in particular, womanly concern began to well within her. These men, like all men, needed to be properly fed. In her mind, Christianity, and southern hospitality, dictated that she should be concerned. Should they die from a bullet, so be it. To suffer from lack of proper food, never....not if Catherine Broun could provide them with the comfort of a good meal.

After a few moments of thought, Catherine had made a decision that would be unpopular with many fellow residents of the occupied community. She, as a woman of compassion, would offer to feed the hungry-looking soldiers who munched their hardtack in the street before her. She stepped back into her foyer for a moment, glanced into the mirror to adjust the silver combs which steadied her neat chignon, wriggled and tugged to adjust her cheerfully yellow gingham dress and summoning her retinue of cleanly-dressed black servants to follow her, marched down the street to the cavalry headquarters at the Methodist Church. She and her trailing staff were startled to find that their progress was blocked by two gruff sentries who denied their access to the commanding officer.

Lieutenant Colonel Greyson, presiding over a map-study session with his officers, heard the challenge voiced by the sentries. He looked up from his work to survey, in surprise, the unusual-looking, white-aproned group who were led by a very determined lady. Mrs. Broun, the hem of her dress fluttering in the freshening morning breeze, stood with her hands on her hips as she demanded to see the officer in charge. The sentries, uncertain of what to do with her, looked across the intervening lawn to Greyson for instructions. He chuckled to his captains. "Looks to me as though those boys have got themselves a situation they can't handle! Excuse me, for a moment." The scene, as he approached, was comical enough to cause him to laugh out loud. Realizing that such laughter would be more than impolite, he managed to contain his merriment. The feisty lady in the yellow dress kept her arms akimbo, but was now impatentiently stamping her foot. The servants, hiding behind her, peeked around her, in fright, at the burly sentries who stood, straight as ramrods, before them. "Ma'am? What may I do for you?"

Catherine's resolution quavered under the gaze of the impressive officer, but she steadied herself to accomplish her mission. "Sir, it is not what you can do for me, but what we may do for you."

"Really? And how so?"

Summoning all of her feminine charm, the lady smiled up at Matthew. "Sir," she looked at the gold insignia on his shoulder, "er, colonel, if you don't mind my saying so, your men look hungry."

Matthew raised his eyebrows and glanced around at the nearby soldiers. The men nudged each other and chuckled among themselves as they watched the unexpected entertainment. "They look all right to me!" He smiled quizzically at her for a moment. "We are carrying rations adequate for our needs. I guess I just don't understand your point."

"The point is, I just don't like the sight of men who are in need of decent food, regardless of the color of their uniforms."

"I see, I think." Greyson scratched the back of his neck as he struggled to understand the conversation. "I'll admit, ma'am, that hardtack and coffee are not the tastiest way to start the day, but we are used to it. Our field rations will just have to do. My men are instructed to avoid burdening you folks with our needs. We have no quarrel with the citizens of Middleburg. Now, may I ask who you are?"

The lady extended her hand. The colonel smiled and bowed as he gently took it. "I am Catherine Broun of the Colonial Inn." She pointed down the street at the hotel, then surveyed the grinning troopers who were assembled to watch the fun. "Forgive me for disagreeing with you, colonel, but your men still look hungry to me. Even though I do not appreciate your presence here, I would welcome the opportunity to feed them, and you. No one, not even you Yankees, should leave Middleburg without a good meal under his belt. 'Southern hospitality' is not just an empty phrase, suh!"

Greyson smiled at her seemingly genuine sweetness. He bowed again, concealing his doubts.

Much as he wanted to do so, he could not dismiss the possibility that Mrs. Broun was simply motivated by the opportunity to sell two hundred hearty meals, and at a handsome profit, should he be motivated to pay her with Federal currency. "You are most kind, Catherine Broun. We would be honored to accept your fine offer. Thank you." He wondered what she would do if he told her that he would not pay, but decided that he did not want to know the answer. "I'll see that you are properly compensated for your trouble."

"No trouble at all, colonel." Catherine self-consciously smoothed her apron. "The matter of compensation is, of course, up to you." She signaled to her servants, and turned to leave. "So! Then we are agreed. If you will, send your men to me, a few at a time throughout the day, and I will see that they are fed plenty of decent food."

The cavalrymen began to cheer, but silenced when Greyson shot them a stern look. Matthew still wondered at the kindness of the gracious lady. If she was just a salesperson, she was a good one. Actually, her motivation did not really matter. A good meal would help to sustain the morale of his troopers.

Mrs. Broun took a few steps away, then returned to look, almost pleadingly, into his eyes. "I trust you will not be staying long?"

"Not long, madam, I promise."

"Very well!" she sniffed, "I'll just hold you to that." Her servants, still very frightened, were nervously shuffling their feet in the desire to retreat to the safety of the inn. "Come along, now. We have soldiers to feed!" Mrs. Broun's retinue marched back to the inn, where pots were immediately set a'boiling and pans a'frying. No one, not even the enemy, would leave Middleburg suffering from hunger should Catherine Broun have her way. She had just proved, once again, what the Middleburg folks already knew. Mrs. Broun usually managed, whatever the situation, to get things to go her way.

Greyson returned his attention to the military business of the day. Patrols were dispatched to scour the countryside, searching for caches of supplies and materiel that might have been hidden there. McEwan's patrol soon returned, burdened with a dozen sawed-off 12 gauge double-barreled shotguns, along with bags of buckshot and powder, that they had found concealed in a hay barn just outside of town. They placed their booty on the church lawn for Matthew's inspection.

Willy was so pleased with his find that he could hardly stand still. "Looky here, colonel. We found us a nice batch of reb cavalry weapons!"

Matt was not particularly impressed. "Looks like a pile of old sportin' shotguns." He rummaged through them. "Some flintlocks, some percussion, and all with their barrels hacked off. Just what do you propose that we do with these, sergeant?"

"I request your permission, sir, to distribute these among the men."

"You do? Why, in heaven's name, would we do that?"

"Well, ah, sir, if you don't mind my opinion, I 'spect that shotguns, along with revolvers, are beginnin' to make sabers pretty doggone obsolete in a cavalry affair." McEwan knew that he was overstepping his bounds, as a mere sergeant, by offering tactical advise. Nevertheless, he continued. "One reason that the reb cavalry is so effective is that they can blow us out of the saddle before we can reach 'em with our sabers. Beggin' your pardon, colonel, but I believe that we have all heard of that happening, of late."

The colonel thoughtfully rubbed his stubbly face. His itchy beard reminded him that he must take the time to shave before searching out the Chandler woman. It wouldn't do to look like a derelict when, and if, he were to finally find the wife of his silenced rebel friend.

Matt believed, as did most classically trained cavalrymen of his day.... except, apparently, the Confederates....that the saber was the weapon of choice. He was, however, flexible enough in his thinking to see the possible merit of the sergeant's words. "Very well, Sergeant McEwan. Kindly inspect, and then distribute, these fierce and terrifying bird guns to those of the men who are most likely to make good use of them. Good work, Will. We are, after all, only lightly armed. We might just put them to good use, and learn a little something about their effectiveness while we are at it!"

McEwan was delighted that he had made his point. He threw the colonel a snappy salute. "Thank you for the opportunity to give these little darlin's a try, Matt."

Matthew condescendingly returned the salute. "Don't mention it, Will. While you play with your new toys, I'm going to give myself a shave and change my shirt. It's near time for us to saddle up and attend to some special business."

Willy's grin was at its proudest, widest, and toothiest. "Understand, sir. What time do you wish to head out?"

"Nine o'clock, sharp. Pick six troopers to go along with us." The colonel disappeared in the direction of the disgustingly overtaxed "necessary shed" that was situated, fragrantly, behind the church.

By 8:55, the six troopers stood to horse in front of the headquarters area. Sgt. McEwan was well aware of the audience of townspeople who stood at a respectful distance across the street.

He had picked his flashiest horsemen to make up the patrol. The horses, curried and brushed until they shone, tossed their heads and danced impatiently. They were firmly held in column of twos, and, sadly for them, just out of reach of the succulent grasses in the church lawn. The mounts longed, mightily, for a taste of the holy grass, but it was not to be. Saber,

164

and McEwan's black gelding, stood at the fore. The Chandler mare stood quietly at the rear.

"Prepare to mount!" bawled McEwan. "Mount!" The men swung smoothly into their saddles. "Draw sabers!" Six sabers flashed in the morning sunlight as they swung in an ark, and then were held upright in their gloved right hands, hands that came to rest just forward of their right hips. The sergeant, still on the ground, spun on his heels and saluted his colonel. "Ready, sir!"

Greyson returned the salute, mounted, and smiled at Willy. "Well done, sergeant!" Then, quietly, "Good show, Will!"

McEwan gave him a clandestine wink. "By column of twos, at the walk, forward, march!" There was a gabble of speculation among the townspeople as the little column turned off the main street and headed north along a small road that lead in the direction of Goose Creek.

Their hand-drawn map proved to be accurate. A small clapboard house, with a well-maintained barn, came into view close by the trail. The fields, that should have been plowed and planted by John Chandler, were, instead, an untended carpet of nodding, wild, white daises. There was, however, a neat little kitchen garden next to the house which contained a nice array of sprouting vegetables. The door yard was surrounded by a whitewashed picket fence, also in good repair, but in need of a fresh coat of white. Several large redbud trees, in full bloom, graced the farmstead with showy clouds of pink.

Matt motioned for McEwan and the six troopers to remain on the trail while he leaned down to unlatch the gate. Swinging it open, he rode into the door yard. Farmers never leave an open gate. He spun Saber and reached to close it behind him. As he did so, the door to the house creaked open, and a tall woman in an homespun dress stepped hesitantly into view. She carried a vintage flintlock squirrel rifle in her hands. Matt was relieved to see that she did not point the ancient piece in his direction. At the same time he noted, to his horror, that the hammer was cocked and that the piece was ready to fire. The mounted men on the road were uncertain as to what action, if any, that they should take. The sight of the weapon caused them to raise the flaps on their holsters and to place their hands on the butts of their revolvers. It was clearly their duty to protect their colonel....

but, from a woman? Not one of them could bring himself to draw his weapon. McEwan raised his hand, unnecessarily, to steady them. The men were already steady....in fact they were not even breathing. If the woman decided to shoot, the colonel would be dead as John Brown, and there would be nothing that they could do about it.

The lady, by all appearances, was calm, fearless, and determined....but her soft voice quavered as she spoke. "You Yankees got no reason to be in my yard. I got nothin' worth your stealin'!"

Matt, still fervently hoping that she would not point her rifle at him, took a good look at her. Her lilting Virginia speech fell pleasantly upon his ears. Frayed and patched as she appeared, she was, indeed, a beauty. She was a high cheek-boned, fresh-faced, young American Indian squaw! She reminded him of the handsome Ojibwa natives whom he had encountered in the upper Great Lakes area when he had restlessly traveled there after his service in the Mexican War. "Excuse me, but I am looking for a Mrs. Chandler. Would she be here?"

Her dark eyes narrowed. "Now, just why would you be askin' for Mrs. Chandler?"

Matt was a little flustered. "Ah, well....well, I got business with her."

"What sort of business?"

"It's about her husband."

The handsome Indian seemed to wilt. Her eyes brimmed with tears in spite of her bravado. A little girl, whom Matthew judged to be ten or eleven years of age, tried to push through the door to stand with her mother. She shoved the child back into the house and reclosed the door. "Just what do you know about her husband?"

"I was there when he died."

The colonel stiffened as he saw her finger reach for the trigger of the rifle. He held his breath, but made no move to defend himself. Captain Paldi, in the light of the present situation, could well have been correct. Perhaps, this really was a stupid mission. Dark thoughts raced through his mind. This could well be a terribly embarrassing way to end a distinguished military career....shot dead by an angry squaw with a squirrel gun! So much for well-meaning projects! However, thankfully, she did not swing the muzzle toward him. Greyson watched, in fascination, as, in slow motion, her thumb reached for the hammer and decocked it. He started to breathe again. She looked at him, questioningly, her eyes searching his face as she tried to understand the nature of his visit. She leaned the rifle against the house without taking her eyes away from his.

"Thank you, God!" Matthew whispered in silent prayer as he rolled his eyes toward the heavens. Then, clearing his throat, "would it be possible that I might speak with Mrs. Chandler?"

"You're speakin' to her." Her voice was so soft that he could hardly hear her words.

Matthew's jaw dropped. "You are Charity Jane Melody Chandler? Really?"

"Really! You didn't expect no injun, did you?"

"Uh, no ma'am. Reckon I didn't."

Mrs. Chandler had begun to size up this splendidly uniformed man who looked down at her from his equally splendid horse. He was not nearly as scary as she had first thought. She gathered her courage. "'Round these parts, it's common courtesy to dismount 'fore you come through the gate into a person's yard. I reckon we can talk, some, if you will kindly remove your horse to the other side of the fence, where he belongs."

"As you say, ma'am." Matthew blushed. He was thoroughly humbled. The men on the road were starting to snicker, relieved that the crisis had passed.

Willy, thinking Matt would not hear, whispered a confidence into the ears of the men, much to their delight. "The colonel never did know how to handle a woman! They always get the best of him. I seen it before."

Greyson could hear enough of their whispers to realize that they were enjoying his discomfort. He gave them an angry look. The men swallowed their chuckles and sat, pokerfaced, while they regained, with difficulty, their military composure. He slid out of the saddle, led Saber back through the gate, and handed the reins to McEwan. He leaned, for a moment, at the sergeant's knee. "You keep these boys quiet, or I'll have you all court-marshaled!" His words were spoken softly, but very firmly. Willy could read the anger that was clearly behind them. It was obvious that the colonel was not in a mood to be taken lightly.

"Yes, sir. Sorry, sir."

"You'd damn well better be! You would be well-advised to spend this moment watching for bushwhackers who could well be creepin' up on us. That, sergeant, is an order. Yesss?" Matt hissed the word, like a snake, as he transfixed the sergeant with a fierce stare.

"Right away, sir!"

"Good!" Matthew strode back through the gate, closed it carefully, and returned to Mrs. Chandler. Will obediently positioned the troopers along the lane, ignoring their ill-disguised smirks. He admonished them to do their duty, to keep a watchful eye for any suspicious activity. He reminded them that they were in enemy territory, and that all of their lives could well be in danger should they not remain alert.

Melody Chandler watched the proceedings with some amusement. "Now that we have your Yankee manners straightened, I'll hear what you have to say." Her dark eyes flashed "Did you kill my husband?" She did not wait for an answer. "I knowed he was dead. Didn't care, 'till now, to know the details. Hurt too much to even think about it."

Matthew, ignoring her cutting appraisal of their Yankee manners, regarded her sympathetically. "I understand. This all must be very difficult for you. I'm sorry to cause you such pain, I didn't mean to do that. Forgive me."

Mrs. Chandler stared at him, giving no evidence of forgiveness.

"Fact is, I didn't kill him. Someone else saw to that, I suppose. Someone under my command, I'll confess." He paused to think, for a moment. His voice, when he continued, was low and reflected a sadness that touched her. "Guess maybe that makes his death my fault, doesn't it?" Matt could no longer meet her gaze.

"I suppose maybe it does make it your fault, but, then again, maybe it don't. If you men got to go killin' each other, then it's all your faults.... including my John's. Fact is, he hated you Yanks so much he probably would have enjoyed shootin' you, had he been given the chance."

168

Matt raised his eyes, giving her a guarded smile. "He even said just that to me when I found him on the battlefield. He said he would have killed me. Didn't say he would have enjoyed it, though!"

Melody still could not guess why this man, whom her husband wanted to kill, was standing before her. "Yank, it's time to tell me just why, in heaven's name, you are here."

"I made your man a promise. He lived only a short time after I found him lyin' in the woods. Just the same, we had time to talk, some. He was....I'm sorry, ma'am....shot through the chest and there was no hope for recovery. The bullet just missed his Book." Matt took the tattered and bloodstained New Testament from his shirt pocket and held it out to her. "He asked me to bring it to you."

She held the little volume with trembling hands. "Why, it is John's Book!" The reality of his death was suddenly upon her. Confederate officers had called upon her to tell her that he was dead, but, somehow, deep in her soul, she could not bring herself to believe that he was really gone. She sobbed openly as she sagged to her knees, clutching John's Bible to her breast. She caressed the torn pages as though she were running her fingers through her husband's hair. "Tell me, mister soldier, did he suffer much.... my John?"

Matt gently helped her to her feet, steadying her. She seemed a little wobbly. "Now, don't you go and faint, Mrs. Chandler." He glanced over his shoulder at the mounted men in the road. Fortunately, they were all looking the other way, watching for bushwhackers as ordered. "I don't need something new for my troopers to chuckle about. Answer is, no. John didn't suffer much, nor long."

Thank God for that." Melody shrugged away from the touch of the hands that sought to steady her. " Want you to know that I could care less whether your soldiers chuckle, spit, or turn green!" She wiped at her eyes with the frayed sleeve of her dress. "I certainly do not intend to faint, thank you very much!"

Matt looked at her as though she might bite. "Whatever you say, Mrs. Chandler." He was beginning to suspect, considering her surly manner, that it might be best if he did not return the mare to her, after all. "We'll be on our way, now. Sorry to have bothered you." He turned his back on her, walked through the whitewashed gate, and turned to close it.

Melody stood with her face covering her hands. "Wait, colonel." He stood with his hand still on the gate. She covered his hand with both of hers. "I'm right sorry for my behavior. Guess it was the shock of hearin' about John, and all." She looked into his steady brown eyes. "Forgive me, suh, if you would. I'm right grateful for what you have done for John and me. Reckon I can't thank you enough for your kindness."

Matt smiled at her for a moment, then laughed. "Considering that it's now clear that neither of us has very good manners, I have something else for you." He whistled to McEwan who was holding the Chandler mare out of sight behind a small thicket at the side of the road. Greyson had instructed the sergeant to keep her hidden, just in case he should change his mind about returning her. His mind was made up. "Bring her on, sergeant!"

Mrs. Chandler's face went from rosy-hued embarrassment to openmouthed amazement as the mare was led into view. Will walked her through the gate and handed the lead to the startled woman. McEwan was beaming. "Reckon if a horse could smile, she'd be doin' it now!"

Matt pretended to look, carefully. "Don't see any smile on that mare, Willy....'cept, maybe, a little around the eyes!"

The girl-child, who had been watching the strange proceedings through a crack in the door, suddenly could control herself no longer. She burst from the house, screaming "Cuppie! Cuppie! Cuppie! You're home! Oh! Cuppie!" She took the horse by the halter and jumped up and down to kiss her repeatedly on the muzzle. "Oh, Cuppie, I never thought I'd see you again!"

Matt glowed. Now he understood why the horse had to be returned. The prayers of a little metis girl had been answered. Even Willy was touched by the scene. His tough, drill sergeant cheek suffered the embarrassment of a little tear that threaded its way down through the freckles and tickled his chin. Greyson could not believe his ears when he heard the girl call out the mare's name. He had been certain that someone would have given this wonderful horse a truly classic, or at least, flashy name. But...."Cuppie"?

"Really, ma'am, her name is, ah, Cuppie?"

170

Melody was short on breath. She struggled to speak. "Yes, it's Cuppie. Stands for Buttercup. My daughter, Mary Sue, named her, as you might guess."

"Aha!" Matt chuckled. "So that's Mary Sue? The one with her lips stuck to that horse's nose?"

Mrs. Chandler smiled through her happy tears. "Yep. That there is Mary Sue and her best friend Cuppie. Her heart was broke when Cuppie had to go to war. My husband wouldn't tell his soldier friends what the horse that he was ridin's' real name was. In fact, he told them that her name was 'Empress', or somethin' silly like that." She smoothed her thick hair. Black as coal on a moonless night, it persisted in flying from the ribbon that tried in vain to hold it in place. "Now y'all know all our names. Can I ask what yours might be?"

"Matthew. Name's Matthew. And this is Will." The colonel was relieved to have this business completed....and quite successfully, he thought. He looked around, remembering their surroundings, and suddenly became a bit nervous. "Pardon me, Mrs. Charity Jane Melody Chandler, but the 'Matt 'n' Willy Show' had best hit the road before somebody gets wind that we are here and decides to use us for target practice. Let's go. Get 'em mounted up, Will."

Greyson paused, for a moment, stroking the mare's silky neck, unconsciously fussing with her mane, as he watched McEwan hurry back to the road. "I have to confess I've become a mite attached to this beast. I'm sure I can count on you to take good care of her."

Mary Sue hugged him, much as she would have hugged her father, had he been there. She craned her neck to look up at him as he towered above her tiny form. "You can bet on that, mister. Thank you for bringing my Cuppie home to me."

"You're most welcome, Mary Sue. A pleasure. Mrs. Chandler, I hope you will be able to use....ah....Cuppie for farming, and not let her get back to your military. I made some promises in that regard."

"Bless you, Matthew." Melody came to him, and shyly reached to touch his cheek. "I can do that. John built a barn 'way out back in the woods. I can hide her there, should the foragers come lookin'. And, we have a light, single-bottom plow she can pull without harm. She might just keep us from starvin' till this awful war is over."

"That's what I had hoped, Mrs. Chandler."

"Call me Melody. That what John called me."

"I know. He told me. I'd like to stay and talk more, but we really must be goin'. Pleasure to meet you, Melody."

As he turned to leave, Melody put her hand on his arm to stop him. Her heart told her that she did not want him to go. Her eyes were so dark that he could not tell if they had any color at all. "Matthew, why? Why did you do such a fine thing for me and Mary Sue?"

"Because John was my friend."

"Your friend? But, how could you tell? You only knew him for a few moments."

The colonel sighed. "A few moments was all we had, but we made do. I looked into his eyes, and I saw friendship there. I'm told that when you look into the eyes of a friend, you can see God smiling back at you. And, it's true."

Melody began to cry. "I swear, I haven't shed so many tears since I was a little girl, size of Mary Sue. Matthew, look into mine. What do you see?"

Matt put his fingers, gently, under her chin and studied her face carefully. "I see God." He smiled. "He is in your eyes, too."

Saber whinnied as Matt carefully latched the little, white gate behind him. Cuppy nickered a soft answer as the blue-uniformed detachment reformed in column, then retraced their steps along the rutted trail back toward Middleburg.

CHAPTER TEN

Across A Stone Bridge

The trail that led between the Chandler farm and town was narrow and seldom traveled. Colonel Greyson was concerned that the Middleburg citizens could well have passed the word to their military that a small detachment of Federal troopers, including their colonel, had left the relative security of their main force and headed, out of town, toward Goose Creek. The possibility of ambush was high....almost a probability.... if enough Confederate soldiers happened to be loose in the area, and were willing to attempt to bag such a tempting prize. Conditions were perfect, fumed Greyson, for an ambuscade. The area was heavily forested. The lush, green, spring growth intruded closely upon the trail, the branches of the trees meeting overhead to form a kind of tunnel through which they had to pass as they hurried, cautiously, to rejoin their unit. Two men rode point, a few rods ahead, and just in sight. Matthew turned to Sergeant Willy, who, as usual, rode at his side. "Will, I don't know how you feel, but I think we did a good thing, and did it well. But, seems to me that we stayed too damned long for our own good."

"Yep, we did a fine thing. Yep, we stayed too long. And, yep, the rebs could be layin' for us, but I don't think so. Our show of force in Middleburg should have scared most of 'em clean out of the county."

"Right now, 'most of 'em' ain't good enough" smiled Matt. The sergeant's words were reassuring. Matt noticed, however, that Will was carrying one of his Johnson pistols in his right hand, cradling the long barrel in the crook of his left arm.

Will leaned forward in the saddle as he peered through the underbrush at the side of the trail. "If you don't mind me sayin' so, Matt, that was a fine-lookin' squaw you picked to be so nice to. Could well be that she'd be happy to see you again, one day."

"Don't matter. Don't expect to ever see her again. Best you wipe such ideas as that clean out of your mind."

"Just the same, you smooth-talked that pretty lady mighty nice. I need to study your methods! Might just be you have given me a new wrinkle as to how to get women to bed with me a little quicker."

Matthew's eyes sparkled, wickedly. "You could be right. Best to follow the example of a master of the art. Of course, you need to have a horse to give away, and you need to learn to be steady in the face of the muzzle of a loaded squirrel rifle!"

The point riders reigned to a halt and drew their revolvers. Greyson raised his hand to halt the rest of the detachment as they also unholstered their weapons. There was a tense moment as they watched the advanced men cock their Colts and point them at an unseen target up the road. "Well, here we go!" muttered Matt.

McEwan spat a brown stream into the roadside bushes. "I can hear somethin' comin'. Don't sound like many, though." To their relief, the advance horsemen straightened in their saddles, reholstered their weapons, and waved. They had determined that the approaching riders wore Federal blue. They turned out to be Captain Paldi and one of his scouts. Paldi had taken the precaution to scatter twenty more troopers along the trail behind him to serve as vedettes.

As they came near, Greyson could see that Paldi's face was grim and unsmiling. "Colonel, enemy cavalry are moving toward us from the east. Right now they're just west of Aldie."

"Ah!" exclaimed Greyson. "Good! They have taken the bait! After all, we're here to find out if there are significant enemy forces in the area. Good! Good! Our lingering in Middleburg has paid off! It would seem that they're advancing to be counted. Have you called in all patrols? Are the men mounted and ready for action?" Captain Paldi saluted. He answered with the confidence of a seasoned leader. "I have, and they are, sir, in anticipation of your orders."

"Well done, Angelo." Greyson breathed a sigh of relief. "Thank you. Let's have the details, if you please." Greyson, Paldi, and the scout dismounted. The scout smoothed a patch in the dust of the road so that he could draw a makeshift map. The troopers, unhappy with the dense underbrush, dispersed as best they could to stand guard. The scout, a cool professional who was weaned on the Mexican War, was precise in his observations. "There's a lot of 'em, sir, well uniformed and equipped, with good horses that are well shod....judging from their tracks. Crack cavalry. Could be Turner Ashby's men from the valley."

Greyson pursed his lips in thought. "Really! Now what would they be doing here? They're supposed to be with Jackson in the Shenandoah."

"Yes sir. But these ain't. They come to pay us a visit, I reckon."

The scout had Greyson's full attention. "Why, do you suppose, that they would be here? What's in Aldie that they might want to protect?"

"Grain and flour, sir, to feed an army. Aldie is a mill town."

Greyson settled his kepi precisely on his head. "You could well be correct! Thank you for your remarkable work. How many are they?"

"About four hundred, sir. I'd guess about twice our number. I 'spect that if they mean to keep us from Aldie, they probably will do just that!"

Matt sensed that the Confederates were offering a challenge. Aldie could be a town well worth the trouble to investigate. "Really! Do they appear to have either infantry or artillery support?"

"No sir. Not as we could see."

"Reserves?"

"No sir. Not as we could see."

"Good. I believe we need to take a look at Aldie."

The scout looked doubtful. "As you say, sir!"

The troops were assembled, and waiting, when Greyson arrived back in town. The horses, sensing the excitement, were pawing and snorting. Some danced nervously, but were well-controlled by the cavalrymen who sat, with the ease of experts, in their McClellan saddles.

The officers, with Sergeant McEwan and the scout, squatted on the church lawn to again study their meager map of the area. A second scout galloped to join them. He was breathless and shaking with excitement. "Colonel, the rebs have picked their ground!" He pointed a sweaty finger to the map at a point on the turnpike that was about midway between Aldie and Middleburg. "They're drawn up in double rank, mounted, and extendin' about a quarter mile on each side of the pike. They've a light barricade 'cross the road. Intend to fight us horse-to-horse in the open....man-to-man. Looks bad, sir. They outnumber us 'bout two to one!"

The colonel's brown eyes were calm and reassuring, but he did not smile. "Interesting! It would seem that they are well officered. They leave us two unpleasant alternatives: A suicide attack, on their ground, and against superior numbers, or to retreat. Gentlemen. We will retreat." The words were spoken quietly....almost as though it made no difference to Greyson, one way or the other.

Captains Acker and Paldi looked at each other in disbelief. Paldi stood to stiffly confront his superior. "Sir! Give us a chance to whip the bastards! We can do it!"

Matthew was still unsmiling. He put a hand on Angelo Paldi's shoulder and patted him, almost paternally. "I'm sure we can, captain....but on our terms....not theirs." He motioned for them to draw close, looking about to see that no one was within earshot. "Here's what we will do." Matthew's face suddenly lost its grim aspect. "We're going to have a party....but on our terms!" He loved a good game of cat-and-mouse. The game was especially appealing since it appeared that he was pitted against a Confederate officer of quality. "Our current position is a dangerous one. Should we get into trouble, our retreat could be bottled into that single stone bridge over the Goose Creek. Sooo....unfurl the colors, and march at parade step to the east. And, oh, have every man salute Mrs. Braun as we pass the Colonial Inn. I'd bet she'll be watching from her door. We'll disappear to the east

176

just long enough for the citizens to dispatch gallopers to the rebs to tell them that we are on our way into their trap. We will then about-face the column, and then canter back through town as though we have just been scared from here to breakfast. We'll look as though we are going to retreat all the way clean across the Shenandoah!"

Captain Acker feared that the colonel had lost his mind. "But, colonel....."

"Hear me out, George. When we cross the stone bridge, we'll be on the west side of the Goose Creek valley. That area is heavily wooded. We will dismount, hide our mounts to the rear, and set up an ambuscade of our own just west of the bridge, covering both sides of the pike. I'll wager they will come galloping across that bridge, chasing us poor, scared Yankees. We'll set up a crossfire across the pike, with Will's shotguns at the fore, and give 'em a dose of lead they won't soon forget. Once they are in retreat, we'll mount up and saber 'em back to wherever they came from. Then, God willing, we'll have a look at Aldie! There's a name for this game, gentlemen. It's called 'even the odds'."

Captain Acker looked sheepish as he apologized to his colonel. "By God, Matt, it might just work!"

"It better work, George. See to it!"

Catherine Braun stood before the door of her inn, as predicted. She could not bring herself to return the smiles of the men whom she had fed. They saluted her, as they passed, to show their gratitude for her kindly hospitality. Men and beasts were well-fed and rested. Her Christian love could do no more. Sadly, In her mind's eye, the smiles of those robust young men seemed to turn into the haunting skeletal grins of shriveled corpses....corpses riding, splendidly, toward their death in the trap that she knew had been set for them. Her knees quivered, and threatened to buckle under her. She was obliged to sit upon the steps of the inn as she watched the Yankees pass. "Why," she thought "would these men, who seemed so gentlemanly, seek to destroy her own butternut and gray-clad friends who sought only to defend their own firesides? Why?" She thought of mothers weeping, and of girls burying their faces in their mother's skirts as they tried to understand the loss of their fathers, or of their brothers. There was no easy answer. God seemed to have turned away, in sorrow, from the foolishness of man. Catherine tried hard to make sense of it all. She sighed a shivering sigh. If only the politicians, on both sides, had ceased their egocentric ravings long enough to think about the unnecessary bloodshed that they themselves would cause, perhaps war could have been averted. If only the fire-breathing orators, be they for "states' rights" or for "preservation of the Union", had cared about the families who would lose loved ones, or who would have to spend the rest of their lives nursing the shattered parts and pieces of soldiers who would be lucky, or unlucky, enough to survive this internecine war, perhaps they would have, instead, led the nation in the direction of peace, and of compromise.

Preserve the Union? That problem could well have resolved itself anyway.... given the hopeful possibility that good sense would eventually prevail. Eliminate slavery? Another extremely noble goal that probably would have been accomplished without war. World opinion had already turned away from the "peculiar institution". Slavery could not have survived long in a world of increasingly reasonable and compassionate men. Only God knows how many leaders on both sides would have backed away from their inflammatory rhetoric had they known that over 600,000 men would die from battle or from disease....or had they known how many mothers, fathers, women, and children would cry, and cry some more, long into the lonely nights of their lives.

Under the stern, but compassionate, leadership of Colonel Greyson, Middleburg had just been briefly occupied by gentleman-soldiers. Catherine Broun had been pleasantly surprised at their behavior. As she sat struggling with her thoughts, she mercifully did not know....yet.... that "modern warfare", in all its horrid glory, was in its infancy. The Confederates, on the one hand, were generally kind to noncombatants, even to the end of the war. Key Union leaders, who far outranked Colonels Brodhead, Greyson, and others like them, were not so kindly. General John Pope started the nastiness by severely punishing citizens who would not declare loyalty to the Union. General Phil Sheridan would unnecessarily scorch the Shenandoah Valley, leaving thousands homeless, and without hope. A certifiable madman, General William Tecumseh Sherman, would cut a swath of inhumane destruction across the south during his "celebrated" march to the sea. The War Between the States produced the end of old-fashioned Napoleonic warfare, the birth of modern weapons of destruction, and the death of compassionate behavior in the hearts of mankind.

At least at first, and for a merciful while, Catherine Broun perceived the war as a kindly one. She did not realize that she was hanging her hat upon an oxymoron. Kindly wars do not exist....and never would, and never will.

$+ + +$

Matthew's plan had seemed to work to perfection. The citizens, in sullen silence, witnessed the Yanks' showy departure to the east. When, after a half-hour interval, the First Michigan thundered back through town, in an obviously hasty retreat, the townspeople scattered out of the way, cheered, and waved their hats. Some were even brave enough to send a few well-chosen epithets after the departing troopers.

The Michigan men cantered their mounts all the way to the stone bridge, crossed, picked their concealment, and planned their fields of fire so that they could pour a murderous hail of lead into the enemy without shooting each other as they fired across the turnpike. Shots angling into the depth of the approaching enemy column would have the most effect. If one missed the first man, one would very likely still pick off the man behind him.

The officers quietly reminded the men to check their weapons. They were to check, and double check, that all six revolver cylinders were loaded, and that percussion caps were in place. Shotguns were fully loaded with buckshot. Sabers were determined to be loose in their scabbards so that they could be easily and quickly drawn. Greyson carried his Colt Walker in his hand. His issue Colt was in its belt holster. McEwan had his horse pistols at the ready. His revolver was on his belt. One shot from each of his flintlocks would surely not be enough for this operation.

They had not long to wait. The sound of four hundred horses approaching at the gallop started as a mere whisper, then gradually escalated to a thunder that shook the earth. The troopers nervously cocked their weapons. Greyson had instructed them to wait for him to fire the first shot. They ducked behind their screens of roadside bushes and trees. The colonel calculated, and hoped, that the enemy would be in column of fours, as they would be planning to crash headlong into his own force on the road. He calculated that the turnpike, and the bridge, were just wide enough to allow such deployment. When the fluttering red, white, and blue of the Stars and Bars came into view across the bridge, they were carried in the midst of four horsemen abreast! The Confederates were closely bunched! Matthew breathed a sigh of relief. Had they been in twos, only half as many would fit into his relatively small ambush area. With four abreast, there would be fewer survivors to deal with after the initial engagement. The colonel waited tensely until the last possible moment, stepped into the road in front of the unsuspecting enemy column, and dropped the flag bearer with a single shot from his Walker. His shot was the signal from Hell. In an instant, the road was filled with the roar of rapid small-arms fire. Smoke bellowed. Horses and men screamed and fell. The rebs on the bridge, and on the approach to it, had no time to react. They collided with their own troops with such force that their mounts reared, plunged, scrambled, and fell. Some rolled down the banks of the creek, or fell off of the bridge and into the water below. The dreadful pandemonium, the shouts, the screams, the curses, seemed to last for an eternity. The First Michigan fired, reloaded, and fired again. The shotguns emptied saddles, and felled horses, by the score. The rebs who were still mounted were pulled from their saddles and subdued by the saber. The action did not slow until the surviving, trapped southerners raised their hands in surrender. The road was littered with the dead and dying. The blood of man and beast mixed together and ran in rivulets across the road, then into the river, becoming a red plume that followed the lazy current.

As the conflict tapered to its conclusion, Colonel Greyson stood, expressionless, in the center of the road and in the midst of the dead, wounded, and dying. A hot, empty revolver was in each hand. He felt grimy tears coursing his cheeks. "Oh," he cried within himself, "what have I done? What have I done?" He stepped over a horse that was lying on its side, paddling its legs and gurgling its last desperate breaths, and walked to the edge of the road to reload his weapons. He kept his back turned.... not wanting his men to see his sorrow, to think him weak.

He tore the paper cartridges with his teeth and seated each ball carefully. A hand was suddenly upon his shoulder. It was McEwan. "Matt--er--sir, are you all right?"

Greyson nodded, but kept his face turned away.

Will patted Matt's shoulder for a moment, then, realizing that his actions should be more militarily correct, stood at attention behind his commander. "Your orders, sir?"

Greyson, his face still averted, continued to see to his reloading. He spoke softly, but firmly, over his shoulder. "Contain and disarm the prisoners. Then, give me a count." He swung to face his sergeant as he regained his composure. "Have Captain Acker mount his men and prepare to pursue the enemy." The colonel was wiping his eyes with the back of his hand. McEwan pretended not to notice. .

"Yes sir!" He turned to his task, shouting instructions in his best fearless and warlike tones. The sergeant was in his element. The victory was a joy beyond belief. "Disarm the prisoners! Now! Captain Acker! Colonel's orders. You are to mount your company and prepare for pursuit!" He spun to face Greyson. "What shall we do with their weapons?"

"Break the sabers, damage the firearms as much as possible, and throw them all in the creek." Matt suddenly smiled. "All except the shotguns."

Will grinned his widest grin. "Thank you, sir! You five....he counted them off....you heard the colonel. Get to it, and you might just earn yourselves your very own shotgun!"

Company I, minus eight casualties, threaded their way through the carnage, deployed their scouts, and cautiously trotted toward Middleburg in the direction of which the escaped enemy had fled. Matthew stopped Captain Acker as he passed. "George, be careful. We are not immune from ambush ourselves!"

"You can bet on that, Matt." Acker was busy reloading his pistol as he looked down from his horse. "What is your plan?"

"You are to reoccupy the town if there is no significant resistance. Send your scouts on to Aldie if that looks reasonable. If possible, I intend to take advantage of our momentum and proceed to Aldie. Send the townsfolk down here with wagons to collect the casualties....including ours. If the rebs have re-formed and are looking to fight, return here immediately. Otherwise, wait there until we join you."

George Acker saluted, and rode to catch up with his men.

Matthew winced as shots rang out. His men were mercifully killing the crippled and dying horses. The waste of the beautiful Virginia animals was appalling. They tended to the wounded men as best they could. The Yanks offered them water. They crudely bandaged critical, hemorrhaging wounds with strips of the injured men's' shirts....be they butternut or blue. The Confederates had suffered eighty-four killed or dying, and two hundred seventeen captured. Of the captured, at least half were wounded. Their colonel, and one captain, were among the fatalities. Another captain, and several lieutenants, were numbered among the prisoners. That left about one hundred enemy cavalryman who were still on the loose....enough to be dangerous, indeed. The First Michigan Cavalry had suffered the loss of twelve wounded enough to be unfit for duty, and nine killed. The prisoners were gathered and marched toward town, leaving the wounded and dead to await the care of the citizens of Middleburg who, hopefully, would soon come to them.

Matthew had no reason to doubt the compassion of the residents of that fair city. A makeshift hospital was already being organized in the Methodist Church. The Union column, herding their prisoners, soon met a column of quite another sort traveling in the opposite direction. It contained an assortment of wagons, buggies and buckboards of all descriptions. The vehicles carried a sizable contingent of women and older men who were bound on their errand of mercy.

Matthew spotted a familiar-looking horse in the midst of the unhappy parade. It was Buttercup. Melody sat sidesaddle upon her. The lady's fine-featured face was stony with anger. She glared at Matt as they passed....her dark eyes blazing into his. She did not speak, nor change her expression. Matt tipped his cap in friendly salute. She, without a word, turned away.

Matt, already saddened by the events of the day, slipped into deeper depression. He leaned to Will, who, of course, rode beside him. "Well! So much for that friendship! Certainly didn't last long did it?"

Will wrinkled his forehead in thought. "Tell you what. You got to look on the bright side. Think how you'd feel now, if we'd lost!"

Matthew shrugged. He was a victorious, but very saddened, man.

They herded the prisoners into a large, empty barn near the edge of town.... filling it to capacity. Greyson posted a small, but heavily armed, contingent to watch over them. Each man brandished a 12 gauge shotgun, some of which were newly captured. Acker reported that the rebels who had managed to escape the ambush had disappeared. The road to Aldie was open. Interrogation of the prisoners, plus the reports of the scouts, soon revealed the importance of that little mill town to the east. A large wagon train was loading grain and flour that was stored at the Aldie mill and was preparing to supply Confederate General Stonewall Jackson's 18,500 man Army of the Valley, who had just crossed the Blue Ridge, and were marching to join General Robert E. Lee's Army of Northern Virginia. It was June 25, 1862, the beginning of Lee's Seven Day's Campaign. Federal forces were about to be chased away from Richmond. Union General McClellan's Peninsular Campaign was soon to come to an ignominious end. Richmond would be safe....for a while.

In their isolated position, Colonel Greyson could not know the details of the unfolding events. He did know, however, that the news of General Jackson's movement to the east could be of the utmost importance. He dispatched gallopers to carry the information to Colonel Brodhead, who was impatiently awaiting a report. By the time the dispatch was wired to Washington, it was too late. The Union forces in the Richmond area were already reeling from the Confederate attack.

Greyson left a small force of occupation in Middleburg and moved rapidly to disrupt the wagon train at Aldie. There was little resistance as they pounced upon the train, sending teamsters and mill workers running for their lives. They proceeded to slash open the neatly loaded sacks of grain and flour, upset the wagons, and set fire to everything that would burn. Jackson's men and horses would have to fight without nourishment from the mill at Aldie.

Unknown to the Michigan men, the gray troopers who had escaped the Goose Creek ambush had reformed on the Leesburg Road north of Aldie. Many were lightly wounded, but still full of fight. When a column of black smoke arose in the distance, from the direction of the mill, they decided that enough was enough. They would destroy the Yankees, now hated more than ever, or die in the trying. The Union scouts had not detected their presence. The gray horsemen charged toward Aldie at the gallop and in column, sweeping Federal vedettes before them. Startled, the mounted sentries fired warning shots, spun their horses, and rode for their lives as the Virginians tried to ride them down with their fast and splendid mounts.

Many of the Union force had no time to mount. They were obliged to take cover as they could, fighting from the ground with saber and revolver. The Confederates were somewhat outnumbered, but they had the element of surprise. Revenge was theirs. Many on both sides died in and around the inferno of burning wagons. Unfortunately for the southern warriors, Colonel Greyson had characteristically left nothing to chance. He, Sergeant McEwan, and fifty troopers stood, mounted and ready, on the turnpike as it rose up a small hill just west of the mill. Recovering quickly from the surprise of the attack, they drew sabers and charged into the fray.

Greyson was not the kind of officer who would send his men into combat without his own personal leadership, whenever possible. Accordingly, he, with his loyal Sergeant McEwan at his side, was the first to smash into the jumble of shouting, cursing men. His reserve force of fifty troopers was close at Saber's heels. The Confederates, realizing that there was a Union officer in their midst, quickly closed around him, and around Will, momentarily isolating them from the rest of the counterattacking troopers. Sabers flashed and clashed. Horses and men, for the second time that fateful day, screamed and fell. Southern saddles emptied all around the dangerous pair as their strong arms, their bloody sabers, did their lethal work. A revolver shot rang out, the sound masked by the uproar of combat. Greyson saw Will reel in his saddle, his right arm suddenly useless, his saber falling to the ground. Matt spotted the shooter, and rushed to intercept him, but the man's second shot caught Will below the shoulder, sending him to the ground. Matt slashed viciously at the man's arm, nearly severing it at the wrist. He thrust, and the man died, but the damage was done. Will lay under the trampling hooves of the frightened horses.

The blue-uniformed men, who had been caught dismounted, recovered sufficiently to pour a withering fire into the southern troopers, causing them to waver in their attack. The Union mounted also pushed them hard. The Confederates fell back, then precipitously withdrew, spurred by the force of the counterattacking Yanks. In an instant, the butternut and gray were gone, necessarily leaving their casualties behind. The sudden silence was punctuated only by the groans and cries of the wounded. A mockingbird, apparently offended by the disturbance, elected to sing a requiem from a nearby laurel.

Matt found Will under the jumble of the fallen. He was alive, but not by much. Blood from his punctured lung frothed his lips. Splinters of his shattered humerus protruded from the fragmented flesh of his arm. Should he, by some miracle, survive, this loyal soldier, this exemplary cavalryman, would very likely never fight again. Matt knelt, and wept, at his side.

McEwan's eyes fluttered open and searched Matthew's face. Even through the pain, he managed his boyish grin. "We got 'em, didn't we, Matt?"

"We got 'em, Will."

They salvaged several of the wagons that had not yet burned and carefully loaded the wounded, both Federal and Confederate, and sent them back toward Middleburg.

Captain Paldi came to Colonel Greyson and saluted. "Shall we fire the mill before we go, sir?"

Greyson was visibly shaken. "I think not, Angelo. I've seen quite enough destruction for one day. How about you?"

Paldi removed his kepi and surveyed the mess. The blood, the fires, the smoke, were enough for anyone. He nodded assent. "Quite enough, sir."

Greyson sheathed his bloodied saber. "Assemble a rear guard. We'll return to Middleburg. I believe our work here is more than finished."

The citizens of Middleburg were aghast when the wagon loads of fresh wounded rumbled into town and stopped at the makeshift hospital in the church. They were already exhausted, but fell immediately to the task of caring for the new batch of bloodied and suffering young men. Teen-aged girls wept as they prepared bandages. Little boys carried buckets of steaming, cleansing water. Old men grimly carried litters of groaning soldiers into the church....a place of safety, and of mercy. Middleburg, that day, became a city of angels.

Colonel Greyson called his captains to his side. "Gentlemen, sort out the wounded. Those who look as though they can stand the journey will go with us. We'll have to leave the rest to the care of the rebs. We don't have enough strength left to withstand another attack. Unless I miss my guess, the enemy will soon bring in a fresh force to finish us off. Agreed?"

Paldi and Acker looked at each other for a moment, then nodded assent. "Agreed!" they chorused.

Matt was grim. "Good! We'll move out as soon as possible. We'll camp on the high ground back at Upperville, then move for the Shenandoah at first light." He left his captains to their tasks and walked quietly into the church, stopping to console each man who would, or could, hear. He found Will propped against a pew, his torso elevated so that he could breathe against the tide of blood in his lung. Melody Chandler was splinting his shattered arm.

She turned to Matt without greeting. "He's your best friend, ain't he?"

"He is." Will was unconscious, his respiration raspy and labored. Matt studied the expressionless face of his fallen comrade. He kept his eyes upon Willy, fearing to look at the dark-haired beauty who was so carefully tending to the shattered arm. He could not stand the reproach that he knew he would see in her eyes. He avoided her gaze, even though he could feel hers upon him. "Melody, I have to leave him."

"I know." Neither spoke while she finished the splinted bandage that stabilized Will's arm. Melody sighed, dropping her shoulders in sadness. She seemed in deep thought for a moment. "Look at me!" she suddenly demanded.

Matthew looked, obediently, into her eyes.

"Melody did not smile. "What do you see now?"

Matt looked, as he had just that morning, into those smoldering eyes that were so dark one could not tell if they had color. "I--I still see God!"

She smiled at him for a moment, took his face gently between her hands, and kissed him fully....and wonderfully long....directly, and meaningfully, on the lips. "I will care for your friend. If God is willing, I will return him to you. Now....you must go."

The interior of the Middleburg Methodist Church was growing gloomy in the fading light. Melody and Matt knelt together at Will's side for a few, long, moments. Candles and lanterns that were carried by the rescue workers cast moving, holy shadows upon the walls and flickered fitfully across their saddened faces. Matt took her hand and held it for a tender moment....savoring the feeling of warmth as she lightly tightened her grip within his. Matt pressed her hand to his lips. He took a long look at the still face of his faithful sergeant, as though memorizing it.

Melody withdrew her hand, and turned to again minister to her patient. Lieutenant Colonel Greyson strode to the open door without saying good-bye. The golden cross upon the altar of the little church amplified the light from the flickering candles and lanterns, glittering its message of hope across the dimness and sorrow of the sanctuary. Shouted orders rang out from beyond the door. The First Michigan Cavalry was moving out.

CHAPTER ELEVEN

In the Dark of A Summer Night

July 4, 1862

Dearest Matthew,

My love, It has been so long since I have received a letter from you. I am nearly crazy with worry.

I pray that you are uninjured, and in good health. Judging from your last letter, I suspect that you are busy campaigning in Virginia and thus probably have not had opportunity to write. I cling to the hope that you have met with success and that soon I will receive word from you.

Even Postmaster Coder looks worried when I stop, each day, to look for mail. The dear man almost cries when he has to tell that he has received nothing for me. I believe that he feels the pulse of the community from the vantage point of his workshop. I live for the day when he will look up from his cobbler's last and give me the smile that says "I have a letter for you!"

You will be pleased to know that patriotism ran rampant in Franklin today....Independence Day! Your name, and the names of Henry Cox and of all the other heroic defenders of the Union, were on everyone's' lips. The red, white, and blue are hung everywhere. The Stars and Stripes were raised on the "Lincoln Pole" that still stands in the orchard next to the road. It was a grand sight to see "Old Glory" raised by Cy Wood while martial tunes were expertly (somewhat) played by a small detachment of musicians who were graciously provided by the Detroit Light Guard. A wonderful picnic followed the ceremony. Oh! How I wish you could have been here!

Dick continues to work, like an inspired demon, to manage the farm. His handicaps seem to be vanishing as he becomes more and more of a man. One scarcely notices his scars these days. Hannah can hardly keep her hands off of him! I suspect that they may even marry some sweet day....but when they are somewhat older, I hope. Would that you were here to watch, and to marvel, at Dick's beautiful metamorphosis! He has even sent a couple of Hannah's would-be beaus packing....one from Farmington, and another from Clarenceville. The Clarenceville lad sported a bloody nose when he departed. My, my!

In spite of all the flag waving, there is an undercurrent of gloom within us all as the war news, which we are receiving, is not good. The rebels seem to be perfectly capable of defending their precious Richmond. Excuse me for saying so, but it does appear that your dashing General McClellan is not as capable a commander as he would like us all to believe. His "Peninsular Campaign" seems to be something of a fizzle, I fear.

We are tired of this ugly war and pray that it will soon end, one way or another, so that you will safely return to my loving arms. Those arms ache to hold you!

I love you.

Bethany

Night had fallen, that hot Forth of July, when Bethany finished her letter, carefully addressed and sealed it, then propped it against a pitcher on the kitchen table so that Dick would not forget to post it in the morning. Dick was off somewhere, celebrating the holiday with Hannah and their young friends. Beth retrieved her knitting and retired to the parlor where she perched, cross-legged, in her favorite chair. Seeking to keep her spirits up, she hummed a medley of her favorite hymns while keeping time with the clicking of her flying needles. Engrossed in her work, she did not hear the quiet hoof beats of a lone horse that turned from the road and approached the house. Held to a slow walk, the hoofs made little sound in the soft earth. She looked up, however, when she did hear the creaking of leather as the rider stealthily dismounted just outside of the open kitchen window.

"Who on earth would be coming here, unannounced, and after dark?" she whispered to herself. Old fears suddenly gripped her in an icy grasp. The thought of the last Pinkerton attack caused her to drop her knitting and to run to the bedroom where she picked up her unwieldy shotgun, cocked it, and aimed it at the kitchen door....just as an unseen hand knocked softly upon it.

"Who is it?" she quavered.

"Miss Dodge?" The voice from the other side of the door was unfamiliar, but not threatening.

Bethany, holding the shotgun at her hip with the muzzle centered on the door, tried to sound brave. "Who are you, sir, and what is your business?"

"Tansy, I am Will McDonald. Cipher name is MacD. Miss, I have an urgent message for you." His quiet voice had a distinctly southern lilt.

"Never heard of you. I must warn you that I am armed."

"Thought you would be, Miss Dodge. You can splatter me all over this porch, if you must, but I surely hope that you won't do that! Leastaways, not 'till you hear what I have to say."

Bethany was beginning to tremble. The thought of what her load of buckshot would do to her visitor, whether or not the door was in the way, gave her some courage. "State your business, sir!"

"Major Dodge has asked that we look after you. I have come from Canada to do just that. I have important words for you."

The use of her father's name convinced her. She lowered the hammer to the safety notch and raised the muzzle of the shotgun toward the ceiling. "Come in, Mr. McDonald."

The door creaked cautiously open and a trimly bearded young man peeked in. He smiled as he extended his empty hands from behind the door for her inspection. "See....I have no weapon. I confess I am just a mite nervous as I have heard what you did to some Pinkerton man unfortunate enough to cause you distress! If you would just put that there smoke pole down, I would feel considerable more comfortable."

Bethany managed a nervous little girlish giggle as she carefully placed the shotgun against the wall. "Well then, do come in and set yourself at the table. Can't have a southern gentleman uncomfortable in my house." Her phrases automatically switched to her native South Carolina inflections. The honeyed phrases slipped off her tongue and seemed to warm her as she spoke. It felt good to speak in her native tongue after talking in clipped Yankee for so long. It was like slipping into an old, soft, and friendly pair of slippers. "May I fix you a cup of tea, Mr. McDonald?"

The visitor pulled out a chair and sat at the table as instructed. "Thank you, no. There is no time for tea. You are in grave danger."

Bethany's face betrayed the return of her fright as she sank into the chair opposite him. "Danger? Oh dear. What danger?"

"Pinkerton style danger! At your father's request we have had an operative keep track of you. Do you remember a nasty little man named Alphaeus Plotkin?"

"No, I think not." Bethany thought for a moment, and her face paled. "Well, yes, perhaps I do know the name. I was told that a fellow named Plotkin was the Pinkerton man who snooped around here for a while, then gave up and went away. In fact," she mused, "I suspect that he could have been the one who trashed my house a while back."

McDonald leaned back in his chair. He was no longer smiling. "You're right. Alphaeus was indeed responsible. You played right into his hands when you didn't report the incident. That convinced him that you were a Confederate agent. He may have gone away, temporarily, but he didn't give up. His greatest hope is to arrest you as a spy, mostly because he didn't take kindly to the fact that you put terminal holes in his friend!"

Bethany shivered at the recollection. "So! I see. Mr. Plotkin was friends with the man who attacked me. I see what you mean. That would make me something other that Mr. Plotkin's favorite person!"

"That's the truth, Miss Dodge. Grossly understated, but the truth. He wants to see you hang as a spy so's he can gloat while he watches you swing. He is one of the meanest little bastards that I have ever laid eyes on, if you will 'scuse my language." Beth waved the impropriety away. She had heard worse. Besides, "bastard" seemed remarkably appropriate when applied to any friend of her deceased attacker.

Will McDonald pushed back his chair and paced nervously to the door where he listened for a moment before continuing. "Do you mind if I put out this lamp?" Bethany wide eyed and mystified, nodded assent. The house was plunged into darkness, save for the single lamp that she had left burning in the parlor. "Our operative, who works out of Windsor but has friendly eyes and ears planted in Detroit, has discovered that Plotkin finally managed to convince the authorities that you should be placed under arrest. The Pinkertons intend to take you either tonight or early tomorrow."

Beth gasped in horror as his words registered in her consciousness. " What must we do?"

"Leave. Now."

His whispered words carried an urgency that frightened her even more. "But, I can't just leave....not now. I promised Matt...."

The Confederate agent pulled back her chair. Gently taking her by the shoulders, he assisted her to her feet. "Never mind about your Matt, right now. My concern is for your safety. Can you pack a small valise and be ready to leave in five minutes?"

"I....I suppose so, but I must leave a note for Dick."

He waggled a finger at her in the near darkness. "No notes. We can't leave any notes. You must simply disappear."

Bethany broke into sobs of despair. Somehow, she had known that something like this must come to pass. She retrieved the parlor lamp, took it to the bedroom, and proceeded to pack as directed. The first thing that she put into her valise was the ribboned packet of Matthew's crumpled letters.

Operative McDonald stepped out on the porch and gave a shrill whistle. Another agent, who had been hidden in a copse just off the Fourteen Mile Road, immediately drove into the door yard in a light one-horse buggy. Bethany wore a heavy veil as she settled next to the driver. Had anyone taken note of them, as they passed on the road, they would have thought that the passenger must have been a delicate woman, veiled against the dusty night air. The horse and rider followed them, casually, as they traveled south on the Inkster Road, then southeast on Grand River Road, to Detroit.

The late holiday parties over, Dick Trick trudged his way home to his little room in the barn. He noted that the farmhouse was dark. He was certain that Bethany had long since gone to bed, and was surely, snugly, asleep. He had no idea that she had just been whisked away. Even if someone had told him, he would not have believed that the fledgling Confederate Secret Service would clandestinely transport his beloved friend through Detroit and Windsor, and all the way across Canada to Halifax, Nova Scotia, where she would take passage on a sleek, fast ship, a blockade runner, that was bound for Charleston, South Carolina.

Blissfully ignorant of all this, Dick's eyes closed almost as soon as he pulled off his boots. Visions of Hannah's lovely cobalt-blue eyes danced in his dreams.

Dawn was still several hours away when Dick suddenly struggled awake, wrinkling his nose at the rancid odor of cigar-laden breath upon his face. He was startled to see the stubbly chin and glinty eyes of one Alphaeus Plotkin hovering over him. He attempted to rise, but was pushed back to his bed by a rough hand placed none-too-gently in the center of his chest.

Dick's sleep-fogged brain was trying to understand. "Take your hands off me! What the hell do you think you are doing?"

Plotkin flashed a grin that pretended to be friendly but, of course, was not. Dick was neither fooled nor soothed in the least. "Relax, little man. I just want you to tell me if the bitch is armed."

"What bitch?"

"Bethany Dodge, you stupid shit! Is she armed?"

Dick's mind was racing. He would not tell about the shotgun. "Don't think so. Her little pistol got stole."

Plotkin's grin faded as he produced Bethany's derringer, cocked it, and placed the muzzle under Dick's nose. "I know that, stupid....'cause I stole it, myself, some time ago."

"You?"

"Yeah. Me." He tried to screw the four-barreled muzzle into Dick's left nostril....a maneuver that enraged Dick to the point of complete loss of caution. He roundhoused a punch into his adversary's face. The blow landed soundly. Plotkin flew in one direction, and landed in a heap. The little pistol discharged near Dick's ear as it flew in a different direction, the bullet fortunately missing his head by a fraction of an inch. Dick did not realize that there were two more Pinkerton men standing in the shadows. They were much larger than the crumpled Plotkin. They pounced on poor Dick. One pulled him upright while the other expertly cracked him on the head with a blackjack. Unconscious, Trick slumped to the floor.

Plotkin staggered to his feet. Blood was running from his mouth as he held his hand to his painfully injured jaw. He staggered to Dick's prostrate form and administered a few well-directed kicks. "Cuff the little shit to the bedpost!" he screamed.

"No need" grinned the blackjack wielder, wiping his weapon on his trousers. "I 'jacked him good. He ain't goin' noplace!"

Plotkin gave Dick another kick. "Well, fine! Leave him, then. Let's go dig out the Dodge bitch."

They smashed through the unlocked door of the farmhouse to find Bethany's bed unslept. She was nowhere to be found. They lost precious time ransacking the house, looking in every corner, under every bed, in the cellar, and in the attic. Unknown to them, Dick was not as thoroughly immobilized as they had thought. Holding his throbbing head, he staggered down the path to town, awakening Mr. Congleton. The alarm spread quickly through the sleepy village. Dick staggered across the road to the Midgley home where he collapsed on the porch with a thump, rousing the household.

Dick remained conscious just long enough to explain the situation to Tom Midgley. Tom immediately grabbed his shotgun and joined the growing group of armed men who were already assembling in the road. Hannah ran to the porch in her nightgown. She sat, sobbing words of comfort, as she cradled the bloody head of the love of her life. Mrs. Midgley ran to bring a basin of cold water, and soft cloths, to compress his wound.

Hastily-clothed women and children ran in all directions through the town to carry the alarm. The Reverend Lanning, awakened by the pounding on his door, and hearing the news, was frustrated that he had no real weapon of defense, let alone of offense. "Turn the other cheek, huh? My ass!" His exclamation was loud enough to cause Mrs. Lanning to nearly fall down the stairs in shocked disbelief that such foul words could be uttered by her saintly husband. Mr. Lanning ran to the wood pile, clutched his ax, and hastened to join the angry men.

Normally soft-spoken George Congleton, sputtering with rage, assumed command of the makeshift force that stood, milling in the lantern light, in the road in front of his shop. They were sleepily trying to understand what was taking place. "Men, Bethany and Dick have been attacked by thugs. Their identity, at present, is unknown. Dick thinks that he might have recognized one as a Pinkerton detective. Dick is wounded, but safe. Bethany may be in their hands. It is our duty to rescue Bethany and apprehend, or destroy, the dirty bastards. Are you with me?"

A mighty cheer was immediately raised as the men and boys waved their collection of rifles, shotguns, pistols, clubs, and axes in the lantern light. "We're with you, George! Let's get the sons-of-bitches!"

"Good! Now, we must move fast. Surround the house. Let's hope that they haven't already gotten away!" No shooting unless I say so. Might endanger Bethany. I'll do the talking, if any is to be done! Agreed?"

"Agreed!" they shouted. "Let's go, George!" The vigilantes ran up the trail to Matthew's farmhouse, their lanterns bobbing and winking in the darkness. Within minutes, they had the house surrounded.

"Come out of there!" called Congleton. "Come out of there! Now! If you show a weapon, you will be shot on sight!"

195

There were muffled exclamations and curses audible from within the house. The three Pinkerton agents swaggered out of the door, but soon lost their bravado when they found themselves looking down the muzzles of more than two dozen shotguns, muskets, and pistols....not to mention the good reverend, who was angrily brandishing his ax, looking for all the world like a peeved knight from Camelot. Protesting loudly, the three hoodlums were disarmed and handcuffed with their own equipment. Charlie Coder was dispatched to summon Constable Snuffy Smith. The townsmen searched, in vain, for Bethany.

Congleton cracked Alphaeus Plotkin on the side of the head with the long barrel of his gun, sending the agent to his knees with the pain of his second injury of the night. "What have you done with Miss Bethany?" Congleton demanded. "Speak, or I will kill you on the spot!"

"Plotkin's courage deserted him. He began to tremble, his voice high with fright. "She ain't here. We came to arrest her. She is a rebel spy!"

"Nonsense!" shouted Congleton. "What have you done with her?" George Congleton, the gentle craftsman, was no longer gentle. He cocked both barrels of his 12 gauge and forcefully jammed the muzzles into the quaking man's chest, his finger hovering over the triggers.

"Its true! Its really true!" whimpered Plotkin.

Congleton was barely able to resist shooting the whining culprit on the spot. Finally, gaining control of himself, he backed away from the sniveling form. "Men, take 'em down to town and shackle 'em to my hitching post. We'll have to let the constable deal with this trash!"

Dick was nursed back to consciousness in time to identify the Sharps derringer, that had been in Plotkin's possession, as Bethany's. There was majority opinion, among the furious men, that the prisoners should be immediately lynched. The big oak tree, down on the corner, could easily accommodate all three, in style. Finally, after much shouting, reason prevailed. George Congleton saw to that. To the great relief of the quaking agents, they were gruffly chained into a wagon and transported to Pontiac by Constable Snuffy Smith. Snuffy was relieved to find himself accompanied by several heavily-armed villagers who were in no mood to take any guff from the prisoners. Angry dispatches would be sent to Alan Pinkerton. His men would be jailed, and at the mercy of the court.

No trace of Bethany was ever found. The Pinkerton men loudly protested that they, themselves, had not been able to locate her. No one would listen to their pleas. It was generally assumed that they had murdered her and hidden her body. Franklin Village was in mourning for their lovely school teacher. The church bell tolled its tearful cry. Bethany was gone.

Pitts Lanning, however, was convinced that all of the pieces of the puzzle were not in place. He and his wife knew Bethany better than anyone else, except, of course, Matthew and Dick. Pitts had a hunch. With his wife in tow, he secretly went to examine the scene of the crime. Mrs. Lanning was the first to discover an unusual circumstance. Bethany's little lace bag containing her silver comb and mirror, hairpins, hair clips, and other miscellaneous feminine essentials, was totally missing. This discovery caused her to snoop even more carefully. Four of Bethany's favorite dresses, along with several blouses and skirts, had vanished. And "Aha!" her valise was nowhere to be found. Mrs. Lanning called to her husband who was busily examining the kitchen. "Pitts, dear, Bethany has packed rather carefully! A trifle unusual for someone who has just been murdered!"

"Hmmm. Indeed!" Pitts had just discovered the torn and tattered letter that Bethany had written, that day, to Matthew. It was lying, under an overturned chair, in a corner of the kitchen. "Look at this, dearest." Together they read the message, their tears staining the paper and causing the ink to run. Pitts took the letter home and penned an enclosure. He addressed a new envelope, and, without informing anyone except his wife, sent it off to Matt.

July 5, 1892

Dear Matthew,

It is with great sorrow that I must inform you that our sweet Bethany has mysteriously disappeared. Several Pinkerton agents are currently incarcerated on suspicion of her murder. It is our belief, however, that she may have fled prior to the arrival of the agents who sought to either arrest her, or to do her other harm.

The Pinkertons are protesting that she is a Confederate spy. We do not feel that this is a likely possibility. We hope and pray that, whatever the reason for her departure, she is alive and well.

For obvious reasons, we have not communicated our suspicions to anyone else lest we endanger her further. Should you be so disposed, and have opportunity to free yourself from your duties, we sincerely hope that you will return here, at the earliest possible moment, to help us search for her. All in Franklin are heart-broken. Our little village cries out in pain, We love Bethany, and we love you. May the spirit of the living Christ strengthen you. May His love return you both safely to us.

Sincerely,

Your dear friends,

The Reverend and Mrs. Pitts Lanning

CHAPTER TWELVE

To Catch a Giraffe

In the early morning hours of July 5, 1862, Bethany had more than ample time to worry about her fate. Neither the warmth of the summer night, nor the protection of her shawl, could keep her from shivering as the light buggy rattled its way down the Grand River Road toward Detroit. There were few travelers on the dark road at that hour, and even fewer lights to light the way, except for the two carriage lanterns that barely illuminated the backside of the horse, let alone the road ahead. The driver's face was hidden by an enormous black beard that concealed any expressions, if there were any, from Bethany's sight. An hour went by, and the man had not spoken a word. She began to worry that, perhaps, she was the victim of a hoax and was actually being kidnapped by persons unknown. Yet, Agent McDonald had seemed genuine enough. She decided to try to get some information from her companion. "Is Mr. McDonald still riding behind us?"

"Reckon so."

"Excuse me, sir, for asking, but....do you have a name?"

"Yep. Joseph."

"Oh, good!" thought Bethany, "now we are getting somewhere." She put on her best smile, but it could not be seen in the darkness. "Where are we going, Joseph?"

"Detroit."

"So I was informed by Mr. McDonald. But, where in Detroit?"

"Detroit Boat Club."

"Why would we be going there? Are we attending a regatta, or are we just stopping in for a friendly visit?"

"Can't say, miss."

"And, why can't you say?"

"Not my job."

"Well, fine!" Glumly, Bethany settled back on the leather seat, arms folded beneath her shawl.

Another bumpy and jiggly half-hour passed. She decided to try again. "Do you think that we may be pursued by the Pinkertons?"

"Can't say, miss."

"I trust that you and Agent McDonald are armed, and ready to fight, should that happen?"

"Can't say, miss."

She was getting exasperated. "For heaven's sake, Joseph, I might just as well be talking to the rear end of your horse." She was expecting, at the least, a chuckle in reply. There was no reaction, whatsoever, to her pointed remark.

Bethany retreated back into the silence of her gloomy thoughts. There was no point in trying to get any more information out of the bearded sphinx. Buildings, faint in the shadows, began to appear with more frequency. She began to detect the dank smells of the city, the dampness of the river. The iron buggy tires began to rattle over cobblestones and brick. They turned several corners. "What road are we on, now?" she asked, forlornly, not expecting an answer.

"Hastings Street. We're almost there." Joseph was suddenly more communicative. He had actually put five words together to form two sentences. He appeared to be relieved that his part of the journey was at an end. A light fog shrouded the river, almost hiding the docks, as the driver pulled the tired horse to a halt. Beth could barely make out the outline of the Victorian clubhouse that squatted in the river, connected to the shore by several docks that were sparsely illuminated by a few lanterns. Sailboats, of all sizes and descriptions, bobbed and tugged at their lines in the gentle swells of the river.

"Well, Joseph, it seems that we are too early for the regatta. Shall we wake the commodore?"

The beard, again, did not smile. "I think not, miss."

Bethany's shivering increased as the dampness of the river penetrated her shawl. "Very well. Thank you for the ride. It was lovely."

There was no answer. A boy stepped out of the shadows and held the bridle while Bethany scrambled out of the buggy, dragging her valise behind her. McDonald rode alongside and dismounted, the boy taking his reins in the other hand. "We're all set, McD."

"Thank you, son." Agent McDonald took Bethany's valise, and offered his arm. They walked to the end of the dock where Beth was startled to see four rough-looking men lounging upon the boards. "Behold, Miss Dodge, your transportation to freedom."

She tightened her grip on his arm. "Sir, I do not behold anything except a bunch of ruffians who are smoking and drinking on the dock."

"Well, look down there." He pointed into the darkness. She peered over the edge of the dock in the direction that he indicated. A large rowboat was tethered to a piling.

"No. No! Let me guess. I'm supposed to get into that thing?"

McDonald chuckled. "You are, indeed."

The ruffians, jolly with the pints of ale with which they had been paid, piled into the boat. Will McDonald followed, and held up his arms to assist Bethany to board. Reluctantly, she did as directed. McDonald helped her down, feeling, with delight, the lithe lightness of her slim body.

Powered by the four oarsmen, the little craft pulled into the darkness of the foggy river.

Bethany huddled in the stern. She could visualize the headlines in the *Charleston Daily Courier.* "Charleston Socialite Drowned by Drunken Sailors in the Detroit River". Her shivering increased to the point where her teeth chattered in a most unladylike manner. Presently, much to her relief, lights appeared through the gloom. McDonald assured her that the lights were in Canada. She was, at last, safe from the Yankee hangman's noose!

Bethany was too frightened to ask any questions while they were on the river. As soon as they clambered onto the Windsor dock, however, she decided that the time had come for an exchange of information. "Mr. McDonald, what....?" He indicated that she should remain silent by putting his finger to his lips and rolling his eyes in the direction of those who might be listening. "Mr. McDonald, could....?" This time he put his finger to *her* lips to emphasize the importance of her continued silence. It was clear that he did not want news of their entrance into Canada to reach any eavesdropping ears, most especially the ears of either the Canadian or the American authorities.

Bethany stopped, suddenly, in her tracks. "Mr. McDonald, stop shushing me!" Her voice was an angry whisper. The agent glanced furtively around. Fortunately, no one seemed to be paying attention to them, at the moment.

"Good heavens, woman, what is it?" he whispered back.

"I have to go to the ladies' room."

"Oh! Why didn't you say so?"

Bethany gave him a wide-eyed look, but made no reply as he led her toward the nearest necessary facilities. Moments later, a hack, its carriage lights winking in the early morning gloom, appeared through the fog. Noticing that neither the agent nor the driver said a word to each other, Beth folded her arms and maintained a gloomy silence. "Quietest damned bunch I ever did see!" she grumped to herself. She would never use such profanity out loud, but felt perfectly free to use it in her thoughts, just as she damned well pleased. Seemingly without direction, the hack circled through the

202

little city. Beth noticed that they were going by the same buildings two or three times. "This seems a little stupid!" she opined. Ignoring her, Agent McDonald kept looking at his watch. Finally, he rapped on the back of the driver's seat. The hack picked up speed immediately and delivered them to the train station where they boarded an eastbound train just before it was to pull away. The cars were nearly deserted. They had no problem in selecting a pair of seats where they would not be overheard if they talked quietly.

"Now, Mr. McDonald...." She was ready to conduct an inquisition.

"Try Will, or William, whichever you prefer."

Bethany took a deep breath. "Now, William, I believe it is time that you tell me where I am going."

"Hopefully, Miss Dodge...."

"Bethany."

He chuckled. "Hopefully, Bethany, you are to be transported back to your home in Charleston. Major Dodge has requested that we make all the necessary arrangements. He has provided the necessary funds. Interestingly, even President Davis has expressed concern for your welfare, and has directed that every precaution be taken to ensure your safety."

Beth giggled, girlishly. "Really? I didn't know I was a celebrity!"

"Apparently, you are. We will all breathe a sigh of relief when you are safely at home and sipping your juleps on your father's verandah."

She pouted. "I've never been in a situation, before now, where folks were so anxious to get rid of me."

"You might as well get used to it, Bethany." He laughed, and patted her hand. "At the moment, you are a high-visibility liability. Here. Perhaps this will help you to get over your wounded pride." He produced a picnic hamper that contained containers of tea, lemonade, sweet rolls, and a nice assortment of sandwiches. "Compliments of the Canadian Confederates. Better eat hearty. It's going to be a long ride."

"A long ride to where?" Bethany lost no time in helping herself to a roll. "Mmmm! Cinnamon!"

"Only the best for you m'lady! We're going to Niagara Falls."

"How nice! This is quite a sight-seeing trip that you've arranged. First, entertained royally at the Detroit Boat Club, a delightful cruise on the river, and now....Niagara Falls! I understand they are lovely this time of year."

Will McDonald pulled a cigar from an inside pocket of his tweed jacket. "Mind if I smoke?"

"Not at all. At least, not at all....unless you can't manage to get the smoke to go in some direction other that at me."

"Haw!" McDonald nearly choked as he lit up. "I'll do my very best, miss. I wouldn't care to have our president angry with me because I asphyxiated one of his favorite daughters of the south. Seriously, while you are enjoying the falls, the rest of us will be trying to figure out what to do with you."

A frown flashed across her face. "I'm truly sorry. I don't mean to be a bother. You mentioned 'the rest of us'. Who might that be?"

The agent settled in his chair and exhaled a cloud of cigar smoke which he pointedly directed out into the aisle, away from Bethany. "Fellow members of the Canadian operation. You'll find them to be quite a charming group of rebels. You'll be well cared for. We have a meeting-place near the falls. The Clifton House. It's a large and fairly luxurious hotel. I believe you'll find it to your liking. You are to stay there until the next stages of your journey are arranged.

Bethany stared out of the window at the Canadian countryside as it swirled by in the morning mist. She was beginning to feel safe from harm as long as she was in the presence of the charming agent. "Where will you be, William?" she asked, sweetly.

"I'll be around. I'm to meet with a pair of important gentlemen who aren't due to arrive until sometime next month. Then, I'll probably go back to Ohio."

"What do you do in Ohio?"

"Secret business. I'm involved with organizing groups of southern sympathizers who live in the north, but who just might be helpful to our cause, one day. The gents who I am to meet, Coxe, from England and Saunders, from Kentucky, are key to that effort."

"*Whom* you are to meet."

"What?"

"Never mind. Your work sounds very dangerous. I do hope you will be careful." William snuffed his cigar. "You bet I'll be careful. I like my neck the length that it is. And, I like your pretty neck the length that it is, too." He smiled at her, looking into the smoky blue of her eyes. "I'm so very glad that you are safe, now. I'll look forward to showing you around Niagara."

Bethany blushed. One could easily become accustomed to having a man like William McDonald around.

They traveled, in awkward silence, for a few minutes. McDonald squirmed in the uncomfortable seat, finally stretching his long legs out into the aisle to keep them from cramping. "You'll need an alias, Bethany."

"Why? I already have one. Tansy."

"That's fine for cipher. Doesn't work in the real world. Anyone who might follow your trail could uncover our network. We can't let that happen. Want to pick a nice name? You pick it, and I will pass the word along so that only our agents will know who you are."

"Very well. How about something slinky, like 'Madame Antoinette LaForche?'"

"That's a touch too dramatic! How about 'Elizabeth Smith'. That way you could still be 'Beth'."

Bethany pursed her lips in thought. "'Elizabeth' is good. 'Smith' is much too common. How about 'Brown', or 'Green', or 'Persimmon?'"

"'Persimmon' would be a little extreme. How about 'Green'? A nice color....as in envy, nausea, or grass?"

Bethany giggled. "Humph! I guess 'Green' will have to do. Nice, really. Besides, 'e.g.' means 'for example'. And, I must be a perfect example of something or other."

McDonald howled with delight, causing the passengers in the forward part of the car to turn and look to see just what it might be that was so humorous. "And, you are, indeed, a perfect example. Of what, I can't imagine."

Bethany clapped her hands in her funny little way. "Thank you, sir, I think."

The two weeks that Bethany, as Elizabeth Green, spent in residence at the Clifton Hotel were an emotional roller coaster for her. She delighted in Agent McDonald's company, but longed for Matthew. She searched the Canadian newspapers for word of the activities of the First Michigan Cavalry, but found nothing. She made many new friends, but missed Franklin, and its dear people, desperately. She wrote letters, daily, to Matthew, and to the Lannings, but had to crumple them and throw them away. William pointed out, firmly, that posting such letters would most certainly endanger the Confederate operatives in Michigan. Bethany cried, but soon was smiling again when William took her to dinner, or promenaded with her on the scenic walk above the falls. She purchased new clothes, and new books, to replace those that she had been forced to leave behind.

Word arrived that Alphaeus Plotkin, and his fellow renegade Pinkerton agents, had been arrested on suspicion of her murder. Beth was delighted with that news, and most grateful to McDonald for her narrow escape. But then, upon learning that Franklin Village was in mourning for her, she cried some more. She could hardly bear the thought that she had caused so much pain to such sweet people.

There was a soft knock at her hotel room door early one morning. It was William. He wore a sad face, that was struggling to be a happy one, for her benefit. "Beth, it's time for you to go. You must catch the train for Quebec in one hour." He handed her a sealed envelope.

Bethany was wrapped in her bathrobe, and barefoot. Her hair was a tousled mess. Will was instantly convinced. Suddenly, tousled hair and all, she seemed to be the most beautiful of all women. A sweet sadness engulfed him. He realized that he was in love with a woman whom he must now send away. "Quebec? Why Quebec?"

"We've arranged passage for you on a ship that is sailing from there day after tomorrow."

"Will you come with me?"

"No. I'd give anything if I could."

Bethany flew into his arms. They held each other for a long, tender moment. She looked into his eyes. "It has to be, doesn't it?"

William could only nod. He kissed her tenderly, then turned and almost ran down the hall, down the stairs, and out into the morning light. His country, the fledgling Confederate States of America, was counting on him to do his duty. He wearily mounted his waiting horse and trotted her in the direction of the nearby little town of St. Catherines. Robert Edwin Coxe, a wealthy and influential man, had moved from his home in the State of Georgia to Europe and now to Canada. Coxe would take charge of their clandestine operations. Agent McDonald threw himself headlong into the complicated planning and organization of the Confederate activities in the north. Busy as he was, and busy as he remained, he could not forget the dark-haired little slip of a girl. She had corrected his grammar, brightened his days, and stolen his heart.

Bethany had stood, blinking back her tears, still feeling the sweetness of his fleeting embrace. She had watched him go, then slid down to the hallway floor, her back against the door jamb. "Why, dear God, dear Jesus, must this happen again? Another wonderful man has run away from me! Oh! How I hate this war!" She tore open the envelope. The message, written in a neat, male hand had no date, salutation, or signature.

> The freighter *Amazon*, a brigantine, will sail from Quebec in two days, bound for Halifax, Nova Scotia. She is a Yankee profiteer, out of New York, engaged in the transportation of Canadian alcohol and Confederate cotton to England. Her master, one Benjamin Briggs, is motivated by money and not by allegiance to any cause. Do not entrust to him any information.

> He will be expecting you, and has been handsomely paid for your passage.

Upon arrival at Halifax please present yourself to Mr. Alexander Keith of the firm of B. Weir and Co. He has been instructed to make further arrangements for you.

Kindly retain your present alias for the remainder of your journey.

Pleasant voyage. Please destroy this message immediately after committing it to memory.

The train ride to Quebec was slow, hot, and tedious. The cars were crowded with a heterogeneous mixture of sailors, rough woodsmen, farmers with their wives and children, well-dressed businessmen, and a few priests in their solemn black suits and clerical collars. A pair of seasoned-looking nuns, who sat immediately in front of Bethany, wore some sort of large, white headgear that looked, to her, like they had geese sitting on their heads. Everyone seemed to be conversing in rapid-fire French. Beth had a reasonable knowledge of the language, but soon gave up trying to understand them as they spoke much too fast for her to translate more than an occasional phrase. Unescorted, and feeling very alone, she retreated into her newly-acquired volume of Shakespeare for the duration of the trip.

When she finally detrained and stood on the platform of the Quebec station, she found it to be teeming with a similar mix of people. "I wonder why it would be," she mused "that all of the Quebecois seem to be going someplace, and all at once!" She wandered out of the station, valise in hand, looking and feeling like a pathetic refugee who had lost her way. Gazing up at the city, resplendent with its towers and spires, she was warmed by a feminine thought. The latest in Parisian fashions were known to be available from the fine clothiers of the city. "Perhaps I should just take a break from this fugitive silliness, and go shopping!" she smiled to herself. Beth made her way to the curb of a very busy street and stood, hands clenched on her hips, as she tried to figure out the proper way for a lady to hail one of the hacks that was passing by. She was impressed that each rig was drawn by proud-looking horses wearing brightly-colored plumes on their heads. Still uncertain what to do, she was startled when a kindly voice spoke into her ear.

"Pardonnez-moi, s'il vous plait, mademoiselle. Comment vous appelez-vous?" She turned to discover a portly gentleman standing by her side. He was dressed in the livery of a hackman, and his face was very red.... apparently resulting from the effort of fighting his way through the crowds to find her in the oppressive heat of the sunny day. She gave him a guarded smile. He did not look in the least bit dangerous.

"Bonjour. Je m'appele Elizabeth Green."

The man beamed as he mopped his dripping brow. "Bon! La Tansy, oui?"

"Oui!" She was relieved to be found, even if it meant the cancellation of her fancied shopping spree.

The gentleman picked up her bag and offered his arm. "S'il vous plait, mademoiselle." He led her to a hack that was parked at the curb, and helped her aboard. The plumed horses were munching their oats from nose bags that hung over their muzzles. The hackman waited for the beasts to finish their snack, removed the bags, climbed up into the driver's seat, and clucked them into action. They threaded their way out onto a broad quay, at which many large sailing ships were docked, and pulled up at the gangplank of a large, two-masted vessel. The Union stars and stripes fluttered high above her stern. The sight of the flag made Bethany perspire. What if she were to be slapped into irons and conveyed back to the U.S.A. to be hanged? She wanted to run. The friendly smile of the plump hackman dissuaded her. He seemed to see the fright in her face. "Come with me, miss. I'll introduce you to the captain. He's a fine fellow." Beth looked at him in amazement. He had spoken in perfect English!"

"Merci, er, thank you!" she stammered.

"Mon plaisir."

The captain, displaying a disarming smile, met her at the top of the gangplank. She decided that he did not look at all sinister. Ben Briggs was an attractive, sunburnt, supple man in a striped sailor's shirt and a cocky mariner's wool cap. He immediately took her to meet his wife, Mary. Mary was as wide as she was tall, and was clad in an unbecoming, faded wool dress from behind the folds of which two freckled children peeped. Bethany stooped to peep back at the shy little boys who did their best to shrink away from her. "What fine little lads!" she exclaimed. "May I ask their names?"

"Claude and Michael" beamed the mother as she attempted to drag them into view. "Say 'hello' to the nice lady, boys." Their lips were sealed.

"I'm very glad to meet you, Claude and Michael" she smiled. "I'm sure that we will be the best of friends."

Ben and Mary, trailed by the boys, showed her to her cabin which was Spartan, but clean and comfortable. "We don't have a lot of passengers, miss, being a freighter, so our accommodations are not very fancy. I hope this will do." Captain Briggs had noticed that her clothing was of fine quality, neatly tailored, and that she had an expensive-looking gold cross suspended from her neck by an equally expensive-looking fine gold chain. He suspected that she might have been more comfortable in a luxury stateroom. However, the *Amazon* was not so equipped.

Bethany instantly put him at ease. She clapped her hands, in her heels-together fashion, in delight. "This will be wonderful, captain. It's very cozy. I'll be most happy here unless, of course, you let the ship rock too much!" She grinned and curtseyed to show that she was joking.

Ben laughed. We'll do our best on that one, won't we, Mary?"

Mary smoothed the quilt that served as a coverlet for the narrow bunk. "We will, indeed. The captain, who, by the way, rarely knows what he is talking about, has promised fine weather and a fair wind for the trip to Halifax. However, what it will really be remains to be seen! I'll go and make us some tea. Ben, why don't you and the boys show Miss Green around the ship?"

"Of course. I'm very proud of the *Amazon*. She was launched just one year ago. Handles like a dream. Guess you can tell I'm in love with her. Are you acquainted with ships, and the sea, Miss Green?"

Bethany decided that it was time to embellish upon her assumed identity. "As a schoolteacher from Ohio, I confess that I don't know about anything but mules, plows, and an occasional riverboat. But, I can learn."

"Good! Bet you can. She's both fore-and-aft rigged, and square rigged. Can run before the wind like a race horse, or sail close to the wind with a bone in her teeth. Y'know what I mean?"

Bethany actually knew exactly what he was saying, but dared not betray her knowledge of things nautical. Her father had taught her well. He had called her his "little wharf rat" because she loved to inhabit the docks and quays of Charleston. She even knew that the rigging was called "hermaphrodite" but dared not expose her knowledge. "How interesting!" she said, blinking owlishly. "How big is your crew?"

"Fourteen, not counting Mary, who is cook, and my boys, who are just a mite young to be much help, as yet. Five of the crew have been with me since launching, the rest are locals who have yet to prove themselves. We should have a good, easy passage. We're part loaded with barrels of Canadian grain alcohol. We'll pick up cotton for the rest of the load."

"And go to where?" Beth already knew the answer, and knew that the cotton was to be transported to England for the benefit of the Confederacy.

"Straight from Halifax to Liverpool."

"How exciting! I'd love to go to England."

Captain Ben patted her on the shoulder. "Well, then! Come with us. All you have to do is to stay aboard."

Beth looked tempted. She, actually, given different circumstances, would have jumped at the opportunity to travel to Europe. "Thank you. I'd love to, but I must meet my father in Halifax." She found, somewhat to her own amazement, that she could lie easily and without discomfort. Rose Greenhow had taught her well. A lovely young woman, properly taught, could get away with almost anything. Mary appeared, waddling across the deck, and invited her to partake of tea and cookies. "I think I'm going to like this!" she thought. "This adventure is not going to be so bad, after all!"

Bethany gazed up at the towering masts with their furled sails. "When do we go, captain?"

"At dawn. The winds promise to be westerly, and fair." He chuckled. "However, as Mary has told you, I really don't know what I am talking about."

Later, as the evening deepened, Bethany, peering through the porthole of her cabin, saw Captain Briggs talking to a well-dressed young man who appeared to be paying for passage. As she watched, the young man produced a wad of bills from his pocket and peeled off a quantity into the waiting hand of the master of the vessel. The transaction completed, the young man picked up his carpet bag and boarded. Beth, ever alert, viewed the proceedings with suspicion. "Now, who might this dandy be?" she wondered. At supper, she was soon to find out. The gentleman was a businessman from Quebec, taking passage to Halifax. He was to be her only fellow passenger. The man, a native Quebecois, but of English extraction, was a livestock dealer who was traveling to Halifax on business. He had a wide, and distinctly affected, smile. Beth disliked him instantly, especially when he proceeded to shower her with unwanted attention. His name, she was told, was Lawrence Martin. She soon tired of his company, excused herself, and retired to her cabin.

The captain, in spite of Mary's disclaimer, was correct about the weather. The *Amazon*, all sails set, cruised into the Gulf of St. Lawrence, then settled into a comfortable beam reach toward Halifax. Bethany and the Briggs family became fast friends. The children finally accepted her. Once they had decided that she was to be trusted, they began to follow her around the ship whenever they had the opportunity, looking for all the world like a pair of playful puppies on an invisible leash. Mary Briggs was delighted to have the boys out from under her feet, giving her more time to look after her cooking and housekeeping duties. Beth, even though she longed to share more of her real life with her new friends, carefully maintained her Elizabeth Green identity.

She discovered that Claude and Michael were sadly lacking in the elementary schooling that they should have been receiving. With Mary's permission, she set up regular school sessions each day and began to teach them the rudiments of the "three R's". Her teaching tasks would have been easier had she had the use of her copy of *McGuffey's First Eclectic Reader* that she had left behind on the bookshelf of Franklin School. There was no library aboard the ship except for a few books on navigation which were of no more help in teaching her very young students than was her volume of Shakespeare. Ever resourceful, she discovered a blackboard which was mounted in the companionway for use as a message center for the crew. Without asking permission, she appropriated it by unscrewing it from the bulkhead. She also found a quantity of chalk and took that, too. School was open! Once she had her pupils' attention, she found them to be bright little boys who could learn their lessons quickly and easily.

A problem did develop, however, which threatened to spoil the pleasant voyage. Lawrence Martin persisted in his efforts to gain her favor. The more that she rebuffed him, the more insistent he became. One evening, just at dusk, the problem took a distinct turn for the worst. She was standing at the rail, near the bow, enjoying the whitecaps as they swept by in the grayness of the dark sea. A sailor, the lookout, dutifully scanned the sea ahead. She loved to hear the whispering sounds of the taut, white sails that towered above her as they, in the failing light, became ghostly images against the twilight sky. "What a lovely symphony!" she exulted, as the cries of a gull, somewhere in the darkness, provided counterpoint to the continuo of the sails. Beth hardly noticed when the seaman left his post and walked aft to where the rest of the four-man watch were gathered near the helmsman. Moments later, she was startled to find Lawrence Martin standing at her elbow.

He spoke quietly, almost in a whisper. "Good evening, Beth."

She turned, instantly, to leave. "Good evening, Mr. Martin. If you will excuse me, I'm going to my cabin."

He grasped her arm firmly, but without causing pain. "Wait! I'd like to go with you. I have a nice bottle of Napoleon brandy. We could have a nightcap, together."

"I think not, Mr. Martin. Please let go of my arm."

He tightened his grasp. "And, I think not, Miss Beth. I wish to be with you, tonight. Just for a drink, you understand."

She tried to pull away. "I understand nothing of the sort, sir. Let go of me, or I shall report you to the captain!"

The whiteness of his wide smile was frightening in the darkness. She pulled away, but he caught her and forced her against the rail. "I wouldn't do that, if I were you."

Panic gripped her, but she remained outwardly calm. "You're not me. Why shouldn't I?"

"Because I know who you are. You are a little rich girl who is a fugitive from Yankee justice."

She pushed at him. "Don't be ridiculous! What makes you think so?"

"Remember the fat hackman? He's my friend. He told me all that he had learned about you through his sneaky Confederate connection. We knew that you were coming to Quebec before you did, Miss Fancy Elizabeth Green!" He leaned toward her, his face close to hers. "How am I doing, so far, missy?"

Bethany turned her face away from him. She was feeling nauseated at the prospect of such a man gaining control of her.

"If I tell the captain that you are a wanted criminal, he will be obliged, as an American master of this vessel on the high seas, to take you prisoner and to deliver you to the Yankee authorities. But, you see, I want to keep you for myself! Your papa might just pay a nice reward for your return! What do you think of that?"

"I think that one scream from me and those sailors, back there," she pointed a trembling finger aft toward the men clustered around the helmsman "will come to rescue me and throw you overboard." Tears of rage were streaming down her cheeks.

Lawrence Martin chuckled. "No, they won't. They are my men."

"Your men?" Beth shuddered as a realization dawned upon her. "Oh, my God! Pirates!"

Martin chuckled. "Call 'em what you want, missy. Now, come with me. We have a pleasant night to look forward to....just you and me. My men have their orders. By the time we are through the ship will be mine."

214

Bethany's mind was racing, looking for a way to escape. It was obvious that the impending rape would be only the first, and far from the last, of his criminal acts against her. Bethany remembered well the lessons that Rose Greenhow had taught her, not so long ago, in Washington. "When all else fails," Rose had said, "go for the privates!" Martin stood before her, his legs braced apart, his hands grasping the rail on each side of her to prevent her escape. His stance was perfect. She caught him in the groin with her knee. He let go of the rail, gasped at the pain, and staggered a step backwards, with the result that she now had room to work. She placed a well-aimed kick in the same spot, and with all the force that she could muster. Martin sank to his knees on the deck, grasping his crotch. Bethany ran to the captain's cabin and thundered upon the door until it opened.

"Ben!" she quavered, breathlessly, "Pirates! They mean to take your ship!" Slamming the door, she jammed a chair under the knob.

Benjamin Briggs was no fool. He knew that on the high seas trouble could appear from any quarter and at any time. The arms cabinet was in his stateroom. The ship's revolvers, Colt Navies, were stored already loaded and capped. He handed one to Mary, who rose, sleepy-eyed from their bed, one to Beth, and cocked one for himself. Mary stuffed the squawking children under the bunk.

When Lawrence Martin forced the door, three .36 caliber balls instantly pronounced his death sentence. His men were standing behind him in the companionway, ready to join in the fray. Seeing their leader fall, and having a modicum of good sense, they instantly abandoned their nefarious project. They ran, but there was no place to go. Diving over the side was not a viable option with no land on the horizon. The culprits soon surrendered when the captain armed the trusted portion of his crew and cornered the piratical scallywags on the foredeck. Little Bethany had saved the ship, the lives of the captain, his family, and the loyal portion of his crew.

Bethany, still quaking and shivering as she tried to get over her fright, told Ben and Mary the whole story. They listened, with sweet understanding, and vowed to protect her forever. Lawrence Martin was unceremoniously buried at sea. The *Amazon* sailed into the Halifax harbor with most of her crew in chains. The Briggs would not soon forget Bethany, nor she, them.

There was a long, low, sleek, slender, sidewheel steamer moored in the harbor. She was painted gray, giving the ghostly impression that she really was not there at all. Air currents, rising from the warmer water of the harbor, further distorted her image. One would think that she was just the spirit of a ship....were it not for the Union Jack which was fluttering, colorfully, above her stern. She was more than a ship. She was the *Giraffe*.

Harper's Pictorial History of the Civil War

CHAPTER THIRTEEN

Second Manassas

By late June, 1862, the great, deadly game of chess was underway. The lead player in the north, the egocentric and confident Union Major General John Pope, blustered from his headquarters in Washington as he sought to concentrate and to strengthen his forces. He had two important goals: (1) Get rid of Union General George McClellan, who was bottled up and skulking in defeat on the peninsula southeast of Richmond, and ensure that the remains of "Little Mac's" Army of the Potomac would be placed under his own command. (2) Search out and destroy the forces of Confederate General Thomas "Stonewall" Jackson which had slipped out of the Shenandoah Valley and were poised to march north toward Washington from Gordonsville, Virginia. He handily accomplished his first goal. His second goal perished on the fields and hills of Second Manassas, where the blood of his command mixed with that of the Confederates....tingeing scarlet, forever....at least in the minds of men, the once placid waters of the little stream called Bull Run.

In Richmond, the great leader of the Confederate forces, General Robert Edward Lee, was busily concocting his own strategies. He too would concentrate his forces. He too had two major goals: (1) Confront, drive from the field, and if possible destroy the "miscreant" General Pope. (2) Carry the war to Union soil so that the north might taste first hand the discomfort of the warfare which had already laid waste to so many farms and towns in the south.

General Lee would cleverly move his knights and pawns in dazzling patterns across the Virginia landscape. This remarkable, and revered, gentleman would accomplish his goals....at least in the short term. President Lincoln would relieve John Pope of his command after the sanguine Union defeat at Second Manassas. Subsequently, Lee would indeed manage to carry the war to Union territory....twice. Unfortunately for the rebel cause, these invasions were generally unsuccessful. The magnitude of the loss of precious, irreplaceable manpower was staggering. Checkmate would forever elude the grasp of "Marse Robert".

In accordance with General Pope's plan for consolidation of his command, General Banks' II Corps left their camp at Middletown, in the Shenandoah Valley, and marched through the summer heat and dust to Culpepper Courthouse. The First Michigan Cavalry, now a part of "Buford's Brigade" were kept busy sweeping and scouting ahead of the sweating column of infantry and artillery. General Banks had hoped to rest his 11,000 man corps at Culpepper after their long march, but it was not to be. He was ordered to move south to confront General Jackson who was already moving north. Jackson had twice as many men as Banks. Stonewall was determined to make good use of his superior numbers by crushing Banks before he could be reinforced. The blue and the gray met with a roar upon the gentle slopes around Cedar Mountain.

Both sides fought hard and well. The outnumbered Yankees very nearly carried the day in spite of the superior numbers of their enemy. They mounted several brilliant charges, driving the rebels from their positions, but could not sustain their gains as they were unsupported by reserves. In the end, by nightfall, the Confederates had chased the Yanks from the field. General Jackson, learning that Union reinforcements had arrived in Culpepper, did not pursue.

It is believed that 3,821 men were lost that day. 1,418 of the killed, wounded, or captured were Confederate, 2,403 were Union. General Nathaniel Banks, though defeated, had carried out his orders. He had stalled the rebel advance long enough for reinforcements to arrive. By mid-August, the Union forces were concentrated north of the Rappahannock River.

Matthew had written several letters to Bethany during those busy weeks, but had no way to post them. His letters were melancholy as they gave witness to the Union defeats and to the losses of his comrades. He continued to be distressed that Will was no longer fighting at his side. He missed the sergeant's strong right arm and his infectious, boyish grin. Surely, his unit would have been more effective had Will been there. But Will, he supposed, was probably dead....never to share a campfire with him again.

They were encamped near Warrenton Junction when the mail finally caught up with them. Matt gave his letters to the courier and received only one in return. It was the letter from Reverend Lanning. He scanned it, his eyes wide with disbelief. He walked quietly away from the bustle of men around the headquarters tent and found a spot where he could sit, alone, with his back to a large oak. It seemed that the strong ,broad trunk of the tree offered him some protection from the horror of the news that he read. He read, and reread, both Lanning's letter and the wrinkled enclosure from Bethany. Matthew finally covered his face with his hands, trying to hide the tears that would not be checked. Presently, he felt a gentle, strong hand on his shoulder. It was Colonel Brodhead.

"What's wrong, Matt? Bad news, I'd guess."

Matt could not raise his eyes, or bring himself to answer. He silently handed the letters to his commander. Brodhead was sputtering with rage before he was halfway through the message.

"This is the damnedest, most outrageous thing I have ever heard! There must be some mistake! Matt, how is this possible?"

Matt could only shake his head.

"That son of a bitch Pinkerton. I'll nail his hide to the wall and then piss on it!" Thornton Brodhead struggled to control himself. He patted Matt on the shoulder. "Let's just look on the bright side. We don't know that she is dead. We'll get to the bottom of this....and real soon!" Brodhead was losing control again. His usually gentlemanly self was shaking with rage. He shouted to the startled group of officers at the headquarters tent. "Hold that mail courier right where he is! Don't let him leave! I have dispatches to send! Matt, I'll write to the provost marshal at Detroit and demand an immediate investigation. I'll write to Pinkerton! He damn well better have some answers. And, damn it, I'll write to Lincoln. He's the one that let that snake Pinkerton suck around the White House in the first place!" Brodhead started to stride toward his tent when Matt caught his arm.

"Colonel, sir, I'd like to go home. I must find her!"

The commander went limp, as though he had just been shot through the heart. He collapsed next to Matt and leaned against the tree. "Please don't ask me that. Please! I can't spare you now. The rebs have built a tremendous force. They may even be circling behind us. We need every single man. Especially you. I can apply some real pressure in the right places. I have a lot of friends both in Detroit and in Washington. I will scream at them until Bethany is found and the perpetrators are behind bars. I promise you I'll see that the bastards hang for this! Don't leave me, Matt. I know your strength. I know that even if I refuse to let you go you might take matters into your own hands and desert. I wouldn't blame you, mind, but please don't. Your country needs you. Your duty is clear!"

Lieutenant Colonel Greyson gulped, wiping his face with the back of his hand. "I understand, Thornton." His misted eyes stared off into the woods for a moment. "I've been a soldier too long to desert in the face of the enemy. I'll stay. I promise. But please help us!"

Brodhead sprang to his feet. "You're damn right I will help, as God is my witness, starting right now!" He stalked to his tent, scattering the incredulous officers who stood before it. He scraped the maps and papers from the scarred field table, depositing them in a jumble on the ground. "Orderly! Bring me paper! Bring me pen and ink! Now!"

Matthew sat without moving through the remainder of the day, and all through the long night that followed. Captains Pauldi and Acker brought him blankets and coffee, and begged him to come to their fire and take some supper. He would not leave the strength of his oak tree.

Bugles blew to assembly before dawn. The troops were ordered to cook three days' rations. Each soldier was issued 150 rounds of ammunition. The cavalry was ordered to make an immediate reconnaissance toward Bristoe Station. A Confederate raiding party had cleverly circled behind them, destroyed the railroad at Bristoe Station, then pillaged and burned the major Union supply depot at Manassas Junction. The true strength of the raiding party was unknown but it was thought to be large. Pope, taking personal command, ordered that the raiders be found and destroyed. He did not understand that 55,000 men in gray, lead by three of the most talented commanders who ever walked the earth....Lee, Jackson, and Longstreet.... were maneuvering to pounce on his 70,000 Yanks.

Saber stood saddled and waiting. His groom tried not to stare at the blanketed form under the oak tree. Instead, the soldier tried to look busy and unconcerned as he combed and primped the handsome creature's forelock and mane. He lifted each hoof for final inspection, removed a few imaginary pebbles, then went around and inspected all four again. The big sorrel stood quietly, enjoying the extra attention.

Matthew startled horse and soldier alike when he suddenly threw his blankets aside and groaned to his feet. He had alternately prayed, cursed, and wept all night. Without a thought for coffee or breakfast, he swung stiffly into the saddle and then spoke quietly to the orderly who stood at attention, holding the reins. "Saber been grained this morning?".

"He was, sir. An' I gave him a little extra." Greyson tugged at the reins to free them from the soldier's grasp, but the man held on. "Sir?"

"What is it, private?"

"We heared 'bout your troubles at home. Good luck, and God bless, sir. We's all pullin' for you."

Matt managed to smile down at the earnest young man. "Thank you, soldier. That means a great deal to me. Please thank the men for their kind thoughts."

"I'll do that, sir."

They exchanged salutes. Greyson whirled Saber and trotted him to the head of the column of horse where Brodhead, Acker, and Pauldi were anxiously awaiting his arrival. The early morning sky to the north was lit by an eerie glow from the flames of the burning supply depot. They moved out cautiously, to seek out the enemy, leaving behind the blue-coated infantry who were still forming into line of march, preparing to follow them into the pages of history. It was the morning of August 28th.

Colonel Brodhead had received orders from his able commander, Brigadier General John Buford, to scout the Bull Run Mountains ten miles to the rear of General Irvin McDowell's III Corps. They made the startling discovery that a major force of Confederates were making their way through Thoroughfare Gap, a natural passage through the mountains, and were headed straight for McDowell's rear. The cavalry deployed to resist their passage, and dispatched the news of the rebel approach to McDowell, who was, regrettably, not particularly impressed. He did, however, send one division of infantry to their aid. Unfortunately, McDowell neglected to inform General Pope of the rebel advance. This left the befuddled General Pope continuing to think that he was dealing with only small enemy forces. He was unaware of the extreme danger to his backside.

Colonel Brodhead, already in a bad mood, was convinced that this oversight was no accident. In his mind, and perhaps rightfully so, General Pope was an idiot, and Irvin McDowell was an out-and-out traitor. Brodhead took out his fury on the approaching rebels, inspiring his men to keep the huge force bottled up in the narrow mountain pass for hours. Lee was finally able to send a flanking force against them. Unable to withstand the mighty army that was thrown against them, the Union soldiers were forced to withdraw. The 30,000 man Confederate column filed through the gap and marched to link with General Jackson who had already opened the festivities by ambushing the balance of McDowell's command.

The battle, known as Second Manassas, or Second Bull Run, raged for three days. By the evening of August 30th, Pope, thoroughly defeated, ordered his Union forces to withdraw to Centreville, a fortified town on the road to Washington. Union casualties would number 16,054. Confederate losses were 9,194. The battlefield was littered with bloating corpses. The requiem was provided by the dying wails of the wounded soldiers who were left to suffer where they lay.

Buford's cavalry did their best to screen the retreat, checking Confederate General Beverly Robertson's aggressive Twelfth Virginia horsemen who were trying to force their way to the rear of Pope's army, disrupt his passage along the Warrenton Turnpike, and prevent the Yankees from crossing the stone bridge to the safety of the Centreville fortifications. The determined resistance demonstrated by Buford's troopers ultimately caused Robertson to abandon his plans and turn away....but the cost was high to the Union cavalry. The rebels sliced and diced them as the running fight carried across Bull Run at Lewis Ford. They found themselves fighting in smaller and smaller groups, often completely surrounded and obliged to fight their way through the determined Confederates in order continue their withdrawal.

Lt. Colonel Greyson, at the head of a small, tattered group of tired men, mounted on even more tired and staggering horses, discovered that Colonel Brodhead had become separated from their unit and was fighting virtually alone, encircled by enemy horsemen....some of whom were fighting dismounted, their own horses having been put out of action. Greyson waved his saber, shouted to his men, and charged toward the colonel. It was too late. As they fought their way toward him, Matthew saw Brodhead drop his saber, reel backward in the saddle, and fall, disappearing from sight into the melee. Matt spurred Saber forward in a desperate attempt to reach his commander, his friend.

Greyson felt Saber shudder in mid stride. The faithful steed reared, his legs buckled, and he stumbled. He sagged to the ground, his great heart pierced by a .58 caliber slug from a rebel trooper's carbine. Matt lost his saber in the fall. His issue Colt revolver was long since empty. He kicked his feet clear of the stirrups and managed to grab his big Walker from the saddle holster where it waited in reserve for just such an emergency. Three dismounted reb troopers converged upon him. Two quick shots from the Walker doomed two of them on the spot. The third, a hulking, bearded man sporting sergeant's stripes, continued toward him, the point of his saber nearly touching Matthew's sweat and bloodstained tunic. Matt fired his third round at pointblank range, his revolver instinctively centered on the man's chest. The Walker, stuffed with (at least) maximum black powder loads, decided at that moment to catastrophically fail. It exploded into lethal chunks of fractured steel. Someone, reeling in anguish within the smoke and the fire, screamed "Sweet Jesus!" The forlorn scream echoed in Matt's ears. He never knew whether it was he, or whether it was the mortally wounded reb, who had uttered the desperate prayer. The Confederate was blown backwards, instantly relieved, forevermore, of duty. Matt's right hand was macerated by the explosion. A jagged piece of metal, that just an instant before had been a part of the cylinder of the big revolver, struck Matt in the right eye, destroying it, and knocking him senseless. The few survivors of his little detachment fought their way clear, and retreated. Matt was left alone among the dead and dying, both blue and gray. American blood was draining into the thirsty Virginia soil. A solemn quiet fell over the killing field as the bloodied, but undaunted, Twelfth Virginia Cavalry galloped away in pursuit of the retreating Federals.

Greyson awoke within minutes, or perhaps within hours, it didn't matter. Time suddenly had no meaning. He was aroused by the sound of the quiet. It was too early for the pain in his head or in his hand to register. He knew only that he could barely see, could barely move. He became aware of the sound of labored breathing....the rasping sounds of lungs filling with blood. Saber! Fumbling blindly, he found the great horse lying quietly nearby. He crawled to the horse's head and gently stroked it. He sensed, rather than felt or heard, Saber's velvety nostrils flutter in recognition of his beloved master who had surely come to save him. Bloody foam bubbled, flew, and spattered with each dying breath.

Matt struggled to remain conscious. He was only dully aware of his own grievous and frightening injuries as blood trickled from what was left of his right eye. He petted the horse lovingly until, with a sigh, Saber's respiration ceased. Matthew rested his head upon the neck of his faithful friend as his own consciousness slipped away. He dreamed that he, riding Saber, was frolicking through a sunny field which was blanketed with the white beauty of nodding spring daisies. They were somewhere in Michigan. Or, perhaps, they were somewhere in Virginia. Somewhere. Somewhere where a man and his horse could ride forever. Even as they joyfully cantered through the fields, Matt could feel that something was wrong. He reached to pat Saber's neck, expecting to feel warmth and sweat, but his hand came away cold. As he slept, and dreamed, he could feel the icy coldness of death seeping into the still form that pillowed his head.

The Union retreat had left the triumphant rebels in gleeful possession of the field of battle. They lost no time in claiming the thousands of Union muskets that had been abandoned, or that were no longer needed by the still hands that clasped them. They gathered the wounded, both blue and gray, and transported them to makeshift field hospitals where most of them, with the help of the crude medical and surgical care available at the time, mercifully died.

The Confederate search parties, working by lantern light, found Colonel Brodhead propped in a sitting position against a dead horse, and struggling to breathe. The colonel was, understandably, in a vile frame of mind and not in the least happy to see them. Nevertheless, they treated him with the respect due his rank and carefully transported him to the stone house, at the corner of the Warrenton Pike and Sudley Road, where a field hospital was being organized.

Several hours passed before a rebel search party stumbled upon Lieutenant Colonel Greyson, who was found lying with his head still resting on the neck of yet another dead horse. The field was littered with dead horses and their dead riders. Greyson and Saber appeared to be just one more gruesome set. They rolled Matthew over and noted, with surprise, his rank. Another Yankee colonel! They at first thought that he was dead, but then were startled to find, considering his mangled appearance, that he was still breathing. The Confederate soldiers dutifully gathered him up and transported him to the same stone house-cum-hospital that already sheltered Colonel Brodhead. However, by the time that they arrived there with Greyson, the house was already full of groaning, wounded men who were in all manner and stages of disrepair. The surplus, for whom there was no room inside, were being placed in pitiful rows in the surrounding meadow. They deposited Matthew there. One of the rescuers had retrieved Greyson's saber, intending to keep it as a souvenir. He wiped the weapon clean with the tail of his butternut shirt. He whistled when he discovered the inscription that was engraved upon the blade:

Presented to Lt. M. Greyson in Honor of His Heroism in Mexico
by Gen'l. Winfield Scott

The inscribed saber was immediately confiscated by the lieutenant in command of the rescue party. He was sorely tempted to keep it for himself, but being a dutiful soldier, carried it to General Jackson's headquarters and turned it over to a Lieutenant Douglas, of the general's staff. He reported to Douglas that two Yankee colonels had been found, more-or-less alive, and had been taken to the stone house. Lt. Douglas gravely accepted the saber, and the news, and hastened to inform General Jackson.

Jackson's tent was carefully guarded. Recognizing the lieutenant, the sentries came to attention at his approach. Their faces were in shadow, while their fixed bayonets gleamed in the glow of the general's lantern. The famous general sat at his table, alone. Needing time to reflect upon the great victory, and upon the great pain and suffering that had bought that victory, he had dismissed his staff....sending them off to attend to the many necessary details of reorganization and re-supply The enemy had disengaged, and had retreated to Centreville. Their would be no further pursuit of the disheartened Federals that night. Tomorrow would come soon enough. Jackson thumbed, absent-mindedly, through the pages of his Bible, his eyes weary and unseeing.

Lt. Douglas nervously cleared his throat as he stood at the open flap of the tent. "Excuse me, general."

"Stonewall" recognized him, but did not smile a greeting. "Ah! Yes, Henry. What may I do for you?"

Douglas saluted. "We have found two more Union officers, sir. Two colonels."

The general leaned back in his chair, not bothering to return the salute. "At ease, lieutenant. Come in, please, and have a seat. Are these two alive, or are you just reporting more corpses?"

"Alive suh. At least the last I heard. They are from the First Michigan Cavalry, of General Buford's brigade. I believe you will be interested in this saber found near one of them."

Jackson took the weapon, turned up the lantern, and held it close to the light. "Well, well! M. Greyson! Matthew! I know him well. Graduate of V.M.I. My comrade, and good friend, in Mexico." He placed the saber on the table, thoughtfully running his fingers over the engraving, then wearily clasped his hands behind his neck. "Good soldier. Good soldier. The inscription speaks well of him....as it should. I recall when he was brevetted to lieutenant during the Mexican War. Brave and talented as he is, he should have been to promoted to general."

Henry Douglas leaned his elbows on the table and rested his chin, thoughtfully, on his cupped hands. "Yes, suh. But, it seems that he only made it to lieutenant colonel. Doesn't seem likely he will get any higher, seeing as now he belongs to us!"

"Astute observation, lieutenant." He rumbled a quiet, deep, and uncharacteristic chuckle.

"Yes, suh. Sorry, suh." Henry was embarrassed that he had belabored the general with the obvious. "I'm told he has a head wound and is unconscious."

"Hmm. Doesn't sound good. What of the other one?"

A Colonel Brodhead, suh. Commander of the Michigan troopers. Shot through the chest."

227

"Commander, eh?" General Jackson sprang to his feet. The lieutenant scrambled to follow suit. "Henry, I want you to make absolutely sure that these gentlemen are made as comfortable as possible. They are to receive the very best in medical care. Please inform Dr. McGuire that he is to give them his personal attention."

"Certainly, suh. As you wish."

"And, I want you with me first thing in the morning. I intend to visit as many of the wounded as possible. Be prepared to show me where the Yanks are. I wish to pay them my respects."

"Yes, suh. I believe they're at the stone house. I'll find them."

"Good. Now, I'm going to rest. Goodnight."

"Goodnight, general." He saluted and turned to leave.

Jackson put a hand on his arm to slow him. "Hold on a minute, Henry. Here. Take Greyson his saber. See that he gets to keep it."

"I will. I'll take care of it. Sleep well, general."

A tiny smile flickered across Thomas Jackson's face, showing, for an instant, a glimmer of teeth through the shaggy beard. "Fat chance of that!"

Lieutenant Douglas muttered to himself as his legs, rubbery with fatigue, carried him away from his general's tent to where his sleeping horse was picketed to a rope that was strung between two trees. A number of other thin and tired horses belonging to the headquarters staff were tied, in a row, to the same rope. The poor beast could hardly open his eyes when the saddle was thumped upon his back and the bit was crammed into his mouth. "Let's go, old fella'!" murmured Henry. "Goin' to be a long night." As he rode down from Stony Ridge, he marveled at the twinkling of hundreds, perhaps thousands, of campfires. The Army of Northern Virginia was turning in for a well-deserved rest. There was no joking, no singing, no spirited card games, no celebration of victory. The men were rolling into their blankets....those that still had them....and thinking of their fallen comrades. They were thinking of tomorrow. Would the Yankees re-engage with new strength and vigor? Would they themselves become

228

blank-eyed members of the piles of grotesque dead that they would have to bury tomorrow?

In contrast, the area in around the stone house was a flurry of weary activity as the hospital teams attempted to triage the hundreds of wounded men. It was a nearly hopeless task.

Every available lantern lighted the gloom, but the feeble lights seemed to serve only to intensify the darkness as they made the suffering more visible. The dead were being unceremoniously dragged to the periphery to get them out of the way of those who still lived. Lieutenant Douglas had no difficulty in locating the surgeon's tent. It was easily identified by the growing piles of severed arms and legs surrounding it.

Henry felt faint from the sights, sounds, and smells of the carnage. He nearly toppled over when he entered the tent and found Dr. Hunter McGuire vigorously sawing the femur of an unfortunate patient who was barely under the influence of chloroform anesthesia. The poor soldier was moaning. His writhing was restrained by two orderlies who had to throw their full weight upon him to keep him on the table. Holding to a tent pole for balance, Henry took a deep breath, and addressed the surgeon. "Dr. McGuire, suh?"

McGuire stopped sawing and looked up at his visitor, his once white apron dripping red. His brow furrowed with disapproval as he viewed the dapper, and very young, lieutenant. "And just what the hell do you want? Can't you see I'm a little busy?"

Henry took a tighter grip on his tent pole. "Yes suh. Sorry, suh. I can see that!"

"Well?"

"I have a message from General Jackson, suh."

The doctor resumed sawing. "What is it? Out with it, boy."

"The general is particularly concerned about two Yankee colonels who are here. He requests that you give them your personal attention."

McGuire finished his sawing and threaded a very large suture needle with some sort of coarse thread. "I'm giving all of these people my personal attention. Why should two damn Yanks be so special?"

"Suh, the general requests...." Douglas, and his tent pole, were standing their ground.

Henry watched, in nauseous fascination, as the doctor expertly sutured the stump. An orderly blithely carried the severed limb outside and pitched it onto the pile. "All right. All right! If Stonewall says so, I'll look at them. That is, I'll look at them if you can find them."

"I'll do that sir. I'll find them." Henry let go of the pole and staggered out into the relatively fresh air. He retched and vomited. "Golly," he thought, as he wiped his chin, "war sure is fun!"

He started his search within the stone house and found Colonel Brodhead within minutes. The Yankee was sitting propped against a wall....still painfully, but so far successfully, engaged in the struggle to continue to breathe against the rising tide of blood within his shattered lungs. "Colonel, suh, I see you are a full colonel. You must be Brodhead."

Brodhead nodded weakly, noting his visitor's rank in the dim light. "You are correct, lieutenant. I am Colonel Thornton Brodhead."

"Thank you, suh. General Jackson sends his compliments."

Brodhead wheezed his surprise. "How very kind of the general! Do you suppose that you, or he, can help me to breathe?"

Douglas examined the wounded man sympathetically. Someone had wrapped his chest in a none-too-clean bandage in an attempt to stem the hemorrhage. The bandage actually did little more than make his respiration more difficult. The blood flowing within his chest continued to fill his lungs, unabated.

"General Jackson has directed our chief surgeon to care for you." Douglas, who had been kneeling at the colonel's side, stood to leave. "I will summon him immediately, suh."

Brodhead coughed painfully. "Thank you, lieutenant. You are very kind. May I ask your name?"

"Henry Kyd Douglas, of General Jackson's staff, suh."

"A pleasure to meet you, Lieutenant Douglas." His voice was weak. He paused to regain his breath before continuing. "Please convey my gratitude to the general." He clutched his chest to ward off the painful coughing. "And, I'm certain that your doctor is very busy, this night. I do not expect preferential treatment. I'm sure that he has many lives to save."

Henry was touched by the brave words. He wavered for a moment, pausing before turning away. "May I say, Colonel, that you are a kind, and brave, man. Were the situation different, I would have been honored to serve under your command."

Colonel Brodhead managed a weak smile. "And, I honored to have you. Pity, that we must fight each other."

There were sounds of new activity outside. When Douglas emerged, he found that a Federal ambulance, under a flag of truce, had arrived in search of their wounded. Lt. Douglas saw to it that the colonel was the first to be loaded. As he took his leave, the lieutenant touched the colonel's hand, and then saluted. "I hope we will meet again, suh."

"Brodhead smiled in the darkness, knowing that his own chances for survival were slipping away with every painful breath. "I hope so too, lieutenant. But don't count on it!" A full load of Union casualties were soon placed aboard, and the ambulance departed for Centreville.

Henry Douglas resumed his search for Colonel Greyson, carrying his lantern further and further toward the periphery of the lines of wounded who were laid out in the meadow. He finally found the still, silent form, his uniform bloody and torn, in a row of the dead and dying. He was cold to the touch, and barely breathing. Douglas had the limp form carried into the light, where Dr. McGuire pronounced him to be severely brain-damaged and unlikely to survive the night. The good doctor, nevertheless, dressed his wounds, shrugged, and walked wearily back to his surgical duties within the tent of pain. He was pleased that the Federals had taken one colonel off of his hands. He feared that the second one would not be alive long enough to matter.

A wagon load of straw, brought for the comfort of the wounded, had arrived. Douglas ordered Greyson carried into the stone house and bedded with an extra ration of the clean, yellow softness. That, he thought, was the best that he could accomplish, considering the circumstances. He decided to carry Matthew's saber back to headquarters as it was certain to be stolen.... especially if the grievously wounded officer should die. Perhaps, General Jackson would see that it was returned to Greyson's family. He would report to the general that Greyson would probably never have further need for it.

Every rock over which the steel-tired ambulance lurched caused Colonel Brodhead intense pain, and made every breath even more difficult. By the time that they reached Centreville, he was more dead than alive, but he rallied when he saw the friendly faces of his officers and men. Strong hands lifted him from the wagon and carried him to a salvaged mattress that was on the floor of a dilapidated house that had been commandeered for use as a temporary officers' quarters. Dr. North, the Federal counterpart of Confederate Dr. McGuire, was soon at his side.

The doctor could see, in an instant, that the situation was hopeless. It was clear that the man would either suffocate on his own blood, or bleed to death....which ever chanced to happen first. "Thornton, let me administer an opiate to lessen your pain, and ease your discomfort. I'm afraid that's about all I can do for you, at present."

"At present, or ever! Keep your narcotic for someone who really needs it!" gasped Brodhead. "Instead, prop me up. Bring me a better light, if you will." He wheezed desperately. "And paper and pen. I have letters to write. I must write them very soon, or not at all."

His requests were quickly accomplished. Captain Acker, bearing the paper and pen, stood beside his bed, cap in hand. "Sir, do you have any news of Matthew Greyson? He is missing, and we fear the worst."

Brodhead's eyes focused slowly as he looked to identify the speaker. "George! Good to see you safe and sound. No. I have no idea what has happened to Greyson."

"Several of our troopers saw his horse shot from under him, but could not come to his aid as they, themselves, were fighting for their lives."

Brodhead's voice was barely audible. "I'm sorry. Very sorry, George."

"I, too, am deeply concerned. The best that we can hope for is that he has been captured. Sir, you should know that Greyson was attempting to come to your aid when he was shot down."

Tears sprang into the colonel's eyes. It took him a few moments before he could speak. "Thank you for telling me, captain." His words were soft with emotion.

Dr. North put a hand on Acker's arm. "George, I don't think the colonel should try to talk more, right now. The doctor sank, wearily, onto a chair in the corner of the room. He would keep a vigil over his patient. There was little that he could do but watch him die.

Brodhead was a man of many talents, not the least of which was his ability to eloquently express himself on paper. He scribbled furiously, page after page, all through the balance of the desperate night. His letter to his wife was filled with Christian love, mingled with the sadness that he must leave her a widow, and their children without a father.

> "Today is Sunday, and to-day I sink to the green couch
> of our final rest. I have fought well, my darling; and I was
> shot in the endeavor to rally our broken battalions...."

To his brother and sister he wrote, in part:

> "I am one of the victims of Pope's imbecility and McDowell's
> treason. Tell the President, would he save the country, he must
> not give our hallowed flag into such hands."

Colonel Brodhead did not live to learn, at least in this life, that President Lincoln would indeed relieve Pope of command shortly after the Battle of Second Manassas. Nor would he know that, subsequent to his charges, General Irvin McDowell's incompetence (but not treason) would be proved in a board of inquiry. Had he known, it would have been easier for Thornton Brodhead to rest peacefully, perhaps at last with a smile, in his "green couch".

One of his last letters was addressed to Mr. D. Trick, Franklin Village, Michigan.

August 31, 1862

Dear Mr. Trick:

As I know not to whom else to write, I regretfully intrust to you the following information: The brave and heroic Lieutenant Colonel Matthew Greyson, my dear friend, has been lost in combat near Centreville, Virginia. It is known that his faithful steed was shot from under him. It is feared that the colonel has been either killed, or captured. His fate is at present unknown.

A few days ago, he asked me, should he be killed, that the title to his farm be conveyed to his beloved Bethany Dodge. In the sad event that she be deceased, the ownership of the farm is to go to you.

I pray that Miss Dodge has been found alive and well. If that is indeed the case, please convey to her my deepest sympathy and that one of my final, and most fervent, prayers will be that Matthew, too, will likewise be found alive and well. I regret that I will be unable to communicate with you further as I expect to die very soon, shot in the defense of our glorious flag.

Respectfully,

Thornton F. Brodhead, Colonel
Army of Northern Virginia

Brodhead was still scribbling as the gray precursor to dawn began to illuminate the broken windows of his room. Finally, the pen faltered, then made an inky trail across the paper as he slipped into a sleep from which he would never awaken. Another great mind was lost. Another great man was sacrificed on the altar of the gods of war. Dr. North took the pen from the stilled hand and gathered the papers to ensure that they would be properly posted and distributed. He paused, for a moment, to listen to his friend's labored breathing. The spark of life would linger for another day but the warrior in blue had already ridden away with the angels. Dr. North went in search of a cup of coffee....and perhaps even a few moments of rest. It had been a very bad day, and an even worse night. He stepped outside and stood alone in the darkness trying to fight the mental and physical fatigue which threatened to overwhelm him. The grayness of the early dawn air was warm and heavy with humidity and smoke. He could hear the muttering and grumbling of the retreating soldiers as they shuffled by him, shadows in the gloom. He raised his eyes to heaven and asked God to grant that there would be no more suffering, no more dying, and that no more of his friends would be lost. Being a practical man, however, he realized that those prayers were unlikely to be answered. "At least," he prayed, "grant me the strength, and will, and expertise to help wherever I can!" Only God, and General Lee, could know what would happen in the wretched days to come....after the sunrise....and the sunrise after that, and after that....

+ + +

When the sun made its appearance on Monday, September 1, 1862, it was obscured by the scudding clouds that presage the coming of a storm. The intensifying light of the new day served only to illuminate the ghastly remnants of the battle. Dead men, dead animals, and shattered ordinance littered the muddy scene. General Lee was determined that he would not lose the initiative. He had defeated Pope, but had not destroyed him. The Confederates set out to finish the task. Jackson's troops were dispatched to cross Bull Run at Sudley Ford. They were to circle to the north around the fortifications at Centreville and to attack Pope as he attempted to move his troops to the safety of the mighty forts that were guarding Washington. Longstreet's command was instructed to bury the dead, collect the wounded, and then to reinforce Jackson's effort to cut off the Union retreat.

Stonewall Jackson dispatched his tired and still hungry troops as ordered, then took the time to visit as many of the wounded as he could before joining the march. He and Lt. Douglas rode to the stone house. The general, Bible in hand, visited and prayed with as many of the wounded as time would allow. The scene in and around the old house was pitiful, but at least basic humanitarian care was being provided. Douglas led the general to Colonel Greyson's prostrate form. He had not moved since the lieutenant had left him the night before. The bandages on his head, and on his hand, were stiff and dark with dried blood. Jackson, sorrow in his eyes, knelt next to him. "Greyson, it is good to see you after all these years, but not under these circumstances! I doubt that you can hear me, but if you can, I want you to know that I am praying for your recovery." To the general's surprise and delight, Matthew's visible eyelids fluttered, but could not quite open. His bandaged right hand twitched as though he wanted to shake the hand of his former professor. Jackson looked up at his lieutenant who was shifting nervously from one foot to the other. The young man was concerned that

Stonewall was urgently needed to join his troops on their muddy march. "Henry, try to stand still for a moment." The general stroked his beard, thoughtfully. "Lieutenant, I believe that this man could recover if we all pray hard enough."

"If you say so, suh." Douglas was not convinced that there was much life left in the body that lay before them.

Jackson took Matthew's good hand in his. "Colonel Greyson, you must get well. That is an order! The world is in need of a man like you." He opened his Bible to his favorite passage, and read softly: "For God so loved the world...."

Douglas had stopped shuffling, but now was twitching impatiently. "Suh, we really must...."

Jackson stood, the better to give the lieutenant a reproachful look. "Henry, at a time like this, when a man is fighting for his life, God's love is focused upon him. Jesus is here, kneeling at this man's side. Don't you feel His presence? Don't you see Him?"

Lieutenant Henry Kyd Douglas was becoming even more uncomfortable. "Sorry, suh. Guess you can see things that I can't." All he could see, in the dim light that filtered into the dark room through the small windows, was a corpse that had not yet been inspired to stop breathing. "Breathing," he thought, cynically, to himself, "could well be a hard habit to break!"

Stonewall chose to ignore his lieutenant's lack of perception. "We must respect His presence, lieutenant. This one man, to our Savior, as important as any one of us....any thousand of us!" Stonewall dropped back to his knees, his hands clasped in prayer. "God, forgive me for those whom I have caused to be killed." He shook his shaggy head. "And, today, more will die." The great general sighed, sorrow touching his soul. "Henry, at this moment He has made time stand still for you, for me, and for Matthew Greyson....so, for God's sake, stop twitching!"

"Yes, suh."

The general seemed lost in thought. Perhaps, indeed, Jackson could see into the bright shadows of spirituality that were beyond the perception of ordinary men. "See that his sword is sent to General Buford with the request that he forward it to Greyson's family for safekeeping.... until he is well."

Douglas, as ordered, had stopped twitching. "As you say, suh."

"And, write a letter of safe conduct for Greyson, over my signature."

"Right away, suh."

"And, see that he is sent to Richmond and placed under the care of the finest doctors available. And...."

"Suh?"

The general's long boots squeaked as he arose from his knees. "Send copies of my order, and of the safe conduct, to President Davis so that they will not be ignored."

"Yes, suh. I'm sure your orders will not be ignored under any circumstances."

"Very well, then. Let's get back to work." He gave Matt a farewell pat on the shoulder. "Good luck, and God be with you, my friend." They strode out of the stone house to their waiting horses. The general's personal mounted guard unit, in splendid gray, was drawn up in column of fours in front of the hospital. The scarlet of their battle flag whipped in the wind of the coming storm. It was just beginning to rain.

CHAPTER FOURTEEN

The Robert E. Lee

It was obvious that careful plans had to be made before the *Amazon* made fast her lines to the Halifax dock. Captain Briggs would be obliged to immediately report the attempted piracy to the authorities so that the prisoners could be turned over to them for trial. There would be inquiries and investigations, both by the British Admiralty and by the American Consulate. Captain Briggs would be facing three major problems: 1. The loading of his cargo of Confederate cotton could come under unwanted scrutiny. 2. His departure for Liverpool could be delayed by the official inquiries. In the shipping business, as in any other, time is money and delay is expensive. 3. Bethany's involvement could lead to an investigation of her identity, and unwanted publicity of her presence. She had hoped to slip through Halifax unnoticed.

Bethany had saved the *Amazon* from the grasping hands of Lawrence Martin and his associated ruffians. Considering what Bethany had done for them, and being informed of her clandestine situation, the Briggs would do whatever was necessary to ensure her safety. Accordingly, Captain Briggs assembled his loyal crew before they docked, delighted them by serving an extra ration of rum, and ordered them to give no indication that anything unusual had occurred on their passage from Quebec. No one was to do or say anything that would attract undue attention to the ship. The men, winking knowingly at each other, savored their rum and complied without question or complaint, and without slip of the lip. They nonchalantly completed their docking chores in silence. The prisoners were chained in the hold, and the hatches closed. They would be neither seen nor heard until Captain Briggs was ready to disclose their presence. The captain took his time as he gathered his ship's papers and strolled slowly to the offices of the Admiralty. Bethany hugged Mary and the boys as they said their tearful good-byes. Followed at a distance by a sailor who carried her valise, Bethany strolled down the gangplank and blended with the busy crowd that thronged the wharf.

During the subsequent inquiry, Briggs would report that his passenger, one Elizabeth Green, had left the ship, gone on her way, and could not be located. The various authorities shrugged. The testimony of the captain, with or without Bethany's presence, was enough to send the luckless pirates to the gallows. Thankfully, for Benjamin Briggs, the matter was quickly settled and justice was swift. Hanging, side by side by their necks the pirates joined their fallen leader in whatever afterlife God has reserved for such souls.

The Halifax firm of B. Weir & Co. had been engaged by the Confederate government to look after cargoes and travelers passing through that port on their way to, from, and for, the Confederate States. Mr. Alexander Keith, a prim and proper Britisher who was a principal agent of that firm, listened in wide-eyed amazement as Bethany recounted her adventure of piracy aboard the *Amazon*. He was galvanized into action, knowing that she must be immediately spirited away, and arranged for her to be speedily transported to the *Giraffe*....that long, low, gray smudge that was anchored in the harbor. "Oh no!" whined Bethany to herself. "Not another silly rowboat!" At least, the sailors who pulled the oars on this one appeared to be perfectly sober. Her passage on the *Giraffe* had been prearranged. Several hours after her arrival, the anchor chain clattered aboard. The *Giraffe's* first scheduled port of call: Charleston, South Carolina. There, she would deliver not only Bethany, but tons of materiel for the rebel army. Her hold was packed with crates of Enfield rifles, hundreds of casks of gunpowder, bullets, cannon projectiles, uniforms and other clothing, and a half-dozen of the fine, English made, Blakely 12 pounder rifled cannon.

As the massive sidewheels churned to clear the harbor, Bethany stood at the rail and wistfully gazed at the *Amazon* as she sat idly at the dock, not yet loading her cargo of cotton. Beth wished the sleeping freighter "Godspeed" on her voyage to Liverpool. Folding her hands in prayer, she leaned against the dull gray of the railing and begged her God to watch over the Briggs family. "Fair winds for them, Father, and snug harbors too, please. Oh, dear Jesus, I already miss them so! Please sail with them, always!"

Bethany's prayers for their safety and happiness were answered....at least for a good while....at least until December of 1872 when the *Amazon*, by then re-christened the *Mary Celeste*, was discovered off of the coast of Portugal sailing alone....really alone. There was no one aboard. Her captain, his family, and her crew had disappeared. Mary had set the table for dinner, but no one was there to eat it. The *Mary Celeste's* cargo of grain alcohol was undisturbed. Some of her sails were set, carrying her wherever the winds decreed that she should go, with no one at the wheel to give her guidance. The cold depths of the Atlantic never yielded an answer to the mystery. Captain Benjamin Briggs, Mary, Claude, and Michael, had simply....vanished. Perhaps, just perhaps, they are still happily sailing, somewhere, under a misty sky upon a misty ocean, sails set for the next port of call that they will never, ever, reach.

Bethany stayed on the deck of the *Giraffe*, trying to stay out of the way, but refusing to go to her cabin for fear of missing anything interesting. Sailors hurried to and fro on the deck as they made ready for sea. The giant paddlewheels stopped their churning and idled slowly. A steam launch pulled alongside and picked up the harbor pilot. The pilot was followed into the launch by a gentleman who wore a black uniform suit with gold trim around the cuffs. Beth learned later that he was the British captain of the vessel. To minimize paperwork and delay, he had been hired so that the *Giraffe* could sail under the authority and Union Jack of the British Admiralty. As soon as the launch pulled away and the sidewheels resumed their churning, a color guard appeared on deck. The men were nattily attired in gray Confederate uniforms. The Union Jack was hauled down. With a drum roll, and with a mighty cheer from the crew the Stars and Bars of the Confederacy swirled and fluttered to the top of the staff. Joy and pride swelled in Bethany's chest. At last! At last she was home! Well, almost home.

Captain John Wilkinson, of the Confederate States Navy and commander of the vessel appeared at Bethany's elbow. He was bowing, apologetically, for his failure to greet her upon her arrival aboard. "Forgive me," he exclaimed, "but the press of business of leaving port on top of the changing of the identity of this ship have kept me quite occupied!"

Bethany offered him her hand, and curtseyed when he took it. "Goodness, Captain Wilkinson, you needn't apologize! I have observed that there has been a good deal of activity since we left the dock. There is no question that you have been very busy!" Her voice slipped into the sweetness of her Charleston accent. "Suh, I confess that I am both overjoyed and confused by what I have seen. Could I trouble you to explain?"

"Of course! I'd be most delighted. With all the flag-waving going on, I can understand your confusion." The captain was a round-faced individual with damp, curly hair that obscured his ears. His upper lip sported a formidable-looking but well-groomed mustache that appeared to her to be quite pickery. "The *Giraffe* has been purchased by our government to serve as a blockade runner. She, as of this moment, is commissioned the *C.S.A. Robert E. Lee*. She is to serve at the forefront of a new fleet that will handily defeat the unlawful Yankee blockade of our ports."

Bethany looked worried. "Are we, then, likely to be intercepted by Yankee warships, captain?"

"Not likely, Miss Green. We are faster than anything the Union has upon the water. With a full head of steam we can make over thirteen knots. We are fast, invisible, and uncatchable!"

"Invisible?"

"Invisible. Gray paint, retractable stacks, and low to the water with no tall rigging. Further, miss, should you care about such things, we burn only anthracite coal. Anthracite burns with little smoke. Most likely, unless we get very unlucky, they will never see us pass. Even our steam is vented underwater so that it doesn't make a sound. The Scottish shipwrights of the River Clyde are experts in the design and fabrication of such vessels as this. We hope to add more of them to our fleet as soon as they can be built."

Bethany applauded in her charming, ladylike way. "Thank you, Captain Wilkinson. I feel most safe and secure."

John Wilkinson bowed. He was dressed in a plain, dark blue suit, white shirt, and dark blue bow tie. The suit was devoid of the gold ornamentation that would befit his rank. "I'm delighted that you feel that way, miss. However, I must speak a word of caution. I don't mean to make you comfortable on the one hand and then to frighten you on the other, but you must understand that even though we are not fitted with heavy ordinance we are a ship of war. The *R.E. Lee* is packed to the gunwales with munitions. Should a fire occur on board, either through act of war or by accident, you must be ready to immediately leave the ship. Be prepared to be thrust into the first boat that goes over the side. Ask no questions, make no complaint. Just go."

Bethany looked a little pale as she comprehended his words. "I understand, and surely will do just as you say." She cleared her throat a bit nervously. "If you will excuse me for saying so, it seems to me that you are telling me that this ship is a, well....a floating bomb!"

The captain chuckled at her discomfort. "Exactly! A very large floating bomb. However, don't let that fact disturb you all that much. The chances of the occurrence of such a nasty problem are really very small."

Bethany did not find Wilkinson's parting words to be comforting. The vision of being lofted into the air by a giant fireball burned in her mind, disturbing her sleep throughout the voyage. She would lie awake listening to every creak, every footstep, every bell. Sleeping on top of tons of explosives does not give one a snug feeling.

The *Robert E. Lee* churned southward along the Atlantic Seaboard, keeping well off of the coast. Once she arrived due east of Charleston, her engines slowed. The paddlewheels stroked the water almost without a sound. Bethany watched as the sailors telescoped the twin smokestacks to their shortest position. Darkness fell, the blackness of the night accentuated by the fact that not one single light glimmered aboard the vessel. Bethany spent the night in a deck chair, fascinated by the danger and excited to be so near her home and her father.

The lights of a Federal warship appeared, dead ahead, her tall rigging etched against the night sky. Silently, the *Lee* veered to port to avoid the blockader. The Yankee ship's bell tolled the watch. One-two, three-four, five-six. The brassy sounds of the bell tinkled across the water. Three o'clock in the morning. They were so close that Bethany could see the

Yankee sailors moving about on the deck of the warship. Yet, no alarm was given and they slipped, silently, past. The Yanks would never know that the *Robert E. Lee* had just paid them a visit.

A half-hour later another ship, off to starboard, emerged from the darkness. She was smaller than the last, and was under sail. Her lookout, who was unusually alert, rubbed his eyes. He had spotted the sparkle of water as it was disturbed by the slowly turning starboard paddlewheel of the *Lee*. He shouted the alarm, and the Federal vessel came to life. Her forward pivot gun, an eleven inch Dahlgren rifle, belched a frightening plume of flame. The ball, fortunately, sailed over them and splashed into the sea beyond.

The *Lee* fairly lept through the waves as the orders for full speed ahead were given. Another flash of flame. The second shot was better aimed, but landed about fifty yards to port, raising a fearful geyser of water. Bethany ran to her cabin, thinking that the wooden structure would afford her some measure of protection. She need not have worried. The Yankee warship was rapidly falling astern. Her last shot was more of a salute than a serious attempt to hit the fleet rebel vessel. Her parting shot fell a full half-mile behind them.

There was no further need for stealth. The *R.E. Lee* made a dash for the harbor, for the protection afforded by the guns of the Charleston forts. The seamen struggled to raise her stacks in order to give maximum draft for her fires. She expertly avoided the bars, and steamed into the harbor at a full thirteen and one-half knots just after dawn. The Confederates stood on the parapets of forts Moultrie and Sumter, waving their hats and shouting cheers of welcome. A cannon salute was fired from Castle Pinkney. Bethany was finally, at last, really home.

Major Jared Dodge, surrounded by a retinue of his household servants, waited on the wharf to greet his beloved daughter. Tears of joy streamed down the tanned face of her father and down the black faces of the devoted servants. Bethany was loved by all. Bethany was the prodigal daughter, returned to her family....both black and white.

+ + +

The respected and well-connected Major Jared Dodge was a very busy man. He was in charge of the procurement and disposition of the vast amounts of powder and projectiles required to satisfy the appetites of the motley collection of seacoast columbiads and miscellaneous smaller cannon that were being mounted for the defense of Charleston. In fact, much of the materiel that was delivered by the *Robert E. Lee* had been ordered over his signature. Much as he loved to be with his daughter, he had little time to spend with her. Attack by the Federal fleet was considered immanent. Consequently, the major had to spend much of his time at the various batteries and forts that defended the harbor.

Bethany was not in the mood for cheerful conversation, anyway. She spent much of her time alone, either in her elegant bedroom, or perched on a wicker chair that rocked upon the spacious porch of her father's Greek-columned mansion. The sun-swept view from the porch, although grand, did little to improve her hopelessly dark mood. Upon her arrival, she had learned of the Confederate victory at Second Manassas. She fretted, and rightfully so, that Matthew could have been involved in the battle that had been such a devastating defeat for the Federals. Over the backs of the monster cannon that were mounted in the White Point Gardens, she could see the dark shape of Fort Sumter squatting in the harbor, far in the distance. She could barely make out the faint, bright dot of color, the Stars and Bars of the Confederacy that floated above the dark bastion.

Life, without Matthew, would barely be worth living. She often tried to read in the hope that her favorite books would soothe her unhappy mind. Sadly, nearly everything that she read seemed to bring more despair. She especially enjoyed the writings of the contemporary poet, John Greenleaf Whittier. Whittier, who was decidedly abolitionist, was far more popular in the north than he was in the south. Not wishing to offend either her father nor her southern friends, she discreetly read Whittier's writings in secret. She did not wish to make an issue of her own private views of the immorality of the "peculiar institution". Her aching heart was drawn like a magnet to one certain passage from Whittier's pen:

> "For of all sad words
> from tongue or pen
> the saddest are these--
> it might have been."

The words rang true to her as she reflected upon the life that she could have enjoyed with Matthew had not the circumstance of war decreed otherwise.

The glowing, crowing accounts of the Confederate victory at Second Manassas, as published in the *Charleston Daily Courier*, were disconcerting. She was proud that the brave southern men had accomplished such a glorious victory. However, she paled and gasped for breath when she read of the Confederate cavalry's rout of the Union horsemen. "Oh! My God!" she cried. Surely, Matthew must have been in the thick of the battle. She feared greatly for his safety. The fright of not knowing of his fate was almost unbearable. She visited the telegraph office daily to watch for the latest news as it clicked off of the wire. She was looking for specific information regarding the involvement of the First Michigan Cavalry, hoping that they had not been heavily engaged. Nothing of the Michigan men was reported. Only the glorious defeat of "John Buford's Cavalry" blazed from the pages.

In desperation, she prevailed upon her father to send a telegraph to Richmond in an attempt to learn whether Matthew's name was on the list of Federal soldiers that were held as prisoners of the Confederacy. Major Dodge patted her hand, stroked her hair, and sympathetically shared her fright. He sent the telegram, with little real hope of success, to his old friend, President Jefferson Davis. Of course, if Colonel Greyson did not appear on the roster of prisoners there was no way to determine whether he was alive or dead. She rather hoped that he would be listed as a prisoner. Then, she would know that he was still alive....and would use her father's influence to rescue him. Otherwise, he could be dead on the battlefield, wounded and lying in a Union hospital, or....God willing....safely retreated to Washington.

Remarkably, her questions were quickly answered. The reply, by return telegram, was amazingly swift. General Jackson's letter referencing Colonel Greyson had been received by the Davis office. Colonel Greyson, protected by Jackson's safe-conduct order, was in Confederate hands, wounded, and being cared for by the surgeons at the Chimborazo Hospital in Richmond. The Chimborazo was the finest hospital facility, north or south, available during the war. The telegram assured them that he was receiving the best of medical care, but gave no further details. Bethany immediately flew into a state of hysteria, the likes of which neither

her Negro servants, nor her father, had ever seen. She insisted that she would go to Matthew, and immediately. She raced around her bedroom, alternately crying and praying, while she stuffed her valise full of an uncharacteristically disorganized selection of clothing. She would go to Richmond if she had to walk, dragging her valise behind her.

Major Dodge poured a shot-glass full of fine Kentucky bourbon and stood with it, his hand trembling a little, in the doorway of her room from whence he disconsolately watched his daughter flit to and fro. "Bethany, you must drink this. It will settle your nerves. Bethany, you *will* please drink this. Now!"

Beth did not even slow her flurry of activity. "I will not, father. I will do no such thing. I need my wits about me!"

"Your wits are far from about you, right now." His voice changed from commanding, to pleading. "Please, Bethany. A little bourbon will help you stop running in circles. You won't help your Matthew by acting like a frantic school girl."

"Will not!" She remained defiant.

The major drew himself to his full height, with a sigh, and entered the room in pursuit. "Daughter, you will do as I say. Drink this before you explode into little pieces!" He was insistent. "If you will not listen to me, I will be forced to send for the paregoric. I will sit upon you, and force you to swallow the opiate until you're calm!"

"I will not drink anything, father! You think that whiskey is the answer to everything!"

"Fine!" He grimly set the glass upon the bureau. "Not quite a fair observation, my dear." She resumed her sobbing, muttering, and flying around the room. "Very well." Jared was not accustomed to being ignored. He turned to the servant who stood, cowering and wide-eyed, in a corner of the bedroom. "Bessie, go and fetch the paregoric." Obediently, the servant ran from the room. The starched skirt of her uniform rustled and fluttered in her haste.

Bethany pulled herself to a sudden halt and looked into her father's eyes. She could see the determination there. She knew that the tincture of opium that he planned to force upon her would not only calm her, but would also interfere, seriously, with her bowel regularity for some time to come. "Humph!" she snorted. "Have it your way!" She snatched the glass from the bureau, and tossed down the contents in one brave gulp. It burned all the way to her stomach. Beth commenced a new dance. She staggered around the room, dramatically clutching at her throat with one hand, while fanning her open mouth with the other.

When she could speak, she croaked at him. "You are trying to kill your only daughter!"

Jared smiled, and held out his arms. "My sweetest little one, never could I seek to harm the one whom I love more than life."

The whiskey had not time to do its work, but the realization of her father's love did. She sank into his arms. The major picked her up and placed her upon the bed. The servant had returned with the bottle of paregoric, and a spoon. He waved the frightened woman away. "Never mind the medicine, Bessie. Please tuck her into bed and watch over her until morning. We will board the first train to Richmond tomorrow. Bessie, you will go with us. Miss Bethany will need your help."

His daughter clung to him as he kissed her on her damp forehead, salty with perspiration. The major then retired to his study, where he poured, this time for himself, another generous shot of the delicious bourbon. Glass in hand, he wandered to the spacious porch of his home and stood looking between the white columns at the beauty of Charleston Bay. "What sadness is this war!" His voice was hushed as he whispered to his God whom he hoped was standing next to him, looking with him at the lovely water and sky. Fort Sumter, its walls dark and barely visible in the twilight, seemed to be brooding and forlorn as it sat alone in the bay. It seemed to be waiting in dread for the next cannonball to fall.

CHAPTER FIFTEEN

Skinny Dippin'

It was late September in Michigan. The days were warm and sunny, but comfortably so, as though the countryside was loath to forget the sweltering August that had just slipped away. The dry, browning grasses voiced small crunching protests when they were trod upon. Overhead, the giant Canada geese squawked to each other as they restlessly practiced their V formations in preparation for their annual journey south. Depending upon their mood, the maples showed scattered splotches of either bright crimson or of burnt orange among the still-prevailing green of the forest, while the cottonwoods echoed the maples' signals of coming winter by decorating their own branches with yellow-gold. Even the poison ivy showed rare good humor by turning its leaves to a dark shade of red, warning passing humans to avoid falling prey to their noxious touch. The war seemed far away....except to those families who wept as they mourned the loss of their young men who had so recently, cheerfully, gone away to serve their country, but who would never return. The tansy, uncaring, glowed with its happy yellow blooms along the roadsides and in the gardens, joyfully spreading its fragrance.

Dick Trick and Hannah Midgley were secretly betrothed. They were deeply and irretrievably in love. However, the uncertainty of war, their hopeless financial condition, the loss of Bethany, the absence of Matthew, and their youth (she was a glowingly beautiful fifteen, he an increasingly handsome, if mildly crippled sixteen-year-old) caused them to delay the announcement of their intentions. They clung to the notion that Bethany could still be alive and that Matthew would return at the end of the war. God willing, Matthew and Bethany were to be the first to learn of their joy. God willing.

The Reverend and Mrs. Lanning took their young friends under protective wings, entertaining them often on their porch, in their parlor, and at their table. The Lannings, in their wisdom, were not fooled in the least by the pretense that their relationship was only casual. They secretly gave their unspoken blessing to the obviously enamored children. The witnessing of the beauty of young love helped the Lannings to remember their own youth....those days, long ago, when their love had first flowered and bloomed. "There is the stuff of a sermon here!" His fertile mind was already composing a message about Christian love for his congregation.

"Hush, my pastor dear!" his wife chuckled as she snuggled her ample self into his arms. "Don't you ever stop working?"

"Probably not. The Lord has told me...."

"I know, dearest." She pressed her fingers to his lips to interrupt his familiar answer. She took him by the hand. "Come with me to the bedroom. I will give you some more 'stuff' for your sermon!" They giggled as they pushed and pulled each other up the staircase. Next Sunday's sermon would be a beauty.

+ + +

On one particularly fine early autumn morning, Dick finished his chores early and hurried to the Midgleys' little home on Franklin Road. He and Hannah had planned, in advance, a special day. When he arrived, Hannah was already industriously packing a picnic basket under the watchful and tenatively disapproving eye of Hannah's sister-in-law. Mrs. Midgley suppressed a laugh as a loaf of fresh-baked bread, a wedge of homemade cheese, slices of beef, apples, and a large container of newly-pressed cider were tossed into the groaning wicker container. "What army you fixin' to feed? Union or Confederate?"

Hannah dismissed her remark with a wave of her hand. "Just us, dear sister. We plan to celebrate this here pretty day with a private little picnic. Just Dick and me."

"And, where would you be goin' for this lovely event?"

"Down by the river."

"I see." Mrs. Midgley stood with arms akimbo. "And....you will be chaperoned, of course?"

Dick blushed. "Hadn't planned on that, ma'am." He shot a sideways look at Hannah as if for reinforcement. She flashed a smile of encouragement back to him. "But we surely promise to behave!"

"And....I'm supposed to believe that?"

"Yes, ma'am. Wish you would!" Dick did his very best to look sincere and virtuous.

Mrs. Midgley smiled to herself as she helped them cover the basket with a clean, white towel.

Well, I guess I'll trust you. You ain't let me down yet....far as I know, anyhow. Now, mind you, don't stay too long. My Tom is almost finished diggin' a well for Mr. VanEvery and should be home soon. I'll send him to find you if you are not back in a couple hours."

Hannah kissed her on the cheek. "Thank you, sister. We won't be long." They hurried up the trail to the Greyson farm where they snitched an old quilt to spread on the ground as a blockade to the ants which would invariably desire to share their woodsy banquet. They had not dared to ask Mrs. Midgley for such a cloth, fearing that she might take it as a sign that their picnic plans might include something more pleasurable than simply dining by the riverside. In fact, that was just what the youngsters intended to do....eat lunch, enjoy each other's company, soak up the warmth of the beautiful afternoon, and perhaps, just perhaps, steal an innocent kiss or two. When they had vowed their love for each other, they had discussed such matters and concluded that they would retain their innocence in honored Victorian fashion until the time was right when they could marry. They sincerely believed in the teachings of their elders, and of their church. Their thoughts were remarkably mature considering that they both were growing up without the benefit of parental guidance. They scampered down the steep slope and spread their anti-ant quilt just at the edge of the stream, a little ways upstream from where it widened into the upper mill pond. The surrounding high banks sheltered them from the rest of the world. A buck and two does were at first startled by their approach, but moved only a short distance to watch, curiously, the strange human behavior. Their noses twitched as the breeze carried the foreign odors of bread and cheese to their sensitive nostrils.

Dick, between bites of bread and quaffs of cider, decided to bring up a subject that was of extreme importance to him. He reached for her hand. "What would you think if I was to jine up with the army and go to fightin' with Matt and the rest?"

Hannah's blue eyes moistened as she looked into his. "I knowed you want to do that. You men must do what you think you have to do. But...." she sighed, "ain't you still too young to be a soldier?"

"There was no hesitation in Dick's answer. "Nope. There's others younger'n me are gone to war already."

The fresh bread upon which Hannah was nibbling suddenly tasted dry and unappetizing. She tossed it into the stream where the minnows had the good fortune of an unexpected feast. "What about the farm? What about me?"

He squeezed her hand. "I just want to go an' do my part, same's Matt an' Will. Matthew will surely understand, 'specially if I 'range for somebody to take care of the place." He gave her a playful peck on the end of her nose. "An', as for you, I hope an' pray that you'd wait for me."

"'Course I would. I'd wait for you forever." Renegade tears streamed down her face. Dick gently dabbed them away with a napkin from the picnic basket. For a long moment they looked, unwavering, into each other's eyes. Their pledge of love, tearful at the thought of parting yet optimistic for the future, unique in themselves yet shared throughout history by millions of other young wartime couples.... was warmer, was brighter than the autumn sun that filtered through the colorful leaves and dappled the freckles on their suntanned faces.

"Do you think they will take me? I mean with my bad arm an' such?" He tried to not look self-conscious but his hand involuntarily rubbed his mildly disfigured arm.

Hannah smiled through her tears. "'Course they will. Nothin' much wrong with you. You can do the work of two men, bad arm or no."

"You really think so?" Dick sprang to his feet and began to posture himself in mock heroic poses for her entertainment. "Not bad, huh?"

"Not bad at all, Dick." She clapped her hands in applause for his clowning.

Thus encouraged, Dick enhanced his posturing with the addition of a little fancy footwork. He became so enamored with his own performance that he forgot his proximity to the river. His dancing foot slipped on the muddy edge and he fell, with a howl, spread-eagled into the water. Hannah, instantly forgetting her sorrow, shrieked and laughed in delight at the ridiculous scene. She leaped to her feet, and without hesitation, launched herself into the water after him. They wrestled, hugged, and splashed in the cool water....tasting each other's kisses in a new and exciting, if very wet, way.

Hannah finally brought the frolic to a dripping halt. She stood in the shallows and surveyed her soaked dress, so recently starched and perky, now hanging limp from her shoulders. "Oh-oh!"

"Oh-oh what?" Dick was sitting submerged with only his head sticking out of the water.

She pushed her hair from her eyes, flashed a mischievous grin, then jumped on him with a mighty splash. He did not resist when Hannah ducked his head under the water. She pulled him up again, and giggled at his sputtering and blowing. "My sister ain't goin' to like this at all. When she sees these wet clothes she'll think we've been bein' bad!"

"Then, don't tell her." Dick put his mouth under the surface and blew some bubbles.

"I 'spose you think she won't notice?"

"Not if we dry out 'fore we go home."

"Now, how do you propose to do that? Oh!" She covered her mouth at the dark thought. "If you think I'm goin' to flounce around naked in these woods while our clothes dry you got another think comin'!"

Dick chuckled. "Guess that would be a lot to ask!" He sidled up to her with the air of a master conspirator. "Here's what we do. We hang our outer clothes on them bushes where the sun is hittin' and they'll dry in no time." As he spoke he stood and was peeling off his sodden shirt.

"But...."

"Now, listen to the rest of the plan 'fore you squawk. Then we can take off our under drawers, put on the dry clothes, and hustle up to the house."

"But...."

"But what?" He unbuttoned the back of her dress and helped her to shimmy out of it.

"Oh....oh....but nothin', I guess." She took his face in her hands, kissed him, then ran her hands over his bare chest. "You got to promise you won't look when I get to the takin'-off-the-underwear part of this plan."

Dick extended his lower lip in a mock pout. He could see the dark circles of her nipples through her wet chemise anyway. "If you insist. But I was really lookin' forward to that part!"

Hannah giggled demurely. "Bet you were!" Her giggles turned to peals of laughter when he dramatically dropped his pants exposing a baggy pair of summer drawers that covered him from waist to knee.

Once the clothing was draped on the sunlit bushes that were conveniently only a few yards away, they returned to dangle their feet into the river while they rinsed the sand and gravel out of their shoes. Hannah pulled her petticoat well up above her knees so that it would not touch the water as they sat on the edge. Actually, it really didn't matter as the garment could not get much wetter than it already was. "I'd guess the plan is to hang our underclothes on the line up at the house?"

"That would be the plan."

"An', just how will you explain such a sight should a neighbor stop by to visit....or worse yet, what if Mr. and Mrs. Lanning should happen by?"

Dick shook his head. "Guess I just can't think of what I'd say, this moment. Reckon we'll just have to kill that chicken if it comes to roost!"

Little did the lovers know that there was a counter-conspiracy afoot. The river flowed on to the east from where they sat, negotiated several oxbows and bends between the tall banks, then opened into the VanEvery's millpond. Well out of sight, but within hearing, three young fishermen were trying their luck at their favorite fishing spot when they were startled to hear the sounds of laughter, and of loud splashing, emanating from somewhere upstream.

Little Jimmy Barnum, the undisputed leader of the group, immediately suspected that some fun was in the offing. Jimmy wasn't quite so little anymore. He had grown a good half-foot since he had been rescued by Sergeant Will McEwan during the parade a year before. His henchpersons were similarly scruffy sub-teens with a similar bent for mischief. They, as though preprogrammed by common evil purpose, instantly cleared for action by winding their lines on their crooked poles and stashing them in the bushes.

The smallest boy spoke respectfully. "What you reckon's goin' on up there, Jim? Skinny dippin'?"

"Might just be." General Jimmy chewed authoritatively upon a blade of grass. He had the steely eyes of a born leader.

"Think we might see some naked ladies?" The plumpest of the lads was jumping up and down in anticipation. "I never seen one. Least not a grown one. Seen my sister, but she ain't much to look at. Her chest is flat as a fence board."

Jim looked at the fat boy pityingly. "What you expect? Your sister is only seven years old. Won't be no good for a few years yet." Their leader was very wise. "Very well, men. Our course of action is clear. We'll sneak up there an' take a look." He fixed them with an authoritative stare. "But," he continued, "you mus'n't sniggle, or snicker, or stumble or you will queer the deal. Understand?"

The troops nodded respectful assent. Silently, the youthful marauders crept single file through the woods, finally reaching a vantage point where they could peek down on the couple below. "Shucks!" whispered the fat one. "They got clothes on!"

The smallest, quietest boy took a careful look and finally ventured a cautious opinion. "Maybe they'll take 'em off. They're down to their underwear already. Maybe if we wait a while they'll do the....you know.... the thing. I'd sure like to see that. Like to know how it's done."

Jimmy signaled for silence. "Shush, boy. You don't know nothin'. They is goin' to just sit there an' kissy kissy. You can sit here all day and wait for them to take their drawers off, if you want, but I think we can have some real fun. Let's slip down there an' grab their clothes. Then, we can hide and watch 'em walk home in their underwear. Could be a real hoot! Watcha think?" The conspirators took a silent vote. "Sure thing, Jim!" was the whispered chorus.

Hannah was getting chilled in her wet clothes. Dick held her close to warm her. His kisses warmed her even more....made her want even more. He slipped his hand under her petticoat and moved it up the increasing warmth of her thigh. A sudden problem developed, however, destining that he would be unable to complete his exploration. The sound of a snapping twig under the foot of a careless raider made his eyes fly open in mid-kiss. He was amazed to see that their clothes had sprouted little legs and were rapidly scurrying up the steep slope.

When the boys crested the bluff, they were startled to discover a tall rider on a very tall horse blocking their escape. The horseman, who had been ambling his mount along the Fourteen Mile Road, had pulled to a stop to see what manner of little apparitions were nosily approaching his vantage point. The young miscreants were comically draped with various articles of adult clothing, and appeared bent upon skittering across the road. Their giggles and snorts of delight at the success of their well-executed military maneuver changed abruptly to little screams and cries of fear when they perceived the mounted menace. Jimmy Barnum's jaw dropped in surprise when he recognized the identity of the rider. It was none other than the Sergeant Willy who had saved him from certain death under the hoofs of the horses in the parade a year previous. The soldier looked very much the same as he had then. Jim, however, was too frightened to note

255

several rather subtle differences. He wore a similar blue uniform, but now his sleeves were embroidered with the impressive multiple stripes of a sergeant-major. His right sleeve was empty. There was no longer a strong arm to fill it. Instead, the cloth was neatly folded and pinned to his tunic to avoid unsightly flapping.

Melody Chandler had made good her promise to Matthew Greyson. She had devotedly bandaged, washed, and nursed Will until he was strong enough to take part in the prisoner exchange that had returned him to his own people. Melody had cried while she saw to it that he was safely loaded onto the Federal vessel that would take him to one of the crowded military hospitals in Washington. She had come to know his broken body better than his own mother ever did. He seemed to take a part of her with him when he was carried away.

Now, sitting his horse in the middle of Fourteen Mile, McEwan struggled to summon enough air into his lungs to speak with authority, while trying to suppress his laughter at the same time. His lungs had been severely damaged, but continued to improve a little every day.

"Hold on there, you three!" he managed to shout. "Stop where you are or I will be forced to shoot!"

The lads skidded to a halt. They had attempted to split their forces and bypass the obstacle, by detouring fore and aft of the horse, when they were arrested by his menacing words.

The fat one was quaking with fear. "Don't shoot, mister! We is only funnin'!"

"That so?" chuckled Will as he wheeled his horse, leaned down, and with his remaining arm deftly caught Jimmy by the back of the frayed rope that kept his trousers in place, and yanked him easily up and onto the front of his McClellan saddle. Jim found himself sitting in an uncomfortable sidesaddle position in front of the rider. "Now, young man, do you make a habit of wearing a pretty pink dress?"

Jim was pale with fright and blushing at the same time. He thought fast. "No sir! I don't wear no lady's clothes, nohow. No sir! I was just carryin' it to the house, yonder, to hang it on the line for the lady what owns it. Seems she got it wet, somehow."

256

"I see. And who might this lady be?"

See for yourself! They is comin' up the hill now!" Jimmy pointed a shaking finger, then tried to hitch himself off of the saddle. His voice turned to a pleading tone. "Please let me go! Them folks ain't goin' to take too kindly to us, should they catch us."

Will contained his mirth and continued to speak sternly. "Well, well, do tell! Tell you what. You leave this dress with me and tell your friends to hand the rest of them clothes up here. That done, you're free to go." Jimmy slipped to the ground, issued the necessary orders, and the three of them vanished in an instant. Will sat with the garments draped across his horse's neck. He nearly fell from the saddle in a convulsion of laughter when he saw Dick appear in his summer drawers, immediately followed by a straggly-looking Hannah, clad only in her feminine undergarments. She, upon seeing Will, immediately hid behind Dick and refused to look at the howling trooper.

Dick's jaw was slack with surprise and his ears were very red with embarrassment. "Uh, that you, Sergeant Willy? I see you're back. How nice!"

The sergeant laughed until his stomach ached. "Looks like I'm back just in time, too. Just in time to save you two from goin' home mostly naked."

Dick was shifting from one foot to the other, not knowing what to do next. Hannah stepped from behind him and wordlessly held out her hand for her dress. She no longer looked embarrassed. Her eyes were no longer just blue. They were, instead, fountains of blue fire flaming at him. Will could see that the fun was over. He cleared his throat and tipped his cap. "Um, reckon we could go on up to Matt's house? My horse and me could use a cool drink of water." As he handed down the dress, he tried to pretend that he did not notice her lovely body. It was only scantily clad with her still wet undergarments, leaving little to the imagination. Their strange procession then made its way the short distance along the road and up to the house. Will led the way, still astride his horse and carrying Dicks clothing. Hannah followed, clutching her dress to her bosom, while Dick, in his drawers and barefooted, padded long at the rear. Dick retrieved his shirt and trousers, then hastened to follow Hannah into the house.

Still not quite believing what he had seen, Will watered his horse, drank from the rusty dipper at the well, and plopped wearily onto a wooden rocker on the porch, comfortably placing his dusty, booted feet upon an adjacent chair. He could surmise, from the sounds and scraps of conversation that escaped through the door to his ears, that Hannah was filching undergarments from Bethany's wardrobe while Dick was stoking the kitchen stove. The iron had to be heated so that Hannah's dress could be restored to some semblance of its former neatness.

Will fought with himself to put aside his disappointment. He had come a long, weary way to visit Hannah. He had dreamed of her, long and often, during the Virginia campaigns when the absence of female companionship had secretly gnawed at him. The visions of her beauty, and the recollection of her veiled promise at their farewell Franklin parade had sustained him. Now, the dreams were gone. Dick had obviously claimed her love. "Fortunes of war!" he sighed. "Well," he thought, "I will just have to find another woman to dance in my dreams!" He would not compete with Dick, his young friend. He found himself thinking wistfully of Melody Chandler. Melody had lovingly cared for him. He began to wish that he had put Hannah out of his mind and stayed in Virginia with the lady who had showed him so much compassion while he had been stupidly blind to her attentions. A dark cloud of disappointment seemed to circle his head and float between his ears. He mentally kicked himself in the pants. "Will McEwan, you are too old to be so stupid!" He stood and stretched, trying to dispel the residual discomfort of his wounds. His mind was racing as if to protect himself from the pain of disappointment. "If you had a brain at all, Will McEwan, you would go back to Middleburg and speak words of love to the lady who saved your sorry ass. Wonder if she'll have me? With my luck, maybe not. Guess I'll just have to go back and find out....if I can find a way to do that. Hmm. Maybe there is a way!" He was so deep in thought that he hardly noticed when Dick creaked open the door and sat nearby on the porch steps.

"Will?"

"What is it, son?" Willy's voice showed no sign of his inner turmoil.

"You reckon you could see your way clear to not mention what happened today?"

Will retrieved his composure and grinned at the discomfited boy. "Not a problem, Dick. We're friends, remember? My lips are sealed. And, I expect those boys ain't likely to dare to talk neither. I scared 'em so bad they may never speak again!"

"Thanks, Will. Glad you're back. Sorry to see you been hurt." Dick could not help but stare at the empty sleeve.

Will shrugged. "I'm lucky to be alive. Have you heard from Matt?"

"Nope. I'm scared somethin' bad has happened to him."

Will moved to sit on the steps next to him, and lit a cigar. "Surely hope he's all right. I hear we took quite a whippin' at Bull Run, but that's all I know. I s'pose you heard that Col. Brodhead was killed?"

Dick stood, walked down the steps, and looked off across the peaceful fields. The sheep were grazing in the distance. "No. Didn't know that. Think Matt got killed too?"

Will went to the saddened boy and put his arm around his shoulders. "Nobody knows, just yet. He 'pears to be missin'. I was hoping you might have heard from him. Guess we'll just have to hope for the best."

Dick nodded, unable to speak. Grown men don't cry.

Will returned to the steps and puffed on his cigar for a moment. "Dick, where's Bethany? It ain't much, but we'll need to tell her what little we know 'bout Matt."

Dick turned to face his soldier friend. His mouth opened, but words would not come. Sadness welled within him, making it impossible to speak without betraying his vulnerability, his sorrow at the loss of his dear friends.

Hannah, who had been keeping track of the conversation from within the house, swept onto the porch and seated herself on a vacant rocker. Her femininity was restored. Her pink dress was perky and ironed, her golden curls springy and neat. "Bethany is gone, Will." Her words were quietly sad.

Will turned to face her, his cigar, forgotten, dangling from his fingers. "Gone where, missy?"

"Gone away, Will....or maybe even dead. We fear the Pinkertons got her."

The sergeant's cigar fell from his fingers. "What? No! Pinkertons? What Pinkertons?"

Dick gained control of his emotions and found himself able to speak. "Three detectives tore up the house and either killed her or scared her away. They said she was a Confederate spy, but nobody else thought so. Them nasty gents are now in jail. Nobody knows what happened to our Bethy....whether she really was a spy and skedaddled, or if they done her in. We hear even Mr. Pinkerton didn't take kindly to his men's' efforts. He fired 'em, and refused to take responsibility for their actions. They're still, far as we know, in military prison. They say they don't know anythin' about Bethany's disappearance."

Will sank to the steps in bewilderment. He lifted his kepi and scratched his head. "I swear I never heard of such a thing. You got any whiskey? I believe I need a serious drink."

"Sorry, Will. Haven't got a drop. Oh, dear!" Hannah spotted a familiar figure walking up the trail from town. "Oh-oh. Its Tom Midgley, my dear brother, come to fetch me." She expected him to be angry at her tardiness in returning home, but he said not a word in that regard. After they exchanged greetings, Tom turned to Dick and produced a letter from his shirt pocket.

"This came for you today, Dick. Postmaster Coder thought it might be important, an' as you didn't stop by the post office today, he asked me to deliver it."

It was addressed in a neat hand. The return address was simply "Surgeon North, Washington." It contained the sadness of the dying Colonel Brodhead's letter. They clustered around him on the steps while Dick laboriously began to read the letter aloud. "Oh, God!" He covered his face with his hands. "Saber is dead, an' so is Matt too!"

Will finished reading for him. "Well! It 'pears we have paid a bitter price, but it seems you have yourself a farm, Dick."

"No! No! Just can't be! Don't want no farm. Want my friends back!" Hannah pulled the sobbing boy to her and sheltered him. She instinctively kissed at his tears, snuggled his head to her neck, and whispered words of strength and love into his ear.

Tom Midgley did not quite know what to do. The depth of the relationship between his little sister and Dick was suddenly apparent, even to a simple digger of wells. He cleared his throat, then stood to leave. "Hannah, supper will be ready soon. You're all invited to eat with us. I'll go tell the wife to set two extra places."

Hannah managed a brave smile. "Thank you, Tom. We'll all be along, right soon."

Will patted Dick's knee. "Come up for breath, boy, quit your blubberin' an' listen to me."

The "blubbering boy" admonishment caused Dick to regain control. He smiled weakly. "Yes sir, Will. I'm stopped....blubberin' I mean. Sorry."

"You needn't be sorry. Any brave man would be touched by such news. Now listen to me. Seein' as Matt is listed as missing, that means that he is probably wounded and is a prisoner someplace. Might just still be alive, and I aim to try and find out. In the mornin' I'm to head back to duty. They're sending me to General John Buford's cavalry. I'm to be assigned to his headquarters staff to help with training seein' as I ain't no good for fightin' anymore." Will hung his head for a moment. It pained him to no longer be physically whole, to be something less than a man.

Hannah and Dick were gazing at him with sympathy and understanding. Dick looked into his eyes with such earnestness that Will had to look away. "They's mighty lucky to get you back, Will. Even with two arms, I ain't half the man you are! Wish I could go with you. I'm thinkin' of goin' to soldierin' anyway."

McEwan chuckled, a little embarrassed, but pleased at the compliment. "Don't be too hasty, son. You got a farm an' a fine lady to look after right here."

It was Hannah's turn to blush a little. She sat as close to Dick as she could and held firmly to his arm. "We'll figger somethin', won't we, Dick?"

"We'll do just that, Hannah. We'll figger somethin' out together. Now, somethin' I don't understand. Will, how ever will you find Matt if he's in enemy hands? Seems impossible to me."

McEwan had come up with a plan that, with a little luck, could bring him both romance and information at the same time. "Well, now, I got an ace in the hole....a pretty lady in Middleberg, Virginia, who will be sure to help me if'n I can get back to her. An', I should be able to do that pretty easy if things don't change much from the way they are now. Far as I know, Buford still has what's left of the First Michigan in his command. That means I'll have some old friends to help me be at the right place at the right time. 'Least I will if there is any of 'em left after the big fight they just had over by Sharpsburg, Maryland."

Dick, the aspiring soldier-to-be, always followed with great interest the events of the war as best he could piece them together. "Heard about that battle just this mornin' when I was down by Congleton's. Folks was sayin' they heard General Lee and his secesh got chased back into Virginia, an' maybe for good!"

Will nodded. "Heard that too. If that's true, that means Buford will be goin' down into Virginia after 'em. And I intend to be ridin' along, arm or no arm! Middleberg ain't too far from where I 'spect they should be. Might just finagle a chance to pay a nice visit to my lady friend. She's the one nursed me back from the dead."

Dick stared at his friend. He was at once hopeful, and skeptical. He wanted to believe that he could count on Sergeant Willy's judgement, but he was having difficulty in understanding the plan. "She must be a fine lady, and all, to take such good care of you, but how can she help? How could she know about Matt? She even know who he is?"

Will threw back his head, laughing heartily, then leaned to Dick and Hannah to speak in a confidential tone. "She not only knows him....she is sweet on him too!" Will beamed at the pair as he savored, in advance, the expected reaction. He was not disappointed.

Hannah jumped to her feet. Will was again delighted to see that lovely ice-blue fire in her eyes. "That can't be, Will! Matt belongs to Bethany!" Hannah stamped her foot loudly upon the wooden stair.

Will tried to look fatherly. "Now, now, little one! That don't mean Matt felt the same."

Hannah frowned, then plopped her fanny back onto the step. She thought a moment, sensing a juicy story. "Tell me more, Will!"

"There's no more to tell!" he teased.

The fire was returning. "Tell me more!" she demanded.

Will left her dangling, disappointed. "There is no more. They met and she liked him. I do believe that if he is in Confederate hands she will find out about him, given the chance."

Dick, who was sitting openmouthed during the exchange, still struggled to understand. "How?"

McEwan resumed his air of confidentiality. "She has some good friends down there. Met one of them who seemed like he knew 'most everything. He's a young cavalryman named John Mosby. Fiery kind of gent. Scary almost. If she asks him to try to find out 'bout Matt, and if Matt is in reb hands, I believe Mosby will pass the word and track him down....'less he's dead and buried on a battlefield, somewhere."

Dick and Hannah shook their heads and clung to each other, there on the porch step, trying to digest all that new and strange information. Dick finally shrugged. "Write us an' let us know soon as you find out anything?"

"Sure will, Dick. I'll let you know right away....good news, or bad." Will stood and took a deep breath to alleviate the discomfort in his chest. "Now, what you say we go down an' sample some of that good Midgley food? I could use a good meal 'fore I go back to hardtack and maggoty beef."

CHAPTER SIXTEEN

Chimborazo

When Bethany, Major Dodge, and Bessie arrived at the Charleston railroad station, the early morning light revealed a study in gray. The gray-painted cars of the North Eastern Rail Road were stuffed to capacity with gray-clad soldiers returning from furlough to duty, and with fresh-faced, very young new recruits in their handsome gray uniforms eager to join in the fight. Gray clouds, gray mist, gray thoughts of what Bethany would find when she, at last, found Matthew. She dreaded the thought of what fearful wounds he might have sustained. Missing arms? Missing legs? Missing whatevers? Hopefully, he would still be alive when she reached him. She was resolved, no matter how severe his wounds, that she would gather him up and, utilizing her father's influence, would gain permission from President Davis to take him home to Charleston so that she might nurse him back to health. She sat and stared blankly out of the dirty windows of the train. Her body and her soul were suspended in time. She refused food or water, and flashed only a scared little smile when her father spoke to her. It took a day, a night, and the good part of another day before they chuffed into the Confederate capitol.

At long last, Major Dodge and his daughter were ushered into the private, second-floor office of the president of the Confederacy. Jefferson Davis rose, and came immediately from behind his small and busily cluttered desk to greet them with a friendly smile. To Bethany, the smile seemed somewhat forced as though the gaunt and sophisticated man had difficulty in putting aside the awesome responsibilities of his position as the leader of the southern nation. The two old soldiers greeted each other warmly. Bethany curtseyed and the president bowed when they were introduced. "My, my, Jared! I might have known you would have such a lovely daughter! Welcome to our home, Bethany. I'll inform Varina of your arrival. I know she will be in to greet you as just as soon as she hears that you have arrived. She is busy with the children at the moment." His one good eye focused intently and sympathetically upon them as Jared explained their plight. Davis already knew, from General Jackson's letter, that Union Lieutenant Colonel Greyson was a person worthy of special consideration. "Major, your expert attention to the Charleston defenses are well known and much appreciated. Miss Dodge, your efforts at espionage in the north are fortunately less well known, but indeed also are much appreciated. Rest assured that I will see to it that you may retrieve your Matthew Greyson with my full cooperation. Please be our guest here at the White House for as long as you deem necessary. There are rooms on the third floor available for your accommodation. And, of course, meals will be served to you whenever you wish. Do you have servants with you, Jared?"

"Just one, Jeff. A female Negro attendant for my daughter."

"Fine. There are comfortable quarters available for her in the basement, next to the pantry." Davis shook his old friend's hand, then bowed to Bethany. "I trust you will be most comfortable. In the morning when you are ready, I'll send you under escort to the Chimborazo Hospital to claim your colonel. I hope and pray that he is not too severely wounded."

Bethany rose from her chair and again curtseyed elegantly. Her words were sweetly seasoned with her native Carolina drawl. "Thank you, Mr. President. You are most kind. I believe y'all have answered my most fervent prayers."

Davis' careworn face cracked into a shy smile. "Let's hope all of our prayers are answered that easily, Miss Dodge." He started to turn away. Struck by a thought, he turned back to her. "By the way, miss, should you desire to continue to work for the 'Cause', you should know that we are constantly improving the Secret Service. It is directly under my, and Secretary Benjamin's, command. We would appreciate the honor of assigning some very interesting work to you, should you be so disposed."

Bethany smiled prettily, melting his heart. "Again, thank you, Mr. Davis. I am honored by your trust." She was actually being foxily deceitful. She really had no further appetite for espionage. "Once my current problem is solved I will attempt to make myself available."

"Thank you. I look forward to good health for your fiancee, to good luck to both of you....to all of us, actually....and to the possibility that we may work together in the near future. Jared, keep me informed. If at all possible, in spite of these busy times, I hope that you both will be able to join Varina and me for dinner before you return to Charleston. We need to swap some lies about the good old days in Mexico! And, Bethany, I know you will enjoy meeting our children." He chuckled proudly. "Those little rascals are the light of my life!"

"And, I'll bet that you are the light of theirs. They are most likely not rascally at all!" A vision of the quiet little Franklin Village school suddenly skipped across Bethany's mind. She settled back into her chair and absent-mindedly picked at the lacy folds of her hooped skirt. "I too am very fond of children. I'm a schoolmistress by profession."

Jeff Davis was delighted. "How wonderful! Perhaps you can give Varina some pointers as to the care and feeding of the little darlin's. They really are something of a handful at times!"

"I'm certain that Mrs. Davis has the situation well in hand."

He walked to her chair and took her hand into his, smiling mischievously. "Well, some times yes, sometimes no. They can raise quite a rumpus when they've a mind to....like most of the time, I fear!"

Beth flashed her beautiful smile. "My goodness! I surely do look forward to meeting your army of little miscreants."

The president was chuckling now, his cares momentarily forgotten. "I'm certain you'll be quite enchanted with them, as I am." He turned to Jared. "Major, your daughter is a delight!"

Major Dodge beamed proudly from his chair. Bethany was her mother, reincarnated. She had the same dark hair, the same fine features, as did his young wife....now gone for so many lonely years. A moment of comfort swept over him. As he watched Bethany so skillfully handling the president

266

of the Confederacy, he could feel his wife's presence, could feel the touch of her soft hand upon his cheek. He remembered the sweet smell of her when she would lean close to him to improve the arrangement of his hair, or to straighten his collar. Jared sighed to himself as his thoughts drifted back to the present. He thanked the Lord that Bethany had come home to him. He wished with all his heart that she would stay with him for a long while. Dodge's reverie was interrupted when a gray-uniformed officer rapped politely on the frame of the open office door. "'Scuse me, suh, for the interruption, but I have a dispatch, just arrived, from General Lee."

Davis' smile faded as he forcibly switched his mind back to the urgent business of a nation at war. "Come in, lieutenant. Please pardon me, friends, a message from Robert Lee is always of greatest importance." He plopped, heavily, into the chair behind his desk and held out his hand for the letter. Bethany and her father quickly bowed and curtseyed their way out of the room.

The Dodges took their supper, alone, in the large dining room which was situated on the lower level of the house. It was a fine meal of salads, soups, roast pork, and tempting pastries for dessert. The major then enjoyed a post-prandial brandy and cigar on the verandah, his daughter on his arm. Yawning, he soon excused himself and went, exhausted, to his bed. Bethany watched him go, and then hurried to her own chambers. She summoned her maid to accompany her. Once safely behind the closed door, Beth stood her servant in the middle of the room and then circled around her, gazing with the critical eye of a fashion expert. She was on an inspection tour.

Bessie was indignant. "Miss Bethany, what on earth is you doin?"

"Hush a minute, Bessie. Hmmm. You look quite nice."

Bessie rolled her eyes and grinned. "You know it too? My menfolks surely don' think I'm too bad 'tall to look at."

Bethany continued to circle. "Yes! Indeed so, Bess. You need to change your blouse, though. Looks a little soiled around the edges from travel."

"Yes ma'am If'n you say so....but I figgered I was just goin' to bed! Planned to look clean an' starched for tomorrow."

Bethany had a firm edge to her voice. "Not bedtime just yet. Please take off your bonnet."

"Why now, must I do that?"

Bethany undid the ribbon under the attractive black lady's chin and took it off herself. "Now....shake your head. Make your hair stand up nice and frizzy."

Bessie, in wonderment, did as she was told.

"Lovely!" Bethany hugged her. "Bessie, you are pretty as a picture!"

Bess giggled. "Well! Mighty nice to be well thought of." She eyed her mistress suspiciously. "Miss Bethy, what in the name of heaven is you up to? I believe you is up to no good! That's what I believe! You is up to no good, ain't you?"

"And, I believe you're right! I'm up to sending you down to charm the stable boys."

"Go to the stable this time of night? 'Sakes! I'd be horsewhipped, sure, if'n I'd get caught at such a thing! Proper ladies, colored or other, don' do no such a thing." She shook her head. "Why would you want me to go there? Them boys down there'll think I want a roll in the hay!"

Bethany giggled. "Well now, you needn't go quite that far. I just want you to sweet-talk one of those gents into hitching up a buggy and driving us to the hospital. I want to find my man. I want to find him tonight!"

"Now, Miss Bethany...." Bessie looked a bit alarmed. "I just don' think we dare do such a thing. Marse Davis might not like...."

"Never mind 'Marse Davis'. I'll handle him as need be. Besides, the whole house has gone to bed. Won't you help me, Bessie? We've been friends since childhood. I never before asked you to do anything you didn't want to do."

Bessie looked at the floor for a moment, then smiled. "Yes'm. You're right, like usual. You and me's special friends. I'll do as you say if you promise I won't get whipped."

Bethany crossed her heart. "Promise!"

Bess grinned. "You better just be right or I ain't never goin' to sneak you no more sweets from your daddy's pantry!" Bessie scampered down the flights of stairs, primped for a moment in the mirror, then slipped out of the back door, and to the stable. Her footsteps made not a sound. Only the faint whisper of her rustling skirts marked her passage.

In a remarkably short time, a hansom cab, twin lanterns shining yellow, pulled up to the front portico. Bethany swept from the house and engaged the corporal of the guard in pleasant conversation. He was pleased and flushed with pride at the attentions of such a pretty lady. "My maid and I have arranged to take some air on such a lovely night. We won't be long."

The corporal bowed, graciously, but somewhat dubiously. "You shouldn't be out alone, ma'am. May I send a mounted escort with you?"

Bethany, lovely in the dim lamplight, devastated him with a girlish smile. "We won't be long, corporal. Just a short ride to clear the cares of the day. An escort will not be necessary. Besides, my servant, and the driver, will look after me. I hear that the streets of Richmond are quite safe these days thanks to you and the other fine-looking men of the provost guard." With her white-gloved hand, she patted his uniformed chest softly, appreciatively, and in a most genteel and ladylike fashion.

He blushed in the lamplight. "Very well, miss. I'll look forward to your return in, I hope, a very short while." He helped her to mount into the cab, and saw to it that she was safely seated next to her maid. Bessie was smiling, impishly, in the darkness.

The corporal saluted as they pulled away. The cab, once out of sight, made straight for the ridge above town called Chimborazo.

Upon their arrival at the Chimborazo Hospital, Bethany began to realize that she had underestimated the task of finding Matthew. The facility was huge. There in the dimly-lit darkness loomed thirty 100'x30' well-constructed and well-ventilated buildings, each designed to accommodate up to sixty patients. Without guidance, her task seemed impossible. Yet, she was determined to try. Bessie, understanding their mission, had brought a "dark" lantern....a single candle, perforated metal affair with a small door that could be opened to emit a feeble shaft of light which could be directed upon any object of scrutiny. They left the driver, chafing nervously on his perch behind and above the cab, and tiptoed into the nearest building. No one seemed to be watching to challenge their presence.

Unbeknownst to them, they had happened to stumble into the very building where Matthew, along with 59 other patients, were sleeping. It was the ward wherein the "brain damaged" had been collected. The first thing they encountered, upon carefully opening the door, was a chorus of sixty snores emanating from the darkness. The smell of men's' bodies was acute, but not entirely displeasing. They walked quietly along the double row of cots looking for someone who was awake. Finally, one patient stirred. They approached, and opened the door of the lantern to illuminate the prostrate soldier's face. Bethany leaned over his bed and gently whispered to him. She wore a black, hooded cloak to shield her from the night air. Only the dim, fair whiteness of her face was visible to the half-asleep man. Her companion, Bessie, was similarly garbed, but only visible as a shadow. "I am looking for Matthew Greyson. Do you know him?" The young man, a battle-addled and double-amputeed teen-ager from the hills of western North Carolina, opened his eyes in surprise. Death, and rightfully so, had been on his mind when he had closed his eyes, and had tried to sleep. He was maimed. His future was too hopeless to even contemplate. Now, suddenly, there before him in the darkness were two angels of death who were obviously seeking a victim. The young man was instantly frightened out of what was left of his wits. He drew a deep, impulsive, breath and screamed a long, high, loud, and bloodcurdling wail that pierced the darkness of the ward like the passage of an artillery shell. There was instant pandemonium as his startled fellow patients flew off of their cots in panic. Men awoke, hollered, and demanded to know what was wrong. The ladies looked at each other, with alarmed uncertainty, for an instant. Bethany tried to shush the youngster by putting a finger to his lips. This produced an even louder wail as the poor fellow flapped and struggled to get away from her touch. Bessie tugged, frantically, at Bethany's sleeve. "Let's go, Miss Bethy! They's goin' to kill us dead if'n we stay here!" She rolled her eyes in fright. Bethany reluctantly agreed. They lifted their skirts and ran, in fear for their lives, out of the nearest door. They vaulted into the cab and shouted to the driver, in most unladylike terms, to get the hell out of there. He did. His sleepy horse, hooves scrambling on the hard-packed road, slid and plunged as the frightened animal tried to do the bidding of the frantically-applied whip.

The two male nurses who had been assigned the responsibility of night duty were sound asleep in a nearby building. When they heard the chorus of shouts, wails, and curses echoing through their open window they struggled awake, yawned, rolled from their cots, lit their lanterns, and proceeded at a leisurely pace to determine the cause of the disturbance. Such incidents were not uncommon occurrences involving the patients in, as the nurses called it, "the looney ward". It took a full quarter-hour for them to calm the participants and to return them safely to their cots. No one seemed to know what had triggered the noisy situation. Several men, however, pointed to the quaking North Carolinian who was "playing possum" by hiding completely under his blanket. The guilty party refused to uncover his head, or to speak. The nurses, unable to determine the cause of the disturbance, suspected that a shriek-generating nightmare might be involved. In any case, the problem seemed to be resolved. They shrugged, loudly bid everyone goodnight, and returned to their own beds. After all, they were convalescents themselves and needed their rest as much as did anyone.

All was quiet, in the darkness, for a few minutes after the attendants' departure. The North Carolinian, after peeking from under his blanket and determining that there were no specters about, whispered to his friend in the next bed. "Pass the word down to Greyson. The death angels is lookin' fer him, figgerin' to carry him off. If I was him, I'd git outa here 'fore they find him an' snuff out his lights for good!" The warning was whispered from cot to cot until it reached Matthew.

Matt shivered in the darkness. "What you gents reckon I should do?" He whispered the query into the inky dark. "Skedaddle!" came back the word from a dozen pairs of nearby lips.

Greyson had received excellent medical and surgical care, considering the limited expertise available at the time. His eye had been syringed clean and most of the metal fragments had been removed. The eyeball, although sightless, had returned to something of its normal shape and size. He had been provided with a black eye-patch to hide his disfigurement. His right hand, although macerated by the detonation of his Colt, had begun to heal. The bones were intact, but the hand would forever be a weak, deformed shadow of its original God-given form. He had an even more significant and lingering problem, however. The Confederate surgeons had diagnosed him as suffering from "contusion of the brain"....and they were essentially

271

correct. His right frontal lobe had been significantly bruised. Fortunately, no acute intra-cranial hemorrhage had occurred. The condition was gradually resolving, albeit very slowly.

The surgeons had noted other symptoms in their reports. He was depressed, confused, and intermittently suffering a mild dementia. His mind had partially shut down in order to protect himself from thoughts of the traumas that he had experienced. He could no longer deal with the visions of the carnage of battle, or of the loss of his comrades. Realization of the permanence of his injuries, and of the shadowy remembrances of who he was, whom he loved, why he was a captive in a hospital, where he had come from, why he could not go home, and where his home really was.... flitted through his head. Sadly, he could not capture his thoughts for long enough to reach any conclusions. Psychiatrists, many years later....after the Vietnam War....would characterize his condition as "Post Traumatic Syndrome Disorder". Chimborazo surgeons listed him as "mentally deteriorated".

Matthew lay on his cot, fretting in the darkness, and trying to decide what to do about the "death angels". Maybe, he should just lie there and let the dark specters claim him. Urgently, those voices in the blackness around him kept whispering "skedaddle!" Eventually, he was able to form a plan. The plan had no depth....but it was, at least, a plan. He felt his way to a storage room at the end of the ward. He had seen clothing there. The Confederates, faced with uniform and underwear shortages, had learned to launder the soiled clothing of the dead and wounded for use by those who could still use them. His Federal uniform and boots had long since been taken from him and had disappeared. Benevolently, the rebels had already provided him with a butternut-hued cotton shirt, a pair of drawers that were once white, shapeless brown trousers of homespun wool, and a pair of worn-out shoes. Groping in the darkness, Matt selected a shell jacket that fit quite well, give or take a size or two, and that seemed to have only a few holes of significant size. He found a disreputable slouch hat that sat, comfortably, upon his head. Thus splendidly outfitted, he slipped out of the "looney ward" without taking the risk of saying good-bye to the many good friends whom he had made during his stay. The angels of death, he decided, would have to get up before breakfast in order to catch Matthew Greyson.

Matt had noted, during the short walks that he had been allowed to take around the hospital area, that there was an adjacent farm containing a large herd of cattle and goats which were kept by the hospital staff and utilized for the feeding of their patients. Next to the farm was a large pasture containing convalescent horses which were suffering from a wide assortment of injuries, sickness, and lameness. The hope was that at least some of them could be returned to duty. The Confederate army, and the cavalry, were already suffering a shortage of good mounts. Matt found the pasture fence in the darkness and then settled unobtrusively into a fence corner to catch a little sleep, and to await the first graying of dawn.

He slept soundly for a while, then began to dream that someone was gently touching his cheek. Bethany! In his dreams, he remembered her beauty, her tenderness. He remembered how much he loved her, but that he knew not where to find her. She had found him! His eyes flew open in the soft, very early light, and focused, with a start, upon the muzzle of an old gray horse which had discovered him hidden in the fence corner and had come to softly nuzzle his face. Matt instinctively sat very still so as to not startle the animal. He struggled, for a moment, to separate his dream from the disappointing reality of the equine kisses. Matthew finally managed to chuckle to himself as he reached to stroke the whiskery nose. Bethany would not be pleased that he had confused her caresses with those of an old gray horse! Once they were acquainted, Matt stood to examine his new friend. The horse was not much to look at. He was a gelding. According to the wear and angle of his teeth, he was a late teenager....thin and bony, but not frightfully so. There was a bit of a problem in the near stifle. "'Spect he stretched the kneecap ligaments in a fall" thought Matt. He had lost much, but his abilities as an expert horseman were still with him. "Bit of shuckin' and grindin' in that knee, old fella! Well now, seein' as you picked me, I guess we'll just have to stick together."

A saucy rooster crowed in the distance to announce to all who might, or might not, be within earshot that he was definitely the #1 bird in the area. Rubbing the sleep out of his eyes, Matt could see the looming shape of an old barn as it materialized in the improving light about fifteen rods distant. He walked to the structure, with the old horse following him as though on lead. The rest of the horses in the pasture looked, but with disinterest, upon their activity. Matt found an old, abandoned length of rope hanging from a peg in the barn. He fashioned it into a halter, fitted it upon his new and mighty steed, and climbed aboard. It was immediately evident that no bridle or bit was necessary. The gray did his bidding with only the slightest pressure upon the improvised reins. Matt rode to the far side of the pasture, let down a fence rail to allow passage, then carefully replaced it. Colonel Matthew Greyson and his new friend disappeared into the surrounding forest.

When breakfast-time arrived at the White House of the Confederacy, Bethany and Bessie were the picture of innocent womanhood. Their foray of the night before had fortunately gone unnoticed. Bessie helped to serve, and Bethany pretended to enjoy, a leisurely and sociable meal of eggs, bacon, ham, fresh-baked muffins, jam, and grits, with Major Dodge, Varina and Jeff Davis, and their tumultuous offspring. In good time, President Davis sent them off to the Chimborazo Hospital in the company of two splendidly-mounted provost guards. The surgeon in charge, Dr. James McCaw, ushered them into the very ward that had been the subject of their surreptitious visit the night before. To everyone's surprise, except for the inmates, of course, Matthew's cot was rumpled, but empty. None of his fellow patients seemed to know where he had gone or what had happened to him. Bethany stood before the empty bed and burst into sobs of anguish. "But....he must be here!" she cried.

The heavily-bandaged fellow in the next bed tried to be sympathetic. "He ain't here, lady! Don't know where he is, but he ain't here. I even looked under the bed. He ain't there, neither!"

She tugged urgently at the lapels of the doctor's frock coat. "Dr. McCaw, please help me find him!" Her broken heart could endure no more. With a sigh, poor, distraught Bethany slumped to the floor, in a deep faint, before anyone could catch her. They gathered her up, placed her on the leathery carriage seat with her head pillowed on Bessie's lap, and sent her back to the White House. The doctor ordered that she be put to bed until such time as her strength would return.

The mysterious disappearance of Matthew Greyson was never explained. Much to the embarrassment of the Chimborazo staff, no one could ever determine what had happened to him. An extensive search was made of the surrounding area. No trace was found. Everyone ignored the prattling of the youth from the hills of North Carolina who insisted, as he peeked from under his protective blanket, that the angels of death had carried Matthew away.

+ + +

Matthew's mind rattled between confusion, depression, and back to confusion again. His was a soul seemingly lost both in space and in time. There was one fluttering bright light, however, that kept entering his thoughts. Bethany. He knew that somehow he must find her. Her face drifted in and out of his remembrance. She had to be somewhere to the north. Northern Virginia? "Aha! Perhaps Middleburg!

That's where!" He would find her in Middleburg.... wherever the hell that might be. "Yep! Someplace north of here. Gaddap there, horse. That's where we'll go, you an' me. North to Middleburg." He patted the gray withers of the old animal as it shambled along. His fevered mind had confused one love with another. In his battle-scarred consciousness, as she emerged from the shadows of his memory, Melody Chandler became one with his beloved Bethany.

Not wishing to be spotted by anyone who might wish to return him to the custody of the dreaded death angels, whom he had so far successfully evaded, he traveled secretively through the forests and meadows of the Virginia countryside. He kept the spires of the Richmond churches to his left for as long as he could see them. After they were gone from sight he navigated by the position of the sun. Unfortunately, he had no watch, and had to guess at the time of the day....an inconvenience that made his northerly course somewhat approximate. He kept to the woods and fields as best he could, but occasionally had to cross railroad tracks and sidings. He congratulated himself that his passage was, so far, unnoticed. Habitation gradually become more sparse. Exhausted and hungry, he paused to lie in the long, sweet grass under the shelter of a huge cottonwood that spread its arms protectively above him. He smiled as he watched his equine companion munch huge mouthfuls of the browning October grass. "At least you ain't goin' hungry, old feller. Wish I could say the same for me!" The sound of a distant train whistle caught his attention. "Hmm! Trains connect towns, and towns have people, and people have food. Worth a try!" He mounted up and headed west toward the sound. The train seemed to be whistling its way to the north. "Good! Horse, we have tracks to follow. Maybe they'll go clear to Middleburg."

After letting himself through a few fences, crossing numerous farm fields, and struggling across various swales, swampy areas, and ditches, he found himself on a well-worn road that seemed to roughly parallel the north-south railroad. The road happened to be, at that particular moment, empty of travelers. After pausing to get his bearings, he gently pointed his shambling steed northward on the road. The weather was turning cold. He buttoned his jacket, and pulled his frayed slouch hat more firmly upon his head to better ward off the chill.

Matt dozed, nearly falling off a few times, as the obedient horse followed the empty road. He was presently, and somewhat rudely, awakened by the shout of a sentry who blocked his progress. "Halt!" A gray-uniformed soldier stood in the center of the road with his rifle leveled at Matthew's chest. The rebel was chewing a large cud of tobacco, and spat a brown stream of juice, expertly, to the side of the road without taking his eyes off of the traveler. "Now, friend, just who might you be?"

Greyson shook the drowsiness from his head and nearly lost his hat in the process. "Just a soldier tryin' to get home, sir."

"Deserter?"

"No, sir. Wounded."

The sentry was a member of a small detachment that had been ordered to man a crude log redoubt that squatted menacingly next to the trail as token protection for the nearby railroad. He looked Matt over carefully. He noted the Confederate shell jacket, the eye patch, the confused manner, and the twisted right hand. "Whar might you be headed, soldier?"

Matthew smiled affably from atop his mount. "North. To Middleburg."

"Middleburg?"

"Yep."

"Virginny?"

"Yep."

"That's a fur piece from here. 'Way north of Fredericksburg. I ain't so sure you and this here broken-down piece of horseshit can make it that far. You furloughed home to get cured up from your wounds?"

"Yep. Reckon."

"Where'd you get wounded, soldier?"

"In my head and my hand." Matt pointed to his eye patch with his crippled hand.

The sentry shook his head sadly. "No, no. I mean....was you in a battle?"

"Yep. Big one. Someplace by a river."

"There is lots of rivers. How 'bout the fight just happened at Antietam Creek?"

"Nope."

The sentry lifted his kepi and scratched his head. "Bull Run, maybe?"

Matthew's unpatched eye slipped out of focus as he concentrated on his answer. "Yep!" he finally answered "That's it! Bull Run."

"Do tell! Manassas. That there was a big 'un. Whipped them damn Yanks good that time, I hear."

"Yes sir. Yes we did." Matt was not really sure of the truth of the matter, but it all sounded reasonable to him.

The sentry's eyes narrowed, suspiciously. "How come you don't speak like no southerner I ever heared? You speak more like a Yankee. How come?"

Matthew was confused by the question, and struggled to devise a plausible answer. "Don't rightly know. I recollect that I was raised, for a while, in the north. Truth is, I'm a rebel, just like you. Honestly, I don't recollect just who I am. Sorry."

The sentry leaned his bayonet-equipped musket against the log wall of the outpost. He decided to accept the confused traveler's explanation. After all, the man was obviously a wounded southern soldier, in spite of the fact that he spoke in a peculiar, Yankee, manner. "Why don't y'all get down and have some grub? We've got 'nuff to share."

"Much obliged. Believe I will." Matt slid off the horse. "Would you have some grain for my friend, here?" He put his arm over the horse's neck. "He could sure use some good feed before his bones poke through his skin."

The sentry patted Matt on the shoulder. "Sorry, soldier. Grain we ain't got, but there is some nice grass, over yonder, and a fine stream to drink from. It's the Chickahominy. She's runnin' clear and sweet, right now."

The rest of the sentries were awakened by the sounds of the conversation coming from the road. They straggled, yawning, from the shelter of their humble emplacement where they had been taking a late-afternoon snooze. Here, at least, was something to break the monotony. A heavily whiskered fellow, who wore corporal stripes and appeared to be in charge, charitably offered a drink from his canteen. The rebels watered Matthew's horse, and picketed the tired animal in the knee-deep, lush grass. They then persuaded Matt to spend the night with them. They shared their hardtack and salt beef for dinner, and again for breakfast. They apologized that they had no coffee. The cool water from the stream would have to do.

After breakfast, they provided matches for Matt to light his campfires along the way, and such rations as they could spare. Greyson accepted their generosity with grateful thanks. "What railroad might that be?" he asked, as he pointed to the adjacent tracks.

The corporal cut a plug of tobacco and offered it to Matt, who politely declined to take it. The rebel stuffed the plug into his own mouth and savored the flavor for a moment, before answering. "The Richmond, Fredericksburg and Potomac Line. This here, where you're standin', is the Telegraph Road. Follow it to Fredericksburg, then go on north from there." He turned to a private who was loitering nearby. "Sam, what did you do with that old saddle you found on that dead horse up the trail?"

"Its on the fence, yonder." He jerked a thumb in that direction.

"You expect you will be havin' need of it?"

"Guess not! Ain't got no damn' horse, this moment! Don't rightly 'spect to git one, neither. Did kind of hope to sell the saddle, though." He looked unhappy. He began to suspect that his prize was about to depart from him, without due compensation. "Don't 'spose this feller has any money to give for it?"

The corporal looked at Greyson. Matthew pulled his pockets inside-out in wordless answer.

"'Pears not!" The corporal chuckled. "Well then, Sam, perhaps you would consider donatin' it to this fine gentleman who has suffered wounds for our cause?"

The soldier shuffled his feet in the dust and looked, unhappily, off into the distance. "'Spect I could do that, corporal, if I must."

"I thank you. Knew you would feel obliged to help." The soldier, grumping and muttering, retrieved the old saddle, complete with a badly decomposed saddle blanket, and helped Matt to outfit his bony steed. Matthew clambered into the saddle and gave them a snappy salute which was promptly, but not quite so snappily, returned. The Johnny Rebs stood beside their modest fortress and sent Matthew on his way with cheers, and with hearty wishes for good fortune, safety, and success on his journey.

Sitting erect and proud upon his newly-acquired saddle, Matt waved a final farewell with his battered hat as the gelding plodded, slowly but determinedly, away. Having no one else to talk to, Matthew jabbered occasional, disjointed, stream-of-consciousness thoughts to his mount. A one-sided conversation with a horse was better than no conversation at all. He noted, with satisfaction, that when he spoke the horse's ears swiveled backwards in order to catch his every word. "You are a nice animal" he observed. "You listen to what I have to say!" He was lost in thought as he swayed comfortably in the saddle for a mile or so. "Seems like you must have a name. Every horse, worth havin', has a name. I 'member a horse I knew once. Didn't know her name, neither. Turned out it was 'Buttercup'. Can you imagine that? 'Buttercup'! Silly name for a nice beast. Don't you think so?" The ears swiveled, but there was no answer. "What might your name be? Hope it's better than 'Buttercup'. Care to tell me what it is?" Again, there was no answer.

"Well then, seein' as you won't tell me, I guess we'll just have to think one up. He switched his position in the saddle, leaving one foot in a stirrup while the other leg curled comfortably across the pommel. "'Bones' would be good, 'cause you got yours stickin' out all over the place. Whatta' ya say, Bones?" There was no reaction, one way or the other. The animal apparently was less than pleased. "Humph! So you don't like that one. Guess I don't blame you. Kind of points out an embarrassin' defect in your appearance." He thought for a moment as he adjusted his hat to a jaunty angle. "Got it! How 'bout Rebel? You're dressed in gray like all the folks around here....including me! What do you think?" To Matt's delight, the ears swiveled back and forth a few times. The gelding, showing a surprising burst of spirit, broke into a shambling trot. Matt took that to be a sign of equine approval. "Rebel it is!" He leaned forward to hug the gray neck. "You and me will have a good time together, Rebel!"

Horse and rider traveled slowly, but persistently, northward. At Massaponax Church, kindly Christians provided him with provisions, and, thank the Lord, with a bar of soap. He moved on and camped at Massaponax Creek where he built a nice fire, enjoyed his new rations, and indulged in a luxurious bath in the chilling water. He now had a warm blanket, thanks to the generosity of the Massaponax congregation. He curled by the fire to enjoy a good night's rest. Matt was lulled to sleep by the sounds that Rebel made as he chewed the tasty grass that carpeted the banks of the stream. His thoughts mixed, confusingly, with his dreams. Bethany pouted as she stroked his growingly luxuriant whiskers. Ellen, his long-departed love, pressed her beautiful breasts against his freshly scrubbed chest. He listened as his father said to him, jokingly but clearly, and in a voice from the distant past, "son, never trust a critter that eats while you sleep!" Matt, a smile on his bearded face, slept until long after sunup. Rebel was a critter that he, indeed, could trust. He guessed that if his father had met Rebel, he would have trusted him, too.

The new day was warm and sunny. The road was dry and good. An occasional southbound traveler would stare at him, mumble a greeting, and continue on his way. The bees were busy at the roadside gathering nectar from the late fall flowers. The locusts buzzed a concerto for his entertainment. Life was good, all things considered, until a rag-tag group of about twenty horsemen blocked his path. Matt's eyes were wide with alarm as he looked them over. Some were dressed in pieces of Confederate uniforms, some were not. They were Confederate irregulars who considered themselves to be soldiers, but who were in actuality nothing more than bandits using the excuse of the war to prey upon the countryside. He turned off of the road to get out of their way, hoping the they would leave him alone. They would not. They spread out to intercept him. One burly fellow grabbed the shoulder of Matthew's jacket and wrenched him from his horse. He had neither the spirit nor the strength to offer any resistance. He landed, with a grunt, upon his back in the dust. The burly one slid from his saddle and placed the sole of his boot on Matt's throat hard enough to make him gasp for breath. The bandit, not content that his victim seemed totally helpless, pressed the muzzle of his revolver against Matthew's nose. "You look like a deserter to me! Reckon we should just put you out of your misery right now!" The horsemen all laughed as a look of horror spread across their victim's face as he struggled to breathe. The burly one spat a stream of tobacco juice into Matt's open, gasping mouth. Matt sputtered in disgust. The mounted men laughed even louder. "Think we might's as well shoot your miserable-lookin' horse, too, while we're at it. He looks useless as you do!" The ruthless bandit removed the muzzle of his revolver from where he had seemingly tried to screw it into Matt's nose, cocked it, and pointed the piece at Rebel's head.

Desperation, fright, and anger suddenly cleared a portion of the cobwebs that shadowed Greyson's mind. A red curtain of rage swept across him as a fragment of his old courage returned. He had, at once, the strength of a madman. Grabbing the booted foot that pressed against his throat, he lifted and twisted it with all of his might. He could hear the man's' bones crack, and his muscles tear. The burly one screamed as he was hurled to the ground. The revolver went flying, harmlessly, into the roadside weeds. Matt pummeled and kicked the shrieking man mercilessly until one of the riders leaned down and cracked the butt of his shotgun solidly onto the top of Matt's skull. Colonel Greyson fell face down in the bloodied dirt of the Telegraph Road. The ruffians gathered up their blubbering comrade. They left their victim where he lay. Buzzards, smelling the freshly spilled blood, were already circling in happy anticipation of the dinner that had just been delivered. They would wait, squawking and impatient, for Matthew to die.

Several hours later, an elderly farmer and his wife, heading for town with a wagon load of produce for the market, found his bleeding and unconscious body. The man pulled his shotgun from under the wagon seat and cocked both barrels. He stood upon the seat and looked carefully in all directions to determine if they, too, would be attacked. His wife, weeping and ringing her hands, sat shivering on the seat....too frightened to voice her normal fountain of opinions and advise. Satisfied that the perpetrators were gone, the farmer climbed down and poked at Matt with the toe of his boot. Greyson responded with a faint groan.

"Well! Durned if this feller ain't still alive!" He turned the victim over for a closer look. "Not alive by much, though, I reckon!" The farmer's wife, controlling her fright as best she could, clambered down to help. Working together, they heaved the bloody and gurgling mess into the back of their wagon and carried him with them to Fredericksburg. It was Matt's good fortune that there were Samaritans on the Telegraph Road that day.

Rebel faithfully limped along behind the rumbling wagon with his tattered reins trailing in the dust. The old horse was not about to be separated from another master, this one a kind friend, if he could help it. His saddle, being the only thing that the bandits could find of value, was gone.

The humble wagon, brakes squealing while negotiating the steeper parts of the grade, traveled down from Marye's Heights, along Hanover Street, and turned left onto Princess Anne. Explaining the circumstances, they delivered their rescued victim to the soldiers who were encamped in and around the Court House. The Confederates, also believing that the still-unconscious man was a fellow rebel, carefully unloaded him and carried him into a spacious room in the Court House. Much of the Court House had been converted into a temporary hospital to accommodate the small number of sick and wounded soldiers who had been brought to that location for care. Fredericksburg, at that time, had been relatively untouched by the horrors of war.

Matt, still covered with blood from his scalp wound, was bedded on a cot that stood, neat and clean, in wait for just such an emergency. A local physician was summoned. The farmer, noticing the old gray gelding following them, was touched by the extraordinary loyalty exhibited by the horse. He led Rebel to a local livery stable and left a small down-payment for his care. He returned to the wagon, which was still loaded with his farm produce, and still presided over by his unhappy wife. He found, somewhat to his discomfort, that his feminine companion had recovered her composure, her tongue, and her opinions. She chattered incessantly about the discomforts and inconvenience that she had suffered during their eventful trip into town. The farmer clucked to his team, and proceeded along Princess Anne Street to attend to their unfinished business at the market.

"A job well done!" he smiled, almost to himself. His wife did not hear.

+ + +

Bethany had aroused from her faint during the short carriage ride from the Chimborazo Hospital to the White House. She had raised her head from Bessie's lap and loudly demanded that she be immediately returned to the hospital so that she might organize an urgent search for her missing fiancé. Bess forced her to lie back down, stroked her forehead, and reminded her that the doctor had ordered her to bed.

"Nonsense!" shouted Bethany. "Driver, turn this rig around, and right now!"

Bessie looked distressed and frightened. She did not know what to do. The driver settled the matter by ignoring Bethany's demands and continuing on course as ordered by Dr. McCaw. Bessie decided that a little pleading was in order. "Please, Miss Bethany! Please lie still! Do that for me. You said we was friends. Lie still just for me!"

The plea struck home. Dramatically, Bethany made herself go completely limp. "As you say, dear Bessie. Now, stop your whining."

"Yes'm."

They arrived at the executive mansion without further incident or protest. Bess, with the help of a squadron of female house servants, undressed Bethany, garbed her in a nightgown, and hustled her into bed. Unfortunately for the worried housemaids, Beth kept popping back out of the bed, crying for Matthew. As often as they stuffed her into the bed, and covered her, she would fly back out....her bare feet landing on the polished floor with a determined plop. Finally, unable to cope with her misbehaving mistress, Bessie nervously and apologetically approached Mrs. Davis for help. Varina Davis took in the situation at a glance, and sent for Dr. McCaw. Summoned by the first lady of the land, the good doctor grabbed his medical bag and traveled at breakneck speed to the White House.

He tried to reason with Bethany. She was too distraught to listen. Words would not quiet her. "Very well, miss." He opened his bag, and sternly ordered her to lie down. Amazingly, she did as she was told. "Now, young lady, you are going to take a nice dose of laudanum."

Bethany shrieked. "Oh no! Not that! It's poison! It makes me constipated!" She flipped over onto her stomach and beat on the mattress with her fists. "Why? Why does everybody want to give me opium? First my father with his stupid paregoric, and now you!"

The doctor had to smile at the clownish, juvenile behavior. "Miss Dodge, if you will take this, and have a good long and restorative sleep, I promise I will come back tomorrow and tell you all I know about Colonel Greyson and his medical condition."

Beth stopped beating on the mattress, and peeked tearfully at him through her now stringy hair that had fallen in disarray around, and over, her face. "Promise?"

"I promise."

Bethany sat up and bravely opened her mouth to receive the bitter medicine. It burned all the way down to her stomach. "Just like my father's poisonous bourbon!" she gasped.

True to his word, Dr. McCaw returned early he next morning to find Beth propped up on her pillows, her hair washed and combed, the very picture of a well-behaved young lady. She was bravely trying to overcome the narcotic-induced fuzziness in her brain. Bessie had brought her a wonderful breakfast, complete with a small vase of roses on the tray, but she had barely touched the food. She clung to the doctor's every word as he described the eye and hand surgery, the depression, the amnesia, the dementia, and the traumatic etiology of the mental impairment. He sympathetically held her hand and dabbed, with his own starched handkerchief, at her tears. "I have sent people to all the sentry posts on the outskirts of the city. I have had the fields and forests searched by the military. No one has seen him. Frankly, I have no idea how he managed to disappear. It would seem that he could not have gotten very far. Yet, he has vanished. I'm sorry."

Bethany gulped. "Would it be all right if I came to your hospital and talked to his friends? They might have some clue as to where he would go."

"Of course. You will always be welcome."

"Do you think I could go and look for him myself?"

"I'm sure that can be arranged with President Davis. You must be properly escorted, of course."

"Of course. Thank you, doctor. You have been more than kind. I'm sorry to have been such a bother." She held out her hand.

He took it graciously. "I truly understand your fears and frustration. Now, I must go. I have several surgeries to do today. Unfortunately, they are mostly amputations." He sighed, unhappily. "I get to see the sadness of combat in a very personal way. I'll look forward to seeing you again, dear lady. Hopefully, under happier circumstances. I will pray for your Greyson, along with my prayers for all the other sick and disfigured boys under my care."

The good doctor snapped shut his bag, gave her a sad smile, a pat on the hand, and a bow, as he excused himself. He would hurry back to the Chimborazo Hospital to resume his merciful ministry.

Bethany, as she watched the door close behind him, suddenly felt ashamed that she had taken him away from his real patients. Patients who would never be whole again. Patients who were asking only to live a while longer. She turned her face into her pillow and wept. "Too many sorrows! Too many sorrows!" she cried.

After a few days, Major Dodge felt that he must return to his military duties in Charleston. He requested that Bethany accompany him back to their home. She resisted, begging him to let her stay in Richmond so that she might continue her search for Matthew. He finally, and reluctantly, agreed. The Davis family were delighted to have her stay on as their guest. She would assist Varina in the education and care of the children. Mr. Davis, showing characteristic understanding and compassion, assigned a pair of his personal, mounted guards to accompany her whenever she traveled around the area looking for clues as to Matt's whereabouts.

Bethany, by means of reading to, and writing letters for, the inhabitants of the "looney ward" finally began to overcome their suspicion and to gain their confidence....with the notable exception of one patient. The young

North Carolinian continued to duck under his blanket at her approach, and would not speak in her presence. To him, she was the "grim reaper" in female disguise. Undaunted, she learned to change bandages, and to wash stinking, purulent wounds....all the while cooing words of encouragement to the unfortunate soldiers. Dr. McCaw noticed that the recovery rate was increased in the "looney ward". Bethany's beauty, and her caring sweetness, was giving hope to the hopeless. With hope came strength. With strength came recovery.

There were two secrets to the success of the Chimborazo: cleanliness, and loving care. The hospital was well ahead of its time....a time when cleanliness was not generally appreciated. Infections were not really understood. Pus was considered "laudable". Further, in those days, few could understand that compassionate care could help to heal a wound, or to soothe a fevered mind. Dr. Steven McCaw understood these things. Under his direction, the Chimborazo was not just a way point on the way to the graveyard. It was a place where men actually healed, and went back to duty, or to their homes.

The heavily-bandaged fellow, who occupied the cot next to the one that had been Matthew's, took a long time to make up his mind as to whether Bethany was to be trusted. One morning, after she had spent a full hour bathing and rebandaging his battered body and his disfigured face, he decided that she must be a true angel, rather than an angel of death, the contrary opinion of the North Carolinian notwithstanding. He watched her as she worked. She hummed hymns that he recognized....hymns that took him back to the remembrance of his childhood when he had perched on the hard pew, between his praying mother and his stern father, in their little country church. He remembered the joy of those holy tunes as they had whined from the choir, wheezed from the old pump organ, and floated, gloriously, out of the windows of the little church so that God might hear.

He nervously cleared his throat. He didn't talk very much, so he was not sure anything would come out when he spoke. "Miss, if you will excuse me askin', but are you an angel that the Lord has sent?"

Bethany tried to smooth the hair that stuck out of the top of his bandage like broom straw. "Nice thought, soldier, but I'm just here to help you get better."

The part of his face that was still intact smiled....under the bandage. "Thought so! You're a real angel! That stupid tarheel don't know nothin'!"

Beth giggled. The girlish music of her laugh warmed him. "You're name is Micah, isn't it?"

"It is. Micah, the dead man."

"I'm pleased to meet you, Micah. You don't look dead to me. It's always fun when an angel gets to talk to a prophet."

Micah clamped his eyes shut. "Don't understand, miss. You talk too fancy for me."

She stroked his hair some more. "Nothing fancy, Micah. You are named after a Jewish prophet, that's all. Why do you say that you are dying? I won't let you do that."

"You won't? Well, now, that's mighty nice of you, miss, but I'm shot through the gut. Union canister. Even if'n I live, my guts'l never work again. Rather, I wish I'd die now, 'stead of slow and miserable."

She took his hands in hers. "Perhaps you will live, Micah." Silently, together, they prayed.

"Miss Angel?"

"Bethany. Miss Bethany." She could see a smile in the saddened eyes that looked through the holes in the bandages that covered his face.

"Miss Angel, why are you lookin' for my friend, Matthew?"

"Because we are to be married, if I can just find him."

"Oh!" Micah was silent for a moment. "If it helps any, he was always talkin' 'bout goin' north, someplace, to find his woman."

"That woman is me" said Bethany. Her voice was an excited whisper.

The soldier squirmed, happily, until pain stopped his movement. "Waal, I'll be dinged! Good for you. Both of you. Tell you what you do. Go and look for him to the north. That's where you are supposed to be, an' that's where he is headed, I reckon."

287

Micah was delighted when Bethany leaned to kiss his bandaged forehead. Now, she had a little piece of information, a small glimmer of hope. She hurried out of the hospital, found her provost guards, requested a side-saddled mount from the Davis stable, and headed north on the Telegraph Road.

"Halt!" commanded the very same sentry who had previously befriended Matthew. "Howdy, ma'am, gents! Don't believe it would be wise for you to go further north from here."

"And why not?" demanded Bethany.

The sentry spat his signature stream of tobacco juice to the side of the road. "Ma'am, word is the Yanks are crossin' a big army over the Potomac north of Fredericksburg. An' Union cavalry are sneakin' around makin' trouble....not to mention the reb ne'er-do-wells who are raisin' a stink 'most every place. Best for you to turn 'round and go back to where you came from. Anyplace south of here will do."

Bethany fixed the soldier with a haughty stare. "Very well. As you say. Tell me, have you seen a man named Matthew Greyson?"

The sentry lifted his kepi and scratched his head. "Huh? Matthew who?"

"Greyson."

"Nope. Not as I recollect. What does he look like?"

"He has a black patch over one eye."

The sentry brightened. "Oh, yeah! He was through here. Spent the night with us. Nice feller. He was ridin' a sorry lookin', broken-down ol' gray horse."

Bethany lost her haughty composure and squealed with delight. "Did he say where he was going?"

"Yep. Middleburg. Middleburg , Virginny. Told him that old nag of his probably couldn't make it that far."

Beth frowned from atop her horse. "Why would he be going to Middleburg?"

288

"He didn't say, ma'am. He really didn't say much at all. Didn't even tell us his name. Did say he was wounded, though, at Second Manassas. We sent him on to Fredericksburg and tol' him to go on north from there. Doubt he'll make it, anyhow." The soldier worked his mouth to spit again, in order to rustically emphasize his words. This time, he remembered his manners and held his cap in front of his face as he spat....in deference to the sensibilities of the lady.

Miss Dodge turned to address her escort. "Couldn't we go on up to Fredericksburg?"

"No, miss. Sorry. Too far. Too dangerous. We got our orders, Miss Dodge."

Beth considered kicking her horse in the ribs and tearing off up the road. However, she quickly thought better of that plan. The guards would certainly ride her down and drag her, gently but firmly, back to the White House. She wanted to cry out in frustration, but controlled herself. "Are the telegraph lines still open to Fredericksburg?"

One of the guards nodded. "Far as I know. They were workin' this mornin'."

"Good!" Bethany set a furious pace back to the Richmond telegraph office. Upon her arrival at the office, she was informed by the telegrapher that the lines to Fredericksburg had just gone down. This, he said, was a nearly sure sign that Union Cavalry, or at least Union sympathizers, were at work in the area between the two cities. The disappointed young woman retreated, sadly, to the solitude of her room at the executive mansion.

Several days later, at Fredericksburg, the commandant of the small CSA force that was garrisoned in that city stopped by the telegraph office to make certain that the wire to Richmond had been repaired, and was functioning. He had sent a mounted squad to find and to repair the downed line. It was obvious that all was in order. The telegrapher's apparatus was sparking and clicking with incoming messages. "Good! It 'pears that the line to Richmond is workin', this mawnin'."

"It is, indeed, suh. Was nice and quiet 'till your boys fixed it." The telegrapher did not have time to look up from his work as he spoke. "Have one for you, colonel. It's from President Davis hisself." He handed the officer the message with his left hand, while his right continued to record the current incoming message.

The colonel leaned against the office counter. "Well, well! From Davis, hey? Probably wants to tell me I'm promoted to general."

The telegraph operator grinned, still without looking up. "Not this time, suh! Maybe next time!"

The colonel walked to where the golden morning light streamed through the flyspecked window. He read, with some difficulty, the scrawled message:

> 9:17 AM 29 Oct 1862
>
> To: Lt. Col. F. Gaillard cmdr. 2nd S.C. Inf. Fredericksburg
> From: President J. Davis Richmond
>
> Searching for wounded soldier black eye patch riding gray horse. Advise if seen your jurisdiction. Detain if found. Name Matthew Greyson.
>
> J. Davis

The colonel strolled back to the desk to address the telegrapher. "Must be some important feller, this Greyson."

The operator nodded, still not looking up from his scribbled messages. "Yep. Surely must be!"

Colonel Gaillard stepped outside to instruct an orderly, who immediately flew onto his horse and galloped away. All sentry posts around the city were subsequently interrogated. No one had seen anyone who fit the terse description. The orderly, however, neglected to check the hospital for the presence of such a man. Further, to search for a certain gray horse would be ludicrous. The town was crowded with horses of every hue....including gray.

> 11:30 AM 30 Oct 1862
> To: Pres. J. Davis Richmond
> From: Lt. Col. F. Gaillard Fredericksburg

Strong enemy activity Warrenton. Invasion this city possible. Request re-enforcement. Preparing to destroy Rappahannock bridges.

Per your last dispatch: No sighting of Greyson this area. Sorry.

F. Gaillard

President Davis summoned Bethany to his private office and handed her Gaillard's dispatch. He watched, his eyes sad, as she read the message. "I regret, Miss Dodge, that your man seems to be lost to us, once again."

Bethany handed the dispatch back to him, and curtseyed bravely. "Thank you, Mr. Davis, for your kindness. I know you have many much more important matters on your mind."

"Indeed, my dear, I do have many important matters to worry me at this time. General McClellan has moved his forces into Virginia. He possibly intends to attack Fredericksburg and then march down here to pay us an unwelcome visit. However," he gave her a fatherly smile, "nothing is more important than two people in love. I will continue to search for word of your elusive colonel."

Bethany's knees suddenly grew weak. She sank, uninvited, into a brocaded chair. "May I stay with y'all for a while, suh, to help with the children?"

Davis settled onto his own chair behind his desk. "Varina and I will continue to be overjoyed by the delight of having you here. You have done wonders with our little dears, already. Please continue to be our welcome guest for as long as you find it convenient to do so."

Beth, shedding her sadness for a moment, giggled politely. "Your 'little dears' are something of a handful, but I believe that they are starting to like me."

Davis waved a finger to correct her. "They are starting to love you, Miss Dodge. Your expertise with children is remarkable."

Bethany giggled again, this time somewhat modestly. "Thank you! Would you mind if I also spent some more time at the hospital, caring for the soldiers? I would like to learn more about being a nurse. There is so much to be done."

"Certainly! I know Dr. McCaw will continue to be delighted to have your help. He's desperately short-staffed. Please come and go as you please. Our home is your home."

The versatile Miss Dodge was destined to spend several months at her dual employment. She brought delight into the eyes of the Davis children, and comfort to the suffering sick and wounded at the Chimborazo. She was no longer mistaken for an angel of death. She was now, not only to Micah, but to all to whom she gave her loving attention, a bright angel of life.

Within weeks, Micah was discharged....scarred, but whole. He would sit again on that hard pew in that little country church, and sing the hymns of praise to his God. When Bethany closed her eyes in prayer, she could almost hear the little choir, the wheezy organ.

Even while she was busily engaged in her duties, Bethany continued to explore every possible opportunity to find Matthew. The renewed Federal activity around and to the north of Fredericksburg continued to make it impossible for her to travel there. On November 7, 1862, Abraham Lincoln, finally exasperated to the breaking point, removed General George McClellan from command of the Army of the Potomac. The removal of the brilliant and popular but overly cautious and slow McClellan was not a happy occasion for his blue-clad troops. Lincoln, making a grievous error, replaced him with General Ambrose Burnside. Burnside was certainly neither overly cautious, nor slow. Instead, he was inept. He was remarkably unqualified, even in his own estimation, to command an army of that size. Nevertheless, the new commander moved quickly to do just what Jefferson Davis had feared. He prepared to move his army, then concentrated at Warrenton, Virginia, to attack Fredericksburg. His intention was to invade that city and then to march south upon Richmond. Thus, he would end the war....personally, and gloriously.

It did not happen quite as the bewhiskered general had fantasized. That campaign, and the career of Ambrose Burnside, were doomed to inglorious failure. The general's ineptitude was bathed in the blood of the thousands of his troops who were soon to be sacrificed needlessly on the slopes of Marye's Heights at Fredericksburg.

Bethany pondered, over and over, the words of the Telegraph Road sentry. Matthew was headed for Middleburg. Middleburg? Why Middleburg?

Why was the name of that obscure northern Virginia town so familiar to her? Finally, while rocking alone on the porch of the Confederate White House, she remembered Matt's letter to her that he had written so many months before. He had mentioned that he had intended to return a captured horse to a widow in Middleburg! A widow? Oh dear! Perhaps a beautiful, young widow! Had a rural Virginia beauty seduced her lover away from her? She cried hot tears of frustration. She might as well be continents away from Middleburg. The fortunes of war prevented her from rushing north to extract her man from the arms of the imagined rival.

Bessie noticed her mistress, alone on the porch, furiously rocking her chair. She brought a nice, steaming cup of tea to her in the hope that it would settle Bethany's nerves. "Somethin' wrong, missie?"

Beth brought the rocker to a sudden halt. "Yes, Bessie. Very wrong. I fear that Matthew has found another woman."

Bess pursed her lips and shook her head. "Just couldn't be, Miss Bethany. You tol' me how deep you was in love with each other. Can't imagine he would do such a thing."

"I can't neither....I mean either....Bess. I suppose I'm letting my imagination run away with itself."

"Yes, missy. That's what you is doin'."

"Funny, though, his going to Middleburg, of all places."

"Yes'm. If you say so." Bessie thought for a moment. "If'n you don't mind me sayin' it, I believe you should just pray he is safe no matter who's got him, right now. If he's kep' alive you will still have a chance to get him back, one way or 'nother."

Beth stared at her treasured servant for a moment. Her gaze began to soften as the truth of the advice sank in. "You are right, of course, Bessie. I'll pray that he makes it to Middleburg, and I'll pray that the mysterious lady, widow or whatever she is, takes good care of him....at least until I can go there to scratch her eyes out!"

Bess nearly dropped her tray. "Yes, Miss Bethany!" she gasped. She had never heard such words from the lips of her usually gentle mistress. "Whatever you say, Miss Bethany! I 'spect I'd best fetch you another cup of tea. Might even slip just a little of Marse Davis' brandy in it just to settle your nerves!"

"Another good idea! Please do just that!" snapped Bethany. She resumed her rocking, the chair squeaking in protest.

Bessie rolled her eyes, in wonderment, and renewed her grip on the silver tray. "Yes'm!" She hustled off toward the pantry, muttering to herself. "'Sakes alive. Uh-huh. White folks do take a strange turn, now and again. Uh-huh! Might need to just sneak a little of that brandy my own self! Seems I have a nerve or two of my own needs calmin'!" Her voice trailed away as she retreated into the quiet interior of the mansion.

Lost in gloomy thought, Bethany did not even notice her loyal friend's departure.

CHAPTER SEVENTEEN

Penelope

The spire of the Fredericksburg, Virginia, Baptist Church was raised to grace the skyline of that charming city in 1855 under the inspired direction and guidance of Pastor William F. Broaddus. Pastor Broaddus was no ordinary minister. He was assigned, some would say, by Jesus himself to shepherd the local congregation of fervent Baptists who proudly shared a heritage dating back to 1767. He guided and inspired them to build their beautiful church at the corner of Princess Anne and Amelia Streets. During the war, Fredericksburg would change hands seven times. Broaddus, the Baptists, and their church would survive it all.

Pastor Broaddus could well be considered a nineteenth century-style activist. He was disturbed by the social inequalities that others dismissed as perfectly reasonable. The most obvious inequality was, of course, slavery. In his wisdom, he did not confront the issues of racial equality and slavery head-on. Had he done so, he would have certainly lost the confidence of his congregation....and his job. Instead, he encouraged his flock to deed their old Sophia Street Church to a black congregation who promptly established the African Baptist Church. The blacks could worship there in peace, and in their own style, without being subjected to the glares of the white bigots who called themselves Christians while, at the same time, they loudly proclaimed that the "niggers" must not be allowed inside the doors of "white" churches unless, of course, it was to do janitorial work.

The pastor was confronted by a virtual smorgasbord of social problems that required his attention. In a male-dominated world, women were considered to be second-class citizens. Therefore, except for the aristocracy who could afford a "finishing school" in Europe, or elsewhere, young women had little access to advanced education. Given that they had a proper education, Broaddus realized, women would eventually find their way to social equality. He established the Fredericksburg Female Academy in the basement of the new, barely completed church. The girls were taught grammar, spelling, penmanship, Latin, French, music, and anything else that the pastor thought would strengthen their young minds.

When the War Between the States began to swirl around Fredericksburg, Pastor Broaddus took the opportunity to teach a new subject to his young female students....compassion....in the form of nursing care for the unfortunate wounded or ill Confederate soldiers who arrived to occupy the limited hospital facilities within the city. The girls were taught to make their own uniforms. These consisted of white aprons, and white scarves with which to tie back, and to demurely cover, their hair. They learned to change disgusting bandages without retching. They learned how to bathe men's' bodies (just the proper parts, of course) without giggling. They learned how to comfort the unhappy patients by reading to them, and by writing letters for them to their loved ones at home. They were providing the same compassionate care that was proving to be so effective at the Chimborazo Hospital. Matthew Greyson, gurgling and unconscious on his cot, had no idea how fortunate he was to have landed in not just one, but two excellent hospitals, one right after the other.

Penelope Barksdale, a tiny, pensive girl, had been enrolled in the academy by her newly widowed mother. Her father, an officer on the staff of General Barnard Bee, had been killed at First Manassas. He had watched, in horror, as General Bee was sniped off of his horse by a Union sharpshooter. Dismounting quickly, and hurrying to the fallen general's side, he too became the recipient of a Yankee bullet....one of the many that had snapped, whined, and zipped around them on the ridge that overlooked the hell of battle. Penelope had been disturbed and distraught since learning that her father would never again return home. Her young little heart simply could not understand the reality of death. Pastor Broaddus had counseled, and had tried to console, the little girl. His efforts were repaid only with angry shakes of the head, and more tears. In her own way, secretly, she was very brave....yet, she refused to be comforted. The pain, the loss, was just too great. No minister that she knew, except, perhaps, Jesus himself could bring her father back to her. "Oh!" she thought, "If only, just one more time, I could sit on daddy's lap and hug his neck! If only, one more time, I could tell him I love him!" She cried, sometimes with her head on her mother's lap, sometimes alone in the quiet of her room, one more tiny victim of a war that never should have blotched the history of mankind.

Early in the gray of a morning, long before classes were scheduled to begin, the pastor found her sitting alone in the sanctuary. Her little frame was huddled under a shawl. She was staring blankly at the cross on the altar as though she expected it to do something to help her.

The pastor slipped quietly into the pew next to her. He was careful that he did not alarm the sensitive child by presuming to sit too close. He spoke softly. "Good morning, Penelope."

She did not acknowledge his presence, or answer his greeting.

"May I pray with you?"

She glanced at him with hurt, angry eyes. "Of course. But it won't do any good."

"Why do you say that? May I presume to ask what you are praying for?"

She burst into tears. "For my father to come home, of course."

"Penny, look at me."

She turned her tearstained face to his. "What?"

"Your father is not coming home. It's time to go on with your life. God has taken him."

Angrily, she shook her light-brown curls. "God didn't take him. A Yankee bullet did!"

"All the same, God took him to his real home in heaven."

Her voice was muffled as she turned away and buried her face in her arms as she rested them on the back of the pew in front of her. She finally spoke, hesitantly, in a little, quavering voice. "Pastor, do you think he is happy there....in heaven, I mean....away from mother and me?"

"Of course he is happy! He is with his Lord. And, of course, he misses y'all....just as you miss him."

Penelope leaned back against the polished wood of the pew. "Then, why does it hurt me so much?"

"It always hurts to be separated from someone you love. Even if it's just for a while. And, Penny, it is just that. Just for a little while."

"Really? Just for a little while?" She wiped at her tears with the back of her hand and attempted a smile.

Broaddus was inwardly relieved. He was finally making some progress. "Really! I promise. The Lord has promised. Just for a little while."

The little girl had skepticism written on her face. "Well now, pastor, Just how long is a little while?"

"Only a blink in the Lord's time."

"A blink?"

He nodded, wisely. "Just a blink. Penelope, can you imagine being invited to two parties at once? Nice parties that you wanted to attend?"

Penny smiled, forgetting, for a moment, her sorrow. "That has really happened to me."

"Did it, now? And, what did you do?"

"Went to one, and then to the other."

"Did you want to leave the first party?"

She shook her head, now completely engrossed in the conversation. The pastor was reaching her level of understanding. "No, suh."

"Did you want to go to the second party?"

"Yes, suh."

"Of course! And that is just exactly what your father did. The Lord spoke to him, and took him by the hand, and led him to the second, more beautiful, party even though he certainly didn't want to leave the first one."

Penny looked puzzled for a moment. "Oh? Oh! The Lord did do that for daddy, didn't He?"

The pastor slapped his knee in delight. "He surely did just that, Penny. And, we will all laugh together about this, someday. You, and me, and your father, and the Lord."

"Really? We will? We'll laugh?"

"We'll laugh. And, we'll cry with joy. Now, Penelope, your father will want to be proud of you. He will want to know what you did with your beautiful life when, in heaven, the two of you are together again."

Penny stared at the cross that gleamed in golden splendor upon the altar. "I want father to be proud of me. I want him to be proud....very much. I want him to know how much I love him. I want him to know that, and to know that right now!" She stamped her foot for emphasis. "Do you think he does?"

Broaddus had to be honest. He really did not know the answer to her innocent question. Questions of his own flashed through his mind. Could her father know, even now, before judgment day? He squirmed, uncomfortably, on the pew. He closed his eyes, and prayed silently that he would say the right thing. "I just don't know the answer for certain, Penny. There are some things that we are not allowed to know, in this life. But, one thing we do know is the depth of the love Jesus has for us. Knowing that, I have a suspicion He would want your father to know how much you miss him." Pastor Broaddus folded his hands and bowed his head. Penny quickly followed his lead, listening silently, gratefully, as he prayed. "Father in heaven, we pray for the soul of Robert Barksdale who has so recently departed this life and gone to the shelter of your loving care. We know not your plan, but we trust in your love. We pray that, if it be your will, Robert's spirit will always be with his daughter, that he may know of her life, and that she may know the comfort of his presence with her. We thank you for the precious years that they spent together, and for the promise of eternity that their spirits will also share....together. Amen."

Penny's eyes reflected a newly-found peace. "You mean my father could always be with me? Like a guardian angel?"

"Well, something like that."

"Will I be able to see him?"

"Not with your eyes. Only with your soul."

Miss Penelope Barksdale scuttled out of the pew and stood, straight as she could, facing her still-seated counselor. She was suddenly inspired, convinced. "Pastor, I know what my daddy would want me to do. I know what I want to do! I want to be a nurse just like the other girls. I just turned fourteen....well, almost fourteen. I know I can do it!"

The pastor stood to give her a good look. She was slender, but with well-developed bosoms for her age. If it were not for her tiny stature, and rather wispy hair, she could have been mistaken for a year or two older. "Very well! Have your mother help you to make a hospital apron. I will expect you to join the other girls at the hospital after classes tomorrow."

Penelope, with a little shriek of delight, ran down the aisle toward the door. Remembering her manners, she skidded to a halt, turned, and curtseyed. "Thank you Pastor Broaddus."

He waved. "You're welcome, dear." When the door closed behind her, he mopped his moistened brow and then turned to the altar. "Whew! Thank you, sweet Jesus! That was a tough one! She is a sweet child, in need of thee." He knew, given the opportunity to heal others, Penelope would soon heal herself. Half of her was still the little girl on her father's knee. The other half was a young woman who was desperately trying to understand the bittersweet ways of the world.

+ + +

The following day, the other girls had arrived at the Court House hospital some time before Penny could get there. She had run home, picked up the white apron and scarf that her mother had just finished sewing, and then hurried to the hospital. She stood, alone, just inside the hospital door, puffing as she tried to catch her breath. She surveyed the scene before her and almost ran, in fright, back out of the door. It seemed that bloodstained bandages and groaning men were everywhere in the room. Uncertainly, she pressed her fingers to her lips. Pastor Broaddus saw her and hurried to take her hand. "Come, Penelope. I want you to read to this man. Here. Take my Bible and read to him." She dragged her feet as the pastor led her to the side of a soldier who lay, very still, upon his cot.

His hands were folded over the clean, white sheet that covered him. His visible eye was closed. The stubble of a beard covered his face, disguising his handsome features. A soiled bandage was wrapped around his head, and covered the other eye. Sadly, no one knew his identity. Penny gave the pastor a frightened look. "Are you sure that he isn't dead?"

Broaddus gave her a reassuring smile. "He's not dead. Just unconscious."

"Then, either way, how can he possibly hear me read?"

"You never know. Sometimes they can hear, sometimes they can't." He opened the Bible. "Please, Penny, read to him from the Gospel of John." Broaddus walked away to help with the other patients. "Call to me if you need me." She reached, hesitantly, to touch the soldier's hands. For a moment her tiny, white hand rested upon his. He was warm! The pastor, indeed, was right. The motionless form beneath the sheet was, in spite of appearances, still among the living. Breathing a sigh of relief that she was not about to waste her time ministering to a corpse, Penny pulled a chair to the bedside and began to read aloud:

> "For God so loved the world, that he gave his only begotten Son, that whomsoever believeth in Him should not perish, but have everlasting life.
>
> For God sent not his Son into the world to condemn...."

Penelope looked up from her reading and was startled, then delighted, to see that the man's lips had begun to move in synchrony with hers as she read the sacred words. She propped the Bible on the bed so that she could both read and watch her patient at the same time. She paused, for a moment, at the end of Chapter 3. The momentary silence seemed to awaken the man. His hands moved a little as though he was anxious for her to continue. His exposed eyelid fluttered and opened. A brown eye, clouded with pain and confusion, looked into hers. He studied her angelic young face for a moment, and struggled to understand the situation. "What

301

do you know about that?" he thought, fuzzily, to himself. "Now, I am dead, and gone straight to heaven!" A smile played across his parched lips as he beheld the little angel. Penelope reached again to gently touch his hands. He tried to speak, his voice barely a whisper. She had to lean close to hear. He could smell a light fragrance in her hair. "Didn't stop to think that angels might smell like lilacs!" he mused, to himself.

"What are you trying to say, soldier? I can't quite hear you."

He cleared his throat, and tried again, a little louder. "Am I dead?"

Penny shook her curls and smiled at him with her pretty, childlike grin. "You're not even a little bit dead. You've been hurt, and just been sleepin', that's all."

"Then, you're not an angel?"

She smiled a sad smile, and patted his hand. "My daddy used to say I was, but he's the only one ever thought so."

"Well, now there's two of us....Me, and your daddy. Reckon I'm mighty tired, little angel. Guess I'll just go back to sleep for a while."

"Wait!" Penny squeezed his hand. "What's your name? Nobody knows who you are!"

"Matthew. Matthew Greyson. An' that's just about all I know." In an instant, he was asleep. Penelope ran to tell Pastor Broaddus of her good fortune.

The rebel "irregular" had delivered a serious blow to his head. Matthew should have died from the resulting swelling and intra-cranial hemorrhage. Somehow, again he survived and gradually regained his strength. Penelope Barksdale helped him to recover with all of her might. She visited him daily, brought him clean clothes, engaged the town barber to shave him whenever she deemed his face to be too stubbly, and even brought her mother to view her very own patient. Pastor Broaddus watched in amazement. There, before his very eyes, a little girl had become a woman. By healing Matthew, she, herself, was healed from the sorrow of the loss of her father. It was time for Penny to transfer her love away from the dead, and to bestow that precious commodity upon the living. She would never forget, nor cease to love, her father.... but within the interval of one or two

302

beats of her youthful heart, her entire being was focused on Matthew, and upon getting him well. Her mother rolled her eyes at the impetuosity, but did nothing to discourage her, nor to dampen her enthusiasm.

As Matthew grew stronger, he and Penny began to take longer, and longer, daily walks up and down Princess Anne Street. Sometimes, they turned down William Street to the river to stand by the old stone warehouse as they watched the soldiers busily preparing to set fire to the bridge across the Rappahannock. Matt listened sadly, and sympathetically, as Penny told him of the loss of her beloved father. Penny was pensive, quiet, and sometimes questioning as he told her of his quest to find his Bethany. He still believed that she was somewhere to the north, in Middleburg. Penny was secretly disappointed that she had to share him with another woman.

There was a November chill in the air on the day that their pleasant walk was unexpectedly interrupted by the sounds of gun fire, the shouts of combat, and the drumming of running feet and hooves. They soon learned that a brash detachment of Federal cavalry was making a raid into the city. Penny's shawled little body was quaking with fear as Matthew pulled her into the nearest doorway, which was that of the old stone warehouse that stood on the corner. His strong arms protected her until the sounds of violence faded away.

Penny had been saving a thought that just had to be spoken. Painful as it was for her, now was as good a time as any. She slid her arms around his neck, and held her head tightly against his chest, face turned away, so that he would not see the sorrow in her eyes when she told him what she knew that she had to say. "Matthew?"

"Yes, Penny?" He kissed the soft brown hair on the top of her head.

She pulled away to look at him. "You must go. You must go to find your Bethany before they burn the bridges!"

Matthew pulled her close. "I know." He stroked her hair. "I know that I must go." He gave her a hug that took her breath away. "But, what will you do?"

"Mother says we must leave this dear place. But, oh, I don't want to! We are to stay with friends in North Carolina where we will be safe from the Yankees. She says we must go soon....like day after tomorrow." She broke into quiet sobs, nestling her face into his neck. "I don't want to go. I don't want to be away from you!"

Matt gently turned her face up to his, and tenderly kissed her quivering lips, innocent and sweet in their youth. "We will always be together in our hearts. We are, truly, special friends."

Penny blushed as the new warmth of sweet love rushed through her. "Will you write to me?"

"Of course. But to where?"

"Durham Station, North Carolina. I will bring you the address."

He kissed her again, savoring the innocence of her response....at first hesitant, then loving, then passionate. They savored their embrace for long moments, feeling the delight of their bodies pressed close together. Matt's mind was racing, dividing his thoughts between the sweet girl in his arms and the struggle to remember something that she had said, something that seemed familiar. "Durham Station?" he said, aloud. "I think I know Durham. Yes, of course I do. I lived there for a while, when I was a lad, before my aunt enrolled me in V.M.I."

Again, she drew back to look at him. "Virginia Military Institute? Did you graduate from there?"

"I think so."

"Then, you must have been a officer." She peered cautiously out of the stone doorway to see if any Union soldiers were still lurking about. Seeing none, she turned the sweetness of her lips back to his. "I wish you could remember!" she murmured, between kisses.

"So do I!"

"Do you think it's safe to go back to the Court House now?" She was beginning to feel the delight, new to her, of a male's body responding to her closeness. She whispered into his ear. "On second thought, maybe I just don't care when we can go back. All of the sudden, I like it right here! Sure was nice of the folks that work here to leave the place to us."

Matthew chuckled. "Was nice of 'em. Reckon they run off to see if they could get a shot at the Yankees."

After long moments of passion, something, a small voice from deep within him, told Matthew to free his lips from Penny's. From the depths of his memory came one word, one face. Bethany. He struggled, with himself, to regain control. "I don't hear any more shootin', Penny." He stroked her hair, kissed her eyelids, and the tip of her nose. "Reckon its safe. Appears the Yankees got chased away."

"Too bad!" she smiled. "Let's stay here, anyway."

"Don't you think the proprietor of this place might object, after a while?"

Penelope pouted. "Who cares? Well, s'pose so." They clung to each other as they made their way back to the makeshift hospital.

+ + +

Early the next morning, Penelope arrived at the Court House with her mother in tow. Mrs. Barksdale presented Matthew with more than enough Confederate currency to buy a nice saddle and bridle for Rebel, even though a premium price had to be paid. Good leather was scarce, and therefore very expensive. Matt was amused by the fact that mother and daughter were so nearly identical in appearance. Were it not for the touch of gray in Mrs. Barksdale's hair, they could have been mistaken for sisters. They were of the same diminutive size, and wore the same shy smile. They both had to look up when they talked to Matthew. "Mr. Greyson," smiled Mrs. Barksdale, "I 'spose you know you are very special to my dear Penelope."

Matthew bowed. "Yes ma'am. And she to me." Matthew was concentrating on his gentlemanly good manners when he was startled to see the little woman reach into her calico handbag and produce a small revolver from its depths. "Good heavens!" he thought. His mind was racing. A vision appeared from the depths of his forgotten past. It was the vision of a dark-haired female pointing a loaded squirrel rifle at his chest. "Here's another woman wants to shoot me!" He tried not to show his concern. He did not have to speak. His startled face, and dropped jaw, were enough to tickle Mrs. Barksdale.

She laughed aloud as she held the weapon out to him, holding it properly by the barrel, and handing it to him butt first. "Don't worry, Mr. Greyson. I won't shoot you. Penelope would never forgive me!" She gave her daughter a sideways hug. "We want you to have this here pistol. Penny and I pray that it will serve to keep you safe on your journey through these troubled times. It belonged to my husband. It was in his belt when he was killed, serving the southern cause, at Manassas. 'Sides, I'd much rather you have it than to leave it for the Yankees. I'm sure they will steal everything they can find if they invade this place."

Matthew hefted the little silver-plated, and engraved, revolver. He was touched that they would entrust such a treasure to him. "Why, thank you, kindly, ma'am. I confess I've never seen a piece quite like this." He squinted to read the fine letters engraved on the top of the barrel. "D. Moore. Patented. Sept. 18, 1860. No wonder I've never seen one. It was patented only two years ago."

Mrs. Barksdale pretended to be quite knowledgeable on the subject. "My husband said it is state-of-the-art, and brand new. From New York. Has brass cartridges attached right to the bullet. Here's a box of those silly things that go in it."

He held out his hand for the box. "Thank you again, ma'am." Matt looked, in wonderment, at the small weapon. He found the lever that opened the cylinder and counted the chambers. "Goodness! It holds seven of these little rounds." He clicked it shut. "I'm honored that you would give it to me. With a little luck, I'll be able to return it to you when the war is over."

Mrs. Barksdale touched his arm. "No need to return it. It's yours." She thought for a moment. "Well, on second thought, maybe you should return it. That way we may have opportunity to see you again."

"God willing, Mrs. Barksdale!"

Penelope clung first to her mother's arm, then to Matthew's, during the conversation. The little girl within her caused her feet to dance as she waited impatiently for her opportunity to speak. Her turn finally came. "Matt, I feel like we're sending a part of my father with you to protect you." Thinking of her father, she absent-mindedly ran her fingers over the shiny engraving while the handgun rested on the palm of Matthew's hand.

306

I hope you never have to use this to protect yourself. But, if you must, you must. I....we....want you to be safe."

Matt put one arm around the mother, and one around the daughter. He drew them both close to him, for a moment. "Believe me, I'm going to avoid any kind of fighting for the rest of my life. It hurts too much!" He smiled as he rubbed his bandaged head. "I just can't thank either of you enough. You've been wonderfully kind to me." He sighed as the sadness of parting momentarily threatened to overcome him. "Surely wish that we didn't have to part. Me goin' north, and you goin' south. Doesn't seem right, somehow."

Mrs. Barksdale gasped, and held her fingers to her lips in surprise, as she watched her daughter brazenly stand on her tiptoes, wrap her arms around Matthew's neck, and kiss him fervently, perhaps even passionately, on the lips. Penny pulled him down to her so that she could whisper in his ear. Her words were for Matthew alone and were not intended for her mother to hear. "I love you, Matt!" she whispered, her lips caressing his ear. Penelope did not wait for a reply. Her greatest fear was that he had not come to love her in the way that she loved him. She was afraid to hear his answer....if there was to be an answer. She slipped out of his arms, turned, and ran as fast as she could down Princess Anne Street. Her tears of parting were at one with the tears of sorrow of a nation at war with itself.

+ + +

Day was just breaking the next morning when Matthew said his good-byes to his new friends at the hospital, paid Rebel's livery bill, saddled and bridled the old gray, and rode across the William Street Bridge. He nodded affably to the sentries who were guarding the bridge, and who were still awaiting the orders to set it on fire. He had been thoroughly briefed by his Confederate friends. Union troops under the direction of their new commander, General Ambrose Burnside, were about to move on Fredericksburg from the northwest. Matthew would travel to the northeast, and thus successfully avoid contacting the main body of troops. He planned to turn to the northwest at Dumfries, toward Centreville, then to Aldie, and then straight west to Middleburg.

Greyson knew that he had to be careful to avoid contacting any military personnel....be they blue or gray. He had no papers of identification and could easily get himself shot as either a deserter, or as a spy. He found it convenient to continue to assume the identity of a Confederate soldier who was attempting to rejoin his unit after convalescence from wounds received at the Second Battle of Manassas. The citizens that he encountered, and casually pumped for information, were happy to give him directions and to inform him of any units, of either persuasion, that might be in the area. When an encounter seemed likely, he would turn Rebel off of the road and into the woods where he would hide until the danger was past. He slipped carefully from hamlet, to village, to hamlet, using the Barksdale's Confederate money to buy necessary provisions. He searched out places to overnight where his small cooking fire would not be seen.

On December 11, 1862, General Burnside's Union troops occupied Fredericksburg. On December 13, his 106,000 troops attacked General Stonewall Jackson's 72,000 man command. The carnage was almost beyond belief. Burnside, paying the price exacted by stupidity, lost 12,000 men. Jackson lost 5,300 soldiers, men that the south could ill-afford to lose.

Far to the north, Matthew Greyson rode, alone and unchallenged, onto the deserted streets of Centreville. Centreville was a shattered ghost of a town that was as yet unable to recover from the devastation caused by the mighty armies that had marched, counter marched, retreated, and fought there during the agonizing battle called Second Manassas that had taken place just four months before. Lt. Colonel Greyson had been there, then. His head began to ache as he surveyed the familiar sights that were so long repressed from his memory. He detoured around the debris on the main street....broken wagons, caissons with crushed wheels, barrels, boxes, and all manner of discarded Union military supplies that lay deteriorating in the December sunlight. He paused for a moment to stare at the burned-out buildings, the smashed windows, and the doors that hung drunkenly from rusty hinges and creaked mournfully in the winter wind. A chill pierced all the way to his heart, in spite of the warm and comfortable coat that Penelope had provided for him. He suspected that the coat had been her father's, but she would not disclose its source. He smiled as he thought of her. He missed her. He missed the sweetness of her. The thoughts of Penny momentarily canceled the winter chill, and provided him with a warmth that no coat could provide. For a moment, he toyed with the idea of pointing poor Rebel's muzzle back to the south, to retrace his steps back to Penelope. But then, he realized, that would not work. She and her mother would be gone....gone to the safety of the deeper south.

"Someday, Rebel, my friend, one fine day when this is all over, you and me will go to find her. Maybe, she'll be at Durham Station. But then, maybe she'll be back in Fredericksburg." He patted the gray neck, noting that the gelding was successfully, and in timely fashion, growing his own winter coat. "Just the same, wherever she is, perhaps we'll just go and find her. You an' me."

Rebel swiveled his ears in approval.

Matt turned left onto the deserted Warrenton Turnpike and presently found himself staring at the shattered remains of the stone bridge over Bull Run. The rebels had built a temporary, ramshackle wooden span in place of the former stonework. He dismounted, and led Rebel across the shaky structure. Matt expected his horse to be frightened, and to balk at the perilous crossing. He did not. It seemed that Rebel was completely unconcerned by the uncertain footing. He plodded, trustingly, along behind his master, completely unmindful of the echo of his hoofs upon the planks. Once safely on the other side, Matt gave the horse a grateful pat, and rubbed his gray ears. "Sometimes, I just don't think you are a real horse!" Rebel was, as usual, unimpressed. Matthew clambered onto the saddle. While Rebel limped along the turnpike, Matt sat and stared as the once familiar sights unfolded before him. It was a road paved with sad, fractured, disjointed, and cloudy memories of pain and death. The frightening remembrances began to aggravate his headache. That ache, that banged around the inside of his head, intensified with every step of Rebel's hoofs along the road. It seemed that he was hearing again the roar of the cannon, the tearing sounds of the massed musketry, and the singing, deadly clash of the sabers. He reeled in the saddle. Possibly, he thought, he would feel better if he found a safe spot, somewhere off of the road, where he could lie down for a while until the pain subsided, and the sounds ceased. He turned Rebel off of the turnpike, to the south, intending to dismount and rest until the headache should cease. He soon found that he had made a frightening mistake. Skeletons of men, some attired in scraps of rotting uniforms, still lay where they had fallen. There was a scattering of the shallow graves of the more fortunate soldiers who had been hastily buried, instead of being left to lie, unloved, upon the comfortless ground. Some of the graves were marked only by a musket ramrod stuck into the hallowed soil. There were a few with crude wooden crosses, mostly without inscription. More than a few had the bones of hands and feet sticking grotesquely out of the weedy soil. The stench of rotting flesh still hung in the air in spite of the December cold. The pain in his head grew steadily more unbearable. Greyson slid from his horse, landed on his hands and knees, and vomited into the dry weeds, decorating them as they rattled in the winter wind. He crawled a few feet, checked to make sure that he had no skeletal company in his immediate vicinity, cradled his head in his arms as if to shut out the world, and slept soundly as he lay in the midst of the killing field. Rebel grazed quietly nearby, waiting for his master to arise, and to resume their journey.

Matt slept for only a few minutes. When he awoke, with a start, he found that, thankfully, the headache and nausea had lessened. He sat, for a while, to collect his thoughts and to fight the depression that cried at him from within. He could recall that he had been there when the carnage had occurred. His coat could not protect him from the chill that had returned to the inside of his body. He shivered. Short snippets of memory brought to him flashes of fighting, with a saber, from the back of a great and beautiful horse. He could not remember, however, whom he was fighting....or even why. He grieved that the skeletons that littered the landscape could be those of his friends, or worse yet, skeletons of those whom he himself had killed! He shuddered, and staggered to his feet. He resolved to leave that place of unbearable sorrow as quickly as possible. Taking Rebel's reins, he led the animal in what he thought was the direction of the Warrenton Pike. The now sunless day, however, confused his sense of direction. He wandered aimlessly for an hour without finding the road. In his wanderings, Matt came upon several large, horrifying, heaps of the mixed bones of men, mules, and horses that someone had dragged together with the apparent intention of burning them in order to sanitize the field. The burning had not taken place. Matt mused that the funereal crews probably lacked the large amounts of coal oil that would have been necessary to fire the corpses. Nature was odorously doing their job for them....albeit a lot more slowly.

Greyson pulled his slouch hat, another gift from Penny, low on his head against the winter cold. The gray discomfort of a sleet storm began to beat on him. It covered his hat with its icy dampness. Rebel was soon soaked, and beginning to shiver, as the cold sleet melted and penetrated his meager, still not completely winterized, gray coat. "Damn! Am I stupid!"

exclaimed Matthew to the horse's ears. "We ain't lost, after all! That wind was coming from the west before we left the road. Probably still is." Changing his course to keep the sleet blowing against the left side of his face, he headed north toward the road.

He came upon another funereal heap that stood directly in his intended path. It was even larger than the rest, and was nauseating to behold. As he led Rebel around it, the horse snorted, planted his hoofs, and came to such a sudden stop that he nearly pulled the reins out of Matthew's hand. His ears were pointed ahead at something just out of sight behind the jumbled pile of bones, skulls, and rotting flesh. Greyson moved a few feet to peer around the obstruction. There, startled and snarling at the sudden interruption, was a pack of large, feral dogs which were taking their dinner, compliments of the corpse of what had been a member of a team of draft horses. The unfortunate horse, and the bones of his teammates, still lay in their traces, attached to the splintered hulk of a supply wagon. The wagon appeared to have been blown apart by a direct hit from an artillery shell.

Matt knew that feral dogs were dangerous. They could be as mean as wolves, and were often even more bold. They were sometimes mad with disease. Warfare often left domestic dogs homeless and unfed. As a result, they frequently banded together in packs, reverting to the wild, in order to do as nature dictated....to survive. Matt attempted to back cautiously away. The alpha male, a huge, brutish-looking beast with a scraggly black coat, snarled and advanced toward him. He knew that if he turned his back and tried to run away the dog would surely attack him and pull him to the ground like a frightened, doomed sheep. Man and beast made eye contact as Matt defiantly stared him to a momentary halt. Then, in frightened desperation, Matthew made the mistake of glancing way from the dog's gaze in the hope that he could find something to use as a club with which to defend himself. Instantly, the beast crouched, and with lightning speed, was upon him. The others, howling with excitement, followed their leader. Some circled to attack man and horse from behind.

Horses normally and instinctively run away from danger. Flight is their natural defense. As Matt had suspected, Rebel was not quite a normal horse. Standing his ground, the old gelding reared and struck out at the attackers. Switching tactics as necessary, he used his hind hoofs to send one flying, howling, through the air.

The alpha male sunk his carrion-stained teeth into Matthew's raised left arm, tearing at his flesh. Nearly knocked from his feet, Matt reached for the little revolver that was tucked under his belt, clumsily cocked it with his crippled hand, and fired point blank into the furry chest. The dog, shot through the heart, released his hold and fell, whining, to the ground. Greyson whirled and emptied his revolver at the circling pack. Three more went down. The rest tucked their tails between their legs and ran away. They could sense that the fun was over. They were no longer the hunters. They had become the prey of two unlikely looking creatures who were, nevertheless, very dominant and very dangerous. They were best left to their own devices.

Rebel stood, quivering and snorting, but uninjured. Matt was not so lucky. His left arm was macerated and almost useless. Using his clumsy right hand, he searched in his coat pocket for the box of .32 Rimfire cartridges. Struggling and cursing, he worked the little ramrod to eject the spent cartridges, and to hastily replace them with unfired rounds. In his haste, he did not notice that the cartridge box had been wrapped in a folded scrap of paper which fell, unseen, to the ground when he had pulled the box from his pocket. He looked warily around, peeking around the cursed bone pile for sign of more canine attackers. The only dogs in sight were those lying about him on the ground. Their glazing eyes stared at him in death.. Dark blood ran from their mouths, and from the bullet wounds that he had inflicted. One was still alive. It whined as it tried to escape, dragging its rear legs, the spine severed by a bullet. Matt knelt in front of the pitiful creature. "Sorry, feller." Tears soaked his black eye patch, and ran down his cheeks as he thumbed back the hammer and fired a merciful shot into its head. Even though they had attacked him, and caused him great pain, they were still dogs. Matt always had a soft spot in his heart for canines. When he fired the merciful shot, it was as though he were firing it into his long departed, beloved Tansy's head. He could kill a man with less remorse than he could kill a dog.

He broke into sobs of despair. Death seemed to be following him around. Death surrounded him in the stillness of the bones, and in the decaying flesh. He raised his eye to the dark heavens. The sleet had been replaced by large flakes of driving, wet snow. "Why, Lord?" he cried. "Why must death surround me when I long only for life? Is it me? I can stand no more, Lord. Now I am even more crippled!" He looked at his newly-injured arm as it hemorrhaged and throbbed. "I don't know who I am. I don't know why I am. I would rather die and take my chances on your heavenly forgiveness than suffer more!" He sighed as he cocked the little weapon and raised it to his temple.

Almost as though he understood, which of course he did not, Rebel nickered to him softly, causing Matthew's finger to relax on the trigger. He turned to look at his equine friend that had so valiantly helped him to fight off the dogs....instead of running away like any normal, frightened horse would do. Matt sorrowfully hugged the animal's neck. "Sorry, old friend. I'm going to leave you now. I nearly forgot to take off your tack so you can run free." He stripped the saddle and bridle off and threw them on the ground. He slapped the old horse on the rear. "Go run away, old friend. Be free. Be free of me! I'm nothing but trouble to everything I touch. Run away, Rebel!" Matt slapped him again and then bounced a stone off of him to make him run. Rebel moved a few rods away, and then stood to look at his master. He would not go. "Well, stay then! Watch me die! Then you will go!" Matt knelt in prayer. "Forgive me, if you will, blessed Lord." As he knelt there, cocked revolver to his temple, his gaze fell upon the scrap of paper that had fallen from his pocket. He lowered the gun and unfolded the paper. It was a note from Penny. It was written in the lovely, proper script that she had learned in penmanship class at the Fredericksburg Female Academy.

Dearest Matthew:

It is my prayer that when you find this you are alive, well, and have found your Bethany. I wish you joy, happiness, and many children. Please tell her, for me, that she is lucky to have you, and that she must love you forever. Please also tell her that if she does not want you any more (which I can not imagine) I do!

If, dear Matthew, for some sad reason you cannot find Bethany, please come back to me. I will be waiting, just in case that should happen.

As I told you, mother and I will stay with her friends near Durham Station, North Carolina, until the war is over. Then, we will surely go back to Fredericksburg. Mother's friends have a tobacco farm far out in the country. Write to me, I beg you, care of Captain

Albert C. Roberts. The captain's wife, Cornelia, is a long time, girlhood friend of my mother's. Surely, they will keep us safe until the war is over. I will go to the post office to look for your letter as often as I am allowed.

If you think that I am just a silly little girl, then you are wrong. I love you with all my heart.

Fondly, desperately,

Your Penelope

Matt sat motionless as he read, and reread, the note. Rebel came to nuzzle him, hoping that his master's madness had passed. Thankfully, the madness was indeed gone. Penelope had seen to that. The joy of life, nurtured by the love of a little girl, had returned. He spent a lot of time alternately begging for forgiveness from his Lord and cursing about the nagging pain in his arm. The pain in his head, pale by comparison, did not seem to matter anymore. The little angel, who had brought him back to life at the Fredericksburg hospital, had saved that life by giving him a reliable weapon with which to defend himself. Now, she had saved it again with the loving letter that she had concealed in his coat. The chill in his heart was gone. He sat, unmindful of the wet snow, and was warmed by her love. He had been a fool. He should have taken the child, so recently turned into a woman, more seriously. He had visions of her traipsing repeatedly to the post office to look for a letter that would not be there. He resolved that he must write to her, but was not quite sure what it was that he wanted to say. As he sat there in the snow, he desperately missed Penny's shy, sweet smile, the soft touch of her little hand. Should he write and tell her that he missed her? Then again, maybe he should not. After all, he was betrothed to Bethany, and Bethany still claimed his heart. Even Ellen still laid claim to his love. Sometimes, in a strangely persistent way, Ellen still called to him. He shook his head. This love business was getting to be too complicated. Oh! If only he could find Bethany! She would hold him close until all of his problems went away. Surely, there was no choice. He must hurry on to Middleburg.

He hastily saddled and bridled Rebel. He endured great pain and difficulty while doing so, but pain did not seem to matter quite so much, anymore. The snowstorm was over. It had left a light dusting of white that covered, like a shroud, the evils of man. He was relieved to find the turnpike. Turning west to where the road crossed Young's Branch of the Bull Run, he found that the former wooden bridge had been reduced to a pile of charred splinters. Fortunately, it was a small stream, easily forded on horseback. Rebel stood in the water and had a long drink. Matthew bathed and bandaged his arm, now purple and swelling, with strips torn from the spare shirt that Penny had given him.

The setting sun had broken through the retreating storm clouds and was shining pale red fire directly into his eyes until he reached the deserted, and damaged, stone house that stood on the corner of the Sudley Springs Road. He turned north, and casually surveyed the structure as he passed. He had seen it before when it was in somewhat better shape. He did not know that, just four months before, he had lain near death at that former field hospital. He did not know that it was only by the grace of God, and of General Stonewall Jackson, that he was still alive.

Matt rode on, Rebel shuffling slowly into the night. He did not care to stop until he was well clear of the main battlefield. Just short of the hamlet of Sudley Springs, he found an abandoned barn that still contained enough straw to make a comfortable and dry bed.

Morning brought the realization that Rebel's lameness was worse than ever. The extra strain caused by the combat with the feral dogs had taken its toll. Overnight, the leg had become so stiff and swollen at the stifle that the animal could barely support his own weight, let alone that of a rider. Most horsemen of the day would have considered the poor creature to be completely useless, and would have abandoned him. Not Matthew. He walked, alone, to Sudley Springs where he found a small, cluttered general store that still had a few supplies. He spent the last of his money to buy a jar of camphorated ointment which he used to massage the painful leg.

Matt was frustrated with the realization that Middleburg was only about fifteen miles away. Nevertheless, he camped in the abandoned barn while Rebel rested, warm and dry, under the protection of the still intact roof. The farmhouse had burned to the ground, but there was still a good well and the remains of a kitchen garden that held a few potatoes and turnips. Matthew's arm was swollen, feverish, and draining. He found an old cast iron pot and heated water in it with which to soak out the infection. In three days, they were on the road again. They took the journey in easy stages, stopping frequently to rest. Matt walked. Rebel followed without being led.

Too weary to build a fire, Greyson camped, for the night, between Aldie and Middleburg. He rolled into his blanket upon the cold, hard ground, but sleep would not come to his feverish eyes. He was certain that he was very near to Bethany, and could not wait to see her. Before dawn, man and horse were on the road, limping toward Middleburg. Memories tugged at Matt as the familiar little town came into view. Unnoticed and ignored, man and horse shuffled down the main street and took the road toward Goose Creek. The infection in his arm was spreading into his bloodstream, leaving him weakened and feverish. He decided to see if Rebel could, now, possibly be strong enough hold his weight. Fortunately, Rebel had healed to the point where he was equal to the task so long as he did not have to move very fast. Matt climbed into the saddle, and promptly fell sound asleep. Rebel followed the road without direction from his rider. The old horse could no longer remember where his real home was, or else he would have hurried....a little....to go there. With nothing else to do, and no place of interest to go, he simply followed the road. With a little luck, there might be some sweet and tasty oats at the end of it. Even an old horse's dreams can come true, sometimes. The hoof of his affected leg dragged lightly, at the toe, with each step, raising a little puff of dust as he walked.

Charity Jane "Melody" Chandler was out and about early that day. She had decided that this would be the day to fix the tired picket fence that separated her door yard from the road. Many of the pickets had fallen, and needed to be re-nailed. Without her husband, John, to attend to them, the hapless pickets lay where they fell. She awakened her grumbling daughter to help with the repair. Bundled against the cold, they were hard at work when Mary Sue spotted the approaching horse and rider. "Mamma, who you 'spose that is comin'?"

Melody stared, hammer in hand. "No idea." She snorted. "Never saw such a sad-lookin' horse 'round here, before. Must be a stranger, but I can't imagine what business he should have on this here dead end road."

Mary Sue tugged at her mother's skirt. "Should we run to the house, mamma?"

"No, sweet. That stranger don't look neither fast, nor dangerous. We'll stay right here, at our work, for now." She took another look. "Why, 'sakes alive, that rider is fast asleep! Wonder if he knows where his horse is takin' him?" The gray horse limped slowly past their gate as it faithfully traveled the road. For a measure of safety, Melody closed the gate and leaned on the inside of it. She raised her voice. "'Scuse me, mister. Do you know where you're headed?"

Matthew's chin raised off of his chest. He tipped he brim of his slouch hat to look at her. "Ma'am?"

Melody gasped in surprise. It was Union Lieutenant Colonel Matthew Greyson, looking a little the worse for wear!

Mary Sue jumped up and down with excitement, "Mamma! I think it's the nice man who brought Buttercup back to us!"

"Well now, so it is!" Melody ran through the gate. Her dreams had come true. The handsome Colonel Greyson had come back to her. Mary Sue took hold of Rebel's reins and petted his velvety muzzle.

Matt frowned, and looked around. Yes, indeed this is the right place! He looked down to stare at the woman who smiled, so happily, up at him. "Bethany?"

Melody's welcoming smile faded in confusion. "No, Matthew. I'm Melody." Her eyes grew moist. "Don't you remember me?"

"No, ma'am. I am truly sorry, but I don't. You see, I'm looking for Bethany."

Clouds of sorrow pressed upon Melody, making her knees weak and her mouth dry. She was beginning to understand that something terrible had happened to her handsome, blue-uniformed colonel since she had last seen him. Yet, he had come back to her. Something had brought him back. Mary Sue stood, openmouthed, not understanding the situation. Melody patted Rebel's neck, her other hand on the stirrup. "It would give me great pleasure, suh, if you would get down and come into the house, where it is warm. We could set for a spell, in front of the fire, and we can talk about Bethany, if you like."

Matt nodded, appreciatively, and tipped his hat. "I thank you kindly, ma'am. I surely don't mean to be a pest, but would you happen to have a little grain for my horse, here? He's a little bit peaked."

Mrs. Chandler stepped back, to better cast a critical eye upon Rebel's protruding bones. "I reckon 'peaked' is as a good word as any! We'll find some grain. Mary Sue, lead the colonel's horse into the door yard so's he can get down and come in."

"Yes, momma. She reached to take hold of the tired horse's bridle.

Matt was disappointed, and confused. Bethany was not at the place where he had dreamed that she would be, waiting with open arms to love and to comfort him. "Oh, God!" he cried to himself "Where could she be?" He looked down at the mother, and her young daughter, who were staring at him with kindness in their eyes. They seemed strangely, and vaguely, familiar.

Mary Sue, skinny in her stained linsey-woolsey dress and frayed jacket, tugged at the bridle. "C'mon, horse! What's his name, mister?"

Matthew, trying to hide his disappointment at not finding Bethany, smiled at her. "Name's Rebel, little missy. He's Rebel 'cause he wears a gray coat."

Mary Sue giggled. "Might have guessed. Seems every gray horse 'round here has the same name, nowadays. C'mon, Rebel." She tugged, again, at the bridle. Rebel was not disposed to move.

Matthew leaned forward in the saddle. "And, what might your name be, child?"

Mary Sue stood, with hands on hips, looking insulted. "Why, don't you remember? I'm Mary Sue. And, please don't call me 'child'! I'm near grown, as you can see."

Melody chuckled at the antics of her daughter. At least, she had said "please". Matt took off his hat and bowed, still in the saddle. "Beg your pardon, miss." She appeared to be two or three years younger than Penelope, but already she showed womanly fire. "With your permission, Miss Mary Sue, I reckon I'd rather dismount out here in the road. I believe it is impolite for a gentleman to ride into a lady's door yard." He slid stiffly to the ground.

Mary Sue was indignant. "Humph! Suit yourself. C'mon, Reb. We've got some oats hid in the barn that we've saved just for you." Rebel, with his rider now safely dismounted, went readily with her.

Melody led Matthew toward the house, looking him over as she did so. "Well," she thought, "he ain't in the best of shape, but he 'pears to 'member some things....like his manners, for instance. Seems I taught him somethin' that stuck when he was here last!" She looked at the bandaged arm that Matt had tied up in a crude sling. "Well now, colonel, looks to me like there is some work for me to do. Reckon we'll start with this." She touched his bandaged arm. He winced and drew it away. "What happened to your arm? Get shot?"

"Nope. Dog bit."

"That could be even worse than a bullet! Think the dog had the madness?"

"Don't know. He was a wild one."

Mrs. Chandler settled him onto a homemade rocker and added a log to the cheerful fire in the fireplace. "Reckon we'd best do some prayin' along with our treatin'."

Matt lay his head back in the tall wooden chair. "Been doin' quite a little of that, lately. Prayin', I mean." He smiled at the pretty, raven-haired lady as she ladled water into the black iron pot that hung from the crane, and swung it over the fire to warm. "What would you have me pray for at this time? The soul of that dog that bit me? Might be he doesn't have one."

She looked at him with a smirk. "I'd rather you prayed that he was as healthy as he was mean. Pray he didn't have the madness. If he did, you ain't worth fixin."

Matt sighed and closed his eyes. "Nothin' like a little sweet encouragement to make a feller feel better."

CHAPTER EIGHTEEN

Blossom

Matthew awoke with a start. He had been dreaming that two fierce yellow eyes were peering at him from the deep shadows that surrounded the glow of his campfire. His own eyes flew open, certain that he was about to be devoured by some stealthy denizen of the forest. Instead, the campfire was really the dying embers of the fire that burned in Melody Chandler's fireplace. But, indeed, the fierce yellow eyes were there, and they were staring into his. Greyson groped for his revolver that should have been tucked under his belt. Fortunately, for the owner of the yellow eyes, the weapon was not in its appointed place or surely bloodshed would have taken place. "Yikes!" exclaimed Matthew.

A quilt-covered form in an adjacent chair stirred. "What's wrong, Matthew?" Melody was sleeping nearby so that she could keep watch over her patient throughout the night.

Matt struggled to clear his sleepy brain. "'Scuse me, Mrs. Chandler, but some yaller-eyed critter is starin' at me!"

She reached to pat his hand. "Relax, colonel. That's just Blossom."

"What the hell is Blossom?"

"Mary Sue's calico cat. Mary Sue named her, of course. Do you remember that she named a horse 'Buttercup'?"

Greyson, a little embarrassed, squirmed in his rocking chair. "Reckon maybe I do."

"Well, then, you shouldn't be too surprised that the scary critter starin' at you is named 'Blossom'." Melody pulled her quilt around her to ward off the December chill that had soaked into the house as the fire had burned down to glowing embers. "Blossom is sittin' on that stool, and lookin' at you, 'cause she is tryin' to decide whether you is friend or foe. Perfectly natural thing for a smart thinkin' cat to do. She is our watch cat."

Matt blinked in amazement. "Never did see a watch cat before. I suppose you are going to tell me that she barks when someone is coming."

Melody pulled her quilt up under her nose and giggled. "Well, almost.... but quieter. Best as a cat can do. She twines around your legs, then runs to the window. If you don't pay attention, she does it again. She can hear a horse on the road a half mile away."

"Pshaw!"

"Really! She can."

A little, wheedling, voice came down from the sleeping-loft which was situated above, and behind, where they were sitting. "Mama?"

"What is it, Mary Sue?"

"I can hear you talkin' 'bout Blossom. Reckon I could come down and tell Colonel Greyson about her? After all, she is my cat, you know."

Melody sighed. "You should be asleep, you sharp-eared little dear. Do you know it's near midnight? Little girls need their rest so's they can grow straight and tall."

"Yes'm, but I'd surely like to tell the colonel about Blossom 'cause he likes animals just like I do." Mary Sue was hanging her head over the edge of the sleeping loft, to better make her point. "Please, please, mama!"

"Very well, dear. Be careful on the ladder. I'll turn up the light a bit." She adjusted the wick on the single lamp that struggled to illuminate the scene through its smoky chimney.

"Thank you, mama." The ladder squeaked as her bare feet hurried to descend. Matt chuckled, to himself, as the little girl emerged into the faint circle of light. She was straight as a stick under her homespun nightgown. Her bare feet stuck out of one end of her shapeless garment, while a mop of curly, jet-black hair stuck out of the other. He was struck by the beauty of her face. She had the high cheek bones of her mother's Indian ancestry tempered by the Scottish genes of her father. There was no question that she would be a fine-looking woman, one day. Mary Sue snatched her cat off of the stool and sat there herself with the cat transferred to her lap. "Want to know why she is named 'Blossom'?"

Matthew tried to find a comfortable position for his arm. It was throbbing painfully. "'Course I do."

Mary Sue assumed a dramatic air. "She is named 'Blossom' 'cause if you put her in a flower garden you can't see her 'cause she has all the colors of the flowers."

"Makes good sense to me."

"Me too" echoed Melody. "Why don't you recite your poem for us. The one about Blossom. I know the colonel would really like to hear it." She shot him a sideways glance, the significance of which was not lost on Matthew.

"'Course I would!" he exclaimed, bravely, and according to the unspoken instruction.

Mary Sue sighed. She put her wrist to her brow in her best, put-upon, manner. "Well, if I must, I must." She slid her skinny fanny from the stool and stood before it, cradling Blossom in her arms.

> "Two little mousies sat upon
> a garden walk, one day.
> You had to listen closely
> to what they had to say.
> It seems they had a worry.
> It seems they had a fret.
> They didn't know which way to run
> to keep from gettin' et!

> Blossom cat, Blossom cat,
> you're hard to tell just where you're at!
> Blossom cat, Blossom cat,
> oh, please just let us be!"

Matthew could not applaud with both hands, so he pounded upon the arm of his rocker with the best of the two. "More! More!" he cried.

"Well, there is more" said Mary Sue, haughtily raising her hand.

"There is?" said Melody, eyebrows raised.

"There is, mother. After all, you don't know everything."

"Very well, dear. Please go ahead."

"Thank you." She curtseyed, grandly, in her nightgown.

> "The little mousies scurried
> to find a safety spot,
> but little did they know, poor things,
> a safe spot there was not!
>
> Blossom cat, Blossom cat,
> you're hard to tell just where you're at.
> Blossom cat, Blossom cat,
> oh, please just let us be!"

Matthew and Melody were laughing uncontrollably. Matt just had to ask. "Do you have a third verse?"

She stood with one arm on her hip, the other holding the cat. The cat was beginning to show a concerned look on her face, as though she were worrying about just how all this confusion and noise was going to turn out. "Well no, actually, not yet. But I do have a dance that goes with the chorus."

"Really?" asked Matthew.

"Really. Want to see it?"

"Of course we do." said Melody, pretending to be serious.

323

Using the poor, terrified cat as a stage prop, Mary Sue launched into her choreographic masterpiece. Her somewhat oversized bare feet flashed in the dim light as they twirled and kicked.

> "Blossom cat, Blossom cat,
> you're hard to tell just where you're at.
> Blossom cat, Blossom cat,
> oh, please just let us be!"

At the end of the verse the *premiere danseuse* sank, exhausted, to the hearth as she reveled in the delight of her audience of two. The cat, having experienced enough of the theater arts for one night, wriggled free and fled. Mother, daughter, and new/old friend howled with delight until tears ran down their cheeks. "Mama?"

"Yes, dear?"

"We haven't laughed like this since pappa died. It feels good."

Melody flew from her chair and knelt to hug her daughter. "It does feel good, thanks to you."

"No, mama. Thanks to Colonel Greyson. He brought happiness back just like he brought Buttercup back. I'm glad he's here."

Melody stroked the black ringlets of her daughter's hair, trying, vainly, to arrange them in some semblance of order. She smiled up at Matthew in the dim light. "Me too."

Matt returned the smile. "Me three!" A new warmth, a new strength coursed through his veins. At last, he was home. At least, to the best of his understanding, he was home. There was love in that little farmhouse....the sweet, healing love of a caring woman and her charming child. "Perhaps," he thought to himself with an inward smile, "I can even get that yellow-eyed cat to like me if she'll let me scratch her under the chin a time or two." Mary Sue and her mother continued to chatter. Matt tried his very best to remain a part of the conversation but his weary body would not cooperate. He was still exhausted from his arduous journey. The combined warmth of fire and companionship wrapped him in an opiate-like blanket of contentment. His eyelids simply refused to stay open. He was sound asleep in an instant.

Melody watched, with alarm, as his head pitched forward, his chin resting uncomfortably on his chest. "This will never do. I fear he will break his poor neck!"

Mary Sue leaned close to his sleeping face to take a good look. "What'll we do, mama?"

"Reckon we'll put him in my bed. Help me get him into the bedroom." The sleeping accommodations in the little house were limited to the one downstairs bedroom plus the loft overhead.

Mary Sue covered her open mouth with her hand, her eyes wide with shock and embarrassment. "Mama! You're not goin' to sleep in there too, are you?"

Melody giggled. "Not hardly. Now, help me get him in there." They shook Matthew partially awake. Then, with considerable pulling, tugging, huffing, and puffing, they managed to stand him on his feet and shuffle him into the bedroom, tip him onto (really into) the feather mattress, and cover him with a thick comforter.

"There!" said Melody, hands on hips, as she viewed the sleeping soldier. "A job well done for tonight."

"There!" echoed Mary Sue, hands likewise on hips, "He should be fine. Got the best bed in the house. Where will you sleep, mama?"

"With you, of course."

The little girl squealed with delight. "Can we cuddle an' stay nice and warm together?"

"Surely, we can do just that. I 'spect you plan to use me as a warmer for those icy feet of yours but I guess I'll live through it."

Mary Sue giggled as she scampered up the ladder. "Hurry, mama. Once you get 'em warm, I promise they will stay that way."

Matthew slept, almost without stirring, until the following evening. He might have slept longer had not Melody awakened him in time to clean up before supper. She shook him gently, but urgently. "Matthew! Matthew!

You must not sleep any longer. You need food, and to have your wounds dressed. Matthew?"

His eyes fluttered open. "Good morning!" he smiled.

Mrs. Chandler tried to look stern. "Morning, indeed! You've slept through a night and an entire day. 'Bout time you got to stirrin' I'd think. I'm startin' to worry that you're goin' to wear out my bed!'"

Matthew blinked, happily. He was refreshed by the long sleep. His mind seemed clearer than it had been at anytime that he could remember. "Sorry! I didn't mean to put you out of your bed! A place in the stable would be just fine if you would allow me to stay on here for a bit." Matthew put his hands under his head as he smiled at his attractive benefactor.

"'Course you can stay on, long's you want. Just the same, December is no time of year for a sick man to be sleepin' in the stable. You'll stay in here where it is nice and warm."

"Thank you....but I'm really not sick."

"Maybe not, but you soon would be if you go back to sleepin' out in the cold." She gave him a wry smile as she reached to gently pat his bandaged arm. "You don't look all that good to me!"

"Thank you! My, you say the nicest things!" chuckled Matthew.

"And I'm goin' to say some even nicer things if you don't get out of that bed and get yourself cleaned up. We need to treat your arm, then have a nice, hot supper. How's fried chicken, biscuits swimmin' in the chicken gravy, vegetable soup, and baked potatoes sound to you?"

"Stand aside, ma'am! I'm hittin' the floor runnin'!"

Melody turned away, speaking over her shoulder. "Soon's you get through with your runnin', kindly land yourself in the chair by the fire so's I can fix your arm."

The water in the black pot that was suspended over the fire was already steaming when Melody removed the bandage from Matthew's mangled arm. The arm was purple, swollen, draining, and purulent. Mary Sue took a quick look, and suddenly had urgent business elsewhere. Melody began to hum, and then to quietly chant, words that Matt did not understand. She produced a small buckskin pouch from which she took a pinch of powder, carefully mixed it into the hot water, and then used the mixture to bathe his arm. Matt was somewhat mystified, but very grateful for the treatment of his painful injury. Anything that could possibly relieve his pain was fine with him....including Indian magic. He studied her face as she leaned over his arm and busily applied the hot compresses. She had beautiful, long, black eyelashes. "What is that song you are singing?"

She looked up, suddenly, and smiled to herself as she caught him staring at her. "Just an Indian chant that helps dog-bit arms to heal."

"Where'd you learn it?"

"From my father, and my father's father, and from my father's grandfather, and from his grandfather."

"I get the idea. Ancient medicine."

"Yes. The ancient medicine of my people. It works. You'll see."

Matt was a little skeptical, but his arm was already feeling more comfortable. Now that she was looking back to her work, he resumed his study of her. Her long, black, shiny hair was carefully tied behind her back with a ribbon of faded blue. "I need you to tell me some things, Mrs. Charity Jane Melody Chandler."

She smiled. "I hope you are not going to go through all of my names whenever you speak to me! Melody will do. What is it you would like to know?"

"I'd like to know who you are. And, I'd like to know who I am. I'm hoping you can fill in some blank spots for me."

"I surely can. Let's do me first, 'cause you will take longer." She began to speak, at some length, in the language of the Chippewa.

Matthew chuckled when she finished. "Now, I hope that you will tell me what you just said."

She looked at him, somewhat skeptically, as she wrung out the hot compress and gently placed it back on his arm. "I'm not sure you will understand the thoughts of the Chippewa."

The magic potion, or perhaps, it was just the moist heat, was lessening the pain in his throbbing arm. "I can learn, given the chance!" he smiled.

Melody absent-mindedly caressed his arm as she held the compress in place. She returned his smile, then raised her dark eyes to the window where the stark trees of the Virginia winter stood gaunt against the twilight sky. Her eyes became moist, causing her vision to blur, as she thought of the northern forests of her childhood that were now so very far away. The dark, lush green of the cedars and white pines swirled down, towering over the sand and cobble-stoned shorelines. An eagle floated in the bright blue of the sky. He had soared to such a height that he could barely be seen had not the sun glinted off of the whiteness of the feathers on his head, and had he not whistled to tell the world of his kingly presence. The softness of her voice matched the sweet longing in her eyes.

"You ask me who I am. If you wish to know, you must seek me in the clouds. I am a bird who rises from the earth, and flies far up, into the skies, out of human sight."

Matthew furrowed his brow. "That's very pretty, but doesn't tell me much about you."

Reluctantly, she struggled back to reality and returned the compress to the water, then to wring it and to place it once again before she answered. "'Bout all you need to know. I'm not very interesting."

"I'm not so sure about that. Did you write those words yourself?"

"No. They are the words of my grandfather. He was a great chief named Keeshkemun. His name means 'sharpened stone'. The British didn't like him much. He favored the Long Knives."

Matthew rubbed his stubbly chin. Who the hell are the Long Knives?"

"Americans, of course. Don't you know anything?"

"Guess not." He slumped in his chair. "Oh, my God!" he thought, "I'm up against another very bright lady. This has happened to me before....

sometime.... somewhere. Someplace." He decided to make the best of the situation. "Well, now!" he said, aloud. "So, you are not very interesting, eh? Except for, and not to mention the fact that you must be some sort of princess!"

Melody threw back her head in a hearty laugh. "A princess of sorts, I suppose. That's stretching it a bit."

"Tell me some more uninteresting things." chided Matthew.

"As you wish. I was born on Mackinac Island."

"Michigan?" She nodded. Matthew began to search his memory. "I thought you looked like a Great Lakes Indian."

"Is that good, or bad?"

He could not conceal his admiration. "That is very, very good!" He was making her blush under the light tan of her skin. "I can remember Mackinac Island being a frequent port-of-call during my sailing days, between wars. Hmmm! I think maybe my memory is getting better."

"Now, that's good news! Let's keep talking. Maybe you'll get it all back if we talk about you instead of about me."

Matthew looked a little stressed. "That would be nice, I'd guess. I'm not yet sure what I want to remember."

"You're afraid of your memories, aren't you?" Melody's eyes brimmed, momentarily, with sympathetic tears.

"Think so?" He paled as he squirmed in his chair. "Let's us just talk about you some more, if you don't mind."

Melody instinctively recognized that Matt needed to be steered away from having to face memories that he was not ready to acknowledge. "Well!" she chirped, pulling a homely ladder backed chair close to his, I'm about to tell you about me....and you will be bored to death."

Matt managed a smile. "Try me."

"I met my husband on Mackinac Island. We were married at Saint Anne's. Did you ever see Saint Anne's Church?"

329

Matt scratched his head for a moment, trying to organize his thoughts. "Yep, I did. Plain little clapboard church with a short steeple. Had a bell in it, though. I remember I could hear it ring while I was 'board ship, at the docks. I never went to the church, but I remember that the sound of the bell made me feel good. It meant that Christ was alive, and well, on Mackinac Island."

Melody touched his cheek and turned his face toward her. "Nice thought. That bell seemed to regulate my life when I was a little girl." She folded her hands on her lap and stared at them for a moment. "I'm real glad to hear you're a Christian, Matthew."

"You are? Why would that matter?"

"'Cause tomorrow is Christmas Eve."

"Pshaw! Really?"

"Really. Will you go to mass with me and Mary Sue?"

Matthew stood to warm his backside before the fire. Something was making him shiver. "Christmas? Good heavens. Christmas. Haven't thought about that for a while. Can we go to church? I mean, well, you can't introduce me as a Yankee colonel. They'd shoot me on the spot....Christmas or no!"

Melody smiled, slyly. "We can tell anyone who asks that you're a shell-shocked rebel soldier that can't even remember his name. You're already pretty good at playin' that role."

Matt favored her with a sweeping bow. "Waal then, y'all, reckon Ah could do just that if'n you feed me enough chitlins an' grits 'for we go to Christmas Eve meetin'."

Giggling, Melody pushed Matthew back into his chair. "That's about as poor acting as I've ever heard, or seen. You act like that and folks will know you're a fake, for sure. Promise you'll behave, and I'll take you to church with us."

"Ah do promise, ma'am. Ah'l try to talk with gentlemanly Virginia good taste."

Melody rolled her eyes. "Guess that will have to do."

Mary Sue had been carefully monitoring the conversation from a safe listening-post in the kitchen where she did not have to look at Matthew's arm. She hustled into the room, and perched on her stool, fearing to be left out. "Mama, ain't you goin' to tell the colonel about daddy, an' about me?"

"I'm not sure he wants to hear all that, dear."

"Surely, he would want to."

Matt settled into the chair, propping his throbbing arm on a pillow. "Surely, I do want to know all about you, Mary Sue."

She sniffed, a little wounded. "Thought so. Can I tell it, mama?"

"Somehow, I doubt there's any stoppin' you. Go ahead, dear."

The little girl needed no further encouragement. Taking a deep breath, to settle herself into a thespian mood, she launched into the telling of their family history. "When my daddy was a young and very handsome man, he heard that there was lots of money to be made by mining for copper up by a place called Lake Superior. North of here, somewheres. Well! He found out he didn't like copper minin' at all 'cause where he had to work it was dusty, and you couldn't see the sky. Sooo....(dramatic pause) he left and caught a ship to Mackinac Island where he found mama. They had a really pretty wedding. Mama was dressed in a pure white buckskin dress with fringes on it. And....they lived happily ever after until...." She wrung her hands in sorrow.

Matthew was caught up in the story. "Until what?"

"This is the sad part. Until my daddy heard that his daddy had died, back here in Virginia. They had to come back here to run the farm. This very farm. And, after while, they had me. That makes me a true Virginian, just like my daddy."

Matthew was captivated by the sweet innocence. "Well you should be proud to be a Virginian. Somethin' I have noticed. Virginia has fine women, wonderful little girls, and magnificent horses."

Puzzled, Mary Sue looked at Matt, and then to her mother. "Is that good, mama?"

Melody held out her arms to hug her child. She kissed her curly black hair. "Just like somebody just said to me, a few minutes ago, 'It's good. It is very, very good.'"

+ + +

Christmas Eve Day dawned bright and cheerful, with a light dusting of snow atop the brown grasses that rustled in the pasture. Buttercup and Rebel grazed side by side, already the best of friends. Matthew, Melody, and Mary Sue strolled across the fields toward a small swale that lay just beyond the far fence. Mary Sue carried a small hatchet to be used for the cutting of evergreen boughs. Matt carried an ax which would be used to harvest a cedar Christmas tree. Melody carried her trusty flintlock squirrel rifle. Matthew looked at her, somewhat askance. "You figger to serve squirrel for Christmas dinner?'

"Nope."

"What, then?"

"You'll see. Somethin' you folks from Michigan know nothin' about."

Matt stopped in his tracks. "Then, you know for sure I'm from Michigan. It's all fuzzy to me, but I guess I knew that all along. How do you know where I'm from?

Melody took him by the elbow and pulled him to restart his progress. "We'll talk about that another time. Right now we've got the Lord's birthday to celebrate."

"Yes, ma'am. Now that we know I'm from Michigan, what else is it that you just mentioned I don't know nothin' about?"

"Mistletoe!" gleefully shouted Mary Sue. "You don't know nothin' 'bout mistletoe!"

Melody cocked the flintlock. "Look to the top of that tree, there." Matthew winced as the squirrel rifle cracked. A wisp of smoke curled from the priming pan, followed, shortly, by a bellowed smoky doughnut that emerged from the muzzle of the long, octagonal barrel. Down at their feet tumbled a small clump of shiny green leaves decorated with white berries. She picked it up for Matthew's inspection. "Mistletoe."

Matt was impressed. "Nice shot! Now that you've got it, what do you do with it?" Mary Sue giggled. Melody held the sprig over Matt's head, then treated him to a warm Christmas kiss. "Mistletoe!" she said, when she was finished with her warmly delicious delivery.

Mary Sue stood, covering her eyes, until the lengthy kiss was completed. "Mother, you didn't have to do it quite that much."

"Hush, Mary Sue" cooed Melody, her arms reluctant to leave Matthew's neck.

Matthew returned her embrace and, too, was reluctant to let her go. "I really like this mistletoe plant. I could almost become a Virginian just to have you hold it over my head."

Melody's arms returned around his neck, her body pressed close to his. "I believe you would make a fine Virginian, should you desire to become one."

That was quite enough for Mary Sue. She walked away to chop some greens with which to decorate the mantle.

+ + +

Christmas Eve was, appropriately, decked in white. A light snowfall, with plump, handsome flakes, and no wind, decorated the evening. Matt harnessed Rebel and backed him into the traces of the Chandler's buckboard. "Time to take a little exercise, old feller. Time to see how that game leg of yours is healing." Mary Sue skipped excitedly about, fastening sprigs of mistletoe on each side of his bridle, and decorating the light, open carriage with cedar boughs and red ribbons.

"There!" Mary Sue stepped back to admire her work. "We'll have the best lookin' rig at church!" A frown crossed her face. "'Cept maybe we would look better if we used Cuppie 'stead of Rebel. Cuppie don't have so many stickin-out bones."

"We'll fatten up Rebel soon enough. You got to remember, little missy, that he needs some easy exercise to keep his leg from stiffening up. Besides, there may be a lot of folks goin' to church tonight....including soldiers. We don't want to show off Buttercup too much. Someone might decide to put her back into the cavalry."

Mary Sue sighed. She flapped her arms in exasperation. "'Spose so. Wouldn't want that to happen. Anyone wants to take her will have to answer to me....and I can be really mean when I have to be."

"No! I don't think you could be mean if you wanted to."

"Oh! Yes I can!" She clenched her teeth and her fists, looking very fierce indeed.

Melody called from the kitchen door. "Mary Sue! Time to change to your good dress. We must go soon, or we'll miss the beginning of the service. The father don't like it when folks come in late."

In minutes, the three of them were snuggled together on the single board seat of the buckboard.

Mary Sue sat in the center, looking up at Matt as he clucked to Rebel and gave the reins a light slap. A heavy wool blanket covered their laps and wrapped around their feet. She wrinkled her nose. The blanket smelled like wet sheep. "Wish my daddy was drivin' us tonight!" she thought to herself. She put her head on her mother's shoulder. Tears moistened the little girl's eyes. She hoped that Matthew wouldn't notice. "Wouldn't want to hurt his feelings," she thought, "but I surely miss my daddy, especially on Christmas." Melody, sensing her feelings, and thinking the same thoughts, put her arm around her daughter and kissed her hair.

The church bells were ringing as they approached the edge of town. Matthew pretended to be unconcerned when he spotted two Confederate mounted riflemen standing watch at the edge of the road. "Hear those bells, Melody? Remind you of Mackinac Island?."

"Surely does" murmured Melody as she too eyed the soldiers.

"Evenin'!" said one. The butt of his rifle rested on his thigh, the muzzle pointed skyward. The daylight was nearly gone. "Oh!" he said, recognizing Melody, "evenin' Mrs. Chandler. Merry Christmas."

"Merry Christmas to you, Ezra, Leonidas."

Matt tipped his hat. "Merry Christmas" he mumbled. The men stared at him, but said nothing more as the buckboard rumbled past their posted position.

There were many buggies and wagons assembled in front of the church, their horses tied to the hitching rails and posts. Matt found an open spot, tied Rebel to the rail, and helped the ladies to descend. There were five or six armed and uniformed Confederates standing near the open door that led to the candlelit sanctuary. Alarmed, he whispered to Melody. "Do you always have armed guards stationed at a church service?"

Melody glanced around. "Not usually. I have to believe they are here for a reason. Most likely, somebody important is attendin'. Maybe Captain Mosby. If he is, then we're in luck. He is our friend."

Matt hoped that his nervousness would be hidden by the gathering darkness. "Well now, I don't know who he would be, but if you say he is a friend, I suppose that he is. I have a bad feelin' I can use all the friends I can get, 'bout now." He could feel small beads of sweat appearing on his forehead in spite of the coolness of the evening.

Melody patted his good arm, then placed her hand on it. "Don't worry. Let's go in." They mingled with the worshipers who were crowding through the door, Mary Sue leading the way.

Matt noticed that several of the rebels had sprigs of mistletoe stuck into the bands of their slouch hats. "I see those boys have mistletoe over their heads. Does that mean that you have to kiss them?"

Melody giggled. "Not unless I want to. And, you don't have to kiss them neither."

Matt snorted. "Thank God for that."

"You can thank Him yourself when you get inside."

"I believe I will."

When they were seated, a gentleman who had been watching them from the back of the church sauntered down the aisle. He had spotted an opening next to Melody and took the opportunity to sit next to her. He took her hand. "Good to see you, Charity Jane. Merry Christmas!"

Melody blushed. "Merry Christmas, John."

Matthew was startled by the unexpected visitor. His eyes flickered over the newcomer in quick appraisal. He was impressed by what he saw. The young man was slender, lithe, and nattily dressed in civilian clothes. He had dark hair and sparkling eyes that darted around as though he never missed anything at all. His smile was handsome and charming. He flashed it at Mary Sue. "Mary Sue, dear, are you having a nice Christmas?"

Mary Sue, for once speechless, was conducting a pointed examination of the ceiling of the little sanctuary. She nodded, and smiled. "Little does he know," she thought, "that no one can have a nice Christmas without a father." She wanted to tell him, but thought better of it. Better to keep her sorrow to herself. She resumed her perusal of the ceiling.

The gent turned his attention to Matthew. "So! Matthew, I'm sure Mrs. Chandler is taking good care of you. He eyed the bandaged arm. "If anybody can get you better, she can. She's a wonderful nurse." Melody blushed again.

Matt looked startled. "Why, yes. She's been very kind to me I'm most fortunate to be under her care." Melody giggled, enjoying the compliments. Matt was puzzled, and showed it. "Excuse me, sir. I could be wrong, but I don't believe we have met before."

"We haven't."

"Then, how do you know my name?"

The fellow laughed and stuck out his hand, reaching over Melody's lap to do so. "Mosby is my name. John Mosby. And yours is Matthew Greyson. I make it a habit to know peoples' names. It's part of my business."

Matt unconsciously rubbed his bandaged arm. "And, what would your business be, Mr. Mosby?"

"Horses."

"Horses?"

"Horses."

Matt was beginning to feel put-upon. Melody put a finger to each of their lips, in turn, to hush them. "Shush! The service is about to begin. Here comes Mary Margaret. Wait 'till you hear her play. She's really good." The organist flounced down the side aisle, her unbuttoned choir robe flapping behind her. She slid onto the stool, pumped the pedals for a moment, then pounced upon the keyboard like a cat upon its prey. Lovely Christmas music filled the room as the acolytes processed down the center aisle bearing their lighted candles. They were followed by the priest who was garbed in his very best cassock and surplice, and who was busily flapping a smoky container of incense toward the congregation as he muttered a blessing.

As the Latin phrases of the high mass droned on, Matthew found his mind wandering. "That organist is very good," he thought, "even better than Bethany. Didn't think that was possible. "His own musings startled him. As he sat inside one holy place he was suddenly able to visualize another.... the little, white church in Franklin. The Reverend Pitts Lanning was in the pulpit describing the Word in his usual, animated style. Matt could almost hear his voice. And there, seated at the organ, was Bethany. Her hair was parted in the middle and pulled back in a severe school teacher's bun, revealing the exquisite whiteness and beauty of her face and neck. Matt sighed audibly, causing Melody to give him a sideways glance. Matt sat still, but suddenly wanted to jump up and shout. He could remember! He could see the faces of his many friends who were sitting in the little Methodist congregation. He could remember!

When the service, the handshaking, and the exchange of greetings were over, Matthew steered Rebel down the dark road toward home. Not, of course, that Rebel really needed steering. He knew perfectly well where home was and needed no guidance whatsoever. His ears were swiveled forward in anticipation of a warm, well-bedded stall and a tasty ration of oats. They stopped to chat, for a moment, with the Confederate sentries who still sat, shivering, at their post. "Gentlemen," chirped Melody, "you can go home now. The service is over."

The two doffed their slouch hats, the courtesy barely discernible in the darkness. "Thank you, ma'am! It's good to be relieved by such a pretty officer! We'll go, Mrs. Chandler. You can bet we will....and right now. Thank you, and Merry Christmas."

Matt noticed that a sadness seemed to settle over his passengers....a sadness that matched the darkness of the road. He could understand that their Christmas was empty. John Chandler, husband and father, was not there. Christmas, he knew, could bring terrible sadness to the recently bereaved, and this was no exception. Immediate intervention, he mused, was a necessity. Without warning, he broke into song at the top of his lungs. "Joy to the world, the Lord is come....!" Rebel swiveled his ears backward in disbelief. Melody and Mary Sue giggled and chuckled, then began to sing along with him. They sang their way, joyously, all the way home.

Matthew had the Christmas "boo-hoos" on the run, and he resolved to keep up the momentum. After tucking Rebel into his warm box stall, he went to the house and insisted that mother and daughter accompany him back to the barn. He had hung several lanterns in the barn to give it both illumination and a warm glow. When the two ladies were standing, rather grumpily, in the barn, he handed each of them a very large, and from a horse's point-of-view, very luscious carrot. "Do you know, ladies, that when Christ was born he was cradled in a manger?" They both nodded, humoring him. "Well," he continued, "did you know that the animals that lived in the stable where Jesus was born crowded around his manger bed so that the tiny baby would be kept warm?" They both wagged their heads to the negative. At this point he could feel that he had their undivided attention....and gloated, inwardly. "And, did you know that, even now, so many years after the holy birth, that at midnight on Christmas Eve, when no human is looking, the animals in stables everywhere bow down to worship the Christ Child?"

Mary Sue, with her incisive mind, had to ask. "What time is it now?"

Matt smiled. "'Bout ten."

"Can I stay here 'till twelve?"

Melody intervened. "I don't think so, dear. 'Sides, the animals probably wouldn't do it if you were watching. I 'spect it is a private....but beautiful.... thing that only animals, and Matthew, understand."

338

"Well, fine." said Mary Sue "But why am I standing here holding this carrot?"

"Now, that," said Matthew, "Is a very good question. And, I shall answer it."

They both stared at him. "Um....well....(he was making this up as he went along) in celebration of the good care that the animals took of the Christ Child, it's only fair that we honor them with their own little Christmas gift. A carrot!" A smile was threatening to turn Melody's lips into a silly grin, but Mary Sue was focused on the lovely tale.

Mary Sue started to jump up and down. "Oh, that's nice! Can we give them the carrots now?" Buttercup and Rebel were hanging their heads out of their stalls in anticipation. They could smell the carrots. "Mama, which one do you want to do?"

Melody handed her the other carrot. "Best if you do them both, dear, as you are their special friend."

Mary Sue planted a heartfelt kiss on each velvety muzzle and presented to each, with a flourish, a crunchy carrot. The ritual completed, they blew out the lanterns and returned to the house where Matthew lit every lamp he could find, to better illuminate the cedar Christmas tree with its homemade bows, and stoked up the fire in the fireplace. As they settled into their chairs in front of the fire, Melody had an inspiration. "Matt, would you be interested in a taste of elderberry wine? The neighbors brought me some last year, and I never tasted it."

Matthew tried, unsuccessfully, to conceal his delight at the suggestion. "Oh, yes!" he cried, "bring on the elderberry!"

Mary Sue was not about to be left out. "Can I have some, too?"

Matthew had a flashback to Bethany. "You may, if you can, little dear."

Mary Sue gave him a crinkle-nosed look, and turned to her mother. "Can I, mama?"

"Yes, dear, you *may*....have a little bit." They sat in front of the fire, chattering gaily, until Melody announced that it was time for all little girls to be in bed.

"Oh, mama, I'm not ready yet. Christmas Eve is too much fun."

Matthew intervened. "Wait! Before you go to bed, Mary Sue, would you please come and sit on my lap for a moment?" She complied, feeling to him for all the world like she was made up entirely of elbows and knees as she obediently plopped upon his lap. "I decided, on the way home from church, that I wanted to give you a Christmas present but realized that I didn't have any money, or anything else, to give....and that made me very sad until I thought of something!"

"What?' The child stared at him, then snuggled her face into his neck. "What did you think of?"

Do you remember the little book of your father's that I brought back from the war and gave to your mother when I brought Cuppie back? I just recently remembered it myself."

"Yep. His Bible. It's right there by the lamp. Mama looks at it every day."

"Well, I have one, too, that I always carry in my shirt pocket. I want you to have it and to learn to read it." He fished the little New Testament out of his pocket and handed it to her.

Mary Sue was almost breathless with excitement. "Oh, thank you! Thank you! I already know how to read it. Mama has taught me good. Mama, look! I have my very own bible! Now, when we read together you can read out of yours and I will read out of mine!" She thumbed through the pages and looked at the inscription in the front. "Um, who is Bethany?"

"She's the one who gave me the book. Her father gave it to her, and she gave it to me. And now, I'm giving it to you. You must promise to take good care of it."

"Did you love her like you love me and mama?" Little girls can be very perceptive.

He glanced at Melody, catching her dabbing at her eyes with her handkerchief as she stared into the fire. "Yes."

"Did you marry her?"

"No. Would have, were it not for the war."

340

"Where is she now?"

Matthew hugged her, for a moment, before he could answer. "She disappeared. I'm told she is dead, but just don't know for sure."

"Oh, how sad! Isn't that sad, mama?"

Melody stood. "Yes, very sad. But, let's not talk about it anymore, tonight. Let's all go to bed thinking about what a wonderful Christmas we've had."

"Are you coming to bed too?"

"Yes. Right now." She leaned down to Matthew and kissed him on the cheek. "Good night." she whispered. "Thank you."

Mary Sue chattered as she climbed the ladder to the loft. "Can I take my new book to bed with me, mama? That way I can start to read it first thing in the morning."

"That would be just fine, Mary Sue."

Matt threw a big log on the back of the fire so that it would still be warm in the morning, then sat before the flaring fire for a while to soak up some heat before he went to bed. They had no candles because of the cost, but the room was resplendent with Christmas decorations anyway. Melody had placed cedar boughs on the mantle and decorated them with white mistletoe and with red dogwood berries. The tree stood in the corner, covered with cheerful bows that were fashioned from bits of bright cloth and with strings of popcorn artfully wound around its bright green and very fragrant branches. With a contented yawn, he blew out the lamps and went to bed. He lay awake, watching the flickering shadows from the fireplace dance across the ceiling while giving thanks to his God that his memory was returning. He couldn't remember much about his military career, but nearly everything else was coming into focus. He thought, wistfully, about Bethany. Perhaps he would only see her again in heaven. When that day came, he would look for her....first thing.

The ladder creaked as someone was coming down from the sleeping loft. "Probably to use the 'necessary shed'." he mused, silently. "Brrr!" That was a cold proposition anytime, but especially so in the middle of a cold winter night. However, no lamp or lantern was lit in preparation for a trip outside. Instead, he heard bare feet padding across the floor and into his room. Melody, in her white nightgown, appeared next to the bed. Her hair was undone and hung over her shoulders, sparkling in the back light from the fireplace in the other room. She pulled back the covers and crawled in next to him, snuggling close to his warm body.

"I'm cold, Matt." she wheedled, "Can you get me warm?"

Matthew smiled in the darkness and drew her close. "You can bet I'll give it a try!" Looking for warmth, her bare feet touched his bare legs. He stifled a cry, and then whispered to her. "My God, woman, you have the coldest feet I have ever felt!"

She clapped a hand over his mouth. "Quiet! You'll wake Mary Sue!" They both snickered and giggled, burying their faces in the pillows to mask the sound. She wrapped her arms around his neck and whispered in his ear. "It runs in the family. Mary Sue has cold feet too. I think it's an Indian trait. Comes from sleeping in cold teepees." Her words set off a new round of muffled snickers, snorts, and giggles.

In the stable, protected from the frosty night, in the darkness of their warmly bedded stalls, the horses bowed their heads.

CHAPTER NINETEEN

Mosby

January and February, 1863, were mostly colored a cheerless brown. There was rarely enough snow to brighten the landscape for more than a day at a time. It was generally cloudy and blustery with rain that sometimes froze, and sometimes did not. The danger of occasional Federal armed occupation, usually by scouting units of cavalry, caused the genteel social activities of Middleburg to be somewhat suppressed. Matthew spent the day times prowling the extensive wilderness along Goose Creek where he harvested rabbits, squirrels, and venison. He supplied many of the neighboring farms with meat which he exchanged for seed corn and wheat, potatoes, apples, and various kitchen garden seeds. The Chandler farm had lost a year of production and was critically short of supplies and seed needed for planting in the spring. Many of the men from neighboring farms had gone to serve in the various armies of the Confederacy, or were members of Captain Mosby's Rangers and were only home occasionally. The neighbors were grateful for the hunting expertise of their mildly crippled, one eyed, pleasant, new neighbor. Whispered discussions occasionally occurred as to who he really was, whether or not he and Melody were living in sin, and why, if he was such a good hunter, he could not go back and fight for the Cause. If he could shoot a rabbit, he could shoot a Yankee. Because of his affable, helpful demeanor, however, serious questions were rarely asked.

"Mama? It's gettin' awful dark in here for sewin'. Can't quite see where my stitches are goin'." Mary Sue's lips seemed to be stuck in an impish pout.

"Maybe you should quit for the day. You can start again early tomorrow right after your lessons."

"But, mama, I do so want to finish. I just know this skirt will look right pretty on me, if I can just get it done."

Melody had been sitting next to her and supervising her work. "Tell you what. You clean both lamp chimneys and turn 'em up bright here on the table. You can work 'till Matthew comes in."

Mary Sue cleaned and lit the lamps, placing them on the table that served, of necessity, as a kitchen table, dining table, and work table....all in one. She resumed her work. "Thank you, mama."

"You're welcome, dear."

"And, thank you for giving me such pretty cloth for Christmas."

"You're welcome again, dear. Watch out! You're gettin' perilous close to the edge with that stitch."

"Yes, mama. Mama?"

"Yes, dear?" There was rarely a lull in the conversation when Mary Sue was around.

"I don't like calling Colonel Greyson 'Colonel Greyson'."

Melody chuckled. "What would you like to call him?"

"How 'bout 'daddy'?" She did not look up from her work.

Melody looked, in surprise, at the little face. "But, you already have a daddy."

"Had."

Her mother sighed. "Well, all right....had. But, nobody has two."

"Could have, if you married Colonel Greyson. Then, I could call him daddy, or papa, or somethin' like that, couldn't I?"

"Yes, yes....I suppose you could." Melody was flustered, her words coming in a slight stammer. "But, there's nothin' goin' on like that."

Mary Sue looked away from her work, then turned to gaze into her mother's eyes. "You love him, don't you?"

Those eyes, shiny with emotion, sparkled in the lamp light. "I don't know, just yet."

Mary Sue delivered one of her best, dramatic sighs and looked back to her stitching. "Is that what you're doin' when you come down to him late at night? Findin' out if you love him?"

Melody's mouth flew open, her face turning bright red. She had no idea that her daughter was monitoring her frequent nocturnal trips down the ladder from the loft. She had waited, each time, until she was sure that the child was sound asleep. She had obviously underestimated her daughter's capacity to keep track of all things of interest. "I....I....I guess that would be somewhat the case." she answered, lamely.

"When will you find out?"

"I don't know."

"What can I call him 'till you do find out?"

Melody thought for a moment, her face still red with embarrassment. "How about 'Uncle Matt'? If that would be agreeable with him, of course."

Another heartfelt sigh. Mary Sue held her work up to the light and admired the evenness of her stitches. "Reckon that 'Uncle Matt' will have to do for now, seems like." She returned to her needle and thread in uncharacteristic silence. When Matthew opened the kitchen door, she flew to hug him with such force that he almost dropped the load of logs he was carrying in for the fireplace.

"Whoa, there!" he laughed, "Let me put down these logs. I don't want to miss such a nice hug!"

"Mama says I can call you 'Uncle Matt' if it's all right with you."

Melody held her breath, fearing that Mary Sue would expound further. The little girl was wise beyond her years, however, and did not bring up the "daddy" subject.

Matthew winked at Melody, noting that her face looked a little redder than usual, even in the lamplight. "Of course! That's just fine with me. And, what shall I call you, little missy?"

"'Mary Sue' will do!" she mumbled, burying her face in his wool jacket.

"Then, Mary Sue it is." He pried her loose and , taking her little hand in his, kissed it ceremoniously. "We have us a deal, you and me! Now then, what time is supper?"

"Right soon. Put away your things and set the table, please, Mary Sue. How hungry are you, Matt?"

"Pretty doggone." He leaned over to look at her. You been settin' too close to the fire or have you got a fever? Your face is red."

Melody turned an even darker shade. It's supposed to be red. I'm an Indian, remember?"

Matt shrugged and went to the basin to wash up. Blossom, her bright calico colors curled snugly on her stool by the fire with her tail covering her nose to ward off any possible chill, suddenly went on alert. She plopped off of the stool, ran to the window, and stared out into the darkness. After a moment of intense watching, she jumped off of the windowsill and hurried to Mary Sue where she rubbed around her legs, then hustled back to the window again. "Uncle Matt....ooo....that sounds nice....Uncle Matt, Blossom says somebody's comin'."

"Pshaw!"

Melody went to the window to see for herself, but could see nothing but blackness. "She's right, Matthew. When Blossom says somebody's comin', somebody's comin'. We'd best be careful. Shouldn't be anybody on this road in the dark 'less they're comin' here. Can't be too careful. Mary Sue, you go up in the loft right now." After barring both doors, she retrieved her squirrel rifle that stood at the ready in the corner by the front door, and placed a percussion cap on the nipple. It was always kept charged with powder and ball....just in case. Matt hurried to retrieve his little revolver from the bedroom and checked to see that all seven chambers were loaded. They blew out the lamps and waited in the flickering light from the fireplace. "Just hope it's not foragers, or bandits!" shuddered the frightened lady.

Matthew put his arm around her. "Don't you worry. If it is we'll fight 'em off. Oh-oh. I hear horses coming....lots of 'em. Darned if the cat wasn't right! We could just have a problem! We can shoot eight without reloading but sounds like a lot more than that."

A whisper wafted down from the sleeping loft. "I can shoot, mama, give me a gun."

"Hush child, and stay where you are. We don't have any more guns." They stood, one on each side of the window, trying to see into the dark night.

"I don't believe how quiet they are. I can hear a lot of hoof beats, but nothing else." whispered Matt. "We might just be in luck. Could be well-disciplined cavalry of one color or another!"

"Shhh. One's comin'." Melody cocked the rifle and stood ready to shoot through the door. They heard the gate creak open. The footsteps of heavy boots could be heard approaching. The footsteps stopped, just short of the door.

A quiet voice broke the silence. "Charity Jane? I know you're in there. It's John Mosby. It would be most appreciated if you wouldn't shoot me."

"Whew!" breathed Melody. "I'm relieved to hear your voice, John. Just a minute." She put the rifle on half cock, stood it back in the corner, and unbarred the door. "My goodness!" The dark shapes of many horses and riders could barely be seen as they crowded in the road along the picket fence. "What did you do, John, bring the whole Confederate Army? I don't have enough teacups!"

Mosby laughed, his face invisible in the darkness. "Reckon the boys can get along without a cup of tea! We're gatherin' to conduct some business tomorrow night. Like to camp down by the creek, if you have no objection."

"Of course I have no objection. Won't you come in, suh?"

"Much obliged." He stepped into the room, bowed, and kissed her hand, but froze, momentarily, when Matthew noisily decocked his revolver and stepped from the shadows. Mosby straightened, slowly, from his bow. He was handsomely dressed in the gray uniform of a Confederate captain, wearing two revolvers, butt forward, one riding at each hip. Matt noted that the captain was not carrying a traditional cavalry saber. His brown felt hat was in his left hand, doffed in the presence of a lady. Mosby came to attention and saluted. "Good evening, Lieutenant Colonel Greyson. A pleasure to see you again. Thank you for not shooting me."

Matt nodded to acknowledge the salute. "Evenin' captain. I wouldn't shoot a man who can train cavalry to move so quietly. I'm most impressed. If they were Federal, you would hear them a mile off!" He tried to hide his nervousness at the open acknowledgment of his Federal rank. "This fellow does, indeed, know everything!" he mused, to himself.

Captain Mosby chuckled. "You see, colonel, we are against a more numerous enemy and have to rely on wit, and sneak attacks. There is no such thing as a noisy sneak attack."

"I thought you told me that your business is horses."

John Mosby laughed, slapping his knee with his hat. "I didn't lie to you. I just didn't mention that they were cavalry horses. I run a small detachment of cavalry under the authority of General J.E.B. Stuart. We operate behind the lines to make life as miserable as possible for you Yanks."

Matt chuckled at the man's candor. "Fair enough!" he said.

Melody intervened in the conversation as she re-lit a lamp. "Why don't you gentlemen sit by the fire while you talk. I will fix some tea, such as it is." Real tea was hard to come by. Hers would be steeped from the dried leaves of wild mint.

Mosby rubbed his behind while he warmed it in front of the fire. "I'll stand, if you don't mind, Charity Jane. I've ridden a long ways, today, and have had just about enough sittin'. Excuse me a moment." He strode out of the door. Matt could hear him deploying sentries at the doors of the little house. He heard him ordering his men to set up camp down by Goose Creek. Vedettes were to be placed in the road, and pickets around the camp. Again, Matt was impressed. He was already certain that he would not enjoy having this man as his opponent on the field of battle.

The captain returned. "Don't be surprised that there will be a number of riders going by tonight. There will be quite a few coming in to join us for a little party we're planning." Now, he was carrying a sheathed saber in his hand. Colonel Greyson stared at it. It looked strngely familiar. Mosby again warmed himself in front of the fire. He partially withdrew the saber from its sheath, admired the engraving on the blade for a moment, returned it into the sheath, and handed it to Matthew. "Here. This belongs to you, I believe."

Greyson blinked in amazement. It *was* his saber! He had forgotten all about it, but there it was! His saber! It was a moment before he could speak. When he did, his voice was husky with emotion. He shivered as memories returned. Melody came to stand behind his chair, rubbed his shoulders, and leaned to press her cheek against his....a move not entirely lost upon Mosby. "Thank you, captain. I guess I lost it. Where did you find it?"

"Got it from a Lieutenant Henry Douglas of General Jackson's staff. He figured you were dead. He intended to send it to your family, but hadn't found out who that might be. He was happy to hear that you survived your wounds, and sends his condolences on the loss of your commander."

"My commander?"

"Yes. A Colonel Brodhead."

"Oh, I see." Memories swirled in his head, seemingly trying to break out and run away. "You seem to have gone to a great deal of trouble on my behalf, but, I confess, I can't imagine why."

John Mosby turned to kick at the logs in the fireplace, his hands on the oaken mantel. "Because, I have an ulterior motive." He turned to smile at Matt. "Want to hear it?"

"Of course." Greyson was totally mystified by the entire encounter, but couldn't help liking the captain. "Please do explain. I admit I am at a loss."

Melody was still stroking Matt's shoulders. "Would you gents like me to leave? I can go in the bedroom 'till you are done talkin'."

John chuckled. "Don't you dare to leave us, Mrs. Chandler. Your beauty warms the whole room for us poor, cold warriors. Besides," he smiled, "the colonel appears to be enjoying your touch."

Matt craned his neck to look up at her. She was blushing again. He reached up to touch her face, then held her hands as they rested upon his shoulders. "Thank you, Melody." He began to wonder if her blushing mechanism wasn't working overtime, that day. "Are you sure you don't have a fever?"

"No, Matt, I don't have a fever." She cleared her throat and made a dash for the kitchen. "I'll get some more tea." She was struck by a better thought. "Or, perhaps, some elderberry wine? I still have some from Christmas."

Both men nodded their heads in the affirmative, allowing that the wine would be a more than appropriate choice over the mint tea.

"Well!" said Captain Mosby as he sank into a chair next to Matthew, "Here goes. Because of the irregular nature of my work, I am well connected with what we call the 'Confederate Secret Service'. This is an organization, you understand, that we deny exists at all. Keep that in mind, please."

Matt nodded. Melody delivered the brimming glasses of dark wine.

"I began to hear rumors, through our underground network, that a wounded Federal officer was wandering around and was headed toward this area. When I heard that Mrs. Chandler was harboring and treating someone of your description, I decided to investigate....not for malice, you understand, but because Charity Jane, my wife Pauline, John Chandler, and myself have been close friends for many years. I didn't want any harm to come to Charity, so I looked into the situation. Pauline and I were concerned for her safety. We decided to determine whether the fellow living here was really a reb, or a Yank in disguise, or even a clever criminal. Make sense, so far?"

Matthew squirmed uncomfortably He was beginning to feel that his quiet arrival at the Chandler farm was about as subtle as a goldfish in a bowl. He cleared his throat, appearing nonchalant. "It does, indeed. Please go on, captain."

"Well, I must confess that I cornered Charity, and pumped her for information, when she was in town and away from you. I found out a very interesting fact. You are a licensed master, navigator, and pilot, with a detailed knowledge of the Great Lakes. You worked, for some time, on commercial vessels that plied those waters before you decided to settle down and take up farming. True?"

"True. I can remember that part of my life very well, now."

"Another interesting fact. Someone, very close to President Davis, is looking for you. Do you know who that might be?"

Matthew thought for a moment. "I have no idea who that might be. Well, maybe, possibly, my Bethany's father. He could, perhaps, have been lookin' for me in case I might have word of his daughter...." Nonchalance was fleeing from Matthew. He choked back his emotion. "He certainly knew that we were betrothed. He's a prominent man. Lives in South Carolina. A major in the Palmetto Guards, I believe. He could be close to your president and could be seeking me in case I have information as to the fate of his daughter." His voice trailed off, for a moment. "Sadly, I would be of no help to him if he found me. She has disappeared. She is probably dead....kidnapped and killed by thugs for some unknown reason."

The captain hung his head as he listened. "I'm sorry, Matt." Melody returned to her post behind Matthew's chair, putting her arms around his neck to comfort him.

Matthew suddenly sat bolt upright in his chair, startling Melody. "Oh! I just thought of something. The letter that I received tellin' me of Bethany's disappearance mentioned that someone suspected her of being a rebel spy. I forgot about that because I thought it to be a ridiculous accusation. Hmmm. I wonder. I wonder if she really *was* connected with your secret service, an' got killed for her trouble. Wonder if her father knows what happened and is lookin' for me to tell me. S'pose?"

"I surely don't know, Matt, but I'll try to find out if I can do so without attracting too much attention." Mosby waved his glass at Melody. "Charity, dear, would you have any more of this? The colonel and I have need of lubrication for the many words that we must share."

Melody gave him a wry smile. She understood males perfectly. "You're in luck, John. I still have another bottle hidden away."

"Bless you, Charity Jane. Matthew, are you acquainted with the harbor at Sandusky, Ohio?"

"I am. A treacherous place, with shifting sandbars."

"Do you know of Johnson's Island?"

"I do. A barren place."

Mosby slid down in his chair, a little mellow from the wine. "It is barren no more. It's a prison island that holds many Confederate prisoners, most of them officers. About 1600 of them."

"Really? So?"

"An acquaintance of mine, a bright young fellow named William Murdaugh, has thought up a way to release those prisoners so that they may return to Confederate service. Murdaugh is a lieutenant in the Confederate States Navy. He is trying to get Navy Department approval of the plan....and, I think it is a good one. It involves capturing the *USS Michigan*."

Matthew looked grim. "I'd be careful, were I you. Last time I saw the *Michigan* she carried only one cannon, but she is made of iron, and is very fast. Fourteen knots, as I recall. She can run rings around most, if not all, Great Lakes vessels. I believe that she is both uncatchable and indestructible. You try to take her and the hunters may become the hunted."

"Murdaugh believes that she can be taken by surprise and boarded with little difficulty."

Greyson rubbed his forehead. The devils of forgotten memories were still banging around in there. "You could be right, captain, given good planning and a measure of luck. However, there is a good chance your Lieutenant Murdaugh will be blown out of the water."

Mosby stood, paced for a moment, then leaned on the arms of Matthew's rocking chair and looked him in the eye. Would you be willing to help us with such a project?"

"Now, why in the world would I do that? Have you taken leave of your senses? I'm a soldier, sworn to serve the United States of America, for heaven's sake."

Mosby straightened. "Granted. But, you are the man we need....a master seaman who knows well the Great Lakes, and is capable of commanding a vessel of war."

"You're out of your mind."

Captain Mosby plopped back into his chair, next to Matthew. "Maybe yes, maybe no. Consider this. Ol' Jeff Davis wants you found....for whatever reason. When Jeff wants something, loyal southern gents bust their asses to get it done. This would include CSS agents. They are hot on your trail. The length of time that you can safely stay here with Charity and Mary Sue is extremely limited. And, I mean days, not weeks or months."

Melody had been sitting quietly to the side of the fireplace, listening intently. "John, what could be so bad? So they find him. He's been hurt. What would they do?"

"Hang him."

"What!" she shrieked, leaping to her feet and grabbing him by the front of his brass-buttoned blouse. "How could you say such a thing?"

He caught her hands. "I'm sorry, Charity, but this is war. If you impersonate a soldier in the other army, you are a spy. In wartime, spies almost automatically hang."

She fell to he knees, her arms clutching Mosby's legs, and sobbed, uncontrollably. "John, I can't stand to lose another man that I love! What can we do? Oh, God, what can we do?"

Matthew knelt beside her, pulled her to him, and stroked her hair. "Don't worry, Melody. We'll think of something."

John Mosby sauntered to the kitchen, found the wine bottle, poured three glasses, and distributed them. "I have, in case you haven't noticed, given this matter a lot of thought. We have three alternatives. Are you ready?"

Melody and Matthew, hugging each other as they sat on the floor before the fire, looked into each other's eyes, or eye, as the case may be. They had lost all thought of hiding their mutual affection. Matt had not realized, until now, how deep the woman's love for him had become. "We're ready, John." quaked Melody.

John leaned against the mantle and looked into the fire. "One. I can arrange to have Matthew rowed across the Potomac in the dark of night so that he may return to his own country with wild tales of his escape from the stupid rebels! However, this is a high risk operation. If you took the Chandlers with you, you would run the risk that they could be shot, captured, or drowned....along with you."

Matthew gave him a wry grin. "I'm following your primrose path, John. I understand what you are saying. Of course, under no circumstances would I put them in danger."

"I knew that." The captain arranged the burning logs with the toe of his boot. "Two. If I were to pass the word to the CSS that you had changed your loyalty, sworn to serve the Confederate States of America, and were engaged in an especially important clandestine operation, your pursuit by CSS agents would end as abruptly as if they had run full-tilt into a stone wall. Jeb Stuart's authority is unquestioned. Therefore, my authority is unquestioned. End of story....except, of course, that you would have to really help us with our project."

Matthew kissed the tears from Melody's cheeks. "I couldn't raise my hand, or my sword, against my brothers in blue."

"I knew that, too. We could do this project with you as a strict noncombatant. You'd be a consultant. And, you'd be helping 1600 gents to return home and to get out of the freezing weather that you folks are used to, but we are not. Done right, bloodshed will be minimal, if at all."

Matt's wry smile returned. "You're good, John, really good....but, you have not convinced me yet. What's the third alternative?"

"I'm surprised you didn't figure it out for yourself." He thought for a minute. "Or, perhaps, you did. I may never know. In any case, you could pretend to go along with my scheme, then blow the whistle on the operation, causing the death or capture of the rebel forces involved."

Matthew pulled Melody to her feet, propelled her to a chair, and gently sat her on it. He sat at her feet, resting his arm on her lap. Melody was dabbing, furiously, at her eyes with her handkerchief, trying to regain her bravery. Matt propped his chin on Melody's knee. It was a while before he spoke. "Captain, I could tell you that I am an honorable man, and that I would not do such a thing. But, that doesn't work, does it?"

No."

"Honor has to be proved, not spoken, doesn't it?"

"It does."

Matt looked up at Melody. "I can't bear to leave you, right now. I want to stay with you, if you'll have me."

Melody tucked her handkerchief into her sleeve. "Surely, I will have you, Matthew....for as long as you would stay."

"Then, I will work with Captain Mosby. When things settle down, after the war, we'll travel to Michigan together. We'll visit your people on Mackinac."

"Oh, Matthew! I'd love that. I'd love that so very much."

"Then, it is done." said Mosby as he stretched and clapped his hat upon his head. "I'm going to turn in. Surely hope my nigger has my tent set up like he is supposed to do. 'Night, y'all. Something makes me believe that you two need to be alone....together. I'll send out the necessary dispatches first thing tomorrow. We'll talk soon, Matt."

"'Night, John. Thanks." Matthew scooched around and sat with his back leaning on Melody's legs. He frowned as he looked into the fire. Now, he had a new problem....and it was not that he was about to become involved in a treasonous project. He could handle that. He was, however, having trouble with the realization that he had now committed his postwar attentions to three different women. One was possibly, but possibly not, dead. The second, at Durham Station, was looking for a letter that he had not yet written. The third woman he had just promised to take to Mackinac Island. "Well, well!" he thought. He genuinely loved the first, had nearly fallen in love with the second, and was busily falling....head over heels....

in love with the third. His thoughts were interrupted by the sound of John Mosby conversing with his sentry, just outside of the front door.

"How's it going, trooper?"

"Fine, thank'y, suh."

"Cold?"

"I'm fine, suh."

"Good. Your horse all fed and watered? We'll need him to be in top shape tomorrow."

"He's fat 'n' sassy, for sure. He an' I will give a good account of ourselves, come the morrow."

"Good! Have a cigar. I have one for the back door sentry, too. Keep a sharp eye. There could be hoodlums in the area, or Yankees trying to do us in before we do them. Keep in mind, too, that no one is to leave the house, either, except to go to the outhouse. Clear?"

"Clear, suh"

Mosby had not told anyone, especially not Greyson, that the surprise attack was to be against Union cavalry who were bivouacked, in strength, near Centreville. He did not, of course, have total confidence in the Yankee colonel, as yet. Time would tell, but for now he would not take any chances. He would leave sentries at the Chandler house, supposedly to keep it safe, but really to keep an eye on Colonel Greyson.

Matt listened to the pleasant way in which Mosby handled his men. It reminded him of his own manner during his own command days. Dark memories began to gnaw at the edges of his mind producing an instant, excruciating headache. "Melody, I guess I have to go to bed. I don't mean to whine, but I don't feel so good." Additionally, the fact that it would now seem that he was again a prisoner of the Confederacy did not help his state of mind.

"You go ahead. I'll go check on Mary Sue. Poor thing has probably fallen asleep with her clothes on trying to eavesdrop on our conversation.

Then, I'll come back to check on you. Maybe I can rub your head, or something."

Matt smiled, in spite of the pain. "I doubt that the 'or something' will respond so good, tonight."

"We'll see."

Matt lay in the darkened bedroom, eyes wide open, holding his head. Mosby's words haunted him. "Lieutenant Henry Douglas sends his condolences on the loss of your commander." He listened to the soft murmurings from the loft as Melody tucked Mary Sue into bed. He tried to keep his eyes open. Every time they closed, the crashing scenes of Second Manassas swirled through his mind, making his head throb even more. Finally, sleep relieved him of the headache, but not of the memories, or of the dreams.

He dug his heels into the great horse's flanks. He fired his 1860 Colts to good effect, one in each hand, until they were empty. He drew his saber and hacked wildly about, emptying rebel saddles, and splitting the heads of those who stood on the ground trying to stop him. "Forward, men. I see the colonel. He's over there! Forward! No! No! Don't turn back! Forward! We can save him!" The great horse shuddered beneath him. "No! No! Saber! Don't go down! Saber!" He drew his Walker from the saddle holster as the horse sagged to the ground. "Oh! No! Saber!" He cocked his giant revolver. "Sweet Jesus!" he screamed.

Melody and Mary Sue nearly broke their necks piling down the ladder to come to his aid. His screams were so loud that the sentries rushed in to see what was the matter. "Never mind!" commanded Melody. "Out!" She shoved them back out of the door and slammed it behind them.

Matthew was covered with sweat and shaking uncontrollably. "What's wrong with him, Mama? He scares me. Is he sick?" Mary Sue stood at the foot of the bed, wringing her hands.

"Yes, he's very sick. Now, go and get a basin of cold water and a clean towel to make a cloth for his head." She lay across him and cooed into his ear. "It's all right, Matthew. It's all right. You had a bad dream, that's all. It's all right."

Matt rolled his head from side to side. "But, the colonel is gone. Colonel Brodhead is gone! He was my friend and I couldn't save him. I wanted to save him....so bad!"

"I know, my love. Listen to me, Matthew. I love you. I love you. I love you! That's all that matters, right now. I love you! Do you hear me?"

Matt stopped shaking, "Yes, Melody, I hear you. I love you too." His voice was a whisper.

Mary Sue had returned to the bedside, where she stood, open mouthed, as she took in the conversation. "Mama?"

Matthew and Melody both looked at her, startled by her presence. She looked like a little dark-haired angel as she stood in her faded, threadbare nightgown, carefully clutching the basin in front of her. Melody was drained by the experience, but managed to answer. "Yes, dear?"

"Does this mean I can call Uncle Matt 'papa' now?"

Melody clutched her own forehead and fell back on the bed. "Not just yet, dear. Now, please set down the basin and wring out the cloth. You can be in charge of placing it on Uncle Matt's forehead, if you wish."

The little angel jumped to the task, carefully placing the cool cloth over Matthew's forehead. "I'd like to be a nurse, someday. Think I would be good at it?"

He smiled, limply, from under his compress. "Mary Sue, you would make a wonderful nurse. I feel better, already, and that's a fact." He reached to hold her hand. "If you will just stay around me, I don't believe I will ever need to be sick again. 'Course, your mother can stay around, too, if she wishes."

Melody, lying on top of the comforter, snuggled to a more comfortable position. "I wishes."

Lieutenant Colonel Matthew Greyson's "Post-Traumatic Stress Disorder" was finally over.

+ + +

Within a week, Captain John Mosby was back. Riding with him was a gentleman in the dark blue, gold trimmed uniform of an officer of the Confederate States Navy. It was Lieutenant William H. Murdaugh. They had good news. The Navy Department had approved his plan. Now, all that was needed was final approval by President Jefferson Davis.

Murdaugh was excited. "We have money. Secretary Mallory has appropriated $25,000.00 for our project. We have a crew. The crew of the CSS Virginia, now burnt and sunk, is assigned to us. We have a captain.... you. Now, all we need is a ship, a few arms, and a few cannon, and the *USS Michigan* is ours!" The gentlemen were seated around Chandler's table, a chart of Lake Erie spread before them.

Greyson leaned on his elbows, eyeing Sandusky Bay. "Lieutenant, I admire your idea, and your pluck. May I ask some questions?"

Murdaugh looked pleased. "Of course, suh. I'm here for your input. Ask away."

"Do you expect to challenge the *Michigan* to combat, ship to ship?"

"No, suh. I don't believe we could win."

"Probably not. What sort of warship do you think you can come up with?"

"We have a passenger vessel that we are quietly converting at St. Catherines, Ontario."

"Wood, or iron hulled?"

Wood."

"Her top speed?

"Not known, for sure. She's a side-wheeler. Former owner estimated that she can reach ten knots. Soon's we get final approval from Richmond, we'll ship six and nine pounder cannon aboard the *CSS Robert E. Lee* to Halifax, then send them overland, concealed of course, to St. Catherines."

"Are your cannon rifled?"

"Ah don't rightly know, suh."

Greyson leaned back in his chair, tipping it on its hind legs. "Your plan, then, is to catch her at anchor, or docked, and board her. Correct?"

"Correct. We hope to catch her at anchor at Sandusky, take her by force of cutlass, and, in cooperation with the prisoners, take Johnson's Island. We will then bring up our little wooden warship, commandeer other vessels, and take off our men. We need you to command both vessels, keeping us out of trouble and off of the sandbars and rocks, be you and the good Lord willin'."

Greyson grinned at them. "Actually, captain, lieutenant, this sounds quite plausible. Almost sounds like fun! How will you get your boarding party to the *Michigan* unobserved?"

"We haven't worked that one out, yet."

"Rather important, don't you think?"

"Aye, suh."

Greyson leaned forward to point to Pelee Island, near the Canadian shore. "This island would be a good place to headquarter. Has some deep water near shore, and is almost unpopulated....just a few hard scrabble farmers and hunters. No one to bother you. You could tow longboats from there to the mouth of Sandusky Bay by dark of night, and let them row, with muffled oars, from there. Your warship could stand off, out of sight and sound, until the boarding party signals that they are aboard, then move up to provide artillery support."

Murdaugh was tickled. "A beautiful plan! They could signal to our ship by firing the *Michigan's* cannon."

"Not a good idea. Use a flare. Might be the wrong party shootin' the cannon, if things go wrong. By the way, if things do go wrong, the boarding party would have to row to the mainland and run like hell. Your warship would have to disappear before the *Michigan* gets up steam, or she would soon be overtaken and blown to bits."

Murdaugh stood, offering his hand to Matt. "Thank you, suh, for your input. We will do exactly as you say. We plan to sail on the *Robert E. Lee*, along with our cannon, as soon as Davis signs his approval. We'll sail from Wilmington." Both men thanked Charity Jane for her hospitality, mounted, saluted, and galloped away.

It was well into the first week of March before a courier cantered up to the Chandler gate. The message was terse:

Dear Sir:

Please report to the aforementioned port and vessel.

WHM

Carrying a letter, provided by John Mosby, identifying him....rather fancifully....as Captain Matthew Chandler of the Confederate States Navy, Matthew kissed the tearful mother and daughter good-bye, clambered aboard his faithful Rebel, and departed for Wilmington, North Carolina. He arrived at that port city just in time to find that the conspiracy had been called off. Jefferson Davis had canceled the project for fear that an unfortunate political situation could develop between the Confederacy and Great Britain. A large Confederate armored cruiser was being built in that country, and Davis did not want to jeopardize its completion and delivery. The clandestine schemers disbanded, vowing to try again as soon as President Davis could be convinced that conditions were favorable for success. Together, Lieutenant Murdaugh and "Captain Chandler" boarded the cars for Richmond. "I'm convinced we'll restart this project soon, Matt" sighed Murdaugh as he settled onto a seat in the crowded car. "I'll send word to you at your farm just as soon as I hear anything."

Matthew clapped his well-traveled slouch hat upon his head and tipped it down over his eyes in preparation for a nap. "Well, lieutenant, it's not really my farm, but I 'spect to be there. I'll look forward to hearing from you. Will you plan to build a fire under Jeff Davis as soon as you get to Richmond?"

Murdaugh grimaced. "Don't reckon I can get right to the president, but at least I can bother the shit out of the Navy Department. Then, *they* can get to the president....if only to shut me up!" They parted at the Richmond station, shaking hands as warm new friends, and wishing each other luck. "Preferably good!" smiled Murdaugh.

Matt laughed, and snapped a salute which was unhesitatingly returned. Neither man could figure just who outranked whom, so the order of salute and response did not matter. Actually, neither was in uniform, anyway. Matthew rode the *Richmond and Potomac Rail Road* to Milford, Virginia, where he had stabled Rebel. Rebel seemed somewhat miffed at being left, but, nevertheless, nickered happily when Matthew reclaimed him. Matthew pointed Rebel's ears not to the north and west toward home, but to the north and east, toward Oak Grove, Virginia, and the Potomac River. He had fulfilled his obligation, if he really had one, to Captain Mosby. He had Mosby's letter of identification in his pocket. That letter would assure him of a dark-of-night ride across the Potomac. The Confederate Signal Corps had established a "secret line" between Richmond and Washington whereby dispatches and personnel could be routinely transmitted between the warring countries. As a Confederate agent he would have no difficulty in arranging transportation. Once across the river, and safely behind Union lines, he could announce his true identity as an officer of the United States Cavalry who had escaped from rebel captivity. Then, he could go home to Franklin Village, his friends, his farm, his memories. He reached to stroke Rebel's neck and to straighten his scrawny mane. "Don't reckon you will be able to come along on this one, old friend, unless you can swim a lot better than I think you can!" Rebel's ears swiveled back toward him as though in disbelief.

Greyson camped on the banks of the Rappahannock river opposite the lights of Smith's Wharf. The faint, yellow lights twinkled from the north shore through the rising mist, giving dimension to the blackness of the river. He unrolled his blanket but did not lie down to sleep. Instead, he covered his shoulders and stared into the crackling flames of his camp fire, trying to organize the contradictions that ached within his heart. Visions danced through his head as he nodded, sleepily, in the darkness. Once in the north, his glittering uniform would be restored to him. He would, no doubt, be honored for bravery by his peers. He would write to Reverend Lanning. He would telegraph the provost marshal at Detroit and demand to know of Bethany. Life would be good, again, just as soon as he crossed the Potomac.

But then, Mary Sue danced across his dreams. "Blossom cat, Blossom cat, you're hard to tell just where you're at...." Blossom stared at him with those piercing yellow eyes...or was it just the lanterns on the other side of the river? Melody Chandler's sweet, firm breasts were pressed against him, seeking the warmth of his body. He could see her, lonely and cold, tossing in her bed and awaiting his return....and waiting....and waiting. And, Bethany waited in a shallow grave, hidden in the woods by her murderers. She was beyond warmth, beyond comfort. Ellen Trick lay in the Franklin Cemetery, awaiting a rose, and a tear. Penelope walked, head bowed and empty-handed, from the Durham Station Post Office. "Good God!" Matthew sprang to his feet, almost falling into his dying campfire. The dampness of the winter night chilled him to the bone. "Goddammit!" he shouted to the dark river, "I'm headed the wrong way!" Love, in the form of a beautiful woman and her little girl, beckoned to him from northern Virginia. They needed him, and he, them. Viciously, he kicked the fire out, rolled his blanket, saddled his startled horse, and headed for Middleburg as fast as poor Rebel could shuffle. Horses, and men, love to go home.

+ + +

Much to Melody's alarm, since Matthew's departure Mary Sue had spent an inordinate amount of time staring out of the window at the empty road. Melody understood the problem but had no idea as to what to do about it. Mary Sue simply could not stand to lose another father, or even a father figure. The war was difficult for mature women, but they could cry, they could understand, they could cope. Not so with children....especially sensitive ones like Mary Sue. Melody feared that her precocious, charming, happy child would be permanently scarred by the sadness of war's separation and death. She could no longer pray for John's return. Her first love was gone forever. But, Matthew? Perhaps Matthew could return. She knelt, childlike, beside her bed each night, her knees cold against the rough board floor, and implored God for his safe return. "Not just for me, Lord, but for Mary Sue. Please, please, Lord." Each morning she gathered Mary Sue to her and, together, they recited the rosary. Each night she took the beads to bed with her, clutching them to her breast, hoping that they would provide the warmth that her empty bed could not.

It was small wonder, then, that Mary Sue spotted Matthew and Rebel before they were anywhere near the picket fence. "Mama! Mama! They're back!" she screamed as she ran through the door, the gate, and down the road. The tired horse endured a kiss on his muzzle. The little girl partly scrambled, partly was lifted, into the saddle with Matthew where she proceeded to attempt to hug him breathless. Melody followed as far as the gate.

Matthew looked down at her. "May I be allowed to come into the door yard, ma'am?"

Melody giggled. "You may, sir, long's you get down off'n that horse first!" They hugged and kissed, and hugged some more, being careful to include Mary Sue in the loving embraces. "Y'all plan to stay for a while, this time?" asked Melody, between kisses.

"For a good while, I reckon. Least 'till new plans are laid, which might be never."

"Never is soon enough for me."

Rebel had survived the journey quite well. His lame leg had seemed to actually strengthen with the exercise, and his fit was still a bit angular, but perfectly acceptable. Mary Sue led him off to the stable (actually, Rebel led Mary Sue) to water, feed, and groom him. As a finishing touch, she tied a pretty bow of bright red ribbon on his forelock as a "welcome home" present.

Matthew helped in the preparation for dinner by peeling potatoes and setting them to boiling in the big, black pot over the fire. Melody chased a chicken around the yard with her hatchet, and soon had chicken pieces deliciously frying in deep fat in the skillet. In-between her culinary duties, she found time to corner Matthew by taking his face between her hands. "Matt, I'm a little worried 'bout Mary Sue."

He was stoking the fire under the potato pot. "Why's that?"

"She's awful attached to you. Been cryin' in the night since you've been gone."

Matt moved to a chair to better supervise the fire. "Sorry. What do you suppose we can do?"

"For a start, don't go away again."

"Can't promise that. Mosby and I have a deal. He keeps me safe, I help him. Gentlemen's' agreement....fair and proper. If they decide to try again I'm honor bound to help."

"Honor, honor, honor! Sometimes I'm sick of you men's' honor!"

Matthew rose and put his arms around her from behind as she was bent over the sizzling skillet. "I'm sorry, Melody, but honor is what makes us different from the savages." The moment that he spoke he realized that he had made a mistake.

She spun around, anger on her face. "By savages, of course, you mean Indians. Well, I beg your pardon, suh, but Indians have honor too....perhaps more than white men do."

"Sorry, Melody. Didn't mean that at all. Oh, damn! Sorry."

She spun back to her frying. "You need to hear a song me an' Mary Sue been singin' since you been gone. Maybe, hearin' it, you'll understand what's more important....love, or honor."

"Did you write it just for me?"

"Almost."

"Almost? What does that mean?"

Melody could sense a problem arising. She decided to be truthful. "We substituted 'Matthew' for 'daddy'. Can you handle that?"

Matthew looked puzzled for a moment as he figured the scenario. "Ah! 'Course I can handle it. Look forward to a special concert after dinner." He turned away, rolling his eyes.

Melody flipped the sizzling chicken parts. "Wish I had some more mulberry wine for you. Think you're going to need it."

Mary Sue, totally recovered from her depression, provided most of the conversation through dinner while Melody and Matthew were less talkative than usual. "Mama, we need to write us a happy new song, now that Uncle Matt's back."

Melody reached across the table to pat her hand. "You're dead right 'bout that. First , though, we need to sing him the song we sang so much while he was gone."

Mary Sue pouted her lips, in deep thought, for a moment. "Reckon that would be fine, mamma, but could we make popcorn, and mint tea, and sit around the fireplace like we used to, first?"

"You bet! We'll do just that....right after we clean up the dishes."

Matthew was growing impatient. "Would you females please tell me what this song might be?"

"It's a lullaby. I think it to be right pretty, if I do say so, myself. It even has a name, doesn't it, dear?"

Mary Sue treated them to her sweetest smile. "It's called *Lullaby for Mary Sue*. Mama wrote it just for me....'cept we can't write it down 'cause we don't know how to write music. Can we learn to do that, one day?"

"Yes, dear. One day we'll learn how to put music on paper. We'll learn together."

Mary Sue was getting excited. Her black curls were sticking out in all directions. "And....and....and....maybe we could just get one of them organs like Miss Mary Margaret plays in church! Bet she could teach us to write music!"

"Might be she could." Melody tried to smooth the renegade black curls. "Now, it's getting late. Let's have our tea and popcorn."

Matthew shook his head to clear his ears from the chatter. "When may I hear this wonderful song, ladies?"

"Bedtime!" they chorused as they washed and dried the dishes, pans, and utensils.

"Could Uncle Matt come up into the loft, on my bed, when we sing my song?"

Melody thought for a moment. "I have a better idea. Why don't we all sleep down here? You and I can take the pillows and Uncle Matt can lie across the foot of the bed." Matt rolled his eyes. Melody chuckled, inwardly. She knew that he had been too long without intimate feminine companionship and would not take kindly to the arrangement.

"That would be just fine!" chirped Mary Sue. "I'm goin' to get ready for bed right now." She hustled up the ladder, reappearing in just seconds wearing her nightie. The corn was soon popped in a long-handled wire basket that was held over the fire in the big fireplace. The popcorn was washed down with steaming cups of mint tea that was lightly sweetened with honey. "You 'spose we could ever get an organ like the one in church?"

Melody looked a little glum. "I think not. Too expensive. Took the church members five years to raise the money for the one they've got. You might be able to take lessons on that one, though."

Mary Sue brightened. "That would be nice. Would you take lessons too?" "We'll see. Time for bed, now."

Matthew's mind was busy as he sat in the dimly-lit little room, staring into the crackling fire. He remembered that he had some money....quite a bit of money....stashed in a bank in Pontiac, Michigan. "Perhaps after the war...." he thought to himself, "Mary Sue will have her organ." Matt carried the lamp into the bedroom and turned it down low. The child propped herself on one pillow and patted the other for her mother to do the same. Matt sprawled across the foot of the bed as previously directed.

"Uncle Matt! Really!"

"What?" his eyebrows were raised.

"You can't go to bed with your boots on."

"Oh. Sorry."

"You go first, mama."

Melody:	Sleep, sleep, don't you weep, mama is right here. Sleep, sleep. don't you weep, you have naught to fear.
Mary Sue:	Matthew's gone to war he has, Matthew's gone away!

Melody: Don't you fret your little head.
               He'll be back, someday.

Both: And through the fields we'll run.
               We'll smile up to the sun.
               Then he will pick us flowers for our hair.
               And we'll wear pretty dresses,
               with ribbons for our tresses,
               and hug him 'till we can not hug no more,
               no more!

Melody: Sleep, sleep, don't you weep,
               mama is right here.
               Sleep, sleep, don't you weep,
               you have naught to fear.

Mary Sue: Matthew's gone to war he has,
               Matthew's gone away!

Melody: Don't you fret your little head,

Both: He'll be back, someday.

At the conclusion of the delightful little lullaby, Melody and Mary Sue looked to their audience, ready to savor his enthusiastic approval.

Matthew was fast asleep.

LULLABY FOR MARY SUE

Page 1

LULLABY FOR MARY SUE

370

CHAPTER TWENTY

Dr. & Mrs. Mortimer Belcher

From mid-December, 1862, to January 5, 1863, President Jefferson Davis was absent from Richmond....and for good reason. Southern morale was slipping. Vicksburg, Mississippi, the important bastion on the bank of the great river, was being threatened by Union troops under the direction of the upstart Union General U.S. Grant. The frightening lists of Confederate casualties were growing at a discouraging rate. His proud country was beginning to show signs of grumbling despair as the southerners viewed the ongoing carnage. With the wounded, but recovering, General Joseph E. Johnston in tow he made a speechmaking, morale-boosting, tour of many of the critical cities in the Confederacy. His, and General Johnston's, impassioned orations successfully re-ignited the fires of southern patriotism. When he returned to the loving arms of his impatiently waiting wife, Varina, his careworn face smiled with the hope that his country was reasonably inspired and solidly united under his leadership.

The executive mansion had been unusually quiet while the president was off on his tour. Bethany greatly enjoyed the company of Mrs. Davis and the children but, nevertheless, had felt isolated and alone. She had longed to sneak off to Middleburg to see if she could find Matthew but could come up with no practical plan to do so. Frustrated and sad, she had thrown herself into the demanding duties at the Chimborazo Hospital. Life was easier if she did not allow herself time to brood. The flow of visitors to the executive mansion had essentially ceased during the president's absence. She had no one to ask as to conditions in Middleburg or as to whether anyone had learned of Matthew's presence there. Even Secretary Benjamin had neither solace to give nor information to offer. She was further disturbed to find that her own father had little time to spare for her. Major Dodge was totally involved in the defense of the City of Charleston. The Federal fleet was attempting to establish a naval blockade of that strategically important South Carolina community....an annoying development that required his full attention.

With the return of the president, however, Bethany's barely-sustained patience began to pay off. As executive luncheons and dinners resumed she had the opportunity to meet many of the important personages of the Confederate high command. She met General Joseph Johnston (a nice little bald sort of man), General Robert Lee (were I a soldier I would follow him anywhere) and General P.G.T. Beauregard (oh, my goodness, what a handsome and charming person!). Davis included both Bethany and Varina in as many executive occasions as he deemed appropriate. The ladies did their work well. The guests, especially the males, were both charmed and relaxed by the perfumed and lacy presence of the lovely women.

Bethany had learned , when she had been in Washington, D.C., under the tutelage of the seductive spy Rose O'Neil Greenhow, that the tuning of one's ears to the various conversations overheard at meetings, receptions, and parties could be of great value. She listened carefully, and catalogued in her mind any scraps of information that might help, even in the remotest way, to lead her to Matthew. She learned, for instance, that the Confederate Army Signal Corps was involved with more than just the sending and receiving of militarily important messages. Hidden within the shadows of the Signal Corps was another organization about which only whispers were heard. It was the Confederate Secret Service.

At their very first meeting, Mr. Davis had casually mentioned that she could perhaps again be of use as an undercover operative should she so desire. Bethany began to give the opportunity some serious thought. Perhaps she did, indeed, so desire! She realized that as a member of the secret organization she would have both access to more information and more freedom of movement than she was allowed within the confines of the executive mansion. Additionally, she was becoming a little bored with the routines of her current positions. She dropped a quiet hint to Davis. He responded only with a wink and said not a word.

Bessie knocked upon the door of Bethany's room early one March morning. She bore a sealed message upon her silver tray. "This just come for you, Miss Bethy."

"Thank you, Bessie. Please come in and tidy up....seeing as you are already here so bright and early." Beth sat at her desk and slit open the envelope while Bessie smoothed the soft sheets and puffed the perky pillows. Bethany uttered a suppressed shriek of delight. The message was from a Captain Norris of the Signal Corps. He wanted to meet with her. She danced around the room holding the penned request. "This is good! This is good! Bessie, I think that I'm finally going to have some fun!"

Bessie turned and sat upon the coverlet that she had just smoothed to perfection. She sighed and shook her head. "Miss Bethany, are you goin' crazy on me again?"

Bethany controlled her glee. "No, dear Bess. Its just that a Captain Norris wants to meet with me."

Bessie pursed her lips. "Who might he be? Some gent wants to make you his woman?"

"No such luck!" came the giggling reply. "I've never even seen the man." She perched confidentially on the bed next to her servant and friend. "In fact, few people have. I understand few folks even know him. Keeps to himself. Seems he doesn't like social occasions very much."

"Sounds like a strange buck to me. You sure you want to meet with him?"

"I'm very sure." Bethany patted her hand. "Don't you worry, Bess."

Bessie vaulted indignantly from her seat on the bed and stood before her mistress with arms akimbo. "Worry? Worry? Me worry? 'Course I worry. I ain't sure you got any sense when it comes to menfolks!"

Bethany's voice was soft. "Why do you say that?"

"Cause when you get through pinin' for a man that's probably already dead you could fall for the first yaller-haired, cigar-smokin' gent that comes along hopin' to give you a ride. Womenfolks get theirselves hurt thataways."

"Don't you worry, my sweet Mother Bessie. I'll always love my Matthew. I'll love him forever. And I'll not let another man near me unless I know for sure that my real and only love is dead....and maybe not even then. Captain Norris may just want to give me employment."

"You already got employment. Lots of It."

"I know. I know something else, too. You're upset because you think that I might leave you behind."

Bess dabbed at her eyes. "Yes'm. Its true."

"Thought so. Don't you worry about that either. I don't expect to go anywhere....and even if I did it would not be for long." Beth gave her a playful crack on the fanny. "Now, why don't you get back to work while I write a reply to the captain?"

Bessie grinned through her tears as she rubbed her smarting backside. "Yes, Miss Bethany."

The Confederate Army Signal Corps was conveniently headquartered just a short distance from the gracefully columned capitol building that stood imposingly atop a hill, overlooking the swirling streets of Richmond. Bethany chose to walk the short distance from the executive mansion to keep her appointment. She was immediately ushered into the cluttered office of the elusive Captain Norris. The uniformed captain arose from his desk and greeted her warmly. Another, younger man who was quite nattily dressed in civilian garb also stood when she entered. The second man's thin face, the goat-like sparse beard that decorated his youthful chin, and the sparkle in his eyes were strangely familiar. Bethany acknowledged the captain's polite greeting with a curtsey. She then turned fix the younger man in her gaze. The cold blue of her eyes made him quake....just a bit. She held out her hand to him. "I believe that we have met before, somewhere."

He bowed and gently took her extended hand. "We have, indeed, Miss Dodge. In Washington. My mother is a friend of Mrs. Greenhow. Mary Surratt."

"Why, of course! You are John. John Surratt Jr. I do remember." She favored him with her dazzling smile. "A pleasure to see you again, John." The blue eyes softened.

He bowed again. "Thank you, Miss Dodge. The pleasure is all mine."

Norris cleared his throat. It seemed that he was taking a back seat in the conversation. "Please have a seat, Miss Dodge. It is my understanding that you are an experienced and well-trained secret agent."

Bethany chuckled. "I don't know who told you that, captain. It would be more accurate to say that I am somewhat experienced and somewhat trained."

"Is it true that you once shot a Pinkerton agent dead while you were on assignment?"

Beth gulped at the frank description of an event that she had hoped to forget. "Yes, that's true. Strictly self defense, you understand."

Surratt sat wide-eyed in his chair. He had not heard this information before. "You really did that, Miss Dodge?"

Beth tried to act callused and matter-of-fact. "I did, Mr. Surratt. I had no choice." Beth smiled to herself. The men were so impressed by the demise, by her hand, of the Pinkerton agent that she did not have the heart to tell them that she also had a one-third interest in the more recent passing, in similarly untimely fashion, of a pirate named Lawrence Martin. It was important, she thought, that she be viewed with respect. It was not necessary, however, that the gentlemen consider her some sort of feminine agent of death.

Captain Norris parked his elbows on the desk and made a little church steeple with his fingers. "Then, you are expert in the use of firearms? I find this unusual in a woman."

Bethany was secretly having a grand time as she coolly looked him in the eye. "Then, sir, perhaps you will find that I am an unusual woman."

Norris exhaled through pursed lips and leaned back in his chair. He was uncertain just what sort of tigress had been foisted upon him. "I suppose it really doesn't matter, but I confess I am indeed curious. Where did you receive your training in weaponry?"

"From my father. He believed that a woman should know how to defend herself. I can tell you that I am surely glad that he did. He taught me to shoot everything from tiny pistols to muskets so heavy that I could barely hold them to my shoulder."

The captain's eyebrows were raised. "Indeed!"

Surratt raised his, too, in silent chorus. "Indeed!" he echoed.

Norris continued his interrogation. "Do you possess a weapon now, Miss Dodge?"

"I do not. Mine was, unfortunately, stolen by another Pinkerton bully."

"What was it?"

"A Sharps derringer."

"Would you like a new one?"

"Certainly."

Norris smiled. "I'll see to it. I must say, Miss Dodge, that I am certainly glad that you are on our side!"

Beth smiled as she coyly played with the folds of her expensively tailored skirt. "Thank you, captain. I am proud to serve the cause."

"Would you be interested in taking an assignment.?"

Bethany again met his gaze. "Depends on what that assignment might be."

Norris looked a little unnerved. "Fair enough. Let me explain. Mr. Surratt, here, is a courier. We need to transport a quantity of gold coin, and Federal greenbacks, to northern Virginia for the use of a Captain Mosby. Have you heard of him?"

She looked puzzled. "Can't say I have. Who is this Mosby, and why does he need gold and Yankee money instead of Confederate currency?"

"An astute question, Miss Dodge. Captain Mosby often has to deal with people who have no faith in Confederate money."

"You mean for bribes, special undercover services, and the like?"

"Precisely."

Bethany stopped petting her pleats and settled squarely in her chair. "Please go on."

Captain Norris swung in his chair to face Surratt. "John, perhaps you, as a courier, could best explain the details."

It was Surratt's turn to nervously clear his throat. "A courier needs to often change his identity to keep from establishing patterns that the enemy might begin to identify and thus lie in wait for his passage. For instance, I intend to change my hair color and shave my beard for this delivery."

Beth chuckled inwardly to herself. That scrawny beard would be no great loss! "I see." she said, quietly. "Please do go on."

Surratt looked at the ceiling as though for inspiration, and cleared his throat again. "It is my thought that if you and I were to travel as husband and wife it would alleviate the suspicions of either Yanks or bandits who might be watching for a delivery of gold, money, dispatches, or whatever."

She wriggled in her chair as she began to comprehend the plan. "What are the chances of getting to our destination without being captured?"

John scratched, thoughtfully, at his fledgling beard. "Perfectly good, I would think, else I wouldn't even try!"

Norris intervened. "The chances of getting through are very good because, for this mission, only the three of us, plus President Davis and Captain Mosby, will know about it. No chance for wagging tongues to give us away."

She nodded her understanding. "Where would we meet this Mosby person?"

The captain leaned back and clasped his hands behind his head. Unbeknownst to either Bethany or John, Jefferson Davis had directed Norris to utilize Bethany should there be a reasonably safe mission to the Middleburg area. "Middleburg. In northern Virginia." Captain Norris smiled, blandly, across his desk as he awaited a reaction from Bethany.

Bethany blinked for a moment as the good fortune registered in her mind. It was almost too good to be true. She sat straight in her chair, as though at attention, and flashed her winning smile. "I'll go. Of course I will go." She batted her dark eyelashes at the men. "Sounds like an exciting way to be of service to our country."

"Fine!" chorused the gentlemen as they rose from their chairs to signal the end of the interview. Norris had been fully informed by the president about Bethany's real motive for going to Middleburg. Nevertheless, he decided against challenging her patriotic outburst. Davis had also assured him that Miss Dodge was deeply loyal to the southern cause. There was no point in exposing her plan to find her fiancé so long as it did not interfere with official business.

"One condition." Bethany waved a finger at them. They plopped back into their chairs. "We will be husband and wife in name only. I shall insist on separate sleeping accommodations."

The men eyed each other in amusement. "Ma'am," said Surratt with a chuckle, "that may be awkward, but I reckon we can manage to make arrangements that you will consider suitable."

"Very well!" said Bethany as she stood to depart. "When do we leave?"

"Tomorrow."

"Tomorrow?"

Norris looked serious. "Tomorrow. I suggest that you say good-bye to no one."

"Yes, suh. I'll be ready." She was already worried about Bessie. The poor, devoted servant would be crushed and dismayed. As she walked back to the White House, Bethany solved the Bessie problem in her mind. She would send her friend back to Charleston with the explanation that Major Dodge had need of her services. Soon, she would promise, they would be reunited.

Beth hoped, with all her heart, that the promise would not be broken.

Early the next morning, Surratt and Dodge boarded the northwestbound train as Dr. and Mrs. Mortimer Belcher. No one was at the station to say good-bye. The alias was Bethany's idea. She firmly insisted upon the name even though her companion whined and protested. He hated the name "Mortimer". "Never you mind." sniffed Bethany. "I won't call you 'Mortimer' very often....'Mort' will do." Surratt offered further objections to the fact that their last name sounded like a gas eruption. Trying to hide a wry smile, Bethany ignored that objection, too. They would travel the westernmost branch of the Confederate "secret line" of communication with the north. They would travel to Gordonsville, then north by rail as far as they could.... depending on which side controlled the right-of-way at that particular time. They were fortunate to be able to take the cars to Culpeper Court House. At that point, they were advised that Federal troops had destroyed the rails to the north. At a prearranged "safe house" they were provided with a single-horse buggy. Chuckling and gleeful at their good fortune, so far, they eventually clip-clopped, unchallenged, into Middleburg....their secret identity undetected, their cover secure.

As far as they could tell, the townspeople seemed to be in a business-as-usual mood. There was a scurry of drays, buggies, and pedestrians bustling hither-and-yon as the citizens of Middleburg went about their daily merchandising, and/or work, and/or pleasure. As with most rural southern communities in 1863, there was a preponderance of women, old men, and small boys. Many of the boys who were driving the heavily loaded wagons looked much too young to be equal to the task. Remarkably, however, Dr. and Mrs. Belcher did not witness any smashups or runaways. "Good thing!" muttered Surratt. "It would be right embarrassing if I got asked to fix some run-over urchin. Wouldn't have the slightest idea what to do."

Bethany tittered. "I'd guess you would think of something, Mortimer."

"Don't call me that."

"Sorry." Even though there were very few men of military age on the street, Bethany noticed a group of five or six gentlemen who were lounging near their horses in front of the Red Fox Tavern. The Red Fox was situated just across a side street from the Colonial Inn, their assigned destination. The men stared at them as they pulled up in front of the inn. Those men are making me nervous, Mort!" whispered Bethany. "Do you suppose they are Mosby's men?"

Furtively, John glanced their way. "If'n they ain't, then they're bandits or some sort of irregulars and we could be in a peck of trouble. Pretend you don't see 'em. Let's get into the inn fast as we can without looking hurried."

"Now, that's a classic contradiction of terms if I ever heard one. I'll try to hurry slowly. Mort, I suspect that you may be an idiot."

"Thank you for your kind words, wifey dear."

A squadron of energetic little black boys emerged, seemingly from nowhere, and descended upon them. They were hopping up and down, fueled by the excitement of having a chance to do the duties to which they had been entrusted by the proprietress, Mrs. Catherine Braun. Catherine, incidentally, still took great pride in serving good meals to soldiers of either uniform, just as she had the year before when Lieutenant Colonel Greyson and the First Michigan Cavalry had come to town. John allowed one of the larger boys to lead the horse and buggy to the stable. To the smaller ones he gave the task of toting his, and Bethany's, personal valises. The two heavy black surgeons bags he chose to carry himself, puffing at the weight of the gold that was concealed beneath their false bottoms. Once inside, they were greeted by Mrs. Braun, herself, who swooped to meet them. She patted an imaginary wisp of hair back into her coiffure as she approached. "Good day, folks! Will y'all be staying with us?"

"We will, if it will be convenient for you to accommodate us." John smiled as he bowed. "We are Dr. and Mrs. Belcher."

Catherine looked a little wide-eyed. "Belcher? Interesting name."

John, embarrassed, began to shuffle his feet. Bethany wanted to kick him to get him to stop, but Mrs. Braun was watching. "It is an interesting name, isn't it?" she smiled. "Mrs. Braun, you may be expecting us."

Catherine stared at Bethany for a moment. "Why, yes, I believe I am.... expecting you. I even have a lovely room that is ready and waiting for you."

"Rooms." Bethany held up two of her carefully manicured fingers. "Rooms. Two rooms, please."

Mrs. Braun raised her eyebrows. "I didn't realize y'all required two rooms. Fortunately, I have another nice room available."

"Thank you." smiled Beth. "May I see them, please?"

"You want to see them before you take them?"

"Yes. I do. Please." She gave the distinct impression that if she did not like the accommodations, she and the doctor would march right out of the door and find lodging elsewhere.

"Very well," sniffed Catherine Braun "but I am sure you will like them. This way, please." She led them up the stairway with the small boys, struggling with the valises, in their wake. In each room, Bethany threw back the neatly-made covers and lifted the pillows on the beds as she looked for the high speed departure of bedbugs that might be lurking there. None were spied.

"These will do just fine!" pronounced Beth. John breathed a sigh of relief. He had carried the doctor's bags quite far enough, for a while. Carrying them up the stairs had been something of a challenge. He dismissed the boys, giving each of them a small coin. He could afford to be generous with Jeff Davis' money.

When the boys had departed, tumbling down the stairs with squeals of delight about their new riches, Mrs. Braun's eyes narrowed as she got right down to business. "Captain Mosby told me to look out for y'all, but he wouldn't say who you were or why you were coming here. Made it hard to figure just who to look out for!"

John pushed back the curtain and looked out of the window. The cluster of horsemen was still in the street. "You did just fine, ma'am. Thank you. We need to meet with Captain Mosby."

"You're in luck, dear. The captain is next door, at the tavern, right now."

"Those are his men down there?"

"I don't even have to look, doctor. There are always gentlemen outside when the captain is inside."

John turned away from the window and, with a groan, picked up the medical bags. "I see. Then, dear wife, let us go and make our delivery that we may be relieved of our responsibility."

Beth waved a hand in front of her face as though annoyed by a fly. "You go. I wish to talk to Mrs. Braun."

"You don't want to meet the handsome captain and his handsome men?"

"Not really, thank you. I do want to talk to Mrs. Braun for a moment. I'm sure that you can handle the rest of the delivery without my further assistance....can't you?" Bethany could sting whenever she thought it appropriate to do so.

Embarrassed again, John's ears and cheeks flushed with color. There was simply no way that he could deal, successfully, with such a woman. "Very well!" was the best reply that he could muster as he departed down the bare wooden stairs, carrying the bags that he had just carried, painfully, in the other direction.

When Surratt arrived at the Red Fox, and identified himself, he was ushered into the tavern where three gray-uniformed men sat before a cheery fire that crackled in the large stone fireplace, their booted feet stretched toward the warmth. A window, to the soldiers' left, gave a clear view of the street, and of the men who were posted thereon. The three stood, politely, when he entered. Their leader, who wore the embroidered insignia of a captain upon the shoulders of his uniform, came forward to shake his hand. "Welcome!" he beamed. "I believe that you have brought us some badly needed supplies!"

"I have. Assuming, of course, that you are Captain John Singleton Mosby."

The captain bowed, graciously. "John Mosby at your service, sir. And your name would be?"

"Don't ask." There was no way that he was going to tell them that his name was Mortimer Belcher.

"Sorry. I should have thought that you would not want to be identified."

"Call me Mort. Suh, there is a quantity of both gold coin and Federal greenbacks under the false bottoms of these bags."

Mosby was beaming again. "Thank you, Mort! A job well done. Ah, is there some sort of signed inventory so that I may know that all of the shipment has arrived? I don't mean to be extraordinarily suspicious, suh, but these are difficult, and sometimes tempting, times."

A peeved look crossed Surratt's face. "Captain, my integrity is beyond question. I am not into skimming funds from my country. You will find an inventory with the money in each bag. The inventories are signed by the president himself. Be assured, it is all there....but, of course, you can see for yourself....unless you or your men are the dishonest ones." Surratt wished that Bethany could have been there to see him stand up like the real man that he was and defy the famous Captain Mosby. John Harrison Surratt Jr. was a quietly brave man who could easily be mistaken for something less. Perhaps it was the weakness of his clean-shaven chin....

John Mosby smiled at the slender rooster who stood before him. "I apologize, Mort. I did not mean to question your loyalty or your honesty. You secret service folks do invaluable, but dangerous, work. Work which is much appreciated by all of us. In case you are wondering, we need the gold and greenbacks to pay off those who have no confidence in the script of the Confederate States of America. Many key people that we depend on fit into this category. I hope you understand that these funds are urgently needed and will be carefully spent to advance various and important undercover activities vital to our cause."

"Indeed I do understand, captain. It's a privilege to work with y'all." He parked his medical bags in front of the fireplace. "If it is convenient, suh, I would much appreciate the return of these satchels along with the medicines and instruments which they contain. We'll need them for cover on our return to Richmond."

"Certainly. Will tomorrow morning be satisfactory?"

"Perfectly. We'll leave as soon as they are returned."

Mosby patted John on he shoulder. "Mort, I heard you say 'we'. You have a woman with you. A pretty one. Who is she, if I may ask?"

"My wife, of course."

"Of course. Your wife, doctor." Mosby grinned. "May wedded bliss visit you on every night of your return trip!"

John returned the grin, albeit a little sheepishly. "Not likely, but thanks for the thought, captain." Surratt strode, abruptly, out of the door. He knew that no miracle, even one straight from heaven, could bring Bethany to his bed. He certainly did not wish to discuss the situation with his grinning new acquaintances.

+ + +

Catherine Braun led Bethany into her private parlor on the upper floor of the Colonial Inn. "Let us sit in here, Mrs. Belcher, and we can talk all you want. You seem a bit edgy about something. Perhaps this undercover work is beginning to tell on you. How about a nice, calming cup of tea? I know! Chamomile Tea!" She summoned a servant who delivered the tea in a remarkably short time. The soothing, fragrant tea was steeped in a rosebud-decorated teapot with matching cups, all on a silver tray with lemon, sugar, and cream all presented in appropriate silver containers. Beth, used to the finer amenities of life, clapped (the heels of her hands delicately together, of course) with delight. "How beautiful! How do you manage to have such lovely things at such an unlovely time of war?"

Mrs. Braun threw back her head in a hearty laugh. "Carefully stored necessities and carefully picked friends. Just because there is a war going on doesn't mean we women can't maintain our simple pleasures." The two women were, instantly, friends. "Now," asked Mrs. Braun as she poured the tea, "what was it that you wanted to talk about?"

"I am trying to locate my fiancé. He is a wounded veteran and is reported to be in this area. His name is Matthew Greyson. Have you heard of him?"

Catherine Braun shook her head, sadly. "No dear, I have not. Well....there was a Yankee officer through here, a year or so ago, who had a name something like that."

Bethany sat straight upright. Her teacup rattled. "Really? That could be him."

"I thought you were talking about a southern boy."

Bethany's mind was spinning. She could be causing problems for Matthew. "Sorry. You are right. Could not be a Yankee. The man that I am looking for is dark haired, very handsome, and is probably wearing a patch over his right eye."

"Oh, dear!" It was Mrs. Braun's teacup's turn to rattle upon its saucer. She almost dropped it. "Yes! It must be he. There couldn't be two men, 'round here, like that. He is working at the Chandler farm outside of town."

"Is Mrs. Chandler a widow?"

"She is. Her husband was killed early in the war."

Bethany turned her eyes toward heaven for a moment. "Is she beautiful?"

"Well, I reckon that she is somewhat attractive, for a squaw."

"A squaw?"

"Yep. She is some sort of an Indian. Don't know much about her as she pretty much keeps to herself. Has a half-breed daughter who seems quite civilized, in my estimation. Don't know the child well, either. Her mother keeps her pretty well separated from the other children 'round here.... probably because of her inferior breeding, I suppose. Also, she appears to be a Catholic. Most folks around here are Protestant, of one sort of another, so she doesn't mix with us at church meetings or socials. The Catholics have their own church, quite a nice one, actually, with nice people who attend."

"I see." Bethany choked back tears as she tried to assimilate all this new information. "Does Matthew....the man with the eye patch....seem well?"

Catherine refilled the cups. "He looks healthy to me. I did notice he has a crippled hand, but that doesn't seem to bother him much. Good heavens, Mrs. Belcher, how did you lose this man, this fiancé?" Mrs. Braun was ignoring, as an obvious farce, the fact that Bethany was supposed to be married to the doctor with whom she had arrived.

Beth buried her face in her hands and started to cry. "The war! The damned war!"

Catherine settled, sympathetically, into her parlor chair. "I'm sorry, dear. How may I help?"

"You can tell me how to get to the Chandler farm."

Mrs. Braun stood and strolled to the window. "I'll do better than that. I'll take you there."

"Oh!" cried Bethany, "Thank you so very, very, very much! You are so understanding and kind. When may we go?"

Mrs. Braun pulled back the crisp lace curtains and stood looking down at the street. "How about first thing tomorrow? Would that be satisfactory?"

"It would. Certainly, it would." Beth tried to conceal that she was shaking with excitement. She offered a silent prayer that she would find Matthew there, and that he would rush into her arms when he saw her.

"Whoops!" Mrs. Braun had noticed something of interest down on the street. "Perhaps tomorrow's visit to the farm will not be necessary. The Widow Chandler is here....right now....obviously to do some shopping at the general store."

"Where? Where?" Beth flew to the window and clawed her way through the curtains. "Where is she? Oh God, where is she? I don't see her!"

"Good heavens, dear, calm down. She just went into the store across the street."

Beth was hyperventilating. "If she has my man I swear I will claw her to pieces! I'm going to march down there and drag her out of that store by the hair!"

"Goodness! Such ferocity from such a sweet little woman!" Catherine took her by the hand and led her back to her chair "Here. Drink some more Chamomile tea. In fact, I think you had better drink a lot of it. Now, listen to me. Charity Jane Melody Chandler is a tall, strong woman. A savage not far separated from the people of the forest. If you are foolish enough to attack her you'll likely find yourself lyin' on your back in the dust of the road with her knee on your chest and a tomahawk whackin' your pretty hair off....along with a nice piece of your scalp! Calm down, Mrs. Belcher. Good God, what the hell is your first name?"

"Bethany."

"Good God, Bethany, calm down! 'Sides, you don't even know if she's got your Matthew, or whoever he is!"

"You are correct, of course." Bethany puffed her cheeks as she caught her breath. She panted until her heart calmed, then drank her cup of tea....and then another. "Well! I am all right, now." She jumped to her feet. "I *will* go to her. Please pray for me."

Catherine Braun set her cup and saucer on the table. "I'm praying now. Do you want me to go with you? I will, if you want me."

"No. Thank you, dear new friend, but I must do this alone." Beth paused at the door. "*However*, should you see her intent upon scalping me, that she might take the pleasure of hanging my hair on her wigwam, would you please avail yourself of some sort of weapon and come to my rescue?"

Mrs. Braun calmly poured herself another cup of tea. "I will, dear, I certainly will! I'll bring a broom. It's a fine, stout one. I will not hesitate to smack her with it."

"Thank you, Catherine!" Bethany, primed for the attack, flounced out of the room, down the stairs, out onto the street, and moved cautiously toward a buckboard to which a handsome bay mare was attached and tied to the rail in front of the store. "I know that mare." muttered Bethany. "I'm certain that I know that mare! It's just like the one that Matthew described to me in his letter. The one that he rescued and returned to that widow. *This widow!*"

Beth was standing, nervously petting the mare's soft muzzle, and gathering the courage to carry out her attack, when the store door jangled open. She looked up to see Charity Jane Melody Chandler standing, with packages in her arms, just outside of the door. She was staring at her. Bethany stared back. The woman was a full six inches taller than Bethany. She was slender, with high cheekbones and long black hair....blacker, even, than her own. "She *is* beautiful, damn it!" she cried, to herself.

Melody smiled. It was a lovely, wide smile full of very white, even teeth. "You like my horse? She's pretty, ain't she?"

Bethany returned the smile while continuing to pet the horse. "Yes, I do. And, yes, she is. What is her name?"

"Buttercup."

"Nice name, Buttercup. Suits her." Beth drew a deep breath. "Mrs. Chandler, could we talk for a moment?"

"Surely. Why not?" Melody placed her packages in the buckboard. "How do you know my name? I never seen you before."

"Sorry. That was impolite of me. " She stuck out her hand. "My name is Bethany Dodge, although, at present, I am supposed to be Mrs. Doctor Belcher. There! I have just exposed myself....but I guess I just don't care, right now. I work for the Confederate government, but that's not what matters. I'm looking for a man named Matthew Greyson. Would you happen to know anything about him?"

The usually unflappable Melody Chandler sagged against the buckboard, using it for support. "Oh, my God!" she thought. "This is the Bethany that Matthew told her about....small, slender, black hair, very fair complexion, blue eyes. Oh, my God!" Her world, that had seemingly once again become secure with her new man, was crashing down around her thanks to the arrival of a woman whom she had secretly hoped was dead.

Inscrutable dark brown eyes met intense, smoky blue as each woman took the measure of the other. Bethany broke the brief silence. "Well, have you seen him....my Matthew?"

Melody stiffened. "I don't know about *your* Matthew, but I have seen Colonel Matthew Greyson. He is quite well, now, and has gone away. I don't know where he might be. Haven't seen him, of late."

Bethany instinctively suspected that the woman was lying, probably to keep her from finding Matthew. She was no longer smiling. "The bitch" she thought "wants to keep him for herself! We'll see about that!" She stopped petting the horse and moved away, stiffly, like a gunfighter getting ready to draw. "Did he stay with you very long, Mrs. Chandler?"

Melody sensed the hostility, but was unimpressed by the little white bird that was trying to look mean, puffing up her feathers. She knew that she could squash that little white bird just like a little white bug, should the occasion arise. "Long enough to heal him, Miss Dodge, just like his friend, Sergeant Will McEwan.".

"Will McEwan? You healed him, too?" Bethany's feathers suddenly lost some of their ruffle.

"'Deed I did. I ain't positive he recovered, but I did put him on a prisoner exchange boat. He was lookin' pretty fair by then. Lost an arm, though, but pretty much of a miracle that he's still breathin' with what's left of his lungs. Far as I know the sergeant is back in the north gettin' ready to come back down here and stir up more trouble for us simple southern folks. Probably Greyson, too. "Spect I should have let 'em both die."

Bethany's eyes sparkled with brimming tears. "Oh no! No! I'm so grateful that you didn't let them die. I'm so grateful that you healed them. I have to thank you for your kindness!" The fight was gone out of Bethany. She pressed her finger to her lips, then turned to absentmindedly stroke Buttercup's neck....a move that at least Buttercup thought was nice. "Um, how did you know how to heal them?"

"The medicine of my fathers, and their father's fathers."

"I see." She did not see, really, but pretended that she understood. "Can you tell me, please, whether Matthew ever got over his brain injury, his confusion?"

"He did. Christmas."

"Did he, then, say anything about me, or about looking for me?"

"No."

"No?"

"No. Not once." Melody, sensing the game, was now lying skillfully.

That was enough. That was all that she could stand. Bethany, totally beaten, sobbing in anguish, with tears streaming down her face, picked up her skirts and flew across the street to the Colonial Inn. Catherine Braun's anxiously awaiting arms caught her as she wailed her way through the door. She sobbed like a little girl who had just broken her favorite doll. When she could speak, her words were punctuated with heartbroken shudders.

"She says Matthew has forgotten me! She says he has gone! She says he doesn't care about me! What shall I do, Catherine?"

Mrs. Braun tried to dry her tears, but it was a fruitless task. They were coming too fast. "First of all, dear, where did she say Matthew is?"

"Gone. Gone! She doesn't know."

"Poppycock!" snorted the proprietress. "The man is still 'round here. Folks see him all the time....'less, of course, he just left in the last couple days, which I doubt. She's probably lyin' about the whole thing, so stop your cryin' and get ahold of yourself."

Beth regained her composure enough to dab at her tears herself. "You really think so? She looked so nice, and she healed those soldiers when she didn't have to. Why would she lie to me?"

"To keep your man away from you, of course."

"Oh, I suppose! I know that I'm not the only woman who has wanted him for her own. It's just that I have always won, before. What else do you know about him?"

Mrs. Braun signaled her servant for more tea and led Bethany back up the stairs to the private parlor where they could talk without being overheard. When they were comfortably seated, Mrs. Braun folded her hands over her bosom and leaned back in her chair. "Well, dear, let me see. I hear he is a good southern boy, raised in North Carolina. Was injured at Second Manassas fighting for the southern cause. Lost one eye and pretty much the use of one hand."

Beth started to cry, again. "I heard that at Chimborazo. Oh, my poor Matthew!"

Catherine waved the servant in who was carrying the freshly filled teapot. "You brought Chamomile, again, didn't you, Iris?"

"Yes'm. Best as I could figure that's what you wanted."

"You were right, as usual, Iris. Thank you."

"Yes'm."

Braun took the cozy off of the pot and neatly laid it aside. "Well, dear, he could not be too bad off, cause he has taken up with Captain Mosby. I wouldn't be surprised to see him ridin' with them."

Beth was aghast. "Really? They are rebels, aren't they?"

"Of course, dear. What do you think they are? Well, maybe you just don't know. Mosby's Rangers! The finest cavalry ever. Work under J.E.B. Stuart."

"So, you think that Matthew is riding with rebel cavalry?"
"That's what I hear."

Beth inflated her cheeks and fluttered her lips. "Now, I've heard everything. Mrs. Braun, this has been quite a day. What else have you heard?"

Catherine poured the tea. "I declare, we're drinking so much tea we're goin' to be running to the outhouse all day and all night! Anyway, I also hear that this man has settled in with Mrs. Chandler and her daughter Mary Sue. I hear Mary Sue loves him like a father."

"How old is she?"

"'Leven, twelve, or so."

Bethany's tears were dry, her attitude was hardening. "Oh! Is that so! Sounds very cozy. I guess that I'll just have to go out to that farm and see for myself. If Matthew is there I will drag him home by the ear!"

Mrs. Braun picked up a fake Japanese fan from the table and fanned herself at the thought. "You had best be careful. I wouldn't put it past that savage to bushwhack you. She does have some backwoods friends who might just think it to be entertaining to make you disappear."

"Pish!" exclaimed Bethany. "I've already done enough disappearing for one lifetime. I do not intend to do any more. Besides, I am armed and dangerous." She lifted her skirt and petticoat to reveal the Sharps derringer that gleamed, menacingly, in its garter holster. She tried to convince Mrs. Braun, and herself, of a bravado that she did not really feel. She did convince Mrs. Braun. "If I go," snarled Beth, with a mock curling of the lip "I won't go easy!"

"Oh, dear!" breathed Mrs. Braun, clutching at her heart. "Whatever you say, dear."

The clatter of hoofs and a gabble of excited shouts suddenly erupted from the street below the window. Both women rushed to see what was taking place. A detachment of Confederate cavalry had galloped into town. They were carrying serious news. A Union reconnaissance-in-force, consisting of five companies of cavalry (about five hundred horse) was approaching Middleburg from the west. No adequate C.S.A. force was available to oppose them. Surely, they would ride into town within the hour.

John Surratt raced up the stairs and into the parlor without knocking. The women turned from the window where they were watching the activity on the street. All military personnel were hurriedly saddling up in preparation for a hasty retreat in the face of impossible odds. "Bethany, where is your cloak?" he panted.

"In my room where it belongs. Why?"

"Captain Mosby has asked us, er, you to carry some dispatches back to Richmond." He waved a packet under her nose. "These here are maps of Yankee fortifications that are drawn on silk." He turned to Mrs. Braun who had returned to the window to watch the show. "Mrs. Braun, could you have one of your servants sew this under the lining of her cloak? I mean, of course, with my wife's permission." He favored Bethany with a sweeping bow.

Bethany ignored his mock demonstration. "Mrs. Braun, how good is your seamstress? I do not want my cloak ruined. Besides, it must not look like it was recently stitched. This will require real skill."

"Indeed, I do have a fine seamstress. Her name is Iris. I'll send for her at once." Mrs. Braun unfolded the maps to take a good look. "Why do they go to the trouble of drawing on such fine silk? Seems such a waste what with silk being almost impossible to get, these days."

"Silk documents are impossible to feel under a lining." explained agent Surratt. "They don't crinkle like paper does. By the way, I assume your seamstress is a darky. Is she trustworthy?"

Catherine Braun recoiled like a wounded snake. "Certainly, she is trustworthy. Her family has been with mine for generations. I love her like a sister, and she, me. She would never betray me, nor the Confederacy, no matter what that silly-ass Abraham Lincoln promises the darkies."

Bethany snickered. "I'd guess that you have made your position, and the maid's loyalty, quite clear!" She spied another, much smaller silk package in John's hand and pointed to it. "What is that, Mortimer?"

"Don't call me Mortimer."

"What would that little package be, Doctor Belcher?"

John, somewhat annoyed, crinkled his nose at her. He held it out for her inspection. It was a document, folded small, and sewn into a silk-covered little package. "It's a dispatch from J.E.B. Stuart to President Davis. Could you possibly find some place on your body to conceal it for the journey home?"

Bethany stared, blushed, then stamped her foot. "Now, just what did you have in mind, John?"

Surratt snorted. "I have no opinion. You can put it wherever you wish, dear wife."

"Well, I suppose that I can hide it in my hair, thank you very much. However, not right now. We cannot leave right now. I have urgent business to which I must attend before I leave Middleburg."

Surratt had a look on his face that was both stern and anxious at the same time. "Beth, these dispatches must get through to Richmond. We just don't dare to take any chances. We can no longer leave to the west. We must leave now, before the Yankee troopers get here. We must run east to Aldie, then south as fast as we can."

"But....but....I cannot go, just now! I believe that I'm close to finding the lost love of my life!" Bethany sank onto a chair and buried her face in her hands. "Don't ask me to do this, John."

John Surratt strode to the window and stood, hands behind his back. "I'm not asking, Bethany. Your country is asking."

Beth stood, with a shuddering sigh, and went to the mirror. She studied her own tear-streaked face for a moment, then pulled the silver tucking comb from her hair, allowing the rich, black tresses to cascade over her shoulders. "Give me the damn package, John." She re-rolled her hair, with the package hidden within, and replaced the tucking comb. "I'll be ready to leave within ten minutes."

Agent Surratt peered anxiously out of the window, trying to see toward the west from whence the Yank troopers would appear. "Thank you, Bethany. Please hurry."

Within minutes the buggy was loaded, valises and medical bags were in place, and Mrs. Braun was waving a tearful good-bye....but it was too late. The Federal advance guard thundered through town, pennants flying and revolvers drawn. Surratt had to hang onto the bridle of the buggy horse. The poor creature plunged in fright as the cavalry cantered past them, kicking up clouds of dust....dust which caused Bethany to become very angry as it settled upon her, soiling her cloak. Her cloak had a hood with which she covered her hair and her face, leaving nothing exposed but her eyes which she kept tightly closed against the swirling dust. The Union horsemen were unopposed, and quickly sealed the city. Sentries were posted at each intersection, and on the roads in and out of the town, within minutes.

Emerging, almost ghostlike, from the swirling dust, three mounted cavalrymen approached the buggy. "Who might you be, sir, and where are you expectin' to go?" The voice sounded strangely familiar to Bethany. She opened her eyes a slit to sneak a look. The speaker was flanked by the other two who sat upon their horses beside him, their carbines at the ready. Even though the weather was still cold, they had rolled their caped overcoats with their blanket rolls, and were wearing their lighter shell jackets. The right sleeve on the spokesperson was empty, the arm missing, but the blue cloth bore the impressive insignia of a sergeant-major. Sandy-colored hair peeked from beneath his kepi. It was Will McEwan!

Bethany felt faint. She shut her eyes. Certainly, should he identify her he would remember that she was under suspicion of being a spy. The only reason that she was not wanted, and subject to arrest, in the north was because the case had been closed. It was considered that she was dead. Capturing her, still very much alive, would earn her a trip north in irons where she would very likely hang. She drew her hood closer around her face and tried to be inconspicuous.

John, still calming the shaking, snorting buggy horse, was quick to answer the cavalryman's question. "Dr. Belcher at your service, suh. We are called to a farm near Aldie. Lady there is havin' berthin' problems. It's my fear that, if we don't get there soon, we might lose both mother and child." His voice was calm and matter-of-fact. No matter what Beth thought of him, John Surratt was a smooth, professional agent.

"I see." Sergeant Willy leaned from his horse to get a better look into the buggy. "Who might that be with you?"

"This here is my wife. She assists me in such matters."

"Midwife, huh?"

"Yes, suh."

Will rode his horse around to the passenger side of the buggy. "Ma'am, I'll have to ask you to uncover your face."

She shook her head. "Can't. Dust chokes me." She drew her hood even closer.

"I'll have to insist, ma'am. We're ordered to look for spies, couriers, an' such that are operatin' in this area. Some of 'em are female. If you don't uncover your face I'll have to do it for you. If you don't cooperate, I'll have to place you under arrest."

A choking feeling, as though the hangman's noose was already tightening around her neck, surged into her throat. She took a deep breath, swung her feet onto the step, and climbed down from the buggy. She stood in the dust, a diminutive figure staring up at her tall interrogator who was mounted on his tall horse. She thought that he looked to be at least two stories high. She flung back her hood. Her eyes shone with ice-blue, defiant fire. She said not a word, waiting for the inevitable arrest.

Sergeant McEwan, stunned, looked as though he had seen a ghost. He, too, was silent. Slowly, almost imperceptibly, one eye drooped in a tiny wink. "Thank you, ma'am. You're not who we are looking for. Sorry to bother you, and sorry about the dust. Couldn't be helped. Better cover up again so's you wont get it in your lungs." He backed his horse away, making him snort and arch his neck, then spun the animal in his tracks. McEwan had not lost his flash. "Corporal! Escort the doctor and his wife east out of town. Toward Aldie. They got them an emergency to attend to!"

At some risk to his military career, Willy McEwan had remained a good friend. His delight in finding Bethany alive, however, caused him to make a grave error. He composed a dispatch which was sent by military courier to the military telegraph, then sent by wire to Pontiac, Michigan, from whence it was delivered, again by military courier, to the Reverend Pitts Lanning:

TAKE HEART. BETHANY ALIVE. STILL LOOKING
FOR MATT. SIGNED SGT MAJ MCEWAN

The message was intercepted by the ever-vigilant Pinkerton agents when it came off of the wire at the Pontiac telegraph office. They copied it, then allowed it to be delivered. Under President Lincoln's suspension of the *writ of habeas corpus*, Alphaeus Plotkin and his henchmen remained in prison even though the murder charges were dropped. Considering the various additional charges against them for breaking and entering, destruction of property, assult, and theft, Provost Marshall Hill decided that the best place for those hoodlums to be was right where they were....behind bars for the duration of the war. Colonel Hill ordered a review of the Bethany Dodge file. Should she be captured she would be subject to immediate arrest and be confined to prison as a spy.

+ + +

John kept the mare at a steady trot after they left their Union escort behind at the edge of town. Bethany immediately started to cry. She cried, pitifully, for about five miles, then sniffed for another three. John ignored her, driving the horse as though she were not in the seat beside him. She finally gulped, and spoke. "I'm coming back here. Right away."

"As you say."

"I will, even if I have to come alone. I can take care of myself!"

"As you say."

"I'll kill them all. Every one of them!"

"Who?"

"Anyone who gets in my way."

"As you say."

"Would you come with me?" The tone of her voice turned from ferocious to pleading.

"Not a chance."

Topping a hill, they spied a line of horsemen blotting out the road about fifty yards distant. "Oh my!" exclaimed Surratt. "It appears we're headed straight into big trouble." But, when they drew closer they saw that the men wore Confederate gray. One of them was Captain Mosby. Mosby greeted them with a doff of the cap and a gallant bow from the saddle. "I see y'all made it out of Middleburg, praise the Lord!"

John Surratt grinned. "Yes we did, captain. 'Deed we did, though I don't understand just how we managed it." Bethany snickered to herself, but kept quiet. She knew exactly just how they had managed their escape, but she was not interested in sharing the details, for obvious reasons.

Mosby replaced his cap and signaled two men, in civilian dress, forward. "These gents are going to escort you, by back roads, to Culpeper Court House where you can catch the cars back to Richmond. Would that be of help?"

"Indeed it would, captain. Thank you." John was delighted by the unexpected assistance.

"You are welcome." He dismounted, with easy grace, and came to take Bethany's hand. "I have not had the pleasure of meeting the lady. I am John Singleton Mosby."

Beth smiled, graciously. She was somewhat awed by the gentleman. "Bethany Belcher, suh. It is a great pleasure to meet you, captain. " Her Carolina accent was sweet as honey. "I pray that you and your men will continue your heroic exploits in great safety."

He bowed. "Thank you miss....er....ma'am. And best of luck to you."

"Thank you captain." she trilled, musically. "'Bye now." She surreptitiously tapped John's leg with her toe. He clucked to the mare, and they moved on, the troopers close behind.

Surratt glared at her. "Don't you think you laid it on a little thick?"

Beth kept her honeyed phrases turned on. "Well, deah, Ah just don't believe that is so. Ah believe that sweet boy enjoyed every minute of our pleasant, if brief, conversation."

"Oh, good heavens." John Surratt, a few minutes before, had almost wanted to put his arm around her to comfort her. Now, he had changed his mind. Miss Dodge was much too complicated, or perhaps, much too devious for his taste.

+ + +

Melody Chandler had watched Bethany run away, back to the Colonial Inn. She could not help but feel sorry for the young, heartbroken woman, but after all, that was life. Bethany had spent her time with Matthew. Now, it was her turn and she would do whatever was necessary to keep Matthew for herself, and for Mary Sue. Neither of their hearts would ever mend if Matthew went away. She simply was not capable of handling the loss of another beloved man, nor was her daughter capable of handling the loss of another father. She hurriedly retrieved the rest of her packages from the store and was about to turn Buttercup toward home when the Confederate cavalry arrived with the news of the Yankee advance. That news gave her increased speed. Now, there was another danger. The Yanks could find Matt and drag him north under one pretext or another. She urged Buttercup into her fastest trot, and kept her there. The wheels of the buckboard fairly sang over the rutted trail as she headed for home. "Matt! Matt! Where are you?" she hollered as she turned off the road, past the picket fence, and toward the barn. "What? What?" He came running from the barn where he had been mending harness. "Good heavens, Melody, what's wrong? I can see you're in a hurry. Buttercup is all lathered."

"Never mind Buttercup! You have to hide. Union troopers are riding into town, and government agents are looking for you!"

Matt looked down the road. "Agents of which government, and how far behind you are they?"

Melody was annoyed that he was not taking her very seriously. "Union cavalry, southern agents, and as far as I know neither is on the way here, yet....but they could be, soon. Matt, I'm scared."

Matthew held her for a moment, stroked her hair, and kissed her ear. "Buttercup is all lathered. Help me cool her down." Together, they unharnessed the mare, rubbed her down with an old towel, and walked her until she was cool to the touch and breathing normally. "Now, who are these agents that are looking for me?"

"I don't know their names, of course, but they are from Richmond and are asking questions about you. I would suspect that they know you are a Yankee officer who should be in Andersonville Prison instead of running loose around the countryside."

"I see. And the Union cavalry?"

"'Bout five hundred, I hear. I don't think they are really looking for you, but if they do see you they might think you are a deserter 'stead of recovering from your wounds. I want you to hide 'till they are all gone."

"Well, I am a Federal officer running loose, out of uniform, in enemy territory, and I am a deserter. Because of my southern upbringing, I have agreed to help the southern cause....at least a little bit. Guilty as charged. What would you have me do?"

"Hide. You an' Buttercup hide in the barn John built back in the woods."

She put her arms around his neck and punctuated her words with kisses. "You will be neither cold, nor lonesome, nor hungry, nor lacking in love, I promise. Make a nice bed in the hay and I will lie in it as often as you like."

Matt's grin was just about as wide as it could get, in anticipation of collecting upon such a promise. "I surely can't turn down an offer like that. When do we start?"

"Right now."

+ + +

Two days later, while Melody and Mary Sue were packing a basket in preparation for a picnic lunch in the woods with Matthew, Blossom suddenly gave the alarm. Within minutes, the road by the gate was filled with blue-uniformed cavalry. Mary Sue hid the picnic basket while Melody stepped out of the front door, her squirrel rifle cradled in her arms. When she recognized Will McEwan at the head of the column, she put down the rifle and ran to him, much to the amusement of the troopers. "Oh Will, Will, I'm so happy to see you looking well!"

"Thanks to you, Melody!" He jerked a thumb toward the mounted men on the road. Those men may be grinning like baboons, but they know how you saved my life. I told 'em. I have come to say thank you. He hugged her with as much might as one arm can hug. The troopers gave three cheers for Melody. Matthew, hearing the hip-hip-hoorays all the way back in the woods didn't know whether to run, or to come out and join the celebration....whatever it might be. He elected to stay where he was and to await developments, if any.

Melody took Sergeant Willy by the hand. "Come in, for a while? I want to hear how you're feeling. You look well."

"Wish I could come in to spend some time with you, Charity Jane, but I'm on patrol. I have to get the men back before my colonel starts to fret." He put his arm around her and walked her toward the house, out of earshot of the troopers. "Have you, by any chance, seen or heard of the whereabouts of Matthew Greyson?"

She had to be careful with her reply. She was certain that loose lips in town had probably already informed him that she had been caring for another wounded soldier. However, she had everyone convinced that the soldier that she had rehabilitated, and who was in her employ, was a reb. However, she was a little concerned as to how much information that Bethany had let slip, or even whether Bethany was still in town. Realizing that Will and Bethany were friends, she felt a chill developing in her spine, a headache developing behind her forehead. "Why do you ask about him?"

"No special reason. I'm trying to figure what happened to him. Nobody knows. Thought, seein' as you and Matt seemed to get on quite nice, that you might have heard from him, should he be still alive."

"No such luck, Will. Sorry." She was becoming more confident that Will did not know very much. "I did try to find out if anyone had heard of him since he last left here. All I could find was that he was thought to have been killed at Second Manassas. That's when I gave him up for lost, Will."

Will McEwan was not a brilliant man. Neither was he stupid. He had been wondering for two days, since he had spotted Bethany, why she should have turned up in the Middleburg area. The answer, finally, became clear in his mind. She certainly was not just a *femme fatale* Confederate agent. Bethany never did anything without purpose. She either knew of Matthew's whereabouts, or had information that he was in the area and was looking for him. Otherwise. it was just too much of a coincidence that she was in Middleburg when he happened upon her. Greyson, he thought, either was here, was expected to be here, or had been here. Obviously, no one was talking, but the inference was that he was alive....if not necessarily well.... and that was good news. "Please stay here, by the door, for a moment." The sergeant strode out through the gate in the picket fence and approached his men. "Gents, form a skirmish line along this road. We're spending a little more time here than I like." Horses pivoted, revolvers were drawn, and carbines came at the ready. A full 100 yards of road were quickly posted for battle. While his men were so occupied, Will untied what appeared to be a dispatch case from behind his saddle and carried it to Melody. Wordlessly, he handed it to her and indicated that she should take it into the house. He turned on his heel and returned to his duties.

She did, without question, as he had indicated. She stood by the window and watched the troopers reform into column and ride away. When they were gone, she opened the dispatch case. Inside was a brand new Colt Model 1860 revolver, a flask of powder, and a cloth bag containing a quantity of .451 caliber ball. There was also a note scrawled on a piece of scrap paper. It said:

M.
Shoot your way home if you have to.
W.

At the bottom of the dispatch case was a fat envelope. On it was written: "You can pay me back after the war!" The envelope contained two hundred dollars in Federal greenbacks in various small, and easily spendable, denominations.

CHAPTER TWENTY-ONE

1863-1864

The buggy ride toward the little village of Culpeper Court House turned out to be reasonably pleasant in spite of the chilly March weather. The spring thaw and rains had left the roads badly rutted and punctuated with a scattering of deep and slippery mud puddles. However, nothing proved impassable as they splashed and jiggled their way along the minor roads and rural trails. John and Bethany took great comfort in the fact that their mounted escorts seemed to know all about the roads, the intersections, and even the occasional farm people whom they encountered along the way. The two troopers were friendly and informative. When they would stop to rest the horses, the men would draw a rough map in the dirt so that their charges could understand that they really were making progress in the right direction. Bethany was totally lost. Eventually, she even gave up looking at the dirt maps. The sun had disappeared behind an overcast sky. Without the sun to guide her, the twists and turns through the farmlands, swamps, and forests confused her sense of direction. She settled into the buggy seat, with a sigh, and refused to get out. She was unaccustomed to having her fate totally in the hands of others. They were traveling almost continually southwest, they informed her. She smiled, nodded, then watched with appreciation as the cavalrymen rode ahead, alert for suspicious hoof prints in the mud, and checking each suspected ambush point before allowing them to proceed. Beth eventually decided that she was, apparently, in good hands and nodded off to sleep. John thought it to be quite humorous that her head rattled around uncomfortably with the jarring and jerking of the buggy. Eventually, he became worried that her neck would be damaged. Summoning all his courage, he delivered a none-too-gentle poke into her ribs. She startled awake and glared at him. "What did you do that for?"

"I was afraid you'd snap your neck."

"Oh. Thanks. Ow!" She rubbed her neck. Do you have to hit every hole in this poor excuse for a road?"

"Yep. Just to make you angry. Here. Use this for a pillow." He handed her the buggy robe from behind the seat. He was rewarded with just the hint of a little smile that lasted only an instant before she drifted back into a sound sleep. John shook his head. "Don't see how she can do that!" he muttered. "I couldn't sleep in this godawful stiff-springed piece of shit if my life depended on it."

They spent the night at a friendly farm near Salem, Virginia. Salem was a nondescript little town that snuggled its shacks and shanties up to the Manassas Gap Railroad right-of-way as though for nourishment. The lady of the house and her daughters greeted them warmly. The troopers knew them well and inquired, anxiously, about the husband and their two boys who were off to war. Thankfully, the farmer and his sons had recently had the opportunity to visit their home and were in robust good health. They were stationed with General Fitz Lee's 800 horse cavalry detachment at nearby Culpeper and had been able to wangle a few days off to visit the female part of the family. When the ladies heard that the cavalrymen and their charges were headed to Culpeper they immediately poked the kitchen stove fire to life, fed it a lot of wood to heat the oven, and set to work making cakes and cookies to be carried to their brothers and father. Bethany rolled up her sleeves, borrowed an apron, and pitched in to help. The delicious aroma of the baking pastries reminded Beth of home. Home....where she and the black kitchen ladies would cook similar aromatic delights for her own father. Wistfully, she resolved to visit Charleston at her first opportunity, hug her father, then to run into the kitchen to do some serious baking of her own. Suddenly, to her own surprise, she was homesick.

After a wonderful supper, which was served to the tune of many giggles by the mother and daughters, Bethany tried to corner the Confederate troopers and to pump them for information about Matthew. But, they were too smart for that. They had sensed a female versus female situation and wanted no part of it. All that she could get out of them was "Sorry ma'am. We just don't know nothin' 'bout that. Seen the man with the eye patch now and again 'round Middleburg but never had the pleasure of meetin' him."

Bethany shook her head in frustration, excused herself, and went to bed. The gentlemen were, appropriately, bedded in the barn....snuggling gratefully into the sweet-smelling straw for a well-deserved night's rest.

The next morning, Tuesday, March 17, 1863, dawned chilly and clear. They bade a tender farewell to their hostesses, loaded the cakes and cookies to be delivered to Culpeper, and started, early, on their way. They still had many miles to travel to the railroad. Early that afternoon the troopers simultaneously held up a hand for them to stop, then indicated the need for silence. They cupped their ears and listened to the southwest. There was a distant rumble from that direction. Artillery fire! The rebs whispered to each other in consternation. Something big must be going on! They hurried forward, followed by the buggy that traveled at its best possible speed over the ruts and grooves. Eventually, the sounds of battle became more pronounced as they approached Culpeper. The sporadic rattle of small arms fire could now be heard interspersed between the bellows of the cannon. They encountered a black man, his ample wife, and a swarm of children who sat atop a mound of belongings in a decrepit wagon drawn by a tired, and very bored-looking, mule.

"What's goin' on 'round heah, boy?"

The Negro ducked his head respectfully. "Don't rightly know, suh. Seems many white men tryin' to kill each other on horseback over to Kelly's Ford, yonder."

"Who you belong to, boy, and where is you headed?"

The head of household smiled a stained, snaggly grin. "We tends a farm west of Culpeper, suh. This mawnin' our massa say to git outa here and don' come back 'till the killin's done. We's goin' as he says, suh."

The rebel troopers grinned. "Well then, git yourselves to goin'. Now, don' y'all forget to come back to where you belong just as soon as you can. Heah?"

"Yessah." The black family had, of course, no intention of coming back. They were headed north....north to Mr. Lincoln's promised land. "Then get on board, little chillen', get on board...."

The rebels promptly dismounted, unrolled their blankets which contained their Confederate uniforms, donned the gray jackets, buckled their sabers into place, checked their revolvers, saluted, wished Bethany and John luck, and galloped away. A good fight was not to be wasted.

"Well, damn!" whistled John Surrat as he watched them depart. "Good thing we don't have far to go! Seems our protection just flew the coop!"

"An astute observation. Wonder what we are to do with all these cakes and cookies? Oh well! We'll think of something. Drive on, Mortimer."

John glared at her. One more "Mortimer" and he was going to pitch her, and the cookies, out of the buggy and leave the whole mess in the mud.

The cavalry battle at Kelley's Ford was an interesting one. The Union horsemen actually won, but did not know it. They withdrew, after a full day of fighting, and abandoned the field to Fitz Lee's whooping Confederates. It was reported that 211 Americans, blue and gray, lost their lives that day. Saddest of all, the men from Salem never had a chance to taste the cookies that were sent to them....with love. When Bethany arrived back in Richmond she found President Davis to be much too distracted by his own problems to take even a moment to hear about her exploits in Middleburg. The people of the southern nation, especially in Richmond, were not getting enough to eat and were beginning to grumble and complain in earnest. Out on the Mississippi, Union pressure on Vicksburg was mounting. The loss of that fortified city would mean the loss of control of the river....and the Confederacy would become split in two. It was not a happy time to be at the Confederate White House. No one in Richmond had time for her. It was time to go home. She hugged Varina and the children, then lost no time in boarding the cars for Charleston where she intended to corner her father and bend his sympathetic ear.

Her plan did not work out quite as well as she had hoped. She arrived on April 7th, just in time to witness, from a great distance, a terrific cannon fight out in the harbor. It was nine Federal ironclads versus forts Sumter and Moultrie. The flashes of fire and bellows of smoke were awesome to behold. She could even hear bell-like clangs as solid cannonballs struck the iron armor of the vessels. The Union gunboats, under the command of Flag Officer Samuel DuPont, unwisely positioned themselves between the two forts and were caught in a murderously accurate crossfire.

The view of the conflict from Major Dodge's porch, which fronted on White Point Gardens, was obstructed by large mounds of earth that the Confederate artillery men had constructed for the protection of their guns and ammunition from enemy fire. Bethany walked to the shoreline to get a better view. The gardens had been transformed into "The Battery", the earthworks of which bristled with cannon, all pointed out into the harbor. The most impressive guns were two monster 10-inch bore Confederate Columbiads that weighed about 15,000 pounds each. Beth watched as the gun crews scurried about with bags of powder, cramming them down the gaping bores, then huffing and puffing to load the largest cannonballs that she had ever seen. A young Lieutenant was supervising the loading. She tugged at his sleeve. "Excuse me, lieutenant. Ah would surely like to know if y'all actually plan to fire these things."

The young officer looked her over with an appreciative eye. "Yes, ma'am. 'Deed we do if'n them Yankees dare to get close enough."

She smiled coquettishly. "Seems to me they must be mighty loud when they go off."

"Yes, ma'am. Mighty loud. They will shake the earth. Might even break windows in those houses over there."

"Oh, deah! That's where we live."

The lieutenant gave her a stern look. "Well then, Ah suggest you gather up your people and head outa' heah right quick if you see the action movin' this way."

"We'll do just that. Thank you!" The "thank you" was flirtatiously musical. As she sauntered away she twirled the little white parasol that protected her from the sun.

The lieutenant watched her until she disappeared from view behind the earthworks. Just as soon as he had the chance, he vowed to himself, he would find out just which residence was hers, and call on her.

"For sure!" he unconsciously exclaimed, aloud, then blushed when all his men turned to grin at him. He cleared his throat to regain his composure. "Back to work men. Get all the ten-inch round shot you can find and stack 'em to the left rear of each gun. Y'all stack 'em neat, now." The men grumbled, but set back to work. The shot was terribly heavy (over 125 pounds) and very awkward to handle. However, it could punch a ragged hole clean through an armored ship, while shell, which was made in various shapes and carried an explosive charge, would bounce off and explode harmlessly....or more often....not explode at all.

The Union ironclad gunboats were badly damaged by the heavy guns of the Confederate forts. They were forced to retreat and one of them, the *U.S.S. Keokuk*, soon sank. She had been hit at least ninety times by rebel cannon projectiles. Consequently, the Federals never came within range of the guns at The Battery, much to the annoyance of the waiting gunners, and much to the delight of Bethany, her staff, and her neighbors.

Bethany had to endure a two-day wait for her father to return home. When he did, Major Dodge was almost unrecognizable. Bessie was the first to see him when he creaked wearily through the door. She clapped her hand to her mouth in amazement. "Why, Massa Dodge, you is blacker than I is!" He was coated, from head to toe, by black soot belched from the victorious cannon at Fort Moultrie. The major extended his lips, which were relatively clean, to his daughter for a kiss....without touching her anywhere else. "Welcome home, dearest daughter! What a lovely, sweet surprise! Bessie, get me a bourbon and draw my bath, please, and in that order."

"Yassah. I swan I never seed so black a white man in my life!" She hollered in the direction of the kitchen. "You darkies fetch pails of hot water and lots of extra soap, an' right this minute!"

The major shrugged out of his heavily soiled uniform jacket and stood looking for a place to put it. "Well, we won, sweetheart."

Beth gingerly took the jacket from him and, holding it at arms length, prepared to carry it out of the room. "I hear you did, daddy. I'm so proud of all of you! For your reward you'll have an extra good dinner tonight, topped off by pies, cakes, and cookies that I have baked myself." She assumed a proud air. "What do you think of that?"

"Pies, cakes, and cookies? All of those? Now I know why I have missed you so much. I can hardly wait!"

The major had not slept in forty-eight hours. Nevertheless, he struggled manfully, during dinner, to stay alert and listen to Bethany's disappointments and frustrations in her search for Matthew. Finally, his eyelids drooped so determinedly that he had to go to bed. We'll talk more in the morning, Bethy, before I have to go back. All the ammunition that we used has to be resupplied....and there's a lot of it. Hope you will stay home for a long time so we can get a new plan going for you just as soon as my duties are caught up."

"I will, father. I will stay a while."

"Good!" Major Jared Dodge retired without even asking for his second bourbon.

Bethany did as she had promised. She stayed with her father for a full month. The fighting was so heavy in Virginia that It was obvious that travel back to Middleburg was impossible. She spent a lot of time with her books, and as much time with her father as he could spare. He took her out to the ruins of Fort Sumter....a perfect mess but still bristling for a fight. From the crumbled parapet she could see the Union blockade vessels in the distance as they respectfully stayed out of range of Sumter's big seacoast cannon.

In early May, the fighting at Chancellorsville produced thousands of casualties. The Chimborazo hospital was crying for help. Bethany returned to Richmond. The mood at the executive mansion had improved with the great Confederate victory at Chancellorsville. However, she had no time to worry about moods. She worked herself to exhaustion, sometimes 24 hours a day, caring for the wounded who were arriving by the trainload.

In June, General Lee fixed his sights upon the untrampled fields and towns of Pennsylvania. He would take the fight to the enemy, thereby taking the pressure off of poor, smoldering, broken Virginia. As the Federal Army of the Potomac, under General Hooker, moved to block the Confederate's northward movement, the fighting in northern Virginia became extremely intense. In Middleburg, as in most communities in the area, the churches again became makeshift hospitals and were packed full of groaning, dying soldiers. Matthew, throwing caution to the winds, came out of hiding.

Together, he and Melody worked endlessly to care for the casualties. Unbeknownst to each other, in a perhaps not a very surprising coincidence, Bethany in Richmond and Melody and Matthew in Middleburg were engaged in a common, merciful purpose....the comfort and healing of their fellow man. Love, in itself, is a hollow word. To find real love, look into the hearts of the healers....those who would endure exhaustion, blood, smells, excrement, vomiting, maggots, crying, sobbing, dying....and who still, their own tears dry because they can cry no more, continue to minister to those who were placed in their care.

+ + +

By autumn of 1863 the fortunes of the Confederacy began to wane. General Lee had suffered a major defeat at Gettysburg, Pennsylvania. Vicksburg, Mississippi, had fallen. As overt military operations became less successful, a greater importance shifted to covert operations. Confederate operatives sought ways to destroy the United States from within. The "Copperheads", a loose organization of southern sympathizers within the Union, began to try to make its strength known. Confederate attention repeatedly focused on Johnson's Island, Ohio, where a large number of captured rebel officers were confined. If only these fine soldiers could be released and armed, they could fight their way south, severely damaging the northern morale. An operation against Johnson's Island was organized under the direction of the famous sea captain and blockade runner John Wilkinson. Sadly for the southern nation, the plot was betrayed before it even started and the effort was abandoned.

In the spring of 1864 a North Carolinian, a lawyer named Jacob Thompson, was named as Confederate commissioner directing the activities of rebel operatives in Canada. Thompson was not without his faults. He tended to have "loose lips", talked too much to too many people, and in general was not ideal as the head of a secret bureau. Nevertheless, he had ambition. He resolved to again try to capture Johnson's Island. In June, 1864, Matthew Greyson was instructed to report to Jacob Thompson in Windsor, Ontario, Canada, before August 1st.

Matthew convened a family conference. Melody, Mary Sue, and Blossom all voted to go north together. The horses did not vote, being in the barn, but were assumed to be in favor of the proposition. Captain....now

411

Colonel....Mosby contributed another two hundred Yankee dollars toward the expenses of the trip. This, with Sergeant Willy's two hundred gave them enough to travel in whatever style they wished. Matt attended to the details of getting under way with military precision. He sold the buckboard and engaged the local wagon shop to construct a covered wagon that had buggy springs for comfortable travel. It was adequately roomy for a family of three, but yet was light enough to be easily pulled by their two horses.

Under Mary Sue's acute supervision, Matthew constructed a deluxe slatted traveling cage for Blossom, complete with holders for water, food, and the obligatory box of sand. Skillfully braiding strips of leather sliced from old horse harness, Mary Sue crafted a tiny harness for the cat complete with a long leather tether so that the animal could, on occasion, enjoy some measure of freedom without becoming lost in some unfamiliar place.

Many of Melody Chandler's treasured possessions had to be left behind due to the limited capacity of the small wagon. Neighbors promised to watch over the place, and Matthew assured her that they would return to her Virginia farm just as soon as the war would allow. Windows and doors were nailed shut. Their mismatched team was harnessed, Blossom was stuffed, with some objection, into her travel abode, and off they went, in high spirits for high adventure, heading north.

Colonel John Mosby was, unquestionably, a genius when it came to covert operations. He had made a marvelous suggestion. They should travel as a poor, Native American family. That way everyone would consider them as harmless, useless, and too poor to bother robbing. Soldiers, north or south, would wave them on....considering their passage to be nothing more than a good riddance. Mary Sue had giggled as Melody dyed Matthew's hair jet black. His skin was already swarthy enough, tanned by the Virginia sunshine. They dressed in suitably ragged clothing. Of course, most of their clothing was somewhat worn and faded, anyway. This made the ragged effect very easy to achieve.

Their disguise worked like a charm. They kept a very low profile, camping out of sight in rural areas and avoiding, where possible, large towns. The only problem that surfaced during their travels was Melody's insistence that she sleep with her squirrel rifle close at hand, ready for action, and under the blankets between her and Matthew. The problem was discovered the very first night on the road when Matt blew out the lantern and crawled under the blankets, feeling for the warmth of his beloved but encountering cold wood and steel. He raised up to glare at her in the darkness. "Charity Jane Melody Chandler?"

"Yes, dearest Colonel Matthew Greyson? How may I help you?"

"By removing the artillery that lies between us."

"Why?"

"Because it is hard to cuddle with one's friends when one has a squirrel rifle in the way." They could hear Mary Sue snickering from her blankets.

"Mary Sue, you go to sleep now! " commanded Melody. "I reckon I'm not in the mood to cuddle anyway, considerin' where we are at alongside some miserable, lonely road."

Matt raised up again, in the darkness, to look in her direction. "It ain't capped, is it?"

"Yep. It is."

"Damn!" exclaimed Matthew as he fell back upon his pillow. Mary Sue giggled louder. "You go to sleep now, Mary Sue." The little girl sounded like she were strangling on her giggles as she tried to suppress them. "You sure it ain't pointed at anybody....like Mary Sue, or the cat, or the horses?"

"Yep."

"You know I can't sleep thinkin' that thing might go off by my ear."

"Yes, dear."

Within seconds, in spite of his pleading pronouncement to the contrary, Matthew's snores serenaded the night. Mary Sue slipped under the blankets, carefully, on the side of her mother opposite the rifle. "I'll snuggle with you, mamma."

"Thank you, dear."

"Don't mind no rifle."

"Thank you, dear." Melody lay, wide awake and a little frightened, as Mary Sue plastered herself against her back and Matt snored on the other side of the rifle. The sounds of Rebel and Buttercup munching the succulent spring grass that grew around the wheels of the parked wagon seemed extraordinarily loud amidst the deep silence of the lonely northern Virginia night.

In spite of Melody's apprehensions, they proceeded north to Lonaconing, Maryland, without incident. There, they booked passage west for wagon, horses, cat, and all on the Baltimore & Ohio Rail Road. After a few transfers and frustrations they arrived at Dayton, Ohio, from whence they were whisked straight north, on the Dayton & Michigan Rail Road, and deposited in Detroit....sound, but not necessarily safe as Matthew was concerned that he might run across someone who would recognize him. Fortunately, no one gave them a second glance. They hitched up and headed northwest along the country roads toward Franklin, breathing a collective sigh of relief once they had traveled beyond the limits of the bustling city.

Matthew timed their travel carefully so that they would arrive in Franklin well after dark. This made for a leisurely trip as they had arrived in Detroit very early in the morning. They stopped to rest, bathe, and picnic on the bank of the River Rouge. It was nearly midnight when they topped the hill, passed the cemetery, and descended the Franklin hill. They could hear the horses' hoofs slide a little, on the gravel, with each step as they worked to hold back the weight of the wagon. Matt leaned on the brake lever, causing the brake to squeal loudly, protesting as the heat built up within it....to the point where they could smell the burning wood of the braking surfaces. "Let's hope she don't catch fire!" muttered Matthew. Mother and daughter hugged each other on the wagon seat, but said not a word. When they reached the bottom of the hill Matt, with a quiet "whoa!" stopped the team and tossed water from their drinking water supply upon the smoking brake. The brake hissed at him for his trouble. They had stopped in front of the school where Bethany had taught. Matt glanced at it, wistfully. It was quiet and dark in the midnight shadows. In fact, the whole town was quiet and dark. They clip-clopped and rumbled quietly up the road through town. To Matt, he was seeing the friendly face of home. To Melody and Mary Sue, it was dark and brooding, and sinister. Once through town, and just before the river, they turned left and the horses strained to climb the

Fourteen Mile Road hill. To their right they could hear the muted splashes as the mill wheel turned, idling, waiting for the morning when it would again have work to do.

Dick Trick startled awake as he heard the sounds of horse's hoofs, the creak and muted rumble of wagon wheels approaching the house. He leaped from bed, grabbed his trusty shotgun, and went to the window where he strained to see who and what was approaching in the darkness. He pulled the hammer to full cock when he heard the sound of booted feet as they climbed the steps and walked across the porch. There was a soft knock upon the door.

"Who's there?" quaked Dick.

"It's me, Dick. Matthew."

"Yeah, sure! If this is some damn fool Pinkerton trick I'll blast you full of holes right through this door!" Dick's finger trembled on the trigger.

"It really is me. Don't you recognize my voice?"

"Well. sort of," Dick took a deep breath to calm himself "but not for sure. You got a lantern?"

"Yep I do, Dick. Right here in the wagon."

"Then get it an' light it so's I can see your face."

Dick watched through the window as a match flared and a lantern was lit. Dimly, he could see a covered wagon, a team of horses, and a familiar-looking man with a patch over one eye. It was! It was indeed Matthew Greyson! Dick unbarred the door and flew out of it to grasp and pump Matthew's hand with as much vigor as he might have used were he filling a fire bucket at the town pump during an emergency. Matt clapped him on the back and gave him a manly hug. "Good to see you, Dick. You're looking well...all growed up and such!"

"Thanks, Matt. You look good, too! Nobody knowed whether you was alive or dead!"

Greyson chuckled. "I like the first choice, thank you. Here, I have some ladies I would like you to meet. Come down from there, girls." Matt helped them to descend. Dick gaped as two pretty smiles sparkled at him in the lantern light. "Melody and Mary Sue, this is my good friend Richard Trick."

Dick maintained his composure very well considering that a friend had returned from the dead, bringing a lovely mother and child with him....all without warning and in the middle of the night. He fired up the kitchen stove and soon had a large pot of coffee brewed. Before it was done, however, the ladies had sleepily retrieved their pillows and blankets from the wagon and had gone to bed. The horses were given generous snacks of fat Michigan oats and turned out to eat grass for the night. Blossom was tucked under the covers with Mary Sue. Dick and Matt settled at the kitchen table and drank coffee until dawn, catching up on each other's experiences since they had last been together two and one-half years previous.

When Dick related the contents of the telegram received by Reverend Lanning from Sergeant Willy informing of the sighting of Bethany, alive, and in northern Virginia, Matthew's jaw dropped and his eyes filled with tears of joy. Dick, while struggling to remain manly, nevertheless shed a quiet tear or two as he watched Matt absorb the welcome news. The sun, rising, flooded the kitchen with its warm light. It was the most beautiful dawn that Matthew Greyson had ever, ever seen.

+ + +

There seemed to be no end to the train and ambulance loads of wounded and sick soldiers who continued to be delivered to the Chimborazo Hospital in Richmond. Bethany worked long hours daily, sometimes seven days a week, to provide care and comfort. Both Varina Davis and Bessie admonished her for working so hard. "'Sakes!" said Bessie, waggling her finger at her mistress, "You is gettin' skinnier by the minute. We needs to go back to Charleston where we can feed you up and rest you good!"

Bethany gave her a tired smile and waved her away. "Not just yet, Bessie. Not just yet."

After a particularly sweltering and exhausting day, Beth returned to the Confederate executive mansion planning to treat herself to a nice warm soak in her bathtub. She was soiled and blood-spattered, having assisted at several horrifying amputations that day. Her hair, barely retained in a soiled bun, stuck out at all sorts of unfortunate angles from her head like the quills of an alarmed porcupine. The last thing that she wanted to see was visitors....but, to her annoyance, three gentlemen were lounging on the verandah and were waiting to speak to her. Viewed from a distance, it seemed that they were more bent upon enjoying the cigars that they were puffing than they were in anything else, but that assumption turned out to be wrong. They were very anxious to talk to her, much to her chagrin considering her unfortunate appearance. She determined, however, to make the best of the situation and approached them with a regal, if somewhat disheveled, sweep, and extended her hand to each to receive the expected bow and kiss. "Gentlemen, I am informed that y'all are waitin' to talk to me. How may I be of service?" Virginia wrens would have sung, spontaneously, had they heard the sweetness of her lilting voice. In spite of the dirt and grime, the men were charmed by her flashing smile. She recognized, instantly, the man in the Confederate officer's uniform. It was Captain Norris of the Signal Corps. The other two she had not seen before. The larger of the strangers seemed humorless, intense, and puppy-like friendly. He was dark-haired, dark-bearded, and quite plain in appearance. He was introduced as a Mr. Jacob Thompson. The other gentleman was quite in contrast. He was very well dressed....actually, almost overdressed in civilian clothes....gray suit, gray broad-brimmed hat, and an expensive silk cravat with a diamond stickpin. He looked, to Beth, as though he was not to be trusted. He could be anything from a wealthy dandy to a riverboat gambler. He was introduced as Captain Charles H. Cole of the Confederate Secret Service.

"Miss Dodge, we have come to ask you to join us at a special meeting in my office tomorrow morning. Would that be possible?" Norris was exceedingly polite and businesslike.

"Ah would be delighted to accommodate you gentlemen, of course, but may I ask the subject of this meeting?"

"That would be a secret, Miss Dodge."

"Oh! Of course! How silly of me to ask!" She tried to pat her sweaty hair into place. "What time would my attendance be required?"

"Would ten o'clock in the morning be satisfactory?"

"That would be just fine." She curtseyed, displaying in the process her bloodstained skirt. "Now, if y'all will excuse me, I would like very much to set myself aright after a trying day in the service of our country."

"Of course." They bowed in unison, then returned to their cigars as soon as she had flounced out of sight.

+ + +

The morning smelled sweet and cool as she walked to Captain Norris' office. The formal greetings were brief. Thompson, Norris, and Cole seemed eager to get down to some serious business. Norris retrieved a key from his desk drawer. "Miss Dodge, I am about to inform you of some secret information. May I assume that you will honor that secrecy? Confidentiality is imperative to the survival of the Confederate States of America."

"Of course, captain. Yes."

Norris unlocked the door to an adjoining room. On the wall was a large map of the United States, the Confederate States, Canada, and Mexico. It was covered with pins which had heads of different colors. Two clerks were working feverishly to update the map as current information was received. The map was the secret nerve center of the Confederacy. It showed troop locations....both Union and Confederate....prisoner locations, secret agent locations, supply locations, naval blockade locations, vessels on the Mississippi and its tributaries, and almost anything else of military importance. "President Davis and Secretary Benjamin come here daily to look at this."

Bethany took a close look at the map. There were several secret agent pins clustered in the Detroit, Michigan, area. Just to the northwest of the city there was a barely discernible hole where another pin had been. "Is that where my pin was?"

"It was."

"Very well. I guess I'm impressed. Now, what is this important secret project?"

Norris pointed to Johnson's Island in Sandusky Bay, Ohio. The island had a varicolored cluster of pins stuck into it. "This island is a prison. It contains a large number of Confederate prisoners....most of them officers. They are the cream of the south. We want them back. And, we want you to help us to get them back."

Beth was becoming a little nervous. This sounded like something big. "Please, suh, if you will, do go on."

Jacob Thompson took up the narrative. "Miss Dodge, the *U.S.S. Michigan* is the only Federal warship on the Great Lakes. She is guarding the prison at Johnson's Island and we need to take her out."

"What does that mean 'take her out'? Sink her?"

"No. Capture her and turn her guns loose on the cities of the Great Lakes. Detroit, Chicago, Milwaukee, wherever."

Bethany took on an air of exasperation. "Mr. Thompson, this is all very lovely, but where do I fit in? I know very little about ships, gunboats, sailors, or even water of any kind except 'bath'." She was being modest, of course. Actually, she knew quite a bit about those things nautical, having been raised in the Port of Charleston under her father's tutelage.

Thompson chuckled. "In case you are wondering where I fit in, I am in charge of Canadian operations. We have a group, now in the process of assembling in Canada, who will board and capture the *Michigan.* However, we need an ace in the hole. That's where you and Captain Cole come in."

Bethany shot a quick glance at Cole who was casually relaxed in a chair, preparing to light his cigar. He did not meet her gaze. She was not sure that she wanted to be paired with him for any purpose, let alone the capture of a Yankee ship. "Please go on, Mr. Thompson."

"Captain Cole is a former member of General Nathan Forrest's cavalry, a former prisoner of war, and a skilled undercover agent. He has been sailing the Great Lakes, as a passenger, and visiting and mapping as many ports as possible. With my approval, he has devised a plan for the capture of the *Michigan.* Basically, the plan is simple. You and he will take up residence in Sandusky, Ohio, as husband and wife...."

Bethany stirred, uncomfortably, in her chair. "You understand, Mr. Thompson, that I could have a problem with that. I have been confronted with this situation before."

"Thompson smiled, condescendingly, and shot a sideways glance at Cole. "I understand, Miss Dodge, but I'm sure that any problems can be worked out amicably. Please listen to the rest of the plan."

"Very well, Mr. Thompson." She had feelings of *deja vu* per her last assignment with John Surrat.

"Mr. Cole will pose as a wealthy oil speculator from Titusville, Pennsylvania. He will have come to town on business, accompanied by his wife. The two of you will meet and charm the officers of the *Michigan*, entertain them, gather all information that you can, and arrange, eventually, to drug those officers so that the then leaderless crew can be easily overcome by a boarding party. The project will require exquisite timing between the efforts of you two and the arrival of said boarding party."

Bethany looked at her hands, for a moment, and absent-mindedly twiddled her thumbs. "Mr. Thompson, I have to be blunt. This has the sound of a far-fetched, little-boy scheme that hasn't a chance of being successful. It is too complicated. It very likely involves too many people who will get drunk and let slip the plans in taverns all over the United States and Canada. Further, I do not relish being in any sort of cozy situation with Captain Cole. Further yet, I am already wanted as a Confederate spy. It would not take the Yankees long to hang me if they caught me in such a scheme. I cannot afford to take a chance like that."

Cole stopped blowing smoke rings into the air and jumped to his feet, eyes blazing. "Really, Miss Dodge, you flatter yourself. I'm sure the Yankees don't think that you are all that important. And, for your information, your highness, I have no interest in you whatsoever, and no interest in violating your privacy, or anything else, for that matter." He plopped back into his chair. "I hope that I have made myself perfectly clear. This is simply a job, risky as it may be, for the Southern Cause. Take it or leave it."

Bethany icily met his gaze. "Thank you, Captain Cole, for clearing up this situation which I could not ever possibly have understood without your help." Her sarcasm was as cutting as was the look from her eyes. Those eyes, catching the blue of the sky through the window, seemed almost luminous. Cole, suddenly, became nervous. Perhaps, he had met his match. This well could be an interesting, and not altogether pleasant, project!.

Beth swiveled in her chair to face Mr. Thompson. Casually, she arranged her skirt to perfection before addressing him. "I'm sorry, Mr. Thompson. It looks like a challenging scheme, but the risks are too high. I am not interested. I'm sorry."

Captain Norris, seeing the project disintegrating, entered the fray. "Even, Miss Dodge, if we could see that you had the opportunity to visit Middleburg, Virginia, again?"

Beth was getting the picture. A bribe! How nice! "Middleburg? Really? Would that be soon?"

"Yes."

"Escorted?"

"Yes."

"And get me back again, safely, to Richmond?"

"Yes."

"Then, I'll do it!" she giggled, girlishly. "You drive a hard bargain, Captain Norris. Mr. Thompson, if I am to enter into this foolishness, I will require a nice undercover name....something other than 'Mrs. Cole', I trust."

Cole was back to blowing smoke rings. He answered for Thompson. "Your name will be Annie. Annie Brown Cole."

"Well! That was a quick answer, Mr. Cole! And who, may I ask, is Annie Brown?"

Cole looked uncomfortable. "No matter. A friend."

Beth had serendipitously found an Achilles heel in Captain Cole. She moved, straight-faced, into the breached wall. "What sort of friend?"

"Just a friend. None of your business, really, miss."

She pressed the attack. "Fiancée? Mistress? What? Wife?"

Cole rolled his eyes. He rose to leave. "Jacob, kindly get another woman for the job, or count me out."

Thompson tapped angrily upon Norris' desk. "Sit down, Charles! Miss Dodge, do you have to know such personal details?"

"I do. If I am to play a man's wife I need to know him."

Jacob Thompson sighed. "Very well, Charles, answer her questions, if you please."

"She's pregnant, isn't she?" triumphantly queried Bethany.

Cole sat, hands behind his head, and puffed his cigar furiously. "Yes, but how did you know that?"

"Woman's instinct. You wouldn't want a fat, pregnant lady to try to impress the officers of the *U.S.S. Michigan*, now would you?" Bethany gave Captain Charles Cole a withering look. "Well, Captain Cole, I'm not Annie Brown, I am not pregnant, and I do not intend to be. Do I make myself clear?"

Cole shrugged and smiled, sheepishly. "Yes, miss. I get the picture."

"Then, I will take the job. However...."

"What?" chorused the three.

"I'll need clothes. Lots of beautiful clothes. Who pays for them, and where do I get them?"

Thompson smiled. Now, here was a woman that he could understand. "Canada, miss. Canada. We'll arrange for clothing straight from Paris."

Bethany tried to look nonchalant, but was inwardly joyous. "That would be just fine, Mr. Thompson. "Thank y'all."

"Very well, Miss Dodge. We have just short of four weeks to get you outfitted, to get you to and back from Middleburg, and to get you in residence with your husband in Sandusky Ohio. You are to be there, checked into the West House....which you will enjoy, by the way....at least by August eleventh. Any problem?"

"No, suh."

Charles Cole flicked his cigar and stood to make his point. "This woman," he said, pointing his cigar at Bethany, "turns her South Carolina accent off and on like the flicking of a jackass's tail. Could she be instructed to assume either one identity or another?"

Jacob Thompson shrugged. "Miss Dodge?"

"I shall be happy to oblige the annoying gentleman. I confess, I have been getting a little careless. What would you prefer? New England? Midwest? West? I can do them all. I can even do a pretty good Mary Todd Lincoln, if you wish. I heard her speak, once. She is midwestern with a little southern drawl thrown in." She illustrated her point by speaking with the proper inflections.

The three men laughed heartily at her antics. Jacob Thompson was entranced. "Whatever you wish, Miss Dodge. Good old Michigan-Ohio-Indiana midwestern would be fine."

"When do I leave for Middleburg?"

"Tomorrow morning. Be on the first train. Your tickets will be waiting for you."

"Thank you, gentlemen!" she trilled. "Good day to y'all....I mean, you all....I mean, to all of you!"

They rose and bowed in unison as she made her dramatic exit, then turned to look at each other, wagging their heads in disbelief There were a few gutsy females out there fighting for the Southern Cause. If Bethany Dodge was not among the best of them, she at least ranked as one of the most interesting.

+ + +

It was about ten o'clock the following morning when Bethany and her valise were deposited at the Richmond train station. The liveried coachman stood at a respectful distance to watch over her until she boarded the cars. Ignoring the bustle around her, she settled on a wooden bench and began browsing through her copy of a collection of poetry by Thomas Gray. She had just begun to read, a little tearfully, *Ode on the Death of a Favorite*

423

Cat, when she was interrupted by a familiar voice. "Are you ready for a new adventure, Mrs. Belcher?"

"Mortimer! Is it really you?" She leaped to her feet, dropping her book. Much to his surprise, she gave him a long and tender hug.

He gently patted the back of her head as they embraced. He desperately wanted to kiss her, but dared not. "Dr. and Mrs. Mortimer Belcher ride again!" They clung to each other as they broke into peals of laughter causing waiting passengers, baggage handlers, and various other passersby to give them sly and curious looks.

Bethany held his face in her two hands. "I thought you told me that you would not come with me."

"I have orders to the contrary."

"Orders or no orders....thank you."

"You are most welcome." He picked up her valise. "Let's get on the train. You realize that this trip could be something of a picnic?"

Bethany settled into the worn seat, removed her bonnet, and primped her hair. "Whatever do you mean? A picnic?"

"General Early is movin' on Washington. There isn't a Yankee in sight in northern Virginia. Our timing is perfect. They've all gone north to try to catch ol' Jubal and his troops. I hear he plans to put the torch to Washington. Hope he does. Then I won't have to go there."

Bethany pouted, her lower lip quivering charmingly. Disappointment glowed in her eyes. "You are going to Washington? I thought you were going to keep me company."

John smiled as he gave her a condescending pat on the hand. "And, that's just what I'm going to do....all the way to Middleburg. Keep you company. After that you're on your own." He put his finger to his lips and glanced about to make sure no one was eavesdropping. His voice dropped to a whisper. I'm assigned to gather intelligence in that hotbed of Yankeedom. Actually, it won't be too bad. I'll get to see my mother. She will like that, and will probably spoil me rotten."

Bethany folded her arms and sighed. She would miss John Surrat. "Your mother is sweet. Be certain to give her my best."

"I will."

"I don't mean to be practical, or self-centered, or anything like that, but who will help me to get back to Richmond if you are gone north?"

Surrat stretched his legs and made himself as comfortable as possible in preparation for a nap. "If you find your Matthew, then he will take care of you. Right?"

"I certainly hope so, but I just don't know." Beth tried to suppress the tears that filled her eyes.

John Surrat removed his hat, scratched his head, and replaced it....but this time it covered his face to keep out the pesky daylight that would interfere with his rest. "Understand. Of course you don't know. Relax. All arrangements have been made. If necessary, Colonel Mosby will provide you with an escort." His sentence faded into a comfortable snore.

"How can you sleep at this time of the morning?"

There was no answer.

The journey to Middleburg was, as predicted, uneventful. They lost no time in collecting Mrs. Catherine Braun from her Colonial Inn and setting out for the Chandler farm. The three of them snuggled onto the buggy seat together, enjoying the warm summer ride. When they reached the farm, Bethany's jaw dropped and she burst into tears. She was ready for a major confrontation and a joyful reunion. Instead, she found a boarded-up farmhouse, a barn with its doors nailed shut, an unkempt door yard with weeds enjoying their new freedom, and far in the distance, someone plowing with a team of mules. She piled out of the buggy, kicked off her shoes, and took off running toward the startled farmer who "whoaed-up" his mules at her approach. His sweaty eyebrows raised in the shade of his grimy, floppy, broad-brimmed hat "Suh! Suh! Ain't this the Chandler place?"

"Yes'm. 'Tis." He ejected a stream of tobacco juice as, suspiciously, he looked her over.

"Are you a Chandler?" she panted, trying to catch her breath.

"Nope. Just farmin' their fields whilst they're gone. 'Till the end of the war, I reckon. Matt said just keep usin' it like my own 'til he gets back. How come you want to know 'bout them?"

Bethany patted the closest of the mules. His long ears did not register appreciation for the attention. "I'm sorry, suh. I'm a friend of the family. Do you know where they have gone?"

"North. That's all I know. North. Said they'll be back after the war's over. "Now, 'scuse me. Me and my friends, here, have a lot of sod to turn 'fore nightfall." The terrible truth hit Bethany with a force that made her knees buckle, almost making her slump onto the freshly turned earth. She wrung her hands, tears of sadness coursing down her flushed cheeks. The farmer looked down on her sympathetically. "Sorry I cain't help you, ma'am. 'Spect you'll find your friends, one day." He clucked to the mules, indicating that the interview was over. "Git up, Maude! Git up Barney, you lazy critters! We'un's got work to do!" Beth was left standing, alone, her bare feet covered by the gentle softness of the gummy Virginia soil.

Bethany remained in Middleburg for a few days to tearfully collect her thoughts, comforted by Catherine Braun and her Chamomile Tea. John Surrat had shyly kissed her, hugged her, and taken his leave. She would never see him again.

John traveled to Washington, D.C., as ordered, and became actively involved within the covert southern community that flourished there under the direction of one John Wilkes Booth. After President Lincoln's assassination in April of 1865, Surrat fled to Canada to avoid arrest. His mother, Mary Surrat, was not so lucky. She was hanged, rightly or wrongly, for her alleged part in the assassination conspiracy. Aware that he could suffer the same fate, he fled to Europe. Somehow ending up in Rome, he enlisted in the Papal Zouave Guards and cut a splendid figure in his red pantaloons, tasseled fez, and his blue jacket emblazoned with the papal cross, his sparse mustache bristling as he guarded the Vatican. Unfortunately for John, a fellow papal guard tipped off American authorities of his presence, hoping to be awarded the $25,000.00 reward that was on his head. John fled to Egypt where he was finally captured and returned to the United States for trial. A jury, apparently composed of southern

426

sympathizers, promptly acquitted him. He lived out his days in Baltimore, quietly and without incident. John H. Surrat died in 1916. One would wonder if through all those years his dreams might have been wistfully pleasured by the image of a slender, brunette girl with mischievous blue eyes.

CHAPTER TWENTY-TWO

Acting Master Bennet G. Burley

By the time Bethany had discovered their departure from Virginia, Matthew, Melody, Mary Sue, Blossom, Rebel, and Buttercup had already made their low profile journey to Michigan, and had arrived at their destination without a single eyebrow having been raised in their direction. The covered wagon was discretely parked behind the barn. Matthew remained out of sight while Dick Trick circulated the cock-and-bull story that he had charitably taken in a widowed squaw and her papoose until such time as they could be properly placed with their own people who lived on the Indian land that was located a ways south of town and over east of the Telegraph Road. The Reverend and Mrs. Lanning looked upon Dick's shenanigan with steamy disapproval, but kept silent. The rest of the villagers wagged their heads knowingly, snickered privately, and kept their distance. The suspicion was, of course, that Dick was taking the woman to his bed in exchange for food and shelter for her and for her daughter. Fortunately, and discretely, no one pressed him for the details of how he had acquired such strange house guests. It was generally assumed that when Dick tired of their company he would eject the inferior savages from his home and return to the good graces of his church and of his community. Only with difficulty could Dick keep himself from bursting into howls of laughter as he witnessed the studied nonchalance of his fellow villagers, especially when he brazenly took the ladies along for the ride as he drove his wagon to the general store, or to the mill. He was thoroughly enjoying the cloak-

and-dagger charade....even though he had no idea what was really going on, or what Matt was up to.

Hannah Midgley was another matter. The feisty beauty could hardly be expected to put up with any female moving in with Dick. Everyone in the village knew that Dick and Hannah intended to marry. They therefore expected a monstrous, screamy scene wherein Hannah would likely tote her brother's shotgun up to the farm and splatter the whole bunch of them all over the front porch.

No such thing happened. Dick had wisely hastened to Hannah, sworn her to secrecy, and let her in on the whole situation....at least as far as he knew it. She slipped up to the Greyson farm, gave Matthew many hugs of joy for his return from the dead, and politely, if icily, greeted Melody and Mary Sue. This accomplished, she smiled sweetly at Matt. "I reckon you have heard that Bethany has been seen, alive, in northern Virginia?"

"I have just learned that from Dick." He glanced nervously at Melody.

Melody did not so much as blink, or flinch. Instead, she stared at him, afraid of what his feelings might be. He did not meet her gaze. Instead, he looked away as though to hide the indecision, the confusion, in his eyes. She felt herself slumping into the white-painted porch rocker in which she was primly and properly seated, her hands folded upon the lap of her somewhat faded and threadbare gingham dress. She stared at her hands for a moment, then closed her eyes in silent prayer. "Oh, dear God! He still loves Bethany! Tell me what to do. If he finds out that I met Bethany in Middleburg and did not tell him he will never forgive me! It is I who loves him now! Oh, whatever should I do?"

Hannah persisted in her campaign to make sure, right up front, that Melody would understand that she was keeping company with another woman's' man. "How do you explain that she disappeared from here and ended up in Virginia?"

"I just don't know, Hannah."

"Do you think Bethany really is a reb spy?"

Matt shuffled his feet, and looked down at them, uncomfortably. "I just don't know."

Hannah shook her golden curls, put her hands in his, and fixed him with a stare that was both piercing and unbelievably blue. He figured that all the ice in the Arctic Ocean must be piled up behind those beautiful eyes to allow them to instantly freeze his soul, and to make him squirm like a schoolboy caught smoking behind the outhouse.

"What are you going to do to find her?"

"Golly, Hannah, I just don't know that, either, right off. If she is a Confederate spy she won't take kindly to being found by anybody."

"Will you try?"

"I'll try." said Matthew, almost in a whisper. Melody was frightened and disappointed by what she had just heard. Gone was the faint hope that he would say: "No, Hannah. I have a new love now." The hoped-for words were not said. The hoped-for love was not expressed. She silently walked into the house, and just as quietly closed and locked the bedroom door behind her. She would not even open it for her daughter who followed, and who knocked and whimpered on the outside of the door.

Hannah looked after her, triumphantly. She had definitely won that round for Bethany. She took Dick by the hand and led him down the path toward town, leaving Matthew standing on the porch trying to figure what to do. Mary Sue gave up on her mother and came to perch on the porch steps. "Do you know what's wrong, Matt? Mama wont let me in."

He sat next to her and patted her head. "Don't you worry, Mary Sue. Sometimes grown-ups need to be alone for a short while. She'll be out directly. How's about you takin' a curry comb to Molly and Moe? Looks to me like they could need some attention."

"Really? They look awful big. Don't think I can reach their backs. Are they nice?"

"Very, very nice. Just snap a lead on and take 'em over by the mounting block. You can stand on that and reach all the way up to their ears."

She smiled her perky smile. "Reckon I'll just do that. Will you call me when mama comes out?"

430

"I will." Colonel Mosby had given him a full dozen of fine cigars that had come from somewhere in the deep south. He scratched a match to flaring life on a stone next to the porch steps and lit one, inhaling the delicious smoke for a few moments. Morosely, he wandered into the kitchen and opened the cupboard. Miraculously, his bottle of select brandy was still there. He poured an ample quantity and returned, glass and cigar in his hands, to the porch steps. Visions of dark-haired Bethany danced in his head. The good cigar, and the good brandy, were of some comfort but did little to resolve the conflict in his mind. Two or three years ago, had someone suggested that either, or both, he and Bethany would become secret agents in the service of the Confederate States of America he would have considered the speaker to be a good candidate for residency in an asylum for the accommodation of the mentally deranged. Now, the unbelievable seemed to be emerging as the truth! He puffed and sipped thoughtfully until Melody, almost without a sound, slipped across the porch and seated herself next to him on the step. She encircled his arm with hers and snuggled her head upon his shoulder.

After a bit, she asked for a sip of his brandy. "What will we do now?" she asked, hesitantly.

"Want to go with me to Canada?" He gently held the brandy to her lips for her to sip. "I am to meet with a gentleman in Windsor. Will you come with me?"

"I will. Mary Sue too?"

"Mary Sue too."

She scooched closer to him on the step and pressed her breast against his arm. "Could I have some more of that, please, whatever it is? Tastes pretty good."

The next morning, before any of the townspeople were awake, they hitched up the wagon and drove to Detroit....to the foot of Woodward Avenue....to board a small, canopied steam launch that chuffed and puffed her way across the Detroit River, depositing them safely in Canada. The only problem with the crossing was a tiny cinder that wafted from the little craft's stack and landed in Mary Sue's eye. The emergency was soon resolved by the application of a little sympathy and with the judicious use of the corner of a handkerchief. Matt had been given the name of one Bennet G. Burley as his

431

contact with the Confederate secret organization in Canada. After lunching in a neat, if somewhat flyspecked little restaurant near the docks, Matthew inquired of the proprietor if he would happen to know Mr. Burley. He did, and was pleased to direct them to Mr. Burley's residence which was just two blocks away. Ben Burley turned out to be a small, friendly, tweedy, and very proper Scottish gentleman who was not only an undercover agent, but also held the rank of acting master in the Confederate Navy. He received them graciously, and insisted that they immediately enjoy a nice cup of tea supplemented with some very delicious home-baked sugar cookies. Melody and Mary Sue, not accustomed to having proper tea and cookies served properly in a very proper parlor, nervously sat on the edge of their seats and did their best to do everything....well....properly. They seemed to have passed the test. Both Matthew and Mr. Burley smiled at them approvingly. "Madam, miss," said Burley as he arose from his chair, "please excuse Captain Chandler and me for a few moments as we have business to which we must attend. Please continue to enjoy the tea and cookies, and ring for the servant if you desire more."

Melody smiled, prettily, in reply. Mary Sue, wholly engaged in balancing her teacup, had a question but had difficulty getting it out. "M-mister Burley?"

"Yes, dear?"

"Is that there a organ you have over there in the corner?"

"No, dear. That is a pianoforte. Do you play?"

"No, suh."

Would you like to try it?"

She beamed. "Yes, suh. Very much."

"Then, please do. The captain and I will be in the library for a short while." He ushered Matthew into the library and closed the door behind them. Mary Sue dived for the piano bench and began to experiment with the keys. Within moments, one-fingered melodies and simple harmonies began to sing from the little spinet.

Mr. Burley motioned to Matt to sit in one of a pair of nicely-crafted maroon leather chairs while he settled into the other. "Mr. Thompson has not yet arrived, so our operation is basically stalled at this moment. However, it is my sense that the plans are proceeding in a perfectly orderly and satisfactory manner."

Matt smiled, getting the measure of the gentleman. "And, just what does that mean, sir?"

Burley laughed. "That means that not a damn thing is happening so far. Hopefully, as soon as Thompson is here we will get underway. Unfortunately, even in the preliminary stages, we have already developed a problem."

"And, that would be....?" Little twinges of skepticism were beginning to trigger alarm bells in the back of Matthew's mind.

"I have been charged with the responsibility of leasing or buying a vessel suitable for our naval operation. The object is to obtain a fast and reliable steamer that we can quietly outfit as a vessel of war. Nothing suitable seems to be readily available. I guess, captain, if we can't buy or lease one, then we will just have to steal one!"

"Oh well!" said Captain Chandler. "We'll have to do what we have to do, I reckon. Sometimes piracy and acts of war are a bit hard to tell apart, aren't they?"

"They are, indeed!" chuckled Ben Burley, "but a little piracy can only add to the fun!" He reached for a silver humidor containing some very nice cigars. They lit up, and for a few moments of silence, watched the smoke rings drift toward the ceiling. "Where shall I find you when we are ready for our combination captain, pilot, and navigator?"

"At my farm in Franklin. I'll be there, but cannot let myself be seen by my fellow villagers. Your couriers must use great discretion."

"They will, of course."

"Further, Mr. Burley, if I am to undertake this responsibility, it will be necessary for me to know, in advance, of your selected vessel....her engines, speed, draft, maneuverability, and proposed armament. If I do not believe that this operation has a good chance of success, I do not intend to participate."

"I understood, sir. You will be kept constantly informed. Believe me. We cannot afford to lose your valuable services. That said, shall we rejoin your charming ladies?"

They returned to the parlor to find pretty notes tinkling from the piano and wafting out of the window into the Canadian sunshine. Melody rose from the piano bench while Mary Sue continued to experiment with the keys. "Mr. Burley?"

"Yes, Mrs. Chandler?" She blushed at the gentleman's mistake as he had naturally assumed that she was Matthew's wife, having been introduced by only her first name.

Mary Sue giggled, knowingly, but kept right on playing. "What a mixed-up world!" she thought. "Right name, wrong daddy!"

Melody shot her a "behave yourself" glance. "How long do you 'spect it will be 'fore Matthew's services will be needed?"

"Mid September."

She clapped her hands in delight. "Oh yes! Oh good! That means that you can take me to Mackinac, Matthew, dear!"

Burley looked puzzled. "Mackinac? That's somewhere in the north woods, is it not? Why would you want to go there?"

"Mackinac Island. I have relatives there that I would like to see."

"Hmmm. Really?"

"Really."

"Hmmm." The little Scotsman's thoughts were whirling. He turned and dove into an unorganized sheaf of papers within his secretary desk. "Yes! Yes! Here it is! Captain, there is a vessel plying these waters that may be suitable for our cause. Perhaps she could convey you to Mackinac Island. Perhaps, also, she could be just what we need."

"I'm listening."

"The *Magnet*. Built in Saginaw, 1856, as a screw steamer. Converted to a side-wheeler. Used to transport lumber and Confederate prisoners to Johnson's Island, Ohio, in 1862."

"Interesting. Then her crew should know something about conditions in Sandusky Bay, right?"

"I would think so." Burley was getting excited. "Matthew, if you were on board this vessel you could ascertain all of the information that we need.... speed, draft, and whatever you need to know."

"Won't the crew think it a little peculiar that I ask so many questions?"

"Not if you tell them that you are associated with the firm of Bennet G. Burley & Co., dealers in fine cork pine lumber....which is the truth. You won't even have to fib! Tell them that we might consider leasing her if she meets our specifications."

"And Burley & Co. would want to lease her for what purpose?"

"Transporting lumber, of course. We wish to buy lumber at the mill in Cheboygan and transport it to ports in Ohio and Illinois. Like Chicago. Like Sandusky. Yes?"

"Yes!" Matt was beginning to admire the little man for his quick mind. "Would this happen to mean that our mutual friend, when he arrives, will pick up the price of the tickets?"

"It does, indeed. Round trip. Our 'mutual friend', as you call him, is well funded."

Matt leaned over Mary Sue to watch her nimble fingers tripping over the keys. "I suppose, now, you want a piano?"

Mary Sue smiled a wicked, hidden smile. "That would be nice, papa. Actually I reckon I'd like both. One of each. One piano and one little organ would suit me just fine!"

Melody winced at the "papa" but kept her composure. "I swear," she thought to herself, "nothing gets by that little girl!"

Matthew gave Mary Sue a little pat on the top of her head. "Greed will get you nowhere, young lady." Come along now. We mustn't bother Mr. Burley any longer." Matt stuck out his hand and Bennet shook it warmly. "Do you have any idea when arrangements can be made for our passage?"

"Not long. Not long. I believe she is due upriver in about a week. You should be ready to leave on short notice. She will be docking at Detroit just long enough to take on firewood and supplies. I'll book your passage under the name Burley & Co. to give further credence to our little plan. I assume Chandler is an alias, right?" Matt nodded. "Good! Identify yourselves as the Captain Matthew Chandler family when you board." He chuckled. "No one needs to know whether the 'captain' is military or is the master of a vessel. We'll all know it means both! By the way, Mrs. Chandler," he bowed to her causing her to execute a very shallow and somewhat awkward curtsey "I have not been aboard the *Magnet* , but I don't believe that she is very fancy in the way of accommodations as she is primarily a freighter. I hope you won't mind."

"Not at all, Mr. Burley. It will be fun to be on any big ship, won't it, Mary Sue?"

"Yes! Yes!" She held her mother's hand and jumped up and down to prove her enthusiasm. All the while, however, she kept casting furtive, longing glances at the piano. She would trade the ship for a pianoforte any day of the week.

They paused on the porch of the plain, but neatly painted, white clapboard home. Burley put his arm around Chandler's shoulder. "I believe we will make great shipmates. God speed to both of us, and....watch your back. There are more Pinkertons snuffling about every day."

As they re-crossed the Detroit River, the only other passenger on the launch was a well-dressed fellow wearing a nice suit and a bowler hat. He ignored them and seemed engrossed in his newspaper until they came in sight of the wharf on the Detroit side. The gentleman lowered his newspaper and frowned. There were three or four uniformed policemen on the dock in the company of two more husky individuals in civilian dress who appeared to be either detectives or inspectors. The gentleman folded his paper, tucked it under his arm, smiled at Matt, and reached into his pants pocket. "It appears," he said "that the authorities have picked today to do some routine inspections of folks crossing the border. They do this just enough to keep everyone on their toes." He pulled two copper pennies from his pocket and held them out for Matthew's inspection. He pointedly flipped them over in his hand until the head side of the coins were up.

Matt smiled. The fellow passenger smiled back. The gentleman was obviously a "Copperhead", a member of the very large secret organization of southern sympathizers in the north. Very likely he had been sent by Mr. Burley to ensure that they had a safe crossing back into the United States. Matthew spoke quietly so that the launch operator would not hear. "Are we in trouble?"

"I don't think so. They don't normally bother much with Indians, but today could be the day." He switched to a loud voice that all could hear.... even the men on the dock who stood watching as the linesmen caught the docking lines and secured them to the cleats. "Young lady, I would like to buy you some candy when you get on shore, but you don't look so good." He handed the pennies to an astonished Mary Sue.

"Is it all right if I take this, papa? Do I look sick, papa?"

Melody rolled her eyes. There she goes again! If the situation were not so tense, Mary Sue's antics would be funny. There was no mistake! Mary Sue longed for Matthew to be her father and intended to take every opportunity to make her position very clear. Melody felt the same way, but dared not bring up the subject to Matthew for fear of rejection....which was an even more likely possibility now that he knew that Bethany was still alive. Now, her body was telling her, in stronger and stronger terms, that the time was near that the subject of marriage would need to be approached....for better or for worse. There was a persistent, frightened feeling in the pit of her stomach.

Matthew was catching on to the Copperhead's ploy. The authorities would be unlikely to detain someone with a sick child who might throw up on them. He whispered into her ear. "Act seasick, Mary Sue. Real seasick."

The child was no dummy either. Realizing the situation, she summoned all of her budding acting skills and put them instantly to work by noisily retching over the side of the launch. She punctuated the retching with pitiful wails. In fact, she got so much into the role that she actually did vomit....much to the disgust of the policemen. They decided that this was an excellent time to be somewhere else. There was a little shop over on Jefferson where coffee and donuts were plentiful. They elected to succumb to the time-honored police tradition of the donut. Much better than watching a sick "injun" child throw up her lunch....and maybe her breakfast, too.

The coast now clear....literally....the Copperhead winked at them and wandered away. Melody mopped Mary Sue's fevered brow, and her messy mouth, with her handkerchief. They hurried away from the wharf and went straight to the candy shop where they purchased the child's reward as prescribed by their mysterious benefactor. Mary Sue made an instant recovery from her dire illness.

They slipped back into Franklin under cover of the dark of the night. The next day, Matt decided that it was time to lose the Indian disguise. Melody was kind enough to wash the black dye out of his hair for him. "My, my!" she trilled. "You have grown old and gray since I last looked at the real you."

"No! What do you mean?"

"Here. Look for yourself." She handed him a mirror. His dark brown hair was liberally peppered with gray flecks.

"Well, damn!"

Melody cackled. "I'm keeping company with an old man!"

"Thank you so much."

Before he had left for war, Matt had arranged to have both Bethany and Dick authorized to withdraw funds from his accounts in a Pontiac bank so that they would be assured of having enough cash available for the operation of the farm. He had also instructed his banker to invest a large portion of his financial assets into the budding Michigan lumber industry. He knew that the northern portion of the state was covered with huge, clear, white pine. The industry had to be a winner. He was right. Even as early as 1864, lumbering was beginning to produce fabulous dividends. His fiscal position was moving from very comfortable to very wealthy without any effort on his part. He sent Dick to Pontiac to withdraw a sizable amount of cash to finance their proposed northern adventure, took Mary Sue and Melody back to downtown Detroit to completely outfit them, and himself, in stylish clothes, packed their valises and trunks, and stood ready to respond to the call to board the *Magnet* when she arrived in Detroit.

Within the week a bewhiskered young man in a threadbare suit trotted his bay horse up the driveway, inquired in a soft southern drawl as to Matthew's identity, and handed him a sealed envelope. "From Canada, Captain Chandler, suh." The courier snapped a salute which was returned by Greyson even though neither was in uniform. In a heartbeat, man and horse were gone. The message was terse and unsigned:

> *Magnet* in port. Will sail tomorrow (Thursday). Board anytime in the morning. Godspeed.

CHAPTER TWENTY-THREE

mitchimakinak

The *Magnet* turned out to be quite impressive when Dick Trick deposited them, their luggage, and their crated....and not very happy....cat on the wharf. They stood and gaped upward at the large paddle wheels which towered above them. Dick whistled. "That's some ship, Matt. Sure wish I was a'goin' with you."

Greyson shook the youth's hand. "Next time, Dick. After the war. I promise. We'll take a trip together. Maybe cruise all the way to Chicago."

"Really? I'll hold you to it, Matt."

"It's a deal, Dick. For sure."

The *Magnet* backed out of her berth with a tremendous splashing from her paddle wheels and a long blast from her bass-voiced whistle. They steamed past *Ile aux Cochons, Ile aux Pesche,* across Lake St. Clair, up the St. Clair River, and emerged into the huge, startlingly blue, Lake Huron which was as waveless and flat as a pancake. Perfect summer weather for steaming, but certainly not for sailing, as there was not a hint of a breeze. They passed several schooners and a large number of sail-powered work boats all sitting idly, their sails flapping, whistling for a wind. After taking their supper with the other passengers and crew, they tucked Mary Sue into her bunk even though she protested, loudly, that she was much too old to have to go to bed so early.

Melody was stern with her. "You must get your rest, dear, so's you don't get sick."

"But mama, I only get sick when papa tells me to!"

Matt howled. "She's got you there, Charity Jane!"

Melody and Matthew went on deck and stood, holding hands, in the bow as they watched the daylight fade over the huge freshwater lake. Dew started to appear on the metal railings. The mild chill of the evening caused them to snuggle together for warmth. Matt offered his jacket, but Melody declined. It was a time of peace, of loving togetherness....but it was not working for Matthew. Thoughts of his beloved Bethany shot across his mind like jagged lightning bolts, destroying the loving moment that Melody so sincerely wanted.

"Matt?"

He wrenched his thoughts away from Bethany. "Lovely evenin' isn't it?" He kissed the top of her head, the lovely black hair.

"Matt, I have to tell you somethin'." She was shaking, but not from the cold. Matt felt the shivers and covered her shoulders with his jacket even though she had said that she didn't need it.

"And that would be what, sweet Melody?"

She took a deep breath. "It appears that I'm carryin' your child."

There was a long, frightening, silence, the moments measured by the noisy splashing of the paddle wheels as they pushed the vessel northward. Matt, strangely, had not considered the possibility of the occurrence of pregnancy, even though he and Melody had shared many wonderful and exciting nights together. "Stupid! Stupid! Stupid!" he cried, silently. "Now, what the hell do I do?"

His answer did not come quickly enough. His stunned silence was too much to bear. Melody shivered even harder, put her head against his chest, and began to cry. "Matt, for God's sake, please say something."

He sighed, smiled, and put his arms around her, holding her in a gentle embrace as though she might break if he squeezed her too much. He struggled, for a moment, to grasp the new world that had just opened to him. Bethany, now, had to step away. He whispered in her ear. "I love you, Charity Jane Melody Chandler Greyson."

They awoke Mary Sue to tell her that they were going to marry. They did not tell her of the pregnancy. That subject could be brought up another time. The little girl's eyes, wide as saucers, looked from one to the other as she suffered an instant of uncharacteristic speechlessness. Then, flying out of her bed, she jumped to hang from Matthew's neck, kissing him repeatedly on the cheeks. "Oh! Papa! Papa! Papa! Now I can really call you papa!" She leaned from Matt's arms to hug and kiss her mother too. "Oh, mama, oh, papa! Oh! When do we get married? When? When? Can I wear my new dress? The one with the big bow on the back? Can we get married real soon?"

Melody giggled, happily, with her daughter. "Yes, dear, we'll marry when we get to the island, and you'll be right pretty in your new dress." She paused for a moment, smiling at Matt. "I'll probably have to do some fast talking to get the priest to marry a Catholic Indian and a heathen Methodist!"

The next day, Matt hastened to make the acquaintance of the captain of the *Magnet,* explained his dreamed-up situation as the master of vessels for Bennet G. Burley & Co., and gently pumped him for information. He found out what he wanted to know. She was fast and strong, 142' long and 24' wide. The captain, a cooperative and friendly fellow, offered to check with the owners of the vessel at his earliest opportunity to ascertain the availability of the vessel for lease in September. He would then contact Mr. Burley, in Windsor, with the result.

Concerning Matthew's questions about Sandusky Bay, the captain urged extreme caution. The shoals and sandbars in the bay constantly shift their position. He advised a slow entry, a constant sharp lookout, and frequent soundings to avoid going aground.

When the *Magnet's* giant paddle wheels slowed, then splashed noisily backward to slow the heavy craft as it turned to starboard and into the harbor at Mackinac Island, Melody and Mary Sue watched, excitedly, from the bow rail as the little town came into view. "It is pretty, just like you said, mama, but I thought it would be whiter than it is."

"You mean the buildings and houses?"

"And the fort. 'Most everything looks kinda gray....like most of the farms down home. Looks like they need a coat of whitewash, or paint, or somethin'. Ain't quite as pretty as I thought it would be from what you said."

Well, sometimes folks are too busy to keep up the paintin', or sometimes they don't just have the money."

"Well, seem like they should take the time. Is that your church over there to the right? Saint Anne's? 'Least *it* looks nice and white."

"Yes it does. Wait 'till you see the hotel we're stayin' at. It's 'way down past Saint Anne's. You can just see it, 'way over there. See? It's real white, with a big long porch in front and a big lawn for you and Blossom to play on."

Mary Sue squinted. "Can't just see it too good. Too far away. Is it a real hotel with a dining room, and servants, and such?"

"It is. Matt says he is treatin' us to the finest. It's called the Mission House. I hear they have lots of people that work there to tend to their guests. Pretty young ladies, and nice clean Negro men in fancy uniforms."

"Ooo! Sounds like it is goin' to cost papa a bunch."

"It is, dear....maybe as much as five dollars a day."

"No. Can't be that much!"

"Yep. That's what he said."

The little girl straightened her pink flowered skirt and smoothed her hair. "Reckon me and Blossom had better be on our best behavior. Where's papa now?"

"He's up in the wheel house watching the captain run the ship."

"Oh. Hope we don't hit the dock. Seems like we are coming in awful fast. Maybe I should go up and help."

"I don't think so, Mary Sue."

"Mama, what's that smell?"

"Fish."

"Yukkk."

Soon after the steamer's paddle wheels had ceased their churning, the little family made their way up the long dock to the shore. Mary Sue skipped, gaily, in the lead. Matthew and Melody followed, hand in hand. In his free hand, Matt toted Blossom's travel cage from whence issued pitiful mews and meows as the occupant protested the indignities of travel. They were met by a handsome black man who was garbed in a fancy gold-buttoned tunic. He was the driver of a capacious two-horse wagon which sported a canvas canopy designed to shelter its passengers from the sun, or from the rain....whichever chanced to be occurring at the moment. "Mission House" was neatly lettered on the sides of the vehicle. Cheerily, and incessantly, the driver chattered to them as he described the sights along the way. Mary Sue ignored his practiced spiel. being much too busy trying to look everywhere at once. "Mama, what are those funny tents along the shore?"

"Those are Indian teepees. The low huts are wigwams. 'Pear to be mostly Chippewa."

Would those be our relatives?"

"Some of 'em. We'll visit them soon to see."

"Oh! There's Saint Anne's Church. That's where you went when you were a little girl, huh?"

"Yes, dear."

The Mission House was as spectacular as Mary Sue had come to imagine. Unlike most of the weather-beaten buildings on the island, it was painted a sparkling white. It had a long, friendly porch upon which one could sit, rock, and look out over the Straits of Mackinac, the view complete with whirling, calling gulls, and a misty, wooded shoreline in the distance. Little boys played stick ball on the lawn while the adult guests lounged on the porch, or upon benches which were scattered here and there upon the neatly groomed grass. The little girl gasped in amazement when she beheld the magnificent ladies who were resplendent in their lovely, full-skirted long dresses. The men, not to be outdone in the fashion department, sported casual suits, perky bow ties, various sorts of yachting caps, and a predominance of handsome mustaches.

The proprietor, a Mr. Franks, greeted them graciously, and personally helped mother and daughter to descend from their conveyance. Matthew had been fortunate to be able to arrange for a pair of the best rooms in the house....second floor, lakeside, with a small but comfortable parlor connecting them. Meanwhile, Blossom's protestations had risen from the pathetic to the urgent. Mary Sue tugged at Matthew's sleeve. He leaned to let her whisper in his ear. "Papa, I think Blossom has to go to the outhouse! 'Spose we can get a pan of sand right quick?" Matt rolled his eyes, but spoke to a nearby lackey who raced out of the lobby to fulfill the cat's urgent needs. Once ensconced in their private parlor, with a fresh pan of sand, the cat voiced no further negative opinions. The staff person went away, smiling, with a nice tip jingling in his pocket. For a few days, however, clean pan and good food be damned.... Blossom did not take kindly to her new surroundings. She had decided, apparently, to walk and/or swim home....all the way to her nice, comfortable farm in Virginia. Fortunately, her every attempted escape was interdicted by her alert young owner. Finally, resigned to her fate, she selected a nice, comfortable spot on the brocaded couch, and settled in to await developments.

Captain and Mrs. Matthew Chandler and daughter soon became accustomed to the luxuries of resort life. As they appeared to possess more than adequate funds, they were treated royally. Even Blossom received special attention. When Mary Sue wished to exercise her cat on the lawn, an attendant was directed to remain nearby in case a marauding dog should show up seeking a furry feline lunch.

Day times, they ambled all over the island exploring the cobbled beaches, and taking an occasional dip in the icy water. In the company of a never-ending supply of tourists, they viewed the natural wonders of the island.... Arch Rock, Sugar Loaf, and Skull Cave. Melody and Mary Sue toured Fort Mackinac with its impressive stone walls, blockhouses, and a parade ground full of drilling Federal soldiers. Not wishing to take a chance on being recognized by some soldier or officer from his past, Matt elected to skip that excursion. They also spent considerable blocks of time visiting the Island's collection of both resident and transient Indians. They visited teepees on the beach and shanty homes in the interior. Word was soon out that an Objibway princess had come home. Word of her visit traveled by canoe as far as St. Ignace, Cross Village, and all the way down the eastern shore of Lake Michigan as far as Petoskey and Charlevoix.

The entire Mackinac experience was exciting and fun, especially for Mary Sue. One of the best parts was bath night...which occurred twice a week whether they needed it or not. Matthew would retire to the lobby to read the two or three-day-old editions of the *Detroit Free Press,* thus allowing the females full run of their rooms. The hotel staff would carry a copper bathtub up to their room, accompanied by steaming buckets of water, soap, and fluffy towels. Mother and daughter enjoyed the feminine camaraderie of their steamy, perfumed rituals. Mary Sue, ever alert, used the occasions to gain valued information. "Mama?"

Melody, naked like her daughter, leaned over the tub and scrubbed the child until she very nearly squeaked. "Yes, love? Hold still while I wash your hair."

"How come your thingies are brown an' mine are pink?"

"What?" Melody blushed. She could sense a significant inquiry on the horizon. "Thingies? You mean nipples?"

"Yes, mama. Will mine turn brown when I get older?"

"No, dear, I don't think so. I'm brown because I'm *Nishnawbe.* An Indian."

Mary Sue splashed, absent-mindedly, in the sudsy water. "I thought I was an Indian too. You told me I was."

"You are, of course, but just half Indian. The other half of you is Scottish, like your father."

There was a thoughtful pause. "Then, do Scottish people have pink thingies?"

Melody shaded her eyes with her hand and shook her head at the frankness of the discussion. "Yes, Mary Sue, I'd guess that they do."

"You used to feed me with those when I was a baby, right?"

446

Melody blushed again and decided that it was high time to put on her robe, "Yes, dear."

"Will I do that? Some day? I mean, feed a baby like you did?"

"God willing. Some day....but a long time from now, I 'spect." Melody nearly decided to terminate the conversation before it became too complicated, but changed her mind, electing to make the most of an almost silly opportunity that had just presented itself. She dried her daughter's skinny body with a soft, fluffy towel. "Mary Sue, I have some extra special good news for you. Want to hear it?"

The child jumped up and down within the towel. "Yes! Yes! Of course, mama. I love special good news when it happens." She wrapped her arms around her mother's neck. "Tell me! Tell me, quick, or I'll just bust!"

Melody knelt before her and stroked her wet hair. "You're goin' to have a baby brother or sister."

Mary Sue almost toppled her mother over backward when she took advantage of her already-established neck-hold and squeezed with all her might. "Oh! Oh! Oh! Mama, that's wonderful! Will it be a boy or a girl? I think a girl. Boys are annoying. What will we name her?"

"Reckon we'll just have to wait an' see." She dreaded the next question, but knew that it was coming.

Mary Sue drew back and studied her mother's deep brown eyes. "I'm so happy for you and me and papa that we have a new baby comin', but, mama, how can that be? You tol' me that folks have to be married to have babies. You an' papa ain't married, as yet, so's how can that be?"

"Well!" Melody cleared her throat as she searched for the right words. "Sometimes....um....God likes to surprise us with special blessings just to show us how much He loves us....like this here baby." She patted her swelling abdomen. "One day, you will understand. Right now, all we have to think about is that God has blessed us with a little brother or sister. Fair 'nuff?"

"Fair 'nuff, I 'spose." She could tell that she was not going to get any more information. She wiggled into her nightgown, leaped upon the bed, and slipped under the covers. "Is papa coming to tuck me in like always?"

"Surely. He should be up directly."

Mary Sue pulled the covers up so that just her eyes showed, concealing her impish grin. She, spurred by her little-girl curiosity, had pieced together all of the bits and shards of information that had come her way through eavesdropping and clever clandestine observation. She had figured out more about sex and its possible link to the production of babies than her mother could ever imagine that she could know. She blinked her eyes, innocently, at her mother. "Can't wait to talk to papa about our new baby. Reckon I'll ask him how come it come so soon....even before we got married. 'Spose he'll know?"

Melody covered her face with her hands to hide both her embarrassment and a very pervasive snicker. "Bet he will! I can't wait, neither, sweet daughter. Should be a mite interestin' to see just what your papa has to say....or doesn't have to say."

+ + +

The next morning, not long after the mists had cleared, and while the leaves still dripped with the night's accumulation of dew, Melody, primped and in a proper sun bonnet, white gloves, and pink layered fashionably hooped dress, descended from the hotel carriage and hurried up the board steps of St. Anne's Church. She headed straight for the confessional where she was greeted by a shadowy priest from behind the screen. "Yes, my child, have you come to confess your sins to the Lord?"

"I have, father, and I got some pretty bad ones, too." She could almost see the priest's ears perk up, in spite of the intervening screen. "Forgive me, father, for I have sinned." She proceeded to tell the entire story of her recent life, trying to hit the high spots and confess only the most important of her transgressions.

When she had finished, there was an awkward silence as the priest digested the abbreviated, but still somewhat lengthy, confession. "Well!" he finally exclaimed, "You have certainly had an interesting series of experiences. Was your real husband, the father of your daughter, a Catholic?"

"No, father."

"And, is the father of your unborn child, your proposed husband, a Catholic?"

"No, father."

"Does he have any faith?"

"He does. He's a Methodist....or Methodist Protestant, or something like that."

The priest sighed, behind his curtain. "Well, I suppose that means that he would not be interested in joining the one true church, our Roman Catholic Church?"

"I serious doubt it, father. He tends to be set in his ways."

"Well then, you have two choices. Leave him, and bring up your children in the Catholic faith, or stay with him and continue to live in sin....may the Lord have mercy on your soul if you choose that route."

Melody's eyes began to sting with anger....anger that was too intense to allow tears to come. "This means, then, that you will not marry us?"

There was another long, awkward silence. "I'm afraid, child, that that is exactly what it means. The decision is up to you. If you will bring your family into the true faith your sins will be forgiven and your family will be blessed with the warmth of God's love."

Melody stiffened. "And, if I can't do that, what then?"

"Then, we will wait, patiently, for your return to the fold."

She jumped to her feet with a suddenness that caused her bonnet to slip off of the top of her head, in spite of the pink ribbon under her chin that was supposed to keep it in place, allowing it to land at the back of her neck. Her ears and checks turned a furious pink that easily rivaled the stylish pink of her bonnet and its attendant ribbon...all collapsed in a heap around her neck. "You would turn me away from my church? The church that taught me my faith?"

The priest sighed again. "I wouldn't look at it that way, child. It is you that has to bend to the laws of the Church, and not the other way around."

Without another word, Melody stormed out of the confessional, slamming the door with a force that made the startled priest's ears ring, ran down the wooden steps, and climbed back into the hotel carriage that had brought her on her hopeful...now dashed...journey of faith. When she had collected herself enough to speak to the driver, which took a moment or two, her voice was barely a whisper. "Do you know where Bela Chapman's house is?"

"'Course I do. Everybody knows where Judge Chapman lives."

"Take me there, please." A deep gloom enveloped her. She blinked her eyes to make the sting go away. It would not. She had been a staunch and enthusiastic Catholic child, blending the teachings of the Objibway spiritual leaders with the teachings of Christ, and had emerged as a staunch believer in both. She had been chosen to receive the power of the shaman by the great eagle that whistled from high in the sky. She had read her catechism carefully and had been received into the flock at Saint Anne's Church. Now, she was abandoned by the Christians and had received no sign from the eagle for many winters. As she sat in the Mission House carriage as it rumbled along the dirt road, splashing through shallow puddles of equine urine and squishing through scattered piles of dung, and as gloom hung over the Straits of Mackinac like a pall, she felt terribly alone and abandoned. Just as her thoughts reached the zenith of their gloom she suddenly sat upright, her eyes brightening. She was far from alone. Perhaps unsettled by the rough ride, or perhaps to give its mother a message of hope, the unborn baby stirred for the first time.

When they pulled up in front of the Chapman residence, the occupants were sitting on the front porch enjoying their morning coffee. Judge Bela Chapman and his ample wife Mary Choret Chapman rose to greet their unexpected visitor. Melody was hoping to find a friend, and advisor, in Mary Chapman who was her half-breed Chippewa aunt, a sister to her own mother. The sisters were daughters of Equameeg, but had different fathers. Equameeg was the daughter of Keeshkenum, a great chief of the Otchipwas, Lac du Flambeau Band, of Wisconsin....the Chippewas....the Objibway.

Her aunt stood at the top of the peeling, whitewashed porch steps, staring at her strikingly beautiful, and stylishly attired, visitor. Suddenly her face broke into a welcome smile, her arms opened wide. "Oh, my goodness!

Welcome, Eagle Song. I have been waiting for you. First, I knew you were coming. Then, I heard you were here. What took you so long to visit me?"

Melody rushed up the steps and into the lady's arms. "Eagle Song! Been so long since I have been called by my real name! Sorry, Aunt Mary. I came as soon as I could." Judge Chapman, a long-faced, big-eared man in his sixties who had a scraggly, graying beard and a sparkling, friendly personality, waited for his turn to be introduced.

"Welcome, child!" he exclaimed when it was his turn to hug her. "Welcome to our home. What did you say your name was?"

Melody laughed and gently placed her hands in his. "Well, dear uncle, you won't believe this, but here goes! My Name is Eagle Song, otherwise known as Charity Jane Melody Chandler, soon to be Greyson. How's that?"

He recoiled in mock amazement. "Oh, my God! How can one beautiful woman have so many names? Does this mean you are some sort of royalty, or just a very confused person?"

"Royalty, Bela." said Mary.

"Confused person." smiled Melody.

"Well, be it as it may, I'm certainly glad I don't have to list you on a legal document. It would take from now until lunch."

Melody looked into his eyes. "Don't be too glad, dear uncle. I may have to ask you to do just that!" It took nearly an hour, sitting on the porch rockers and sipping coffee, to tell what had transpired since she had left the island as the bride of a Virginian of Scottish ancestry, one John Chandler, now deceased. "Humph!" grunted her aunt. "Since you have been gone doing all those things, we have needed you here. Do you still have the power? Are you still a medicine woman, a shaman?"

Melody sat with her eyes downcast, her hands folded upon her lap. "Mary, I'm just not sure. The eagle has not come to me, to sing of the power of the Great Spirit, for a long time. I fear he may be unhappy with me as I chose to leave the land of my ancestors."

451

Mary patted Melody's folded hands. "I do not have your power, but I do have some insight into the spiritual. The eagle has watched over you....all the way to Virginia."

Melody lifted her eyes. "You really think so, Mary? Oh! Of course! The eagle sang to me when Matthew came to me, injured and sick in his mind. The eagle gave me the power to heal him and I didn't even thank him for it. Aunt Mary, I'm ashamed."

"Well, you needn't be. Important thing is you are back. You have much to do. We have many sick people that white man's medicine does not help. Will you heal them?"

"I'll try, Aunt Mary. I'll do as best I can. Perhaps the Great Spirit will allow me. The Christians certainly have no interest in my welfare, or, I 'spect, in the welfare of the Chippewa Nation." There was a bitterness in her voice that startled even herself. "Maybe Jesus does....in spite of 'em. I just don't know, right now." She sighed a deep sigh. "Bring the sick to me, or take me to them, and I'll do what I can." Tears of frustration coursed down her cheeks as she lifted her gaze from the peeling porch rail, to the dung-splattered street, to the misty gray of the Straits of Mackinac.

Mary Chapman swiveled in her rocker to address her husband who was sitting, rocking, sipping his coffee, and quietly enjoying the conversation. "Bela, dear?"

The rocking stopped. "Yes, dearest?"

"Would you excuse us for a few moments? We have feminine subjects to discuss."

Bela sighed and heaved to his feet. "Of course. I'll finish my coffee in the study. I have legal matters to consider, anyway." He was obviously irritated that he would not be a party to the gossip that was about to ensue.

Mary giggled. "Bela's a real snoop. That's what makes him a good lawyer and judge. But, then, he don't have to know everything. Somethin's bothering you, Eagle Song. What is it?"

"The priest at Saint Anne has refused to marry me to the man who is the love of my life."

"What about the other love of your life? The man who fathered your first child?"

"As I told you, he's dead."

"How many loves of your life can one woman have?"

Melody looked embarrassed. "From my point of view at least two, I'd guess."

Mary Chapman folded her hands and pursed her lips. She was actually quite a formidable-looking woman whose severely drawn-back hair style and bulldog appearance made Melody just a little nervous. She was heavyset, with bold features that did not smile easily. Her black hair, speckled with gray, was drawn back so tightly that she looked almost bald. Melody hoped that she had not made a mistake by confiding in such a stern and no-nonsense person. Mary rocked, silently, as she stared into space....apparently deep in thought. Eventually, her visage softened as she reached, again, to touch Melody's hands. "You're carrying this man's child, aren't you?"

Melody, who...enduring the silence and wishing that she had not come.... gulped, and blinked in surprise, at the lady's insight. "Yes, Aunt Mary. I am."

"Well," the lady sighed, resuming her rocking with a little more vigor, "it would be best if you were to be married both in the Catholic Church and by the Objibway ritual, but I expect we will have to make do with what we have available to us. Leave it to me. You will be married." She turned in her chair and hollered through the open door into the house. "Bela! When can you marry this woman?"

There was a pause as the judge, ensconced in his study, ruffled through his calendar. "How about a week from Friday, dears?"

Mary and Melody looked at each other and nodded in agreement. Melody, following her aunt's example, hollered through the door. "That would be just fine, Uncle Bela!"

The women turned and both resumed their rocking, looking out over the rutted street. Melody was still a little nervous. "When do you think the sick and injured will come to me?"

"Ask the eagle."

+ + +

Five evenings later, Matthew returned from his walk to report a new happening to Melody and Mary Sue. Across the darkness of the water, on the usually dark Round Island, campfires were glowing. The next morning they all walked to the shore to investigate. There, in the distance, they could see many canoes pulled up on the sandy beach of the island. Smudges of smoke from cooking fires rose into the air like smeared gray pencil sketches. The conical , white forms of teepees were evident. Wigwams were also scattered along the beach, their low forms blending with the tree line. "What do you make of that, my little Indian princess?" asked Matthew. He stood behind her and held her close, kissing her hair as they stared across the water.

"That's easy. My people have come." Just that morning, Melody had appeared in a fawn-colored doeskin dress that was fringed, lovely, beaded, and in considerable contrast to the fashionable apparel to which the hotel management, guests, and her family had grown accustomed. "Come wade with me." She slipped off her moccasins and waded into the water, relishing the clean sand as it squished between her toes. Mary Sue lost no time in joining her mother. Matthew retired to a nearby grassy hummock to light his cigar. As he looked over the flame of his match, he noticed a birch bark canoe being launched from the beach of the island. Manned by two braves, it seemed to be headed directly toward them.

As Matthew shook out his match he suspiciously eyed the approaching craft through a drifting cloud of cigar smoke. "Melody, are you expecting visitors?"

Melody, holding hands with her daughter and splashing their feet in the shallow water, looked up to give him a smile. "Not really, Matt."

Matt flicked an imaginary ash from the end of his newly-lit cigar. "Well, expected or not, a couple of buckos are surely headed this way, 'less I'm mistaken. Do you think they are friendly, or do I have to shoot 'em on arrival?"

Melody gave him a nose-crinkled look. "Keep your pistol in your pocket, Matt. I'm sure they mean no harm. "Maybe they're just paddling around. They're allowed to paddle wherever they please, you know." She was wrong. The canoe continued in their direction.

Mary Sue watched, with more than a little interest, as the two lithe, teen-aged, Indians pulled their birch bark craft onto the sand. One approached Melody while the other stayed to keep the canoe from drifting away. "Eagle Song?"

"Yes." Melody acted as though she were not surprised in the least that the boy knew her name. Matthew and Mary Sue, however, stared at each other in wide-eyed amazement.

The young brave handed her a birch bark cone from which protruded a bouquet of eagle feathers. "Wasagunabi, chief of Lac Du Flambeau Objibwe, sends his greeting."

"Thank you." smiled Eagle Song, dropping her eyes as she took the proffered gift.

The young man stood stiffly in the water, his paddle in his hand. Mary Sue, standing quietly next to her mother, did not miss an ounce of his physique, right down to the intriguing loincloth that concealed (almost) his private parts. "Wasagunabi asks that you join him at his council fire. Tonight at moonrise."

"Alone?"

"Alone."

"Will he send a canoe for me?"

"He will."

Matthew snuffed his cigar into the moist sand....as though clearing for action....and stood as tall as he could, effectively towering over the young Indians. He strode purposefully toward them. "Now, wait a minute." The boys looked frightened, but stood their ground....or, actually, water....in this case. "If, er, Eagle Song is coming to your camp, then I am coming too, to ensure her safety. Is that clear?"

Mary Sue, sensing the momentum, chimed in. "And me, too!"

The young men, trying to look like their escape was unhurried, pushed their canoe off of the sand and stepped effortlessly into the fragile craft without causing a wobble or a ripple. "Chief Wasagunabi said 'alone'. If he does not agree that you all come then we will not return for you."

Melody stared after the departing canoe and silently handed the chief's gift to Mary Sue for her inspection. "Matt, we mustn't ruffle the chief's feathers. I want him to marry us."

"How come? I thought Judge Chapman is goin' to tie the knot."

Melody patted his cheek. "He is, dear. We'll be married twice."

Matt whistled. "Whew! Reckon we'll be good and married! Don't 'spose there will be any danger that it won't last, what with the knot tied that tight." Suddenly, to his surprise and for the briefest of moments, a vision of Bethany appeared before his eyes. She was dancing up Fourteen Mile Road and wiggling her hips as he trudged after her carrying his sick dog. Matt smiled an inward, secret smile and blinked his way back to reality.

That night, as the silver full moon arose from Lake Huron, the braves were back, standing quietly on the shore, holding a much larger canoe, and awaiting their three passengers. The Chandlers boarded the *bateau,* which was large enough to handle several more passengers, and were paddled without a sound from either the paddles or the young men to the island were teepees glowed in the flickering, orange light of the Objibway fires. Chief Wasagunabi sat cross-legged in the sand, staring into his fire. He was puffing on a long wooden pipe that had several feathers fastened to its long shaft. He neither stood nor offered a word of greeting. Instead, he simply waved for them to sit near his fire. To Matthew's discomfort, numerous male forms seemed to be lurking just outside of the flickering shadows. Ever so casually, he moved his hand to be near the butt of the little revolver that nestled beneath his belt. The chief offered the pipe to Matthew. "Welcome to my fire." The chief's lined face cracked with a quiet smile.

"Thank you." said Matthew, relieved. "We are privileged to be here."

The chief did not acknowledge Matt's reply. Instead, he turned to Eagle Song, who sat quietly in the sand next to her daughter, and addressed her in rapid-fire Objibway tongue. She answered him in such a positive manner that even Matt and Mary Sue, rolling their eyes at each other, could recognize that Eagle Song was asserting her authority, even though they understood not a word.

A young Indian stepped into the circle of light to add a log to the fire. Melody leaned to Matthew to speak quietly. "He says that he will marry us. He also asks that I heal those who are sick. Is this acceptable for you?"

"Of course it is! Any way that you can be my wife is fine. Right, Mary Sue?"

"Mary Sue, somewhat frightened by the whole scenario, discovered that she really had to go to the outhouse. Unfortunately, there were no such facilities on Round Island. She crossed her legs. "Yes, papa." She tried not to look distressed. "Whatever you say, papa."

Two plump young women, pretty in their buckskin dresses which were adorned with feathers and colorful beads, shuffled, hesitantly, into the firelight. One, obviously the spokesperson, bravely stepped a little closer. "Chief Wasagunabi, it is our understanding that there is to be a wedding."

The chief nodded, gravely. "This is true."

The women giggled. "Would we be allowed....?"

The chief held up his hand for silence. After a few studied puffs on his pipe he spoke to Matthew, his voice gravelly and quiet. The squaws fidgeted nervously. "These women wish to make clothing for the bride and her daughter. May they do this? It would be a gift from our people to Eagle Song and her family. Is this acceptable to you?"

Matt was becoming at ease with the situation. He no longer sensed danger. "Of course! We will be pleased and honored by the gifts of your people."

The chief cracked a rare smile in his leathery face. "My people are about to become your people. After all, your adopted child and your unborn child are Chippewa." The chief puffed the pipe back to life with a coal from the fire and handed it back to Matt.

Matthew drew on the pipe in a manner that he hoped signified his sufficiently solemn concentration. He let the acrid smoke curl around his nose for a dramatic moment. ""I am honored to be warmed by your fire, Chief Wasagunabi."

"Then, you shall become one of us."

"Thank you. I would be honored to be considered a Chippewa."

"Good!" The chief waved a dismissal to the squaws who reached out with friendly hands to Melody and Mary Sue. As they arose to go with them, Mary Sue whispered to her mother. "Mama? Do you suppose that they could possibly have an outhouse? I just gotta go."

Melody chuckled, placed her hand on her daughter's back, and propelled her out of the firelight. "We'll take care of that problem right directly, Mary Sue."

When they were gone, the chief pulled a blanket over his shoulders to ward off the evening chill. "You are a warrior. I can tell."

Matt sensed that there was no point in playing games of deceit with such a wise man. "I am. A horse soldier."

"Where, then, is your horse?"

"Dead. Killed in battle."

"Was your eye killed in the same battle?"

Matt shrugged and involuntarily touched his fingers to his black eye patch. "Yes. It was."

"Did you win the battle?"

"No. But we fought well. We fought nobly and without surrender."

The chief puffed the pipe and stared into the fire for what seemed a very long, silent time. Finally, he spoke. "If you are to be Objibwa then you must have an Objibwa name. Your name, forever more, is 'Warrior-who-rides-a-dead-horse'. You loved that horse, didn't you?"

"I did."

"His name?"

"Saber."

There was another long silence. Chief Wasagunabi grunted as he scrambled to his feet. "One day you will ride him again....across fields of waving flowers."

Matt shuddered. It was the dream that he had dreamt as he lay, unconscious, on the bloody field of Second Manassas.

The chief grinned. "Enough of serious talk. Come inside. I have a bottle of white man's brandy. We will drink together and talk of happy things."

There were many giggles coming from a nearby teepee where Melody and Mary Sue had been stripped bare and were being expertly fitted with pure white doeskin, soon to become the royal garments of matrimony.

+ + +

Bela Chapman's "week from Friday" was not long in coming. It was a lovely, simple ceremony in the judge's study. Ignasius Pelotte, a local fisherman of some wealth and his Chippewa wife, Rosalie, served as witnesses. They were relatives of the Chapman's and were delighted to be a part of the ceremony. A certain amount of secrecy had to be maintained, however, as Melody and Matthew were already considered to be husband and wife, name of Chandler, by the hotel staff and by anyone who might be inordinately interested in their identity. Mary Sue was allowed to wear her new dress from Detroit....the one with the enormous white bow at the back. The child virtually glowed with pride and love for her parents. After the wedding they elected to send the carriage back to the Mission House empty, much to the disappointment of the liveried driver. They walked back, Mary Sue and Melody carrying their flowers, and enjoyed the scene of the fort with its glowering cannon, the peeling buildings along the shoreline, the deep blue water, the cries of the gulls, and....a new sound.... the sound of drums from across the water at Round Island....the sound of Objibway drums....the sound of preparation for a royal wedding.

Just at dawn the following morning, Melody was startled awake by a shrill whistle. Matthew lay by her side, snoring gently. The whistle came again, seeping through the open window of their hotel room. Quietly, so that she would not disturb her husband's slumber, she slipped from under the covers and leaned from the second story window, looking up to the cobalt blue of the sky which sported a few wispy clouds....clouds tinged with the gold of the sunrise. Just below, or perhaps just above the scattered clouds an eagle wheeled, only a speck against the sky. The golden sunrise glinted white against the feathers of his head, neck, and the under layer of his tail. He whistled again as though to call her to fly to him. Kneeling there in the window, she raised her arms to the heavens. She could feel a warmth on the top of her head. She took three breaths through her flared nostrils and exhaled them through pursed lips. She dreamed that a golden shaft of light came from the eagle, or perhaps from the sky, or perhaps from the Great Spirit. The shaft of light seemed to break, from the golden, into splinters of a rainbow. She instinctively curled her hands and arms inward so that her fingers touched the top of her head.

When she awoke, Matthew was gently shaking her. "Melody? Melody? why are you lying here by the window? You feel cold. Come back to bed with me and I will warm you."

She smiled at him, stretched, yawned, and complied with his request, snuggling securely against the hardness of his muscular, but gentle, body. "I love you, Matthew."

"I love you too, Melody. Where have you been?"

"To the sky with an eagle."

Matt scratched his private parts absentmindedly. "Would this be a male eagle or a female eagle?"

She stretched, her naked breasts lovely before his eyes. "A male eagle, of course."

"Do you suppose your eagle friend would share you with me?"

She gathered him close. "Oh yes. He would, indeed." She pulled him, ever nearer, that he might dance within her. The eagle whistled no more that morning.

Final preparations for their Objibwa wedding were nearly complete. Far to the south, in Windsor, Canada, Bennet Burley penned an urgent message to Matthew.

CHAPTER TWENTY-FOUR

Eagle Song,
Heals-With-Flowers

They came by the scores. The word had been carried up and down the coasts, up the cold, sparkling rivers, and deep into the piney forests. Eagle Song had come. Eagle Song had come back, at last, to heal her people. They came by *bateau*, they came by birch bark canoe, by rowboat, by two-masted, gaff-rigged Mackinac boat. They came, hope glowing in their eyes. There were no social services, nor drugs, and only the occasional inept physician to comfort them. In 1864, if you were sick or crippled, you usually died. If you did not die right away, you suffered a lot, and then you died anyway.

Had Norman Rockwell been alive in 1864, he would have tripped over his easel in his haste to grab his brushes and to paint Mary Sue as she intently watched her mother try to heal the crippled and the sick. The little girl sat, barefooted and bare-assed, on the summer sun-warmed beach as she watched her mother give comfort to those in need. Mary Sue's body, including her skinny bottom that rested in the sand, was properly covered, but only by a feather-decorated and very simple buckskin dress that was kept free from the pull of gravity by slim leather thongs that were neatly tied across her shoulders. Her thick, curly, jet-black hair swirled around her head and cascaded over her shoulders. Her feet were supposed to wear moccasins, but she had kicked the plain, buckskin shoes off, leaving them to lie beside her, helter-skelter. Appreciatively, she wiggled her toes into the soft sand, and sniffed the sweet smoke from the cedar smudge that Eagle Song waved around her patients to cleanse the air. Even though her pregnancy was beginning to be obvious, her mother still moved with lithe grace as she circled her patients. "Hmmm!" thought Mary Sue, "Mama's thingies seem to be growing. Hmmm. She's got lots and I don't hardly have any." She sighed audibly enough to have her mother glance at her to see if she was all right. The little girl continued her silent thoughts as she played with a piece of a clam shell, using it to dig a miniature excavation in the sugary sand as she continued her private thoughts. "Mama says I'll have some one day. Hope so. Hope so, and soon! I believe it's 'bout time I was a woman." She shot a few furtive glances around, assessing the young, male Chippewa population. "Well, now! Sure would like to get a good look under them skimpy loincloths those boys is wearin'." She had an inspiration that was so brilliant that it was worth chancing a reprimand for interrupting Eagle Song's work. "Mama, can I do the smudge when you are through with it?" Maybe, she thought, if she had the smudge she could walk around with it....and get nearer to the gaggle of boys who were standing in the background and giggling, quietly, among themselves.

Her mother played right into her hands. Eagle Song blew on the little bundle of cedar boughs to keep it smoking, and handed it to her daughter. "Walk around us in a circle to keep the air clean. An' while you are at it, tell those boys to keep quiet."

"Yes, mama." she said gravely, and with an inward smile, as she took the smudge and headed straight for the boys to give them a piece of her mind....and to take a closer look at their bronzed, lean physiques.

There were a full dozen subjects, that day. Eagle Song carefully attended every one without ever touching them. Holding her palms several inches from them, she scanned for hot or cold spots in their auras. When she detected a spot that had sickness she deftly pushed the evil away....still without touching. Chief Wasagunabi sat quietly on the foot-high sandy ledge that marked the upper edge of the beach where the white sand began to give way to grasses and flowers. He puffed upon his long hand-carved pipe, not missing a thing that transpired. As Eagle Song's patients began to leave, he noticed that those who came limping in pain left showing no evidence of discomfort. Those who had sickness in their bodies left feeling better. If they were not completely healed, at least their spirits were lifted in the hope that their health would soon be improved. They all thanked Eagle Song as they left, their dark eyes sparkling in gratitude.

The medicine woman, suddenly exhausted, was glad to see the last of them go. Just as she was about to gather up her daughter and to request a canoe ride back to Mackinac Island where her husband awaited their return, a canoe, paddled by two elderly men, beached on the shore. They chattered to her in the Objibway tongue, asking for her help. They were sorry that they were late, but they had paddled all the way from St. Ignace against the wind, and had done the best that they could. Eagle Song squatted on the sand and motioned for them to come closer. Obliging, they bent over the canoe and lifted an old, toothless woman who was wrapped in a colorful trading blanket. They struggled through the sand and placed her, prostrate and unresponsive, at the shaman's feet. Eagle Song stood and turned to leave. There was nothing that she could do. The woman was already dead. Suddenly, the woman....who seemed to resent being prematurely pronounced dead....opened her eyes, spied the medicine woman, and began to shriek for help. Eagle Song, a bit embarrassed, knelt by her side to comfort her. The shrieking soon stopped and the blubbering began. Dying was not the problem. She knew that she had not long to live. The problem was the terrible pain in her distended abdomen that had been worsening for months, to the point where it was constantly unbearable.

Eagle Song threw off her exhaustion and quietly chanted ancient words of comfort to her, gently stroking her forehead. "Mary Sue! Light a new smudge and come to help me." Her daughter came running, trailing a stream of smoke and flame from the newly-lit bundle. Blowing out the flames and encouraging the smolder, she skidded to a stop, dropped to her knees next to the whimpering woman, and burst into tears. "Mama, what can we do for her? Oh mama, please help her. She looks so sad."

The woman turned to look at Mary Sue, then reached her gnarly hand to gently touch the child's tear-streaked face. "Is this your daughter, or is this an angel that has come for me?"

Eagle Song smiled. "This is my daughter who has come to help me drive away your pain. Also, I believe she is an angel, 'specially to me."

"Thought so. An angel. Oh!" She clutched at her distended, misshapen abdomen as barbs of intense pain shot through her. "I have prayed to the

464

Great Spirit, and to Jesus, but neither has helped me. Oh!" She writhed in pain, urinating involuntarily in her blanket.

Wasagunabi, still in the same spot, relit his pipe. Mary Sue's tears of sympathy flowed even harder. She threw the smudge onto the sand and wrung her hands in anguish.

Eagle Song rose to her feet and beckoned Mary Sue to do the same. "Perhaps both Jesus and the Great Spirit have brought you here. "Mary Sue, hold your hands over your head, wide apart, reaching toward heaven as I do. Pray to the Great Spirit that he might help us." The little girl complied. They stood, unmoving, for several minutes. "Do you feel anything?"

Chief Wasagunabi's pipe dropped from his hand. Mother and daughter were glowing with a subtle, golden aura. He looked to heaven and thanked the Great Spirit for His intervention. Now, the tribe had two medicine women to care for them! "Yes, mama. The top of my head feels hot. An'.... an' my feet feel hot where they touch the sand."

"Good. Now do as I do." They again knelt next to the old woman, one on each side, and passed their hands, palms down, over...but not touching her abdomen. "What do you feel now?" she asked her daughter.

Mary Sue blinked away her tears. "I feel hot all around the edges of her tummy and cold in the middle."

"That's right. You're doing well. Now, do as I do. Concentrate on pushing the bad spirits out of her with the palms of your hands, but do not touch her." In unison, they pushed mightily against the evil area within the woman's aura. When they were through, even though the huge tumor in her abdomen remained, the pain was gone....and the patient was smiling gratefully at them. Mary Sue ran to the edge of the woods where the wild blue flag iris was in full bloom, standing like little blue Federal soldiers along the edge of the sand. She picked a handful and brought them back to the woman who received them with tears and smiles of joy, and clutched them to her bosom.

"Thank you, beautiful angel. Thank you, Eagle Song. I believe I will go home now." She motioned to the men who came to help her to her feet and walk her to the canoe where they made her comfortable. Climbing in, they raised their paddles in salute, then began their long journey back across the waters to the Upper Peninsula.

Chief Wasagunabi groaned to his feet with some difficulty. He had been sitting in the same spot for some time. He put one hand on Mary Sue's head and lifted her chin with the other so that she would look into his eyes. "Your name is 'Heals-with-flowers'." Without another word he turned and walked away, ducking into his wigwam. The Objibwa were now blessed with two shamans....one a little young, as yet, but sure to follow in her mother's footsteps.

A few rods inside the woods stood the skeleton of a giant, dead white pine. Unnoticed, an eagle silently preened himself as he sat on an upper branch, then, just as silently, flew away.

The old woman, a smile on her lips and clutching her blue bouquet, lulled by the quiet sound of paddles swirling the water, died....silently and without pain....before they reached St. Ignace.

+ + +

Matthew was happy that he, "'Warrior-who-rides-a-dead-horse'", had been accepted by the Chippewa. He was happy that he and Chief Wasagunabi had become good friends. He was also happy that Melody and Mary Sue seemed to be known and loved by every Native American that they met. Spoiling all the happiness, however, was the fact that he had to leave his pregnant wife, and his daughter, and book passage south to assist in the Confederacy's ambitious Great Lakes naval project. He had received a letter from Ben Burley requesting that he return to Windsor two weeks sooner than planned. Not trusting in the privacy of the mails, of course, Agent Burley had simply alluded to a slight change of plans which required his presence as early as possible, certainly no later than September 1st. Not surprisingly, Matthew was no longer certain that he wanted to go at all. The excitement and allure of the interesting rebel undertaking had faded in his mind. But, he was a man of his word. A promise is a promise.

The summer was slipping by at an astonishing rate. Their wedding celebration, as decreed by Chief Wasagunabi, was only a week away. In two weeks he would have to be on his way back to the war. Matt began to toss and turn at night, spending most of his nights worrying about leaving his family, and worrying about the baby who appeared to be due sometime in December. What if the lakes froze and he couldn't get back in time? What if he were captured or killed while helping his friends to free their friends from Johnson's Island? What if? What if? He arose early one morning, leaving his sleeping females undisturbed in their beds. He tiptoed out of their room, put on his shoes in the lobby, and set off on a counterclockwise walk all the way around the island, appreciating the beauty of the dawn over the Straits of Mackinac while he tried to gain control of his gloomy thoughts.

When he reached town, after walking most of the distance around on the lake shore road, the streets were still deserted. The only discernible activity was the fishermen raising the sails on their Mackinac boats to catch the morning breeze. He recognized Ignasius Pelotte in the distance and waved to him. The fisherman, just climbing into his boat, squinted for a moment, recognized him, and waved back shouting a friendly "Halloo, Matt!" He passed Saint Anne's Church, still silent, but holding aloft its cross to sparkle in the early morning sunlight. Walking on, he came to Mission Church. The door was open, revealing the white-painted sanctuary which was cheerfully illuminated by the sun streaming through the side windows....in surprising contrast to the gray and peeling clapboards of the exterior. A lone gentleman was seated at the top of the tall front stairway, apparently deep in thought....or prayer....and, like Matt, enjoying the quiet of the morning.

"Mornin'!" said Matt as he walked past, tipping his hat.

The man stood, smiled, waved, and came down the steps to intercept him. "It's a good morning, indeed, sir. I see you walking by quite frequently. Are you a resident nearby?"

Greyson smiled and stuck out his hand. Just temporary. Name's Chandler. Matthew Chandler."

The gentleman shook his hand. "Pleased to meet you, Matthew. I'm Bill Ferry, the pastor here."

"Pleasure, Reverend Ferry." Matt was edging away, hoping to continue on to the Mission House where he knew hot coffee would be waiting for him in the dining room.

"Care to come sit on a nice, hard step with me? A little pleasant conversation never hurt anyone on such a fine morning."

Matt laughed. He was certain that the minister was trying to catch a new member. At least, he was pleasant about it. "Surely. I'll sit with you for a short spell."

William Ferry was a very friendly and outgoing man. He was clean-shaven, had neatly-groomed graying brown hair of medium length, and wore a starched white shirt with a tall, winged clerical collar. His sleeves were already rolled up in anticipation of a hot day. "Are you staying at the Mission House?"

"Yep. With my wife, daughter, and a new baby comin'."

"How nice. Will you and your family be staying with us long?"

Matthew was finding it easy to talk to the cheerful preacher. "Well now, that's a problem. My family will be staying on but I have to go away on business. Scares me, some, to be away at this time with the wife expectin' and all."

"Must be important business."

Matt shrugged. "It is."

They sat in silence for a moment, soaking up the warming rays of the rising sun. Pastor Bill put his hand on Matt's shoulder. "If it'll help, Matthew, I'll be happy to look after your family while you are gone. As you are staying right next door at the Mission House, it would be real convenient for you to bring them to the Sunday morning service. That way I could meet them." Reverend Ferry chuckled. "Besides, you might even get something out of the service. My sermons are not always bad, and the choir is not always flat."

Matt laughed with him. "Very kind of you, sir, but I have to be truthful. My wife and I are not too pleased with Christian churches in general, right now."

The reverend's eyes went round with alarm. "Oh my! How so?"

Matt lost no time in venting his displeasure regarding the priest at Saint Anne's who had refused to marry them....even though Charity Jane had been born, christened, and raised under the protective wings of that church.

Bill propped his elbows on his knees and held his head in his hands in exasperation. "Well, the Catholics have their rules. I guess we have to admire them for sticking to them, no matter the cost. However, If God had sent you to me I would have married you in a minute."

"Even though Charity Jane was pregnant with my child before marriage?"

"Even though your wife was pregnant with your child before marriage. We're not into guilt like the Catholics. Instead, we're into joy. Tell me, where did the older child come from?"

"Melody's former marriage. Her first husband is dead."

The reverend was looking a little confused, trying to take in all the information that was being thrust upon him so early in the morning, before, even, he had had his coffee and flapjacks.

"Melody?"

Matthew chuckled. "Sorry. That's Charity Jane, my wife. She has a lot of names."

"I see, I think. Sooo, I gather you are truly married now?"

"Yes, sir. By Judge Chapman. And, just to make sure it sticks, we're to be married by Chief Wasagunabi in one week."

"The Objibway chief from Wisconsin? Is he here?"

"He is. And he brought a lot of Indians with him. They are all camped on Round Island."

"You don't say! Why?"

"To marry us, of course."

"Why would he do that? Is there something special about you that you haven't told me?"

"No. There is nothing special about me. It's my wife."

The reverend leaped to his feet and staggered up and down the steps, holding his head. Suddenly he stopped, on all fours, on the steps below Matt. "All right, Matthew. You have had your fun with me. Are you going to tell me who your wife is?"

"Eagle Song. A Chippewa princess. A medicine woman. A shaman. She heals people."

Bill Ferry's eyes were round again. "She does? Really?"

"She really does. I've seen her at work. It's truly amazing."

"Really?"

"Really."

The minister, prostrate on the stairs, folded his arms on the step below Matt and cradled his own head on them. His voice was muffled. "If I wasn't a minister of God, I would say, well, I'd say 'I'll be damned!'"

Greyson snickered. "Hope not, sir."

Bill Ferry climbed back to the same step that Matt was sitting upon, clasped his hands between his knees, and bowed his head. "Let me tell you something, Matthew."

Matt shot him a sideways glance, beginning to fear that the reverend was a little "tetched".

"God has sent you here. This church....meaning all the people in it....will welcome and assist you and your family if you will let us."

"Thanks, Bill. Your kindness is much appreciated and needed, actually, what with me goin' away and such."

"Good! Tell you one more thing."

"What would that be?"

"I'm not about to wait until Sunday to meet your family. When may I meet them?"

Matthew grinned, stood and stretched, and prepared to resume his journey. "How about in one hour, for breakfast at the hotel? On me, of course."

"How kind! Thank you. I'll be there. I've never had the opportunity to meet a real princess before, especially one with the power of healing."

"I have two princesses."

"You do? Aw, c'mon now!"

"I do. Mary Sue is the other one. You'll see. Meet you at the hotel in an hour."

The reverend, now properly attired in his black suit coat, presented himself at the dining room in forty-five minutes. Matthew was right. He did have two princesses, both of whom were enchanting....especially the smaller one who talked incessantly, except when hushed by her parents, and who seemed to have an opinion on, and an observation about, just about everything.

CHAPTER TWENTY-FIVE

Longknives Come!

"Sir?"

"Something wrong with your hearing, lieutenant? I said, take a detachment over to Round Island and see what all the fuss is about! The constant drumming is getting on my nerves!"

"Yes, sir!" An embarrassed blush pinked the cheeks of the young lieutenant as he stood stiffly at attention before his commanding officer. "If you please, Captain Pratt, I have heard that the Indians are just having a big wedding for some princess or other."

Pratt snorted and leaned back in his chair. "Princess be damned. There's a whole flock of savages camped on United States property and raising some kind of hell. I want them to know that they're being watched, just in case they get drunked up on firewater and decide to get rascally. Clear?"

"Yes, sir."

"At ease, lieutenant. Have a seat."

"Thank you, sir."

"Something else you should know in case you don't already." The lieutenant, perched uncomfortably on a bare wooden chair, raised his eyebrows. "Garrison troops get bored. When they get bored, they get troublesome. They got nothing to do except drill and polish, polish and drill."

"Yes, sir?"

"You're going to give them something to do....something to talk about. Take the three Mackinac boats we have at our disposal, load them with eight fully-armed men each and sail or row, depending on the wind, for Round Island. Go to the east side, out of the wind, form in column....with bayonets mounted....and march in good order up the beach to the Indian encampment. I make there could be upwards of two hundred of them on that island."

"Do you think that that kind of show of force might frighten them into armed resistance?"

The commandant of Fort Mackinac chuckled. "I think not. In fact the contrary. If they do resist it will go badly for them, won't it lieutenant?"

Lieutenant Smalley coughed, nervously. "Of course. As you say, captain." He paused to gather courage. "Could I ask one thing, sir?"

"Ask away!"

"Could we beach closer to their camp? I'm not sure my leg can march that far through the sand....and several of my men are walking wounded in the same fix."

Captain Pratt twiddled his thumbs, hands resting upon his blue, brass-buttoned tunic, as he considered the request. "I apologize for forgetting that I'm in command of a gaggle of cripples, fuzzy-faced boys, and old graybeards. Sorry. Beach as close as you must. It would be embarrassing to us, and worse, amusing to the Indians to have you crawl back to your boats if your legs give out."

"Thank you, sir." He grinned to hide his dislike for his commander. "I have an idea."

Pratt sank back in his chair with an indulgent sigh. "Which is....?"

"Let's train the cannon, all of 'em on both the upper and lower parapets, on the island. Then, if anything goes wrong, we can blow their red asses right into the happy hunting ground!"

They both had a good laugh. "Lieutenant, your sarcasm is duly noted. However, this could be a good idea! It will give our gunners something to do. When you have returned from your mission we can have them lob a few solid shot into the Strait. Give 'em a show."

"That would do it, sir. Scare the feathers right off 'em!" Lieutenant Smalley stood to leave. "With your permission, sir, I'll get to it. Kindly be certain those artillery men don't get itchy trigger fingers until my boats are well clear of the area."

"I'll see to it. Don't you worry one bit!" Captain Pratt softened a bit, dropping, for a moment, his strict military manner. "By the way, son, tell me about your wound. How did you get that gimpy leg?"

"Second Bull Run, sir. Musket ball passed through my thigh and killed my horse. At least I'm better off than he is."

+ + +

Melody kissed Matthew awake in the gray of the dawn, then bounded into Mary Sue's room to do the same to her. "Awake, my loves! It's our wedding day!" There was no breakfast to be had as the hotel waitstaff had not yet put in an appearance in the dining room. Even the seagulls were still sleeping, their heads tucked under their wings as they stood in their sandy beds, and did not start their noisy squawking and calling until disturbed by the little family's shuffling and shivering approach. The same two young braves who usually met them were already there, standing motionless on the cold sand and watching over their large *bateau* which bobbed in the shallows, its gunwales decorated for the occasion with varicolored flowers and dyed feathers.

"Good morning!" chirped Eagle Song. The boys smiled shyly and managed to nod in reply.

Matthew, just getting his circulation going under his warm jacket, marveled at the lean youths who did not seem chilled in the least by the unseasonably cold morning even though their legs and feet were bare. In deference to the cold, however, they were wearing long-sleeved fringed buckskin shirts that he thought looked quite nice. Each wore a headband over his thick, long, black hair. The headbands each held several eagle feathers which were obviously worn in Eagle Song's honor.

Mary Sue, aka Heals-with-flowers, thought that they looked very nice, too. Even though she kept her eyes averted, and pretended not to look at them as she climbed into the big canoe, their closeness still made her skin tingle a bit.

"Sorry to get you up so early." Eagle Song smiled at them. "Ain't you cold?"

"Not too early. Usually up to fish, anyhow." Indian #1 climbed into the bow while Indian #2 shoved off.

Indian #2 looked up at the cloudless sky. "Not be cold long. Soon be too hot!"

Matt stood at the edge of the water, the tiny waves lapping at the toes of his boots. "Don't forget to come back for me, and don't forget I will be bringing two friends."

"Not forget." The stern man raised his paddle in salute. "Chief Wasagunabi say bring big canoe back for you when sun high in sky."

"Good! Thank you." Matthew watched as they grew smaller in the distance. Melody turned and waved to him. As he returned the wave, the sweetness of Bethany's face, dim in the distance, flashed into his consciousness. He ducked his head and shaded his eyes. Bethany was dancing up Fourteen Mile Road, waving and clowning. The warmth of the vision was deeply disturbing. His eyes became wet with tears....tears that he could not quite understand. Not very manly! He looked around to make sure that no one saw him. Impatiently, he brushed the rogue tears away and strode to the road, following it to the tall steps of the Mission Church. He sat on the top step, chin cupped in his hands, as he stared without seeing over the beautiful blue waters of the Straits of Mackinac. Bethany would forever be the love hidden in his heart.

Within minutes, the Reverend Bill Ferry was sitting by his side, a steaming mug of black coffee in each hand. "Mornin' Matthew! I could tell, even through the window, that you are overdue for your morning coffee!"

Matt smiled a reply and gratefully took the cup. "Thanks, friend."

"You are most welcome." The smile did not fool the reverend. "Why so glum? You getting cold feet on your wedding day? Might as well not bother, with the cold feet I mean, because it's too late to run now....seeing as you're already married!"

Matt laughed. "Yeah, yeah. I know, Bill. Besides, I ain't got cold feet.... exactly."

"Well, what then?"

The bridegroom sighed. He wanted to talk about Bethany, to bring her out into the open, but he dared not. He decided to cover his sadness by discussing another subject that was only mildly bothersome to him. "You think I should be married by an Indian chief? I mean, they seem to be nice people and all, but they are savages, ain't they?"

"For what the word 'savage' is worth, I guess they are."

"It's obvious, ain't it? I mean, they live in the woods, beat each other's brains out with clubs, skewer each other with arrows, blow each other away with firearms, slice scalps off of living victims, sink axes into each other's skulls, drag each other's women and children off by the hair to serve as slaves. Ain't that a pretty good definition of savages?"

Reverend Ferry took a swig of coffee. "Actually, quite a good and thorough definition. Now, consider this: We, the civilized and non-savage white men, steal their land through silly treaties and buyouts that, taking advantage of their ignorance, totally cheats them of their rightful heritage. We shoot them like vermin, infect them with European diseases that kill them by the thousands, and cram them....weeping and crying.... onto pitiful reservations where they cannot possibly live a quality life. While we are engaged in doing all these nice things to the Indians, we are also taking the time to fight the War Between the States, where brother is shooting brother and thousands are dying by the saber, by the musket ball, and by

476

being blown to bloody bits by canister and shell. Now, excuse me, my dear friend, but just exactly who are the savages?"

Matthew was a little off balance from the fusillade of words. "I see, I think. Um....very well, Bill. I stand corrected. So, we are all savages! Now, what about their gods? They worship wolves and eagles and all sorts of things."

Ferry smiled. That's because they know more than we do."

"What? Aw, c'mon now."

Mrs. Ferry, attractive in her white lace-trimmed bonnet, appeared in the doorway. "You gents are much too serious for such a fine wedding day!" She held a blue enameled, smoke-smudged coffee pot in her hands. "I have made a fresh pot. Are you ready?" In unison, they held out their mugs for her to fill. Matthew," she chattered, "I am so looking forward to the wedding this afternoon. I have never seen an Indian wedding before!"

Matthew gestured flippantly and sipped his coffee. "Neither have I. Should be interesting for all of us. Thank you for the coffee. Much appreciated."

"William, what do you think I should wear this afternoon?"

"Something simple, my love. You will be climbing in and out of canoes and sitting in the sand."

"Oh dear! That does present a challenge!" She set the coffee pot on the steps and flounced away to examine her wardrobe.

Ferry shook his head, lovingly, as he looked after her. "I don't know what I would do without her to keep things lively around here! Now, where were we?"

"We have dispensed with the 'savage' problem and are talkin' 'bout native gods."

"Oh yes. Native God. One God. They have only one. Same as us. Same God. The Creator who provides life here and life after death. Matthew, I have been blessed to have been sent to this place because it has given me the opportunity to study the native people. They aren't nearly as ignorant as they seem. Their beliefs are real and genuine. They see God in all the creatures and features of their wilderness world."

Matt shook his head. "You mean like the wolf god, eagle god, frog god, what-have-you god?"

"These are not gods. They are spirits. They, in their ancient faith, can see them, where we cannot. Kind of like the Catholics with all their saints. They can see them and we cannot! Some would say that the Indians...and the Catholics....worship a pantheon of gods, but they do not. They worship God and they revere the spirits and the saints."

"You mean that Melody's carrying on about her eagle friend could be true?"

"Of course it could. We must keep an open mind and an open heart. You could learn from her what we all should learn....God is in the earth, the sky, the waters, the creatures....and we must treat them all with respect, and care for them as gifts from the Supreme Being. Matthew? You're staring into space. Have I lost you in the muddle of my theological enthusiasm?"

Matt patted the reverend on the shoulder. "No, of course not. I appreciate your words. You are opening my eyes to Melody's world."

Bill's eyes danced with delight. He retrieved the coffee pot and refilled their mugs. "Good! Now, talk to me. There is something else bothering you, I can tell. What is it? Out with it!"

Matthew smiled at his friend. "You're right, of course. You always are. But, I can't talk about it today. Some other day, perhaps, we can talk. Today is Eagle Song's and Heals-with-flowers' day."

"I'll be waiting." There was a moment of silence as they both stared into their coffee mugs. "How about telling me how you met Melody? I confess I'm a bit curious."

"It's a very long story."

"I have no place to be all morning except right here on this very hard wooden step that is giving me corns on my ass! Nevertheless, I will sit here while you tell it to me. I'd like to hear your long story."

"Very well." Matthew, brightening, giggled. "It's your ass." He told of finding Confederate trooper John Chandler dying on the battlefield, and how they had become fast friends in the few moments that they had had together. He told of praying with John when he died. When he glanced at Reverend Bill, he was startled to see tears streaming down the preacher's cheeks. "Well," thought Matthew, "perhaps tears are not so unmanly after all!!"

"Sorry!" said Ferry, wiping his eyes with the sleeve of his shirt. "It's a beautiful story. Please go on." When Matt had finished telling how Melody had nursed him back to health, the minister was almost quivering with joy. "A love story! A real love story! I see material for several sermons in it! May I use it from the pulpit some day?"

"If you wish, but please don't connect me with it in any way."

"Because you are a dead lieutenant colonel who isn't?"

Matt smiled. "Right. That makes me at best a convalescent and at worst a deserter. I have lost an eye, the part of a hand, a part of my life, and a beautiful woman in the service of the United States of America. That is quite enough." He neglected to mention the Confederate connection. That would add "traitor" to the descriptive list.

Ferry cackled. "Beautiful woman, huh? Now I'm getting the picture! Still don't want to talk about her, huh?"

Matt smiled a shy, pensive smile. "Not today. Like I said, today is Melody's day. Tomorrow, maybe."

Reverend Ferry shrugged. "As you wish, of course. I want you to know I am bringing my Bible and my prayer book to your 'savage' wedding. Maybe the chief will let me chime in."

Matthew feigned exasperation. "Oh, how fine! Now it's a triple knot! I'll never get out of this marriage!"

Ferry looked him in the eye and stuck out his hand. "That's right. Keep that in mind! Shake on it?"

Matt took the proffered hand. "You got a deal, friend."

+ + +

Mrs. William Ferry's perky little nose twitched, bunny-like, under the lacy leading edge of her sun bonnet. "I smell food! Good food!" The *bateau* rocked gently through the choppy waves in response to the muscular paddle strokes of the familiar young Indians who, seated fore and aft, propelled the craft toward Round Island.

Bill Ferry, clutching his Bible and his prayer book, agreed. Smells like lunch! Good thing. I'm famished."

Matthew, seated just behind them, could not decide whether or not he was looking forward to the festivities. In any case, he was happy to have the Ferrys along for company.

When the canoe gently touched the sandy shore, The Reverend Ferry hopped into the ankle-deep water and scooped up his wife while she clung to his neck, squawking and giggling with delight....and with the fear of being dropped, butt first, into the water. Chuckling, snorting, and pretending to groan from her weight, he managed to deposit her safely upon the dry sand.

Matt stood on the shore and looked out over the beautiful water. He was surprised to see an entire flotilla of canoes and boats, some of which were mere specks on the horizon, all paddling, rowing, or sailing, converging on the camp. The fishermen had obviously been watching for his arrival. He whispered a little prayer of thanksgiving for having so many friends. The encampment was bustling with cooking activity. Three full venisons, on three separate fires, sizzled and browned as the spits were turned by squabbling broods of urchins who constantly argued with each other as to whose turn, literally, it was. Cornbread emitted delightful odors as it baked in large cast iron frying pans that were precariously propped over the fires. Cast iron hanging pots contained a mysterious, boiling concoction that appeared to be composed of various meats and vegetables of undisclosed, and possibly suspicious, origin. "Probably 'coon, fish, grouse, and various other leftovers not to be reflected upon!" thought Matt. Beneath the embers of the cooking fires whitefish and lake trout, carefully wrapped in wet leaves, steamed to a fall-off-of-the-bone state of perfection.

Chief Wasagunabi approached, hand raised in greeting. He presented each of the new arrivals with beaded headbands decorated with the obligatory feathers. The chief was trailed by a pretty little slip of a girl whose hair was done in long, fetching, braids. She was carrying a special gift for Matthew.... a wedding gift from the entire tribe. It was a beautifully tanned and fringed buckskin shirt. It was decorated down the front with four parallel, vertical rows of hand-crafted mother-of-pearl buttons, each painstakingly carved from the clamshells which were so abundant in the area. All watched, with smiles of encouragement, as Matt struggled into the shirt and donned his headband. "There!" he cried when he was finished, twirling for all to admire.

"Good Heavens!" exclaimed the reverend. "You could pass for a genuine Indian if you hair was just a tad blacker!"

Matt indulged in an inward grin, thinking of his long journey northward masquerading as a 'genuine' Indian. Mrs. Ferry went off to find Melody while the gentlemen sat cross-legged near the chief's fire, smoking in turn as the ceremonial pipe passed between them. They sat in silence as they watched the boatloads of fisherman arrive at the beach.

Their peaceful reverie and silent companionship was startlingly disturbed by the approach of a giggling gaggle of squaws and girls of all ages. Encircling and dancing around Eagle Song and Heals-with-flowers, they propelled the guests of honor toward the waiting men at the chief's fire. At some predetermined signal, the circle faded away, leaving mother and daughter standing by the fireside. They were beautiful. Matthew's heart jumped in his chest at the sight of his loved ones. Both were dressed in plain, startlingly white doeskin dresses. They were devoid of ornamentation except for the exquisite beadwork on their matching moccasins. Eagle Song's hair fell over her shoulders in seductive straight lines. By contrast, there was nothing seductive about little Heals-with-flowers. The ringlets and curls of her long black hair, barely tamed by brushing and primping, cascaded over her shoulders and down her back in ferocious elegance, threatening to stand straight up, or out, or to fly away without a moment's notice.

Tribal men, seemingly appearing from nowhere, encircled the chief's fire, pressing close....but silent....in response to Wasagunabi's upraised hand. Gravely, the chief joined hands with Matthew, Melody, and Mary Sue, forming a circle within the restless layers of braves who in turn encircled them. "Eagle Song, do you wish this man, Warrior-who-rides-a-dead-horse, to be your husband?"

Eagle Song smiled into Matthew's eyes. "I do."

"Heals-with-flowers, do you take this man to be your father?"

Mary Sue jumped up and down, still holding hands. "Oh, I do! I do!"

"Go then, and live together in peace. May the warmth of the fire in your hearts warm your wigwam forever." A premature whoop issued from the back row by a brave who was hungry for his supper. "Wait! White holy man would speak."

Reverend Ferry stepped forward. "There is little that I need to add to this beautiful ceremony except to pray that our Lord Jesus, son of the Great Spirit, will add his blessing to the union of this family." From between the leaves of his prayer book he produced two golden crosses, each attached to finely braided horsehair necklaces which he presented to mother and daughter. When they had tied them in place, the plain little crosses sparkling at their necks, he bowed his head in prayer. "Let us pray the prayer that Jesus has taught us." In unison they prayed....including, surprisingly, nearly all of the assembled Indians. "In the name of the Father, Son, and Holy Spirit, I now pronounce you man, wife, and daughter!" There was an instant bedlam of whoops, yelps, and howls filling the air as the braves danced around the wedding party.

Ironically, the chorus of whoops coincided almost exactly with the instant that Lieutenant Smalley and his detachment of soldiers beached their Mackinac boats on the shore just out of sight of the party. "Ohmygod, lieutenant! They've spotted us!" cried a young private.

"They're gonna rip us to pieces!" whined another, even younger, teenager.

"Nonsense! Fall in! Dress up that line there!" He winced when he spotted a dark urine stain at the crotch of the youngest boy's light blue trousers. "Poor, scared little bastard!" he thought, with a smirk. They all fidgeted nervously as they fell in. "Load and cap your weapons. Affix bayonets!" The click of ramrods and the musical clink of bayonets being drawn from their scabbards followed his orders in quick succession. "In column of two, forward march!" Even though some of them immediately began to suffer the reawakened pain of their old wounds, they shuffled determinedly through the deep sand, along the beach, and toward the noise of the celebration.

Chief Wasagunabi held aside the leather door of the nuptial tent and motioned for Melody and Matthew to enter. Blushing, Mrs. Ferry led Mary Sue away. Together, they sat on the sand while friendly women brought to them the sumptuous banquet which steamed deliciously at them from improvised birchbarkware. A new chorus of whoops crescendoed as the chief closed the door behind them. Out of sight on the beach, several trembling soldiers pleaded that they were grossly outnumbered and therefore should return immediately to the boats. Smalley waved his saber at them. "I will run any man through who breaks ranks! We have our orders! Forward! March!"

Inside the teepee, Matthew's eyes became accustomed to the dim light and focused on piles of blankets and soft, cuddly bearskins. "Now what? What the hell are we supposed to do in here?"

"Make love, silly." Melody undid the thongs at her shoulders and let her dress drop to the ground.

Matt gaped at her sudden nakedness. "With all those people whoopin' and yellin' and dancin' 'round out there? I'm not sure I can do that!"

She caressed him, concentrating her attention upon his important part. "You never had trouble before."

Matthew spluttered. "But, but, it's different when all those men are watching."

She pulled him down to the softness of a bear rug, and kissed him. "They ain't watchin'. They're eatin'! The wedding feast! Remember?"

Matt sat up. "The feast! Yes! And, I'm hungry!"

"You have to earn your supper." She pulled him back down to her. After only one or two tender moments there was a sudden cessation of the laughing, whooping, and hollering that had been going on outside the tent as the wedding guests helped themselves to the ample food. At once, there was no sound at all. Matt and Melody looked at each other, wide-eyed.

"Now what? Is this a new part of the ceremony?"

Melody was mystified. "I have no idea!" Fumbling at the door flap warned them that they were about to have a visitor. Hastily, they covered themselves with a blanket.

Chief Wasagunabi stuck his head in. "Longknives come!" He motioned to Matt. You better come out and talk!"

Melody snuggled under the trade blanket and giggled. "Well! That certainly gets you off the hook! How did you work that?"

"Hush!" Matt pulled on his trousers. "I don't know what's goin' on, but it might be somethin' serious to have soldiers show up here. I'm not likin' the sound of this." He peeked out of the teepee without showing himself. "Yep. We got us a problem." Flanked by two very large warriors who stood with their arms defiantly folded, Chies Wasagunabi stood facing the detachment of soldiers who were lined up on the beach with their backs to the water and their weapons at present arms. Matt noted that each soldier's thumb was on the hammer of his rifle, but the rifles were not cocked to fire. The fixed bayonets made an impressive show of determination. He could hear soft rustlings and muted clicking sounds issuing from the forest behind the row of teepees. "Yikes!" thought Matt, "The braves are getting ready to take the soldiers down!" He took another look at the soldiers. Their lieutenant was face to face with Wasagunabi. "Well now," he muttered to himself, "that is one stupid officer! He has his men standing like targets in a shooting gallery, with no place to retreat to unless they want to swim for the fort! His men could well pay with their lives for the lieutenant's stupidity." He turned and whispered to Melody who sat, wide-eyed, hiding her naked body under her bearskin coverlet. "I can't let this happen. I've got to go out there!"

"Be careful, Matt. It wouldn't be fair to lose you on our nuptial day."

He grinned at her and stepped out into the afternoon sunlight. "On *one* of our nuptial days, love." He took off his feathered headband and pulled his slouch hat low over his eyes. It was at least a slight possibility that he could have previously served with one of the soldiers. He did not want to take the risk of being recognized. Strolling casually, and wearing a big smile, he made his way to the side of the chief. Neither he, nor the Indians, displayed any weapons except for the sheath knives which they all wore on their belts. They had nothing with which to annoy twenty-four soldiers with rifled muskets and fixed bayonets. The warriors hidden on the fringe of the woods just behind the camp were, however, quite another matter. Matt surveyed the collection of greybeards and wet-crotched boys who were arrayed in front of him. "I hope they won't get too sassy." thought Matthew. "They won't last a minute against a determined force."

Chief Wasagunabi's voice was low in pitch, quiet, and betraying no sense of anxiety or fear. "What can we do for you, Longknife? I know of no quarrel between us."

The young lieutenant stood, defiantly, with his unsheathed saber in his hand. His voice was high-pitched with excitement. "I hope not. Our commandant wants to know what you people are doing here, and how long you intend to stay. You are on federal land and are not allowed to establish any sort of long-term camp without government permission."

Matt stepped forward, still wearing his smile. The soldiers remained in their rigid position without a quiver. The odds still looked good to them. Twenty-five to four was to their liking. "I can speak for the chief, if he wishes." He turned to the chief, his eyebrows raised. Wasagunabi nodded assent. "First, lieutenant, this is a friendly, non-hostile gathering. If we are to talk, I'll thank you to sheath your saber and put your men at ease."

The officer was not quite as inexperienced as Matt had hoped. He shook his head in the negative. He had begun to sense the danger of ambush. "Tell the rest of the savages to come out where I can see them. Then, maybe we can talk friendly."

Matt smiled even wider. "Well!" he thought. "The boy does have some promise." He turned to the chief. "Chief Wasagunabi, should you feel that this would be a wise move, I would suggest that you have your men stack their arms and come forward. These soldiers mean us no harm." Matthew was anxious to defuse the situation. One nervous, itchy trigger finger and all hell would break loose.

The chief looked at him, concern in his eyes. "You are sure of this, Warrior-who-rides-a-dead horse?"

"I give my word, Chief Wasagunabi."

"Then, so be it." He raised his hand, waving a silent signal. The lieutenant's eyes grew large as he perceived at least a hundred warriors file silently out of the forest, sit cross-legged on the ground, and lay their assortment of bows, spears, and rifles before them in the sand. Only then did Lieutenant Smalley realize what danger he and his men had unknowingly faced. Matthew winced. The sand would not hurt the bows and spears, but it certainly would bugger up the rifles. He wanted to tell them to pick them up again, but restrained himself.

"Order arms!" barked the lieutenant. "At ease!"

Matthew still wore his smile, which he began to feel was frozen to his face. He stepped forward, hand extended. "I'm Captain Matthew Chandler. May I have the pleasure of making your acquaintance?"

Lieutenant Smalley sheathed his saber and accepted the handshake. "Lieutenant Henry Smalley at your service, sir."

"Pleased to make your acquaintance. Lieutenant Smalley, all we are doing here is having a wedding. My wedding. When it is over....which is by tomorrow....camp will be broken and we will all go away. Does that satisfy your inquiry?"

Smalley's eyes studied Matthew's face which was darkly tanned and barely visible under the generous brim of his slouch hat, and further hidden by his black eye patch. "It does indeed, thank you. Er....captain, what sort of captain are you? Somehow you look familiar to me. And, if I may say so, sir, you have the distinct bearing of a military officer. Have we met before?"

Matt's smile faded. The young man did look vaguely familiar. "I don't believe so, Lieutenant Smalley. I am a master of Great Lakes commercial vessels and rarely visit these islands. Most of my work is out of the mainland ports....Bay City, Alpena, Rogers City, Cheboygan, and such. The firm I work for hauls lumber."

Smalley shook his head. "Sorry. I must be mistaken." He was not mistaken. Before being wounded at the Battle of Second Bull Run, in Virginia, he had been a trooper in General Buford's command. He had often seen Matthew,

486

as Lieutenant Colonel Matthew Greyson, astride his magnificent horse as he officered the First Michigan Cavalry. Fortunately for Matthew, the lieutenant could not quite reconcile his recollections with the face before him.

The chief, who had stepped aside from the conversation between the two white men, reasserted himself. "Soldier, I invite you and your men to join us at the wedding feast. We have plenty for all."

Smalley was not an unreasonable man, but sitting down to sup with a bunch of near-naked savages was not his idea of fun. "I respectfully and gratefully decline, chief, sir. I must get my men back to the fort, if you will excuse us. Thank you for your proffered hospitality."

"Huh?" said the chief.

"You are most welcome!" smiled Matthew. "Perhaps another time."

The short journey from Round Island to the ramshackle docks that languished before the equally ramshackle town, which in turn languished below the imposing fort, gave Lieutenant Smalley a few minutes for reflection as the crews of the three boats pulled at their oars. "I know I have seen that man someplace before!" he mused. "He must be, or have been, a Federal officer....I'm sure of it." Smalley was not ungrateful that Captain Chandler had very probably saved the lives of his men...not to mention himself.... as he, dumb Lieutenant Smalley, had stupidly (he mentally kicked himself in the pants) placed his soldiers like shooting ducks before a probably hostile force, and with no way to retreat. "Maybe that's why Chandler is a captain and I'm a lieutenant." he mused, further. "Maybe the man is a colonel, or a general, or something." A flash of brilliance illuminated his mind. He would send a courier to Captain Chandler, at first light on the morrow, to invite him and his bride to dine with himself, the commandant, and the commandant's wife! Brilliant! Given a lengthy social situation, a lot of nice, red wine, and a snifter or three of the commandant's carefully hoarded Napoleon brandy, tongues would wag and he would solve the mystery. "Probably," he thought, "the gentleman was wounded in the eye and retired from the service of his country. But....then again....he could be on a secret mission for the Union, or, he could even be a deserter. Or, he could even be a spy!" The excitement of the chase was making the lieutenant's humdrum existence more bearable. He was a man without enough to do, making him, of course, one of the most insufferable forms of humanity. He would pursue his Captain Matthew Chandler until he took him to ground or brought him to bay.

+ + +

With the dinner invitation neatly stowed in his black leather dispatch case, a uniformed courier was rowed through the rising mist to Round Island early the next morning. He lept from the boat and strode toward the campsite as soon as the bow touched the sand. He paused in mid-stride. The campsite was empty. There was simply no one present. There were no teepees, no wigwams, no boats, no canoes, no anything except a few still-smoldering fire pits. It was as if the Chippewa Nation had never set foot on Round Island. They had vanished back into the spirit world from which they had come. Shaking his head in disbelief, he trudged back to the waiting boat. As though to add to his discomfort, there was a shrill whistle from somewhere high in the sky that made the hairs on the young soldier's neck stir and stand erect. An eagle, ghostly above the morning mist, circled....and said things to him that he could not understand.

CHAPTER TWENTY-SIX

Mr. & Mrs. Charles Cole

On August 11, 1864, the Confederate plot to free the rebel prisoners on Johnson's Island was officially underway. As the train carrying the bogus Mr. and Mrs. Charles H. Cole rumbled into Sandusky, Ohio, Bethany wrinkled her nose at the sight of the plain little city. Small, ramshackle manufactories, businesses, stables, and pens of cattle crowded the rail right-of-way. Peering through the smoke-smudged windows, she found the view to be much less than inspiring. Beth coquettishly patted her companion's arm. "Well, Charles, my beloved husband, this town looks like a perfectly awful dump. I'm glad I did my shopping elsewhere!"

Charley Cole laughed, brushing an imaginary lint from the sleeve of his expensive suit. "It's really not as bad as it looks along the tracks, Annie. Actually, Sandusky has a quite charming little business district down near the bay. And, my dearest," he smiled at her condescendingly, "I believe that you, in spite of your prejudices, will like the West House. It's a very nice little hotel with good, clean accommodations. I checked it out a few weeks ago."

Bethany, aka Annie Brown Cole, looked charmingly grumpy. "I'll like it as long as there aren't too many spiders, or rats, and *noooo* bedbugs....and, as long as I have a good strong lock on my bedroom door."

Captain Cole shrugged, yawned, and stretched. "Don't flatter yourself, lady. I have no intention of going anywhere near your bedroom door."

"Good!"

"You can even leave it open in perfect safety."

"Not a chance."

"I find myself wishing, more and more, that I could have brought Annie Brown instead of you."

"Humph! Perhaps if you would have been a little more careful in your lovemaking she would be here instead of me."

"You don't know that."

Beth noticed, with hidden glee, that the man was actually blushing. "I didn't think you would admit it. Women can sense these things, you know."

"Really? Pardon me if I'm not impressed with your womanly deductive powers. It may put you at ease to know that we have a nice two bedroom suite, fancy enough to please a wealthy Pennsylvania oil speculator and his charming wife." He picked up his top hat and clapped it upon his head with a chuckle. "You *can* be charming, can't you, if you put your mind to it?"

"Only when I'm with someone I like!" she sniffed.

He ignored her unkind inference. "You'd better gather up your things. We're almost at the station."

"I guess that means that I have to start being sweet." she sighed. "How painful! By the way, what did you say is the name of the oil company you are supposed to be founding? You told me, but I forgot."

"Mount Hope. Mount Hope Oil Company. And, we're from Titusville, Pennsylvania. Kindly do not forget again. It could be most embarrassing if someone noticed that my dear wife doesn't even know where she is from."

"Don't you worry your little head, Charles. I'll be the best wife you've ever had. Just stay out of my bedroom."

"You have already made that very clear, Mrs. Cole."

Annie giggled, chiding him. "Oh! Sorry! I forgot."

Upon arriving at the West House, Annie performed her habitual search for bedbugs lurking in the covers, and for spiders in residence in the closets and corners. Finding neither, she pronounced the accommodations to be satisfactory. A quick exploratory walk along the main street, punctuated with a few perfunctory pokes into the few shops that looked at least a bit interesting caused her to evaluate the Sandusky shopping as somewhere between backwoods and nonexistent. She congratulated herself on having the foresight to bring ample clothing and accessories with her, thanks to the funds provided to her for that purpose by the Confederacy. Additionally, thanks to the good graces of the gentlemen in Richmond, they also had at their disposal a nice, fat $60,000.00 credit in a Sandusky bank, thoughtfully provided in advance, in Cole's name, by Mr. Jacob Thompson.

The Coles lost no time in getting into action. Charles quickly built a reputation as a substantial and very generous businessman who loved to give fine parties and expensive dinners, all of which featured the finest wines and the most expensive cigars....all imported, of course. Annie was breathtaking in her fashionable gowns and glittering jewelry, causing men to treat her like royalty and women to turn green with envy. Men swam in the beauty of her blue eyes, feasted their eyes on what they could see of her shapely bosoms, and longed to touch her cascading, raven hair. Women hoped that she would not stay in town very long.

The officers of the *U.S.S. Michigan*, charmed by the Coles, and seduced by their glittering parties, had no idea that they were targeted to be victims of the Confederacy. The friendship of the charming midwestern couple was something to be cultivated. The Coles smiled as the moths came fluttering to the candle flame. Commander J.C. Carter became a frequent guest. Within days, Charlie was invited aboard the ship, and even was allowed to take frequent tours of the prison facilities on Johnson's Island where he generously handed out cigars to the rebel inmates as a gesture of goodwill to all men. No one seemed to notice that the prisoners did not immediately light up their cigars, seeming to prefer to save them and smoke them later. Actually, inside the cigar bands were tiny handwritten messages giving details of the plan to secure the release of the prisoners by force, thus assuring a coordinated effort between the prisoners and the party which was to board and take over the *Michigan*.

The iron hulled *Michigan* was the only real obstacle standing in the way of the liberation of the waiting rebel prisoners. If fact, she was the only armed Federal vessel on the Great Lakes. The 582 ton three-masted side wheel steamer constituted a significant threat as she stood guard over the Johnson's Island prison. Mounting fourteen cannon, she would not be an easy mark for conventional attack. Clever subterfuge would even the odds.

Charles and Annie were good at their craft. The officers of the *Michigan* tumbled pell-mell into the trap that was laid for them. It was no surprise to the Coles when they were invited to an evening of dining and wine drinking aboard the ship on the evening of September 19th. After all, it was only good manners to repay such charming hosts with a reciprocal invitation. When the invitation was received, the Coles celebrated by drinking an entire bottle of chilled, expensive French champagne between the two of them. Charles then hastened to the telegraph office where he sent an encoded message to the naval wing of the conspiracy at their lair in Windsor, informing them of the target date. The trap was set, the plan was simple. Captain Cole and Annie would provide enough fine wine to produce a satisfactory level of inebriation of the officers, then slip drugs into their beverages to seal the deal. Once leaderless, the ship's crew could be easily overcome when attacked by the boarding party.

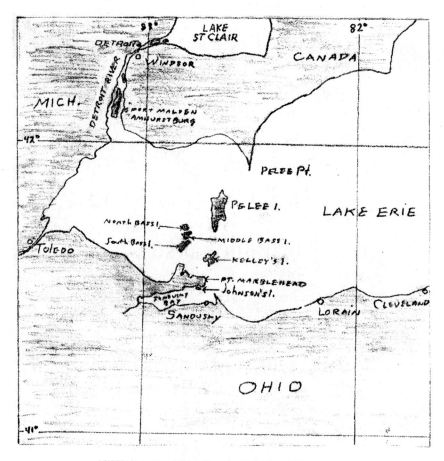

WESTERN LAKE ERIE AND THE DETROIT RIVER

SOURCE: NOAA

CHAPTER TWENTY-SEVEN

The Philo Parsons

Matthew's hasty departure from Mackinac Island had worked out beautifully. First, he had freed himself, at least for the present, from the scrutiny of the nosy Lieutenant Smalley. Second, he had managed to rap on the door of Ben Burley's residence in Windsor, Ontario, a full day before his requested time of arrival. Chief Wasagunabi's Chippewas had paddled him across the Straits of Mackinac to the lumber mill city of Cheboygan where he was able to arrange passage on a screw and sail lumber schooner that was, fortunately, already loaded. She sailed southbound on Lake Huron that very night, providing Matt with a quick, clean, and very tidy exit from the area..

On September 2, 1864, a clandestine meeting of the principals involved in the Johnson's Island conspiracy was arranged by Burley in a small hotel in Sandwich, a small village on the outskirts of Windsor. Confederate Commissioner to Canada Jacob Thompson presided over the meeting. Matt disliked him instantly. The man struck him as pompous, loose-lipped and possibly dangerously incompetent at the secret service game. Thompson seemed almost resentful when he was asked questions or received suggestions. "Bad sign!" thought Matthew. A second attendee at the meeting also made Matthew nervous. He was a tall, gaunt man with darting eyes and a quiet, but surly, disposition....one Godfrey Hyams. He had been assigned to procure the small arms that were necessary for the success of the operation. Apparently, he had adequately performed his assigned task. Still, the shifty-appearing Arkansan impressed Matt as being suspicious and untrustworthy.

Thompson introduced Matthew to the man whom he had appointed to be commander of the maritime portion of the operation, Acting Master John Yates Beall. Matt was thrilled to have the opportunity to serve under Beall. The man was already a legend for his highly successful raids on Union shipping on the Chesapeake Bay earlier in the war. Beall was the perfect man for command of the operation. He was intelligent, energetic, fearless, and possessed unrestrained enthusiasm for the Confederate cause.

The affable Scotsman, Acting Master Bennet G. Burley, was, of course, also present at the meeting. Burley had been given two assignments. He was to provide a vessel that would be fitted as a warship for the operation. This he had failed to accomplish. He was also charged with the responsibility of assuring that the required crew members would be available for duty at the proper times and locations. For one reason or another, there were many southern ex-soldiers who were hiding in Canada, and whom, one would think, would jump at the chance to again serve the southern cause. Not so. It required a lot of bribery, and a lot of wheedling, begging, and appealing to their latent sense of honor to get enough crew. They were a rough-looking lot, but seemed generally reliable....especially considering that they would be paid in gold *after* the project was finished.

As Burley had been unable to lease or to buy a suitable vessel, he had elected to hijack one and to impress it into the service of the Confederate States of America. He, Beall, and Charles Cole did not have far to look. They picked the *Philo Parsons*, a 135 foot wooden sidewheeler displacing 222 tons. Conveniently, she was engaged in the regular transport of passengers and small freight between Detroit, Sandusky, and points in between. Relatively slow and fragile, she was an unlikely candidate for a vessel of war. However, she would just have to do, given the urgency of the moment.

Jacob Thompson presided over the meeting, making certain that his officers understood every detail of the plan. First, the *Philo Parsons* would be hijacked on the last leg of her regular run to Sandusky. She would then steam to the mouth of Sandusky Bay where she would lie in wait for a signal from Charles Cole which would signify that he and his female companion had successfully drugged the *Michigan's* officers. The crew, thus leaderless, would be easy pickings for the boarding party to overcome. After seizing the vessel, the Confederates would train one of the *Michigan's* cannon on the Union officer's barracks on the island, and gleefully blow a hole in it. "That should be quite a wake-up call, don't you reckon?" chortled Thompson. "The Ohio National Guard are not much to be concerned about, anyway. Mostly greybeards and boys unfit for war. I dare say they will be easy to scare into surrendering considering that we will be in good position to blow them to kingdom come! Besides, the cannon shot by previous arrangement accomplished by Captain Cole will be the signal for the reb prisoners to rise up and overpower their captors."

Matthew cleared his throat and fidgeted in his seat as though desiring to speak. Thompson, ignoring him, continued with the plan outline. "Once the prisoners are freed, we will transport them to Sandusky where they will join forces with a large army of Copperheads and fight their way south, devastating Yankee materiel as they go." Thompson was so pleased with himself, and with the plan, that he began to quiver with excitement. "The *Michigan*, now under Confederate command, will immediately commence a leisurely and unopposed tour of the major ports on the Great Lakes, shelling the cities into submission and frightening the wits out of the inhabitants!" Thompson puffed out his ample chest. "Gentlemen, Captain Cole and I have designed a wonderful plan that cannot help but succeed!"

Matthew again cleared his throat. This time he kicked back his chair and stood at attention.

"Captain?" Thompson was already looking irritated at the interruption of his grand speech.

"If you will excuse my saying so, drugging the entire cadre of officers of a United States vessel of war sounds like an unusually risky operation upon which to base the success or failure of the operation. What do you 'spose are the chances of his success?"

"Very high. Charlie is a skilled undercover agent and impersonator. And, he is not acting alone. His accomplice is a very attractive young woman who is also a skilled secret service agent. She is playing the role of his wife....and if I might say so, will charm the pants off the Yankee officers!"

Thompson indulged himself with a little chuckle at his own witticism as he tried to wave Matthew back to his seat.

Matt stood firm. "Seems to me the Yankee sailors will probably put up a good fight....officers or no officers."

Thompson stiffened. "Seems to me you worry too much. There are always risks when you are at war. Are you afraid, Captain Chandler?"

Matt's face and neck turned very red. "Not for myself, sir, but for the success of the operation. I believe the risk of failure is very high. And, what about this woman? Ain't we giving her a lot of responsibility, not to mention putting her in danger?"

"Not a problem with her, Chandler. She knows if she gets caught she will likely go to the gallows as a spy. She, apparently unlike you, thinks primarily of the gallant Confederacy instead of her own safety."

Insulted, and rightly so, Matt toyed with the idea of walking out of the door, but thought better of it and sat down. If he walked, Thompson would seem to win the exchange. If he walked, the lack of adequate leadership might be disastrous, and men could surely die. Harebrained scheme or not, he decided to see it through. "I believe that remark was uncalled for, Commissioner Thompson."

Jacob Thompson's grin was insincere. "You 're right, Chandler. I apologize. I simply want you to know this woman is not to be worried about. She has already killed at least one, maybe two, men. Mrs. Cole is very lovely, very dedicated, and very dangerous. She is perfectly capable of doing her job and taking care of herself all at once."

Matt was aghast at the thought of such a woman who could so easily combine beauty, lethality, and subterfuge to achieve the success of her mission. "Does she have a name? I'd like to know it so's I can stay away from her."

"In these days of loose tongues there is no reason for you to know her true identity."

Matt shrugged. "Reckon you are right there, sir. I really don't need to know her name. She is in enough danger without that information getting out."

"Thank you, Captain Chandler. Now, where was I....?" Matt stood again. Thompson was losing his composure. "Now what, captain?" Beall and Burley squirmed in their seats and repressed snickers at the continuing unexpected entertainment. Godfrey Hyams sat quietly in the corner, his face expressionless.

"Are you concerned that they have fourteen cannon and we have none, and that they have an iron hull and ours is of wood?"

"Not in the least. We are to take them by surprise! Captain, those guns will soon be ours! They will never have a chance to use them against us. Are you through with your questions?"

"No."

"What? Sir, this is an outrage. I'll have to ask you to take your seat!"

Defiantly, Matt remained standing. "You have accused me of being afraid and undedicated to our cause. Let me ask you another question. Will you be aboard during this operation?"

"No. I am needed at my headquarters in Toronto."

"Then, your neck will not be at risk at all. As you do not see fit to personally share the risks, then you should indulge us when we seek to ensure our safety and the safety of our crew."

Thompson folded his arms and stared at the ceiling for a moment, struggling to repress his anger. Finally, he lowered his gaze to Burley and Beall. The look in his eyes was one of exasperation. "Gentlemen, do you agree with Chandler's concerns?"

They both nodded in the affirmative. "Jacob, Burley and I have discussed the risks....and they are great. I wish you would let Matthew continue. I believe he is on the right track."

Thompson blew a long breath through pursed lips as though letting off steam. He turned a chair around and sat facing them, nodding stiffly at Matthew. "Kindly continue."

Matt plopped back onto his chair. "At the very least, we need a second vessel to be available as backup to the *Parsons*. Depending on what happens, she can be used to help transport the freed prisoners to the mainland. Or, she could be used, if necessary, to ram the *Michigan*. Or, in the worst case, she could be used to fish our survivors out of the water and make an escape."

"Bravo!" shouted Burley, leaping to his feet. "A capital idea! Only thing is, I'm not sure we have enough crew for two vessels."

Beall grinned up at the Scotsman "Think you can get some more?"

Burley's arms were akimbo. "Do you have any idea how hard I had to work to get what we've got?"

"I know. I know. You have my sympathy. Can you get some more or not?"

With a sigh, Ben resumed his seat. "Oh, I guess so. On such short notice they will have to be locals. Do we have enough gold for more crew, Jacob?"

Commissioner Thompson was becoming convinced that the trio's concerns and ideas were worthy of his consideration. "Y'all get the men. I'll see they get paid. How will you arrange command of two vessels, Mr. Beall?"

Beall fairly dripped confidence. "That's easy. Burley and I will take the *Parsons*. Chandler and Hyams can officer the second. By the way, that brings up another little sticky point. Now we have to find another vessel to commandeer....and we don't even have the first one yet! Watch'a think, Burley?"

Ben Burley displayed an air of put-upon elegance. "Well, my friends, O ye of little faith, believe it or not I do have another vessel for you. She is readily available and ripe for the picking by a stout crew of Johnny Rebs. The *Island Queen*."

Incredulous, Thompson, Chandler, and Beall leaned toward him. "What's the *Island Queen*?"

Burley twiddled his mustache. "I had her picked as a second choice to the *Philo Parsons*. She's a 173 ton, 123 foot, wooden sidewheeler. Fairly fast. Makes daily runs from the Bass Islands to Sandusky and back carrying passengers and light freight like the *Parsons*."

"Well!" smirked Beall as he stood to stretch the kinks out of his back. "You are a right quick little Scotsman."

"I'm not that little!" chuckled Burley.

John Beall gave him a sideways look. "Be that as it may, you wouldn't happen to have something in an iron hull in your pocket, would you? If we have to ram the *Michigan* with a wooden ship I suspect the Yanks will not come out second best."

Commissioner Thompson, looking somewhat defeated, sat up straight and looked each of the three pointedly, individually, in the face. "Gentlemen, I believe y'all to be just a little daft. Perhaps that's what will likely make this mission a great success."

"Or, a very messy failure!" chimed Matthew.

"He's right. Y'ave to be a wee crazy to attempt such a scheme in the first place."

"Amen!" intoned Beall

Godfrey Hyams sat in his corner, saying not a word. Only his eyes moved.

Thompson stood, gathered his papers and prepared to leave. "Crazy or not, I wish y'all God speed and good luck. I will pray for your safe return and look forward to your report of the success of your mission. I must return to Toronto." He shot a defiant stare at Chandler. "And not because I would be afraid to go with you....I have many other important projects in the wind to which I must attend." He headed for the door of the room. Before opening it, he swung around and cracked a wide, toothy smile. "I believe that if those Yank swabbies knew that you gents had them in your sights they would immediately take steps to save their asses by striking their colors right now!" He returned to shake each of their hands, then spun on his heel and was gone.

The officers stared after him for a moment. Beall finally spoke. "Speakin' of saving asses, Matt, I believe you might just have saved ours. I believe our chances of success have greatly improved."

"Hope so." smiled Matt.

"One question, though. Do you really believe that if you have to ram an iron ship with a wood one that the wood one will survive and the iron one won't?"

Matt smiled again. "No, and yes. I don't believe either ship will survive. The wood ship will, of course, be smashed and what's left of her will sink. Now, with 173 tons of wooden ship, traveling at full speed, striking the *Michigan* at right angles and amidships, chances are that she will roll on her beam-ends and fill with water. She has almost no keel, her deck is leaky, and her hatches will probably be open. I doubt that she will be able to right herself." He thought a moment. "In fact, we can go one better. I could light the *Island Queen* on fire before ramming if you gentlemen would prefer something really spectacular!"

Ben Burley shook his head. "By God, Chandler, Thompson is right. You are more than slightly insane."

Matthew laughed. "Remember Mr. Thompson included you in his assessment."

"You're right. But I'm not daft enough to volunteer to take a ride on a doomed fireship! What would you and your crew do? Jump overboard just before being crushed and incinerated....or incinerated and crushed....as the case may be?"

"Exactly. Remember, this is a last resort scenario. The Yanks will see us coming and be throwing everything at us that they've got. We'll have to lash the wheel 'cause they'll be shooting at the pilot house. We will also jam the rudder so it wont turn even if they do destroy the wheel. Then we'll light her off. Then we'll dive overboard and swim away like hell. Kindly don't forget to pick us up."

Hyams, still in his corner, finally stirred. "'Scuse me, y'all. Who is 'we'?"

The three turned and smiled at him. Matt spoke. "Welcome to the meetin' Godfrey. It'll be you and me."

"Do I have anythin' to say 'bout that?"

"No!" chorused the three.

"I cain't swim."

"I 'spect you'd better learn right quick!" drawled Matt.

"How come a man your age never learned to swim?" asked Ben, incredulously.

"Ain't much water in my part of Arkansas."

"I see." said Beall, scratching his head. "Arms-master Hyams, do you have any other comments or suggestions?"

"No, suh."

"Is your arms chest in proper order?"

"Yes, suh."

"Good!" said John Beall. "Now, lets all go and have a nice supper and a bottle of wine."

"How about four bottles of wine?" suggested Matt, jumping to his feet.

"Agreed!" shouted Ben. "You coming, Godfrey?"

"Thank you, suh. No, suh. I must carry the arms chest to Malden. The crew are just now gatherin' there, waitin' for your orders."

Beall patted Hyams' bony shoulder. "Very good, Hyams. Carry on and keep up the good work. You'll hear from us very soon, I hope."

Godfrey waited until the trio had disappeared, laughing and backslapping, into the rustic saloon of the little hotel. He hurried out of the back door to the nearby stable, saddled his horse, and headed, not for Malden, but toward Windsor which lay in the opposite direction. After an impatient wait for the chuffy little craft to arrive, he took the ferry across the river to Detroit..

Union Lieutenant Colonel Bennet H. Hill was at his desk in his Detroit hotel room when he heard a quiet rap on his door. "Come in! It's open!" he called. "Ah! Hyams. Do come in. Do you have something for me?"

"Shore do, colonel." He doffed his cap. "There's goin' to be a secesh raid on the *Michigan*."

"At Johnson's Island?" Godfrey nodded. "Do tell! Have a seat, Hyams, and give me the details. Hyams was delighted to do so, in detail, hoping for some extra gold to jingle in his pockets. Godfrey J. Hyams was a double agent working for both the Confederates in Canada and for B.H. Hill, the Union assistant provost marshal general of Michigan. "Sooo! What is the planned date of this far-fetched little scheme?"

"That I don't know yet, suh. They's awaitin' fer Cole to tell 'em when he's goin' to drug the ship's officers."

"I see." Hill stroked his beard thoughtfully. "Well! Good work, Hyams!" He rummaged in his desk for a small velvet bag of gold coins, fished out two, and handed them to the delighted double agent. "You'd better get back to your arms-master duties. Be certain to advise me the minute you get a date certain for the raid." Hyams slipped out of the hotel and into the gathering darkness just as the twinkling gas street lamps were being lit. Colonel Hill soon followed, heading for the nearest telegraph office where he dispatched a lengthy message to Commander J.C. Carter, advising that he bring his ship to full alert, but conceal his actions so as to make it possible to bag all of the raiders and conspirators before they could do any damage.

Commander Carter had received such warnings before and nothing had ever happened. This time appeared to be different. He was first incredulous, then embarrassed to learn that his new friends, Mr. and Mrs. Cole, were actually the enemy. He quietly doubled the watches and loaded his cannon, but did not bother to get up steam.

The days slipped by while the combatants on both sides waited for Cole's signal. Finally, on September 18, 1864, John Beall received the coded message. The "dinner and wine-drinking" was to take place aboard the *Michigan* on the evening of the 19th. Beall sent out the word. All personnel were to be at their stations, ready to board the *Philo Parsons* on the morrow.

Godfrey Hyams slipped away and made a lathered trip to Colonel Hill's office in the middle of the night, then returned, undetected, to his post at Malden. Hill telegraphed Commander Carter, suggesting that Mr. and Mrs. Cole should be arrested immediately.

On the morning of the 19th, Ben Burley and Matt Chandler boarded the *Philo Parsons* at Detroit's Trowbridge, Wilcox & Co. dock. Down river at Sandwich, Ontario, John Beall and a well-dresswed trio of his men boarded. Further down river at Malden, twenty-five tough-looking men came on board dragging a very heavy, beat-up steamer trunk. If any of them would cause suspicion it would be these buckos....but no one gave them a second glance. The riverbanks were crawling with "skedaddlers", draft evaders from the northern states who seemed to be continually crossing the river in one direction or the other.

None of the conspirators acknowledged that they knew each other until the *Parsons* left Kelley's Island, in Lake Erie, on the last leg of her voyage to Sandusky. First Mate D.C. Nichols and Wheelman Mitchel Campbell were in the wheelhouse when a well-dressed gentleman let himself in. "Can we help you, sir? Passengers are not allowed in the pilot house." Nichols turned to confront the man and found himself looking down the barrel of a Colt pocket revolver. It was cocked and aimed right between his eyes.

John Beall smiled. "I have the honor to inform you, suh, that this vessel is now in the possession of the Confederate States of America. You and your crew are prisoners of war. Kindly turn around and maintain your course." Shouts and pistol shots rang out. The rebel ruffians had retrieved their collection of pistols, hatchets, knives, and clubs from their steamer trunk. Under Matthew's and Bennet's direction, they manhandled any passenger or crewman who resisted, searched them for weapons, and locked the entire wide-eyed bunch into the hold. Several female passengers swooned with fright, but no one was really hurt. Matthew then took the helm while Beall and Burley organized their new warship and their roughneck crew.

The *Parsons* was a wood-burner and was low on fuel. Matt steered her to Middle Bass Island where she pulled in to the fuel dock and took on a full load of wood, thanks to the forced labor of the captured crew. In the naiveté of the time, they paroled the passengers and crew, leaving them on the island after making them swear that they would refrain from talking about the hijacking for 24 hours. This done, they prepared to go in search of the *Island Queen*, then sail on to Sandusky.

Dame fortune suddenly smiled upon them. As they were preparing to cast off, to their amazement, none other than the *Island Queen* hove into view and innocently paddled in to tie up next to them at the fuel dock, herself being low on firewood. She was an easy mark. The people on board had no idea that the familiar *Parsons* was now a Confederate vessel of war. The raiders pounced, easily subduing the crew, passengers, and a small group of unarmed soldiers in only a few minutes. The uniformed soldiers offered little resistance as they were very young and inexperienced recruits who were returning from furlough. The *Queen's* crew was, of course, impressed to load the necessary firewood, after which passengers and crew were sent onto the island to join the forlorn-looking group from the *Parsons*.

The raiders found several casks of coal oil in the hold of the *Queen*. They brought them on deck to have them at the ready should Matt's fireship plan need to be implemented. Axes to broach the casks, twisted newspaper torches, and an ample supply of matches were stashed nearby. Lines and cargo nets were draped over her sides in case sea rescue would become necessary. Matthew, at the helm, was satisfied that his little vessel was as ready for action as she was going to get, come what may. The scarlet battle flags of the Confederacy were hoisted at the fantail of each vessel and flapped bravely in the Lake Erie breeze as the ships steamed for the mouth of Sandusky bay, arriving just at nightfall.

The boarding crew checked and rechecked their weapons, standing impatiently by their boats, awaiting the signal flare that would tell them that the Coles had successfully incapacitated the officers. The *U.S.S. Michigan* remained a dark silhouette against the dark shadows of Johnson's Island. No signal ever came.

+ + +

Annie Brown Cole was absolutely stunning as she appeared from her boudoir, ready for the gala dinner party aboard the *Michigan*. Charles, standing before the foyer mirror working to tie his black formal tie, glanced her way and then couldn't take his eyes off of her. "My God, woman! You are beautiful!" he blurted, in spite of himself.

She curtseyed, sweetly. "Thank you, kind sir. That's quite a complement, coming from gruff old you." Ignoring the bustles and hoops of high fashion, Annie's slender, shapely form was clothed in an emerald green satin gown that was trimmed, tastefully, in exquisite black lace. The bodice was low-cut, revealing just enough cleavage. The sleeves were short, and off the shoulder, while the black lace traveled alluringly down her arms to terminate in fanciful flares at her wrists. She wore short, black, silk gloves, each decorated by a single pearl button at the wrist and carried a black lace fan that matched, exactly, the rest of her outfit. Under all of the folds of satin dress and silk petticoats, her trusty Sharps derringer nestled in a garter holster. She, Charles, and the Confederacy would triumph, at last, at this last....literally last....party to end all parties.

Charles had sent six cases of expensive French wine ahead to the ship. It was already spiked with the careful addition of the dissolved white powder that would send the sailor officers to dreamland in no time. They would awaken as prisoners of war. He checked his Colt pocket revolver, slipped it into the back of his waistband, and pulled on his formal black coat. He was reaching for his top hat when, without warning, the door burst open and uniformed sailors rushed into the room and grabbed him before he could react. They lost no time in finding and confiscating his revolver. A junior officer followed, pointing a cocked Colt Navy revolver at him. "You are under arrest, sir and madam. You are prisoners of the United States Navy!" Resistance was useless. Wordlessly, Cole held out his wrists to receive the shiny manacles carried by one of the sailors. Annie started to cry....not in fear, but in frustration. They had been so close to success! She held out her hands to receive her set of manacles. As the sailor started to lock them onto her delicate wrists, the officer ordered him to take them back off. "Not becoming a fine lady, even if she is a rebel Take them off. Just hang on to her arm."

"Aye, sir."

The last light was just fading from the sky when they were pushed into a carriage, transported to the ship, and hustled on board. Standing to receive them, arms folded in the dim lantern light, was Commander Carter. His cap was pulled low over his eyes so that, in the gloom, they could not see his face. The gold on his shoulders, buttons, and cap glinted authoritatively. "I want you two to know that I have the authority to hang you both from the yardarm right now....and I'm severely tempted to do so. You are guilty of conspiracy to aid in the pirating of a United States vessel."

Charles Cole stiffened. ""We are not pirates, sir. We are soldiers of the Confederate States of America."

Carter laughed a strained, low chuckle. "At best, you are spies. You can be hung for that too, and probably will. Take them below to the brig and lock them up."

"Aye, sir."

They started to walk toward the companionway, Charles in the lead, still in irons, with a brawny sailor on each side. Annie followed, propelled by her own brace of seamen, when she suddenly stopped. "I'm sorry. Excuse me. My heel is caught in my hem." The men stood by as she bent to correct the problem. They were completely unprepared when she straightened, stepped back a step, and pointed the four menacing barrels of her little derringer in their direction. She cocked the weapon with a faintly audible click. "Stand away!" she ordered as she backed toward the seaward rail. Maintaining her deadly aim, and managing her skirts with remarkable dexterity, she slid over the rail and stood on the ledge on the other side, facing them. The men were paralyzed with surprise. Commander Carter, sensing a problem, swung around, his jaw dropping in disbelief. Annie gave them all a brave little smile, then disappeared....jumping backward into the darkness, still clutching her little gun. It was a long ways down, so there was a bit of a delay before they heard a very unladylike splash as she hit the dark, frigid water. Amid shouted orders and muttered curses, the boats were launched immediately. Lantern light searched the blackness of the water to no avail. The little lady was gone to meet her maker amongst the tangling seaweed at the bottom of Sandusky Bay.

Out in the bay, facing a mutiny if he attacked without the reassuring signal from Cole, Beall reluctantly ordered his ships to slip away in the darkness.

The next morning torn petticoats, bits of lace, and a pair of shoes were found pitifully floating to and fro in the waves. Annie Cole, or whatever her real name might have been, was presumed drowned. Even a strong swimmer could not have lasted very long is such frigid water.

"Just as well." said Carter. "Saved us the trouble of hanging her."

Captain Charles H. Cole spent the rest of the war in Federal prison. Annie Brown (the real one) sent numerous tearful requests to Jacob Thompson in Toronto, pleading for him to arrange for, or buy, his release. Perhaps he could even arrange for his escape. She received no answer. Somehow, he was eventually released after the war when, by rights, he should have been hanged. Perhaps then, Jacob Thompson had made some arrangements after all. Cole disappeared immediately after his release and was never seen or heard from again. It is hoped that he collected his Annie Brown (again, the real one) and took her with him to live happily ever after.

Bennet Burley was captured by Canadian authorities shortly after the raid and clapped into irons while he awaited extradition to the United States. Because of his British citizenship he became a political football and was eventually released.

John Yates Beall would never give up. He was finally captured at Niagara City, New York, while engaged in another Confederate clandestine operation. On February 24, 1865, he was hanged on Governor's Island. Beall was charged, not surprisingly, with piracy and spying.

Matthew stayed with his shipmates until, under orders from Beall, the *Philo Parsons* and the *Island queen* were scuttled. The Confederate Great Lakes Navy was no more. He traveled back to Windsor, took the ferry across the river, rented a saddle horse in Detroit, and slipped back into Franklin under cover of darkness. Dick Trick was not quite as startled this time. He was getting used to Matt's mysterious comings and goings in the night. It was not until Dick offered him food that Matthew realized that he had not eaten for at least twenty-four hours. Suddenly famished, he dove into a huge plate of cold sliced beef, beans, and potatoes. By the time Dick had the stove hot enough to make coffee it was too late. Matt's eyes were already going shut. Sleepily, he headed for a bedroom. "Take care of my horse will you, Dick? He'll need a day's rest like I do."

"Surely. Don't 'spose I can turn him out?"

"Nope. Hide him in the barn like usual. He's pretty tired. A nice hot bran mash would do him a world of good."

"I'll give him a good rub down too. Have a good sleep and don't worry 'bout a thing."

Matt smiled and clapped him on the shoulder. "Thanks, Dick. I can always count on you. Do me another favor."

"Just name it."

"Get Hannah up here tomorrow. I need to talk to you both. I'll leave again after dark tomorrow." Matt slept until noon. When he awoke, Hannah was already there. The table was set with a lunch so sumptuous that they could have been entertaining royalty. "My goodness, Hannah, you have really outdone yourself!"

Hannah looked pleased. "I hope you'll like it. Baked a nice apple pie this mornin' for dessert. I don't get to have two handsome men to myself very often! You think this here is good, wait 'till you see supper!"

"Dick, I sure hope you're plannin' to marry this girl real soon." He gazed at Hannah admiringly. "My, my! All that beauty an' a good cook besides. You'd better get hitched before somebody steals her."

Hannah blushed and took Dick's hand. "We'll marry soon's the war is over. An' I hope that's right soon." She stood on tiptoe to kiss Dick's cheek. It was his turn to blush.

Matt chuckled at the snuggly pair. "Let's hope that silliness will soon be done with. The south 'pears to be weakening some. Might not be too long to the end." When lunch was done, and the pie and coffee served, Matthew swore them to secrecy and launched into a explanation of his visit. "First of all, I'm still on the run. Can't give you any more details except that soldiers from both sides could be lookin' for me."

Jaws dropped in amazement, Hannah and Dick looked at each other. "How'd you work that, Matt?" queried Dick.

"Can't tell you. Military secret. Anyhow, if anybody comes snoopin' 'round here don't let on that you know anything about me. That would be neither Lieutenant Colonel Matthew Greyson nor Captain Matthew Chandler. If you have to contact me, do it by writing to Judge Bela Chapman or Reverend William Ferry on Mackinac Island. Don't use either of my names, and use a big post office, like Detroit, to mail from. Got all that?"

"Got it!" they chorused.

"Next thing. This one might be a shock to you. Charity Jane Melody Chandler is now Charity Jane Melody Greyson." He paused to watch the announcement sink in. "And, we're goin' to have a baby come winter."

Hannah gasped. "But what about Beth...." She clapped her hand over her own mouth, her eyes brimming with tears. She ran around the table to hug and kiss Matt, wetting his cheeks with her tears while Dick hustled over to pump his hand in congratulation. "I'm so happy for you both!" she gave him a final kiss on the cheek, then ran from the room.

That night Dick and Hannah stood hand in hand on the porch and watched him ride away into the darkness. Back in Windsor, Matt booked the first available passage northbound to Mackinac Island.

The news of Bethany's drowning in the dark waters of Sandusky bay was eventually communicated, with heartfelt regrets, to her father in Charleston by means of a letter from Commissioner Jacob Thompson. Major Dodge sat on his verandah with a light robe tucked around him and rocked, staring out to sea, for days. He barely ate or drank, and spoke to no one....not even to his faithful servants who hovered around him with tears in their eyes and sobs in their throats. Bessie, the favored servant and Bethany's dear friend, took to her bed and refused to get up again, burying her face into her pillow whenever anyone tried to talk to her. Finally, the Major wearily heaved himself from his chair and went to his desk.

November 14, 1864

The Reverend Pitts Lanning
Franklin Village, Michigan

Dear Reverend:

It is with unimaginable sorrow that I must inform you, and through you her friends, that my beloved Bethany has died in the service of her country, the Confederate States of America. I realize that you all suspected that she was already dead, killed by the hands of Pinkerton bullies. It is time to set the record straight. She escaped them and lived, unhappily sighing for her missing Matthew, until September 19th of this year when she drowned, still serving the Southern Cause, in Sandusky Bay, Ohio.

She was a beautiful, fine, loyal, and wonderful daughter whom I shall miss to the end of my days. It was my privilege to be her father and to share her short, remarkable life. She was one of God's angels sent to earth to give us joy.

Sincerely, Your Obed. Servt.,

Major Jared Dodge, CSA

There would be gasps of disbelief, wails of anguish, and tears of sorrow at the worship service of the Franklin Methodist-Protestant church on the next Sabbath morning.

For a second time, Assistant Provost Marshall General Bennet Hill closed his file on Bethany Dodge.

USS MICHIGAN
Painting by Charles Peterson located at Dossin Great
Lakes Museum, Belle Isle, Michigan. Photograph
courtesy of Naval Historical Foundation.

CHAPTER TWENTY-EIGHT

Patience

The snoopy Lieutenant Henry Smalley became considerably miffed when he was informed that Captain Chandler and his Chippewa friends had flown the coop right from under his very sensitive nose. He sniffed, disdainfully, dusting that prominent protuberance with the edge of a very white and uncomfortably starched handkerchief. Undaunted, he was still determined to investigate the mysterious captain. He found it most interesting when his informants passed along the information that the noticeably pregnant Mrs. Chandler and her daughter had moved out of the Mission Hotel and had taken up residence in the comfortable home of Judge Bela Chapman for some undetermined reason. " Aha!" That meant that Captain Chandler would very likely return, at some point, to reclaim his family. Greasing their palms with a little silver, Henry alerted his informants at the docks to watch for the captain's reappearance. While awaiting that event, the lieutenant proceeded with his investigation. The fort commandant, Captain Pratt, viewed both Henry Smalley and his compulsive investigation as somewhat humorous. However, at the very least, it was something to do. In any case, most probably just to shut off the lieutenant's whining requests, he agreed to write a letter to Provost Marshall Hill in Detroit requesting any information he might be able to uncover about this mysterious, and perhaps sinister, Captain Chandler.

If one could ignore his shortcomings, it was fairly easy to discern that Lt. Smalley had a pretty good mind and a very sharp memory....especially concerning the Battle of Second Bull Run where he had received his own debilitating wound. His recollections associated Captain Chandler with the First Michigan Cavalry....not by name, but by the remembrance of seeing a similarly handsome officer on a splendid horse commanding cavalry under a colonel named Brodhead and a General named Buford. Colonel Hill's office could not find any reference to a Captain Chandler anywhere in General Buford's command. With a bulldog's tenacity, Smalley requested a roster of the First Michigan Cavalry at the time of Second Bull Run. "Eureka!" he cried as his finger stopped on the list by the name of Lieutenant Colonel Matthew Greyson. "It's him! It's him. I bet that's him!" Exultation! Delight! Lowly Henry Smalley had caught him a high-class deserter.

Quivering with excitement within his lonely stonewalled room in the fort, Smalley dispatched another inquiry regarding Greyson. Sadly for the lieutenant, the results were disappointing, confusing, and not as anticipated. Greyson had been seen by witnesses of the battle lying dead among the pitiful, twisted bodies on the battlefield. One retreating Union cavalryman had even reported that he was seen lying with his arm around the neck of his dead horse. By all reports, he had been fatally shot in the head. It was supposed that his body had been carried off by the victorious rebels. Another trooper, while heavily engaged nearby, had seen Greyson fall. That witness noted that Colonel Greyson was unhorsed while he was furiously hacking his way through overwhelming numbers of enemy cavalry in an attempt to save his commander, Colonel Brodhead.

Smalley, disappointed....in a way....but unbowed, decided to search for further information. He convinced Captain Pratt, who convinced Provost Marshall Hill, that an official inquiry regarding the missing Lieutenant Colonel should be sent to the Confederate capitol at Richmond by military courier under flag of truce. As though to compound Henry Smalley's annoyance, General Buford had recommended that Greyson be posthumously awarded a commendation for extreme bravery under fire. Further, he was to be posthumously promoted to the rank of full colonel, an action which would provide more postwar compensation for his family. Subsequent investigation revealed that Greyson simply had no family to benefit from his heroism. Of course, the army investigators had no idea where to look. Smalley smirked at their inadequacy as he sat on his cot in his dimly-lit stone room trying to decide what, if anything, to do next.

He had not found a spy, or even a deserter. He had, instead, found a very much alive dead hero. "Ohmygod, now what do I do?" moaned Smalley. He pulled off his boots, flung them against the wall, and flopped onto his cot for a refreshing nap.

It was not long before Colonel Greyson, aka Captain Chandler, slipped undetected....or so he thought....back onto Mackinac Island. Glancing about to make sure that no one was watching (they were, of course, but he did not spot Smalley's observers), he headed straight for Bela Chapman's house where he was joyously greeted by his wife, daughter, and the Chapmans. Matthew cast an appreciative eye over Melody's increased bulbousness and patted her tummy. "How are you feeling, my Eagle Song Melody?"

"Fat."

"Figured when you're due?"

"'Bout January."

Mary Sue pulled on his sleeve. "Me an' mama been cryin' every night 'cause we ain't heared from you. Been prayin', too. See, mama? I told you God would help bring papa back!"

Melody saw the earnestness in the little girl's eyes and hugged her tightly. "Yes, you did....an' yes, He did."

"Mr. Ferry said so, too." The last comment came from the corner of her mouth because that was all that Mary Sue could free from her mother's smothering hug.

"Yes, sweet little daughter, the preacher said just that." Melody freed one hand from hugging the child and gently touched Matt's face as though to assure herself that he was real. "Reverend Ferry's been right kind to us, Matthew."

"Bill's a good friend." smiled Matthew. "Reckon I'll sneak down to see the Ferrys first chance I get and tell 'em how much we appreciate them bein' so caring, an' nice, an' all."

+ + +

October is unbelievably lovely in northern Michigan. The trees display such a riot of color that it almost hurts one's eyes when the sun shines.... reds, greens, and yellows that harmonize with the deep, deep blue of the Straits of Mackinac. Matt sat in the Chapman's front window and gazed admiringly, wistfully, through the wavy glass, letting the lacy curtain drop in place when someone passed the house who might spot him. He wished that he could take his family for a buggy ride around the island, or could sit on the beach with Mary Sue, in the warmth of the midday sun, and skip flat stones into the water. However, he dared not show himself, especially considering that that upstart lieutenant up at the fort would likely be looking for him. Greyson would really have been nervous had he known that Lieutenant Smalley knew perfectly well that he was there, and that he was keeping a low profile at the judge's house....for whatever reason. "What if the little shit finds out that I'm a deserter?" mused Matthew. "Or, God forbid, that I have been connected with the abortive raid on the *USS Michigan*? Damn! I don't even dare contact Doc Bailey to find out if it would be safe for Melody to travel. If I knew it was safe, I'd get us out of here in a minute!" Doctor John Bailey, the only physician on the island, maintained a good rapport with the soldiers at the fort, providing them with medical care when needed. The good doctor could hardly be expected to keep his mouth shut about Matthew's presence on the island.

Safely after dark, the three of them (actually, the four of them) would take long walks in the light of the harvest moon, watching the moon-path sparkle across the waters. Eagle Song would tell them how the eagle would sometimes awaken in his lofty nest on a moonlight night and take flight, circling and whistling as he spoke to the god of the moonlit waters, and to the fishes who swam just below the sparkling surface. Heals-with-flowers would listen in rapt attention. Matt would shrug her stories off as Indian fairy tales and puff on his cigar. Passing ships, showing faint yellow, red, and green, clanked, chuffed, and splashed as they slid by in the night, giving another dimension to the darkened, silvered waters.

+ + +

By the middle of November, the island was decorated with a foot of fresh, drifted snow. The horse-drawn wooden v-plows struggled to keep a narrow path along the village streets, the horses snorting puffs of smoky breath as their ice-calked hooves struggled to keep a footing. The whiteness of the

516

snow seemed to accentuate the blue of the waters, turning them into an even deeper, more vibrant hue. "Blue! Blue!" Muttered Matthew from his window perch, the silent thoughts loud within him. "Blue!" Blue eyes. Beautiful smoky blue eyes that he dared not think nor to dream about anymore. He left the window and traipsed into the judge's study where his distinguished host was studying a sheaf of legal papers. Matt went to the sideboard and poured himself, and the judge, a nice stiff drink into the delicate stemware of Bela's brandy set.

The judge looked over the rim of his glasses. "Something wrong, Greyson? It's a mite early in the morning for spirits, is it not?"

"It is, Bela." They clinked glasses. "Shall we drink to feeling blue?"

Chapman's eyebrows raised, but he asked no questions. "As you wish, Matthew."

That same day, one of the last steamers of the season docked at Mackinac Island. She carried a military courier who hastily disembarked and hurried up the hill to the fort, taking his dispatches straight to the commandant. Pratt perused the message, whistled under his breath, dismissed the courier, and called for Lieutenant Smalley. When the Lieutenant arrived in his office, Pratt tipped back in his desk chair. "Henry, I can't believe you pulled this one off."

"Sir?"

"Take a look."

> Judah P. Benjamin
> Secretary of War
> Confederate States of America
> Richmond, Virginia
>
> October 17, 1864
>
> Lieutenant Colonel Bennet H. Hill
> Assistant Provost Marshall General of Michigan
> Detroit, Michigan

Dear Sir:

We have received your inquiry regarding a Lieutenant Colonel Matthew Greyson who was wounded and captured by our forces during the Second Battle of Manassas, Virginia, in August of 1862. Normally, in these chaotic times, records of such a man [one of hundreds or thousands like him] would be forever lost.

However, I personally recall Greyson because he was accompanied by a letter from our General Thomas Jackson requesting that he receive special and preferential care. Accordingly, he was hospitalized in our Chimborazo Hospital and received the finest care available. I understand that he was suffering, primarily, from wounds to the eye, head, and brain, with resulting dementia and amnesia. He subsequently disappeared from that facility. His current condition and whereabouts are unknown.

Would that we could locate all of our fallen heroes, on both sides, and comfort their families. I hope I have been of assistance.

Respectfully,

Judah Benjamin

+ + +

Matt sat quietly on the upholstered rocker in the corner of the parlor, gently rocking as he sipped his morning coffee and listened to Melody giving Mary Sue her arithmetic lessons. The child was reciting her multiplication tables, corrected when necessary by her mother, when they all became gradually aware of an approaching disturbance which seemed to be coming down the street from the center of town. The disturbance turned out to be a martial drumbeat sounding in the distance, growing louder as it approached. The day was clear, and quite sunny for November. Mary Sue peeked through the curtains. "Papa! There are soldiers coming up the street!"

"Really!" said Matthew from his chair. "What fun!" He was accustomed to the soldiers from the fort practicing parade formations through the streets of town just to remind the populace that they had a serious military presence in their midst.

"Papa! They're stopping here!"

"Oh-oh!" exclaimed Matt as he put down his coffee and went to look for himself. The little girl was right. Not only had they stopped in front of the Chapman house, they were drawn up in double rank. As he watched, they ordered arms, dressed up their ranks, and stood at rest. The two mounted officers dismounted, handed their reigns to orderlies, and climbed the front steps. One was Commandant Pratt, the other was the annoying Lieutenant Smalley. Matt ducked out of sight while Melody answered their knock on the door.

"Good morning, ma'am. We request the honor of speaking to Colonel Matthew Greyson. Is he in?"

Melody fixed the men in a terrible stare. She fervently wished that she had her old squirrel rifle, but, of course, it was back in Franklin where she had left it. "I know no Matthew Greyson."

Lieutenant Smalley grinned. "Of course you do, Mrs. Greyson. We would like to speak to him, please."

Matt discreetly viewed the scene from behind the window curtain. "Damned if this isn't the fanciest arrest detail I ever saw! Clean boots, clean uniforms, white gloves, stars and stripes, regimental flag, the whole shebang! Darling," he patted Mary Sue affectionately, "I believe we are in deep trouble."

Judge Chapman stalked from his study and shouldered his bulky frame through the doorway, gently nudging Melody aside. "Captain Pratt, Lieutenant Smalley." He bowed. "To what do I owe the honor of this visit?"

Captain Pratt returned the bow, his epaulets sparkling and the polished hilt of his sheathed sword gleaming in the sunlight. "We wish to speak to Colonel Greyson, if you will, sir."

Bela drew himself to his full height. "Colonel Greyson? I'm not sure I know...."

"Never mind. Thank you, Bela," Matt stepped onto the porch and stood stiffly at attention. "I am Lieutenant Colonel Matthew Greyson. How may I serve you gentlemen?" Matt knew, of course, that he was about to be clapped into irons.

"Squad! Attention!" bawled the sergeant who stood in his appointed place ahead of the double rank of blue-clad soldiers. He was a man of extraordinary lung-power. The volume of his commands caused neighbors to run out of their houses to see what was the matter. "Support arms!" Every time he shouted the word "arms" he pronounced it with an "h" in front of it so that the word would come out louder. In snappy three-motion cadence, the men tucked their rifles, vertically, against their left shoulder, left hand on their breast, right hand at their side. "Present arms!" They moved their rifles to the salute position, vertically and directly in front of them. Pratt and Smalley snapped to attention and saluted, waiting for Greyson to return the salute. Bewildered, he did so, trying to keep his jaw from developing an un-military sag of amazement.

Captain Pratt approached him. "Colonel Greyson, I have the honor to present you with the insignia of full colonelcy, and with a written commendation from the Congress of the United States of America honoring you for extreme bravery under fire in the service of defending the integrity of the Union. Brigadier General A.T.A. Torbert, your new comander, is delighted to learn of your survival, and of your recovery from your wounds. He sends his best wishes. I have here a letter from him requesting that you will, at your earliest convenience, report to his command for reassignment as soon as you are completely recovered."

Tears glistened in Colonel Greyson's eyes but through sheer manly force refused to course down his cheeks. "Thank you, gentlemen." His voice was barely above a whisper as he gazed at the commendation which had been placed in his hands.

"A great pleasure, sir!" grinned Smalley as he spun on his heel and marched down the wooden steps, the tip of his sword scabbard clinking on the stairs behind him as he descended and followed Captain Pratt to their waiting horses. "Damn!" he thought to himself. "Too bad this fancy-pants wasn't a famous reb spy or somethin' such. Could have got a promotion out of snappin' the irons on him! Oh well!" he sighed. "Better luck next time, Smalley!"

"Squad! Ordah harms!" barked the sergeant. "Shouldah harms! Right face! In column of twos, forwaaard, harch!" And they were gone, the drumbeat fading as they marched back up the incline to the fort. A cannon on the parapet belched smoke as it fired a three-gun salute. Matt, aghast, collapsed onto a frosty wicker porch rocker while Melody and Mary Sue piled onto his lap.

"Papa! Papa! You're a hero!"

Matt mopped his brow in spite of the cold air. "Hero? I don't think so. They should have dragged me off and shot me. However," he brightened, "I like this a lot better!"

Three days later a nattily dressed young man in a business suit and carrying an expensive valise knocked at the Chapman's door. Mrs. Chapman answered the door with all the welcoming appearance of an oversized bulldog. "Yes?" She obviously thought that she was addressing some kind of shyster salesman or other.

The young man did not seem afraid. "Good afternoon, madam. I have a message for a Matthew Chandler. Do I have the right address?"

"Depends."

"Depends on what, madam?"

"On who you are."

In a smooth motion, almost like a magician pulling a rabbit out of a hat, he produced a business card from an inner pocket and held it out, suspended between two extended fingers, to Mrs. Chapman.

"My card, madam. If you will kindly tell Mr. Chandler that a Mr. Burley sent me, I'm certain he will want to speak to me." She squinted at the card. It read: John Singer, agent, Ajax Shipping Company, Ltd, Windsor, Canada. Within moments, he and Matt were seated in the parlor while Melody produced a couple of brandies from the sideboard, then politely took her leave. "Captain Chandler, I have to apologize. Acting Master Burley did not actually send me here. He is in jail at this moment."

Matt looked distressed. "Bennet in jail? Damn!"

"Yes, suh. He was arrested in Canada right after the Johnson's Island thing."

"Well, what, then?"

The young gentleman sipped his brandy. "My message is from Jacob Thompson, but first, I must congratulate you. You are one of the most difficult people to locate that I have ever been assigned to find....and I have been assigned to find some beauties."

"That's good, I assume?"

"That's very good. Now, the message from Commissioner Thompson is that the reason our mission at Johnson's Island failed was because we were betrayed by a double agent named Godfrey Hyams."

Matthew jumped to his feet. "I knew it! I knew it! Goddammit, I knew I didn't trust that slimy bastard!"

The courier laughed. "Of course, suh, y'all were right. Too bad y'all didn't see fit to shoot him, if only just on general principles."

"Should have!" moaned Matt, sinking back into his chair.

"Yes, suh. Now, I have nothing but dummy papers in this valise. My messages from Thompson are all verbal, for obvious reasons."

Matt retrieved the brandy decanter from the sideboard and refilled the glasses. "Of course. Dammit! Stupid me!"

The courier giggled....a bit unprofessionally. "As you say, suh. Anyway, Commissioner Thompson advises extreme caution as Hyams has alerted the authorities to be looking for you even though they have no positive identification for you, nor location where you might be hiding."

"Shit! Ain't that just fine!" Matt clapped his hand to his forehead, visibly upset.

"Yes, suh. As you say, suh. One more thing. Commissioner Thompson requests that you contact him, at your earliest convenience, for reassignment. We lost several important agents during and after the Johnson's Island project, and are in need of expert personnel. He would be most appreciative if you would contact him, at your earliest convenience, for reassignment. As we speak, a new ship of war is being outfitted in Canada."

Matt stroked his chin. "You don't say! Really? Hmm." For a moment he was tempted by the thought of new, high adventure, but thought better of it. "Well, I reckon not. Got my plate full right now with a new baby comin'." He paced the parlor, pulling back the curtains and looking out of the windows for a long moment, trying to adjust to all the new information. "What agents did we lose?"

"Cole, captured. Burley, captured, and a female agent, drowned. Acting Master Beall, fortunately, has escaped and is again busily at work for the Confederacy."

"A female agent was drowned? How'd that happen?"

"Apparently in an escape attempt. She jumped to her death off the deck of the *Michigan*. Sad thing. She was one of the best agents we had." The courier bowed his head for a moment as though struggling for words. "She was a close friend of mine." His voice was quietly sad.

Matt reacted sympathetically to the sorrow of the young Confederate and reached to pat him on the shoulder. "I'm so sorry. War is an even more unspeakable horror when women have to be lost doing their patriotic duty.

"This brings us to my second reason for visiting you. I doubt if you have already heard. The agent's name was Bethany. Bethany Dodge."

Matthew's hand tightened around the stem of Bela Chapman's delicate brandy glass so tightly that it shattered, the shards piercing his hand. Unnoticed, crimson blood ran onto the arm of the parlor chair.

The courier stared at the blood as it soaked into the upholstered arm, then began to drip upon the faux oriental carpet. "Sorry, suh. I had hoped to find you for her, but not like this. My heart cries out when I think of her."

Matt's voice was hoarse, his words almost intelligible. "As does mine." He rose to find a napkin to wrap around his hand and pressed it tightly to staunch the flow. "Tell Mr. Thompson that I am dead."

"What?"

"Dead. Killed and scalped by a nasty band of Objibway Indians in northern Michigan when they caught me takin' immoral liberties with their squaws."

The rebel, recovering his composure, smiled. "As you say, suh. Nice story. I will enjoy communicating it. Well! I guess I'd best be on my way." He picked up his valise and headed for the door. "Sorry to be the bearer of sad news. For what it's worth, now, she never stopped loving you. Her heart was broken when she found that you had left Middleburg with another woman....your wife, I presume. Good day, and good luck, suh."

Matthew followed him to the door, holding his hands above his head to avoid further drips on Mrs. Chapman's carpet. "Thank you for your perseverance in finding me. Are you certain that you were not followed?"

"Very certain, suh. I have been in the undercover business for some time. If I hadn't learned to keep my eyes open I would have been dead long ago."

"I am indebted to you for your great expertise." Matt's voice quivered with supressed emotion. "Am I allowed to ask your name?"

"Of course, as long as y'all don't communicate it to anyone!" The courier grinned, knowing that the caution was unnecessary. "I'd shake your hand, but I can see both of them are busy keeping you from bleeding to death. Just call me John. John Surrat. Perhaps, one fine day, we will have the opportunity to work together."

+ + +

December passed quickly for everyone except Melody who was, naturally, getting more uncomfortable as her time neared. The strait froze solid enough for horse-drawn sleighs and dog-drawn sleds to cross from St. Ignace with mail and supplies. One of the snowy deliveries produced a bundle addressed to Colonel Matthew Greyson. Compliments of General Torbert, it was a complete new uniform, resplendent with the gold-framed eagle shoulder straps that befitted his new rank. Snow covered the island with a mantle so white that one could imagine that only virgins dwelt there....three feet in depth on the level, eight or nine feet in the drifts.

Matt, Melody, and Mary Sue passed the Christmas season bathed in the warmth of their friendships with the Ferrys, the Chapmans, and their new friends Captain and Mrs. Pratt up at the fort. Melody organized a lady's' knitting club which produced prodigious amounts of warm woolen mittens, socks, and scarves for the soldiers....soldiers who longed to be home with their families instead of being stuck in a Godforsaken stone fort perched on top of a frozen, snow-covered hill. Ste. Anne's Catholic Church and the Protestant Mission Church were located just a few short blocks from each other on the same street. On Saturday evening, Christmas eve, the windows of both churches glowed with their candlelight celebrations of the blessed arrival of the Christ Child. Christmas Day, being Sunday, produced larger than usual crowds of worshippers at the morning services. Protestants, Catholics, soldiers, Indians, and other residents of all shapes, sizes, and beliefs milled together in the street, heartily wishing each other the joys of the season. Melody, however, bypassed the Catholics and their church without even acknowledging their presence. She directed Matthew to drive their rented one-horse sleigh past Ste. Anne's without slowing, not even a little bit, to exchange greetings with the Roman Catholics who gave them friendly smiles, then turned away, unacknowledged.

Mary Sue, on the other hand, was far more cosmopolitan with the distribution of her Christmas greetings. Late on Christmas Eve, she lugged a half-bushel of carrots to the local livery stable, which was just down the street from the Chapman house, and presented each and every creature with a treat. Even the stable cats were favored with bits of fish that she had filched from the Chapman kitchen and wrapped in a napkin. She had desperately wanted to wait until midnight to see if the animals really would bow down in honor of the Christ Child, like she had been told that they did in Virginia, but her papa said that she must not be out in the darkness at such a late hour. With a sigh, she had returned home, well before that special time, and was tenderly tucked into bed by her mama and papa, kissed, and wished a merry Christmas. As soon as her eyes closed, she dreamed of the stable and of the steamy animals that stood, unattended, in the darkness within. She watched in amazement as all of the horses, mules, and even the cats, bowed at midnight while a brilliant star shone through the dirty windows of the humble stable.

+ + +

January, 1865, was a symphony of howling white. Even the tough, fur-clad French-Indians dared not take their dog sleds across the ice for fear of freezing to death on the way to the island. It was at such a time that the Greyson child decided to make its way into the world. Doctor Bailey and a brace of Chippewa midwives struggled through the drifts to be in attendance. Matthew and Mary Sue cuddled by the parlor stove to await developments. And they waited, and waited, and waited, wincing at the occasional cry of pain from Melody as she lay in an adjacent bedroom while murmurs from the attendants and light from the many lamps within seeped under the closed door.

Finally, in the snowy gray of the dawn, there was a cry...the cry of a new person in the world who was very upset at being disturbed and evicted from its comfortable, warm quarters. "Good set of lungs!" grinned Matt as he hugged Mary Sue. "What do you think we got? Brother or sister?"

Mary Sue snuggled. "Sister."

"Now, how would you know that?"

"The eagle told me."

Matt pulled her onto his lap and held her at arms length so that he could look into her eyes. "Are you telling me the eagle talks to you, too?"

"Yes, papa."

"Since when?"

"Since the day on Round Island when mama taught me."

"Omygod!" exclaimed Matt. "I'm surrounded by Injuns!"

"Lucky you!" said Mary Sue, snuggling back into his neck.

"Lucky me." smiled Matt, kissing the top of his daughter's pretty black hair.

Before long the black enameled doorknob clicked softly as it turned, and Doctor Bailey appeared, framed in the bright light from within the bedroom. "Mary Sue, you have a lovely sister!" Mary Sue rushed to take her bundled sister in her arms, struggling to see her reddened little face in the dim morning light."

"Told you, papa!"

"You're right, of course, Mary Sue." He bent to look, a tender smile on his face. "Thank you, doctor. Doctor, how is Melody? Is she all right? The delivery took such a long time. May I see her now? I want to be with her.... to hold her hand."

Bailey's professionalism was immaculate. "Of course, Matthew. Come, sit with me for a moment. First of all, the baby is fine. She was breech presentation and is a little bruised, but with no significant damage. Melody, of the other hand, is of concern. She has hemorrhaged excessively, and her color is poor. I fear that the uterus may have ruptured."

Matt shuddered. "What does this mean? What can you do?"

"We have packed her with gauze and pressure-bandaged her abdomen. I'm confident that the hemorrhage will stop, unless...."

"Unless, what?"

"Unless, if the uterus has indeed ruptured, then there is extreme danger of sepsis."

"How will we know?"

"We'll know."

Twenty-four hours later Melody had developed a high fever. Forty-eight hours later Charity Jane Melody Chandler Greyson was dead.

"Papa?" Mary Sue's eyes were wet with tears of sorrow that just would not cease to flow.

Yes, dear."

"I wish I could give milk like that Ojibway lady you hired to nurse my sister. I'd do it for her."

"It's not your time, love. One day you will nurse your own child, God willing."

"Yes, papa." She looked at the slumbering, swaddled infant in her arms. "Papa? How come we ain't named her yet?" Gently, she placed the sleeping baby into her cradle.

"I just can't bring myself to think about that right now. Maybe after the funeral."

"But God took mama an' gave us her to love instead. I want to be able to call her by name when I hold her an' tell her I love her."

Matthew started to cry. Mary Sue hugged him for all she was worth and cried too. It was a while before he could speak. "Mary Sue, you'll just have to have patience with me."

His daughter jumped off of his lap, stared at him through her tearstained reddened eyes, then took his big hand in her two little ones. "Papa! That's it!"

"That's what?"

"Her name! Patience!"

Matt wiped his own eyes with the back of his free hand. "Of course! You are right, child. Patience. How 'bout Patience Melody Greyson?"

"Yes! Yes! Yes! Mrs. Chapman! Judge Chapman! The baby's got a name!" she shouted, then ran from the room to find them to deliver the good news personally.

+ + +

Reverend Ferry called at the rectory of Ste. Anne's Church to bring the sadness of Melody's passing to the attention of the priest. After several cups of tea, and the swapping of many stories, the priest offered to conduct the funeral service provided that she would be interred in the Catholic cemetery. "What would you think if she were to be buried in the military cemetery, father?"

The priest thought for a moment, then nodded assent. "But, how could that happen? She was not a soldier."

Ferry smiled, thinking to himself that she was not really a Catholic, either. "We'll see about that. I think she was."

Leaving the rectory, Ferry trudged up the snowy path that inclined across the bluff and into the fort. He noticed that the flag that fluttered over the whitewashed stone of the fort was at half-mast. Captain Pratt greeted him cordially at the door of the large and comfortable commanding officer's house. "You look chilled, reverend. Would you care for some spirits to revive---oh no, I suppose not. How about a coffee, or some hot chocolate?"

"A cup of hot coffee would be wonderful."

"Come into the kitchen. Mary has a fresh pot already on the stove." Once seated at the kitchen table, they also discovered that she had a pan of blueberry muffins almost ready to come out of the oven.

Mrs. Mary Pratt, swathed in a very businesslike white and pink apron, whisked the muffin pan out of the oven and set it on the top of the big, black, cast iron wood burning range. "Reverend, you timed your arrival perfectly. How did you know I was baking muffins?"

"God told me. I have special communications with heaven, you know. He told me that your blueberry muffins are not to be missed....so, here I am!"

The captain guffawed. "So! That's why you trudged all the way up here in the snow and cold....to eat Mary's muffins! Whew! I thought maybe we were in trouble with the Lord, or something."

"Well, Henry, you probably are, but that's not why I'm here, either. I want to talk about Melody Greyson."

Mary looked sad. "Can I listen?"

Ferry jumped to his feet and pulled out a chair for her. "Of course you may. Would I be silly enough to tell the world's best muffin-maker to go away? I think not!"

The reverend took a big swig of coffee. "Melody was not, of course, a sworn soldier. She, however, really was one....a soldier with the rank of angel. She was very quiet about her accomplishments. I'll wager you don't know that, down in Virginia, she worked tirelessly to save the lives of soldiers, be they blue or gray. Matthew was one of them. She actually produced miracles of healing, using the healing methods of the Chippewa. She was often on the scene of battle before the shooting stopped, bandaging, comforting, healing. She cared not the color of the uniform. A wounded man was a wounded man to her and she would do her very best to save them. Many that she saved had been given up as hopeless by battlefield surgeons. One Union sergeant, I forget his name, was so badly shot up that even Matthew gave him up for dead. It took months, but Melody saved him, getting him well enough to send him back north."

Mary sat, her hands folded on her lap, for a moment. "Bill, you are absolutely right. The woman was a soldier of mercy. Oh! I'm so sorry that she is gone!" She burst into tears and fled from the room.

The men looked after her for a moment. With a sigh, Henry Pratt heaved to his feet and retrieved the coffee pot for refills. "Well now, reverend, when are you going to tell me where all this is headed?"

"Right now. What would you say to a military funeral with burial in the military cemetery?"

"Um, I guess I don't see why not. Would be good for Colonel Greyson, wouldn't it? Also, she was a favorite of the troops. She was always providing them with comforts that made them feel more at home.... cookies, mittens, scarves, helping them write letters, bandaging scrapes and bruises, whatever. I believe they would really like to honor her, too. I think burial with full military honors would be totally appropriate. And, happily, there is no way that I can request permission from headquarters.... even if I wanted to....which I don't. Communication, at the moment, is impossible. You got a deal, William."

Ferry jumped to his feet. "Wonderful! Thanks, Henry. I'll head right down to Chapman's to give Matthew the news. I'm sure this will be a comfort to him."

"How about one more muffin before you go?"

"Well, if you insist. May I get a little more coffee, too?"

Pratt sighed as he reached for the pot. "You're a greedy sinner, reverend."

"Only when it comes to blueberry muffins."

Within the hour, Lieutenant Smalley, complete with cemetery map and a detail of soldiers, slogged their way up to the cemetery. They found the grave site selected by Captain Pratt on the map, shoveled the snow away, and fanned out into the woods collecting firewood. The fire, built on the grave site, would be tended all night to drive the frost from the ground so that digging could commence in the morning. The v-plows also worked all night clearing the way to the military cemetery which was situated on the high ground of the island, lonely but for the stars and stripes that fluttered in the center of the small, fenced area. Immediately adjacent, and snuggled up to the military cemetery as though for protection, were two other cemeteries. The shady plot just across the trail to the west was reserved for the Catholic faithful. To the north, a rolling meadow was reserved for the remains of everyone else.

+ + +

The day of the funeral was a grand one. The sky was ice-blue and cloudless, the snow blinding white. "See, papa, God even sent us a pretty day for mama." She tried, unsuccessfully, to stifle the sobs that welled from within her young, broken heart. She was a brave little girl, and helping to care for the baby was a godsend, giving her a purpose for living even though her mama was gone and life had crashed around her in a fearful wreck. "Oh, papa, what will we do?"

Matt dabbed at her tears and hugged her close. "Patience is a part of your mama left on earth, just like you are. Together, we'll raise her up, and care for her, and get her the best education money can buy. Then, one day, it will be her turn to care for us just like mama did. You'll see."

Mary Sue brightened. "Does that mean I'll get the best education money can buy too?"

"It certainly does. You can even go to Europe to study if you want to....or to one of those fancy schools out east....if you want to. 'Course, I'd just as soon you stayed with me and Patience and love us both full time."

"I'll do that."

"I know you will, much as you can. The future is bright and exciting for a girl smart and pretty as you. And I'm goin' to help you find your way, least 'till you find your own man to love. Then, me and Patience will have to share you with him."

"Oh, papa, you make is sound so nice."

531

"It will be nice."

"Even without mama?"

"She'll always be with us, Mary Sue. Trust me."

The procession started at the fort, led by a single mounted color bearer. A bow of black silk ribbon graced the top of the staff. Behind the colors rode Captain Pratt and Lieutenant Smalley, the two Henrys riding side by side in full dress uniform, epaulets gleaming gold in the sunlight. Next came the nine-member honor guard, three abreast in the narrowed road, with rifles shouldered and bayonets mounted. Next came the hearse in the form of a large, black bunting-bedecked bobsled pulled by a stout, matched pair of dapple gray horses with black cockades on their bridles. Melody's coffin was draped with the flag of the United States. Matt thought that the flag of the Confederate States of America would be more appropriate, but wisely did not offer an opinion on the subject.

The drummer followed the hearse, beating a muffled, solemn, slow cadence for the rest of the garrison who marched in ten ranks, three abreast, behind him. Then, in sleighs, came the handsomely uniformed Matthew, seated next to Mary Sue who was so wrapped in a large blanket that only her reddened tear-stained eyes were exposed; then came the Ferrys with Father Mazzuchelli, then the Chapmans, then the balance of the island population crowded onto bobsleds and sleighs, or slipping and sliding along on foot.

At the cemetery gate, waiting for the procession, was a surprise honor guard....about fifty buck-skinned, blanketed, and heavily feathered Chippewa Indians who had somehow, and at great peril, made their way across the treacherous ice and snow to the island. No one seemed to know how they had learned of Eagle Song's passing. When asked, Chief Wasagunabi only smiled, and said nothing.

Father Mazzuchelli and Reverend Ferry shared the interment service. The Father, swinging his incense burner on its gold chain, intoned the Mass For The Dead. "Requiem aeternam dona eis, Domine: Et lux perpetua luceat eis...."

Mary Sue tugged at her father's sleeve. He bent down to hear her whisper. "Papa, he's doing the same thing mama did with the cedar smudge to drive away the evil spirits!"

"Reckon you're right. Shhh!" he whispered.

"Absolve, Domine, animas omnium fidelium defunctorum a omni vinculo delictorum...." Father Mazzuchelli was now sprinkling holy water from its golden dispenser upon the casket.

"Papa? What's that?"

"Holy water."

"Ojibwas don't have that."

"Shhh. I know. You have to be Catholic."

"But, where do you get...?"

"Shhh."

Reverend Ferry took over at the homily, delivering a touching sermon about the soldier with the rank of angel to whom they were bidding good-bye that day. Good-bye for now, of course, but not forever.

The honor guard fired three volleys in salute, the blue-grey smoke drifting between the mourners, the snow-draped cedars, and the crisp winter sun. Taps, a new tune just born in a Union camp on southern soil, echoed its message of sadness across the island. Another soldier was dead, but another soldier was never to be forgotten.

As they walked, hand in hand, from the cemetery, Mary Sue whispered. "Papa, can I talk now?"

"Yes, love."

"I've been looking and looking into the sky. I don't see any eagles. Where do you suppose mama is?"

That one stopped Matthew cold in his tracks. He dropped to his knees in the snow to bring his face down to her level. "Mama is in heaven with Jesus. I guess I don't know for sure, but I 'spect in a little while she will fly with the eagles. Give her a little time, sweet daughter. She will always be with us."

"I'll feel better when I see her flying, circling, telling us she loves us."

"Give her time, child. Give her time." Warrior-who-rides-a-dead-horse was beginning to understand the sweetness and comfort of the Chippewa spirit world.

Matthew engaged a local craftsman to inscribe a headstone made of the local, soft limestone. The inscription read:

> Charity Jane Greyson
> loving mother of
> Mary Sue and Patience
> born March 12, 1829
> died January 19, 1865
> Love Eternal

Matthew vowed that as soon as they could go south in the spring he would purchase a headstone made of enduring granite to replace the crude marker on her grave. In spite of his good intentions, many springs would pass before his return. The crumbling limestone seemed forgotten, its loving inscription slowly weathering away. It stood, sadly awaiting him, comforted only by the simple markers on the graves of the soldiers which were arranged in neat rows close by.

CHAPTER TWENTY-NINE

"The Old Flag Will Triumph Yet"

The Reverend Pitts Lanning frowned when he spotted the military courier dismounting in front of the parsonage. The soldier, looking frosty in spite of his woolen overcoat and kepi, tramped the snow off of his boots on the porch steps and knocked on the door. "Oh-oh!" thought the reverend. "News of more casualties. Oh, how I hate this damned war!" Lanning answered the door with his heart skipping in fear of what the message might be. "Good afternoon, soldier. Sorry you had to come out in the cold."

"No trouble." grinned the young man. "They give me a nice warm horse to sit on."

"Who's dead now?"

"Don't rightly know that anybody is, reverend. This 'spatch come from Fort Mackinac. Don't think there is any shootin' goin' on up there! It's from a Colonel Greyson."

Lanning's trepidation was replaced with a warm glow. "Thank the Lord, and thank you, soldier. This may be the news of a new life beginning instead of one ending. How in the world did a dispatch get here from Mackinac in the dead of winter?"

"Snowshoes and horseback, sir. Come with other communications from the Fort to our office in Detroit. Sorry it took so long. Took about a month to reach us."

"Thank you, son. Stay warm." Pitts turned up the lamp on his desk against the gathering gloom of the late February afternoon. There were two letters in the envelope. One was addressed to him, and one to Dick Trick. As soon as he began to read, his eyes filled with tears, making it difficult to make out the message.

> January 26, 1865
>
> The Reverend Pitts Lanning
> Franklin, Michigan
>
> Dear Pitts,
>
> I trust this finds you and Mrs. Lanning well. I make the assumption that Dick Trick has by now advised you of my various adventures and misadventures during the last couple of years, and how we ended up on Mackinac Island, the land of my wife's people. It is with the greatest sadness that I must inform you that my beautiful wife, Melody, who unfortunately you never had a chance to meet, has died in childbirth. The sadness of her loss is nearly tearing me, and my adopted daughter, to pieces. I wish that you were here, or we there, that you might help us. We are fortunate to have a good friend, Reverend William Ferry of the Presbyterian faith, to help us find the strength that Jesus promised. So far, that strength seems to have evaded us.
>
> Now, on the bright side, we have a lovely, healthy little baby daughter and sister name of Patience Melody. She gives us joy in a time of sadness. We will bring her to you for her baptism in the spring when the ice is gone and passenger service resumes. I can't wait to return to Franklin and resume the sweet life of a farmer!
>
> Please give the enclosed message to Dick. Thank you.
>
> Matthew

The Franklin villagers had been saddened and touched by the news of Matthew Greyson's misfortunes....Bethany Dodge's untimely death, and now Melody Greyson's passing from complications of childbirth....not to mention his severe and debilitating war wounds which had almost taken the life of Matthew himself. Dick Trick had received a letter from Matthew, in the previous October, informing him of the good news that Matt had been reinstated in the Army of the United States, and promoted to full colonel. Dick, no longer restrained by Matthew's order for secrecy, had indeed lost no time in telling the story, much as he knew, of Matt's painful journey back from Richmond, and back from the dead. Now, Dick had said, the lady who had saved Matt's life was his wife, and they were about to have a child come winter! He knew not, of course, of Greyson's brief service in the Confederacy. That was a secret that could never be told.

Now, all was changed. Melody was dead. Dick shuddered as he finished reading the letter to Mr. Lanning and opened his own. It was dark and blustery outside of the Greyson farmhouse. Pitts Lanning had pulled on his hat, coat, and mittens, had twined his long wool scarf around his neck, and trudged down the road and up the path to deliver the letter, and the news, to Dick.

January 26, 1865

Dear Dick,

I am certain that Reverend Lanning has informed you that we have lost Melody and gained Patience! Fortunately, the baby leaves us little time for sorrow, but sorrow there is....a lot of it.

I plan to be home as soon as the ice is out, and in time for planting. Please be sure to have plenty of seed on hand. Please also be certain that the house is clean and that the guest room is freshly painted and set up for a little girl and her baby sister. We will be bringing with us the Chippewa woman who has been helping us with the infant. She will be staying with us for a while, but not too long as she will not want to be away from her family any great length of time. Probably, when the time comes, we can find us a war widow there in town who would like work. We'll worry about that later. The Indian lady will require a place to sleep. Please fix up the upstairs garret room. Do whatever is necessary to provide her with comfortable quarters there.

Please also go down to Detroit, to Whittemore's Music Store, and order up a spinet-size piano and have it delivered into the parlor. Get a good one. There should be plenty of money in the bank to do this. Expect it to be expensive, though. I read an advertisement in the *Detroit Advertiser* last fall by Mr. Whittemore. I copied it down at the time. It said:

> "Attention 1st Michigan Cavalry--Form *en masse*, charge!--not upon the enemy, but upon the music store of J. Henry Whittemore, where can be found that noble song in memory of your late gallant leader, Col. Brodhead, entitled, 'The Old Flag Will Triumph Yet.'"

I intend to get Mary Sue to learn to play and sing it. There is one lady here on the island who teaches piano so I signed her up. She has already learned some of the basics and is starting to play quite decent. The piano is to be a surprise "welcome home" gift when we get there. We'll go back down and get her some more sheet music then.

Hope your winter is going well. Got all the harness mended? There's three to ten foot of snow up here. See you in the spring. There will be four of us if you count the cat.

Matt

Lanning was leaning his elbows on the kitchen table, chin cupped in his hands, while he listened to Dick laboriously read the letter. "Sounds like you have your work cut out for you, Dick my boy. You might as well start right now by giving this poor old minister a nice hot cup of black coffee to get me back down the hill and home without freezing up!"

+ + +

In late April, 1865, steamers were again plying the open waters of the Great Lakes, delivering limited cargoes and passengers to the ice which still choked the majority of the northern ports. With them came the news: April 12, General Robert E. Lee surrendered the Army of Northern Virginia to General U.S. Grant at Appomattox Court House, Virginia. The war was essentially over; on April 14, John Wilkes Booth shot President

Abraham Lincoln at Ford's Theater in Washington; April 15, Lincoln died and the nation went from the joy of victory to the black buntings of mourning; April 26, General Joseph E. Johnston surrendered his 30,000 man Confederate army to General William T. Sherman at Durham Station, North Carolina. At Fort Mackinac the garrison lowered the flag to half-mast, then proceeded to celebrate the end of the war with the rest of the island population.

It was early May before the ice was sufficiently thin to allow vessels to dock at Mackinac Island. Matthew had to wait, albeit a bit impatiently, until a passenger vessel arrived that had heated staterooms available. The weather was still cold, and no one wanted baby Patience to take a chill.

On May 10, Confederate President Jefferson Davis was captured by the 4th Michigan Cavalry near Irwinville, Georgia. On May 29, to Matthew's great delight, United States President Andrew Johnson issued a proclamation of general amnesty affecting most of those who had participated in the rebellion. Matthew felt as though a great weight had been lifted from him, but resolved never to tell of his part in the *Philo Parsons* affair. Considering the possible charge of piracy, there was a good chance that the amnesty would not apply is his case. Best to keep his mouth shut forever!

On Friday, June 2nd, Matthew and his family disembarked at Detroit. They were met by Dick Trick driving Matthew's two-horse buggy, and George Congleton driving one of his famous wagons in anticipation of a large quantity of luggage. He was not disappointed.

To Greyson's surprise, Dick was wearing the uniform of the Federal army, emblazoned with the insignia of company E, 30th Michigan Infantry. Matt returned the young man's salute, then hugged him and slapped him on the back. "Dick! You made it! You're a soldier!"

A smile of pleasure and pride persisted on Trick's face. "Yes, sir. Sort of, sir."

"Sort of? What do you mean 'sort of'?"

"Well, they gave me this uniform an' handed me a musket and sent me with the rest of my company to stand guard at the river down by Wyandotte. By the time they got around to doin' my paperwork they said not to bother 'cause the war was about to be over....and so it was!"

Matt pumped the boy's hand. "Sure sounds like you're a soldier to me. Congratulations!"

Dick blushed. "Thanks, Matt....er,....sir."

As they descended the steep grade into Franklin, the squealing of the brakes on George's wagon alerted the populace who immediately rushed out to greet their returning hero. Matthew, resplendent in his uniform, saluted the villagers as they waved their flags and shouted greetings. Mary Sue and the Indian woman were wide-eyed with amazement. Dick Trick sat ramrod-straight and struggled to drive the team and salute snappily at the same time. Blossom meowed her horror of the frightening noises while she cowered at the back of her travel crate. Rebel and Buttercup, swiveling their ears in all directions, were giving serious consideration to running away....were it not for Trick's strong hands on the reins. The Franklin Church bell pealed its brassy song of joy from the belfry of the little white house of worship.

"Thank God for Michigan!" The war was really over.

When they reached the farm, Matt hugged his daughter as he lifted her from the buggy. "Are you going to like it here, Mary Sue?"

Still carefully holding Blossom's travel crate, she took a moment to refresh her memory of the place....the big red barn, the freshly painted white house, the huge oak trees, Molly and Moe looking over the board fence, the sheep off in the distance. "You built all this, didn't you papa?"

"I did."

"I can tell. I can see your love in it."

"You can?" Matt had not expected or anticipated, that comment. He had simply hoped that she would be happy in her new home, and would put away her thoughts of the farm in Virginia.

"Yep. Every stick. You made it with love, didn't you?"

Matt, taken aback, thought a moment. "Well, child, now that you mention it, I guess I did."

"Thought so. How, then, could I not love it, papa?"

"Good!" exclaimed Matt. "Now come inside. I have something to show you, but you will have to close your eyes at first." Matt had a feeling that he had just been outmaneuvered by a thirteen year old. He was not certain that she had really answered his question....which, of course, she had not. When they reached he parlor door, he made her close her eyes and promise not to peek. Leading her by the hand, he took her to the shiny new piano bench and told her to sit. "Now, open your eyes."

It took a moment for her eyes to understand what they were seeing.... the gleam of polished cherry, the stark black and white of ivory keys, the fancy gold letters that said "Chickering, established 1823". She took in a deep breath. Matthew feared that she might forget to breathe again. She didn't forget. She let the breath out with a low whistle through pursed lips. Oh, papa! You did this for me?"

"I did. It's yours. Yours to keep for ever, if you like it."

She jumped up and hugged his neck. "Like it? Of course I do. I love it! Oh, papa, I don't deserve a papa like you!" She tried a few notes, then played a few tentative snatches of the "Minuet in G" that she had begun to learn on the island. Matt beamed, and wiped at his eyes. They must have been irritated by the dust of the long journey from Detroit, he thought.

By the next day, as though by reflex, a steady stream of ladies began bringing steaming soups, stews, pies, cakes, cookies, and all manner of comforting foods and goodies to the Greyson household. Mary Sue, already charmingly schooled in etiquette, curtsied prettily and graciously thanked each of their culinary benefactors as they arrived. She even made notes as to whose plate or dish belonged to whom so that they could be promptly and properly returned. The ladies were duly impressed by the little girl and whispered among themselves that she had been well "brung up". Actually, the "little girl" was not so little anymore. Just turned thirteen, she was blossoming into a woman. Her breasts were beginning to swell, fetchingly, beneath the bodice of her modest gingham dress. A matching ribbon tied back the thickness of her curly, shoulder length black hair. Her black Indian eyes glowed at one like smoldering coals....just like her mother's. Word of her beauty and charm circulated through the village like wildfire. Within days, "little Jimmy Barnum", now grown to a gangly but quite handsome teen-ager, came to call. Jim just had to see for himself what this supposedly wonderful young lady was all about. If took about fifteen minutes of their rocking on Greyson's side porch rockers for him to fall desperately in love.

For Matthew, love was not quite so simple as it was for the young people. Love, among young adults, could be terribly intense. However, if a relationship did not happen to work out another choice could soon be just around the corner....and be just as intense....and the previous relationship would soon be forgotten as a new love blossomed forth. Not so for Matthew. He was older now. He had fallen in love four times in his life. Three of those loves were, sadly, deceased.

The shadows of the losses within his heart were devastating, causing him to toss and mumble in his restless sleep, just like had happened when he lost Ellen in the tragic fire years before. It was the reoccurrence of a depression that had smoldered within him, each new loss adding fuel and causing the smolder to gain in intensity, threatening to burst into unrestrained flame. He even began to doubt his faith. He had learned, and believed, that Jesus was with him every day, at every turn, watching and helping lest he should dash his foot upon a stone. Yet, he had met that stone, and the stones had won. Darkly brooding, he made his way to Reverend Lanning's office in the little white church and flopped into the chair across from the minister's desk. "Like I told you in my letter, Pitts, I'm not sure I am strong enough to survive all this."

Lanning walked around the desk and held out his hands to Matthew. "Take my hands, Matt. Let us pray together. Dearest Jesus, help us to understand the trials that we share. We know that you are with us, hour to hour, day to day, but sometimes we just don't understand. Help us, we pray. Amen."

"Amen."

Pitts returned to his desk and took out a pad of blank paper and a pencil. "Now, tell me what it is that you cannot bear. We'll make a list."

"It won't be a long one, rev."

"So much the better. Talk to me....and bear in mind that the Lord is hearing every word."

"It's very simple. I loved Ellen and she died, horribly, in a fire. I loved Bethany and she drowned in Sandusky Bay doing what she perceived to

542

be her duty of country. I loved Melody and she died in childbirth. No one could save her. I loved my friends in the war, and many of them died.... especially heart-wrenching was the loss of my friend Colonel Brodhead. I loved my dog, Tansy, and she died. I loved my horse, Saber, the best any man could ever have, and he died with rebel .58 caliber mine balls in his chest while doing his best for his master....me. Now, reverend, tell me I shouldn't be depressed."

Lanning tapped his pencil on the paper pad. He had not written anything. "You should not be depressed."

Angrily, Greyson sat bolt-upright in his chair. "What? How can you possibly say that?"

"Angry, disappointed maybe, but not depressed."

"Easy for you to say. You haven't suffered any damn losses."

Lanning tipped back in his worn oaken desk chair which protested, squeakingly. "Not fair, Matt. The people of this community are my family. I have cried, for the last four years, every time one of our young men has been killed, or maimed, or disappeared forever into some battlefield of rotting bones. I cry too, Matthew....more than I care for you to know. I cry for the young widows, for the young wives who must care for the men who return to them shell-shocked and without arms or legs. I deal with this on a daily basis. You and I have the same problem, and we will lick it together."

Greyson, sobered, took a deep breath. "The common problem, I 'spose, is sadness from all the bad things. Right?"

"Wrong. The common problem involves controlling that sadness and not allowing it to become depression. There's sadness just around the corner in every life. Some is caused by natural events, like Melody's passing. Much is caused by people who must solve their differences by shooting and stabbing each other. For one reason or another, life is not necessarily kind, or fair. Sad events are a part of the beautiful package of life. Jesus teaches us to rise above sadness, that the only thing that really matters is that we love Him, and love each other. Knowing that, all other things will fall into place. There is no sadness in the Lord. Only joy."

Matt rose from his chair, walked to the window, and stared out at the road, hands clasped behind his back. "Why, then, doesn't He control war? Strike down those who would cause it....or at least change their minds?"

"I think you already know the answer to that one."

"Probably, I do. Just want to hear it from you."

"In the recent conflict, both sides prayed to the same God for victory, and claimed that God was on their side!"

"Tough spot to put God in, hey?"

"Unquestionably. Whose prayers would you answer if you were God?"

Matt chuckled. "The Union ones, of course." He sounded decisive with his answer, but in his mind he pictured his many friends in the south.

"Wise decision seeing as we already won!" smirked the reverend. "See, the Lord can't control all the vagaries of mankind. If he did, we wouldn't have the will to make decisions on our own. Free will. If we had no free will, no right to choose our course, He would have had a mob of unfeeling mannequins to worship him. Don't you think He deserves more than mannequins, this Creator God?"

Greyson sighed. "'S'pose so." He thought for a moment. "So, what, then, does our Lord do for us, day to day, like you say? I don't feel him doing anythin', right now."

"First of all, your question should be 'what can we do for Him?', not 'what can He do for us?' But, we can talk about that later. Matt, He likes to remain anonymous. He can work better that way within this 'free will' thing. Do you think that it was strictly by chance that you found and comforted the dying Confederate soldier? That you were led to your beloved Melody, the woman who saved your life, and then sacrificed her own to bear you a daughter? We are not allowed to know His plan. That doesn't mean that He doesn't have one. He knew what would happen, what you would do, who you are, long before you were even conceived."

Matt came back to his chair. He had not thought about life in such grand terms before. "Go on, please, rev."

"Now that Melody is safely in heaven, how do you know that there is not another woman waiting to love you, another dog waiting to lick your hand, another splendid horse waiting to serve you? Persons and animals that will not only love you, but more importantly they will benefit from your love! Count your blessings and take your inventory, Matthew. What blessings you have! Mary Sue! Patience Melody! Now, go home. You are one of the strongest men that I know. I feel with great certainty that you will not disappoint Jesus our Lord, or me."

Without speaking, Matt reached to shake the minister's hand. Head bowed, he shuffled out of the door, down the steps, and turned west on the German Mill Plank Road. At Franklin Road he stood, for a moment, at the intersection, weaving on his feet like a drunken man, then turned left and lifelessly climbed the hill, turning into the wrought-iron gate of the cemetery. His brain was on overload. He had heard the reverend's words before, but had never really listened until now. Finding Ellen's grave, he threw himself upon it and tried to sort out his thoughts in the shadow of her stone.

He awoke when the chill of the night awakened him. Somehow, though shivering cold, he felt warmed. He could not shake the feeling that his beloved Ellen had caressed him awake. He hurried home in the darkness, then cried, unashamedly, when Mary Sue leapt into his arms, hugged his neck, and wet his cheeks with her tears. "Papa! Papa! Where have you been? I have been so afraid!"

Matthew hugged the child with all his might....well, some of his might, lest he hurt her. The warmth of her young, sobbing body made him understand. "I'm sorry, Mary Sue. I will never leave you again."

She leaned back from his arms to look into his eye. "Promise?"

"Promise. I love you with all my heart and will protect you until my dying day."

She wiped her tears with the sleeve of her dress. "Really? Thank you papa. That's more than I could ever ask. I love you, papa."

"I love you, Mary Sue."

Matthew Greyson finally understood something that his daughter already knew. If there was, indeed, a master plan like Lanning said, within the strength of his renewed faith he need not worry about it. He needed only to trust in his God and await the next joy or the next sadness with confidence and thanksgiving. Silently, he thanked God for allowing him to share the lives of Ellen, Bethany, and Melody....if only for a little while.

When morning came, Matt took Mary Sue by the hand. Together they walked up to the cemetery to visit Ellen's grave. They sat there, Mary Sue resting her tousled head upon his shoulder while he related the story of love, of terror, of horrible separation. Heals-with-flowers' black eyes looked into his. Without a word, she arose and walked to the base of the wrought-iron fence at the perimeter of the cemetery where spring violets grew. Still silently, she held the delicate little blue bouquet to his lips for him to kiss, then laid them at the base of Ellen's stone.

High overhead, almost just a speck in the blue, an eagle whistled, and a second answered. Wheeling together, they added their blessing. Ellen Trick could finally rest in peace. Matthew Greyson could really be free to love again.

That night, after Mary Sue and Patience had been tucked into bed, Matt sat before the crackling fire in the parlor fireplace, his stocking feet extended toward its warmth. "Amazing what a person can learn if he has the opportunity to live long enough." he thought, reveling in the comfort of the warm fire and the warmth of the brandy in his glass. "Well now, let's just see, Greyson. Four loves, all genuine. Three gone. Hmmm. Do the arithmetic." He heaved to his feet, retrieved pad, inkwell, and pen from the desk, and after some deliberation began to write.

June 14, 1965

Miss Penelope Barksdale
c/o Captain Albert Clark Roberts
General Delivery
Durham Station, North Carolina

Dearest Penelope,

It is my hope, and prayer, that you and your dear mother have survived the vagaries of war and have returned, or are preparing to return, to your home in Fredericksburg. I pray that you are safe, and that your home has not been too severely damaged in spite of the repeated and severe battles which took place in that city during the recent unpleasantness. Since you, my blessed angel, brought me back to life so long ago, many things have happened. I have never found my Bethany. She is, I fear, dead. Subsequent to Bethany, I have lost another loved one, through childbirth. I now have an adopted daughter, aged 13, and a real daughter in her infancy.

I can't help but look back upon the good times we had together when you, a kind and sweet angel, looked after, and it seems, loved me....while you were saving my life. For all of this I am eternally grateful to you. At the time, your age was very close to the present age of my adopted daughter, Mary Sue. She is sweet. You would like her. She sustains my life and comforts my soul. Patience Melody, her infant sister, is equally charming and beautiful....although she has yet to display her true personality aside from screaming for milk or objecting to someone changing her soiled underwear!

We live on a nice farm near a little country town called Franklin, situated on a small river that runs much clearer and colder than the Rappahannock. I may have told you about the farm before, but my mind is a little fuzzy about much that went on when I was with you in Fredericksburg. Please forgive me. I believe that you would like it here, should you be so disposed, and situation allow. In any case, I would be delighted to hear from you, now that the postal service seems to be restored.

Should you care to write, the address is: Col. Matthew Greyson, Franklin, Michigan. Guess you never knew my full name before, until now!

Yours truly and sincerely,

Matthew Greyson

For almost three years, every time she was conveyed into town....Durham Station....Penelope had visited the post office in hopes that the anticipated letter from Matthew would arrive. In early July of 1865, it was there.

547

Matt glanced at the Gilbert octagon clock that ticked on the mantle, its ticks strangely comforting....like the purr of a kitten on your lap. 2:15 A.M. "Well!" he muttered. "Might just as well keep goin' and get my letters done." An expression of condolence to Bethany's father was long overdue. Dipping his pen into the inkwell that was perched, precariously, on the arm of his chair, he launched into the second letter. He had no problem with recalling Bethany's father's name and place of residence that she had confided to him in the early days of their romance before Matt had left to serve with the 1st Michigan Cavalry.

June 15, 1865

Major Jared Dodge
Charleston, South Caroloina

Dear sir:

I regret that, due to the unfortunate circumstances of war, that I have been unable to communicate with you sooner. First, I must tell you that I loved your daughter with all my heart, and she, me. She was, truly, the love of my life. In fairness, I must confess that there were more women before and since, but none....absolutely none....who could hold a candle to her.

You may well not know that I was severely wounded by your gallant and victorious forces at the Battle of Second Manassas/ Bull Run. My brain was so addled from my injuries that I had no idea that Bethany was still alive, let alone looking for me. I have learned, too late, otherwise. She had dedicated herself to finding me. I was, like an idiot, unaware.

Finally, she gave her sweet life for the Southern Cause that she loved, yielding it to the cold waters of Lake Erie. I applaud her bravery and determination. I only wish that she were still alive that I could tell her of my love.

Thank you for making it possible for me, even if just briefly, to share in the life of this woman. She will be in my heart to the end of my days....and, perhaps, beyond.

I have two daughters to care for, now. One is an infant. I wish Bethany were here. She could tell me how to care for them.

Now that your military responsibilities are over, perhaps you would consider traveling north to visit us. Please consider doing so. It would be a privilege to have you as a guest in our house for as long as you can stand to be in our frosty Yankee land!

I will never, ever, forget your daughter. My soul still cries in the night for her. Thank you for Bethany. I am forever in your debt.

Col. Matthew Greyson

In a remarkably short time, about a month, Greyson received an answer to his second letter. There was no response from Penelope Barksdale, but Major Dodge had responded immediately.

June 29, 1865

Col. Matthew Greyson
Franklin, Michigan

Dear Sir:

Thank you for your comforting letter of June 15. I cannot tell you how good it is to know that the person Bethany cried for was you. You are obviously worthy of such devotion. I want you to know that she cried, and cried, and did every thing in her power to find you. But, it was not you who was at fault. It was the stupid war that was at fault. I hope that we all have learned our lesson so that Americans may never again die because of their disagreements.

Yes, perhaps I will visit you, one day. I not only wish to talk at length with you. I would like to see for myself where Beth spent so many happy days. Your town must be a beautiful place. Do you really have a river that runs as cold as ice and as clear as gin? She told me that you do, but then, she could exaggerate sometimes.

Now, let me communicate to you an interesting twist. One of Bethany's best and most devoted friends was her servant, name of Bessie. She is a Negro. I had decided to set my servants free even before your late President Lincoln decreed that it must be so. I have done that, but none of them will leave. This premises is their home. I now pay them a wage in addition to their free room and board, and they are more than content. Bessie, strangely, is not. I showed her your letter. Bessie, by the way, can read. Contrary to the former law down here, Bethany taught her, and the other servants, the basics of education.

Now, when I showed her your letter I saw something that I had never witnessed before. A Negro turning pale. She said "Massa, I wants to go up there in the cold. I wants to care for them chillin'. Miss Bethany's spirit is up there, somewhere in that nasty, Yankee cold lake. I will find her, and, when the time come, I will bring her home to where she belong."

Laugh, if you will, Colonel Greyson. Bessie may or may not know things that we do not. If you want her, she is yours. All you must do is care for her. She is a very fine darky who is part of our family here. I would, reluctantly, entrust her to your care should you so desire, and if you will pledge to return her if she becomes unhappy up there.

I look forward to your reply.

Respectfully,

Major Jared Dodge

Greyson immediately responded in the affirmative. Within weeks, Bessie, struggling with hatboxes and frayed valises, was on the cars heading toward the scary, cold north. Fortunately, she was warmed by the hugs, sandwiches, and good wishes from her fellow servants, and by the heartfelt tears of Major Dodge.

CHAPTER THIRTY

Plotkin's Revenge

Sunday, October 24, 1865

"By God, he even looks like a flamin' pirate!" exclaimed Alphaeus Plotkin under his breath as he perched uncomfortably on one of the unpadded pews in the Franklin Methodist-Protestant Church. That all might see his piety, his head was bowed and his eyes mere slits as though lost in contemplation and prayer. Actually, his clandestine gaze was focused like the eyes of a circling hawk upon Matthew's black eye patch. The Greysons sat in the second pew at the front of the sanctuary (Methodists occupy the first pew only when there is no reasonable alternative such as when all other pews are crowded to capacity leaving no chance to squeeze in) unaware of the admiring glances of their fellow villagers and especially unaware of Detective Plotkin's malicious stare. Matt, Mary Sue, and baby Patience who lay peacefully sleeping in her sister's arms, were all tastefully dressed in their Sunday best. Sitting next to them, Bessie felt like a queen. In fact, she almost looked like a queen in the nice new dress and hat that Mary Sue and Matthew had picked out for her. She held her head regally high, knowing full well that she was pretty as a picture. "Too bad there ain't some nice, handsome men of color here 'bouts. They'd be crawlin' on their hands and knees to get a close look at me!" She smiled to herself, glancing furtively around to see if perhaps there might be some blacks in the congregation. "Mercy!" she thought, aghast. "Not a blessed one. Didn't even see none outside carin' fo' the folk's horses. Shame to look so nice and have only white folk to see me. Don't reckon any blacks would care to live this far north. Reckon I'll just have to get used to it." Such fine, "store bought" clothes were rarely seen in the rural village where, of necessity, most residents made their own garments. Plotkin, too, was looking quite spiffy, especially considering his former grungy appearance. He wore an almost-new suit, an almost-white shirt, a black ribbon tie, a nicely trimmed and stylish droopy mustache, and an improbably slick toupee which blended less than seamlessly with his own fringe of real hair.

Alphaeus had convinced himself that the townspeople had forgotten all about him, dismissing him without further thought, even though they had nearly lynched him only a few years previous. He was certain that his new, clean image provided an adequate disguise so that his appearance would not jar unpleasant thoughts in their memory. Besides, he had his own collection of unpleasant thoughts which persistently churned over and over in his mind. The near-lynching was one thing....at least they did not really dangle him by the neck from some convenient tree. The villagers did, however, wrongfully cause him to be incarcerated for the disappearance and presumed murder of Bethany Dodge along with a host of other trumped-up associated charges. He and his friends sat out the war in jail....which was right where Provost Marshall Hall wanted them to be.... out of the way and unable to cause more trouble for him or anybody else. When the war ended, so did the suspension of the writ of *habeus corpus*. Rather than go to the bother of a trial for the creeps, Hill had decided that they had served enough time and signed for their release. Without so much as an explanation, or a fare-thee-well, the surprised Plotkin had found himself blinking in the sunshine outside of the door of the county jail that had been his home for the past three years.

Much to his chagrin, he had found that the Pinkerton Detective Agency had ceased to be the major investigative unit for the Federal forces. The catalyst for the change from private agency to a military one was clear. Alan Pinkerton had received his government contracts for investigative work largely because of his good friend, General George McClellan. In 1864, McClellan had decided to run against Abraham Lincoln for the presidency of the United States. This action helped to make the general decidedly unpopular with Lincoln and his cabinet. Happily for Lincoln, sadly for McClellan, George lost the bid for the presidency. Not surprisingly, his mentor gone, Alan Pinkerton had lost his job. In his place, the Union had developed the U.S. Secret Service to better combat the Confederacy's skilled and expansive clandestine network.

Undaunted, Pinkerton had withdrawn back into his private gumshoe operation. As a man of remarkable business skills, Alan guided his agency to such great successes that the business has persisted into modern times, long after Pinkerton's death. It remains viable 140 years later. However, back in 1865, and perhaps not consistent with his usual good judgment, Pinkerton re-hired Alphaeus Plotkin. Attempting to keep the compulsive snoop under control, he restricted his activities to chasing errant husbands, unfaithful wives, and runaway children. Plotkin soon became bored with all that, yearning to be involved instead with the more entertaining counterspy activities.

The thought had persisted in his fevered brain that there was still something fishy in Franklin...Bethany or no Bethany. If there was one secesh spy in Franklin, would it not be logical that there were more hiding in the village as respectable citizens? And, would it not be fun to root them out, one by one, and to see them hanged? Such revenge would be sweet! But then, President Andrew Johnson had dropped the bombshell. He had proclaimed a general amnesty to most Confederate combatants. However, that amnesty did not necessarily include those accused of criminal activity....murder, bank robbery, piracy, etc. Piracy? So much for chasing down minor spies. But.... piracy? A new light had glowed in Detective Plotkin's darting eyes. In his spare time (of which he had no shortage), Alphaeus had met with, drank with, smoked with, and in general fraternized with his fellow members of the private intelligence community. One can glean a lot of information that way. One of the most common topics of conversation involved the late, aborted, Johnson's Island caper. The most expert on the subject was ex-double agent Godfrey Hyams who was still hanging around, seeking ways to earn more monetary rewards within the framework of the alleged piracy of the *Philo Parsons* and the *Island Queen*. Specifically, Hyams was trying to catch the mysterious, one-eyed, Captain Matthew Chandler, the only unaccounted for officer of the expedition. There was a problem hindering his investigation, however. No one seemed to know whether the Johnson's Island affair was a bona-fide military action for which there would now be no punishment, or whether it was an act of piracy. Piracy, of course, was a capital crime usually punished by hanging. The United States and Canada continued to toss poor Ben Burley back and forth across the border trying to decide whether his British citizenship and/or his former commission in the Confederate States Navy made him immune to the piracy charges.

Plotkin had been fascinated by the whole affair, particularly when he heard that this Captain Chandler had been seen on numerous occasions by informants on the docks of both Windsor and Detroit. His conspicuous eye patch had made him easy to spot and to remember. He had been seen embarking and disembarking on various vessels sailing to or from the north, and boarding ferries to or from Canada. Alphaeus decided, on a lark, to check with his friends at the livery stables near the Detroit docks, something that Hyams had not been smart enough to do. He hit the jackpot. Chandler had rented various rigs and several saddle horses from the same stable. The detective quizzed the stable master over a friendly beer or three at the local watering hole and found that the rentals had been for differing lengths of time and that the animals were always returned in as least as good a condition as they had been in when they left the stable. The shortest rental had been two days. "One out, one back!" snickered Plotkin under his breath. "Got him now!" The stable master's tongue had been loosened not just by the free beer, but also by the promise of a coin or two from Plotkin. To no one's surprise, the promised reward was never received.

In the privacy of his cluttered, cheap hotel room, Detective Plotkin had pushed an accumulation of dirty dishes, cups, laundry, and papers off of his table and onto the floor with one sweep of his arm. Unfolding his map, he had drawn a twenty-five mile circle with its center at the livery stable. Twenty-five miles was about as far as one could ride in a day without wearing out his horse. Oh, joy! It came as no surprise to him that the circle included Franklin Village. He would start his investigation there for old time's sake. If the mystery sailor were not found he would then search in such communities as Farmington, North Farmington, Clarenceville, Piety Hill, and so on. Nose to the ground, the hound had lost no time in getting to the scent. The only delay had been the time required to take a bath, get a shave, and to purchase a cheap wig.

Plotkin had been wrong about one supposition....that he would be unrecognized by the Franklin populace. He had registered at the Franklin Hotel and let it be known that he was a traveling farm equipment salesman with a catalog of harnesses, plows, hay rakes, and so on, and who would soon be calling upon the local farmers to explain his wares. So far, so good. But, at that Sunday morning Franklin Church worship service, to Plotkin's misfortune, Dick Trick happened to be standing at the back of the sanctuary serving as an usher. Dick did not notice him come in, what with the rush of the arriving congregation. Once the service had started, however, he had time to look around, noticing a man who was unfamiliar to him. It was an infrequent, but welcome, occurrence to have strangers stop to worship in the little church. Curious, Dick moved to the rear of the side aisle for a better look. The man looked, somehow, familiar. He stared some more. When recognition dawned, it caused a cold chill to trickle down Trick's spine. It was Alphaeus Plotkin! The man who had sought to harm Bethany and who had trashed her house and whose thugs had beaten him! How dare he come back here? Richard Trick seethed. There were now four ears in the congregation that were deaf to the eloquent messages of peace and love that flowed from the lips of Pastor Lanning.

When the benediction was pronounced and the service ended, Plotkin made another mistake. He remained seated for a few moments too long, engrossed in watching Matthew and Mary Sue showing off the baby to their fellow parishioners. He did not notice Trick slip into the now-empty pew behind him. When he started to rise, two strong hands clamped on his shoulders and pushed him back down. He opened his mouth to voice a loud protest when Dick's voice hissed into his ear. "Sit quiet, you swine, or I'll tell who you are and the men of this village will take you apart, piece by piece! Alphaeus shuddered, realizing that he had been recognized, and sat still as he was instructed. His thoughts whirled, thinking of a way to escape this most unfortunate situation. The hands tightened, painfully, on his shoulders. The whispering voice continued. "I'd like nothing better than to drag you outside and beat the livin' shit outa you." The strong hands released his shoulders and moved to the base of his throat. But this bein' the House of the Lord an' all, I ain't goin' to do that, just now." The voice paused to let the message sink in. "You will walk quietly out of here and be out of this town within the quarter hour, even if'n you have to walk all day and night to get someplace else...anyplace else. Understan'?" Plotkin nodded. "You know who I am? The detective wagged his head in the negative. "Name's Dick Trick. Remember me?" An affirmative nod. "I'll be watchin' your every move. If you don't do as I say, or if I ever see you again, I will kill you on the spot. Clear?"

Alphaeus cleared his throat, his voice a bit husky. "Clear." He fingered the pistol in his pocket as he considered putting it to good use by blowing his tormentor full of holes.... but thought better of it. Too many witnesses. He arose, shuffled quietly out of the pew, and looking straight ahead while ignoring the curious stares of the few remaining parishioners, left the church and strode rapidly toward the hotel. Dick waited a few hours, making certain that the miscreant was well out of town then marched up to the path to inform Greyson of the incident.

"What?" Matt leaped to his feet. "Why didn't you tell me? I would have strangled the bastard on the spot!"

Dick grinned. "That's why I didn't tell you."

Matthew was livid. "You're protecting that piece of shit?"

Trick plopped into a chair. "Not protecting him, Matt. Protecting you an' me. I'm sure, given the opportunity, you and me separately or together could make sure he never bothered anybody again. But, what's done is done. Ain't worth either of us goin' to jail for."

Mathew made a sound like the letting off of steam, then dropped into his own chair. "You're right, of course, Dick. Just when in hell did you suddenly get so all-fired wise?"

"Reckon kind of gradual. Person can't help growin' up a bit. Besides, bein' with Hannah has made growin' up easier. Her sweetness kind of grows on a person. Makes me better for knowin' her."

Greyson chuckled. "For God's sake, Richard, like I keep telling you, marry that woman before she finds out what an oaf you are and changes her mind."

"Promise I'll do that 'for she figures me out. " Dick snickered and wiggled in his chair. "What say we have a touch of tansy bitters? Seems we should celebrate gettin' rid of that thug so easy. There's still a jug stashed in the cold cellar."

"Good idea!" exclaimed Matt, leaping to his feet. He walked to the window and stared out for a moment. "Wonder why Plotkin came back here. Wonder what he was lookin' for." He felt a bit uneasy in the pit of his stomach. He thought he knew the answer. Captain Chandler. "Dick, let's load up the shotguns and pistols just in case our friend is stupid enough to come back."

"Good idea! I'll get the tansy. You load up. My shotgun is already ready and rarin'!"

+ + +

The days after Plotkin's ejection from town passed quietly with no sign of trouble. Matt and Dick kept a vigilant, armed watch and alerted several trustworthy male villagers to keep watch too. It was an excellent year for hay, the weather remaining warm into late October, and the Franklin area farmers worked furiously to harvest the third cutting and to store it in the barn lofts before the fall rains would come and spoil it. Shortly after sundown, and supper, both Matt and Dick tumbled, exhausted, into bed.... Matt into his now lonely bed in the farmhouse, Dick in his equally lonely bed in the tack room in the barn. The night was soft and warm as the last of the summer breezes sighed through the oaks and gave way to the autumn chill that would soon follow.

A bit after midnight, in the wee small hours of Friday, October 29th, it took Dick Trick a few moments to arouse from his slumber to realize that something was amiss. The animals, secured in their stalls and pens in the barn, were stirring, making small stomping, mooing, neighing, and bleating sounds that indicated that something was disturbing their slumber. The chickens were squawking little panicky squawks as though something were stalking their precious chicks. "Damn fox is here again, the bastard. I'll get him this time." Trick pulled on his trousers, lit his lantern, and picked up his shotgun. "Maybe I'll get the furry little bugger 'for he can grab another chicken!" he muttered, emerging from his tack room quarters. Walking into the stable area, he held the lantern high in one hand, his shotgun, capped, cocked and ready, in the other. The meager yellow light of the lantern revealed nothing amiss. As he walked the center aisle of the stable area, he noted that all of the stall doors were securely closed, and that the animals were peering back at him, sleepily, in the gloom.

A flash passed before his eyes. A biting pain compressed his windpipe. The smell and curse of a body pressed against him from behind. A garrote!" He dropped the lantern, shattering the glass. The flames from the spilled coal oil spread across the wooden floor, igniting it. His precious shotgun fell from his grasp, firing with a roar of shot and flame as it hit the floor. He felt the wire of the garrote twist. There was no way that he could get it off. Reaching behind him with both arms, his strong hands found the head and neck of his adversary. Grasping him behind the neck, Dick flipped his attacker over his shoulders and flat on the ground before him. It was Alphaeus Plotkin. Dizzy from pain and lack of oxygen, Dick picked up his shotgun and, with the butt, pounded Alphaeus Plotkin's head into a bloody, and very dead, pulp. With his last, fading consciousness, Dick staggered from stall to stall letting chickens, horses, sheep, and cows run away from the crackling, spreading flames that spread from the shattered lantern to the wooden floor, to the hay, and then exploded throughout the barn with indescribable fury. Dick Trick, for the second time, was seared by flame, this time unto death. Alphaeus Plotkin, his head a shapeless mass, never knew that his useless body was finally incinerated by the justice of the flames.

Matthew came running, alerted by the shotgun blast. It was too late. The alarm bell rang in the town, and villagers, with their fire buckets, arrived. It was too late to save anything but the house, which they doused with buckets of water to keep it from igniting from the radiant heat of the incandescent, collapsing barn. Alphaeus Plotkin would never again bring hate to the world. Richard Trick would never again bring love.

+ + +

Hannah wept bitter tears and prayed bitter prayers. The Lannings, the Midgleys, and the Greysons stayed with her, held her, and cried with her. "Why? Why? Why?" she sobbed. "Why, Mr. Lanning, why? You call yourself 'reverend'....then tell me why my future husband had to die."

"I don't know, just yet, Hannah. Jesus is not obligated to tell me all of his Father's plans, right off. Sooner or later it will be clear....trust me. And, one day, we will all be together again in heaven. Then His plan will be known to us. Please, let's all of us lay our hands on Hannah's hands, that we may share our strength with her. God of heaven, we pray that Dick did not suffer when he died. Please accept our heartfelt thanks that we could share his beautiful life. He farmed our sweet earth and fed us by his labor. He defended us from an evil man who might have caused festering wounds among the people of this village. He served his church.

He loved his Hannah with a love that was so pure and sweet that it will stand forever in our memories. And, Lord, have mercy on the soul of Alphaeus Plotkin...."

"No!" screamed Hannah. "Let the bastard burn in hell!"

"....and Jesus has taught us to forgive, to love the fallen, to go on with his work. And we will, together, go on."

Mary Sue, in tears, ran out of the parlor, off of the porch of the Midgely home and out into the road, searching for an eagle in the sky. There were no circling specks against the blue.

Hannah Midgley abruptly ceased her sobbing. She looked at each in the circle of friends and smiled, her face still wet with tears. She thanked them each with a kiss on the cheek then walked out of the door to join Mary Sue who stood in the middle of Franklin Road scanning the sky. The two women, one very young, one in full flower, held each other's hands and looked into each other's eyes. Without a word, Hannah returned to the house, excused herself, and made her way up the stairs to the spacious loft that was her room. Hannah Midgley had seen the face of God. She had seen God in the eyes of her friend.

The Midgley's served tea to their guests. In about an hour, Hannah returned down the stairs, a paper in her hand. She handed it to the reverend. ""Reverend Lanning, I apologize for being a bother, but could you please see that these words are read at the funeral and inscribed on Richard's stone?"

"Of course I will, Hannah." Adjusting his spectacles, the reverend read the words....the words that would still be legible, if one would dig a bit, and pull the grass a bit, one hundred forty years later.

> WE LOVED HIM; YES,
> NO TONGUE CAN TELL
> HOW MUCH WE LOVED HIM
> AND HOW WELL.
> GOD LOVED HIM TOO
> AND HE THOUGHT WELL
> TO TAKE HIM HOME
> WITH HIM TO DWELL

Tender hands had scooped up Dick's charred remains and stuffed them into his beloved uniform for burial. The coffin was closed and sealed. There was no point in allowing any viewing of the deceased. The sheriff had removed the twisted wire from Richard's neck to keep as evidence just in case there was ever any question as to the cause of death. They nailed the skeletal remains of Alphaeus Plotkin into a rude, county-supplied coffin and hauled him off to be buried in the potter's field, interring him not far from the remains of his former Pinkerton associate whom Bethany had dispatched a few years before.

Nearly every village resident, and many from the surrounding area, attended the funeral service, filling the pews, standing in the aisles, and spilling out through the door when there was no more room inside. The service was rather lengthy as many of his friends stood to speak kind, admiring words about their deceased friend and fallen hero. Afterward, the long cortege walked up the cemetery hill following the flag-draped coffin that was transported on a Congleton wagon pulled by Rebel and Buttercup. Waiting at the grave site, in precise line and at parade rest, was a squad of soldiers consisting of six members of Dick's unit: Company E, 30th Michigan Infantry.

Colonel Greyson, handsome in his impeccable blue uniform, marched up the hill with Mary Sue on his arm. The soldiers came to attention and saluted when the Greysons approached. "Good God, Mary Sue!" he whispered in her ear, "This is the worst-looking bunch of warriors I have ever seen! Good thing the war's over and we don't much need 'em anymore!" Mary Sue giggled. The soldiers did look a bit pathetic. Two of them were graybeards in their eighties. Three more looked relatively normal, but somewhat jaded. The last was a slender youth of short stature who sported a ferocious black mustache that must have taken a good deal of concentration to grow. Matt chuckled and looked around, making certain that no one but his daughter was close enough to hear. Again, he whispered in her ear. "See that little soldier? He looks like he should still be suckin' his mama's tit." Mary Sue exploded into laughter, which she quickly subdued when the rest of the assembled mourners glared at her, including Reverend Lanning who raised his eyebrows at her impropriety. Matthew, a little red-faced that he had caused the incident, silently tried to focus his gaze upon the distant trees while Reverend Lanning intoned the final words.

Regaining his composure, Colonel Greyson returned his gaze to the soldiers who stood in a precise line on the opposite side of the gravesite from where he and Mary Sue stood. Matt held Mary Sue's hand as she dabbed at her tears with a handkerchief held in her free hand. Mary Sue had not known Richard Trick for very long, but she had liked him a lot. When he looked again upon the soldiers, he caught a flash of the young man's eyes staring at them. When it became time for the infantrymen to fire their traditional three round salute, Matt watched with the professional eye of one who had commanded many. He held his breath when he noticed that the smallest soldier required two quivering thumbs working in concert to cock his Springfield. The muzzle of the weapon wavered unsteadily when the shots were fired. Strangely, possibly because of his colonel's insignia, the diminuitive soldier seemed to glance their way each time he tore the cartridge for the next round with his teeth and tamped the charge home. Actually,The squad performed quite admirably. As the blue smoke from the volley drifted up to the upper branches of the ancient spruces, a bugler sounded taps, echoed by a second bugler down the hill. Each year, ever after, the echoed taps would be repeated, on Memorial Day, by generations of villagers who would remember the departed heroes who had preserved their freedom.

"Mary Sue looked up at her father. "Papa? That littlest soldier is a girl."

"Pshaw! Never did see a lady with that much mustache. A few fuzzes I could understand....but not one like that!" He glanced at the soldier out of the corner of his eye so as not to be caught staring. "What makes you think he's a girl, anyway? 'Pears to me to be a lad of fifteen or sixteen."

"He's a girl!" Mary Sue stamped her foot for emphasis. "She has a very strong aura, like she's a very strong person." She, too, cast furtive glances at the soldier. "A very female aura."

Matt grinned. "How 'bout one of those queer boys who wishes he was a girl?"

"Nope."

"As you say, Heals-with-flowers. I know better than to argue with you. You have certainly inherited your mother's mystical powers." He tenderly lifted her chin and looked into those lovely dark eyes. For a moment It was a though Melody was looking back at him. "I'm very proud of you Mary

Sue Heals-with-flowers Greyson." They paused at Ellen Trick's grave, which was just a few steps north of Dick's, and watched as the sexton rolled up his sleeves and commenced filling in the grave. The dirt rang hollowly upon the coffin at first, then became silent as the work progressed.

Mary Sue wiped some more tears and looked sympathetically at her father's saddened face.

"Papa? Would you like to take the long way home, just you an' me?"

"Surely. A good idea. Just you an' me." They walked west along the trail that followed the high ground all the way to the Inkster Road, then circled back toward home along Fourteen Mile. Mary Sue was unusually quiet, deep in thought. They startled a covey of bobwhite quail that thundered into the air at their approach, lifting her from her reverie. "Maybe I'd like to be a soldier like that girl when I grow up."

"Don't think so. Soldierin' is a man's' job, though I admit there's been a few ladies found in both armies pretendin' to be men for some crazy reason or another."

"How'd they get found out?"

Matt chuckled. "Usually when they got themselves wounded and somebody took their clothes off."

"That would do it."

"And some even got caught when they had to pee, if you know what I mean."

Mary Sue howled. "I get the idea. Maybe I'd rather be a doctor like Dr. Cox. Then I could do both real medicine and faith healin' for the Chippewas."

"That's surely a better idea, but not an easy one either. Doctors are mostly men, though that could change."

"Maybe I could change It. Men have all the fun. I could be one of the first."

Matt gave his daughter a playful, sideways hug. "I reckon if anybody could do that, it would be you. First you need to finish your education here. Then, if the money keeps coming in, maybe we can send you out east or even to England to finishing school."

She frowned. "Sounds nice, but I don't want to be away from you and Patience."

"Would only be for a little while. Then, when you are all grown, there's a medical school not far from here at the University of Michigan. You could try for that if you're still of a mind to. Fact is Henry Cox is plannin' to go there to finish his own learning. Might be he would give you some pointers."

"Mmmm. Guess I got lots of thinkin' to do." They stamped the dust from their feet on the porch. "I'll get us some lemonade. Want some, Bessie?"

Bessie was snugged into a porch rocker, rocking slowly, humming softly, and knitting a baby blanket for the coming winter. No, thank you, Miss Mary Sue." She shivered. "I declare I'm cold enough already without no cold drink. Wish I could send some South Carolina sunshine thisaway."

Matt leaned against a porch post and stared out at the still-smoldering ruins where his barn once stood. "Did you want to go home for the winter, Bessie?"

Bessie rocked at a faster pace. "No suh! No suh! Yesterday maybe, but not today. No suh!"

Matt turned to look at her. She would not look up from her knitting. He was puzzled to see an impish grin that tried to hide itself on her face. "What changed your mind between yesterday and today?"

"Don't rightly know." She quickly changed the subject. "Sad, sad thing" she drawled, "That y'all had to put that nice young man in the col' ground." She had the grin under control.

Mary Sue swooped onto the porch carrying a tray with two tinkling glasses of lemonade and a plate of cookies. "Here you go, papa. Care for a cookie, Bessie?" "No thank you, missie. My hind end is gettin' too big for me to go eatin' no cookies." The impish grin was back.

Mary Sue snickered into her lemonade. "Very well, Bessie. We'll just cut off your cookies! Papa, Jimmie Barnum asked me to go down to the river fishin' with him this afternoon. That be all right?"

"Of course it's all right. You catch some nice pan fish an' bring 'em home for supper, hear?"

"Yes, papa."

"And best you change out of that nice dress into some gingham or homespun."

"Yes, papa. Oh! Here comes Jimmie now." She flew in the door, hollering over her shoulder as she went. "You talk to him while I change!"

After Jim and Mary Sue left for the river carrying their crude poles, bent pins for hooks, and a can of worms for bait, Matt wandered into the house in search of a brandy to calm his soul. In the center of the kitchen table he spied a large bouquet of tired-looking greenery that sported a lemony smell and a display of fading yellow flowers. Matt stuck his head back out of the door. "Bessie! How come you put that stinky tansy on the table?"

Bessie's grin was now at its widest and was accompanied by a little giggle. "Didn't."

He made a puzzled face. "Then, who did?"

The giggle was getting louder. "Just don' know, suh. Just know I didn't do it. Can't imagine who would do such a thing. Them tansys is uglier than ugly this time of year. What the frost ain't killed is near dead anyhow."

"Mary Sue must have done that for a prank."

"You think? Might be you're right, Massa Greyson!" The giggle was totally out of control.

"And, you are in on it. You and Mary Sue are up to somethin', ain't you? I can tell by the look in your eyes. I never should have let you two get together. If you and she have played some sort of mean trick on me I swear I will turn you both over my knee!"

Bessie stayed put in her chair, but set aside her knitting and erupted into shrieks and whoops of laughter, alternately covering her face with her hands, and then fanning her hands in front of her face to relieve the heat that was building there. "You ain't seen it all yet, Massa Greyson!"

Matt took a sip of his brandy. "What does that mean?"

"Means you better take a look in your bedroom!" Bessie erupted into more shrieks and whoops.

Matt was starting to giggle too. It was infectious. "Tell me you didn't put tansy in my bed. I hope not. That plant has bugs on it." He was convinced that he was the butt of a devious prank and might just a well go along with it. He half expected Mary Sue to pop out of hiding from somewhere and join in the laughter, but she did not appear.

He took an exaggerated gulp of brandy for Bessie's amusement, and made a face at her. "All right!. This has got to be good. Let's get it over with." He gave her a wink and headed for his bedroom. The door was closed. He turned the knob and cautiously peeked in, half expecting something to jump out at him, or at the very least to find a clump of tansy stuffed under his comforter.

There was Tansy in his bed, all right. The kind that certainly had no bugs on it. It was the little soldier sitting cross-legged on the bed, the false mustache gone, the kepi off, revealing short-cropped raven hair. She held out her arms to him. "Matthew, I love you. Will you take me back?" It was no prank. It was a miracle. It was Bethany.

She had hidden under the dock at Johnson's Island until the searchers gave up, stolen uniforms and a valise from the quartermaster's stores, and masqueraded as a soldier ever since, buying and bribing her way with the Confederate gold that she had stashed in her undergarments. In fact, the gold had been so heavy that it nearly drowned her....a circumstance, she thought, that would have been a really unfortunate state of affairs had she not been a strong and plucky swimmer.

Down at the river, Jimmy Barnum and Mary Sue sat in the sunshine on the soft, aromatic autumn grass. Their fishing lines dangled mostly unheeded as they chatted of children's' things....school, homework, friends, and such. Mary Sue lay back in the grass, looking so beautiful that Jim could barely restrain himself from touching her breasts that swelled, so modestly and prettily, under her gingham jumper. Mary Sue shaded her eyes, then pointed skyward. "That's my mother up there."

Jimmie flopped backward in despair, squinting upward to where her finger pointed. Mary Sue, why do you tell me dumb things like that? I may be stupid, but not that stupid. You ain't no eagle."

"Don't be too sure. I'm a Chippewa Indian."

He raised on one elbow to look at her. "Naw, I don't believe that. You ain't no Indian and you ain't no eagle. "Sides, there is two birds up there. Which one is your ma?"

"Don't know. Wish I did." Jim could stand it no longer. He leaned over and kissed her, fully, gently, and innocently on her lips. She responded, sweetly stroking his hair. For each of them, it was their first kiss.

Time was drawing toward evening, and the sun was casting long shadows upon the golden grass. The cardinals chirped their happy "pit, pit, pit" as they found their evening meal. A tiny screech owl sang his warbley, spooky little song as he sat in the shadows amidst the top branches of a big white pine that presided over all things that were just upstream. Following their standard evening choreography, little tendrils of mist tried to hug the river as it coursed past the mill and squeezed under the bridge.

Seven hundred miles to the south, Penelope Barksdale and her mother prepared to board the cars at Durham Station. With many hugs and kisses, Captain Roberts consigned them to the mercies of the newly repaired railroad. Service had been restored. Their hatboxes and valises were safely stored aboard. A huge hamper of sandwiches, lemonade, candies, cookies, and other goodies too numerous to mention was hauled aboard to make certain that they would not suffer hunger during their long journey. As the train chuffed out of the station the conductor came to examine and to punch their tickets. "My, my!" he exclaimed. "Y'all are goin' a long ways up into Yankeeland!" His punch clicked through the tickets. There were transfers and layovers, but the last destination, on the last ticket, read "Detroit, Michigan".

VAN EVERY GRIST MILL - 1837
Courtesy Franklin Historical Society
Artist: Max Altekruse

BIBLIOGRAPHY

Atwood, Mary Dean: Spirit Healing; Sterling Publishing Co. Inc.

Barkless, John: Spies of the Confederacy; Dover Publications Inc.

Booth, John Wilkes: Right or Wrong, God Judge Me; University of Illinois Press

Cannon, Bettie Waddell: All About Franklin; Franklin Historical Society

Civil War Times Illustrated:
>Volume XIV #4 July 1975: Gaday, David W.: Gray Cloaks and Daggers
>Volume XVIII #3 June 1979: Levin, Alexnder Lee: The Canadian Contact: Edwin Gray Lee Volume XXII #5 September 1983: Pelzer, John & Linda: Hijack! The Fate of the Philo Parsons; Volume XXII #9 January 1984: Trimble, Tony: A Quiet Sabbath; Reflections From Johnson's Island;
>Volume XXX # 3 July/August 1991: Grimsley, Mark: We Will Vindicate the Right; an Account of the Life of Jefferson Davis; Volume XXXIV August 1995: Antonucci, Michael: Code-Crackers; Volume XXXVII #1 March 1998: Long, Roger: Out of a Frozen Hell (Johnson's Island) Volume XL #3 June 2001: Special Issue! Rebel Secret Agents and Saboteurs in Canada.

Deur, Lynne: Nishnaube; River Road Publications Inc.

Echoes of Glory: Arms and Equipment of the Confederacy; Time-Life Books

Garrison, Webb: Civil War Hostages; White Mane Books

Great Civil War Heroes and Their Battles: Abbeville Press

Handbook of Historic Fredericsburg Virginia; Historic Fredericsburg Foundation Inc.

Harper's Pictorial History of the Civil War; The Fairfax Press

Hershock, Martin J.: The Mighigan Historical Review Volumg 18 #1: Copperheads and Radicals; Michigan Partisan Politics During the Civil War Era; Central Michigan University Press

Horan, James D.: Confederate Agent; Crown Publishers Inc.

Mackinac, an Island Famous in these Regions: Mackinac State Historic Press

Michigan History Magazine Volume 82 #4: Civil War Collector's Issue

McMillan, Loyal: A Walk With History (Middleburg, Va.)

Mosby, Col. John S.: Mosby's Memoirs; JB Sanders & Co.

Petersen, Eugene T.: Mackinac Island, Its History in Pictures: Mackinac Island State Park Commission

Ripley, Warren: Artillery and Ammunition of the Civil War; Promontory Press

Rodgers, Bradley A.: Guardian of the Great Lakes: University of Michigan Press

Sharf, J. Thomas: History of the Confederate States Navy; The Fairfax Press

Smith, Rockne P.: Our "Downriver" River

Spencer, Herbert Reynolds: USS Michigan, USS Wolverine; Erie Book Store

Stern, Philip Van Doren: Secret Missions of the Civil War; Rand McNally & Co.

The Civil War Almanac: WH Smith Publishers Inc.

Thomason, John W., Jr.: Jeb Stuart; University of Nebraska Press

Tidwell, William A.: Come Retribution; University Press of Mississippi

Tidwell. William A.: Confederate Covert Action in the American Civil War; Kent State University Press

Voices of the Civil War--Second Manassas: Time-Life Books

Wiley, Bell Irvin: The Life of Billy Yank; Louisiana State University Press

Wood, Bert D.: Franklin's Yesteryear; Edwards Brothers Inc.

Woodford, Frank B. and Arthur M.: All Our Yesterdays (Detroit); Wayne State University Press

ABOUT THE AUTHOR

Dr. David Roberts has been a veterinarian for 47 years and a resident of the Village of Franklin, Michigan, for 39 years. During those years he has managed to pursue a number of varied interests. He is interested in history and in antiques, particularly antique firearms. He served as a firefighter, instructor, and Deputy Chief of the Franklin-Bingham Fire Department for many years, actively supported the Franklin Community Church, and directed plays and musicals for the Franklin Village Players.

Married for 49 years, David and wife Jane have raised 2 sons and are enjoying four grandchildren.

Dr. Roberts has written four plays which have been presented locally. This is his first novel.

Printed in the United States
51669LVS00003BA/4-9